Why Do You Need this New Edition?

If you are wondering why you should buy this new edition of *Reading Across the Discipline*, here are six good reasons!

1. **An all-new chapter on career fields.** With a tough job market, preparing for a successful career is crucial. A new Chapter 20, "Career Fields," addressing three high demand career fields—education, criminal justice, and travel and hospitality—has been added to Part Two of the text, providing instruction on how to read specialized materials within these fields.

2. **An all-new Chapter on Visual Literacy.** Textbooks as well as print and electronic media are becoming increasingly visual, and the ability to read a wide variety of visuals is becoming ever more important in college and the workplace. A new Chapter 5, "Reading and Thinking Visually," provides vital instruction in how to read and analyze photographs, tables, graphs, pie charts, diagrams, maps, timelines, and infographics.

3. **New Coverage of Visual Literacy in Every Reading in Part Two.** To provide you with additional practice opportunities for reading visuals, every selection in Part Two now includes at least one visual and in a section titled "Reading and Thinking Visually" several questions that guide you in analyzing and interpreting how it contributes to the reading.

4. **Expanded Coverage of Main Ideas.** Grasping the main idea of a short passage, article, textbook chapter, or work of fiction is essential to college success. Section 3b in Chapter 3 offers expanded instruction and practice on identifying topics, stated main ideas and topic sentences; and section 3c offers additional instruction on understanding and expressing implied main ideas, which can often be more difficult to identify.

5. **Increased Emphasis on Contemporary Issues.** Keeping up-to-date with issues in your field is important for success in college and the workplace. To help you achieve this, contemporary issue readings dealing with topics like citizen journalism, E-waste, medical ethics, species extinction, and alternative energy options have been integrated throughout the Chapters in Part 2.

6. **New Reading Selections.** Interesting, current readings make it easier to concentrate, learn, and practice skills. Twenty-six new readings taken from textbooks and other sources you would be expected to use have been added to this edition of the text. New topics include homeless camps, camera surveillance of private citizens, Superbowl advertising, hot jobs in the future, and cell phones as teaching tools.

Reading Across the Disciplines

College Reading and Beyond

Fifth Edition

Kathleen T. McWhorter
Niagara County Community College

PEARSON

Boston Columbus Indianapolis New York San Francisco Upper Saddle River
Amsterdam Cape Town Dubai London Madrid Milan Munich Paris Montreal Toronto
Delhi Mexico City São Paulo Sydney Hong Kong Seoul Singapore Taipei Tokyo

Editor in Chief: Eric Stano
Senior Acquisitions Editor: Nancy Blaine
Senior Development Editor: Gill Cook
Executive Marketing Manager: Tom DeMarco
Senior Supplements Editor: Donna Campion
Senior Media Producer: Stefanie Liebman
Production Manager: S.S. Kulig
Project Coordination, Text Design, and Electronic Page Makeup: PreMediaGlobal

Cover Designer/Manager: John Callahan
Cover Art: Top left: BIOS/Photolibrary; Top right: Arctic Images/Alamy; Middle: Monty Rakusen/ Photoshot; Bottom: Shepard Fairey, Revolution Girl. Outdoor location, Los Angeles. Obey Giant Art, CA.
Senior Manufacturing Buyer: Roy Pickering
Printer/Binder: Quad/Graphics-Taunton
Cover Printer: Lehigh-Phoenix Color Corp.

Credits and acknowledgments borrowed from other sources and reproduced, with permission, in this textbook appear on the appropriate page within text [or on pages 674–681].

Library of Congress Cataloging-in-Publication Data

McWhorter, Kathleen T.
Reading across the disciplines: college reading and beyond / Kathleen T. McWhorter.—5th ed.
   p. cm.
Previous ed.: 2009.
Includes index.
ISBN 978-0-205-18476-7
1. College readers.   2. Reading (Higher education)   3. Interdisciplinary approach in education.   I. Title.
PE1122.M37 2011
428.6—dc23

2011025297

Student ISBN 10: 0-205-18476-6
Student ISBN 13: 978-0-205-18476-7
AIE ISBN 10: 0-205-20949-1
AIE ISBN 13: 978-0-205-20949-1

www.pearsonhighered.com

Brief Contents

Detailed Contents

PART TWO   Readings for Academic Disciplines 233

Preface

Reading Across the Disciplines, Fifth Edition, is designed to improve college students' reading and thinking skills through brief skill instruction and extensive guided practice with academic discipline–based readings. The text is structured around 11 academic disciplines. The 33 readings—all of which aim to motivate students—are selected from college textbooks as well as from books, periodicals and popular magazines, newspapers, and Internet sources. The objective is to show the relevance of college studies to events and issues in everyday life through the use of engaging readings.

PURPOSE

The primary purposes of the text are to teach essential college reading skills and to guide their application in each of 9 academic disciplines and 2 workplace related. The text develops basic vocabulary and comprehension skills, as well as inferential and critical-reading and -thinking skills. In addition to developing overall reading skills, the text also introduces students to content-specific reading skills. Each chapter in Part Two, "Readings for Academic Disciplines," begins with a tip list for applying reading and thinking skills to text with the unique characteristics of academic and career fields. Questions and activities that precede and follow each reading demonstrate the application of vocabulary, comprehension, and critical-reading and -thinking skills to the particular discipline.

Another important goal of the text is to demonstrate to students the relevance and utility of college courses to their daily lives. The book attempts to answer the long-standing question frequently asked by students, "Why do I have to take a course in history, biology, etc.?" The book presents readings that show students how academic disciplines embrace and investigate topics of interest and concern to everyday human experience.

NEW TO THE FIFTH EDITION

The goals of this revision were to provide tips for and practice with reading in rapidly expanding career fields, improve students' visual literacy skills, and expand coverage of stated and implied main ideas.

NEW Chapter on Career Fields. Because career field courses are growing on college campuses and many students are now faced with reading specialized materials within their chosen career field, a new Chapter 20, "Career Fields," has been added to Part Two. Three high-demand career fields are represented in this chapter: education, criminal justice, and travel and hospitality.

NEW Chapter on Visual Literacy. In recognition that textbooks, as well as both print and electronic media, are becoming increasingly visual, a new Chapter 5, "Reading and Thinking Visually," has been added to Part One. Topics covered include reading and analyzing photographs and how to approach reading graphics in general. Graphics covered in detail include tables, graphs, pie charts, diagrams, maps, time lines, and infographics (combined photographs, charts, and diagrams).

New Coverage of Visual Literacy in Each Reading in Part Two. Each reading selection in Part Two now includes at least one visual that contributes meaning to the reading. In the questions following each reading is a new section titled "Reading and Thinking Visually" that guides students in analyzing and interpreting the visual.

NEW Integrated Emphasis on Contemporary Issues. To enhance the coverage of contemporary issues, Chapter 14 from the previous edition, "Public Policy/Contemporary Issues," has been replaced by contemporary issue readings that have been integrated throughout the Chapters in Part Two and are identified by an icon. Contemporary issues include citizen journalism, e-waste, medical ethics, species extinction, and alternative energy options.

Contemporary
Issues Reading

Expanded Coverage of Main Ideas. Part One, Chapter 3b offers additional instruction and practice on identifying topics, main ideas, and topic sentences.

Expanded Coverage of Implied Main Ideas. Part One, Chapter 3c offers additional instruction on understanding and expressing implied main ideas.

New Reading Selections. Twenty-three new readings have been added to this edition of the text. Each academic discipline chapter contains at least one new reading; some contain all new readings. An effort was made to choose readings from textbooks within the discipline as well as other sources students may have contact with as they study within the discipline. New topics include homeless camps, camera surveillance of private citizens, Super Bowl advertising, hot jobs in the future, and cell phones as teaching tools.

CONTENT OVERVIEW

The book is organized into three parts:

- **Part One, "A Handbook for Reading and Thinking in College,"** presents a brief skill introduction. Written in handbook format (1a, 1b, etc.), this part introduces students to essential vocabulary, comprehension, and critical-reading skills.
- **Part Two, "Readings for Academic Disciplines,"** has 11 chapters, each containing readings representative of a different academic and career fields. Each chapter has three reading selections. The readings in each chapter are chosen from textbooks, books, periodicals,

newspapers, and Internet sources that contain material relevant to the discipline. The readings in each chapter vary in length as well as difficulty. Within each chapter, readings are arranged from least to most difficult, providing students with the opportunity to strengthen their skills, experience success, and build positive attitudes toward reading. Each reading is accompanied by an extensive apparatus that guides student learning.

- **Part Three, "Textbook Chapter Reading,"** contains an excerpt from a psychology textbook chapter. This excerpt enables students to practice skills on a larger piece of writing and to apply the skills they have developed in the preceding parts. Apparatus is provided for both major section of the excerpt.

FEATURES

Reading Across the Disciplines guides students in learning reading and thinking skills essential for college success.

Students Approach Reading as Thinking

Reading is approached as a thinking process—a process of interacting with textual material and sorting, evaluating, and reacting to its organization and content. The apparatus preceding and following each reading focuses, guides, and shapes students' thought processes.

Students Develop Active Reading Skills

Students learn to approach reading as a process that requires involvement and response. In doing so, they are able to master the skills that are essential to college reading. The reading apparatus provides a model for active reading.

Students Learn Essential Reading Skills

Vocabulary, comprehension, and critical-reading skills are presented concisely in Part One, "A Handbook for Reading and Thinking in College," and are accompanied by several exercises.

Students Learn Discipline-Specific Reading Skills

The high-interest readings in Part Two are grouped according to academic discipline and career fields. Each chapter begins with a brief list of tips for reading and learning within the particular discipline. Students are encouraged to apply these techniques as they read the selections within the chapter.

Students Learn as They Work

Unlike many books, which simply test students after they have read a selection, this text teaches students as they work. Some of the apparatus provides new material on vocabulary, methods of organizing information, transitions, and reading/study strategies.

Students Understand the Importance of Academic Disciplines to Their Daily Lives

Through the high-interest topics selected, students will come to understand the relevance of various academic disciplines to their daily lives, careers, and workplace.

Students Learn Visually

Increasingly, college students are becoming visual learners, and visual literacy is critical to success in today's world, so this text includes an entire chapter on how to read and interpret photographs, graphics, graphic organizers (maps), charts, and diagrams.

Students Appreciate Consistent Format

Because students often need structure and organization, this text uses a consistent format for each reading selection. Students always know what to expect and what is expected of them.

Students Refer to Part One, "A Handbook for Reading and Thinking in College," to Get Help Answering Questions

The activities following each reading parallel the topics in Part One of the book, which presents a brief skill overview in a handbook format. For example, if students have difficulty answering inferential questions, they may refer to the section in Part One that explains how to make inferences. The handbook also includes section on reading and evaluating electronic sources.

Format of the Apparatus

The apparatus for each reading selection follows a consistent format. The sections vary in the number of questions and the specific skills reviewed. Each reading selection has the following parts:

- **Headnote.** A headnote introduces the reading, identifies its source, provokes the students' interest, and most important, establishes a framework or purpose for reading.
- **Previewing the Reading.** Students are directed to preview the reading using the guidelines provided in Part One and to answer several questions based on their preview.
- **Making Connections.** This brief section encourages students to draw connections between the topic of the reading and their own knowledge and experience.
- **Reading Tip.** The reading tip is intended to help students approach and work through the reading. A different reading tip is offered for each reading. For example, a reading tip might suggest how to highlight to strengthen comprehension or how to write annotations to enhance critical thinking.

- **Reading Selection/Vocabulary Annotation.** Most reading selections contain difficult vocabulary words that are essential to the meaning of the selection. Often these are words that students are unlikely to know and cannot figure out from context. These words are highlighted, and their meanings are given as marginal annotations. Preferable to a list of words preceding the reading, this format allows students to check meanings on an as-needed basis, within the context of the selection. Annotations are also used occasionally to provide necessary background information that students may need to grasp concepts in a reading.

- **Understanding the Thesis and Other Main Ideas.** This section helps students figure out the thesis of the reading and identify the main idea of selected paragraphs.

- **Identifying Details.** This section focuses on recognizing the relationship between main ideas and details, as well as distinguishing primary from secondary details. The format of questions within this section varies to expose students to a variety of thinking strategies.

- **Recognizing Methods of Organization and Transitions.** This part of the apparatus guides students in identifying the overall organizational pattern of the selection and in identifying transitional words and phrases within the reading. Prompts are provided that serve as teaching tips or review strategies.

- **Reviewing and Organizing Ideas.** Since many students are proficient at literal recall of information but have difficulty seeing relationships and organizing information into usable formats for study and review, this section emphasizes important review and organizational skills such as paraphrasing, mapping, outlining, and summarizing.

- **Reading and Thinking Visually.** Since textbooks and electronic media are becoming incresingly visual, students need to be able to interpret and analyze visuals. This section guides students in responding to the visual(s) that accompanies the reading.

- **Figuring Out Implied Meanings.** The ability to think inferentially is expected of college students. This section guides students in making inferences based on information presented in the reading selection.

- **Thinking Critically.** This section covers essential critical-thinking skills including distinguishing fact from opinion, identifying the author's purpose, recognizing bias, evaluating the source, identifying tone, making judgments, and evaluating supporting evidence.

- **Building Vocabulary.** The first part of this section focuses on vocabulary in context, while the second is concerned with word parts. Using words from the reading selection, exercises are structured to encourage students to expand their vocabulary and strengthen their word-analysis skills. A brief review of the meanings of prefixes, roots, and suffixes used in the exercise is provided for ease of reference and to create a meaningful learning situation. The third vocabulary section focuses on a wide range of interesting features of language, drawing upon unusual or striking usage within the reading. Topics such as figurative language, idioms, and connotative meanings are included.

- **Selecting a Learning/Study Strategy.** College students are responsible for studying and learning what they read; many use the same study method for all disciplines and all types of material. This section helps students to choose appropriate study methods and to adapt their study methods to suit particular academic disciplines.
- **Exploring Ideas Through Discussion and Writing.** Questions provided in this section are intended to stimulate thought, provoke discussion, and serve as a springboard to writing about the reading.
- **Beyond the Classroom to the Web.** These activities draw on the skills students have learned by directing them to the Internet, where they are asked to read particular articles. These activities also demonstrate the relevance of the academic discipline beyond the classroom and provide guidance in using Web sources.

BOOK-SPECIFIC ANCILLARIES

- **Annotated Instructor's Edition.** The Annotated Instructor's Edition is identical to the student text, but it includes answers printed directly on the pages where questions and exercises appear. ISBN 0-205-66278-1
- **Test Bank.** This supplement contains numerous tests for each chapter, formatted for easy distribution and scoring. It includes content review quizzes and skill-based mastery tests for Part One and a discipline-based test and two discipline-based mastery tests for Part Two. ISBN 0-205-66276-5
- **Instructor's Manual.** The manual includes teaching suggestions for each section of Part One. For each reading in Part Two, the manual provides numerous suggestions for introducing the reading and offers a variety of follow-up activities designed to review and reinforce skills. ISBN 0-205-66277-3
- **Expanding Your Vocabulary.** Instructors may choose to shrink-wrap *Reading Across the Disciplines* with a copy of *Expanding Your Vocabulary*. This book, written by Kathleen McWhorter, works well as a supplemental text providing additional instruction and practice in vocabulary. Students can work through the book independently, or units may be incorporated into weekly lesson plans. Topics include methods of vocabulary learning, contextual aids, word parts, connotative meanings, idioms, euphemisms, and many more interesting and fun topics. The book concludes with vocabulary lists and exercises representative of ten academic disciplines. To preview this book, contact your Pearson sales consultant for an examination copy.

ACKNOWLEDGMENTS

I wish to express my gratitude to my reviewers for their excellent ideas, suggestions, and advice on the preparation and revision of this text:

Bonnie Arnett, Washtenaw Community College; Susan Banach, South Suburban College; Kathleen S. Britton, Florence-Darlington Technical College; Laraine Croall, South Louisiana Community College; Kimberly S. Hall, Harrisburg Area Community College; Tracy Harrison, Valencia Community College; Anne Hepfer, Seattle University; Debra Herrera, Cisco Junior College; Valerie Hicks, Community College Beaver County; Lisa Jones, Pasco Hernando Community College; Diane Lerma, Palo Alto College; Linda Maitland, Lone Star; Dianne Miller, Phoenix College; Cindy Ortega, Phoenix College; Lynette D. Shaw-Smith, Springfield College Illinois/Benedictine University; Jeffrey Siddall, College of DuPage; Ursula Sohns, LSC North Harris; Maria Spelleri, Manatee Community College; Kitty Spires, Midlands Technical College; Rakesh Swamy, Ohlone College; Michelle Van de Sande, Arapahoe Community College; Michael Vensel, Miami Dade College; Carl Vinas, Nassau Community College; and Sylvia D. Ybarra, San Antonio College.

I also wish to thank Gill Cook, my development editor, for her creative vision of the project, her helpful suggestions, and her assistance in preparing and organizing the manuscript. I am particularly indebted to acquisitions editor, for her enthusiastic support and valuable advice, Nancy Blaine.

KATHLEEN T. McWHORTER

STRATEGIES

Ten Success Strategies for Learning and Studying Academic Disciplines

SUCCESS STRATEGIES FOR LEARNING AND STUDYING ACADEMIC DISCIPLINES

Each academic discipline has a specialized approach for studying the world. To illustrate, let's choose human beings and consider how various disciplines might approach their study.

- An **ARTIST** might consider a human being as an object of beauty and record a person's fluid, flexible muscular structure and meaningful facial expressions on canvas.

- A **PSYCHOLOGIST** might study what human needs (love, safety, etc.) are fulfilled by various behaviors.

- A **HISTORIAN** might research the historical importance of human actions and decisions—their decisions to enter wars or form alliances with other countries.

- An **ECONOMIST** might focus on the supply of and demand for essential human goods (food, clothing, transportation) and the amount of business they generate.

- A **BIOLOGIST** would categorize a human as *Homo sapiens*.

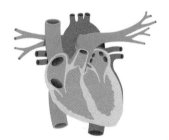

- A **PHYSIOLOGIST** would be concerned with human bodily functions (breathing, heart rate, temperature).

- A **MATHEMATICIAN** might calculate human life expectancies based on lifestyle, gender, race, and so forth.

Each academic discipline, then, approaches a given object or event with a different focus or perspective. Each has its own special purposes and interests that define the scope of the discipline. You will find that each discipline also has its own methodology for studying the topics with which it is concerned. Because each discipline is unique, each requires somewhat different study and learning strategies. The purpose of this introduction is to show you how to modify and adapt your learning, thinking, and study strategies to best apply them to a variety of specific academic areas.

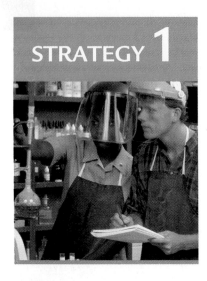

STRATEGY 1

Develop New Skills for Each Academic Discipline

In college, you are likely to encounter disciplines with which you have little or no prior experience. For example, sociology, political science, and chemistry may be new to you. At first, you may feel lost, confused, or frustrated in such courses. These feelings may result from unfamiliarity with the specialized language of the discipline; with the types of learning and thinking that are expected of you; or with the conventions, approaches, and methodology of the discipline. One student described this feeling as "being on the outside looking in," watching other students participate in the class but being unable to do so himself.

STRATEGIES FOR READING IN NEW DISCIPLINES

When approaching a new field of study, try the following:

1. **Understand the baseline for success in the course.** Each discipline uses a specific set of tools. Identifying and understanding these tools is essential. If you do not use them, you will not learn the material properly. For example, in business courses, case studies are common, so you need to develop a system for identifying and summarizing their key points. In economics, you must understand how to create and analyze graphs.

2. **Establish an overview of the field.** Study your textbook's table of contents; it provides an outline of the course. Look for patterns, progression of ideas, and recurring themes, approaches, or problems. Before you read each chapter, preview the material at the end of the chapter, which often includes study questions. Then use these questions to guide your reading of the chapter.

3. **Overlearn until you discover what is expected.** Until you discover what is important in the course and figure out the best way to learn it, learn more information than you may need. That is, err on the side of learning too much rather than too little. As an example, consider a criminal justice class. Until you know whether the instructor's focus is on trends, patterns, and theories— or on facts, research findings, and specific laws—it is safer to learn both.

4. **Use several different methods to learn the same information.** For example, in an anthropology course, you might learn events and discoveries chronologically (according to occurrence in time) as well as comparatively (according to similarities and differences among them). In a sociology

course you might highlight textbook information (to promote factual recall) as well as write outlines and summaries (to interpret and consolidate ideas). You might also draw diagrams to map the relationships between concepts and ideas.

5. **Look for similarities between the new subject matter and other academic fields that are more familiar to you.** If similarities exist, you may be able to modify or adapt learning approaches and strategies with which you are already familiar. For instance, if you are familiar with mathematics, some of the learning strategies you use in math courses may apply to physics and chemistry.

6. **Develop a support network.** Ask students who've taken the class about their experiences. What Web sites are helpful as study tools? What kinds of questions does the instructor tend to ask on exams? Which chapters in the textbook are the most important?

7. **Think in new ways.** Many college courses ask you to change your fundamental way of thinking. For example, many economics instructors say they want their students to "think like an economist," which means understanding the trade-offs involved in choices. Geography instructors ask students to "think geographically," which means looking at how human beings interact with their locations.

EXERCISE 1 . . . THINKING IN NEW WAYS

Sociologists often discuss two different perspectives on society. The *functionalist perspective* maintains that social institutions (such as the education system and the family) work in society's best interests. The *conflict perspective* maintains that these same institutions set up systems in which certain people benefit at the expense of others.

Think about the idea of arranged marriages, in which parents arrange their children's marriages to suitable partners. What would sociologists with a functionalist perspective say about these marriages? What would sociologists with a conflict perspective say about the same topic?

FOR FURTHER INFORMATION AND STUDY

Part Two of this book, "Readings for Academic Disciplines," provides readings from a wide variety of subject areas. Use the suggestions outlined above, as well as the tips at the start of each chapter, as you begin reading in each new discipline.

STRATEGY 2

Acquire the Right Tools

To be successful in any discipline you need the right tools. These include:

The Textbook

Some students try to get through a course without the text-book. This is never a good idea. The textbook provides essential information, along with many study aids to help you learn and prepare for tests. Most textbooks also come with a free companion Web site that provides additional learning aids. If your instructor requires a textbook, buy it and use it.

A Collegiate Dictionary

All college students need a collegiate dictionary. Many are available in inexpensive paperback editions. Online dictionaries are also available, and many of them offer an audio function that allows you to hear a word's pronunciation. Here are two useful online dictionaries:

- **Dictionary.com** (http://www.dictionary.com). This site provides definitions from different sources and allows you to compare them. Below is a sample for the word *metabolism.*

Dictionary.com Unabridged (b1.1)

me·tab·o·lism <u>Audio Help</u> [m*uh*-**tab**-*uh*-liz-*uh* m] <u>Pronunciation Key</u> – <u>Show IPA Pronunciation</u>

–noun

1. *Biology, Physiology.* the sum of the physical and chemical processes in an organism by which its material substance is produced, maintained, and destroyed, and by which energy is made available. Compare <u>ANABOLISM</u>, <u>CATABOLISM</u>.

2. any basic process of organic functioning or operating: *changes in the country's economic metabolism.*

[Orgin: 1875–80; < Gk metabol ē change (meta– <u>META</u>– + bol ē a throw) + –<u>ISM</u>]

- **Merriam-Webster Online** (http://www.m-w.com). This site allows you to enter a word or phrase and check the site's dictionary, thesaurus, Spanish-English dictionary, and/or medical dictionary for its meaning.

Subject-Area Dictionaries and Glossaries

Many academic fields have specialized dictionaries that list most of the important words used in that discipline. The field of nursing, for instance, has *Taber's Cyclopedic Medical Dictionary.* Other subject-area dictionaries include *A Dictionary of Anthropology, The New Grove Dictionary of Music and Musicians,* and *A Dictionary of Economics.* Most libraries have copies of these specialized dictionaries in the reference section, and you can also access numerous subject-area dictionaries online.

Most textbooks also include a **glossary,** which is a sort of mini-dictionary of the key terms used in a specific discipline. In introductory courses, the end-of-book glossary is a useful substitute for a longer, specialized subject-area dictionary.

Web Sites

The Internet is home to a wealth of information on learning and studying each academic discipline. For example, the site http://apphysicsb.homestead.com/study.html contains useful information on how to study physics. Look at the syllabus your instructor gives you on the first day of class; many syllabi include lists of helpful Web sites. Be sure to use the textbook's companion Web site, too.

Documentation Guides

Most academic fields have preferred methods of crediting the sources used when writing essays or term papers. Find out what documentation style your instructor requires, and then obtain the appropriate style guide in print or locate a reliable Web site that summarizes the guidelines. The most common documentation styles are:

- **MLA** (Modern Language Association). Used in English, some humanities, and foreign languages. (http://www.mla.org/style)
- **APA** (American Psychological Association). Widely used in the social sciences. (http://www.apastyle.org)
- **CSE** (Council of Science Editors). Used in the life sciences, physical sciences, and mathematics. (http://www.councilscienceeditors.org)
- **Chicago Style.** Commonly used in history, art history, philosophy, and some humanities. (http://www.chicagomanualofstyle.org)

EXERCISE 2 . . . USING ONLINE DICTIONARIES

Use an online dictionary to look up the meanings of any unfamiliar words, and then rewrite these sentences.

My somnolence increases when I experience pleasurable olfactory and auditory sensations.

After suffering from years of ennui, the writer's amanuensis decided to write a bildungsroman of her own.

FOR FURTHER INFORMATION AND STUDY

To take advantage of the many additional resources offered on this textbook's companion Web site, visit http://www.myreadinglab.com.

STRATEGY **3**

A white blood cell ingests bacteria using phagocytosis.

Learn the Language of the Discipline

Each academic discipline has a set of specialized words that allow precise communication through accurate and concise descriptions of events, principles, concepts, problems, and occurrences. One of the first tasks you face in a new course, then, is learning that course's specialized language. You cannot learn a new discipline without being able to use its terminology!

This task is especially important in introductory courses in which the subject is new and unfamiliar. In an introductory psychology course, you must learn many new terms—*assimilation, autonomic nervous system, conditioning, reinforcement, defense mechanism,* and *extinction* are a few examples. You will encounter this specialized vocabulary in class lectures and in textbooks and will be expected to use it in assignments and on exams.

Class Lectures

Often, the first few lectures in a course are devoted to acquainting you with the nature and scope of the field and introducing you to its vocabulary. Use the following tips to keep track of and learn new terms during lectures.

- **Read Chapter 1 of your textbook before the first lecture.** The textbook's first chapter usually introduces key terminology that will be used throughout the course. For example, in a widely used psychology textbook, 34 new terms are introduced in the first two chapters (40 pages), and in a popular chemistry book, 56 vocabulary words are introduced in the first two chapters (28 pages). Understanding some of the key terms before you go to class will make that first class much easier.
- **Record each new term for later review and study.** If you don't fully understand a word during the lecture, look up its meaning in the textbook or ask your instructor for clarification.
- **Pay attention to your instructor's clues about what terms are important.** Some instructors make a habit of writing key vocabulary on the board. Others emphasize new terms and definitions by slowing down, almost dictating, so that you can record definitions in your notebook. Still other instructors may repeat a word and its definition several times. Following each class, compare notes with a classmate to ensure that you haven't missed any key terms.
- **Develop a consistent way of easily identifying new terms and definitions recorded in your notes.** You might (1) circle or draw a box

around each new term, (2) underline each new term in red as you review your notes, or (3) write "def." in the margin near each term and its definition. The particular mark or symbol you use is your choice; the important thing is to find some way to mark definitions for further study.

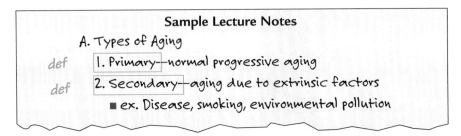

> - **Never stop learning.** In some courses, key vocabulary can be learned in just the first few weeks of class. But in most courses—especially those in the sciences—you will be learning new vocabulary in just about every class, from the first week of the term until the last. Adjust your expectations accordingly!

Textbook Assignments

Some of the terms you'll encounter in your textbooks are words common in everyday usage that have specialized meanings when used in a specific discipline. For example, the word *drive* is commonly used to mean "to control a vehicle," but in psychology it means a biologically based motivation. *Ground,* commonly used to refer to the solid surface on which we stand, means background—the area around and between figures—in the field of visual arts. Other technical terms are used only in a specific subject area. For example, the terms *distal tubing, endodermis,* and *photosynthesis* are unique to biology-related fields.

Most textbooks use various methods to emphasize and explain new terminology. These include:

> - **Typeface variations.** *Italic* type, **boldfaced** type, or **colored print** often identify important terms and/or definitions.
> - **Marginal definitions.** New terms are sometimes defined in the margin of a page next to where they appear in the text.
> - **Key terms lists.** These appear at the beginning or end of each chapter, often with a page number to indicate the page on which the term is defined.
> - **Glossaries.** These comprehensive lists of the terms in the textbook are usually found at the end of the book. They list all the key terms alphabetically, along with their definitions and sometimes the page number on which the term is introduced.

An excellent way to test your vocabulary is to make and use flash cards. Write the word on one side of an index card and the definition on the other side. (Just writing the word and its definition will help you learn them.) Test yourself or a classmate. Many textbook Web sites include electronic flash cards to help you study.

EXERCISE 3 . . . LEARNING ACADEMIC VOCABULARY

In the following chart are five terms used often in sociology courses. Using the online sociology dictionary at http://www.webref.org/ (or any other dictionary of sociology), match each term with its correct definition.

_____	1. altruistic love	a. the role we perform in relation to a particular audience
_____	2. social script	b. nonconformity to social norms
_____	3. lifeboat ethics	c. placing another's happiness before one's own
_____	4. deviance	d. marriage between a man and more than one woman
_____	5. polygyny	e. the idea that providing food to countries in crisis does not address the problems that caused the need for food aid

FOR FURTHER INFORMATION AND STUDY

Chapter 2, "Vocabulary Building," offers additional tips for building your vocabulary. In addition, each reading in this book includes vocabulary exercises to help you master academic vocabulary.

STRATEGY 4

Communicate and Network

In college as in life, success is often determined by your ability to build a support network and to communicate and work with others. Developing strong networks can help you in even the most challenging courses.

In most courses, your classmates and instructors are your most valuable and important resources. Talking with classmates in person or by phone was once the primary form of communication. Now computers and the Internet offer convenient ways of communicating, sharing information, and studying.

Tips for Communicating with Classmates

Here are some tips for communicating electronically with classmates.

- **E-mail.** Try to get the e-mail addresses of some classmates the first week of class. If you miss a class or are confused by an assignment, you can contact a classmate for help. If you are taking an online class, you may be able to communicate directly with your classmates through the course Web site. To make e-mail communication easy, keep your e-mail address simple. For example, FirstName.LastName@gmail.com is much better than h0tRv3rGur1@gmail.com.

- **Instant Messages (IMs) and Text Messages.** Instant messaging allows you to talk back and forth with classmates through your computer, as long as you are both online at the same time. With an IM partner, you can discuss assigned readings, collaborate on a presentation, or quiz each other in preparation for a test. Choose an IM partner who is serious and respectful of your time constraints, and keep the discussion focused on your studies. It is too easy to waste valuable time chatting about nonessentials! Because there are many different chat programs, try one that operates on multiple networks, like Trillian or Meebo, which support AOL Instant Messenger, MSN Messenger, Yahoo! Messenger, Windows Live, Facebook, and/or IRC simultaneously. You'll still need separate accounts with each service, but you'll have fewer programs running.

  In general, text messages (brief messages usually sent from one cell phone to another or from a computer to a cell phone or personal communication device such as an iPhone or Android) are much less effective for substantive communication. Typing on a cell phone can be very time-consuming—which can make it difficult to convey information efficiently. Never answer or talk on a cell phone in class!

- **Online Study Groups.** If everyone in your group takes notes on a computer, sharing them is easy. Instant messages, e-mail, and programs like Skype make it easy to share notes and ideas. Group chat rooms that offer text and audio are often preferable to walking a mile in the rain to participate in a study group. Many of the course management systems now used on college campuses have built-in chat rooms.
- **Professor-Operated Message Boards.** In some courses, your professor may create a message board where class members can post and share information. Remember that anything you post here is public and available for anyone to read. Avoid posting complaints about assignments or the workload. Instead, use the message board positively: get other students' points of view on topics and issues, or share study tips, information sources, or course deadlines.
- **Social Networks.** Many students communicate through social networks such as MySpace or Facebook, posting photographs, status updates, or party announcements. Use these networks with caution, and be sure not to provide information that may jeopardize your safety or security. If you are using a public network, remember that what you post now may hurt you later. Many employers check these networks to learn about potential employees' backgrounds. You would not want a potential employer to see a photo of you in embarrassing or inappropriate poses, for example.

  While social networks are often used for nonacademic purposes, they can be quite useful in building a network. At some schools, students list all their current and past classes on Facebook; this allows them to create a support community. A freshman can ask a junior for tips on how to succeed in the course, and friendships developed through Facebook in this way have led to many job offers!

Tips for Communicating with Instructors

The best way to communicate with instructors is in person, before or after class or during their office hours. But many instructors now make themselves available through e-mail and other electronic means.

- **E-mail.** Most instructors give students an e-mail address at which to contact them. You can generally find the instructor's e-mail on the course syllabus. Some professors check their e-mail several times a day; others may check it as little as once a week. Until you are certain an instructor checks e-mail frequently, do not e-mail time-sensitive questions or information.

  Although e-mail is more informal than other types of writing, use a more formal level of communication with professors than you would with friends. Use correct grammar, spelling, and punctuation; avoid slang. Try to keep your e-mails short and focused; get to the point quickly. Do not be overly familiar, and don't send attachments or pictures unless requested. Some professors won't discuss grades or other personal information over e-mail. And an e-mail should never be a substitute for attending class.

- **Phone.** Be cautious with professors' phone numbers, and always ask about appropriate calling times. It's OK to call an office number at two A.M., but not a home number. If an instructor has provided a cell phone number, do not text him or her without permission.
- **Instant Messages (IMs).** Most professors do not communicate with students via instant messages. Online courses can be the exception; instructors and students may communicate in real time via IMs and chat rooms. If you have an instructor who allows IMs outside of class time, treat his or her screen name as you would a home phone number. Do not make it available in any public forum unless you have permission to do so.

The culture of the Internet has made many people expect immediate responses to their e-mails or messages. Be aware that most instructors are not "on call" 24 hours a day, so your messages may go unanswered longer than you would like. Plan accordingly: don't wait until the last minute to ask important questions or get essential information.

EXERCISE 4 . . . COMMUNICATION SKILLS

Suppose you are preparing for an exam that will take place next week. You have decided to assemble a study group of five students. You have identified five possible ways of getting together to study:

- Meeting at the library for a two-hour study session
- Sitting in front of your computers with Skype
- Texting each other on your cell phones
- Setting up a chat room that you all attend
- Starting an e-mail chain in which one person asks a question and everyone else answers

What are the pros and cons of each method?

FOR FURTHER INFORMATION AND STUDY

Chapter 12 of this text provides additional tips for effective communication via readings from the Communication and Speech disciplines.

STRATEGY 5

Demonstrate Academic Integrity

Academic integrity is a code of honest and ethical academic conduct. It applies to both students and instructors, and it means:

- Doing your own work,
- Not representing the work of others as your own, and
- Conducting yourself in class in a serious, respectful manner.

Cheating

There are many forms of cheating—some obvious, some subtle. Obvious forms of cheating include sharing homework assignments, buying term papers online, exchanging information with other students during exams, or getting answers from students who've taken the class before you. Less obvious, but still very serious, forms of cheating include (but are not limited to):

- Using unauthorized notes during an exam
- Changing exam answers after grading and requesting regrading
- Falsifying or making up results for a lab report
- Submitting the same essay or paper for more than one course without instructor authorization
- Not following rules on take-home exams
- Using someone else's work or ideas as if they are your own (plagiarism)

Most colleges have very strict anticheating policies. Getting caught cheating just once can cause you to fail a course. In some cases, college officials may ask cheaters to leave the school entirely.

Plagiarism

Plagiarism means borrowing someone else's ideas or exact words without giving that person credit. If you take information about Frank Lloyd Wright's architecture from a reference source (such as an encyclopedia, scholarly journal, or Web source) but do not specifically indicate where you found it, you have plagiarized. If you take the six-word phrase "Peterson, the vengeful, despicable drug czar" from an online news article on the war on drugs, you have plagiarized.

Plagiarism can be intentional (planned) or unintentional (done by accident or oversight). Either way, it carries the same academic penalty—failing the course or dismissal from the college. If you buy a paper from an Internet site or copy and paste a section from a Web site into your paper, your plagiarism is intentional. If your essay or paper uses the exact same words as something that has been previously published and does not enclose those words in quotation marks, your plagiarism is unintentional.

Here are some guidelines to help you understand exactly what constitutes plagiarism.

WHAT IS PLAGIARISM?

- **Plagiarism** is the use of another person's words without crediting that person.
- **Plagiarism** is using another person's theory, opinion, or idea without listing the source of that information.
- **Plagiarism** results when another person's exact words are not placed inside quotation marks. Both the quotation marks and a citation (reference) to the original source are required.
- Paraphrasing (rewording) another person's ideas or words without credit is **plagiarism.**
- Using facts, data, graphs, and charts without stating their source(s) is **plagiarism.**
- Using commonly known facts or information is **not plagiarism,** and you need not provide a source for such information. For example, the fact that Neil Armstrong set foot on the moon in 1969 is widely known and does not require documentation.

To avoid plagiarism, do the following:

- **Use quotation marks.** When you take notes from any published or Internet source, place anything you copy directly in quotation marks.
- **Separate your ideas from those of the sources you use.** As you read and take notes, separate your ideas from ideas taken from the sources you are consulting. You might use different colors of ink or different sections of a notebook page for each. Separating ideas this way will prevent you from mistakenly presenting other people's ideas as your own.
- **Keep track of all the sources you use,** clearly identifying where each idea comes from.
- **When paraphrasing someone else's words, change as many words as possible and try to organize them differently.** Be sure to credit the original source of the information.
- **Write paraphrases without looking at the original text** so that you rephrase information using your own words.
- **When writing an essay or paper, use quotation marks to designate exact quotations.**
- **Use citations to indicate the source of quotations and all information and ideas that are not your own.** A **citation** is a parenthetical notation referring to a complete list of sources provided at the end of the paper. (For more information on citation, see "Documentation Guides" in Strategy #2, page 7.)

Avoiding Cyberplagiarism

Cyberplagiarism is a specific type of plagiarism. It involves using information from the Internet without giving credit to the Web site that posted the information. It is also called *cut-and-paste plagiarism,* due to the ease of copying something from an Internet document and pasting it into an essay or paper. Cyberplagiarism can also refer to buying prewritten papers from the Internet and submitting them as your own work. Because many instructors have access to Web sites that can easily identify shared or purchased papers, they can easily identify plagiarism.

Use the following suggestions to avoid unintentional cyberplagiarism.

- **If you cut and paste information from an Internet source into your notes, add quotation marks at the beginning and end of the excerpt.** Also record the author's name, the name of the Web site or page, the date you accessed the material, and the exact URL (no matter how long it is). Consult a documentation manual for details on how to format your sources and citations.
- **Keep source information for *all* the information you have taken from the Internet** regardless of whether it takes the form of direct quotes, paraphrases, facts, opinions, ideas, theory, data, or summaries of someone else's ideas.
- **Never copy and paste directly from a Web site into your essay or paper** without enclosing the words in quotation marks and listing the source.

As you encounter new disciplines, you may ask yourself, "How can I possibly write a paper without using someone else's ideas? I don't know enough about the subject!" The good news is that it is perfectly acceptable to use other people's ideas in your research and writing. The key thing to remember is that you must *credit* all information taken from any published or Internet source, and you must provide a specific citation for the publication from which you took your information. Identifying your sources serves two important purposes. First, it credits the person who originally wrote the material or thought of the idea. Second, it helps those who want to explore the subject further locate the sources you've used.

EXERCISE 5 . . . AVOIDING PLAGIARISM

Read the following passage from the sociology textbook *Sociology for the Twenty-First Century* by Tim Curry, Robert Jiobu, and Kent Schwirian. Place a check mark next to each statement that follows that is an example of plagiarism.

Mexican Americans. Currently, Mexican Americans are the second-largest racial or ethnic minority group in the United States, but within two decades they will be the largest group. Their numbers will swell as a result of continual immigration from Mexico and the relatively high Mexican birth rate. Mexican Americans are one of the oldest racial-ethnic groups in the United States. Under the terms of the treaty ending the Mexican-American War in 1848, Mexicans living in territories acquired by the United States could remain there and be treated as American citizens. Those who did stay became known as "Californios," "Tejanos," or "Hispanos."

_____ a. Mexican Americans are the second-largest minority in the United States. Their number grows as more people immigrate from Mexico.

_____ b. After the Mexican-American War, those Mexicans living in territories owned by the United States became American citizens and were known as Hispanos, Californios, or Tejanos (Curry, Jiobu, and Schwirian, 207).

_____ c. "Mexican Americans are one of the oldest racial-ethnic groups in the United States."

_____ d. The Mexican-American War ended in 1848.

FOR FURTHER INFORMATION AND STUDY

As you work through this textbook, note how for each reading selection specific information is provided regarding the author and the publication from which it was taken. The "Credits" at the end of the book are the equivalent of the "Works Cited" page in an academic essay or paper.

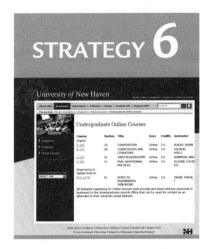

STRATEGY 6

Become Familiar with Online Courses

Many colleges now offer students the opportunity to take online courses. Rather than attending class in person, students complete all or most of the course requirements electronically. Some of these courses are "hybrid courses," a mixture of occasional trips to campus with a strong online component.

In an online course, instructors post reading assignments, sponsor and monitor discussions, and interact with individual students by e-mail, instant messages, or chat rooms. Some online classes are conducted in **real time,** meaning that the instructor and students are online together at given times. Other classes permit students to work independently, choosing the times they want to participate, work, and study.

Many online courses make use of sophisticated electronic systems, such as BlackBoard or WebCT. These **course management systems** allow the instructor to control the course, set deadlines, post announcements, provide specific resources and assignments, and give exams. They also allow students to submit assignments, organize discussion groups, send e-mail, and post announcements. Many of these systems also provide additional resources for student learning, such as test-yourself quizzes, electronic tutorials, and electronic flash cards.

While online courses may seem easy, they require a great deal of self-discipline and the ability to work alone. Use the following tips to maximize your success in online courses.

1. **Avoid taking online courses your first year of college.** Your first year of college is likely to be transitional. You'll go from a world in which you're very comfortable (especially if you go to college right after high school) to one in which you are expected to manage your own education. Attending traditional on-campus classes makes it easier to learn what is expected in college. Once you have learned how to manage your time and workload, you will be better prepared to take online courses.

2. **Take online courses for distribution requirements or other courses not required for your major.** While scheduling concerns may require you to take online courses for your major, it is better to attend majors courses in person. Your major is your area of specialty, and the benefits of being on campus for these courses are strong. You'll forge a stronger relationship with your instructors and network live with other students, which can help you when you begin looking for a job in your field.

3. **Read, read, read.** Whether you attend a class on campus or take an online course, reading is your primary source of information. In fact, the reading requirements for an online course may be heavier than for a lecture course, simply because your professor isn't physically present to reinforce textbook concepts. If you aren't a strong reader or need personal contact with instructors and other students, online courses may not be appropriate for you.

4. **Keep up with the work and meet all due dates.** Most students who fail online courses do so because they fall hopelessly behind with the required reading assignments and cannot catch up. The course's home page usually provides a list of what is due and when. Due dates for papers and other assignments are not flexible just because the course is online. If the course home page indicates that a paper is due on March 15th, be sure to submit that paper no later than March 15th.

5. **Treat your online course exactly as you would treat other courses.** Prepare a work/study schedule and follow it, just as you would for any other class.

6. **Focus.** Turn off music, your cell phone, instant messaging, and e-mail.

7. **Make use of optional resources.** With online courses, consider the computer your study partner. Use the resources provided by the textbook's Web site or the course's home page to help you learn and quiz yourself. Take advantage of built-in learning aids such as chapter quizzes and test reviews, even if your instructor does not officially assign them.

8. **Take screen breaks.** Your eyes can become tired and dry if you spend hours staring at a computer screen. To keep yourself alert, take occasional breaks from the screen. Use this time to have a healthy snack or to work with the printed textbook. If you are using an e-book, you may find it helpful to print out important pages and work with those instead.

USING COURSE MANAGEMENT WEB SITES

When using a course management Web site, be sure you do not submit materials until you have finalized them. Once you click "send," your work is submitted. Take the time to be sure your work is top quality and does not need further revision.

Make sure you're using the latest version of your Web browser and have the most recent plug-ins for Quicktime, Flash, Adobe Reader, and anything else the site requires. (Usually, links will be provided to safe, reliable Web sites where these plug-ins can be downloaded and installed.) While most course management Web sites work with Firefox and Safari, some are still Internet Explorer–only. Be sure you use the recommended browser.

Be cautious about using real-time instant messages or other chat features included with the system. It is easy to get distracted from course materials if you are chatting or socializing with friends.

Finally, keep backups of all your work. Most course management systems are reliable, but they can be prone to technological glitches. Save a copy of your work on your own computer or on a flash drive. Write down the system's technical support phone number and e-mail in a safe place, or store this information in your cell phone. Don't hesitate to contact tech support if you need it. Most calls to tech support involve lost usernames and passwords, so be sure to keep track of that information.

EXERCISE 6 . . . WORKING WITH ONLINE COURSES

The best way to understand the demands of an online course is to talk to other students who've taken them. At the student center or some other location, try to find students who've taken an online class and ask them about their experiences. What do they see as the pros and cons of online courses? Report your findings to a small group or to the class.

FOR FURTHER INFORMATION AND STUDY

A relevant Web site or Web search for each reading in this book is included as part "K" following the reading. Be sure to check out the additional resources offered by these sites.

STRATEGY **7**

Develop and Use New Study Resources

While print textbooks, instructor handouts, and print library sources are still important primary sources of information, you also need to be familiar with newer information delivery systems, including e-books, online class notes, and online information sources.

Reading E-books. E-books are textbooks that you can purchase in electronic form. E-books have one major advantage—they are usually cheaper than print textbooks. They are also convenient, portable via computer, and much lighter than traditional textbooks. However, they do have their drawbacks. Some can be difficult to read outdoors on a sunny day, and most are sold through a subscription model. This means that you have access to the content for a limited period of time (usually one semester), after which the content disappears. If you need the textbook to serve as a reference in later courses or your career, it may be better to purchase the printed textbook. Finally, reading e-books can be tough on the eyes, though some new e-book readers allow you to increase the size of the type or adjust the screen contrast.

Here are some suggestions for reading and using e-books:

- **Use the search function.** If the e-book is in PDF format, you can use the search function to find useful information (such as key terms) not only in the chapter you're currently studying, but also elsewhere in the text.
- **Experiment with the toolbar.** Many e-books have premium features that may come in handy, such as the ability to highlight, type notes in the margin, and click on key terms for their definitions. Use whichever tools work with your personal learning goals and styles.
- **Sometimes paper is just better for the task at hand.** Feel free to print out what you need.

Reading/Using Online Notes

Some instructors post online notes on their personal Web sites. The notes may be guides to upcoming lectures, summaries of previous lectures, or Microsoft PowerPoint presentations they used in their lectures. All of these resources are useful because they identify what the instructor feels is important and necessary to learn. Here are a few tips for reading and using online notes.

1. **Do not skip the lecture and rely only on online notes.** Online notes are intended as an outline or summary of a particular course or lecture. They are a tool for review, not a substitute for the full lecture. Missing a lecture also means missing the class discussion, one of the best ways to understand new concepts.

2. **Do not use online notes as a substitute for taking your own notes in class.** Lectures often cover different aspects of the material and go into greater detail than the notes do. In addition, because notes are often prepared *prior* to class, they will not always include the answers to questions that come up in class.

3. **Devise a system for placing your own notes beside the online notes.** Use a split screen or a different color to add your notes to the online notes. If you are annotating a PowerPoint presentation, print the slides and write in the white spaces, or type your notes into the "Notes" section at the bottom of each slide.

4. **Test yourself on the content of online notes.** Reading online notes is not enough to ensure that you have learned the material. Unlike notes that you have taken yourself, you have little ownership of them. You have not thought about the material, condensed it, and expressed it in your own words. To learn the material, try to interact with the notes by summarizing, rewriting, reorganizing, or testing yourself on the contents.

Lecture Capture

New **lecture capture** software allows instructors to record their lectures and place them online afterward. While watching recorded lectures, you will not only see and hear your instructor, but also be able to see what has been written on the board. This new technology can be extremely helpful in subject areas that require a lot of board work, such as mathematics, statistics, and the sciences. Because the lectures are captured in real time, you're able to hear all the questions asked by the class, as well as the instructor's answers.

Lecture captures are extremely useful for review sessions. You can "rewind" the video as many times as you like, or watch the same mathematical problem get solved until you understand the solution. Remember, though, that watching a lecture video is mostly a passive process. To get a good grade in the course, you must still do all the reading, complete all the assignments, and participate in class. Like online notes, lecture captures are a helpful review but not a substitute for attending class.

EXERCISE 7 . . . WORKING WITH NEW TECHNOLOGIES

If you haven't seen an e-book, visit the campus library and ask the librarian to demonstrate one for you. What do you see as the benefits of e-books? The drawbacks?

FOR FURTHER INFORMATION AND STUDY

Chapter 16 of this book, "Technology/Computers," offers a series of readings on new and developing technologies, along with a discussion of their benefits and drawbacks.

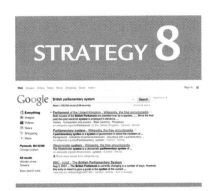

Focus Your Research

STRATEGY 8

Twenty years ago, anyone who conducted research had to sit in a library, sort through a card catalog, and wander the stacks looking for the books and journals they needed. The Internet has changed all that. Today's students can conduct research and work on assignments anywhere that has a computer and an Internet connection.

Although convenient, the Internet contains a vast amount of information that is not organized in any particular way. It becomes important, then, to limit or qualify your information search to yield the best results.

Starting with Google and Wikipedia

While many Internet search engines are available, most information searches today start with Google (http://www.google.com). No matter what your topic, Google is likely to return highly relevant results on the first try, which is what has made this search engine so popular.

It often helps to use Google's "Advanced Search" feature, which is located to the right of the search bar on Google's home page. After clicking on "Advanced Search," type your search term in the box labeled "this exact wording or phrase," then hit the "Advanced Search" button. This type of search allows you to find the phrase that corresponds *exactly* to your search term. For example, if you search for the novelist "Stephen King" on the Google home page without doing an advanced search, you're likely to find information not only about the writer, but also about other people named Stephen and various kings!

Wikipedia (http://www.wikipedia.org) is an online encyclopedia that has no specific author. Rather, anyone is permitted to adjust, change, or add to any entry. For this reason, Wikipedia is almost never acceptable as a source in a term paper or project. However, many of the discussions in Wikipedia come with footnotes that cite credible sources. Clicking on the relevant citations can take you to credible Web sites with good information. The best overall guideline for using Wikipedia is: Use it as a place to start or to develop a general understanding, but be cautious anytime you see a statement labeled "Citation needed." This means that the statement has not been verified by an expert. In general, remember that you need at least two credible sources to confirm any piece of information.

If Google doesn't deliver the results you need, try one of these other search engines:

- Dogpile (http://www.dogpile.com)
- Mamma (http://www.mamma.com)
- Yippy (http://www.yippy.com)

Remember to keep track of every URL you have visited so that you do not engage in unintentional plagiarism. Also remember that it is difficult to get full books online, unless you purchase them. Because many instructors require a combination of sources in term papers—including books, articles, and Web sites—you will likely end up taking a trip to the library at some point.

Focus

In a world of information overload, it's easy to get distracted by all the materials coming at you on the Web. In general, you can ignore the results that appear in the right-hand column of a Google results page. These are paid ads, usually from businesses that are trying to sell a product or service. In other search engines, you will see a list of "sponsored results" at the top or bottom of the results page. *Sponsored results* is another term for *advertisements,* so you can ignore these results, too.

Many Web sites, even those managed by credible information sources, have begun to accept advertisements as well. Often these advertisements are placed at the top, bottom, left, or right of the screen. Ignore the advertisements and focus on the center of the screen, which is where you're likely to find the best information.

Finally, remember that, in general, you are likely to get the best information from Web sites that end in *.edu* (indicating a college or university domain), *.org* (indicating a nonprofit organization), or *.gov* (indicating a government Web site that is home to reliable information and data).

EXERCISE 8 . . . CONDUCTING AN ONLINE SEARCH

List the courses you are taking this term. Conduct a Google search to identify at least three helpful Web sites for each course. How did you find these Web sites? Were they included on the first page of your Google results page, or did you have to dig deeper to find them?

FOR FURTHER INFORMATION AND STUDY

Once you find information on a Web site, be sure to evaluate its purpose, content, and accuracy using the suggestions provided in Chapter 10, "Reading and Evaluating Electronic Resources."

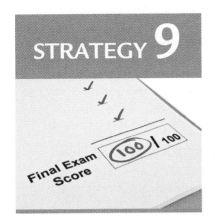

Learn to Take Tests

STRATEGY 9

Quizzes, midterms, and final exams are often the basis on which grades are awarded. But they are also valuable thinking and learning experiences. Quizzes force you to keep up with reading assignments, while longer exams require you to consolidate and integrate concepts and information. Exam questions fall into two general categories: objective (multiple-choice or true/false) and essay exams.

Multiple-Choice and True/False Questions

Here are some tips for answering multiple-choice and true/false questions on exams.

- **Read the directions thoroughly.** The directions may contain crucial information you need to answer the questions correctly.
- **Leave nothing blank.** Even if you guess at the answer, you have nothing to lose.
- **Watch for absolute words such as** *all, none, always,* **and** *never.* Absolute statements tend to be false or incorrect.
- **Read two-part statements carefully in true/false questions.** If both parts are not correct, then the answer must be "false."
- **Read all choices before choosing your answer,** even if you think you have found the correct one. In multiple-choice tests, remember that your job is to choose the *best* answer.
- **Avoid selecting answers that are unfamiliar or that you do not understand.**
- **When you have to guess at an answer, pick the one that seems complete and contains the most information.** Instructors are usually careful to make the best answer completely correct and recognizable. Such a choice often becomes long or detailed.
- **Play the odds.** In a multiple-choice test, if you can eliminate a couple of choices that are absolutely incorrect, you greatly increase your chances of getting the answer right.
- **If two of the answer choices are opposites, it is likely that one of them is the correct answer.**
- **If two similar answer choices are presented, one is likely to be correct.**
- **Don't change answers without a good reason.** When reviewing your answers before you turn in your exam, don't make a change unless you

have a good reason for doing so. Very often your first impressions are correct.

- **Mark any item that contains unfamiliar terminology as false.** If you have studied the material thoroughly, trust that you would recognize as true anything that was part of the course content.
- **When all else fails, it is usually better to guess true rather than false.** It is more difficult for instructors to write plausible false statements than true statements. As a result, many exams have more true items than false.
- **Choose a midrange number.** When a question asks you to select a number, such as a percentage or other statistic, choose a midrange number. Test writers often include choices that are both higher and lower than the correct answer.

Essay Exams

Here are some tips for preparing for and taking essay exams.

- **Determine the likely questions on the exam.** You can do this by reviewing your lecture notes, thinking about the topics your instructor emphasized in class, rereading parts of your textbook, or talking with your classmates about possible questions. Write up the possible questions and practice answering them.
- **Remember that an essay exam requires an essay with a good topic sentence and adequate support.** Before you start writing, quickly outline your answer so that your essay has form and structure.
- **Keep your eye on the time.** Bring a watch to class, and plan how much time you will spend on each question. You must answer each question to get a good grade.
- **Read the directions carefully before you start the exam,** looking for clues that will tell you what the instructor is looking for.
- **If you have a choice of questions, select carefully.** Read all the questions first, and then choose the questions on which you will be able to score the most points.
- **If you don't know the answer, do not leave the page blank; write something.** In attempting to answer the question, you may hit upon some partially correct information. However, the main reason for writing something is to give the instructor an opportunity to give you at least a few points for trying. If you leave a blank page, your instructor has no choice but to give you zero points.

Be sure to begin studying for each major exam at least a week before the test. Research has shown that early preparation leads to higher grades than an all-night cram session the day before the test. Show up for the exam a few minutes early, sit at the front of the room (to minimize distractions and be one of the first to get the exam), and bring the necessary materials (including pens, pencils, and erasers).

EXERCISE 9 . . . ANALYZING TEST QUESTIONS

The following multiple-choice items appeared on a psychology exam. Study each item and use your reasoning skills to eliminate items that seem incorrect. Then, making an educated guess, select the best answer.

_____ 1. If a psychologist were personally to witness the effects of a tornado on the residents of a small town, what technique would she be using?
    a. experimentation
    b. correlational research
    c. observation
    d. none of the above

_____ 2. A case study is a(n)
    a. synonym for a longitudinal study.
    b. comparison of similar events.
    c. study of changes and their effects.
    d. intense investigation of a particular occurrence.

_____ 3. Approximately what percentage of men are color blind?
    a. 1 percent
    b. 10 percent
    c. 99 percent
    d. 100 percent

_____ 4. Jane Goodall has studied the behavior of chimpanzees in their own habitat. She exemplifies a school of psychology that is concerned with
    a. theories.
    b. mental processes.
    c. human behavior.
    d. naturalistic behavior.

FOR FURTHER INFORMATION AND STUDY

Many of the questions in this book are multiple-choice or true/false. Use the techniques you learned here to help you determine the correct answers.

STRATEGY 10

Choose a Major

As pages 2–3 show, each academic discipline has a specialized approach to studying the world. At some point in your college career, usually your second year, you will need to declare a major. Before doing so, it's important to have a sense of what each discipline *is* and what each discipline *does*. For example, many students believe that psychology is the study of the human mind and human problems. Psychology does consider those areas, but it also has very strong biology, anatomy, and physiology components. Many students who take Psych 101 are surprised when they spend three or four weeks studying the brain and spinal column!

If you haven't chosen your major yet, here are some suggestions.

- An old saying goes, "Do what you love, and success will follow." Since you'll be spending a lot of time (and effort) in your major courses, *liking* the field of study is essential.
- Some majors have the reputation for being "practical," such as business, allied health, and science. Other majors are reported to be "impractical," such as sociology and English. Remember that no matter what your major, you will be learning skills that are in demand in the workplace, especially writing skills, critical-thinking skills, and collaboration skills. For many first jobs, employers are looking for enthusiasm, ambition, and a positive attitude. These factors are just as important as, and sometimes more important than, your major.
- If your college allows you to choose a minor, consider doing so. A minor can provide a good balance to your studies, while also making you more desirable in the job market. For example, suppose you are an accounting major but love theater. Spending some of your college credits acting, building sets, and directing plays can be a very nice balance to the hours you'll spend with numbers in the accounting major. In addition, all theaters need accountants to help manage the business, so the two areas of study are not as far apart as they may seem to be.

The following table summarizes some of the key academic majors and what is expected of the people who study them. Use it to help determine if the major you're considering is right for you.

SUBJECT AREA	DISCIPLINES	WHAT IS EXPECTED OF MAJORS IN THESE AREAS?
Business	■ Accounting ■ Finance ■ Management ■ Marketing	■ You should be competitive. ■ You should enjoy teamwork. ■ You should not be afraid of mathematics. ■ You should be willing to develop people skills. ■ You should understand how to save, use, and invest money.
Liberal Arts, Humanities, and Education	■ Art history ■ Communication ■ Education ■ English ■ History	■ You should enjoy reading and writing. ■ You should be able to see the world from multiple perspectives. ■ You should have a good eye for detail, as well as an ability to see the "big picture." ■ You should be able to think critically.
Life and Physical Sciences	■ Allied health ■ Biology ■ Chemistry ■ Physics ■ Geology	■ You should have a high degree of proficiency in math. ■ You must enjoy experimentation, lab work, and fieldwork. ■ You must be a strong team player. ■ You must understand the importance of memorization. ■ You must be patient, with a long-term orientation.
Social Sciences	■ Criminal justice ■ Economics ■ Psychology ■ Sociology	■ You should be able to handle a heavy reading load. ■ You should have an adequate grounding in math. ■ You should be organized and good at keeping records. ■ You should write and communicate effectively. ■ You should be able to think critically and analytically.
Technical and Applied Fields	■ Automotive ■ Child care ■ Computer information systems ■ Hotel and restaurant management ■ HVAC	■ You should enjoy working with your hands. ■ You should like solving problems. ■ You should be comfortable working with instruments, equipment, and tools. ■ You should enjoy meeting and interacting with people.

EXERCISE 10 . . . CONDUCTING RESEARCH INTO YOUR MAJOR

Visit the campus counseling center and ask to take a career aptitude test. What careers do the test results say you are best suited for? Which major and/or minor will best prepare you for those careers? Were the test results surprising to you?

FOR FURTHER INFORMATION AND STUDY

Reading Across the Disciplines is intended to be a buffet . . . it provides you with samples of reading materials from almost every college course to help you determine what you like best and what you might like to major in. Enjoy!

PART ONE

A Handbook for Reading and Thinking in College

1 Active Reading and Thinking Strategies

LEARNING OBJECTIVES

1 Learn to read actively
2 Preview before reading
3 Activate your background knowledge
4 Check your comprehension
5 Strengthen your comprehension

What does it take to do well in biology? In psychology? In history? In business? In answer to these questions, college students are likely to say:

- "Knowing how to study."
- "You have to like the course."
- "Hard work!"
- "Background in the subject area."
- "A good teacher!"

Students seldom mention reading as an essential skill. In a sense, reading is a hidden factor in college success. When you think of college, you think of attending classes and labs, completing assignments, studying for and taking exams, and writing papers. A closer look at these activities, however, reveals that reading is an important part of each.

Reading stays "behind the scenes" because instructors rarely evaluate it directly. Grades are based on production: how well you express your ideas in papers or how well you do on exams. Yet reading is the primary means by which you acquire your ideas and gather information.

Throughout this handbook you will learn numerous ways to use reading as a tool for college success.

1a ACTIVE READING: THE KEY TO ACADEMIC SUCCESS

LEARNING OBJECTIVE 1
Learn to read actively

Reading involves much more than moving your eyes across lines of print, more than recognizing words, and more than reading sentences. Reading is thinking. It is an active process of identifying important ideas and comparing, evaluating, and applying them.

TABLE 1.1 ACTIVE VERSUS PASSIVE READING

ACTIVE READERS . . .	PASSIVE READERS . . .
Tailor their reading to suit each assignment.	Read all assignments the same way.
Analyze the purpose of an assignment.	Read an assignment because it was assigned.
Adjust their speed to suit their purpose.	Read everything at the same speed.
Question ideas in the assignment.	Accept whatever is in print as true.
Compare and connect textbook material with lecture content.	Study lecture notes and the textbook separately.
Skim headings to find out what an assignment is about before beginning to read.	Check the length of an assignment and then begin reading.
Make sure they understand what they are reading as they go along.	Read until the assignment is completed.
Read with pencil in hand, highlighting, jotting notes, and marking key vocabulary.	Read.
Develop personalized strategies that are particularly effective.	Follow routine, standard methods. Read all assignments the same way.

MyReadingLab

To practice active
reading skills, go to

▼ Study Plan
　▼ Reading Skills
　　▼ Active Reading
　　　Strategies

Have you ever gone to a ball game and watched the fans? Most do not sit and watch passively. Instead, they direct the plays, criticize the calls, encourage the players, and reprimand the coach. They care enough to get actively involved in the game. Just like interested fans, active readers get involved. They question, challenge, and criticize, as well as understand. Table 1.1 above contrasts the active strategies of successful readers with the passive ones of less successful readers. Not all strategies will work for everyone. Experiment to discover those that work particularly well for you.

EXERCISE 1-1 ACTIVE READING

Consider each of the following reading assignments. Discuss ways to get actively involved in each assignment.

1. Reading two poems by Maya Angelou for an American literature class.

_____

_____

2. Reading the procedures for your next biology lab.

_____

3. Reading an article in *Newsweek* magazine assigned by your political science instructor in preparation for a class discussion.

_____

1b   PREVIEWING

LEARNING OBJECTIVE 2
Preview before
reading

Previewing is a means of familiarizing yourself with the content and organization of an assignment *before* you read it. Think of previewing as getting a "sneak preview" of what a chapter or reading will be about. You can then read the material more easily and more rapidly.

How to Preview Reading Assignments

Use the following steps to become familiar with the content and organization of a chapter, essay, or article.

1. **Read the title.** The title indicates the topic of the article or chapter; the subtitle suggests the specific focus of, or approach to, the topic.
2. **Check the author and the source of an article and essay.** This information may provide clues about the article's content or focus.
3. **Read the introduction or the first paragraph.** The introduction or first paragraph serves as a lead-in, establishing the overall subject and suggesting how it will be developed.
4. **Read each boldfaced (dark print) heading.** Headings label the contents of each section and announce the major topic covered. If there are no headings, read the first sentence of each paragraph.
5. **Read the first sentence of each paragraph.** This sentence is often the topic sentence, which states the main idea of the paragraph. By reading first sentences, you will encounter most of the key ideas in the article.
6. **Read the first sentence under each major heading.** The first sentence often states the central thought of the section. If the first sentence seems introductory, read the last sentence; often this sentence states or restates the central thought.
7. **Note any typographical aids.** Colored print, boldfaced font, and italics are used to emphasize important terminology and definitions, distinguishing them from the rest of a passage. Material that is numbered 1, 2, 3; lettered a, b, c; or presented in list form is also of special importance.
8. **Note any graphic aids.** Graphs, charts, photographs, and tables often suggest what is important. Be sure to read the captions of photographs and the legends on graphs, charts, or tables.
9. **Read the last paragraph or summary.** This provides a condensed view of the article or chapter, often outlining the key points.
10. **Read quickly any end-of-article or end-of-chapter material.** This might include references, study questions, discussion questions, chapter outlines, or vocabulary lists. If there are study questions, read them through quickly because they tell you what is important to remember in the chapter. If a vocabulary list is included, rapidly skim through it to identify the terms you will be learning as you read.

A section of an interpersonal communication textbook chapter discussing the breakup of a relationship is reprinted here to illustrate how previewing is done. The portions to focus on when previewing are shaded. Read only those portions. After you have finished, test how well your previewing worked by completing Exercise 1-2, "What Did You Learn from Previewing?"

Ending a Relationship

1   Some relationships, of course, do end. Sometimes there is simply not enough to hold the couple together. Sometimes there are problems that cannot be resolved. Sometimes the costs are too high and the rewards too few, or the relationship is recognized as destructive and escape is the only alternative. As a relationship ends, you're confronted with two general issues: (1) how to end the relationship, and (2) how to deal with the inevitable problems that relationship endings cause.

The Strategies of Disengagement

2   When you wish to exit a relationship you need some way of explaining this—to yourself as well as to your partner. You develop a strategy for getting out of a relationship that you no longer find satisfying or profitable. The table (p. 38) identifies five major disengagement strategies. As you read down the table, note that the strategies depend on your goal. For example, you're more likely to remain friends if you use de-escalation than if you use justification or avoidance. You may find it interesting to identify the disengagement strategies you have heard of or used yourself and see how they fit in with these five types.

Dealing with a Breakup

3   Regardless of the specific reason, relationship breakups are difficult to deal with; invariably they cause stress. You're likely to experience high levels of distress over the breakup of a relationship in which you were satisfied, were close to your partner, had dated your partner for a long time, and felt it would not be easy to replace the relationship with another one.

4   Given both the inevitability that some relationships will break up and the importance of such breakups, here are some suggestions to ease the difficulty that is sure to be experienced. These suggestions apply to the termination of any type of relationship—between friends or lovers, through death, separation, or breakup.

Break the Loneliness-Depression Cycle

5   The two most common feelings following the end of a relationship are loneliness and depression. These feelings are significant; treat them seriously. Realize that depression often leads to serious illness. In most cases, fortunately, loneliness and depression are temporary. Depression, for example, usually does not last longer than three or four days. Similarly, the loneliness that follows a breakup is generally linked to this specific situation and will fade when the situation changes. When depression does last, is especially deep, or disturbs your normal functioning, it's time for professional help.

FIVE DISENGAGEMENT STRATEGIES

Think back to relationships that you have tried to dissolve or that your partner tried to dissolve. Did you or your partner use any of the strategies listed here?

STRATEGY	FUNCTION	EXAMPLES
Positive tone	To maintain a positive relationship; to express positive feelings for the other person	I really care for you a great deal but I'm not ready for such an intense relationship.
Negative identity management	To blame the other person for the breakup; to absolve oneself of the blame for the breakup	I can't stand your jealousy, your constant suspicions, your checking up on me. I need my freedom.
Justification	To give reasons for the breakup	I'm going away to college for four years; there's no point in not dating others.
Behavioral de-escalation	To reduce the intensity of the relationship	Avoidance; cut down on phone calls; reduce time spent together, especially time alone.
De-escalation	To reduce the exclusivity and hence the intensity of the relationship	I'm just not ready for so exclusive a relationship. I think we should see other people.

Take Time Out

6   Resist the temptation to jump into a new relationship while the old one is still warm or before a new one can be assessed with some objectivity. At the same time, resist swearing off all relationships. Neither extreme works well.

7   Take time out for yourself. Renew your relationship with yourself. If you were in a long-term relationship, you probably saw yourself as part of a team, as part of a couple. Now get to know yourself as a unique individual, standing alone at present but fully capable of entering a meaningful relationship in the near future.

Bolster Self-Esteem

8   When relationships fail, self-esteem often declines. This seems especially true for those who did not initiate the breakup. You may feel guilty for having caused the breakup or inadequate for not holding on to the relationship. You may feel unwanted and unloved. Your task is to regain the positive self-image needed to function effectively.

9   Recognize, too, that having been in a relationship that failed—even if you view yourself as the main cause of the breakup—does not mean that you are a failure. Neither does it mean that you cannot succeed in a new and different relationship. It does mean that something went wrong with this one relationship. Ideally, it was a failure from which you have learned something important about yourself and about your relationship behavior.

Remove or Avoid Uncomfortable Symbols

10   After any breakup, there are a variety of reminders—photographs, gifts, and letters, for example. Resist the temptation to throw these out. Instead, remove them. Give them to a friend to hold or put them in a closet where you'll not see them. If possible, avoid places you frequented together. These symbols will bring back uncomfortable memories. After you have achieved some emotional distance, you can go back and enjoy these as reminders of a once pleasant relationship. Support for this suggestion comes from research showing that the more vivid your memory of a broken love affair—a memory greatly aided by these relationship symbols—the greater your depression is likely to be.

Seek Support

11   Many people feel they should bear their burdens alone. Men, in particular, have been taught that this is the only "manly" way to handle things. But seeking the support of others is one of the best antidotes to the unhappiness caused when a relationship ends. Tell your friends and family of your situation—in only general terms, if you prefer—and make it clear that you want support. Seek out people who are positive and nurturing. Avoid negative individuals who will paint the world in even darker tones. Make the distinction between seeking support and seeking advice. If you feel you need advice, seek out a professional.

Avoid Repeating Negative Patterns

12   Many people repeat their mistakes. They enter second and third relationships with the same blinders, faulty preconceptions, and unrealistic expectations with which they entered earlier ones. Instead, use the knowledge gained from your failed relationship to prevent repeating the same patterns.

13   At the same time, don't become a prophet of doom. Don't see in every relationship vestiges of the old. Don't jump at the first conflict and say, "Here it goes all over again." Treat the new relationship as the unique relationship it is. Don't evaluate it through past experiences. Use past relationships and experiences as guides, not filters.

—from De Vito, Joseph A. *The Interpersonal Communication Book*, 9e

---

EXERCISE 1-2 WHAT DID YOU LEARN FROM PREVIEWING?

Without referring to the passage, answer each of the following true/false questions.

_____ 1. To end a relationship you need to find a way to explain the breakup to yourself and to your partner.

_____ 2. The breakup of a relationship almost always causes stress.

_____ 3. The two most common feelings following the end of a relationship are anger and fear of desertion.

_____4. After a breakup occurs, it is important to keep letters and photographs as reminders of the relationship at its best.

_____ 5. One mistake people often make after a breakup is to enter into a new relationship too soon.

You probably were able to answer all (or most) of the questions correctly. Previewing, then, does provide you with a great deal of information. If you were to return to the passage from the textbook and read the entire section, you would find it easier to do than if you hadn't previewed it.

Why Previewing Is Effective

Previewing is effective for several reasons:

- **Previewing helps you to make decisions about how you will approach the material.** On the basis of what you discover about the assignment's organization and content, you can select the reading and study strategies that will be most effective.
- **Previewing puts your mind in gear and helps you start thinking about the subject.**
- **Previewing also gives you a mental outline of the chapter's content.** It enables you to see how ideas are connected, and since you know where the author is headed, your reading will be easier than if you had not previewed. Previewing, however, is never a substitute for careful, thorough reading.

EXERCISE 1-3 PREVIEWING

Assume you are taking a sociology course. Your instructor has assigned the following article from the Utne Reader, *a periodical that focuses on current issues reported in a variety of alternative and independent presses. Preview, but do* not *read, the article using the procedure described on p. 36. When you have finished, answer the questions that follow.*

Treating Wounded Soldiers: Polytrauma
Joan O'C. Hamilton

1   Corporal Jason Poole was 17 when he joined the U.S. Marine Corps in 2000. On his third tour of duty in Iraq in 2004, Poole was in a group patrolling near the Syrian border when an improvised explosive device detonated, killing two Marines and an interpreter, and ripping off the top left part of Poole's head. He had surgery to repair

and seal his skull and remained in a coma for almost two months. When he finally awoke to see the excited face of his twin sister, he was frightened and disoriented—although he laughs at the memory of reaching immediately for his head. "I thought I'd have some big Afro after two months," Poole says, "but my head was shaved."

2   Five years after that horrific blast, he sits in a visitors' lounge at the Veterans Affairs Palo Alto Health Care System. He is blind in his left eye, deaf in his left ear. His right side is weak and his right arm heavily scarred. His hands and arms still contain scores of faint, freckle-sized black specks of shrapnel. But many subsequent surgeries have given Poole back a friendly and good-looking face whose scars do not overshadow his easy, bright smile. That in itself is something of a miracle. Not to mention the fact that he has relearned how to speak, how to eat, how to read, how to walk.

Jason Poole at his home in Atherton, California.

What Is Polytrauma?

3   There is no official definition for polytrauma in most dictionaries, although it's easy enough to figure out: *Trauma* is bodily shock or emotional injury; *Poly* is from the ancient Greek for *many*. But at the VA Palo Alto's Ward 7D, the Polytrauma Rehabilitation Center (PRC), the idea of "many" shocks and injuries barely does justice to reality. Palo Alto is one of four PRCs—along with those in Minneapolis, in Tampa, Florida, and in Richmond, Virginia—chartered in 2005 to address what the U.S. military acknowledges is a signature injury of its operations in Afghanistan and Iraq: traumatic brain injury (TBI) in combination with other combat wounds. Service members patrolling debris-strewn streets and crowded areas are vulnerable to booby-trapped roadside bombs that not only hurl shrapnel into and through body tissue at tremendous force and create burns, but also produce a shock wave that can severely damage the brain without any visible sign of injury.

4   Veterans with polytrauma often return with profound physical disfigurements, missing limbs, and serious organ damage. But their TBIs also produce myriad neurological symptoms, which can include amnesia, headaches, dizziness, vision problems, and the inability to concentrate, swallow, speak, or read. They also suffer from insomnia and nightmares. And they battle other common symptoms of

posttraumatic stress disorder, such as a lack of impulse control, flashbacks, and irritability. Together, these issues affect their ability to think, to sleep, to see, to interact normally with others—even to recognize their spouses and children.

5   In March 2009 Pentagon officials reported that more than 350,000 service members that returned from deployment in Iraq and Afghanistan might have suffered some form of brain injury. (This includes mild TBI, or concussion.) The Department of Veterans Affairs estimates that it has treated 8,000 brain injuries in this group. So far about 700 of the most gravely injured have been treated in the four PRCs, almost 200 of them in Palo Alto.

Treatment at the Polytrauma Research Center

6   Patients spend an average of 42 days in Ward 7D. Those who are in a coma spend at least 90 days, most at least six months. During that time, an extraordinary number of specialists work with them. When program director Sandy Lai settles into a chair at her team's biweekly meeting to discuss cases, she joins about 20 team members from physiatry, rehabilitation nursing, blind rehabilitation, neuropsychology, psychology, speech-language pathology, occupational therapy, physical therapy, social work, chaplaincy, nutrition, therapeutic recreation, and prosthetics. Virtually everyone has an opinion and a therapeutic or diagnostic angle on the patients under discussion; they comment on everything from the growing strength in one person's injured leg to how to convince another person to take his medications. All are encouraged to contribute any insight or observation that may help. A speech pathology aide, for example, shares her discovery that one of the patients is particularly interested in basketball. These are the seemingly small but significant insights that can provide a window on motivating someone in a new way.

7   One aspect of these patients' lives that demands a new approach is their youth. Before the wars in Afghanistan and Iraq, the VA facilities mostly were dealing with Vietnam veterans, who are much older, Lai explains. The Afghanistan and Iraq service members "do not want to play bingo as rehabilitation," Lai says. "They have more energy, they are more technology oriented. They even have bigger appetites. We have redesigned the kitchens so they and their families can access food more easily; we have brought in Wii systems and personal computers for their recreational therapy."

Family-Centered Care

8   Because of their youth, these veterans also have families who are far more involved in their care than many older veterans' families, and those families have expectations for recovery that the staff have to both support and manage. Lai, whose background is in family medicine, was instrumental in developing the four PRCs' "family-centered care" philosophy, which from day one strikes a partnership with the injured service members' families, including parents and, often, very young spouses who are overwhelmed by the tragedy. "We always try to focus on the possibilities," Lai says. "When we admit the patient, he or she may have a serious disfigurement. We try to focus on what we know

is possible, that a prosthetic, for example, will eventually restore a normal-looking head to the patient, and that young people's ability to heal is quite amazing."

9   Jason Poole's sunny demeanor masks the lingering consequences of his brain injury. He has no memory of the explosion that changed his life. He sometimes has trouble finding the right words, and it's hard to concentrate when he reads. As we talk, a slight, pale young man who has been standing a bit uncomfortably near us suddenly pulls up a chair and announces, "I find when I join a group, the group stops functioning as it has been."

10   Such jarring comments are not uncommon here. TBI robs many patients of the ability to empathize, read social situations, or interact as expected. Poole's compassion and social skills are intact. He leans toward the anxious young man with genuine concern and reassures him that we're simply in the middle of a conversation we need to finish. No hard feelings, nothing to worry about. In fact, he says, "I'll catch up with you later, man."

—*excerpted from* Stanford *(Nov.–Dec. 2009), the eclectic bimonthly magazine of the Stanford Alumni Association.* www.stanfordmag.org

1. What is the overall subject of this article?

2. What caused Jason Poole's injuries?

3. What is polytrauma?

4. Why do recovery expectations differ for these veterans?

5. On a scale of 1 to 5 (1 = easy, 5 = very difficult), how difficult do you expect the article to be? _____

1c   ACTIVATING BACKGROUND KNOWLEDGE

LEARNING OBJECTIVE 3
Activate your background knowledge

After previewing your assignment, you should take a moment to think about what you already know about the topic. Whatever the topic, you probably know *something* about it: This is your background knowledge. For example, a student was about to read an article titled "Growing Urban Problems" for a sociology class. His first thought was that he knew very little about urban problems because he lived in a rural area. But when he thought of a recent trip to a nearby city, he remembered seeing the homeless people and crowded conditions. This recollection helped him remember reading about drug problems, drive-by shootings, and muggings.

Activating your background knowledge aids your reading in three ways. First, it makes reading easier because you have already thought about the topic. Second, the material is easier to remember because you can connect the new information with what you already know. Third, topics become more interesting if you can link them to your own experiences. Here are some techniques to help you activate your background knowledge.

- **Ask questions, and try to answer them.** If a chapter in your biology textbook titled "Human Diseases" contains headings such as "Infectious diseases," "Sexually transmitted diseases," "Cancer," and "Vascular diseases," you might ask and try to answer such questions as the following: What kinds of infectious diseases have I seen? What caused them? What do I know about preventing cancer and other diseases?
- **Draw on your own experience.** If a chapter in your business textbook is titled "Advertising: Its Purpose and Design," you might think of several ads you have seen and analyze the purpose of each and how it was constructed.
- **Brainstorm.** Write down everything that comes to mind about the topic. Suppose you're about to read a chapter in your sociology textbook on domestic violence. You might list types of violence—child abuse, rape, and so on. You might write questions such as "What causes child abuse?" and "How can it be prevented?" Alternatively, you might list incidents of domestic violence you have heard or read about. Any of these approaches will help to make the topic interesting.

EXERCISE 1-4 ACTIVATING BACKGROUND KNOWLEDGE

Use one of the three strategies listed above to discover what you already know about injuries veterans have sustained in the wars in Iraq and Afghanistan.

1d   CHECKING YOUR COMPREHENSION

LEARNING OBJECTIVE 4
Check your comprehension

What happens when you read material you can understand easily? Does it seem that everything "clicks"? Do ideas seem to fit together and make sense? Is that "click" noticeably absent at other times?

Table 1.2 lists and compares common signals to assist you in checking your comprehension. Not all the signals appear at the same time, and not all the signals work for everyone. But becoming aware of these positive and negative signals will help you gain more control over your reading.

TABLE 1.2 COMPREHENSION SIGNALS

POSITIVE SIGNALS	NEGATIVE SIGNALS
You feel comfortable and have some knowledge about the topic.	The topic is unfamiliar, yet the author assumes you understand it.
You recognize most words or can figure them out from context.	Many words are unfamiliar.
You can express the main ideas in your own words.	You must reread the main ideas and use the author's language to explain them.
You understand why the material was assigned.	You do not know why the material was assigned and cannot explain why it is important.
You read at a regular, comfortable pace.	You often slow down or reread.
You are able to make connections between ideas.	You are unable to detect relationships; the organization is not apparent.
You are able to see where the author is leading.	You feel as if you are struggling to stay with the author and are unable to predict what will follow.
You understand what is important.	Nothing (or everything) seems important.

EXERCISE 1-5 CHECKING YOUR COMPREHENSION

Read the article titled "Treating Wounded Soldiers: Polytrauma" that appears on page 40. Be alert for positive and negative comprehension signals as you read. After reading the article, answer the following questions.

1. On a scale of 1 to 5 (1 = very poor, 5 = excellent), how would you rate your overall comprehension? _____

2. What positive signals did you sense? List them below.

   _____

   _____

   _____

3. What negative signals did you experience, if any? List them below.

   _____

   _____

   _____

4. In which sections was your comprehension strongest? List the paragraph numbers. _____

5. Did you feel at any time that you had lost, or were about to lose, comprehension? If so, go back to that part now. What made it difficult to read?

_____

_____

1e   STRENGTHENING YOUR COMPREHENSION

LEARNING OBJECTIVE 5
Strengthen your
comprehension

Here are some suggestions to follow when you realize you need to strengthen your comprehension.

1. **Analyze the time and place in which you are reading.** If you've been reading or studying for several hours, mental fatigue may be the source of the problem. If you are reading in a place with distractions or interruptions, you might not be able to understand what you're reading.
2. **Rephrase each paragraph in your own words.** You might need to approach complicated material sentence by sentence, expressing each in your own words.
3. **Read aloud sentences or sections that are particularly difficult.** Reading out loud sometimes makes complicated material easier to understand.
4. **Reread difficult or complicated sections.** In fact, at times several readings are appropriate and necessary.
5. **Slow down your reading rate.** On occasion, simply reading more slowly and carefully will provide you with the needed boost in comprehension.
6. **Write questions next to headings.** Refer to your questions frequently and jot down or underline answers.
7. **Write a brief outline of major points.** This will help you see the overall organization and progression of ideas.
8. **Highlight key ideas.** After you've read a section, go back and think about and underline what is important. Underlining forces you to sort out what is important, and this sorting process builds comprehension and recall. (Refer to 8a for suggestions on how to highlight effectively.)
9. **Write notes in the margins.** Explain or rephrase difficult or complicated ideas or sections.
10. **Determine whether you lack background knowledge.** Comprehension is difficult, or at times impossible, if you lack essential information that the writer assumes you have. Suppose you are reading a section of a political science text in which the author describes implications of the balance of

power in the Third World. If you do not understand the concept of balance of power, your comprehension will break down. When you lack background information, take immediate steps to correct the problem:

- Consult other sections of your text, using the glossary and index.
- Obtain a more basic text that reviews fundamental principles and concepts.
- Consult reference materials (encyclopedias, subject or biographical dictionaries).
- Ask your instructor to recommend additional sources, guidebooks, or review texts.

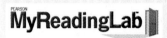

For Further Practice
For support in meeting this chapter's learning objectives, log in to http://www.myreadinglab.com, go to the Study Plan tab, click on **Reading Skills** and choose **Active Reading Skills** from the list of subtopics. Read and view the videos and resources in the Review Materials section, and then complete the Recall, Practice, and Test exercises in the Activities section. You can check your scores and overall progress by using the Gradebook.

Vocabulary Building

LEARNING OBJECTIVES

1 Use context clues

2 Use prefixes, roots, and suffixes

Your vocabulary can be one of your strongest assets or one of your greatest liabilities. It defines and describes you by revealing a great deal about your level of education and your experience. Your vocabulary contributes to that all-important first impression people form when they meet you. A strong vocabulary provides both immediate academic benefits and long-term career effects. This chapter describes two methods of strengthening your vocabulary: using context clues and word parts.

2a   USING CONTEXT CLUES

LEARNING OBJECTIVE 1
Use context clues

Read the following brief paragraph in which several words are missing. Try to figure out the missing words and write them in the blanks.

Rate refers to the _____ at which you speak. If you speak too _____, your listeners will not have time to understand your message. If you speak too _____, your listeners' minds will wander.

Did you insert the word *speed* in the first blank, *fast* in the second blank, and *slowly* in the third blank? Most likely you correctly identified all three missing words. You could tell from the sentence which word to put in. The words around the missing words—the sentence context—gave you clues as to which word would fit and make sense. Such clues are called **context clues.**

While you probably won't find missing words on a printed page, you will often find words that you do not know. Context clues can help you to figure out the meanings of unfamiliar words.

MyReadingLab

To practice
vocabulary skills
go to

▼ Study Plan
    ▼ Reading Skills
        ▼ Vocabulary

Example

Phobias, such as fear of heights, water, or confined spaces, are difficult to eliminate.

From the sentence, you can tell that *phobia* means "fear of specific objects or situations."

Here's another example:

> The couple finally **secured** a table at the popular, crowded restaurant.

You can figure out that *secured* means "got or took ownership of" the table.

There are four types of context clues to look for: (1) definition, (2) example, (3) contrast, and (4) logic of the passage.

Definition Clues

Many times a writer defines a word immediately following its use. The writer may directly define a word by giving a brief definition or a synonym (a word that has the same meaning). Such words and phrases as *means, is, refers to,* and *can be defined as* are often used. Here are some examples:

> **Corona** refers to *the outermost part of the sun's atmosphere.*
>
> A **soliloquy** is *a speech made by a character in a play that reveals his or her thoughts to the audience.*

At other times, rather than formally define the word, a writer may provide you with clues. Punctuation is often used to signal that a definition clue to a word's meaning is to follow. Punctuation also separates the meaning clue from the rest of the sentence. Three types of punctuation—commas, parentheses, and dashes—are used in this way. In the examples below, notice that the meaning clue is separated from the rest of the sentence by punctuation.

1. **Commas**

> *Five-line rhyming poems,* or **limericks,** are among the simplest forms of poetry.
>
> **Equity,** *general principles of fairness and justice,* is used in law when existing laws do not apply or are inadequate.

2. **Parentheses**

> **Lithium** (*an alkali metal*) is so soft it can be cut with a knife.
>
> A leading cause of heart disease is a diet with too much **cholesterol** (*a fatty substance made of carbon, hydrogen, and oxygen*).

3. **Dashes**

> Our country's **gross national product**—*the total market value of its national output of goods and services*—is increasing steadily.
>
> Ancient Egyptians wrote in **hieroglyphics**—*pictures used to represent words.*

Facets—*small flat surfaces at different angles*—bring out the beauty of a diamond.

EXERCISE 2-1 . . . USING DEFINITION CLUES 1

Read each sentence and write a definition or synonym for each boldfaced word or phrase. Use the definition context clue to help you determine word meaning.

1. The judge's **candor**—his sharp, open frankness—shocked the jury.

   _____

2. A **chemical bond** is a strong attractive force that holds two or more atoms together.

   _____

3. Hearing, technically known as **audition,** begins when a sound wave reaches the outer ear.

   _____

4. A **species** is a group of animals or plants that share similar characteristics and are able to interbreed.

   _____

   _____

5. Many diseases have **latent periods,** periods of time between the infection and the first appearance of a symptom.

   _____

EXERCISE 2-2 . . . USING DEFINITION CLUES 2

Read the following paragraphs and use definition clues to help you determine the meaning of each boldfaced word or phrase.

During **adolescence** (the period of growth from childhood to maturity), friendship choices are directed overwhelmingly to other students in the same school. Adolescent students may be involved in an informal network of friendship subsystems that operate primarily within the boundaries of the school world.

Cliques are relatively small, tightly knit groups of friends who spend considerable and often exclusive time with each other. Although cliques are the most common and important friendship structure for adolescents, not everyone belongs to one; in fact, fewer than half of adolescents do. About 30 percent of students are **liaisons**—individuals who have friends from several different cliques but belong to none. The remaining students are **social isolates**—individuals with few friends. Schools also contain **crowds,** which are loose associations of cliques that usually get together on weekends.

—adapted from Rice and Dolgin,
The Adolescent: Development, Relationships, and Culture, pp. 250–251

1. adolescence _____

2. cliques _____

   _____

3. liaisons _____

   _____

4. social isolates _____

5. crowds _____

Example Clues

Writers often include examples that help to explain or clarify a word. Suppose you do not know the meaning of the word *toxic,* and you find it used in the following sentence:

> **Toxic** materials, such as arsenic, asbestos, pesticides, and lead, can cause bodily damage.

This sentence gives four examples of toxic materials. From the examples given, which are all poisonous substances, you could conclude that *toxic* means "poisonous."

Examples

> Perceiving, learning, and thinking are examples of **cognitive** processes.

Cognitive processes, then, are mental processes.

> **Legumes,** such as peas and beans, produce pods.

Legumes, then, are vegetable plants that produce pods.

> Many **pharmaceuticals,** including morphine and penicillin, are not readily available in some countries.

From the examples of morphine and penicillin, you know that pharmaceuticals are drugs.

EXERCISE 2-3 . . . USING EXAMPLE CLUES 1

Read each sentence and write a definition or synonym for each boldfaced word or phrase. Use the example context clue to help you determine word meaning.

1. The child was **reticent** in every respect; she would not speak, refused to answer questions, and avoided looking at anyone.

   _____

2. Instructors provide their students with **feedback** through test grades and comments on papers.

   _____

3. Clothing is available in a variety of **fabrics,** including cotton, wool, polyester, and linen.

   _____

4. **Involuntary reflexes,** like breathing and beating of the heart, are easily measured.

   _____

5. The student had a difficult time distinguishing between **homonyms**— words such as *see* and *sea, wore* and *war,* and *deer* and *dear.*

   _____

EXERCISE 2-4 . . . USING EXAMPLE CLUES 2

Read the following paragraphs and use definition and example clues to help you determine the meaning of each boldfaced word or phrase.

Freshwater lakes have three life zones. The **littoral zone,** nearest to shore, is rich in light and nutrients and supports the most diverse community—from cattails and bulrushes close to shore, to water lilies and algae at the deepest reaches of the zone. Inhabitants include snails, frogs, minnows, snakes, and turtles, as well as two categories of the microscopic organisms called plankton: photosynthetic **phytoplankton,** including bacteria and algae, and nonphotosynthetic **zooplankton,** such as protists and tiny crustaceans.

The **limnetic zone** is the open-water region of a lake where enough light penetrates to support photosynthesis. Inhabitants of the limnetic zone include cyanobacteria, zooplankton, small crustaceans, and fish. Below the limnetic zone lies the **profundal zone,** which is too dark for photosynthesis. This zone is inhabited primarily by decomposers and detritus feeders, such as bacteria, snails, and insect larvae, and by fish that swim freely among the different zones.

—adapted from Audesirk, Audesirk, and Byers, *Life on Earth,* pp. 622–624, 632

1. littoral zone _____

   _____

2. phytoplankton _____

   _____

3. zooplankton _____

   _____

4. limnetic zone _____

   _____

5. profundal zone _____

   _____

Contrast Clues

It is sometimes possible to determine the meaning of an unknown word from a word or phrase in the context that has an opposite meaning. Notice, in the following sentence, how a word opposite in meaning from the boldfaced word provides a clue to its meaning:

> One of the dinner guests **succumbed** to the temptation to have a second piece of cake, but the others resisted.

Although you may not know the meaning of *succumbed*, you know that the one guest who succumbed was different from the others who resisted. The word *but* suggests this. Since the others resisted a second dessert, you can tell that one guest gave in and had a piece. Thus, *succumbed* means the opposite of *resist*; that is, "to give in to."

Examples

> Most of the graduates were **elated,** though a few felt sad and depressed.
> (The opposite of *sad and depressed* is joyful.)

> The old man seemed **morose,** whereas his grandson was very lively.
> (The opposite of *lively* is quiet and sullen.)

> The gentleman was quite **portly,** but his wife was thin.
> (The opposite of *thin* is heavy or fat.)

EXERCISE 2-5 . . . USING CONTRAST CLUES 1

Read each sentence and write a definition or synonym for each boldfaced word. Use the contrast context clue to help you determine word meaning.

1. Some city dwellers are **affluent;** others live in or near poverty.

   _____

2. I am certain that the hotel will hold our reservation; however, if you are **dubious,** call to make sure.

   _____

3. Although most experts **concurred** with the research findings, several strongly disagreed.

   _____

4. The speaker **denounced** certain legal changes while praising other reforms.

   _____

5. When the couple moved into their new home, they **revamped** the kitchen and bathroom but did not change the rest of the rooms.

   _____

EXERCISE 2-6 . . . USING CONTRAST CLUES 2

Read the following paragraph and use contrast clues to help you determine the meaning of each boldfaced word. Consult a dictionary, if necessary.

The Whigs chose General William Henry Harrison to run against President Martin Van Buren in 1840, using a **specious** but effective argument: General Harrison is a plain man of the people who lives in a log cabin. Contrast him with the suave Van Buren, **luxuriating** amid "the Regal Splendor of the President's Palace." Harrison drinks ordinary hard cider with his hog meat and grits, while Van Buren **eschews** plain food in favor of expensive foreign wines and fancy French cuisine. The general's furniture is **unpretentious** and sturdy; the president dines off gold plates and treads on carpets that cost the people $5 a yard. In a country where all are equal, the people will reject an **aristocrat** like Van Buren and put their trust in General Harrison, a simple, brave, honest, public-spirited common man. (In fact, Harrison came from a distinguished family, was well educated and financially comfortable, and certainly did not live in a log cabin.)

—adapted from Carnes and Garraty, *The American Nation,* p. 267

1. specious _____

2. luxuriating _____

3. eschews _____

4. unpretentious _____

5. aristocrat _____

Logic of the Passage Clues

Many times you can figure out the meaning of an unknown word by using logic and reasoning skills. For instance, look at the following sentence:

> Bob is quite **versatile;** he is a good student, a top athlete, an excellent car mechanic, and a gourmet cook.

You can see that Bob is successful at many different types of activities, and you could reason that *versatile* means "capable of doing many things competently."

Examples

> When the customer tried to pay with Mexican **pesos,** the clerk explained that the store accepted only U.S. dollars.

Logic tells you that customers pay with money; *pesos,* then, are a type of Mexican currency.

> We had to leave the car and walk up because the **incline** was too steep to drive.

Something that is too steep must be slanted or have a slope; *incline* means a slope.

> Since Reginald was nervous, he brought his rabbit's foot **talisman** with him to the exam.

A rabbit's foot is often thought to be a good luck charm; *talisman* means a good luck charm.

EXERCISE 2-7 . . . USING LOGIC OF THE PASSAGE CLUES 1

Read each sentence and write a definition or synonym for each boldfaced word. Use information provided in the context to help you determine word meaning.

1. The foreign students quickly **assimilated** many aspects of American culture.

_____

2. The legal aid clinic was **subsidized** by city and county funds.

_____

3. When the bank robber reached his **haven,** he breathed a sigh of relief and began to count his money.

_____

4. The teenager was **intimidated** by the presence of a police officer walking the beat and decided not to spray-paint the school wall.

_____

5. If the plan did not work, the colonel had a **contingency** plan ready.

_____

EXERCISE 2-8 . . . USING LOGIC OF THE PASSAGE CLUES 2

Read the following paragraphs and use the logic of the passage clues to help you choose and circle the correct meaning of each boldfaced word or phrase.

The map of the geography of languages is not **static.** The use of some languages is expanding because the speakers of those languages are **diffusing** around the world, are gaining greater power and influence in world affairs, or are winning new **adherents** to their ideas.

For international **discourse,** English is the world's leading **lingua franca,** partly because of its widespread use in science and business. Many multinational corporations have designated English their corporate language, whatever the languages of their home countries might be.

—adapted from Bergman and Renwick, _Introduction to Geography,_ p. 263

_____ 1. static
    a. difficult
    b. unchanging
    c. unfit
    d. unlikely

_____ 2. diffusing
    a. spreading
    b. revealing
    c. being eliminated
    d. causing confusion

_____ 3. adherents
    a. opponents
    b. meanings
    c. supporters
    d. power

_____ 4. discourse
    a. communication
    b. problems
    c. currency exchange
    d. society

_____ 5. lingua franca
    a. international currency
    b. form of negotiation
    c. language held in common by many countries
    d. corporate policy

CONTEXT CLUES

CONTEXT CLUE	HOW TO FIND MEANING	EXAMPLE
Definition	1. Look for words that announce that meanings are to follow (*is, refers to, means*).	Broad, flat noodles that are served with sauce or butter are called **fettucine.**
	2. Look for parentheses, dashes, or commas that set apart synonyms or brief definitions.	Psychologists often wonder whether **stereotypes**—the assumptions we make about what people are like—might be self-fulfilling.
Example	Figure out what the examples have in common. (Peas and beans both are vegetables and both grow in pods.)	Most **condiments,** such as pepper, mustard, and catsup, are used to improve the flavor of foods.
Contrast	Look for a word or phrase that is the opposite in meaning of a word you don't know.	Before their classes in manners, the children were disorderly; after "graduation" they acted with more **decorum.**
Logic of the Passage	Use the rest of the sentence to help you. Pretend the word is a blank line and fill in the blank with a word that makes sense.	On hot, humid afternoons, I often feel **languid.**

<hr>

2b   LEARNING PREFIXES, ROOTS, AND SUFFIXES

LEARNING OBJECTIVE 2
Use prefixes, roots, and suffixes

Suppose that you came across the following sentence in a human anatomy textbook:

> Trichromatic plates are used frequently in the text to illustrate the position of body organs.

If you did not know the meaning of *trichromatic,* how could you determine it? There are no clues in the sentence context. One solution is to look up the word in a dictionary. An easier and faster way is to break the word into parts and analyze the meaning of each part. Many words in the English language are made up of word parts called **prefixes, roots,** and **suffixes.** These word parts have specific meanings that, when added together, can help you determine the meaning of the word as a whole.

The word *trichromatic* can be divided into three parts: its prefix, root, and suffix.

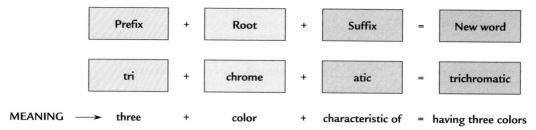

| Prefix | + | Root | + | Suffix | = | New word |

| tri | + | chrome | + | atic | = | trichromatic |

MEANING ⟶ three + color + characteristic of = having three colors

You can see from this analysis that *trichromatic* means "having three colors."

Here are two other examples of words that you can figure out by using prefixes, roots, and suffixes:

> The parents thought the child was **unteachable.**
>
> **un-** = not
> **teach** = help someone learn
> **-able** = able to do something
> **unteachable** = not able to be taught

> The student was a **nonconformist.**
>
> **non-** = not
> **conform** = go along with others
> **-ist** = one who does something
> **nonconformist** = someone who does not go along with others

The first step in using the prefix-root-suffix method is to become familiar with the most commonly used word parts. The prefixes and roots listed in Tables 2.1 and 2.2 (pages 60–62) will give you a good start in determining the meanings of thousands of words without looking them up in the dictionary. Before you begin to use word parts to figure out new words, there are a few things you need to know:

1. **In most cases, a word is built upon at least one root.**
2. **Words can have more than one prefix, root, or suffix.**
    a. Words can be made up of two or more roots (*geo/logy*).
    b. Some words have two prefixes (*in/sub/ordination*).
    c. Some words have two suffixes (*beauti/ful/ly*).
3. **Words do not always have a prefix and a suffix.**
    a. Some words have neither a prefix nor a suffix (*read*).
    b. Others have a suffix but no prefix (*read/ing*).
    c. Others have a prefix but no suffix (*pre/read*).

4. **The spelling of roots may change as they are combined with suffixes.** Some common variations are included in Table 2.2 (p. 62).

5. **Different prefixes, roots, or suffixes may have the same meaning.** For example, the prefixes *bi-, di-,* and *duo-* all mean "two."

6. **Sometimes you may identify a group of letters as a prefix or root but find that it does not carry the meaning of that prefix or root.** For example, the letters *mis* in the word *missile* are part of the root and are not the prefix *mis-,* which means "wrong; bad."

Prefixes

Prefixes appear at the beginnings of many English words. They alter the meaning of the root to which they are connected. For example, if you add the prefix *re-* to the word *read,* the word *reread* is formed, meaning "to read again." If *pre-* is added to the word *reading,* the word *prereading* is formed, meaning "before reading." If the prefix *post-* is added, the word *postreading* is formed, meaning "after reading." Table 2.1 lists 62 common prefixes grouped according to meaning.

EXERCISE 2-9 . . . USING PREFIXES 1

Read each of the following sentences. Use your knowledge of prefixes to fill in the blank and complete the word.

1. A person who speaks two languages is _____ lingual.

2. A letter or number written beneath a line of print is called a _____ script.

3. The new sweater had a snag, and I returned it to the store because it was _____ perfect.

4. The flood damage was permanent and _____ reversible.

5. I was not given the correct date and time; I was _____ informed.

6. People who speak several different languages are _____ lingual.

7. A musical _____ lude was played between the events in the ceremony.

8. I decided the magazine was uninteresting, so I _____ continued my subscription.

9. Merchandise that does not pass factory inspection is considered _____ standard and is sold at a discount.

10. The tuition refund policy approved this week will apply to last year's tuition as well; the policy will be _____ active to January 1 of last year.

TABLE 2.1 COMMON PREFIXES

PREFIX	MEANING	SAMPLE WORD
Prefixes referring to amount or number		
mono-/uni-	one	monocle/unicycle
bi-/di-/du-	two	bimonthly/divorce/duet
tri-	three	triangle
quad-	four	quadrant
quint-/pent-	five	quintet/pentagon
dec-/deci-	ten	decimal
centi-	hundred	centigrade
homo-	same	homogenized
mega-	large	megaphone
milli-	thousand	milligram
micro-	small	microscope
multi-/poly-	many	multipurpose/polygon
nano-	extremely small	nanoplankton
semi-	half	semicircle
equi	equal	equidistant
Prefixes meaning "not" (negative)		
a-	not	asymmetrical
anti-	against	antiwar
contra-/counter-	against, opposite	contradict
dis-	apart, away, not	disagree
in-/il-/ir-/im-	not	incorrect/illogical/irreversible/impossible
mal-	poorly, wrongly	malnourished
mis-	wrongly	misunderstand
non-	not	nonfiction
un-	not	unpopular
pseudo-	false	pseudoscientific
Prefixes giving direction, location, or placement		
ab-	away	absent
ad-	toward	adhesive
ante-/pre-	before	antecedent/premarital
circum-/peri-	around	circumference/perimeter

(continued on next page)

(continued from preceding page)

PREFIX	MEANING	SAMPLE WORD
com-/col-/con-	with, together	compile/collide/convene
de-	away, from	depart
dia-	through	diameter
ex-/extra-	from, out of, former	ex-wife/extramarital
hyper-	over, excessive	hyperactive
hypo-	below, beneath	hypodermic
inter-	between	interpersonal
intro-/intra-/in-	within, into, in	introduction
post-	after	posttest
pre-	before	preview
re-	back, again	review
retro-	backward	retrospect
sub-	under, below	submarine
super-	above, extra	supercharge
tele-	far	telescope
trans-	cross, over	transcontinental

EXERCISE 2-10 . . . USING PREFIXES 2

Read the following paragraph and choose the correct prefix from the box below to fill in the blank next to each boldfaced word part. One prefix will not be used.

multi	uni	pseudo
tri	bi	sub

Neurons, or nerve cells, can be classified structurally according to the number of axons and dendrites that project from the cell body. (1) _____ **polar** neurons have a single projection from the cell body and are rare in humans. (2) _____ **polar** neurons have two projections, an axon and a dendrite, extending from the cell body. Other sensory neurons are (3) _____ **unipolar** neurons, a (4) _____ **class** of bipolar neurons. Although only one projection seems to extend from the cell body of this type of neuron, there are actually two projections that extend in opposite directions. (5) _____ **polar** neurons, the most common neurons, have multiple projections from the cell body; one projection is an axon, all the others are dendrites.

—adapted from Germann and Stanfield, *Principles of Human Physiology*, p. 174

TABLE 2.2 COMMON ROOTS

COMMON ROOT	MEANING	SAMPLE WORD
anthropo	human being	anthropology
archaeo	ancient or past	archeology
aster/astro	star	astronaut
aud/audit	hear	audible
bene	good, well	benefit
bio	life	biology
cap	take, seize	captive
cardi	heart	cardiology
chron(o)	time	chronology
corp	body	corpse
cred	believe	incredible
dict/dic	tell, say	predict
duc/duct	lead	introduce
eco	earth	ecological
fact/fac	make, do	factory
fem	female	feminine
gen	create	generate
geo	earth	geophysics
graph	write	telegraph
gyneco	woman	gynecology
log/logo/logy	study, thought	psychology
mit/miss	send	permit/dismiss
mort/mor	die, death	immortal
neuro	nerve	neurology
path	feeling	sympathy
phono	sound, voice	telephone
photo	light	photosensitive
port	carry	transport
pulmo	lungs	pulmonary
scop	see	microscope
scrib/script	write	inscription

(continued on next page)

(continued from preceding page)

COMMON ROOT	MEANING	SAMPLE WORD
sen/sent	feel	insensitive
spec/spic/spect	look, see	retrospect
tend/tent/tens	stretch or strain	tension
terr/terre	land, earth	territory
theo	god	theology
ven/vent	come	convention
vert/vers	turn	invert
vis/vid	see	invisible/video
voc	call	vocation

Roots

Roots carry the basic or core meaning of a word. Hundreds of root words are used to build words in the English language. Forty of the most common and most useful are listed in Table 2.2. Knowledge of the meanings of these roots will enable you to unlock the meanings of many words. For example, if you know that the root *dic/dict* means "tell or say," then you have a clue to the meanings of such words as *dictate* (to speak for someone to write down), *diction* (wording or manner of speaking), or *dictionary* (book that "tells" what words mean).

EXERCISE 2-11 . . . USING ROOTS 1

Use the list of common roots in Table 2.2 to determine the meanings of the following words. Write a brief definition or synonym for each, checking a dictionary if necessary.

1. photocopy

_____

2. visibility

_____

3. credentials

_____

4. speculate

_____

5. terrain

_____

6. audition

_____

7. astrophysics

_____

8. chronicle

_____

9. autograph

_____

EXERCISE 2-12 . . . USING ROOTS 2

Read the following paragraph and choose the correct root from the box below to fill in the blank next to each boldfaced word part. One root will not be used.

graph	scope	mit
astro	photo	logy

You might think that the easiest way to discover extrasolar planets, or planets around other stars, would be simply to (1) _____ **graph** them through a powerful (2) **tele** _____. Unfortunately, current observational (3) **techno** _____ cannot produce such images. The primary problem arises from the fact that any light that an orbiting planet might (4) **trans** _____ would be overwhelmed by light from the star it orbits. For example, a Sun-like star would be a *billion times* brighter than the reflected light from an Earth-like planet. Because even the best telescopes blur the light from stars at least a little, finding the small blip of planetary light amid the glare of scattered starlight would be very difficult. For now, (5) _____ **nomers** must rely on techniques that observe the star itself to find indirect evidence of planets.

—adapted from Bennett, Donahue, Schneider, and Voit,
The Cosmic Perspective, p. 218

Suffixes

Suffixes are word endings that often change the tense and/or part of speech of a word. For example, adding the suffix *-y* to the noun *cloud* forms the adjective *cloudy*. Accompanying the change in part of speech is a shift in meaning (*cloudy* means "resembling clouds; overcast with clouds; dimmed or dulled as if by clouds").

Often, several different words can be formed from a single root word by adding different suffixes. If you know the meaning of the root word and the ways in which different suffixes affect the meaning of the root word, you will be able to figure out a word's meaning when a suffix is added. A list of common suffixes and their meanings appears in Table 2.3.

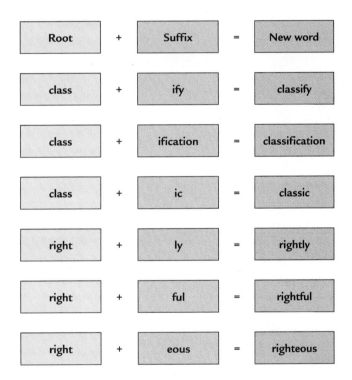

You can expand your vocabulary by learning the variations in meaning that occur when suffixes are added to words you already know. When you find a word that you do not know, look for the root. Then, using the sentence the word is in, figure out what the word means with the suffix added. Occasionally you may find that the spelling of the root word has been changed. For instance, a final *e* may be dropped, a final consonant may be doubled, or a final *y* may be changed to *i*. Consider the possibility of such changes when trying to identify the root word.

TABLE 2.3 COMMON SUFFIXES

SUFFIX	SAMPLE WORD
Suffixes that refer to a state, condition, or quality	
-able	touchable
-ance	assistance
-ation	confrontation
-ence	reference
-ible	tangible
-ic	chronic
-ion	discussion
-ish	girlish
-ity	superiority
-ive	permissive
-less	hopeless
-ment	amazement
-ness	kindness
-ous	jealous
-ty	loyalty
-y	creamy
Suffixes that mean "one who"	
-an/-ian	Italian
-ant	participant
-ee	referee
-eer	engineer
-ent	resident
-er	teacher
-ist	activist
-or	advisor
Suffixes that mean "pertaining to or referring to"	
-ac	cardiac
-al	autumnal
-ary	secondary
-hood	brotherhood
-ship	friendship
-ward	homeward

Examples

The article was a **compilation** of facts.

> **root + suffix**

compil(e) + -ation = something that has been compiled, or put together into an orderly form

We were concerned with the **legality** of our decision to change addresses.

> **root + suffix**

legal + -ity = pertaining to legal matters

Our college is one of the most **prestigious** in the state.

> **root + suffix**

prestig(e) + -ous = having prestige or distinction

EXERCISE 2-13 . . . USING SUFFIXES 1

For each of the words listed, add a suffix so that the new word will complete the sentence. Write the new word in the space provided. Check a dictionary if you are unsure of the spelling.

1. converse

   Our phone _____ lasted ten minutes.

2. assist

   The medical _____ labeled the patient's blood samples.

3. qualify

   The job applicant outlined his _____ to the interviewer.

4. intern

   The doctor completed her _____ at Memorial Medical Center.

5. eat

   We did not realize that the blossoms of the plant could be

   _____.

6. audio

   She spoke so softly that her voice was not _____.

7. season

   It is usually very dry in July, but this year it has rained constantly. The weather isn't very _____.

8. permit

   The professor granted her _____ to miss class.

9. instruct

   The lecture on Freud was very _____.

10. remember

    The wealthy businessman donated the building in _____ of his deceased father.

EXERCISE 2-14 . . . USING SUFFIXES 2

Read the following paragraph. For each pair of words in parentheses, underline the word that correctly completes the sentence.

How do new species form? Most evolutionary (1) (**biologists** / biological) believe that the most common source of new species, especially among animals, has been geographic isolation. When an (2) (**impassable** / impassor) barrier physically separates different parts of a population, a new species may result. Such physical separation could occur if, for example, some members of a population of land-dwelling organisms drifted, swam, or flew to a remote (3) (oceany / **oceanic**) island. Populations of water-dwelling organisms might be split when (4) (**geological** / geologist) processes such as volcanism or continental drift create new land barriers that divide previously (5) (**continuous** / continuation) seas or lakes. You can probably imagine many other scenarios that could lead to the geographic subdivision of a population.

—adapted from Audesirk, Audesirk, and Byers, *Life on Earth*, p. 237

SUMMING IT UP

WORD PARTS

WORD PARTS	LOCATION	HOW TO USE THEM
Prefixes	Beginnings of words	Notice how the prefix changes the meaning of the root or base word. (How does meaning change when *un-* is added to the word *reliable?*)
Roots	Beginning or middle of words	Use roots to figure out the basic meaning of the word.
Suffixes	Endings of words	Notice how the suffix changes the meaning of the root or base word. (How does meaning change when *-ship* is added to the word *friend?*)

PEARSON
MyReadingLab

For Further Practice

For support in meeting this chapter's learning objectives, log in to http://www.myreadinglab.com, go to the Study Plan tab, click on **Expanding Your Vocabulary** and choose **Vocabulary Development** from the list of subtopics. Read and view the videos and resources in the Review Materials section, and then complete the Recall, Practice, and Test exercises in the Activities section. You can check your scores and overall progress by using the Gradebook.

3 Thesis, Main Ideas, Supporting Details, and Transitions

LEARNING OBJECTIVES

1 Identify the thesis
2 Find main ideas
3 Find implied main ideas
4 Recognize supporting details
5 Recognize transitions

Most articles, essays, and textbook chapters contain numerous ideas. Some are more important than others. As you read, your job is to sort out the important ideas from those that are less important. For exams, your instructors expect that you have discovered and learned what is important in assigned chapters. In class, your instructors expect you to be able to discuss the important ideas from an assignment. In this chapter, you will learn to identify the thesis of a reading assignment and to distinguish main ideas and supporting details. You will also learn about transitions that writers use to link ideas together.

3a   IDENTIFYING THE THESIS

LEARNING OBJECTIVE 1
Identify the thesis

The **thesis** is what the entire reading selection is about. Think of it as the one most important idea that the entire article or assignment is written to explain. In articles and essays the thesis is quite specific and is often stated in one sentence, usually near the beginning of the article. In textbook chapters the thesis of the entire chapter is much more general. Individual sections of the chapter may have more specific theses. A psychology textbook chapter on stress, for example, may have as its thesis that stress can negatively affect us, but there are ways to control it. A section within the chapter may discuss the thesis that there are five main sources of stress. A magazine article on stress in the workplace, because it is much shorter, would have an even more specific thesis. It might, for instance, express the thesis that building strong relationships with coworkers can help to alleviate stress.

Now look again at the article from *Stanford* magazine on the topic of polytrauma that appears on p. 40.

The thesis of this reading is that polytrauma involves numerous physical and emotional injuries. The remainder of the article presents details that explain this thesis.

EXERCISE 3-1 ... IDENTIFYING THESIS STATEMENTS

Underline the thesis statement in each group of sentences.

1. a. Monotheism is a belief in one supreme being.

   b. Polytheism is a belief in more than one supreme being.

   c. Theism is a belief in the existence of a god or gods.

   d. Monotheistic religions include Christianity, Judaism, and Islam.

2. a. Vincent Van Gogh is an internationally known and respected artist.

   b. Van Gogh's art displays an approach to color that was revolutionary.

   c. Van Gogh created seventy paintings in the last two months of his life.

   d. Van Gogh's art is respected for its attention to detail.

3. a. The Individuals with Disability Education Act offers guidelines for inclusive education.

   b. The inclusive theory of education says that children with special needs should be placed in regular classrooms and have services brought to them.

   c. The first movement toward inclusion was mainstreaming—a plan in which children with special needs were placed in regular classrooms for a portion of the day and sent to other classrooms for special services.

   d. Families play an important role in making inclusive education policies work.

4. a. Stress can have a negative effect on friendships and marital relationships.

   b. Stress can affect job performance.

   c. Stress is a pervasive problem in our culture.

   d. Some health problems appear to be stress related.

3b   FINDING STATED MAIN IDEAS

LEARNING OBJECTIVE 2
Find main ideas

A paragraph is a group of related sentences. The sentences are all about one thing, called the **topic.** A paragraph expresses a single idea about that topic. This idea is called the **main idea.** All the other sentences in the paragraph support this main idea. These sentences are called **supporting details.** Not all details in a paragraph are equally important.

MyReadingLab

To practice your skills
identifying main ideas
go to

▼ Study Plan
  ▼ Reading Skills
    ▼ Main Idea

In most paragraphs the main idea is expressed in a single sentence called the **topic sentence.** Occasionally, you will find a paragraph in which the main idea is not expressed in any single sentence. The main idea is **implied;** that is, it is suggested but not directly stated in the paragraph.

You can visualize a paragraph as shown in the accompanying diagram.

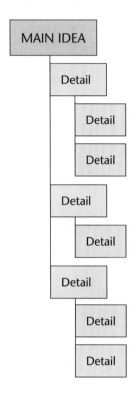

Distinguishing Between General and Specific Ideas

A *general* idea applies to a large number of individual items. The term *television programs* is general because it refers to a large collection of shows—soap operas, sports specials, sitcoms, and so on. A *specific* idea or term is more detailed or particular. It refers to an individual item. The term *reality TV,* for example, is more specific than the word *program.* The title *Survivor* is even more specific.

Examples

General:	Continents	General:	Parts of Speech
Specific:	Asia	Specific:	noun
	Africa		verb
	Australia		adjective

EXERCISE 3-2 . . . IDENTIFYING GENERAL IDEAS

For each list of items, select the choice that best describes that grouping.

_____ 1. dodo bird, tyrannosaurus rex, wooly mammoth, stegosaurus
   a. extinct animals
   b. animals
   c. endangered animals
   d. zoo animals

_____ 2. single-parent, divorced, two-career, married
   a. children
   b. incomes
   c. families
   d. societies

_____ 3. for money, for experience, to meet people
   a. reasons to attend a party
   b. reasons to get a part-time job
   c. reasons to apply for loans
   d. reasons to date

_____ 4. U.S. Constitution, Bill of Rights, Federalist Papers, Twenty-fifth Amendment
   a. policies
   b. historical events
   c. historical documents
   d. party politics

_____ 5. Mars, Saturn, Jupiter, Mercury
   a. asteroids
   b. solar systems
   c. galaxies
   d. planets

Now that you are familiar with the difference between general and specific, you will be able to use these concepts in the rest of the chapter.

Finding the Topic

We have defined a paragraph as a group of related ideas. The sentences are related to one another, and all are about the same person, place, thing, or idea. The common subject or idea is called the **topic**—what the entire paragraph is about. As you read the following paragraph, you will see that its topic is elections.

> Americans elect more people to office than almost any other society. Each even year, when most elections occur, more than 500,000 public officials are elected to school boards, city councils, county offices, state legislatures, state executive positions, the House of Representatives and the Senate, and of course, every fourth year, the presidency. By contrast with other countries, our elections are drawn-out affairs. Campaigns for even the most local office can be protracted over two or three months and cost a considerable amount of money. Presidential campaigns, including the primary season, last for at least ten months, with some candidates beginning to seek support many months and, as noted earlier, even years before the election.
>
> —Baradat, *Understanding American Democracy,* p. 163

Each sentence of this paragraph discusses or describes elections. To identify the topic of a paragraph, then, ask yourself: *"What or who is the paragraph about?"*

EXERCISE 3-3 . . . IDENTIFYING THE TOPIC

After reading each of the following paragraphs, select the choice that best represents the topic of the paragraph.

_____ 1.   Magazines are a channel of communication halfway between newspapers and books. Unlike newspapers or books, however, many of the most influential magazines are difficult or impossible to purchase at newsstands. With their color printing and slick paper (in most cases), magazines have become a showplace for exciting graphics. Until the 1940s most consumer (general) magazines offered a diverse menu of both fiction and nonfiction articles and miscellany such as poetry and short humor selections. With television providing a heavy quotient of entertainment for the American home, many magazines discovered a strong demand for nonfiction articles, their almost exclusive content today.

—Agee, Ault, and Emery, *Introduction to Mass Communication,* p. 153

    a. magazine graphics

    b. magazines

    c. entertainment

    d. communication

_____ 2.   Businesses do not operate in a vacuum, but rather exist within a business environment that includes economic, legal, cultural, and competitive factors. Economic factors affect businesses by influencing what and how many goods and services consumers buy. Laws and regulations have an impact on many activities in a business. Cultural and social factors influence the characteristics of the goods and services sold by businesses. Competition affects what products and services a business offers, and the price it charges.

—Nickerson, *Business and Information Systems*, p. 30

a. business environment

b. economic factors in business

c. business activities

d. competition in business

_____ 3.   The process of becoming hypnotized begins when the people who will be hypnotized find a comfortable body position and become thoroughly relaxed. Without letting their minds wander to other matters, they focus their attention on a specific object or sound, such as a metronome or the hypnotist's voice. Then, based on both what the hypnotherapist expects to occur and actually sees occurring, she or he tells the clients how they will feel as the hypnotic process continues. For instance, the hypnotist may say, "You are feeling completely relaxed" or "Your eyelids are becoming heavy." When people being hypnotized recognize that their feelings match the hypnotist's comments, they are likely to believe that some change is taking place. That belief seems to increase their openness to other statements made by the hypnotist.

—Uba and Huang, *Psychology*, p. 148

a. hypnosis results

b. relaxation

c. hypnosis process

d. suggestion during hypnosis

_____ 4.   Although there were unions in the United States before the American Revolution, they have become major power blocks only in the last 60 years or so. Directly or indirectly, managerial decisions in almost all organizations are now influenced by the effect of unions. Managers in unionized organizations must operate through the union in dealing with their employees instead of acting alone. Decisions affecting employees are made collectively at the bargaining tables and through arbitration, instead of individually by the supervisor when and where the need arises. Wages, hours, and other terms and conditions of employment are largely decided outside of management's sphere of discretion.

—Mosley, Pietri, and Magginson, *Management: Leadership in Action*, p. 317

a. union membership

b. history of unions

c. power of unions

d. establishment of unions

_____ 5. Automated radio has made large gains, as station managers try to reduce expenses by eliminating some of their on-the-air personnel. These stations broadcast packaged taped programs obtained from syndicates, hour after hour, or material delivered by satellite from a central program source. The closely timed tapes contain music and commercials, along with the necessary voice introductions and bridges. They have spaces into which a staff engineer can slip local recorded commercials. By eliminating disc jockeys in this manner, a station keeps its costs down but loses the personal touch and becomes a broadcasting automaton. For example, one leading syndicator, Satellite Music Network, provides more than 625 stations with their choice of seven different 24-hour music formats that include news and live disc jockeys playing records.

—Agee, Ault, and Emery, *Introduction to Mass Communication,* p. 225

a. satellite radio

b. radio costs

c. local radio commercials

d. automated radio

Stated Main Ideas

The **main idea** of a paragraph is what the author wants you to know about the topic. It is the broadest, most important idea that the writer develops throughout the paragraph. The entire paragraph explains, develops, and supports this main idea. A question that will guide you in finding the main idea is *"What key point is the author making about the topic?"* In the paragraph about elections on page 70, the writer's main idea is that elections in the United States are more numerous and more drawn out than in other countries.

Often, but not always, one sentence expresses the main idea. This sentence is called the **topic sentence.**

Finding the Topic Sentence

To find the topic sentence, search for the one general sentence that explains what the writer wants you to know about the topic. A topic sentence is a broad, general statement; the remaining sentences of the paragraph provide details about or explain the topic sentence.

In the following paragraph, the topic is the effects of high temperatures. Read the paragraph to find out what the writer wants you to know about this topic. Look for the one sentence that states this.

Environmental psychologists have also been concerned with the effects that extremely high temperatures have on social interactions, particularly on aggression.

There is a common perception that riots and other more common displays of violent behaviors are more frequent during the long, hot days of summer. This observation is largely supported by research evidence. C. A. Anderson reported on a series of studies showing that violent crimes are more prevalent in hotter quarters of the year and in hotter years, although nonviolent crimes were less affected. Anderson also concluded that differences in crime rates between cities are better predicted by temperature than by social, demographic (age, race, education), and economic variables. Baron and Ransberger point out that riots are most likely to occur when the outside temperature is only moderately high, between about 75° and 90°F. But when temperatures get much above 90°F, energy (even for aggression) becomes rapidly depleted, and rioting is less likely to occur.

—Gerow, *Psychology: An Introduction*, p. 553

The paragraph opens with a statement and then proceeds to explain it by citing research evidence. This first sentence is the topic sentence, and it states the paragraph's main point. High temperatures are associated with aggressive behavior.

Tips for Locating the Topic Sentence.   Here are some tips that will help you find the topic sentence.

1. **Identify the topic.** Figure out the general subject of the entire paragraph. In the preceding sample paragraph, "high temperatures and aggressive behavior" is the topic.
2. **Locate the most general sentence (the topic sentence).** This sentence must be broad enough to include all of the other ideas in the paragraph. The topic sentence in the sample paragraph ("Environmental psychologists have also been concerned with the effects that extremely high temperatures have on social interactions, particularly aggression.") covers all of the other details in the paragraph.

The topic sentence can be located anywhere in the paragraph. However, there are several positions where it is most likely to be found.

Common Positions for the Topic Sentence

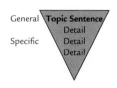

Topic Sentence First.   Most often the topic sentence is placed first in the paragraph. In this type of paragraph, the author first states his or her main point and then explains it.

There is some evidence that colors affect you physiologically. For example, when subjects are exposed to red light respiratory movements increase; exposure to blue decreases respiratory movements. Similarly, eye blinks increase in frequency when eyes are exposed to red light and decrease when exposed to blue. This seems consistent with intuitive feelings about blue being more soothing and red being more arousing. After changing a school's walls from orange and white to blue, the blood pressure of the students decreased while their academic performance improved.

—DeVito, *Interpersonal Communication,* p. 182

Here the writer first states that there is evidence of the physiological effects of color. The rest of the paragraph presents that evidence.

Topic Sentence Last. The second most likely place for a topic sentence to appear is last in the paragraph. When using this arrangement, a writer leads up to the main point and then directly states it at the end.

> Is there a relationship between aspects of one's personality and one's state of physical health? Can psychological evaluations of an individual be used to predict physical as well as psychological disorders? Is there such a thing as a disease-prone personality? Our response is very tentative, and the data are not all supportive, but for the moment we can say yes, there does seem to be a positive correlation between some personality variables and physical health.

—Gerow, *Psychology: An Introduction,* p. 700

In this paragraph, the author ponders the relationship between personality and health and concludes with the paragraph's main point: that they are related.

Topic Sentence in the Middle.   If it is placed neither first nor last, then the topic sentence appears somewhere in the middle of the paragraph. In this arrangement, the sentences before the topic sentence lead up to or introduce the main idea. Those that follow the main idea explain or describe it.

> There are 1,500 species of bacteria and approximately 8,500 species of birds. The carrot family alone has about 3,500 species, and there are 15,000 known species of wild orchids. Clearly, the task of separating various living things into their proper groups is not an easy task. Within the insect family, the problem becomes even more complex. For example, there are about 300,000 species of beetles. In fact, certain species are disappearing from the earth before we can even identify and classify them.

—Wallace, *Biology: The World of Life,* p. 283

In this paragraph, the author first gives several examples of living things for which there are numerous species. Then he states his main point: Separating living things into species is not an easy task. The remainder of the paragraph offers an additional example and provides further information.

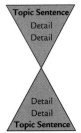

Topic Sentence First and Last.   Occasionally the main idea is stated at the beginning of a paragraph and again at the end, or elsewhere in the paragraph. Writers may use this organization to emphasize an important idea or to explain an idea that needs clarification. At other times, the first and last sentences together express the paragraph's main idea.

Many elderly people have trouble getting the care and treatment they need for ailments. Most hospitals, designed to handle injuries and acute illness that are common to the young, do not have the facilities or personnel to treat the chronic degenerative diseases of the elderly. Many doctors are also ill-prepared to deal with such problems. As Fred Cottrell points out, "There is a widespread feeling among the aged that most doctors are not interested in them and are reluctant to treat people who are as little likely to contribute to the future as the aged are reputed to do." Even with the help of Medicare, the elderly in the United States often have a difficult time getting the health care that they need.

—Coleman and Cressey, *Social Problems*, p. 277

The first and last sentences together explain that many elderly people in the United States have difficulty obtaining needed health care.

EXERCISE 3–4 . . . FINDING TOPIC SENTENCES 1

Underline the topic sentence of each of the following paragraphs.

Paragraph 1

Sociologists have several different ways of defining poverty. *Transitional poverty* is a temporary state that occurs when someone loses a job for a short time. *Marginal poverty* occurs when a person lacks stable employment (for example, if your job is lifeguarding at a pool during the summer season, you might experience marginal poverty when the season ends). The next, more serious level, *residual poverty*, is chronic and multigenerational. A person who experiences *absolute poverty* is so poor that he or she doesn't have resources to survive. *Relative poverty* is a state that occurs when we compare ourselves with those around us.

—adapted from Carl, *Think Sociology*, p. 122

Paragraph 2

The symbols that constitute language are commonly referred to as words—labels that we have assigned to concepts, or our mental representations. When we use the word *chair* as a symbol, we don't use it to label just one specific instance of a chair. We use the word as a symbol to represent our concept of chairs. As symbols, words need not stand for real things in the real world. We have words to describe objects or events that cannot be perceived, such as *ghost* or, for that matter, *mind*. With language we can communicate about owls and pussycats in teacups and a four-dimensional, time-warped hyperspace. Words stand for cognitions, or concepts, and we have a great number of them.

—Gerow, *Psychology: An Introduction*, p. 250

Paragraph 3

Body mass is made up of protoplasm, extracellular fluid, bone, and adipose tissue (body fat). One way to determine the amount of adipose tissue is to measure the whole-body density. After the on-land mass of the body is determined, the underwater body mass is obtained by submerging the person in water. Since water helps support the body by giving it buoyancy, the apparent body mass is less in water. A higher percentage of body fat will make a person more buoyant, causing the underwater mass to be even lower. This occurs because fat has a lower density than the rest of the body.

—Timberlake, *Chemistry,* p. 30

Paragraph 4

Early biologists who studied reflexes, kineses, taxes, and fixed action patterns assumed that these responses are inherited, unlearned, and common to all members of a species. They clearly depend on internal and external factors, but until recently, instinct and learning were considered distinct aspects of behavior. However, in some very clever experiments, Jack Hailman of the University of Wisconsin showed that certain stereotyped behavior patterns require subtle forms of experience for their development. In other words, at least some of the behavior normally called instinct is partly learned.

—Mix, *Biology, The Network of Life,* p. 532

Paragraph 5

With so many people participating in social networking sites and keeping personal blogs, it's increasingly common for a single disgruntled customer to wage war online against a company for poor service or faulty products. Unhappy customers have taken to the Web to complain about broken computers or poor customer service. Individuals may post negative reviews of products on blogs, upload angry videos outlining complaints on YouTube, or join public discussion forums where they can voice their opinion about the good and the bad. In the same way that companies celebrate the viral spread of good news, they must also be on guard for online backlash that can damage a reputation.

—adapted from Ebert and Griffin, *Business Essentials,* p. 161

Paragraph 6

Elections serve a critical function in American society. They make it possible for most political participation to be channeled through the electoral process rather than bubbling up through demonstrations, riots, or revolutions. Elections provide regular access to political power, so that leaders can be replaced without being overthrown. This is possible because elections are almost universally accepted as a fair and free method of selecting political leaders. Furthermore, by choosing who is to lead the country, the people—if they make their choices carefully—can also guide the policy direction of the government.

—adapted from Edwards et al., *Government in America,* p. 306

Paragraph 7

A gunnysack is a large bag, usually made of burlap. As a conflict strategy, gunnysacking refers to the practice of storing up grievances so we may unload them at another time. The immediate occasion for unloading may be relatively simple (or so it might seem at first), such as someone's coming home late without calling.

Instead of arguing about this, the gunnysacker unloads all past grievances. As you probably know from experience, gunnysacking begets gunnysacking. When one person gunnysacks, the other person often reciprocates. Frequently the original problem never gets addressed. Instead, resentment and hostility escalate.

—DeVito, *Human Communication*, p. 217

Paragraph 8

As just about everyone today knows, e-mail has virtually become the standard method of communication in the business world. Most people enjoy its speed, ease and casual nature. But e-mail also has its share of problems and pitfalls, including privacy. Many people assume the contents of their e-mail are private, but there may in fact be any number of people authorized to see it. Some experts have even likened e-mail to postcards sent through U.S. mail: They pass through a lot of hands and before a lot of eyes, and, theoretically, many different people can read them.

—adapted from Ebert and Griffin, *Business Essentials*, p. 64

Paragraph 9

Patrescence, or becoming a father, usually is less socially noted than matrescence. The practice of **couvade** is an interesting exception to this generalization. Couvade refers to "a variety of customs applying to the behavior of fathers during the pregnancies of their wives and during and shortly after the births of their children." The father may take to his bed before, during, or after the delivery. He may also experience pain and exhaustion during and after the delivery. More common is a pattern of couvade that involves a set of prohibitions and prescriptions for male behavior. Couvade occurs in societies where paternal roles in child care are prominent. One interpretation views couvade as one phase of men's participation in parenting: Their good behavior as expectant fathers helps ensure a good delivery for the baby. Another interpretation of couvade is that it offers support for the mother. In Estonia, a folk belief is that a woman's birth pains will be less if her husband helps by taking some of them on himself.

—adapted from Miller, *Cultural Anthropology*, pp. 144–145

Paragraph 10

Everything moves. Even things that appear at rest move. They move relative to the sun and stars. As you're reading this you're moving at about 107,000 kilometers per hour relative to the sun. And you're moving even faster relative to the center of our galaxy. When we discuss the motion of something, we describe motion relative to something else. If you walk down the aisle of a moving bus, your speed relative to the floor of the bus is likely quite different from your speed relative to the road. When we say a racing car reaches a speed of 300 kilometers per hour, we mean relative to the track. Unless stated otherwise, when we discuss the speeds of things in our environment we mean relative to the surface of the earth; motion is relative.

—adapted from Hewitt, *Conceptual Physics*, p. 39

EXERCISE 3-5 . . . FINDING TOPIC SENTENCES 2

Underline the topic sentence of each of the following paragraphs.

Symbols and Superstitions

On the surface, many marketing images have virtually no literal connection to actual products. What does a cowboy have to do with a bit of tobacco rolled into a paper tube? How can a celebrity such as basketball star Michael Jordan enhance the image of a cologne? The meanings we impart to these symbols are largely influenced by our culture, so marketers need to take special care that the symbol they use in a foreign market has the meaning they intended. Even the same product may be used quite differently and take on a different meaning to people. In parts of rural India, for example, the refrigerator is a status symbol, so people want a snazzy-looking one that they can keep in the living room to show off to visitors.

For assistance in understanding how consumers interpret the meanings of symbols, some marketers are turning to a field of study known as **semiotics,** which examines how people assign meanings to symbols. For example, although the American cowboy on packs of Marlboro cigarettes is a well-known symbol of the frontier spirit in many countries, people in Hong Kong see him as a low-status laborer. Philip Morris has to make sure he's always pictured riding a white horse, which is a more positive symbol in that country. Even something as simple as a color takes on very different meanings around the globe. Pepsodent toothpaste found this out when it promised white teeth to people in Southeast Asia, where black or yellow teeth are status symbols.

Marketers also need to be concerned about taboos and superstitions. For example, the Japanese are superstitious about the number four. *Shi,* the word for "four," is also the word for "death," so Tiffany sells glassware and china in sets of five in Japan. In some Arab countries, alcohol and pork are forbidden to Islamic consumers (even stuffed pig toys are taboo), and advertisers may refrain from showing nudity or even the faces of women in photos, which some governments prohibit.

—Solomon and Stuart, *Marketing: Real People, Real Choices,* p. 108

EXERCISE 3-6 . . . FINDING MAIN IDEAS

After reading the following passage, select the choice that best completes each of the statements that follow.

Picking Partners

Just as males and females may find different ways to express emotions themselves, the process of partner selection also shows distinctly different patterns. For both males and females, more than just chemical and psychological processes influence the choice of partners. One of these factors is *proximity,* or being in the same place at the same time. The more you see a person in your hometown, at social gatherings, or at work, the more likely that an interaction will occur. Thus, if you live in New York, you'll probably end up with another New Yorker. If you live in northern Wisconsin, you'll probably end up with another Wisconsinite.

The old adage that "opposites attract" usually isn't true. You also pick a partner based on *similarities* (attitudes, values, intellect, interests). If your potential partner expresses interest or liking, you may react with mutual regard known as *reciprocity*. The more you express interest, the safer it is for someone else to return the regard, and the cycle spirals onward.

Another factor that apparently plays a significant role in selecting a partner is *physical attraction*. Whether such attraction is caused by a chemical reaction or a socially learned behavior, males and females appear to have different attraction criteria. Men tend to select their mates primarily on the basis of youth and physical attractiveness. Although physical attractiveness is an important criterion for women in mate selection, they tend to place higher emphasis on partners who are somewhat older, have good financial prospects, and are dependable and industrious.

—Donatelle, *Health: The Basics,* p. 105

_____ 1. The thesis of the entire selection is
    a. several factors influence choice of partners.
    b. physical attraction is more important to men than for women.
    c. proximity is the key to mate selection.
    d. opposites attract.

_____ 2. The topic sentence of the first paragraph begins with the words
    a. "For both."
    b. "One of these."
    c. "The more."
    d. "Just as."

_____ 3. The topic of the second paragraph is
    a. physical attraction.
    b. interaction.
    c. the old adage.
    d. similarities.

_____ 4. In the second paragraph, the topic sentence begins with the words
    a. "You also pick."
    b. "The more you express."
    c. "If your potential."
    d. "The old adage."

_____ 5. The topic sentence of the third paragraph is the
    a. first sentence.
    b. second sentence.
    c. third sentence.
    d. fourth sentence.

3c   UNDERSTANDING IMPLIED MAIN IDEAS

LEARNING OBJECTIVE 3
Find implied main ideas

MyReadingLab

To practice your skills identifying main ideas go to

▼ Study Plan
 ▼ Reading Skills
  ▼ Main Idea

Study the cartoon below. What main point is it making? Although the cartoonist's message is not directly stated, you were able to figure it out by looking at the details in the cartoon. Just as you figured out the cartoonist's main point, you often have to figure out the implied main ideas of speakers and writers. When an idea is **implied,** it is suggested but not stated outright. Suppose your favorite shirt is missing from your closet and you know that your roommate often borrows your clothes. You might say to your roommate, "If my blue plaid shirt is back in my closet by noon, I'll forget it was missing." This statement does not directly accuse your roommate of borrowing the shirt, but your message is clear—Return my shirt! Your statement implies or suggests to your roommate that he has borrowed the shirt and should return it.

Roadkill

EXERCISE 3-7 . . . UNDERSTANDING IMPLIED MAIN IDEAS

For each of the following statements, select the choice that best explains what the writer is implying or suggesting.

_____ 1. Jane's hair looked as if she just came out of a wind tunnel.

    a. Jane needs a haircut.

    b. Jane's hair is messed up.

    c. Jane needs a hat.

    d. Jane's hair needs coloring.

_____ 2. Dino would not recommend Professor Wright's class to his worst enemy.

    a. Dino likes Professor Wright's class.

    b. Dino dislikes Professor Wright's class.

    c. Professor Wright's class is popular.

    d. Professor Wright's class is unpopular.

_____ 3. The steak was overcooked and tough, the mashed potatoes were cold, the green beans were withered, and the chocolate pie was mushy.

    a. The dinner was tasty.

    b. The dinner was nutritious.

    c. The dinner was prepared poorly.

    d. The dinner was served carelessly.

When trying to figure out the implied main idea in a paragraph, it is important to remember the distinction between general and specific ideas. (see p. 68). You know that a *general* idea applies to many items or ideas, whereas a *specific* idea refers to a particular item. The word *color,* for instance, is general because it refers to many other specific colors—purple, yellow, red, and so forth. The word *shoe* is general because it can apply to many types, such as running shoes, high heels, loafers, and bedroom slippers.

You also know that the main idea of a paragraph is not only its most important point but also its most *general* idea. *Specific* details back up or support the main idea. Although most paragraphs have a topic sentence, some do not. Instead, they contain only details or specifics that, taken together, point to the main idea. The main idea, then, is implied but not directly stated. In such paragraphs you must infer, or reason out, the main idea. This is a process of adding up the details and deciding what they mean together or what main idea they all support or explain.

What general idea do the following specific sentences suggest?

> The doctor kept patients waiting hours for an appointment.
> The doctor was hasty and abrupt when talking with patients.
> The doctor took days to return phone calls from patients.

You probably determined that the doctor was inconsiderate and managed her practice poorly.

What larger, more general idea do the specific details and the accompanying photograph on the next page point to?

> The wind began to howl at over 90 mph.
> A dark gray funnel cloud was visible in the sky.
> Severe storms had been predicted by the weather service.

Together these three details and the photograph suggest that a tornado has devastated the area.

EXERCISE 3-8 . . . WRITING GENERAL IDEAS

For each item, read the specific details. Then select the word or phrase from the box below that best completes the general idea in the sentence that follows. Make sure that each general idea fits all of its specific details. Not all words or phrases in the box will be used.

different factors	genetic	contributes	nonverbal messages
store's image	advertisers	characteristics	
process	problems	dangerous effects	

1. a. Major life catastrophes, such as natural disasters, can cause stress.

   b. Significant life changes, such as the death of a loved one, elevate one's level of stress.

   c. Daily hassles, such as long lines at the drugstore, take their toll on a person's well-being.

   General idea: A number of _____ contribute to stress.

2. a. Humorous commercials catch consumers' attention.

   b. Fear emphasizes negative consequences unless a particular product or service is purchased.

   c. "Sex sells" is a common motto among those who write commercials.

   General idea: _____ use a variety of appeals to sell products.

3. a. Acid rain may aggravate respiratory problems.

   b. Each year millions of trees are destroyed by acid rain.

   c. Acid rain may be hazardous to a pregnant woman's unborn child.

   General idea: Acid rain has _____.

4. a. Facial expressions reveal emotions.

   b. Hand gestures have meanings.

   c. Posture can reveal how a person feels.

   General idea: The body communicates _____.

5. a. The smell of a store can be appealing to shoppers.

   b. Colors can create tension or help shoppers relax.

   c. The type of background music playing in a store creates a distinct impression.

   General idea: Retailers create a _____ to appeal to consumers.

6. a. Creative people are risk takers.

   b. Creative people recognize patterns and make connections easily.

   c. Creative people are self-motivated.

   General idea: A number of different _____ contribute to creativity.

How to Find the Implied Main Ideas in Paragraphs

When a writer leaves his or her main idea unstated, it is up to you to look at the details in the paragraph and figure out the writer's main point. The details, when taken together, will all point to a general and more important idea. Use the following steps as a guide to find implied main ideas:

1. **Find the topic.** As you know from earlier chapters, the *topic* is the general subject of the entire paragraph. Ask yourself: "What is the one thing the author is discussing throughout the paragraph?"

2. **Figure out what is the most important idea the writer wants you to know about that topic.** Look at each detail and decide what larger idea is being explained.

3. **Express this main idea in your own words.** Make sure that the main idea is a reasonable one. Ask yourself: "Does it apply to all of the details in the paragraph?"

Here is a sample paragraph; identify the main idea.

Severe punishment may generate such anxiety in children that they do not learn the lesson the punishment was designed to teach. Moreover, as a reaction to punishment that they regard as unfair, children may avoid punitive parents, who therefore will have fewer opportunities to teach and guide the child. In addition, parents who use physical punishment provide aggressive models. A child who is regularly slapped, spanked, shaken, or shouted at may learn to use these forms of aggression in interactions with peers.

—Newcombe, *Child Development*, p. 354

The topic of this paragraph is punishment. The author's main point is that punishment has negative effects. You can figure out this writer's main idea even though no single sentence states this directly. You can visualize this paragraph as follows:

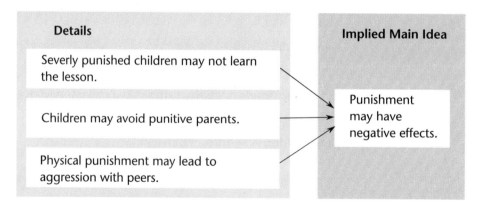

Details	Implied Main Idea
Severly punished children may not learn the lesson.	Punishment may have negative effects.
Children may avoid punitive parents.	
Physical punishment may lead to aggression with peers.	

EXERCISE 3-9 . . . FINDING IMPLIED MAIN IDEAS 1

After reading each of the paragraphs, complete the diagram that follows by filling in the missing information.

Paragraph A

The average American consumer eats 21 pounds of snack foods in a year, but people in the West Central part of the country consume the most (24 pounds per person) whereas those in the Pacific and Southeast regions eat "only" 19 pounds per person. Pretzels are the most popular snack in the mid-Atlantic area, pork rinds are most likely to be eaten in the South, and multigrain chips turn up as a favorite in the West. Not surprisingly, the Hispanic influence in the Southwest has influenced snacking preferences—consumers in that part of the United States eat about 50 percent more tortilla chips than do people elsewhere.

—adapted from Solomon, *Consumer Behavior*, p. 184

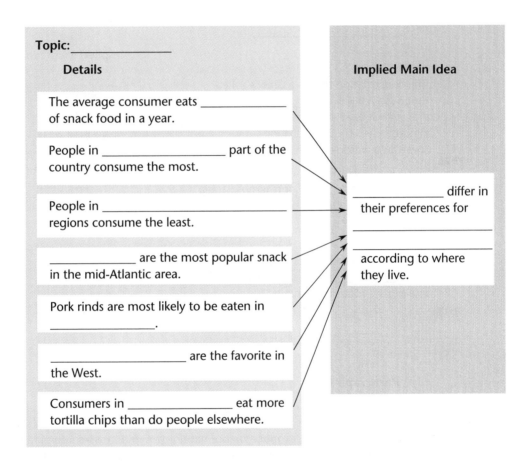

Topic:_____

Details

The average consumer eats _____ of snack food in a year.

People in _____ part of the country consume the most.

People in _____ regions consume the least.

_____ are the most popular snack in the mid-Atlantic area.

Pork rinds are most likely to be eaten in _____.

_____ are the favorite in the West.

Consumers in _____ eat more tortilla chips than do people elsewhere.

Implied Main Idea

_____ differ in their preferences for

_____

_____ according to where they live.

Paragraph B

The constellation [group of stars] that the Greeks named Orion, the hunter, was seen by the ancient Chinese as a supreme warrior called *Shen*. Hindus in ancient India also saw a warrior, called *Skanda*, who rode a peacock. The three stars of Orion's belt were seen as three fishermen in a canoe by Aborigines of northern Australia. As seen from southern California, these three stars climb almost straight up into the sky as they rise in the east, which may explain why the Chemehuevi Indians of the California desert saw them as a line of three sure-footed mountain sheep.

—adapted from Bennett et al., *The Cosmic Perspective*, p. 28

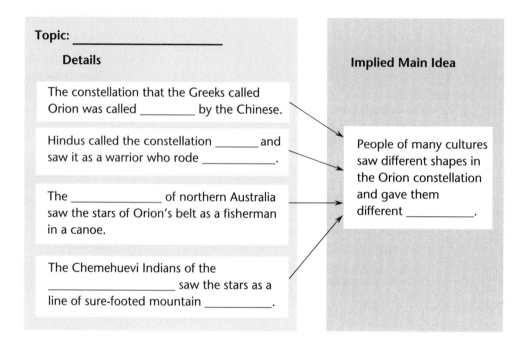

Topic: _____

Details

The constellation that the Greeks called Orion was called _____ by the Chinese.

Hindus called the constellation _____ and saw it as a warrior who rode _____.

The _____ of northern Australia saw the stars of Orion's belt as a fisherman in a canoe.

The Chemehuevi Indians of the _____ saw the stars as a line of sure-footed mountain _____.

Implied Main Idea

People of many cultures saw different shapes in the Orion constellation and gave them different _____.

Paragraph C

More than 30 percent of all food borne illnesses result from unsafe handling of food at home. Among the most basic of precautions are to wash your hands and to wash all produce before eating it. Avoid cross-contamination in the kitchen by using separate cutting boards and utensils for meats and produce. Temperature control is also important; hot foods must be kept hot and cold foods kept cold in order to avoid unchecked bacterial growth. Leftovers need to be eaten within 3 days, and if you're unsure how long something has been sitting in the fridge, don't take chances. When in doubt, throw it out.

—adapted from Donatelle, *Health: The Basics*, p. 280

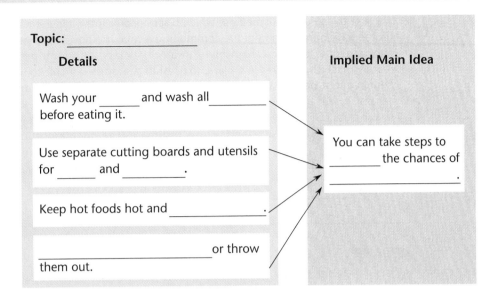

Topic: _____

Details

Wash your _____ and wash all _____ before eating it.

Use separate cutting boards and utensils for _____ and _____ .

Keep hot foods hot and _____ .

_____ or throw them out.

Implied Main Idea

You can take steps to _____ the chances of _____ .

EXERCISE 3-10 . . . FINDING IMPLIED MAIN IDEAS 2

Write a sentence that states the main idea for each of the following paragraphs.

Paragraph 1

During the 1960s, police went from walking "beats" [regular routes] to riding in squad cars. While squad cars provided a faster response to emergency calls, they also changed the nature of social interaction between police officers and the public. Much police work had been highly personal, as officers strolled the sidewalks talking to storekeepers and homeowners, but it became much more impersonal, with less contact between officers and citizens. Since the 1960s, technological advances have provided more elaborate means of communication and surveillance, better-equipped squad cars, and more sophisticated weaponry. Unfortunately criminals have benefited from increased technology as well. This increased technology and other developments have led many city leaders to question contemporary policing practices and some to accentuate the need to reemphasize police–community relations.

—Thompson and Hickey, *Society in Focus*, p. 162

Main idea: _____

_____

Paragraph 2

In order to measure social class standing, sociologists may use the *objective* method, which ranks individuals into classes on the basis of measures such as education, income, and occupational prestige. Sociologists may also use the *reputational* method, which places people into various social classes on the basis of reputation in the community. A third method, *self-identification,* allows people to place themselves in a social class. Although people can readily place themselves in a class, the results are often difficult to interpret. People might be hesitant to call themselves upper-class for fear of appearing snobbish, but at the same time they might be reluctant to call themselves lower-class for fear of being stigmatized. The net result is that the method of self-identification substantially overestimates the middle portion of the class system.

—Curry et al., *Sociology for the 21st Century,* p. 138

Main idea: _____

_____

Paragraph 3

In 1970 the federal government passed the Comprehensive Drug Abuse, Prevention and Control Act (also known as the Controlled Substance Act). That act did not contain a rigid penalty system but rather established only upper bounds for the fines and prison terms to be imposed for offenses. In 1984 the act was amended in order to impose fixed penalties, particularly for dealers. For anyone caught with more than 1 kilogram of heroin, 50 grams of cocaine base, or 1,000 kilograms of marijuana, the applicable penalty was raised to imprisonment from 10 years to life plus a fine of $4 million. A variety of other prison penalties and fines were outlined in that amendment. Another amendment passed in 1988 included the death penalty for "drug kingpins."

—Miller, *Economics Today,* p. 513

Main idea: _____

_____

Paragraph 4

As recently as 20 years ago, textbooks on child psychology seldom devoted more than a few paragraphs to the behaviors of the neonate—the newborn through the first 2 weeks of life. It seemed as if the neonate did not do much worth writing about. Today, most child psychology texts devote substantially more space to discussing the abilities of newborns. It is unlikely that over the past 20 years neonates have gotten smarter or more able. Rather, psychologists have. They have devised new and clever ways of measuring the abilities and capacities of neonates.

—Gerow, *Psychology: An Introduction,* p. 319

Main idea: _____

_____

EXERCISE 3-11 ... FINDING IMPLIED MAIN IDEAS 3

After reading each of the following paragraphs, select the choice that best answers each of the questions that follow.

Paragraph A

John Kennedy, the first "television president," held considerably more public appearances than did his predecessors. Kennedy's successors, with the notable exception of Richard Nixon, have been even more active in making public appearances. Indeed, they have averaged more than one appearance every weekday of the year. Bill Clinton invested enormous time and energy in attempting to sell his programs to the public. George W. Bush followed the same pattern.

—adapted from Edwards et al., *Government in America,* p. 422

_____ 1. What is the topic?

    a. the presidency

    b. the effects of television

    c. President Kennedy

    d. public appearances of the president

_____ 2. What main idea is the writer implying?

    a. U.S. presidents all enjoy being in the public eye.

    b. The successors of President Kennedy have tried to imitate him.

    c. Presidents have placed increasing importance on making public appearances.

    d. Presidents spend too much time making public appearances.

Paragraph B

When registering for online services under a screen name, it can be tempting to think your identity is a secret to other users. Many people will say or do things on the Internet that they would never do in real life because they believe that they are acting anonymously. However, most blogs, e-mail and instant messenger services, and social networking sites are tied to your real identity in some way. While your identity may be superficially concealed by a screen name, it often takes little more than a quick Google search to uncover your name, address, and other personal and possibly sensitive information.

—Ebert and Griffin, *Business Essentials,* p. 188

_____ 3. What is the topic?

    a. online identity

    b. screen names

    c. online services

    d. Google searches

_____ 4. What is the writer saying about the topic?

    a. Google searches offer clues to your identity.

    b. People write things on the Internet they would never say face-to-face.

    c. Your identity is not secret on the Internet.

    d. Screen names help conceal your identity.

Paragraph C

All the nutrients in the world are useless to humans unless oxygen is also available. Because the chemical reactions that release energy from foods require oxygen, human cells can survive for only a few minutes without oxygen. Approximately 20% of the air we breathe is oxygen. It is made available to the blood and body cells by the cooperative efforts of the respiratory and cardiovascular systems.

—adapted from Marieb, *Anatomy and Physiology*, p. 9

_____ 5. What is the topic?

    a. humans

    b. nutrients

    c. oxygen

    d. the respiratory system

_____ 6. What main idea is the writer implying?

    a. All chemical reactions require oxygen.

    b. Oxygen is vital to human life.

    c. Less than a fourth of the air we breathe is oxygen.

    d. The respiratory system and the cardiovascular system work together.

_____ 7. Which one of the following details does *not* support the paragraph's implied main idea?

    a. All the nutrients in the world are useless to humans.

    b. The chemical reactions that release energy from foods use oxygen.

    c. Plants release oxygen into the air through the process of photosynthesis.

    d. The respiratory and cardiovascular systems supply oxygen to the blood and body cells.

Paragraph D

People's acceptance of a product may be largely determined by its packaging. In one study the very same coffee taken from a yellow can was described as weak, from a dark brown can as too strong, from a red can as rich, and from a blue can as mild. Even your acceptance of a person may depend on the colors worn. Consider, for example, the comments of one color expert: "If you have to pick the wardrobe for your defense lawyer heading into court and choose anything but blue, you deserve to lose the case. . . ." Black is so powerful it could work against the lawyer with the jury. Brown lacks sufficient authority. Green would probably elicit a negative response.

—adapted from DeVito, *Messages: Building Interpersonal Communication Skills*, p. 161

_____ 8. What is the topic?

    a. packaging

    b. marketing

    c. colors

    d. dressing for success

_____ 9. What is the writer saying about the topic?

    a. Colors influence how we think and act.

    b. A product's packaging determines whether or not we accept it.

    c. A lawyer's success depends on the color of his or her wardrobe.

    d. Color experts consider blue to be the most influential color.

_____ 10. Which one of the following details does *not* support the paragraph's implied main idea?

    a. The same coffee is judged differently depending on the color of the coffee can.

    b. The colors a person is wearing may influence your opinion of that person.

    c. Lawyers who wear blue in court deserve to be defeated.

    d. Green is not considered a good color to wear in the courtroom.

EXERCISE 3-12 . . . FINDING STATED AND IMPLIED MAIN IDEAS

Turn to the article titled "Treating Wounded Soldiers: Polytrauma" on p. 40. Using your own paper, number the lines from 1 to 10, to correspond to the ten paragraphs in the article. For each paragraph number, if the main idea is stated, record the sentence number in which it appears (first, second, etc.). If the main idea is unstated and implied, write a sentence that expresses the main idea.

3d   RECOGNIZING SUPPORTING DETAILS

LEARNING OBJECTIVE 4
Recognize supporting details

Supporting details are those facts and ideas that prove or explain the main idea of a paragraph. While all the details in a paragraph do support the main idea, not all details are equally important. As you read, try to identify and pay attention to the most important details. Pay less attention to details of lesser importance. The key details directly explain the main idea. Other details may provide additional information, offer an example, or further explain one of the key details.

MyReadingLab

To practice your skills
on implied main ideas,
go to

▼ Study Plan
  ▼ Reading Skills
    ▼ Supporting
       Details

Figure A shows how details relate to the main idea and how details range in degree of importance. In the diagram, more important details are placed toward the left; less important details are closer to the right.

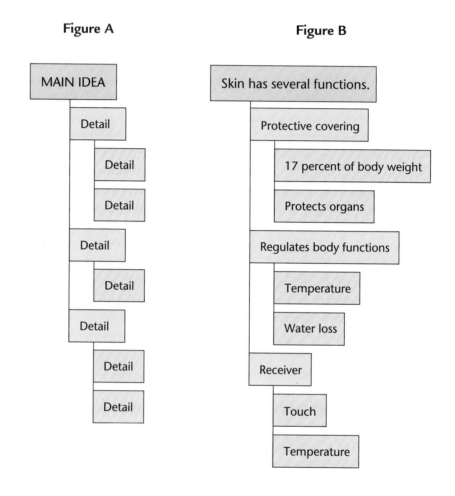

Figure A

Figure B

Read the following paragraph and study Figure B.

The skin of the human body has several functions. First, it serves as a protective covering. In doing so, it accounts for 17 percent of the body weight. Skin also protects the organs within the body from damage or harm. The skin serves as a regulator of body functions. It controls body temperature and water loss. Finally, the skin serves as a receiver. It is sensitive to touch and temperature.

From this diagram you can see that the details that state the three functions of skin are the key details. Other details, such as "protects the organs," provide further information and are at a lower level of importance.

Read the following paragraph and try to pick out the more important details.

Many cultures have different rules for men and women engaging in conflict. Asian cultures are more strongly prohibitive of women's conflict strategies. Asian women are expected to be exceptionally polite; this is even more important when women are in conflict with men and when the conflict is public. In the United States, there is a verbalized equality; men and women have equal rights when it comes to permissible conflict strategies. In reality, there are many who expect women to be more polite, to pursue conflict in a nonargumentative way, while men are expected to argue forcefully and logically.

This paragraph could be diagrammed as follows (key details only):

Many cultures have different rules for men and women engaging in conflict.

Rules in Asian cultures

Rules in the United States

EXERCISE 3-13 . . . RECOGNIZING SUPPORTING DETAILS 1

Each of the following topic sentences states the main idea of a paragraph. After each topic sentence are sentences containing details that may or may not support the topic sentence. Read each sentence and put an "S" beside those that contain details that support the topic sentence.

1. **Topic Sentence:** An oligopoly is a market structure in which only a few companies sell a certain product.

    _____ a. The automobile industry is a good example of an oligopoly, even though it gives the appearance of being highly competitive.

    _____ b. The breakfast cereal, soap, and cigarette industries, although basic to our economy, operate as oligopolies.

    _____ c. Monopolies refer to market structures in which only one industry produces a particular product.

    _____ d. Monopolies are able to exert more control and price fixing than oligopolies.

    _____ e. In the oil industry there are only a few producers, so each producer has a fairly large share of the sales.

2. **Topic Sentence:** *Mens rea,* a term that refers to a person's criminal intent when committing a crime, or his or her state of mind, can be evaluated in several ways.

_____ a. Confessions by criminals are direct evidence of their criminal intent.

_____ b. Circumstantial evidence can be used to suggest mental intent.

_____ c. *Actus rea* is a person's actions that make up a crime.

_____ d. A person may unknowingly commit a crime.

_____ e. Expert witnesses may offer an opinion about a person's criminal intent.

3. **Topic Sentence:** Food irradiation is a process in which food is treated with radiation to kill bacteria.

_____ a. Gamma radiation is made up of radioactive cobalt, cesium, and X-rays.

_____ b. The radioactive rays pass through the food without damaging it or changing it.

_____ c. The newest form of irradiation uses electricity as the energy source for irradiation.

_____ d. Irradiation increases the shelf life of food because it kills all bacteria present in the food.

_____ e. *E. coli,* salmonella, and listeria cause many illnesses each year.

4. **Topic Sentence:** Overtraining is the most common type of fitness-related injury, and it can be easily avoided.

_____ a. A physical fitness program will improve your health and well-being.

_____ b. Our bodies usually provide warning signs of potential muscle damage.

_____ c. People often injure themselves by doing too much too soon when they exercise.

_____ d. To avoid injury, do not rely solely on repetitive motion activities like running or step aerobics.

_____ e. Varying an exercise program can allow muscles time to rest and recover from strain.

5. **Topic Sentence:** Frank Lloyd Wright was a radically innovative architect.

_____ a. Wright believed that buildings should fit their surroundings.

_____ b. He popularized the use of steel cantilevers in homes at a time when they were only used commercially.

_____ c. He built the Kaufmann Residence over a waterfall without disturbing it.

_____ d. Wright had plans to build a mile-high skyscraper but died before he could do so.

_____ e. Wright designed the Guggenheim Museum.

EXERCISE 3-14 . . . RECOGNIZING SUPPORTING DETAILS 2

Underline only the most important details in each of the following paragraphs.

Paragraph 1

Physical dependence is what was formerly called addiction. It is characterized by *tolerance* and *withdrawal*. *Tolerance* means that more and more of the drug must be taken to achieve the same effect, as use continues. *Withdrawal* means that if use is discontinued, the person experiences unpleasant symptoms. When I quit smoking cigarettes, for example, I went through about five days of irritability, depression, and restlessness. Withdrawal from heroin and other narcotics is much more painful, involving violent cramps, vomiting, diarrhea, and other symptoms that continue for at least two or three days. With some drugs, especially barbiturates, cold-turkey (sudden and total) quitting can result in death, so severe is the withdrawal.

—Geiwitz, *Psychology*, p. 512

Paragraph 2

The two most common drugs that are legal and do not require a prescription are caffeine and nicotine. *Caffeine* is the active ingredient in coffee, tea, and many cola drinks. It stimulates the central nervous system and heart and therefore is often used to stay awake. Heavy use—say, seven to ten cups of coffee per day—has toxic effects, that is, it acts like a mild poison. Prolonged heavy use appears to be addicting. *Nicotine* is the active ingredient in tobacco. One of the most addicting of all drugs and one of the most dangerous, at least when obtained by smoking, it has been implicated in lung cancer, emphysema, and heart disease.

—Geiwitz, *Psychology*, p. 513

Paragraph 3

Hypnosis today is used for a number of purposes, primarily in psychotherapy or to reduce pain, and it is an acceptable technique in both medicine and psychology. In psychotherapy, it is most often used to eliminate bad habits and annoying symptoms. Cigarette smoking can be treated, for example, by the suggestion that the person will feel nauseated whenever he or she thinks of smoking. Sufferers of migraine headaches treated with hypnotic suggestions to relax showed a much greater tendency to improve than sufferers treated with drugs; 44 percent were headache-free after 12 months of treatment, compared to 12 percent of their drug-treated counterparts.

—Geiwitz, *Psychology*, p. 229

Paragraph 4

There are four main types of sunglasses. The traditional *absorptive* glasses soak up all the harmful sun rays. *Polarizing* sunglasses account for half the market. They're the best buy for knocking out glare, and reflections from snow and water, but they may admit more light rays than other sunglasses. *Coated* sunglasses usually have a metallic covering that itself reflects light. They are often quite absorptive, but a cheap pair of coated glasses may have an uneven or nondurable coating that could rub off after a short period of time. New on the market are the somewhat more expensive *photochromatic* sunglasses. Their chemical composition causes them to change color according to the brightness of the light: in the sun, they darken; in the shade, they lighten. This type of sunglasses responds to ultraviolet light only, and will not screen out infrared rays, so they're not the best bet for continual exposure to bright sun.

—George, *The New Consumer Survival Kit,* p. 14

Paragraph 5

In simplest outline, how is a President chosen? First, a candidate campaigns within his party for nomination at a national convention. After the convention comes a period of competition with the nominee of the other major party and perhaps the nominees of minor parties. The showdown arrives on Election Day. The candidate must win more votes than any other nominee in enough states and the District of Columbia to give him a majority of the electoral votes. If he does all these things, he has won the right to the office of President of the United States.

— "ABC's of How a President Is Chosen," *U.S. News and World Report,* p. 45

EXERCISE 3-15 . . . RECOGNIZING SUPPORTING DETAILS 3

Reread the article "Treating Wounded Soldiers: Polytrauma" on p. 40 and underline the most important supporting details in each paragraph.

3e   RECOGNIZING TRANSITIONS

LEARNING OBJECTIVE 5
Recognize transitions

Transitions are linking words or phrases used to lead the reader from one idea to another. If you get in the habit of recognizing transitions, you will see that they often guide you through a paragraph, helping you to read it more easily.

In the following paragraph, notice how the underlined transitions lead you from one important detail to the next.

The principle of rhythm and line also contributes to the overall unity of the landscape design. This principle is responsible for the sense of continuity between different areas of the landscape. One way in which this continuity can be developed is by extending planting beds from one area to another. For example, shrub beds developed around the entrance to the house can be continued around the sides and into the backyard. Such an arrangement helps to tie the front and rear areas of the property together. Another means by which rhythm is given to a design is to repeat shapes, angles, or lines between various areas and elements of the design.

—Reiley and Shry, *Introductory Horticulture,* p. 114

TABLE 3.1 COMMON TRANSITIONS

TYPES OF TRANSITIONS	EXAMPLES	WHAT THEY TELL THE READER
Time or Sequence	first, later, next, finally	The author is arranging ideas in the order in which they happened.
Example	for example, for instance, to illustrate, such as	An example will follow.
Enumeration	first, second, third, last, another, next	The author is marking or identifying each major point (sometimes these may be used to suggest order of importance).
Continuation	also, in addition, and, further, another	The author is continuing with the same idea and is going to provide additional information.
Contrast	on the other hand, in contrast, however	The author is switching to a different, opposite, or contrasting idea than previously discussed.
Comparison	like, likewise, similarly	The writer will show how the previous idea is similar to what follows.
Cause and Effect	because, thus, therefore, since, consequently	The writer will show a connection between two or more things, how one thing caused another, or how something happened as a result of something else.

Not all paragraphs contain such obvious transitions, and not all transitions serve as such clear markers of major details. Often, however, transitions are used to alert you to what will come next in the paragraph. If you see the phrase *for instance* at the beginning of a sentence, then you know that an example will follow. When you see the phrase *on the other hand*, you can predict that a different, opposing idea will follow. Table 3.1 lists some of the most common transitions used within a paragraph and indicates what they tell you.

EXERCISE 3-16 . . . RECOGNIZING TRANSITIONS 1

Select the transitional word or phrase from the box below that best completes each of the following sentences.

another	however	more importantly
for example	because	

1. The function of taste buds is to enable us to select healthy foods. _____ function is to warn us away from foods that are potentially dangerous, by detecting a sour or bitter taste.

2. Michelangelo considered himself to be primarily a sculptor; _____, the Sistine Chapel ceiling painting is one of his best known works of art.

3. Failure to floss and brush teeth and gums can cause bad breath. _____, this failure can also lead to periodontal disease.

4. Businesses use symbols to stand for a product's qualities; _____, the golden arches have come to represent the McDonald's chain.

5. In the 1800s, the "Wild West" was made up of territories that did not belong to states. _____ there was no local government, vigilantes and outlaws ruled the land, answering only to U.S. marshals.

EXERCISE 3-17 . . . RECOGNIZING TRANSITIONS 2

Select the transitional word or phrase from the box below that best completes each of the following sentences. Two of the transitions in the box may be used more than once.

on the other hand	for example	because	in addition
similarly	after	next	however
also			

1. Typically, those suffering from post-traumatic stress disorder are soldiers after combat. Civilians who have experienced events such as the World Trade Center destruction can _____ experience this syndrome.

2. Columbus was determined to find an oceanic passage to China _____ finding a direct route would mean increased trading and huge profits.

3. In the event of a heart attack, it is first important to identify the symptoms. _____, call 911 or drive the victim to the nearest hospital.

4. In the 1920s, courtship between men and women changed dramatically. _____, instead of paying calls at the woman's home with her parents there, men now invited women out on dates.

5. Direct exposure to sunlight is dangerous because the ultraviolet rays can lead to skin cancer. _____, tanning booths also emit ultraviolet rays and are as dangerous as, if not more dangerous than, exposure to sunlight.

6. Lie detector tests are often used by law enforcement to help determine guilt or innocence. _____, because these tests often only have an accuracy rate of between 60 percent and 80 percent, the results are not admissible in court.

7. The temporal lobes of the brain process sound and comprehend language. _____, this area of the brain is responsible for storing visual memories.

8. The theory of multiple intelligences holds that there are many different kinds of intelligence, or abilities. _____, musical ability, control of bodily movements (athletics), spatial understanding, and observational abilities are all classified as different types of intelligence.

9. During World War II, Japanese Americans were held in relocation camps. _____ the war was over, the United States paid reparations and issued an apology to those who were wrongfully detained.

10. Support continues to grow for the legalization of marijuana. _____, legalization has not yet been passed in any state and it is unlikely this will happen anytime soon.

EXERCISE 3-18 . . . RECOGNIZING TRANSITIONS 3

Many transitions have similar meanings and can sometimes be used interchangeably. Match each transition in column A with a similar transition in column B. Write the letter of your choice in the space provided.

Column A	Column B
_____ 1. because	a. therefore
_____ 2. in contrast	b. also
_____ 3. for instance	c. likewise
_____ 4. thus	d. after that
_____ 5. first	e. since
_____ 6. one way	f. finally
_____ 7. similarly	g. on the other hand
_____ 8. next	h. one approach
_____ 9. in addition	i. in the beginning
_____ 10. to sum up	j. for example

EXERCISE 3-19 . . . RECOGNIZING TRANSITIONS 4

Each of the following beginnings of paragraphs uses a transitional word or phrase to tell the reader what will follow in the paragraph. Read each, paying particular attention to the underlined word or phrase. Then, in the space provided, describe as specifically as you can what you would expect to find next in the paragraph.

1. Price is not the only factor to consider in choosing a pharmacy. Many provide valuable services that should be considered. <u>For instance</u> . . .

   _____

2. There are a number of things you can do to prevent a home burglary. <u>First,</u> . . .

   _____

3. Most mail order businesses are reliable and honest. <u>However,</u> . . .

   _____

   _____

4. One advantage of a laptop computer is that all the components are built into the unit. <u>Another</u> . . .

   _____

5. To select the presidential candidate you will vote for, you should examine his or her philosophy of government. <u>Next</u> . . .

   _____

   _____

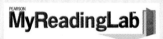

For Further Practice

For support in meeting this chapter's learning objectives, log in to www.myreadinglab.com, go to the Study Plan tab, click on **Stated Main Idea** and **Supporting Details** from the list of subtopics. Read and view the videos and resources in the Review Materials section of each, and then complete the Recall, Practice, and Test exercises in the Activities section. You can check your scores and overall progress by using the Gradebook.

4 Organizational Patterns

LEARNING OBJECTIVES

In this chapter, you will learn how to

1 Recognize definition

2 Recognize classification

3 Recognize order or sequence

4 Recognize cause and effect

5 Recognize comparison and contrast

6 Recognize listing/enumeration

7 Recognize mixed patterns

8 Recognize other patterns of organization

MyReadingLab

To practice using organizational patterns, go to

▼ Study Plan

  ▼ Reading Skills

    ▼ Patterns of Organization

Most college students take courses in several different disciplines each semester. They may study psychology, anatomy and physiology, mathematics, and English composition all in one semester. During one day they may read a poem, solve math problems, and study early developments in psychology.

What few students realize is that a biologist and a psychologist, for example, think about and approach their subject matter in similar ways. Both carefully define terms, examine causes and effects, study similarities and differences, describe sequences of events, classify information, solve problems, and enumerate characteristics. The subject matter and language they use differ, but their approaches to the material are basically the same. Researchers, textbook authors, and your professors use standard approaches, or **organizational patterns,** to express their ideas.

In academic writing, commonly used organizational patterns include definition, classification, order or sequence, cause and effect, comparison and contrast, and listing/enumeration. Other important patterns include statement and clarification, summary, generalization and example, and addition.

These patterns can work for you in several ways:

- Patterns help you anticipate the author's thought development and thus focus your reading.
- Patterns help you remember and recall what you read.
- Patterns are useful in your own writing; they help you organize and express your ideas in a more coherent, comprehensible form.

The following sections describe each pattern listed on the previous page. In subsequent chapters, you will see how these patterns are used in specific academic disciplines.

4a **DEFINITION**

LEARNING OBJECTIVE 1
Recognize definition

Each academic discipline has its own specialized vocabulary. One of the primary purposes of introductory textbooks is to introduce students to this new language. Consequently, definition is a commonly used pattern throughout most introductory-level texts.

Suppose you were asked to define the word *comedian* for someone unfamiliar with the term. First, you would probably say that a comedian is a person who entertains. Then you might distinguish a comedian from other types of entertainers by saying that a comedian is an entertainer who tells jokes and makes others laugh. Finally, you might mention, by way of example, the names of several well-known comedians who have appeared on television. Although you may have presented it informally, your definition would have followed the standard, classic pattern. The first part of your definition tells what general class or group the term belongs to (entertainers). The second part tells what distinguishes the term from other items in the same class or category. The third part includes further explanation, characteristics, examples, or applications.

You can visualize the definition pattern as follows:

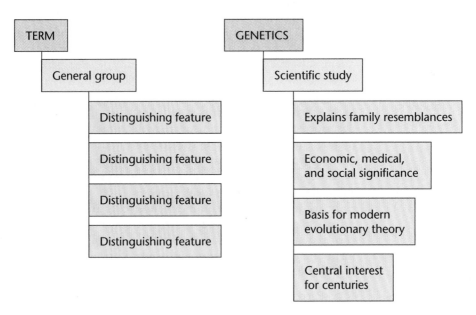

See how the term *genetics* is defined in the following paragraph, and notice how the term and the general class are presented in the first sentence. The remainder of the paragraph presents the distinguishing characteristics.

Genetics is the scientific study of heredity, the transmission of characteristics from parents to offspring. Genetics explains why offspring resemble their parents and also why they are not identical to them. Genetics is a subject that has considerable economic, medical, and social significance and is partly the basis for the modern theory of evolution. Because of its importance, genetics has been a topic of central interest in the study of life for centuries. Modern concepts in genetics are fundamentally different, however, from earlier ones.

—Mix, Farber, and King, *Biology: The Network of Life*, p. 262

Writers often provide clues called **transitions** that signal the organizational pattern being used. These signals may occur within single sentences or as connections between sentences. (Transitional words that occur in phrases are italicized in the box below to help you spot them.)

TRANSITIONS FOR THE DEFINITION PATTERN

genetics *is* . . .
bureaucracy *means* . . .
patronage *refers to* . . .
aggression *can be defined* as . . .
deficit is *another term* that . . .
balance of power *also means* . . .

EXERCISE 4-1 . . . USING DEFINITION

Read each of the following paragraphs and answer the questions that follow.

A.   A pidgin is a contact language that emerges when different cultures with different languages come to live in close proximity and therefore need to communicate. Pidgins are generally limited to highly functional domains, such as trade, since that is what they were developed for. A pidgin therefore is no one's first language. Many pidgins of the Western hemisphere developed out of slavery, where owners needed to communicate with their slaves. A pidgin is always learned as a second language. Tok Pisin, the pidgin language of Papua New Guinea, consists of a mixture of many languages, some English, Samoan, Chinese, and Malayan. Tok Pisin has been declared one of the national languages of Papau New Guinea, where it is transforming into a creole, or a language descended from pidgin with its own native speakers and involving linguistic expansion and elaboration. About two hundred pidgin and creole languages exist today, mainly in West Africa, the Caribbean, and the South Pacific.

—Miller, *Cultural Anthropology*, pp. 308–309

1. What term is being defined?

_____

2. Explain the meaning of the term in your own words.

_____

_____

3. Give an example of the term. _____

B.   The integumentary system is the external covering of the body, or the skin. It waterproofs the body and cushions and protects the deeper tissues from injury. It also excretes salts and urea in perspiration and helps regulate body temperature. Temperature, pressure, and pain receptors located in the skin alert us to what is happening at the body surface.

—Marieb, *Essentials of Human Anatomy and Physiology*, p. 3

4. Define the integumentary system in your own words.

_____

5. List three things the integumentary system does.

_____

_____

4b   CLASSIFICATION

LEARNING OBJECTIVE 2
Recognize classification

If you were asked to describe types of computers, you might mention PCs, laptops, and BlackBerries. By dividing a broad topic into its major categories, you are using a pattern known as **classification.**

This pattern is widely used in many academic subjects. For example, a psychology text might explain human needs by classifying them into two categories: primary and secondary. In a chemistry textbook, various compounds may be grouped and discussed according to common characteristics, such as the presence of hydrogen or oxygen. The classification pattern divides a topic into parts, on the basis of common or shared characteristics.

Here are a few examples of topics and the classifications or categories into which each might be divided.

- **Movies:** comedy, horror, mystery
- **Motives:** achievement, power, affiliation, competency
- **Plants:** leaves, stem, roots

Note how the following paragraph classifies the various types of cancers.

The name of the cancer is derived from the type of tissue in which it develops. Carcinoma (carc = cancer; omo = tumor) refers to a malignant tumor consisting of epithelial cells. A tumor that develops from a gland is called an adenosarcoma (adeno = gland). Sarcoma is a general term for any cancer arising from connective tissue. Osteogenic sarcomas (osteo = bone; genic = origin), the most frequent type of childhood cancer, destroy normal bone tissue and eventually spread to other areas of the body. Myelomas (myelos = marrow) are malignant tumors, occurring in middle-aged and older people, that interfere with the blood-cell-producing function of bone marrow and cause anemia. Chondrosarcomas (chondro = cartilage) are cancerous growths of cartilage.

—Tortora, *Introduction to the Human Body*, p. 56

You can visualize the classification pattern as follows:

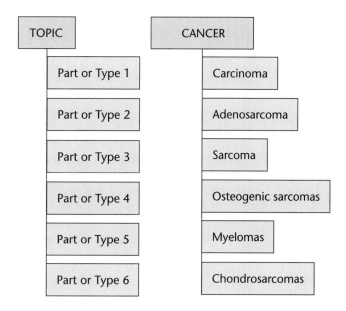

TOPIC

Part or Type 1

Part or Type 2

Part or Type 3

Part or Type 4

Part or Type 5

Part or Type 6

CANCER

Carcinoma

Adenosarcoma

Sarcoma

Osteogenic sarcomas

Myelomas

Chondrosarcomas

TRANSITIONS FOR THE CLASSIFICATION PATTERN

There are *several kinds* of chemical bonding . . .
There are *numerous types of* . . .
Reproduction can be *classified as* . . .
the human skeleton is *composed of* . . .
muscles *comprise* . . .
one type of communication . . .
another type of communication . . .
finally, there is . . .

EXERCISE 4-2 . . . USING CLASSIFICATION

Read each of the following paragraphs and answer the questions that follow.

A.   The reptiles made one of the most spectacular adaptive radiations in all of Earth history. One group, the pterosaurs, took to the air. These "dragons of the sky" possessed huge membranous wings that allowed them rudimentary flight. Another group of reptiles, exemplified by the fossil *Archaeopteryx,* led to more successful flyers: the birds. Whereas some reptiles took to the skies, others returned to the sea, including fish-eating plesiosaurs and ichthyosaurs. These reptiles became proficient swimmers, but retained their reptilian teeth and breathed by means of lungs.

—Tarbuck and Lutgens, *Earth Science,* p. 309

1. List the classification of reptiles included in this paragraph.

   _____

2. Highlight the transitional words used in the paragraph.

B.   From the hundreds of billions of galaxies, several basic types have been identified: spiral, elliptical, and irregular. The Milky Way and the Great Galaxy in
Andromeda are examples of fairly large spiral galaxies. Typically, spiral galaxies
are disk-shaped with a somewhat greater concentration of stars near their centers,
but there are numerous variations. Viewed broadside, arms are often seen extending from the central nucleus and sweeping gracefully away. One type of spiral
galaxy, however, has the stars arranged in the shape of a bar, which rotates as a
rigid system. This requires that the outer stars move faster than the inner ones,
a fact not easy for astronomers to reconcile with the laws of motion. Attached
to each end of these bars are curved spiral arms. These have become known as
barred spiral galaxies. The most abundant group, making up 60 percent of the
total, is the elliptical galaxies. These are generally smaller than spiral galaxies.
Some are so much smaller, in fact, that the term dwarf has been applied. Because
these dwarf galaxies are not visible at great distances, a survey of the sky reveals
more of the conspicuous large spiral galaxies. As their name implies, elliptical galaxies have an ellipsoidal shape that ranges to nearly spherical, and they lack spiral
arms. Only 10 percent of the known galaxies lack symmetry and are classified as
irregular galaxies. The best-known irregular galaxies, the Large and Small Magel-
lanic Clouds in the Southern Hemisphere, are easily visible with the unaided eye.

—Tarbuck and Lutgens, *Earth Science*, pp. 620–621

3. What are the three primary classifications of galaxies?

   _____

4. What determines how a galaxy is classified?

   _____

5. Highlight the transitional words used in the paragraph.

4c   ORDER OR SEQUENCE

LEARNING OBJECTIVE 3
**Recognize order or
sequence**

If you were asked to summarize what you did today, you probably would mention key events in the order in which they occurred. In describing how to write
a particular computer program, you would detail the process step-by-step. In
each case, you are presenting information in a particular sequence or order.
Each of these examples illustrates a form of the organizational pattern known
as *order* or *sequence*. Let's look at several types of order.

Chronology

Chronological order refers to the sequence in which events occur in time. This pattern is essential in the academic disciplines concerned with the interpretation of events in the past. History, government, and anthropology are prime examples. In various forms of literature, chronological order is evident; the narrative form, used in novels, short stories, and narrative essays, relies on chronological order.

You can visualize the chronological order pattern as follows:

The following paragraph uses chronology to describe the sinking of the *Lusitania*.

At 12:30 on the afternoon of May 1, 1915, the British steamship *Lusitania* set sail from New York to Liverpool. The passenger list of 1,257 was the largest since the outbreak of war in Europe in 1914. Six days later, the *Lusitania* reached the coast of Ireland. The passengers lounged on the deck. As if it were peacetime, the ship sailed straight ahead, with no zigzag maneuvers to throw off pursuit. But the submarine U-20 was there, and its commander, seeing a large ship, fired a single torpedo. Seconds after it hit, a boiler exploded and blew a hole in the *Lusitania's* side. The ship listed immediately, hindering the launching of lifeboats, and in eighteen minutes it sank. Nearly 1,200 people died, including 128 Americans. As the ship's bow lifted and went under, the U-20 commander for the first time read the name: *Lusitania*.

—adapted from Divine et al., *America Past and Present*, p. 596

> ## TRANSITIONS FOR CHRONOLOGICAL ORDER
>
> *in* ancient times . . .
> *at* the start of the battle . . .
> *on* September 12 . . .
> the *first* primate species . . .
> *later* efforts . . .
> Other chronological transitions are *then, before, during, by the time,*
> *while, afterward, as, after, thereafter, meanwhile,* and *at that point.*

EXERCISE 4-3 . . . USING ORDER OR SEQUENCE

*Read each of the following textbook excerpts and answer the questions
that follow.*

A. Railroads: Pioneers of Big Business

Completion of efficient and speedy national transportation and communications networks encouraged mass production and mass marketing. Beginning in
1862, federal and state governments vigorously promoted railroad construction
with land grants from the public domain. Eventually, railroads received lands one
and a half times the size of Texas. Local governments gave everything from land
for stations to tax breaks.

With such incentives, the first transcontinental railroad was finished in 1869.
Four additional transcontinental lines and miles of feeder and branch roads were
laid down in the 1870s and 1880s. By 1890, trains rumbled across 165,000 miles
of tracks. Telegraph lines arose alongside them.

—Nash et al., *The American People,* pp. 611–613

1. What events does the excerpt detail?

   _____

2. What is the importance of these events?

   _____

3. Highlight the transitional words used in the excerpt.

B. U.S. Intervention in Vietnam

The pretext for full-scale intervention in Vietnam came in late July 1964. On
July 30, South Vietnamese PT (patrol torpedo) boats attacked bases in the Gulf of
Tonkin inside North Vietnamese waters. Simultaneously, the *Maddox,* an American
destroyer, steamed into the area to disrupt North Vietnamese communication facilities. On August 2, possibly seeing the two separate missions as a combined
maneuver against them, the North Vietnamese sent out several PT boats to
attack the destroyer. The *Maddox* fired, sinking one of the attackers, then radioed
the news to Washington. Johnson ordered another ship into the bay. On August 3

both destroyers reported another attack, although somewhat later, the commander of the *Maddox* radioed that he was not sure. Nonetheless, the president ordered American planes to retaliate by bombing inside North Vietnam.

—Wilson et al., *The Pursuit of Liberty*, p. 493

4. What events in history does this paragraph describe?

_____

_____

5. Highlight the transitional words used in the paragraph.

Process

In disciplines that focus on procedures, steps, or stages by which actions are accomplished, the process pattern is often employed. These subjects include mathematics, natural and life sciences, engineering, and many career fields. The pattern is similar to chronology, in that the steps or stages follow each other in time. Transitional words and phrases often used in conjunction with this pattern are similar to those used for chronological order. You can visualize the process pattern as follows:

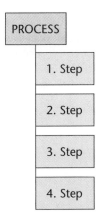

Note how this pattern is used in a paragraph explaining what occurs in the brain during sleep.

Let us track your brain waves through the night. As you prepare to go to bed, an EEG records that your brain waves are moving along at a rate of about 14 cycles per second (cps). Once you are comfortably in bed, you begin to relax and your brain waves slow down to a rate of about 8 to 12 cps. When you fall asleep, you enter your *sleep cycle,* each of whose stages shows a distinct EEG pattern. In Stage 1 sleep, the EEG shows brain waves of about 3 to 7 cps. During Stage 2, the EEG is characterized by *sleep spindles,* minute bursts of electrical activity of 12 to 16 cps. In the next two stages (3 and 4) of sleep, you enter into a very deep state of relaxed sleep. Your brain waves slow to about 1 to 2 cps, and your breathing and heart rate decrease. In a final stage, the electrical activity of your brain increases; your EEG looks very similar to those recorded during stages 1 and 2. It is during this stage that you will experience REM sleep, and you will begin to dream.

—Zimbardo and Gerrig, *Psychology and Life,* p. 115

EXERCISE 4-4 . . . USING PROCESS

Read each of the following textbook excerpts and answer the questions that follow.

A.   Should you eat less fat? Scientists doing medical research think you probably should; they recommend no more than 30% fat in our diets, whereas the average American diet is estimated to contain 34% fat. Perhaps you're convinced that you should cut down on fatty foods, but you can't imagine watching the Super Bowl without a big bag of chips at your side. The chemists at Procter & Gamble have been trying to resolve your dilemma by developing an edible substance with the rich taste and smooth texture of fat molecules but without the calories. Olestra seems to meet these criteria.

Fat digestion is an enzyme-mediated process that breaks fat molecules into glycerol and fatty acids, which are then able to enter the bloodstream. Olestra is a hexa-, hepta-, or octa-ester of fatty acids (derived from vegetable oil, such as soybean oil or cottonseed oil) and sucrose. Because the body contains no digestive enzymes that convert Olestra's fat-like molecules into their smaller components of sucrose and fatty acids, and because Olestra is too large to enter the bloodstream undigested, the compound passes through systems unchanged.

—Bishop, *Introduction to Chemistry,* p. 749

1. What process does this passage explain?

   _____

2. Why is Olestra not digested?

   _____

   _____

B.   BMI [body mass index] is an index of the relationship of height and weight. It is one of the most accurate indicators of a person's health risk due to excessive weight, rather than "fatness" per se. Although many people recoil in fright when they see they have to convert pounds to kilograms and inches to meters to calculate BMI, it really is not as difficult as it may seem. To get your kilogram weight, just divide your weight in pounds (without shoes or clothing) by 2.2. To convert your height to meters squared, divide your height in inches (without shoes) by 39.4, then square this result. Sounds pretty easy and it actually is. Once you have these basic values, calculating your BMI involves dividing your weight in kilograms by your height in meters squared.

$$BMI = \frac{\text{Weight (in lbs)} \times 2.2 \text{ (to determine weight in kg)}}{(\text{Height [in inches]} \div 39.4)^2 \text{ (to determine height in meters squared)}}$$

Healthy weights have been defined as those associated with BMIs of 19 to 25, the range of the lowest statistical health risk. A BMI greater than 25 indicates overweight and potentially significant health risks. The desirable range for females is between 21 and 23; for males, it is between 22 and 24. A body mass index of over 30 is considered obese. Many experts believe this number is too high, particularly for younger adults.

—Donatelle, *Access to Health*, p. 264

3. What process is being described in this paragraph?

_____

4. How do you convert height in inches to meters squared?

_____

5. What does BMI measure and why is it useful?

_____

_____

Order of Importance

Ideas can be organized in a pattern that expresses order of priority or preference. Ideas are arranged in one of two ways: from most to least important, or from least to most important. In the following paragraph, the causes of the downward trend in the standard of living are arranged in order of importance.

The United States' downward trend in standard of living has many different causes, of which only a few major ones can be identified here. Most important is probably deindustrialization, the massive loss of manufacturing jobs as many U.S. corporations move their production to poor, labor-cheap countries. But deindustrialization hurts mostly low-skilled manufacturing workers. Most of the well-educated, high-skilled employees in service industries are left unscathed. Deindustrialization alone is therefore not enough to explain the economic decline. Another major factor is the great increase in consumption and decrease in savings. Like their government, people spend more than they earn and become deeply in debt. Those who do practice thrift still have an average rate of savings significantly lower than in countries with fast-growing economies. The habits of high consumption and low saving may have resulted from the great affluence after the Second World War up until the early 1970s.

—Thio, *Sociology*, p. 255

Order of importance is used in almost every field of study.

TRANSITIONS FOR ORDER OF IMPORTANCE

is *less* essential than . . .
more revealing is . . .
of *primary* interest is . . .
Other transitions that show the order of
importance are *first, next, last, most important, primarily,*
and *secondarily*.

EXERCISE 4–5 . . . USING ORDER OF IMPORTANCE

Read the following paragraph and answer the questions that follow.

Media resources are being reassembled in a new pattern, with three main parts. The first is the traditional mass media that will continue to be for a long time the most important element in the pattern in terms of their reach and influence. The second consists of the advanced electronic mass media, operating primarily within the new information utility, and competing increasingly with older media services. Finally, there are newer forms of personal electronic media, formed by clusters of like-minded people to fulfill their own professional or individual information needs. Internet chat rooms and personalized Web pages are fast-expanding examples of this development. Each of these parts of the evolving mass-communications pattern deserves separate scrutiny.

—Dizard, *Old Media, New Media*, p. 179

1. What does this paragraph describe?

   _____

2. Write the transitional words used in the paragraph.

   _____

3. Why is traditional mass media the most important type of resource?

   _____

4. Which type of media resource competes the most with the traditional mass media?

   _____

5. What are some examples of personal electronic media?

   _____

Spatial Order

Information organized according to its physical location, or position or order in space, exhibits a pattern that is known as **spatial order.** Spatial order is used in academic disciplines in which physical descriptions are important. These include numerous technical fields, engineering, and the biological sciences.

You can see how the following description of a particular type of blood circulation relies on spatial relationships.

> Pulmonary circulation conducts blood between the heart and the lungs. Oxygen-poor, CO_2-laden blood returns through two large veins (venae cavae) from tissues within the body, enters the right atrium, and is then moved into the right ventricle of the heart. From there, it is pumped into the pulmonary artery, which divides into two branches, each leading to one of the lungs. In the lung, the arteries undergo extensive branching, giving rise to vast networks of capillaries where gas exchange takes place, with blood becoming oxygenated while CO_2 is discharged. Oxygen-rich blood then returns to the heart via the pulmonary veins.
>
> —Mix, Farber, and King, *Biology: The Network of Life,* pp. 663–664

Diagramming is of the utmost importance in working with this pattern; often, a diagram accompanies text material. For example, a diagram makes the functions of the various parts of the human brain easier to understand. Lecturers often refer to a visual aid or drawing when providing spatial descriptions.

TRANSITIONS FOR SPATIAL ORDER

the *left side* of the brain . . .
the *lower* portion . . .
the *outer* covering . . .
beneath the surface . . .
Other spatial transitions are *next to, beside, to the left, in the center,* and *externally.*

EXERCISE 4-6 . . . USING SPATIAL ORDER

Read the following paragraph and answer the questions that follow.

> Skeletal muscle tissue is named for its location—attached to bones. Skeletal muscle tissue is also *voluntary* because it can be made to contract by conscious control. A single skeletal muscle fiber (cell) is cylindrical and appears *striated* (striped) under a microscope; when organized in a tissue, the fibers are parallel to each other. Each muscle fiber has a plasma membrane, the sarcolemma, surrounding the cytoplasm, or sarcoplasm. Skeletal muscle fibers are multinucleate (more than one nucleus), and the nuclei are near the sarcolemma.
>
> —Tortora, *Introduction to the Human Body,* p. 77

1. Briefly describe skeletal muscle tissue.

_____

_____

_____

2. Highlight the transitional words in the paragraph.

3. How are skeletal muscle fibers or cells arranged in a tissue?

_____

4. Where can the sarcolemma (or plasma membrane) be found in muscle fibers?

_____

5. Where are the nuclei in the skeletal muscle fibers located?

_____

4d   CAUSE AND EFFECT

LEARNING OBJECTIVE 4
Recognize cause and effect

The **cause-and-effect** pattern expresses a relationship between two or more actions, events, or occurrences that are connected in time. The relationship differs, however, from chronological order in that one event leads to another by *causing* it. Information that is organized in terms of the cause-and-effect pattern may:

- explain causes, sources, reasons, motives, and action
- explain the effect, result, or consequence of a particular action
- explain both causes and effects

You can visualize the cause and effect pattern as follows:

Cause and effect is clearly illustrated by the following passage, which gives the sources of fashions or the reasons why fashions occur.

> Why do fashions occur in the first place? One reason is that some cultures, like ours, *value change:* what is new is good, even better. Thus, in many modern societies clothing styles change yearly, while people in traditional societies may wear the same style for generations. A second reason is that many industries promote quick changes in fashion to increase sales. A third reason is that fashions usually trickle down from the top. A new style may occasionally originate from lower-status groups, as blue jeans did. But most fashions come from upper-class people

who like to adopt some style or artifact as a badge of their status. But they cannot monopolize most status symbols for long. Their style is adopted by the middle class, maybe copied or modified for use by lower-status groups, offering many people the prestige of possessing a high-status symbol.

—Thio, *Sociology*, p. 534

The cause-and-effect pattern is used extensively in many academic fields. All disciplines that ask the question "Why" employ the cause-and-effect thought pattern. It is widely used in the sciences, technologies, and social sciences.

Many statements expressing cause-and-effect relationships appear in direct order, with the cause stated first and the effect following: "When demand for a product increases, prices rise." However, reverse order is sometimes used, as in the following statement: "Prices rise when a product's demand increases."

The cause-and-effect pattern is not limited to an expression of a simple one-cause, one-effect relationship. There may be multiple causes, or multiple effects, or both multiple causes and multiple effects. For example, both slippery road conditions and your failure to buy snow tires (causes) may contribute to your car sliding into the ditch (effect).

In other instances, a chain of causes or effects may occur. For instance, failing to set your alarm clock may force you to miss your 8:00 a.m. class, which in turn may cause you not to submit your term paper on time, which may result in a penalty grade.

TRANSITIONS FOR THE CAUSE-AND-EFFECT PATTERN

stress *causes* . . .
aggression *creates* . . .
depression *leads to* . . .
forethought *yields* . . .
mental retardation *stems from* . . .
life changes *produce* . . .
hostility *breeds* . . .
avoidance *results in* . . .
Other cause-and-effect transitions are *therefore,*
consequently, hence, for this reason, and *since.*

EXERCISE 4-7 . . . USING CAUSE AND EFFECT

Read each of the following paragraphs and answer the questions that follow.

A.   All objects continually radiate energy. Why, then, doesn't the temperature of all objects continually decrease? The answer is that all objects also continually absorb radiant energy. If an object is radiating more energy than it is absorbing, its temperature does decrease; but if an object is absorbing more energy than it is emitting, its temperature increases. An object that is warmer than its surroundings emits more energy than it receives, and therefore it cools; an object colder than its surroundings is a net gainer of energy, and its temperature therefore increases. An object whose temperature is constant, then, emits as much radiant energy as it receives. If it receives none, it will radiate away all its available energy, and its temperature will approach absolute zero.

—Hewitt, *Conceptual Physics*, p. 272

1. Explain why some objects that radiate energy increase in temperature.

_____

_____

2. What happens to an object that radiates energy but does not absorb any?

_____

3. Highlight the transitional words used in the paragraph.

4. What causes an object's temperature to remain constant?

_____

5. What is the effect of an object being warmer than its surroundings?

_____

B.   It's the end of the term and you have dutifully completed the last of several papers. After hours of nonstop typing, you find that your hands are numb, and you feel an intense, burning pain that makes the thought of typing one more word almost unbearable. If you are like one of the thousands of students and workers who every year must quit a particular task due to pain, you may be suffering from a repetitive stress injury (RSI). These are injuries to nerves, soft tissue or joints that result from the physical stress of repeated motions. One of the most common RSIs is carpal tunnel syndrome, a product of both the information age and the age of technology in general. Hours spent typing at the computer, flipping groceries through computerized scanners, or other jobs "made simpler" by technology can result in irritation to the median nerve in the wrist, causing numbness, tingling, and pain in the fingers and hands.

—adapted from Donatelle, *Access to Health*, p. 516

6. What is the cause of RSIs?

_____

7. What kind of damage causes carpal tunnel syndrome?

_____

8. What do students often do that can cause RSIs?

_____

9. What kinds of symptoms can result from RSI?

_____

10. Highlight the transitional words used in the passage.

_____

LEARNING OBJECTIVE 5
Recognize comparison and contrast

The **comparison organizational pattern** is used to emphasize or discuss similarities between or among ideas, theories, concepts, or events, whereas the **contrast pattern** emphasizes differences. When a speaker or writer is concerned with both similarities and differences, a combination pattern is used. You can visualize these three variations of the pattern as follows:

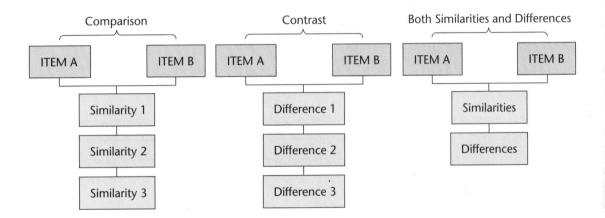

The comparison-and-contrast pattern is widely used in the social sciences, where different groups, societies, cultures, or behaviors are studied. Literature courses may require comparisons among poets, among several literary works, or among stylistic features. A business course may examine various management styles, compare organizational structures, or contrast retailing plans.

A contrast is shown in the following paragraph, which describes the purchasing processes of small and large businesses.

Small businesses are likely to have less formal purchasing processes. A small retail grocer might, for example, purchase a computer system after visiting a few suppliers to compare prices and features, while a large grocery store chain might collect bids from a specified number of vendors and then evaluate those bids on pre-established criteria. Usually, fewer individuals are involved in the decision-making process for a small business. The owner of the small business, for example, may make all decisions, and a larger business may operate with a buy-ing committee of several people.

—Kinnear, Bernhardt, and Krentler, *Principles of Marketing*, p. 218

Depending on whether a speaker or writer is concerned with similarities, differences, or both similarities and differences, the pattern might be organized in different ways. Suppose a professor of American literature is comparing the work of two American poets, Walt Whitman and Robert Frost. Each of the following organizations is possible:

1. **Compare and then contrast the two.** That is, first discuss how Frost's poetry and Whitman's poetry are similar, and then discuss how they are different.
2. **Discuss by author.** Discuss the characteristics of Whitman's poetry, then discuss the characteristics of Frost's poetry, and then summarize their similarities and differences.
3. **Discuss by characteristic.** For example, first discuss the two poets' use of metaphor, next discuss their use of rhyme, and then discuss their common themes.

TRANSITIONS THAT SHOW CONTRAST

unlike Whitman, Frost . . .
less wordy *than* Whitman . . .
contrasted with Whitman, Frost . . .
Frost *differs from* . . .
Other transitions of contrast are *in contrast, however, on the other hand, as opposed to,* and *whereas.*

TRANSITIONS THAT SHOW COMPARISON

similarities between Frost and Whitman . . .
Frost is *as powerful as* . . .
like Frost, Whitman . . .
both Frost and Whitman . . .
Frost *resembles* Whitman in that . . .
Other transitions of comparison are *in a like manner, similarly, likewise, correspondingly,* and *in the same way.*

EXERCISE 4-8 . . . USING COMPARISON AND CONTRAST

Read each of the following paragraphs and answer the questions that follow.

A.   When considering the relationship of Congress and the president, the basic differences of the two branches must be kept in mind. Members of Congress are elected from narrower constituencies than is the president. The people usually expect the president to address general concerns such as foreign policy and economic prosperity, while Congresspersons are asked to solve individual problems. There are structural differences as well. Congress is a body composed of hundreds of independent people, each with a different power base, and it is divided along partisan lines. Thus, it is difficult for Congress to act quickly or to project unity and clear policy statements.

—Baradat, *Understanding American Democracy*, p. 300

1. What two branches of the government are discussed?

   _____

2. Does this paragraph mainly use comparison, contrast, or both?

   _____

3. Explain how the two branches are similar and/or different.

   _____

   _____

4. Why is it difficult for Congress to act quickly?

   _____

   _____

5. Highlight the transitional words in the paragraph.

B.   What are the main characteristics of this new postindustrial society? Unlike the industrial society from which we are emerging, its hallmark is not raw materials and manufacturing. Rather, its basic component is *information*. Teachers pass on knowledge to students, while lawyers, physicians, bankers, pilots, and interior decorators sell their specialized knowledge of law, the body, money, aerodynamics, and color schemes to clients. Unlike the factory workers in an industrial society, these workers don't *produce* anything. Rather, they transmit or use information to provide services that others are willing to pay for.

—Henslin, *Social Problems*, p. 154

6. What two things are being compared or contrasted?

   _____

7. What is the postindustrial society based upon?

   _____

8. What did most workers in the industrial society do at their jobs?

   _____

9. How is information connected to money in the postindustrial society?

   _____

10. Highlight the transitional words used in the paragraph.

4f   LISTING/ENUMERATION

LEARNING OBJECTIVE 6
Recognize listing/
enumeration

If asked to evaluate a film you saw, you might describe the characters, plot, and technical effects. These details about the film could be arranged in any order; each detail provides further information about the film, but they have no single order in which they must be discussed. This arrangement of ideas is known as **listing** or **enumeration**—giving bits of information on a topic by stating them one after the other. Often there is no particular method of arrangement for those details.

You can visualize the listing/enumeration patterns as follows:

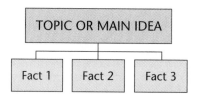

The following list of managers' difficulties in problem solving could have been presented in any order without altering the meaning of the paragraph.

> Although accurate identification of a problem is essential before the problem can be solved, this stage of decision making creates many difficulties for managers. Sometimes managers' preconceptions of the problem prevent them from seeing the situation as it actually is. They produce an answer before the proper question has ever been asked. In other cases, managers overlook truly significant issues by focusing on unimportant matters. Also, managers may mistakenly analyze problems in terms of symptoms rather than underlying causes.
>
> —Pride, Hughes, and Kapoor, *Business*, p. 189

This pattern is widely used in college textbooks in most academic disciplines. In its loosest form, the pattern may be simply a list of items: factors that influence light emission, characteristics of a particular poet, a description of an atom, a list of characteristics that define poverty.

Somewhat tighter is the use of listing to explain, support, or provide evidence. Support may be in the form of facts, statistics, or examples. For instance, the statement, "The incidence of white collar crime has dramatically increased over the past ten years" would be followed by facts and statistics documenting the increase.

TRANSITIONS FOR LISTING

one aspect of relativity . . .
a second feature of relativity . . .
also, relativity . . .
there are *several characteristics of* . . .
(1) . . . , *(2)* . . . , *and (3)* . . . ,
(a) . . . , *(b)* . . . , *and (c)* . . . ,
Other transitional words and phrases are *in addition, first, second, third, finally,* and *another.*

EXERCISE 4-9 . . . USING LISTING

Read each of the following paragraphs and answer the questions that follow.

A. Minorities come into existence, then, when, due to expanded political boundaries or migration, people with different customs, languages, values or physical characteristics come under control of the same state organization. There, some groups who share physical and cultural traits discriminate against those with different traits. The losers in this power struggle are forced into minority group status; the winners enjoy the higher status and greater privileges that their dominance brings. Wagley and Harris noted that all minorities share these five characteristics: (1) They are treated unequally by the dominant group. (2) Their physical or cultural traits are held in low esteem by the dominant group. (3) They tend to feel strong group solidarity because of their physical or cultural traits—and the disabilities these traits bring. (4) Their membership in a minority group is not voluntary but comes through birth. (5) They tend to marry within their group. Sharing cultural or physical traits, having similar experiences of discrimination, and marrying within their own group create a shared identity—sometimes even a sense of common destiny. These shared experiences, however, do not mean that all minority groups have the same goals.

—Henslin, *Social Problems,* p. 252

1. What does this paragraph list?

   _____

2. How do minority groups come into existence?

   _____

   _____

   _____

B. Voters make two basic decisions at election time. The first is whether to vote. Americans' right to vote is well established, but in order to do so citizens must go through the registration process. America's unique registration system is one major reason why turnout in American elections is much lower than in most other democracies. The 1996 election was another in a long string of low-turnout elections. Second, those who choose to vote must decide for whom to cast their ballots. Over a generation of research on voting behavior has helped political scientists understand the dominant role played by three factors in voters' choices: party identification, candidate evaluations, and policy positions.

—Edwards, *Government in America,* p. 330

3. What does this paragraph list?

   _____

   _____

4. Highlight the transitional words used in the paragraph.

5. What is the major reason why voter turnout is low in America?

_____

4g   MIXED PATTERNS

LEARNING OBJECTIVE 7
Recognize mixed patterns

Organizational patterns are often combined. In describing a process, a writer may also give reasons why each step must be followed in the prescribed order. A lecturer may define a concept by comparing it with something similar or familiar. Suppose an essay in your political science textbook opens by stating, "The distinction between 'power' and 'power potential' is an important one in considering the balance of power." You might expect a definition pattern (where the two terms are defined), but you also might anticipate that the essay would discuss the difference between the two terms (contrast pattern).

EXERCISE 4-10 . . . USING ORGANIZATIONAL PATTERNS 1

For each of the following topic sentences, anticipate what organizational pattern(s) the paragraph is likely to exhibit. Record your prediction in the space provided.

1. The Enlightenment celebrated the power of reason; however, an opposite reaction, Romanticism, soon followed.

   Pattern: _____

2. Psychogenic amnesia—a severe and often permanent memory loss—results in disorientation and the inability to draw on past experiences.

   Pattern: _____

3. Several statistical procedures are used to track the changes in the divorce rate.

   Pattern: _____

4. The GNP (gross national product) is an economic measure that considers the total value of goods and services that a country produces during a given year.

   Pattern: _____

5. Large numbers of European immigrants first began to arrive in the United States in the 1920s.

   Pattern: _____

6. There are sources of information about corporations that might help an investor evaluate them. One of the most useful is the Value Line Investment Survey.

   Pattern: _____

7. Diseases of the heart and blood vessels—cardiovascular diseases—are the leading cause of death in the United States today.

   Pattern: _____

8. The spinal cord is located within the spinal column; it looks like a section of rope or twine.

   Pattern: _____

9. Think of the hardware in a computer system as the kitchen in a short-order restaurant: It's equipped to produce whatever output a customer (user) requests, but sits idle until an order (command) is placed.

   Pattern: _____

10. The purpose of a résumé is to sell the qualities of the person writing it; it should include several important kinds of information.

   Pattern: _____

EXERCISE 4-11 . . . USING ORGANIZATIONAL PATTERNS 2

Read each of the following paragraphs and identify the primary organizational pattern used in each.

Paragraph 1

Ours is an ethnically, religiously, and racially diverse society. The white European Protestants, black slaves, and Native Americans who made up the bulk of the U.S. population when the first census was taken in 1790 were joined by Catholic immigrants from Ireland and Germany in the 1840s and 1850s. In the 1870s, Chinese migrated to America, drawn by jobs in railroad construction. Around the turn of the twentieth century, most immigration was from eastern, central, and southern Europe, with its many ethnic, linguistic, and religious groups. Today, most immigration is from Asia and Latin America.

—Greenberg and Page, *The Struggle for Democracy*, p. 71

Pattern: _____

Paragraph 2

Anthropology is the study of human beings from their origins to the present time. It is concerned with humans as both natural and social beings, and, as such, overlaps with other academic disciplines such as sociology, psychology, biology, and history. Because the field of anthropology is so complex and diverse, it is commonly divided into four branches. Cultural anthropology focuses on the behavior of human beings in social groups. Archaeology is the study of people who lived in the past; it concentrates on material goods that humans left behind. Physical anthropology studies the biological development of human beings. Anthropological linguistics is the study of human language, both historical and modern, and focuses on the development, change, and use of language.

—Tortora, *Introduction to the Human Body*, p. 77

Pattern: _____

Paragraph 3

The process of digestion begins at the upper end of the gastrointestinal tract. The *mouth* is where food enters and where the processes of mechanical breakdown and digestion begin. In the mouth, food is chewed (a process called mastication) and mechanically broken down into smaller particles by the cutting and grinding actions of the teeth. The food is also mixed with saliva, which lubricates it and contains an enzyme which begins the digestion of carbohydrates by breaking down starch and glycogen.

From the mouth, the food-saliva mixture is propelled by the tongue into the pharynx (commonly known as the *throat*), a common passageway for food and air. From the pharynx, the passageways for food and air diverge. Whereas air enters the larynx and trachea and proceeds toward the lungs, food enters the esophagus, which runs parallel to the trachea.

The esophagus is a muscular tube whose primary function is to conduct food from the pharynx to the stomach. It can easily stretch to accommodate food as it is swallowed; when food is not present, however, it is normally collapsed.

—adapted from German and Stanfield, *Principles of Human Physiology*, pp. 606–607

Pattern: _____

Paragraph 4

By far the most important committees in Congress are the standing committees. Currently 16 standing committees in the Senate and 22 in the House receive the bills that are introduced in Congress. The standing committees are assigned subject-matter jurisdiction by the rules of their respective house, and their titles reflect their general area of expertise. Hence, we have the Senate Finance Committee, the House Agriculture Committee, the Senate Budget Committee, the House Judiciary Committee, and so on. The authority of the standing committees includes the power to study legislation, to subpoena witnesses or information, to remand bills to subcommittees, to vote bills dead, to table bills (putting them aside, thus allowing them to die quietly at the end of the congressional term), to amend bills, to write bills (amending a bill or writing an entirely new version of a bill is called marking-up), or to report the bill to the floor.

—Baradat, *Understanding American Democracy*, p. 202

Pattern: _____

Paragraph 5

Not all tumors are malignant (cancerous); in fact, most are benign (non-cancerous). Benign and malignant tumors differ in several key ways. Benign tumors are generally composed of ordinary-looking cells enclosed in a fibrous shell or capsule that prevents their spreading to other body areas. Malignant tumors, in contrast, are usually not enclosed in a protective capsule and can therefore spread to other organs. Unlike benign tumors, which merely expand to take over a given space, malignant cells invade surrounding tissue, emitting clawlike protrusions that disrupt chemical processes within healthy cells.

—adapted from Donatelle, *Health*, p. 324

Pattern: _____

4h OTHER PATTERNS OF ORGANIZATION

LEARNING OBJECTIVE 8
Recognize other patterns of organization

Although the patterns presented in the previous sections are the most common, writers do not limit themselves to these six patterns. Especially in academic writing, you may also find statement and clarification, summary, generalization and example, and addition. Transitions associated with these different patterns are listed in the "Summing It Up" table on pages 134–135.

Statement and Clarification

Many writers make a statement of fact and then proceed to clarify or explain that statement. For instance, a writer may open a paragraph by stating that "The best education for you may not be the best education for someone else." The remainder of the paragraph would then discuss that statement and make its meaning clear by explaining how educational needs are individual and based on one's talents, skills, and goals. Here is a sample paragraph about sex ratios.

Sex ratios in the poor countries do not show a consistent pattern. In some poor countries men outnumber women, but in others, in tropical Africa, for example, women outnumber men. In fact, variations in sex ratios can be explained only by a combination of national economic and cultural factors. In the countries of North America and Europe and in Japan, women may suffer many kinds of discrimination, but they are not generally discriminated against when it comes to access to medical care.

—Bergman and Renwick, *Introduction to Geography*, p. 185

Notice that the writer begins with a statement about sex ratios in poor countries and then goes on to clarify this fact. The author uses the transitional phrase *in fact*.

Summary

A summary is a condensed statement that provides the key points of a larger idea or piece of writing. Frequently, summaries at the end of each chapter provide a quick review of the chapter's contents. Often writers summarize what they have already said or what someone else has said. For example, in a psychology textbook you will find many summaries of research. Instead of asking you to read an entire research study, the textbook author will summarize the study's findings. Other times a writer may repeat in condensed form what he or she has already said as a means of emphasis or clarification.

In the following paragraph about the magazine industry, the author uses the summary method of organization.

> In summary, the magazine industry is adapting to the new world of electronic multimedia information and entertainment, with formats that will be quite different from the familiar ones. Computer-generated publishing has become the norm in the magazine business, expanding beyond its uses in producing newsletters and other specialized publications. Most general circulation magazines already rely heavily on desktop computers, interacting with other electronic equipment to produce high-quality, graphics-filled products.
>
> —Dizard, *Old Media, New Media,* p. 169

Notice that the author summarizes many facts about how the magazine industry uses electronic multimedia information and that the transitional phrase *in summary* is used.

Generalization and Example

Examples are one of the best ways to explain something that is unfamiliar or unknown. Examples are specific instances or situations that illustrate a concept or idea. Often writers make a general statement, or generalization, and then explain it by giving examples to make its meaning clear. In a social problems textbook, you may find the following generalization: Computer theft by employees is on the increase. The section may then go on to offer examples from specific companies in which employees insert fictitious information into the company's computer program and steal company funds.

In the following paragraph about dreams, the writer uses generalization and example.

> Different cultures place varying emphases on dreams and support different beliefs concerning dreams. For example, many people in the United States view dreams as irrelevant fantasy with no connection to everyday life. By contrast, people in other cultures view dreams as key sources of information about the future, the spiritual world, and the dreamer. Such cultural views can influence the probability of dream recall. In many modern Western cultures, people rarely remember their dreams upon awakening. The Parintintin of South America,

however, typically remember several dreams every night and the Senoi of Malaysia discuss their dreams with family members in the morning.

—Davis and Palladino, *Psychology*, p. 210

Notice that the author begins with the generalization that different cultures place different emphases on dreams and then goes on to give examples of the way specific cultures treat dreams. Note the use of the transitional phrase *for example.*

Addition

Writers often introduce an idea or make a statement and then supply additional information about that idea or statement. For instance, an education text-book may introduce the concept of home schooling and then provide in-depth information about its benefits. This pattern is often used to expand, elaborate, or discuss an idea in greater detail.

In the following paragraph about pathogens, the writer uses addition.

> Some pathogens [disease-causing organisms] evolve and mutate naturally. Also, patients who fail to complete the full portion of their antibiotic prescriptions allow drug-resistant pathogens to multiply. The use of antibiotics in animal feed and to spray on fruits and vegetables during food processing increases opportunities for resistant organisms to evolve and thrive. Furthermore, there is evidence that the disruption of Earth's natural habitats can trigger the evolution of new pathogens.
>
> —Bergman and Renwick, *Introduction to Geography*, p. 182

Notice that the writer states that some pathogens mutate naturally and then goes on to add that they also mutate as a result of human activities. Note the use of the transitional words *also* and *furthermore.*

EXERCISE 4-12 . . . USING ORGANIZATIONAL PATTERNS 3

For each of the following statements, identify the pattern that is evident and write its name in the space provided. Choose from among the following patterns: process, statement and clarification, summary, generalization and example, addition, and spatial order.

1. If our criminal justice system works, the recidivism rate—the percentage of people released from prison who return—should decrease. In other words, in a successful system, there should be a decrease in the number of criminals who are released from prison and become repeat offenders.

   Pattern: _____

2. Students who are informed about drugs tend to use them in moderation. Furthermore, they tend to help educate others.

   Pattern: _____

3. A successful drug addiction treatment program would offer free or very cheap drugs to addicts. Heroin addicts, for example, could be prescribed heroin when under a physician's care.

   Pattern: _____

4. In conclusion, it is safe to say that crime by women is likely to increase as greater numbers of women assume roles traditionally held by men.

   Pattern: _____

5. The pollutants we have just discussed all involve chemicals; we can conclude that they threaten our environment and our well-being.

   Pattern: _____

6. Sociologists study how we are socialized into sex roles, the attitudes expected of males and females. Sex roles, in fact, identify some activities and behaviors as clearly male and others as clearly female.

   Pattern: _____

7. Patients often consult a lay referral network to discuss their medical problems. Cancer patients, for instance, can access Internet discussion groups that provide both information and support.

   Pattern: _____

EXERCISE 4-13 . . . USING ORGANIZATIONAL PATTERNS 4

Read each of the following paragraphs and identify the predominant organizational pattern used. Write the name of the pattern in the space provided. Choose from among the following patterns: statement and clarification, summary, generalization and example, and addition.

1. Managing Emotional Responses

Have you gotten all worked up about something you thought was happening only to find that your perceptions were totally wrong or that a communication problem had caused a misrepresentation of events? If you're like most of us, you probably have. We often get upset not by realities but by our faulty perceptions. For example, suppose you found out that everyone except you is invited to a party. You might easily begin to wonder why you were excluded. Does someone dislike you? Have you offended someone? Such thoughts are typical. However, the reality of the situation may have absolutely nothing to do with your being liked or disliked. Perhaps you were sent an invitation and it didn't get to you.

—Donatelle, *Access to Health*, p. 81

Pattern: _____

2.   A serious problem with some drugs is addiction, or drug dependence. That is, people come to depend on the regular consumption of a drug in order to make it

through the day. When people think of drug addiction, they are likely to think of addicts huddled in slum doorways, the dregs of society who seldom venture into daylight—unless it is to rob someone. They don't associate addiction with "good," middle-class neighborhoods and "solid citizens." But let's look at drug addiction a little more closely. Although most people may think of heroin as the prime example of an addictive drug, I suggest that nicotine is the better case to consider. I remember a next-door neighbor who stood in his backyard, a lit cigarette in his hand, and told me about the operation in which one of his lungs was removed. I say "I remember," because soon after our conversation he died from his addiction.

—Henslin, *Social Problems*, p. 93

Pattern: _____

3.   In short, the view that a drug is good or bad depends not on objective conditions but on subjective concerns. It is a matter of how people define matters. People's definitions, in turn, influence how they use and abuse drugs, whether or not a drug will be legal or illegal, and what social policies they want to adopt. This is the central sociological aspect of drug use and abuse, one that we shall stress over and over in this chapter.

—Henslin, *Social Problems*, p. 91

Pattern: _____

4.   Human migration has by no means come to an end. Large-scale migrations still make daily news. The United Nations' Universal Declaration of Human Rights affirms anyone's right to leave his or her homeland to seek a better life elsewhere, but it cannot guarantee that there will be any place willing to take anyone. As in the past, the major push and pull factors behind contemporary migration are economic and political. Also, people are trying to move from the poor countries to the rich countries and from the politically repressed countries to more democratic countries. In addition, millions of people are fleeing civil and international warfare. Pressures for migration are growing, and in coming years they may constitute the world's greatest political and economic problem.

—Bergman and Renwick, *Introduction to Geography*, p. 197

Pattern: _____

5.   Be careful not to evaluate negatively the cultural differences you perceive. Be careful that you don't fall into the trap of ethnocentric thinking, evaluating your culture positively and other cultures negatively. For example, many Americans of Northern European descent evaluate negatively the tendency of many Hispanics and Southern Europeans to use the street for a gathering place, for playing Dominoes, and for just sitting on a cool evening. Whether you like or dislike using the street in this way, recognize that neither attitude is logically correct or incorrect. This street behavior is simply adequate or inadequate for *members of the culture.*

—DeVito, *Human Communication*, p. 103

Pattern: _____

SUMMING IT UP

PATTERNS AND TRANSITIONS

PATTERN	CHARACTERISTICS	TRANSITIONS
Definition	Explains the meaning of a word or phrase	Is, refers to, can be defined as, means, consists of, involves, is a term that, is called, is characterized by, occurs when, are those that, entails, corresponds to, is literally
Classification	Divides a topic into parts based on shared characteristics	Classified as, comprises, is composed of, several varieties of, different stages of, different groups that, includes, one, first, second, another, finally, last
Chronological Order	Describes events, processes, procedures	First, second, later, before, next, as soon as, after, then, finally, meanwhile, following, last, during, in, on, when, until
Process	Describes the order in which things are done or how things work	First, second, next, then, following, after that, last, finally
Order of Importance	Describes ideas in order of priority or preference	Less, more, primary, first, next, last, most important, primarily, secondarily
Spatial Order	Describes physical location or position in space	Above, below, beside, next to, in front of, behind, inside, outside, opposite, within, nearby
Cause and Effect	Describes how one or more things cause or are related to another	*Causes:* because, because of, for, since, stems from, one cause is, one reason is, leads to, causes, creates, yields, produces, due to, breeds, for this reason *Effects:* consequently, results in, one result is, therefore, thus, as a result, hence
Comparison and Contrast	Discusses similarities and/or differences among ideas, theories, concepts, objects, or persons	*Similarities:* both, also, similarly, like, likewise, too, as well as, resembles, correspondingly, in the same way, to compare, in comparison, share

(continued on next page)

(continued from preceding page)

PATTERN	CHARACTERISTICS	TRANSITIONS
		Differences: unlike, differs from, in contrast, on the other hand, instead, despite, nevertheless, however, in spite of, whereas, as opposed to
Listing/Enumeration	Organizes lists of information: characteristics, features, parts, or categories	The following, several, for example, for instance, one, another, also, too, in other words, first, second, numerals (1., 2.), letters (a., b.), most important, the largest, the least, finally
Statement and Clarification	Indicates that information explaining an idea or concept will follow	In fact, in other words, clearly, evidently, obviously
Summary	Indicates that a condensed review of an idea or piece of writing is to follow	In summary, in conclusion, in brief, to summarize, to sum up, in short, on the whole
Generalization and Example	Provides examples that clarify a broad, general statement	For example, for instance, that is, to illustrate, thus
Addition	Indicates that additional information will follow	Furthermore, additionally, also, besides, further, in addition, moreover, again

For Further Practice

For support in meeting this chapter's learning objectives, log in to http://www.myreadinglab.com, go to the Study Plan tab, click on **Reading Skills** and choose **Patterns of Organization** from the list of subtopics. Read and view the videos and resources in the Review Materials section, and then complete the Recall, Practice, and Test exercises in the Activities section. You can check your scores and overall progress by using the Gradebook.

5 Reading and Thinking Visually

LEARNING OBJECTIVES

In this chapter, you will learn how to

1 Read and analyze photographs
2 Approach graphics
3 Analyze tables
4 Analyze graphs
5 Analyze charts
6 Analyze diagrams
7 Analyze maps and time lines
8 Analyze infographics

If you preview this (or any other) textbook, you will probably notice many photos, figures, tables, and other learning aids. **Visual aids,** such as photographs, graphs, and illustrations, are common not only in college textbooks, but also in other reading materials, from magazines to Web sites to newspapers.

All visual aids share one goal: to illustrate concepts and help you understand them better. As a reader, your key goal is to extract important information from them. Visual aids work best when you read them *in addition to* the text, not *instead of* the text.

5a   READING AND ANALYZING PHOTOGRAPHS

LEARNING OBJECTIVE 1
Read and analyze photographs

An old saying goes, "A picture is worth a thousand words." Photographs can help writers achieve many different goals. For example, photos can be used to

- **spark interest.**
- **provide perspective.**
- **elicit an emotional response.**
- **introduce new ideas.**
- **offer examples.**

Just as you can learn specific techniques to improve your reading comprehension, you can use a process for reading and analyzing photos.

1. **First read the text that refers to the photo.** Photos are not a substitute for the text. They are meant to be examined *along with* the text. In fact, most textbooks will include specific references to each photo, usually directly after a key point. For example:

> A common term for a shantytown, especially in Latin American countries, is *favela* (Figure 5-1).

Examine the photo as soon as you see the reference. The photo will help you visualize the concept, making it easier to remember.

2. **Read the photo's title and/or caption.** The **caption** is the text that accompanies the photo. It is usually placed above, below, or to the side of the photo. The caption generally explains how the photo fits into the discussion.

3. **Ask: What is my first overall impression?** Because photos can be powerful, they are often chosen to elicit a strong reaction. Analyze your response to the photo. Ask yourself: Why has the author included this photo?

FIGURE 5-1 PHOTOGRAPH FROM A GEOGRAPHY TEXTBOOK

A favela in Rio de Janeiro. Shantytowns are common in South American countries, where they often develop close to wealthy neighborhoods in big cities with large populations. These shantytowns are called *favelas, barrios, colonias,* or *barriadas.*

Source: http://www.travel-images.com/photo-brazil78.html.

4. **Examine the details**. Look closely at the picture, examining both the foreground and the background. Details can provide clues regarding the date the photograph was taken and its location. For example, people's hairstyles and clothing often give hints as to the year or decade. Landmarks help point to location. If you saw a photo of a smiling couple with the Eiffel Tower in the background, you would know that the photo was taken in Paris, France.

5. **Look for connections to the textbook, society, or your life**. Ask yourself how the photo relates to what you are reading or to your own experiences. Putting the image in context will help you learn the concepts *and* help you prepare for exams.

    Now apply this method to Figure 5-1.

1. **Read the text that refers to the photo.** Note that this photo is from a geography textbook. The text it illustrates might read as follows:

> On the outskirts of many cities in developing countries are large shantytowns with no access to utilities or running water (see photo).

Note that the reference comes directly after a key point.

2. **Read the caption.** In reading the caption, you learn where the photo was taken (Rio de Janeiro, Brazil). You also learn key vocabulary terms: *favelas, barrios, colonias,* and *barriadas*.

3. **Examine your first impression**. This is clearly a settlement of some sort. The homes are built on a hill, and the surrounding area looks quite pleasant, with trees. But would you want to live here? Why or why not? (Most people probably would not want to live in a shantytown.)

4. **Examine the details.** In examining the details, you may notice the absence of power lines. What does this suggest about the income level of the people who live in a favela? Notice too the crowded conditions and the size of the houses. What do these details suggest about the people who live there? (All these details suggest the people are probably poor.)

5. **Look for connections.** Thinking about connections to American society or your life, you might contrast the way poor people live in a favela to the way poor people live in the United States. How is this favela similar to low-income neighborhoods in U.S. cities? How is it different? It is similar in that many people live in a small area. It is different in that the setting is natural rather than urban.

EXERCISE 5-1 . . . ANALYZING A PHOTOGRAPH

Analyze the photo and answer the accompanying questions.

1. What does the term "culturally diverse society" mean?

_____

_____

In a society as culturally diverse as the United States, companies try to ensure that their advertising is appealing to as many people as possible.

2. Which culturally diverse groups are represented in this photo?

   _____

   _____

3. What do the hairstyles and clothing of the people in the photo tell you about their income level? (Also notice the type of car being driven.)

   _____

   _____

4. What audience do you think the advertiser is trying to reach with this photo? For example, is this ad trying to appeal to senior citizens? To recent college graduates?

   _____

   _____

5. Can you think of any groups *not* represented in this photo?

   _____

   _____

5b   A GENERAL APPROACH TO READING GRAPHICS

LEARNING OBJECTIVE 2
Approach graphics
In addition to photographs, you will encounter many other types of graphics in your reading materials. These include

- tables
- graphs
- charts
- diagrams
- maps
- time lines
- infographics
- cartoons

Here is a step-by-step approach to reading graphics. As you read, apply each step to the graph shown in Figure 5-2.

FIGURE 5-2 A SAMPLE GRAPH

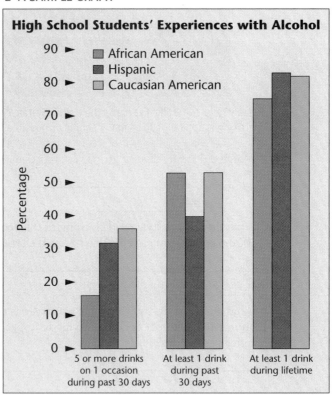

High School Students' Experiences with Alcohol

■ African American
■ Hispanic
□ Caucasian American

Percentage

5 or more drinks on 1 occasion during past 30 days

At least 1 drink during past 30 days

At least 1 drink during lifetime

Caucasian American high school students are more likely than African American or Hispanic students to have had five or more alcoholic drinks on one occasion during the past 30 days.

Source: Fabes and Martin, *Exploring Child Development*, p. 454

1. **Look for the reference in the text.** The textbook author will refer you to each specific graphic. When you see the reference in the text, finish reading the sentence, then look at the graphic. In some cases, you will need to go back and forth between the text and the graphic, especially if the graphic has multiple parts.
2. **Read the title and caption.** The title will identify the subject, and the caption will provide important information. In some cases, the caption will specify the key take-away point for the graphic.
3. **Examine how the graphic is organized.** Read all headings and labels. Sometimes a label is turned sideways, like the word "Percentage" in Figure 5-2. Labels tell you what topics or categories are being discussed, and they are important. For example, if Figure 5-2 did not specify "Percentage," you might incorrectly think that the numbers along the left side are *numbers* of students instead of *percentages* of students.
4. **Look at the legend.** The **legend** is the guide to the colors, terms, and other important information in the graphic. In Figure 5-2, the legend appears at the top and shows blue for African Americans, orange for Hispanics, and green for Caucasian Americans.
5. **Analyze the graphic.** Based on what you see, determine the graphic's key purpose. For example, is its purpose to show change over time, describe a process, present statistics? The purpose of Figure 5-2 is clear: it compares high school students from three ethnic groups in terms of their alcohol consumption.
6. **Study the data to identify trends or patterns.** If the graphic includes numbers, look for unusual statistics or unexplained variations. For instance, note that while Caucasian high school students are more likely than African American students to have had *five or more* alcoholic drinks on one occasion during the past 30 days, Caucasian and African American students are *equally likely* to have had at least *one* drink during the past 30 days. What conclusion can you draw from this observation?
7. **Make a brief summary note.** In the margin, jot a brief note summarizing the graphic's trend, pattern, or key point. Writing will help cement the idea in your mind. A summary note of Figure 5-2 might read, "Most adolescents have had some experience with alcohol, and about one-third have engaged in heavy consumption in the last month."

EXERCISE 5-2 . . . READING GRAPHICS

Choose any graphic or visual aid from this chapter and go through it step-by-step, following the seven-step process outlined above.

5c   TABLES

LEARNING OBJECTIVE 3
Analyze tables

A **table** lists factual information in an organized manner, usually in rows or columns. Tables are often composed of numbers (Figure 5-3), but they can also contain words (Figure 5-4). Tables condense or summarize large amounts of data into

FIGURE 5-3 A SAMPLE TABLE: NUMBERS

ESTIMATED DAILY CALORIE NEEDS

	Calorie Range		
	Sedentary	→	Active
Children			
2–3 years old	1,000	→	1,400
Females			
4–8 years old	1,200	→	1,800
9–13	1,600	→	2,200
14–18	1,800	→	2,400
19–30	2,000	→	2,400
31–50	1,800	→	2,200
51+	1,600	→	2,200
Males			
4–8 years old	1,400	→	2,000
9–13	1,800	→	2,600
14–18	2,200	→	3,200
19–30	2,400	→	3,000
31–50	2,200	→	3,000
51+	2,000	→	2,800

Source: Donatelle, *Health,* p. 257

an easily readable format, but they can sometimes seem overwhelming because they include so much information. To understand tables, follow a step-by-step process:

1. **Look for the reference in the text.**
2. **Determine how the information is divided and arranged.**
3. **Look for key data points, make comparisons, and determine trends.**
4. **Draw conclusions.**

EXERCISE 5-3 . . . READING TABLES

Use Figures 5-3 and 5-4 to answer the following questions.

FIGURE 5-3

Indicate whether each statement is true (T) or false (F).

_____ 1. Starting at age 4, males require more calories than females.

_____ 2. In general, those who lead more active lifestyles tend to need fewer calories.

_____ 3. The highest calorie requirements are needed by active females in the 14–30 age range.

FIGURE 5-4 A SAMPLE TABLE: WORDS

MAJOR STORE RETAILER TYPES

TYPE	DESCRIPTION	EXAMPLES
Specialty stores	Carry a narrow product line with a deep assortment, such as apparel stores, sporting-good stores, furniture stores, and florists.	Tiffany, Radio Shack, Williams-Sonoma
Department stores	Carry several product lines—typically clothing, home furnishings, and household goods—with each line operated as a separate department managed by specialist buyers.	Macy's, Sears, Neiman Marcus
Supermarkets	Relatively large, low-cost, low-margin, high-volume, self-service operations designed to serve the consumer's total needs for grocery and household products.	Kroger, Safeway, A&P, Stop & Shop, Hannaford
Convenience stores	Relatively small stores located near residential areas, open long hours seven days a week, and carrying a limited line of high-turnover convenience products at slightly higher prices.	7-Eleven, Wawa, Circle K, Sheetz
Discount stores	Carry standard merchandise sold at lower prices with lower margins and higher volumes.	Walmart, Target, Kohl's, Kmart
Off-price retailers	Sell merchandise bought at less-than-regular wholesale prices and sold at less than retail, often leftover goods, overruns, and irregulars obtained at lower prices from manufacturers and other retailers. This category also includes retailers that sell items in bulk.	Home Goods, T.J. Maxx, Marshall's, Sam's Club, BJ's Wholesale Club
Superstores	Very large stores aimed at meeting consumers' total needs for routinely purchased food and nonfood items.	Walmart Supercenter, BestBuy, PetSmart

Source: Armstrong and Kotler, _Marketing,_ p. 346.

FIGURE 5-4

1. What type of store is a bookstore? _____

2. Into what category of store would factory outlets fall? _____

3. Provide an additional example of each of the seven types of stores in the table.

   _____

   _____

   _____

4. At which type of store are you likely to pay a higher price for a gallon of milk: a supermarket or a convenience store? _____

5d   GRAPHS

LEARNING OBJECTIVE 4
Analyze graphs

A **graph** shows the relationship between two ideas, sometimes called *variables* because they can change depending on the circumstances. Graphs are extremely common in business and science textbooks and fall into two general categories:

- bar graphs
- line graphs

To understand a graph, do the following:

- **Read all the labels, which identify the variables.**
- **Read the legend, which explains how the information is presented.**
- **Summarize the graph's key points in a few sentences.**

Bar Graphs

Bar graphs illustrate relationships with thick bars. They are often used to make comparisons between amounts, and they are particularly useful for showing changes over time. In a well-constructed bar graph, it is easy to see key differences.

The bars shown on a bar graph can be either horizontal or vertical. Figure 5-5 is a simple vertical bar graph showing the importance of small business in the United States. Part (a) of the graph shows that almost 86 percent of all U.S. companies have fewer than 20 employees. Part (b) shows that 25.6 percent of U.S. workers work at a company with fewer than 20 employees. Note a special feature of this graph: the author has included a built-in note summarizing the key point.

FIGURE 5-5 A SAMPLE BAR GRAPH

THE IMPORTANCE OF SMALL BUSINESS IN THE UNITED STATES

*Almost 86 percent of all U.S. businesses have **no more than 20 employees**. The total number of people employed by these businesses is approximately one-fourth of the entire U.S. workforce. Another 29 percent work for companies with **fewer than 100 employees**.*

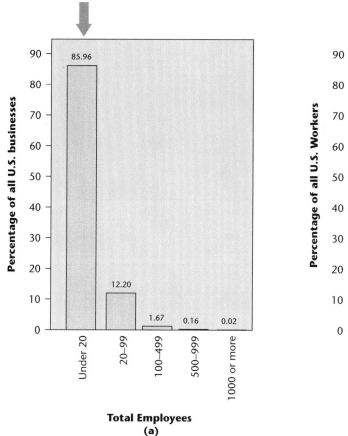

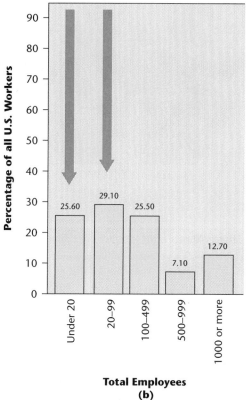

Total Employees
(a)

Total Employees
(b)

Source: Ebert and Griffin, *Business Essentials*, p38.

In a **multiple bar graph,** two or three comparisons are made simultaneously, which makes reading the labels and the legend particularly important. Figure 5-6 shows the breakdown of the elderly population in the United States by race and ethnicity. Note that two bars are included for each racial and ethnic group: the actual percentages for 1990, and the estimated percentages for 2050.

FIGURE 5-6 A SAMPLE MULTIPLE BAR GRAPH

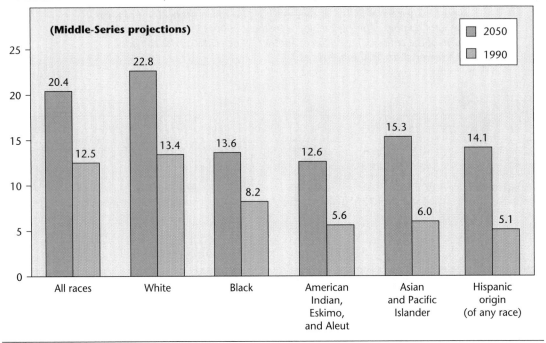

PERCENTAGE OF ELDERLY, BY RACE AND ETHNICITY, 1990 AND 2050

Source: Kunz, *THINK Marriages and Families*, p. 173

FIGURE 5-7 A SAMPLE STACKED BAR GRAPH

DAY CARE ARRANGEMENTS, BY ETHNICITY

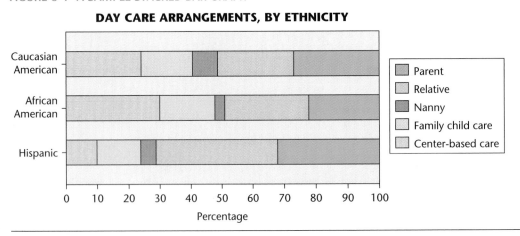

Source: Fabes and Martin, *Exploring Child Development*, p. 196

In a **stacked bar graph,** the bars are placed one on top of another rather than side by side. The goal is often to emphasize whole/part relationships (that is, the relationship of one part of the bar to the entire group or class). Figure 5-7 is a stacked bar graph showing the day-care arrangements made by people of three ethnic groups: Caucasians, African Americans, and Hispanics. By looking at the colors of the graph, you can see that nannies are employed much more by Caucasians than by African Americans, while African Americans make more use of center-based care than the other two groups.

Line Graphs

Line graphs connect data points along a line. Connecting points in this manner often gives a sense of trends or changes over time. Sometimes only one variable is shown in a line graph, but it is common to see line graphs with multiple variables, as in Figure 5-8, which shows how Americans' answer to the question "How much of the time do you think you can trust the government?" changed over the period 1958–2006.

FIGURE 5-8 A SAMPLE LINE GRAPH

THE DECLINE OF TRUST IN GOVERNMENT, 1958–2006

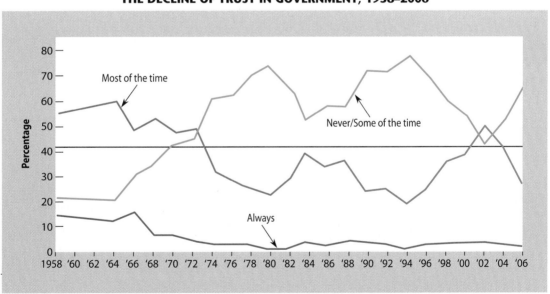

The graph shows how people have responded to the following question: How much of the time do you think can trust the government in Washington to do what is right—just about always, most of the time, or only some of the time?

Source: Edwards, Wattenberg, and Lineberry, *Government in America,* p. 201

EXERCISE 5-4 . . . READING GRAPHS

Use Figures 5-5 through 5-8 to answer the following questions.

_____ 1. What is the best summary statement for **Figure 5-5** (p. 145)?

    a. Most U.S. businesses employ a minimum of 500 workers.

    b. Small businesses are more common in the United States than in Europe.

    c. Only about 2 percent of U.S. companies employee 100 workers or more.

    d. People in the United States enjoy working for small, family-owned businesses.

_____ 2. What is the best summary statement for **Figure 5-6** (p. 146)?

    a. The Hispanic population is growing significantly in the United States.

    b. The Hispanic population in the United States is expected to decrease between 1990 and 2050.

    c. There were roughly the same numbers of American Indians and Hispanic people in the United States in 1990.

    d. Regardless of race or ethnicity, the U.S. population is getting older, and elderly people will make up much larger chunks of the population in 2050 than in 1990.

3. Using **Figure 5-7** (p. 146), write a statement summarizing the use of relatives for child care by Caucasian, African American, and Hispanic families.

_____

_____

_____

4. Use **Figure 5-8** (p. 147) to complete this statement:

The number of people saying they trust the government most of the time reached its peak in _____, while the number of people saying that they trust the government never or only some of the time reached its peak in _____. Absolute trust in government was the highest in _____; that was the year that the most people said they always trust the government to do what is right.

5e   CHARTS

LEARNING OBJECTIVE 5
Analyze charts

Unlike graphs, which illustrate two or more variables, a **chart** often focuses on illustrating just one variable or concept.

Pie Charts

Pie charts, also called *circle graphs,* show whole/part relationships. The pie or circle represents the whole (or 100 percent), and each "slice" of the pie represents a smaller part. Figure 5-9, a pie chart illustrating world religious affiliations, indicates that Christianity has more adherents than any other world religion.

FIGURE 5-9 A SAMPLE PIE CHART

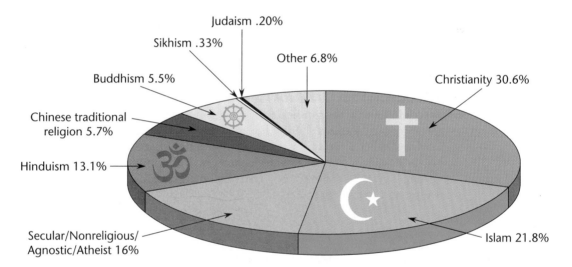

WORLD RELIGIOUS AFFILIATIONS

Judaism .20%
Sikhism .33%
Other 6.8%
Buddhism 5.5%
Christianity 30.6%
Chinese traditional religion 5.7%
Hinduism 13.1%
Secular/Nonreligious/ Agnostic/Atheist 16%
Islam 21.8%

Note: Total equals more than 100% due to rounding. I think it should be added back.

Source: Carl, *Think Sociology*, p. 271

Organizational Charts

Organizational charts divide an organization (such as a corporation, university, or hospital) into its administrative departments, staff positions, or lines of authority. Figure 5-10 shows an organization chart for a typical U.S. corporation. In general, bosses and other higher-ups appear higher in the chart, while lower-level workers appear lower on the chart.

FIGURE 5-10 A SAMPLE ORGANIZATIONAL CHART

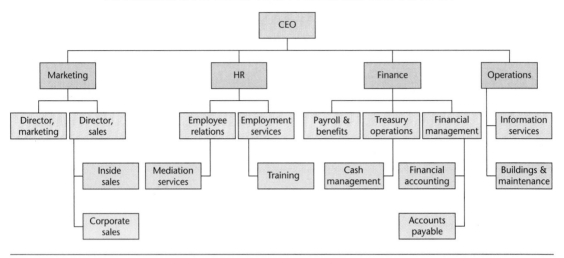

ORGANIZATIONAL CHART OF A TYPICAL U.S. CORPORATION

Source: Solomon, Poatsy, and Martin, *Better Business,* p. 205

Flowcharts

A **flowchart** shows how a process or procedure works, often from beginning to end. Lines or arrows indicate the direction in which to follow steps through the procedure. Various shapes (boxes, circles, rectangles) enclose what is done at each step. You could, for example, draw a flowchart to describe how to apply for a student loan or how to locate a malfunction in your car's electrical system. Figure 5-11 shows a flowchart for emergency medical technicians illustrating how to care for patients who have chest pain.

FIGURE 5-11 A SAMPLE FLOWCHART

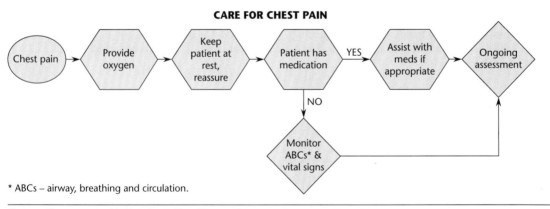

CARE FOR CHEST PAIN

* ABCs – airway, breathing and circulation.

Source: Bergeron and LeBaudour, *First Responder,* p. 257

Many flowcharts flow from left to right, and some (such as Figure 5-11) have junction points at which you choose which path to follow based on your answer to a specific question. To check that you fully understand the process outlined in a flowchart, summarize it in your own words.

EXERCISE 5-5 . . . READING CHARTS

Use Figures 5-9 through 5-11 to answer the following questions.

_____ 1. According to **Figure 5-9** (p. 149), which of the following is not one of the world's top three religions in terms of the number of people practicing that religion?

    a. Judaism

    b. Islam

    c. Christianity

    d. Hinduism

_____ 2. According to **Figure 5-10** (p. 150), which of the following departments has the lowest rank in the company?

    a. payroll and benefits

    b. information services

    c. accounts payable

    d. employee relations

_____ 3. Which of the following is not part of caring for someone who has chest pain, according to **Figure 5-11** (p. 150)?

    a. keeping the patient at rest

    b. providing oxygen

    c. assessing whether the patient has medication or not

    d. applying pressure to the area of pain

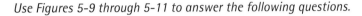

5f   DIAGRAMS

LEARNING OBJECTIVE 6
Analyze diagrams

A **diagram** is a simplified drawing showing the appearance, structure, or workings of something. Diagrams can have many purposes, including

- **to introduce key vocabulary.**
- **to show the parts of a system.**
- **to illustrate relationships.**

Diagrams are common in technical and scientific books. They often correspond to fairly large segments of text, requiring you to switch back and forth frequently between the text and the diagram. Consider the following excerpt from a human anatomy textbook and the diagram that illustrates it:

> A **nail** is a scalelike modification of the epidermis that corresponds to the hoof or claw of other animals. Each nail has a *free edge*, a *body* (visible attached portion), and a *root* (embedded in the skin). The borders of the nail are overlapped by skin folds, called *nail folds*. The thick proximal nail is commonly called the *cuticle* (Figure 5-12). The *stratum basale* of the epidermis extends beneath the nail as the *nail bed*. Its thickened proximal area, called the *nail matrix,* is responsible for nail growth. The region over the thickened nail matrix that appears as a white crescent is called the *lunula.*
>
> —Mareib, *Essentials of Human Anatomy and Physiology,* p. 106

Because diagrams and their explanations are often complicated, plan on reading these sections more than once. Read first to grasp the overall process or structure. In subsequent readings, focus on the details or progression.

One of the best ways to study a diagram is to redraw it in as much detail as possible without referring to the original. Or, test your understanding and recall of the process outlined in a diagram by explaining it, step-by-step, in your own words.

FIGURE 5-12 A SAMPLE DIAGRAM

THE STRUCTURE OF A NAIL

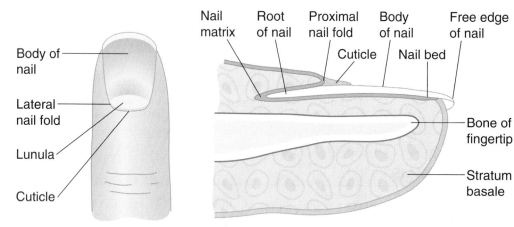

Structure of a nail. Surface view (left) and longitudinal section of the distal part of a finger (right), showing nail parts and the nail matrix that forms the nail.

Source: Mareib, *Essentials of Human Anatomy and Physiology,* p. 106

EXERCISE 5-6 . . . READING A DIAGRAM

Use Figure 5-12 (p. 152) and the accompanying text discussion to answer the following questions.

Indicate whether the following statement is true (T) or false (F).

_____   1. The human fingernail is similar to a horse's hoof.

Select the best answer.

_____   2. Most men cut their fingernails when the _____ extends beyond the finger.

    a. lunula

    b. cuticle

    c. free edge

    d. nail matrix

_____   3. Which of the following is not a part of the human fingernail?

    a. stratum basale

    b. free edge

    c. root

    d. body

5g   MAPS AND TIME LINES

LEARNING OBJECTIVE 7
Analyze maps and time lines

Maps and time lines are used to show how information is related in terms of place and time.

Maps

Maps describe relationships and provide information about location and direction. They are commonly found in geography, history, and economics texts. They can cover a very small area (for example, just one block in a city) or an area as large as the entire world.

While we often think of maps as showing distances and place names, they are also used to show the distribution of all kinds of data—public opinion, population concentration, area in which a particular language is spoken, and so on. When reading maps, use the following steps:

1. **Read the title and caption,** which will identify the subject of the map.
2. **Use the legend or key to identify the symbols or codes used.**
3. **Note the *scale*, which explains how distances on the map correspond to distances in the real world.** For example, a map may be scaled so that one inch on the map represents one mile.

FIGURE 5-13 A SAMPLE MAP

MILLIONAIRES IN THE UNITED STATUS IN

More wealth is located on the coasts – Washington, California, New York, Pennsylvania, Florida, and New Jersey have the highest number of millionaires.

New York
• 368,388 millionaires live in New York
• Has the 15th highest poverty rate in the United States, which could be related to Wilson's claim that urban areas are prone to higher poverty.

Texas
• One of the richest states with the 9th highest poverty rate. Why might this be?

Number of millionaires in the United States, by State

0-49,999   50,000-99,999   100,000-199,999   200,000-700,000

Source: Carl, *Think Sociology,* p. 122

4. **Study the map, looking for trends.** Often the text accompanying the map states the key points.
5. **Write, in your own words, a statement of what the map shows.**

Figure 5-13 is a map showing the U.S. states with the highest numbers of millionaires. Note that the person who created the map has built in study questions to help you read and analyze it.

Time Line

A **time line** is a graphic representation of the passage of time as a line. Very common in history textbooks, time lines can help you keep track of key dates, social movements, and trends. Time lines usually focus on major events and are extremely useful for learning the "big picture," but they generally do not provide a lot of detail. To fully understand what is happening in a time line, you must read the accompanying text. Figure 5-14 is a time line showing the birth and development of feminism (women's rights) in the United States.

FIGURE 5-14 A SAMPLE TIME LINE

The History of Feminism

First Wave Feminism

1848
Activists such as
Elizabeth Cady
Stanton and
Susan B. Anthony
fought for women's
right to vote

1917
Groups such
as the Silent
Sentinels
came together
to support
women's
suffrage

1960s
The
Women's
Liberation
movement
began

1960s and 1970s
Women began to
go to college and
pursue careers

Mary Wollstonecraft
Shelley's *A
Vindication of the
Rights of Woman*
was published,
which argued for
a woman's
right to vote
1792

Women in
Wyoming
were
permitted
to vote
1869

19th Amendment
was ratified,
which gave all
women in the
United States
the right to vote
1920

Betty Friedan
published
*The Feminine
Mystique*, which
helped further
ignite the
Women's
Lib movement
1963

**Second Wave
Feminism**

Third Wave Feminism

Early 1990s
The third wave of
feminism begins
to address the
failures of the
second wave

Early 1990s
Bands like
Bratmobile,
Bikini Kill, and
Huggy Bear
communicated the
message of third
wave feminism

The National
Organization for
Women—the leading
feminist organization—
was founded
1966

Feminist leaders
Gloria Anzaldua,
bell hooks, Maxine
Kingston and Audre
Lorde promote
feminist cause
Early 1990s

Groups such as
Take Back the
Night and Dress for
Success emerged
1990s

**Second Wave
Feminism**

Source: Carl, *Think Sociology*, pp. 200–201

EXERCISE 5-7 . . . READING MAPS AND TIME LINES

Use Figures 5-13 (p. 154) and 5-14 above to answer the following questions.

_____ 1. According to **Figure 5-13,** which of the following states has the smallest number of millionaires?

    a. New Jersey

    b. Montana

    c. Florida

    d. Texas

2. According to **Figure 5-13,** Texas is one of the richest states in the United States, but it also has the ninth highest poverty rate.

    a. What might explain the wealth?

    _____

    b. What might explain the poverty?

    _____

    _____

_____ 3. According to **Figure 5-14,** feminism began in

    a. 1792.

    b. 1860.

    c. 1920.

    d. 1966.

_____ 4. According to **Figure 5-14,** the earliest feminism was concerned with

    a. equal pay for men and women.

    b. women's right to vote.

    c. women's right to attend college.

    d. women's right to inherit wealth from their parents.

_____ 5. Which was not a key event in the history of feminism, according to Figure 5-14?

    a. the publication of *The Feminine Mystique*

    b. the founding of the National Organization for Women

    c. the ratification of the 1st Amendment

    d. women's attending college and pursuing careers

5h   INFOGRAPHICS: COMBINED PHOTOS, CHARTS, AND DIAGRAMS

LEARNING OBJECTIVE 8
Analyze infographics

Graphic designers are always looking for new, visually interesting ways to present information. In recent years, a new type of visual aid called an *infographic* has become popular. While the definition is not precise, **infographics** usually combine several types of visual aids into one, often merging photos with text, diagrams, or tables.

Unlike other graphics, infographics are sometimes designed to stand on their own; they do not necessarily repeat what is in the text. Consider the following excerpt from a health textbook:

> Different cultures have unique languages and dialects, as well as different ways of expressing feelings and using body language. Some cultures gesture wildly; others maintain a closed and rigid means of speaking. Some are offended by direct eye contact; others welcome a steady look in the eyes. Men and women also tend to have different communication styles, which are largely dictated by culture and socialization (see Figure 5-15, "He Says/She Says").
>
> —Donatelle, *Health*, p. 129

Figure 5-15 lists many differences in male and female communication styles, which are *not* listed in the text. To understand this material, you must carefully read and learn the infographic, because the information cannot be found in the text.

FIGURE 5-15 A SAMPLE INFOGRAPHIC

HE SAYS/SHE SAYS

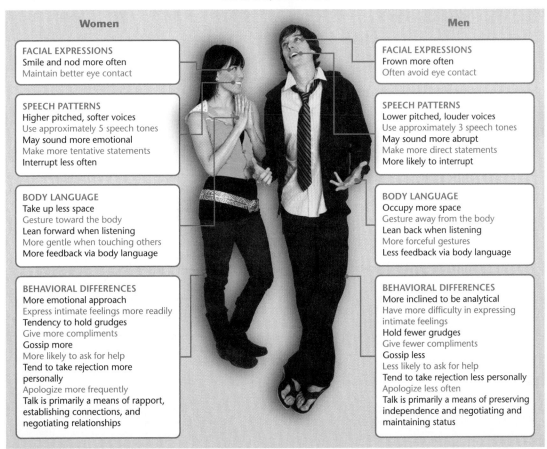

Women	Men
FACIAL EXPRESSIONS Smile and nod more often Maintain better eye contact	**FACIAL EXPRESSIONS** Frown more often Often avoid eye contact
SPEECH PATTERNS Higher pitched, softer voices Use approximately 5 speech tones May sound more emotional Make more tentative statements Interrupt less often	**SPEECH PATTERNS** Lower pitched, louder voices Use approximately 3 speech tones May sound more abrupt Make more direct statements More likely to interrupt
BODY LANGUAGE Take up less space Gesture toward the body Lean forward when listening More gentle when touching others More feedback via body language	**BODY LANGUAGE** Occupy more space Gesture away from the body Lean back when listening More forceful gestures Less feedback via body language
BEHAVIORAL DIFFERENCES More emotional approach Express intimate feelings more readily Tendency to hold grudges Give more compliments Gossip more More likely to ask for help Tend to take rejection more personally Apologize more frequently Talk is primarily a means of rapport, establishing connections, and negotiating relationships	**BEHAVIORAL DIFFERENCES** More inclined to be analytical Have more difficulty in expressing intimate feelings Hold fewer grudges Give fewer compliments Gossip less Less likely to ask for help Tend to take rejection less personally Apologize less often Talk is primarily a means of preserving independence and negotiating and maintaining status

Source: Donatelle, *Health,* p. 130

EXERCISE 5-8 . . . READING INFOGRAPHICS

Use Figure 5-15 to complete the following table. Check off which characteristics are more common in men and which are more common in women. The first answer has been provided for you.

CHARACTERISTIC	MORE COMMON IN MEN	MORE COMMON IN WOMEN
1. Apologizing		√
2. Leaning forward while listening		
3. Using approximately 3 speech tones		
4. Asking for help		
5. Interrupting		
6. Frowning		
7. Providing feedback through body language		
8. Taking rejection personally		

5i   CARTOONS

Cartoons express an idea and make a point with humor. They can be very broad and easy to understand, or very subtle and complicated. Analyzing cartoons requires you to pick up on unstated messages. For more information about unstated messages, see Chapter 6, Section 6c, "How to Make Inferences,' p. 162.

For Further Practice

For support in meeting this chapter's learning objectives, log in to http://www.myreadinglab.com, go to the Study Plan tab, click on **Reading Skills** and choose **Graphics and Visuals** from the list of subtopics. Read and view the videos and resources in the Review Materials section, and then complete the Recall, Practice, and Test exercises in the Activities section. You can check your scores and overall progress by using the Gradebook.

6 Making Inferences

LEARNING OBJECTIVES

In this chapter, you will learn how to

1 Make inferences from facts
2 Make inferences from written material
3 Make accurate inferences

MyReadingLab

To practice making
inferences, go to

▼ Study Plan
   ▼ Reading Skills
      ▼ Inference

Look at the photograph below, which appeared in a psychology textbook. What do you think is happening here? What is the man's occupation? What are the feelings of the participants?

In order to answer these questions, you had to use any information you could get from the photo and make guesses based on it. The facial expression, body language, clothing, and other objects present in this photo provided clues. This reasoning process is called "making an inference."

6a   MAKING INFERENCES FROM THE GIVEN FACTS

LEARNING OBJECTIVE 1
Make inferences
from facts

An **inference** is a reasoned guess about what you don't know made on the basis of what you do know. Inferences are common in our everyday lives. When you get on an expressway and see a long, slow-moving line of traffic, you might predict that there is an accident or roadwork ahead. When you see a puddle of water under the kitchen sink, you can infer that you have a plumbing problem.

The inferences you make may not always be correct, even though you based them on the available information. The water under the sink might have been the result of a spill. The traffic you encountered on the expressway might be normal for that time of day, but you didn't know it because you aren't normally on the road then. An inference is only the best guess you can make in a situation, given the information you have.

EXERCISE 6-1 . . . MAKING INFERENCES 1

Study the photograph below. Use your skills in making inferences to write a statement explaining what is happening in this photograph.

_____

_____

_____

_____

_____

EXERCISE 6-2 . . . MAKING INFERENCES 2

Read each of the following statements. Place a check mark in front of each sentence that follows that is a reasonable inference that can be made from the statement.

1. Twice as many couples seek marriage counseling as did 20 years ago.

_____ a. There are more married people now than 20 years ago.

_____ b. There has been an increased demand for licensed marriage counselors.

_____ c. Marriage is more legalistic than it used to be.

_____ d. Couples are more willing to discuss their differences than they were 20 years ago.

2. More than half of all Americans are overweight.

_____ a. Many Americans are at high risk for heart disease.

_____ b. Teaching children about nutrition and exercise should be a high priority in public schools.

_____ c. Americans place great emphasis on appearance.

_____ d. The weight-loss industry is an important sector of business.

3. Many courts now permit lawyers to file papers and handle some court work over the Internet.

_____ a. Courtrooms will no longer be needed.

_____ b. Attorneys will be able to check the status of their cases from their home computers.

_____ c. Some cases may proceed more quickly now.

_____ d. More lawyers will carry laptops.

6b   MAKING INFERENCES FROM WRITTEN MATERIAL

LEARNING OBJECTIVE 2
Make inferences from written material

When you read the material associated with your college courses, you need to make inferences frequently. Writers do not always present their ideas directly. Instead, they often leave it to you to add up and think beyond the facts they present. You are expected to reason out or infer the meaning an author intended (but did not say) on the basis of what he or she did say. In a sense, the inferences you make act as bridges between what is said and what is not said, but is meant.

6c   HOW TO MAKE ACCURATE INFERENCES

LEARNING OBJECTIVE 3
Make accurate
inferences
Each inference you make depends on the situation, the facts provided, and your own knowledge and experience. Here are a few guidelines to help you see beyond the factual level and make solid inferences.

Understand the Literal Meaning

Be sure you have a firm grasp of the literal meaning. You must understand the stated ideas and facts before you can move to higher levels of thinking, which include inference making. You should recognize the topic, main idea, key details, and organizational pattern of each paragraph you have read.

Notice Details

As you are reading, pay particular attention to details that are unusual or stand out. Often such details will offer you clues to help you make inferences. Ask yourself:

- **What is unusual or striking about this piece of information?**
- **Why is it included here?**

Read the following excerpt, which is taken from an essay about a young Polish immigrant to the U.K., and mark any details that seem unusual or striking.

An Immigration Plan Gone Awry

Due to her own hardship, Katja was not thrilled when her younger brother called her from Warsaw and said that he was going to join her in the U.K. Katja warned him that opportunities were scarce in London for a Polish immigrant. "Don't worry," he said in an effort to soothe her anxiety. "I already have a job in a factory." An advertisement in a Warsaw paper had promised good pay for Polish workers in Birmingham. A broker's fee of $500 and airfare were required, so her brother borrowed the money from their mother. He made the trip with a dozen other young Polish men.

The "broker" picked the young men up at Heathrow and piled them in a van. They drove directly to Birmingham, and at nightfall the broker dropped the whole crew off at a ramshackle house inside the city. He ordered them to be ready to be picked up in the morning for their first day of work. A bit dazed by the pace, they stretched out on the floor to sleep.

Their rest was brief. In the wee hours of the night, the broker returned with a gang of 10 or so thugs armed with cricket bats. They beat the young Polish boys to a pulp and robbed them of all their valuables. Katja's brother took some heavy kicks to the ribs and head, then stumbled out of the house. Once outside, he saw two police cars parked across the street. The officers in the cars obviously chose to ignore the mayhem playing out in front of their eyes. Katja's brother knew better than try to convince them otherwise; the police in Poland would act no differently. Who knows, maybe they were part of the broker's scam. Or maybe they just didn't care about a bunch of poor Polish immigrants "invading" their town.

—Batstone, "Katja's Story,"

Did you mark details such as the $500 broker's fee, the promise of a well-paying job despite scarce job opportunities for Polish immigrants, and the beating and robbery of the boys?

Add Up the Facts

Consider all of the facts taken together. To help you do this, ask yourself such questions as the following:

- **What is the writer trying to suggest with this set of facts?**
- **What do all these facts and ideas seem to point toward or add up to?**
- **Why did the author include these facts and details?**

Making an inference is somewhat like assembling a complicated jigsaw puzzle; you try to make all the pieces fit together to form a recognizable picture. Answering these questions will require you to add together all the individual pieces of information, which will enable you to arrive at an inference.

When you add up the facts in the article "An Immigration Plan Gone Awry" you realize that the brother is the victim of a scam.

Be Alert to Clues

Writers often provide you with numerous hints that can point you toward accurate inferences. An awareness of word choices, details included (and omitted), ideas emphasized, and direct commentary can help you determine a textbook author's attitude toward the topic at hand. In the foregoing excerpt, the "ramshakle" house, the men "piled" into a van, and sleeping on the floor are all clues that something is amiss.

Consider the Author's Purpose

Also study the author's purpose for writing. What does he or she hope to accomplish? In "An Immigration Plan Gone Awry" the writer seems critical of immigrant brokers and of the police.

Verify Your Inference

Once you have made an inference, check that it is accurate. Look back at the stated facts to be sure that you have sufficient evidence to support the inference. Also, be certain that you have not overlooked other equally plausible or more plausible inferences that could be drawn from the same set of facts.

EXERCISE 6-3 . . . MAKING INFERENCES 3

Study the cartoon below and place a check mark in front of each statement that is a reasonable inference that can be made from the cartoon.

_____ 1. The cartoonist thinks workers are physically abused.

_____ 2. The cartoonist is critical of those in management.

_____ 3. Many conflicts exist between workers and supervisors.

_____ 4. The cartoonist believes that people change when they become managers.

_____ 5. The cartoonist is a labor relations specialist.

"We get it, Tom—you're management now."

EXERCISE 6-4 . . . MAKING INFERENCES 4

Read each of the following statements. Place a check mark in front of each sentence that follows that is a reasonable inference that can be made from the statement.

1. Political candidates must now include the Internet in their campaign plans.

_____ a. Political candidates may host online chats to assess voter opinion.

_____ b. Informal debates between candidates may be conducted online.

_____ c. Internet campaigning will drastically increase overall campaign expenditures.

_____ d. Television campaigning is likely to remain the same.

2. Half of the public education classrooms in the United States are now hooked up to the Internet.

_____ a. Children are more computer literate than their parents were when they were in school.

_____ b. Students now have access to current world news and happenings.

_____ c. Books are no longer considered the sole source of information on a subject.

_____ d. Teachers have become better teachers now that they have Internet access.

3. The Internet can make doctors more efficient through the use of new software and databases that make patient diagnosis more accurate.

_____ a. The cost of in-person medical care is likely to decrease.

_____ b. Doctors may be able to identify patients with serious illnesses sooner.

_____ c. Doctors are likely to pay less attention to their patients' descriptions of symptoms.

_____ d. Information on the symptoms and treatment of rare illnesses is more readily available.

EXERCISE 6-5 . . . MAKING INFERENCES 5

Read each of the following passages. Using inference, determine whether the statements following each passage are true or false. Place an X next to each untrue statement.

A.   The United Nations Population Division predicts that by 2025, world population will increase to about 9 billion people. More disturbing, whereas the United Nations earlier predicted that the world population would stabilize at around 10 billion, it has revised its estimate to close to 11 billion, or even as high as 14 billion. These projections have prompted concerns that overpopulation and food scarcity are the principal threats to the planet's future. The United Nations sponsored an International Conference on Population and Development held in Cairo in 1994. There, a World Programme of Action was developed to shift the focus of dismal demographic projections toward concern about a gender-sensitive, humanistic approach to population control.

—Thompson and Hickey, *Society in Focus*, p. 544

_____ 1. If the projections are inaccurate, the world community no longer needs to be concerned about overpopulation.

_____ 2. Previous approaches to population control have not been gender sensitive.

_____ 3. If population increases more rapidly than predicted, there will be even greater food shortages.

_____ 4. The United Nations has developed adequate responses to food scarcity.

_____ 5. By 2050, world population will have increased to 20 billion.

B.   Blowfish is one of the most prized delicacies in the restaurants of Japan. This fish is prized not only for its taste, but for the tingling sensation one gets around the lips when eating it. In blowfish TTX (a neurotoxin) is concentrated in certain organs, including the liver and gonads. Its preparation takes great skill and can only be done by licensed chefs who are skilled at removing the poison-containing organs without crushing them, which can lead to contamination of normally edible parts. The toxin cannot be destroyed by cooking. Lore has it that the most skilled chefs intentionally leave a bit of the poison in, so that diners can enjoy the tingling sensation caused by blockage of nerve signals from the sense receptors on the lips.

—adapted from Germann and Stanfield, *Principles of Human Physiology*, p. 185

_____ 6. Consuming TTX has potentially dangerous consequences.

_____ 7. The United States has strict rules about the preparation of blowfish.

_____ 8. Japanese diners enjoy blowfish partly because of the sense of danger involved.

_____ 9. TTX causes blockage of signals from nerves.

_____ 10. Blowfish is always unsafe to eat.

C.   Through your parents, teachers, and the media, your culture instills in you a variety of beliefs, values, and attitudes—about success (how you define it and how you should achieve it); the relevance of a person's religion, race, or nationality; the ethical principles you should follow in business and in your personal life. These teachings provide benchmarks against which you can measure yourself. Your ability to, for example, achieve what your culture defines as success, will contribute to a positive self-concept. Your failure to achieve what your culture teaches (for example, not being married by the time you're thirty) will contribute to a negative self-concept.

—DeVito, *Essentials of Human Communication*, pp. 36–37

_____ 11. People with positive self-concepts often have achieved their culture's notion of success.

_____ 12. Most cultures do not believe that race or religion are relevant.

_____ 13. People often ignore their culture's beliefs about ethical principles.

_____ 14. Self-concept is affected by both success and failure.

_____ 15. Your self-concept can never change.

EXERCISE 6-6 . . . MAKING INFERENCES 6

Read each of the following paragraphs. A number of statements follow them; each statement is an inference. Label each inference as either:

PA—Probably accurate—there is substantial evidence in the paragraph to support the statement.

IE—Insufficient evidence—there is little or no evidence in the paragraph to support the statement.

A.   While working for a wholesale firm, traveling to country stores by horse and buggy, Aaron Montgomery Ward conceived the idea of selling directly to country people by mail. He opened his business in 1872 with a one-page list of items that cost one dollar each. People could later order goods through a distributed catalog and the store would ship the merchandise cash on delivery (COD). The idea was slow to catch on because people were suspicious of a strange name. However, in 1875 Ward announced the startling policy of "satisfaction guaranteed or your money back." Contrasting with the former retailing principle of caveat emptor (Latin for "buyer beware"), this policy set off a boom in Ward's business.

—Frings, *Fashion: From Concepts to Consumer,* p. 11

_____ 1. Aaron Ward had experience in sales before he began his own business.

_____ 2. Country people were targeted because they do not have access to stores in cities.

_____ 3. Ward's mistake was to give every item on the list the same price.

_____ 4. Other stores in operation at the time did not offer money back guarantees.

_____ 5. Other mail order businesses quickly followed Ward's success.

B.   Artist Georgia O'Keeffe was born in Sun Prairie, Wisconsin, and spent her childhood on her family's farm. While in high school, she had a memorable experience that gave her a new perspective on the art-making process. As she passed the door to the art room, O'Keeffe stopped to watch as a teacher held up a jack-in-the-pulpit plant so that the students could appreciate its unusual shapes and subtle colors. Although O'Keeffe had enjoyed flowers in the marshes and meadows of Wisconsin, she had done all of her drawing and painting from plaster casts or had copied them from photographs or reproductions. This was the first time she realized that one could draw and paint from real life. Twenty-five years later she produced a powerful series of paintings based on flowers.

—adapted from Preble and Preble, *Artforms,* p. 34

_____ 6. O'Keeffe's artistic style was influenced by her high-school art teacher.

_____ 7. O'Keeffe's paintings from plaster casts were unsuccessful.

_____ 8. O'Keeffe was deeply influenced by nature.

_____ 9. O'Keeffe was not influenced by modern art.

_____ 10. O'Keeffe never copied flowers from other paintings.

EXERCISE 6-7 . . . MAKING INFERENCES 7

Read the following paragraphs and the statements that follow. Place a check mark next to the statements that are reasonable inferences.

August Vollmer was the chief of police of Berkeley, California, from 1905 to 1932. Vollmer's vision of policing was quite different from most of his contemporaries. He believed the police should be a "dedicated body of educated persons comprising a distinctive corporate entity with a prescribed code of behavior." He was critical of his contemporaries and they of him. San Francisco police administrator Charley Dullea, who later became president of the International Association of Chiefs of Police, refused to drive through Berkeley in protest against Vollmer. Fellow California police chiefs may have felt their opposition to Vollmer was justified, given his vocal and strong criticism of other California police departments. For example, Vollmer publicly referred to San Francisco cops as "morons," and in an interview with a newspaper reporter, he called Los Angeles cops "low grade mental defectives."

Because of his emphasis on education, professionalism, and administrative reform, Vollmer often is seen as the counterpart of London's Sir Robert Peel and is sometimes called the "father of modern American policing." Vollmer was decades ahead of his contemporaries, but he was not able to implement significant change in policing during his lifetime. It remained for Vollmer's students to implement change. For example, O.W. Wilson, who became chief of police of Chicago, promoted college education for police officers and wrote a book on police administration that reflected many of Vollmer's philosophies. It was adopted widely by police executives and used as a college textbook well into the 1960s.

Vollmer is credited with a number of innovations. He was an early adopter of the automobile for patrol and the use of radios in police cars. He recruited college-educated police officers. He developed and implemented a 3-year training curriculum for police officers, including classes in physics, chemistry, biology, physiology, anatomy, psychology, psychiatry, anthropology, and criminology. He developed a system of signal boxes for hailing police officers. He adopted the use of typewriters to fill out police reports and records, and officers received training in typing. He surveyed other police departments to gather information about their practices. Many of his initiatives have become common practice within contemporary police departments.

—Fagin, *Criminal Justice*, p. 195

_____ 1. Vollmer did not have a college degree.

_____ 2. Most police officers of Vollmer's time had limited educations.

_____ 3. Vollmer believed police should be held accountable for their actions.

_____ 4. Sir Robert Peel dramatically changed policing procedures in England.

_____ 5. Vollmer received support from most police officers on the street.

_____ 6. Vollmer would support technological advances in policing.

_____ 7. Police departments of Vollmer's time were run with a careful eye toward accuracy.

_____ 8. Vollmer outlawed billy clubs.

For Further Practice

For support in meeting this chapter's learning objectives, log in to http://www.myreadinglab.com, go to the Study Plan tab, click on **Reading Skills** and choose **Inference** from the list of subtopics. Read and view the videos and resources in the Review Materials section, and then complete the Recall, Practice, and Test exercises in the Activities section. You can check your scores and overall progress by using the Gradebook.

7 Critical Reading

LEARNING OBJECTIVES

In this chapter, you will learn how to

1 Distinguish fact from opinion

2 Identify the author's purpose

3 Evaluate tone

4 Identify bias

5 Evaluate data and evidence

6 Understand connotative language

7 Interpret figurative language

MyReadingLab

To practice thinking critically, go to

▼ Study Plan
  ▼ Reading Skills
    ▼ Critical
      Thinking

In college you will be reading many new kinds of material: research articles, essays, critiques, reports, and analyses. Your instructors expect you to be able to do much more than understand and remember the basic content. They often demand that you read critically, interpreting, evaluating, and reacting to assigned readings. Specifically, an instructor may expect you to do all of the things listed above. To meet these expectations, you'll need to distinguish facts from opinions, identify the author's purpose, recognize the author's tone, detect bias, evaluate data and evidence, understand connotative language, and interpret figurative language.

7a IS THE MATERIAL FACT OR OPINION?

LEARNING OBJECTIVE 1
Distinguish fact from opinion

When working with any source, try to determine whether the material is factual or an expression of opinion. **Facts** are statements that can be verified—that is, proven to be true or false. **Opinions** are statements that express feelings, attitudes, or beliefs and are neither true nor false. Following are examples of each:

Facts

1. More than one million teenagers become pregnant every year.
2. The costs of medical care increase every year.

Opinions

1. Government regulation of our private lives should be halted immediately.
2. By the year 2025, most Americans will not be able to afford routine health care.

Facts, once verified or taken from a reputable source, can be accepted and regarded as reliable information. Opinions, on the other hand, are not reliable sources of information and should be questioned and carefully evaluated. Look for evidence that supports the opinion and indicates that it is reasonable. For example, opinion 2 is written to sound like a fact, but look closely. What basis does the author have for making that statement?

Some authors are careful to signal the reader when they are presenting an opinion. Watch for words and phrases such as:

According to	It is belived that	Presumably
Apparently	It is likely that	Seemingly
In my opinion	One explanation is	This suggests
In my view	Possibly	

In the following excerpt from a social problems textbook, notice how the author carefully distinguishes factual statements from opinion using qualifying words and phrases (shown here underlined).

Economic Change, Ideology, and Private Life

It seems clear that there has been a major change in attitudes and feelings about family relationships since the eighteenth century. It is less clear how and why the change came about. One question debated by researchers is: In what social class did the new family pattern originate—in the aristocracy, as Trumbach believes, or in the upper gentry, as Stone argued, or in the working class, as Shorter contended? Or was the rise of the new domesticity a cultural phenomenon that affected people in all social categories at roughly the same time? Carole Shammas has found evidence of such a widespread cultural change by looking at the kinds of things people had in their homes at various times in the past, as recorded in probate inventories. She found that in the middle of the eighteenth century all social classes experienced a change in living habits; even working-class households now contained expensive tools of domesticity, such as crockery, teapots, eating utensils, and so on. Thus, according to Shammas, the home was becoming an important center for social interaction, and family meals had come to occupy an important place in people's lives.

—Skolnick, *The Intimate Environment,* p. 96

Other authors do just the opposite; they try to make opinions sound like facts, as in opinion 2, or they mix fact and opinion without making clear distinctions. This is particularly true in the case of *expert opinion,* which is the opinion of an authority. Ralph Nader represents expert opinion on consumer rights, for example. Textbook authors, too, often offer expert opinion, as in the following statement from an American government text.

> Ours is a complex system of justice. Sitting at the pinnacle of the judicial system is the Supreme Court, but its importance is often exaggerated.
>
> —Lineberry, *Government in America,* p. 540

The author of this statement has reviewed the available evidence and is providing his expert opinion as to what the evidence indicates about the Supreme Court. The reader, then, is free to disagree and offer evidence to support an opposing view.

The article "Treating Wounded Soldiers: Polytrauma," reprinted in Chapter 1, uses expert opinion, as well. The opinions of Sandy Lai, program director of the Palo Alto Polytrauma Rehabilitation Center are given as evidence.

EXERCISE 7-1 . . . DISTINGUISHING FACT AND OPINION 1

Read each of the following statements and identify whether it is fact (F), opinion (O), or expert opinion (EO).

_____ 1. United Parcel Service (UPS) is the nation's largest delivery service.

_____ 2. United Parcel Service will become even more successful because it uses sophisticated management techniques.

_____ 3. Americans spend $13.7 billion per year on alternative medicine.

_____ 4. The best way to keep up with world news is to read the newspaper.

_____ 5. A community, as defined by sociologists, is a collection of people who share some purpose, activity, or characteristic.

_____ 6. The Bill of Rights comprises the first ten amendments to the Constitution.

_____ 7. Archaeologists believe that the stone monument known as Stonehenge was built to serve a religious purpose.

_____ 8. According to Dr. Richard Sobol, a communication specialist, conflict in interpersonal relationships is not only inevitable, it can also be beneficial.

_____ 9. The finest examples of landscape photography can be found in the work of Ansel Adams.

_____ 10. The symbol of Islam—a crescent and star—appears on the flags of nations that have a Muslim majority, such as Turkey and Pakistan.

EXERCISE 7-2 . . . DISTINGUISHING FACT AND OPINION 2

Each of the following paragraphs contains both facts and opinions. Read each paragraph and label each sentence as fact (F), opinion (O), or expert opinion (EO).

A.   1. Almost half of all Americans drink coffee every day, making it the most widely consumed drug in the United States. 2. Some people believe its popularity can be explained by the "wake-up" effect of caffeine, a critical element of many people's morning ritual. 3. A five-ounce cup of coffee contains between 65 and 115 milligrams of caffeine, depending on the brand of coffee and the strength of the brew. 4. In addition to enhancing mental alertness and reducing fatigue, the stimulant effects of caffeine include increases in urinary output, insomnia, irregular heartbeat, and indigestion. 5. Apparently, these rather unpleasant side effects are not enough to deter millions of Americans from their daily caffeine "fix."

—adapted from Donatelle, *Health,* p. 215

Sentences: 1. _____ 2. _____ 3. _____ 4. _____ 5. _____

B.   1. Harriet Tubman was born a slave in Maryland in 1820 and escaped to Philadelphia in 1849. 2. Her own escape presumably required tremendous courage, but that was just the beginning. 3. Through her work on the Underground Railroad, Harriet Tubman led more than 300 slaves to freedom. 4. During the Civil War, Tubman continued her efforts toward the abolition of slavery by working as a nurse and a spy for the Union forces. 5. Today, Americans of all races consider Harriet Tubman one of the most heroic figures in our country's history.

Sentences: 1. _____ 2. _____ 3. _____ 4. _____ 5. _____

C.   1. Smokeless tobacco is used by approximately 5 million U.S. adults, most of whom are young males. 2. One explanation for the popularity of smokeless tobacco among young men is that they are emulating professional athletes who chew tobacco or use snuff. 3. In any major league baseball game, more than a few players with chewing tobacco bulging in their cheeks apparently believe the myth that smokeless tobacco is less harmful than cigarettes. 4. In reality, smokeless tobacco contains 10 times the amount of cancer-producing substances found in cigarettes and 100 times more than the Food and Drug Administration allows in foods and other substances used by the public. 5. Smokeless tobacco has been banned from minor league baseball, a move that should be extended to all professional sports to help discourage the use of smokeless tobacco products.

—adapted from Donatelle, *Access to Health,* pp. 372–373

Sentences: 1. _____ 2. _____ 3. _____ 4. _____ 5. _____

D.   1. Managed care plans have agreements with certain physicians, hospitals, and health care providers to give a range of services to plan members at a reduced cost. 2. There are three basic types of managed care plans: health maintenance organizations (HMOs), point-of-service plans (POSs), and preferred provider organizations (PPOs). 3. The PPO, in my opinion, is the best type of managed care plan because it merges the best features of traditional health insurance and HMOs. 4. As in traditional plans, participants in a PPO pay premiums, deductibles, and co-payments, but the co-pay under a PPO is lower (10 percent or less compared to the 20 percent co-pay under a traditional plan). 5. The best part of a PPO, though, is its flexibility: participants may choose their physicians and services from a list of preferred providers, or they may go outside the plan for care if they wish.

—adapted from Pruitt and Stein, *HealthStyles*, pp. 572–573

Sentences: 1. _____ 2. _____ 3. _____ 4. _____ 5. _____

E.   1. Some sociologists believe that if any nation deserves the "pro-family" label, it is Sweden. 2. The typical Swedish family today consists of two working parents, with the majority of women working part-time and more than 90 percent of men working full-time. 3. To support women's and men's dual roles in the family and work, the state has devised a benefit package that *all* families receive, regardless of class or income. 4. Benefits include public-supported child care, parental leave insurance for both men and women, a basic child allowance per year of around $900, and a housing allowance that is based on income and number of children in the family. 5. Despite deficiencies (for example, women occupy only 5 percent of upper management positions), the way Sweden combines family and employment appears to be far superior to the situations in most other countries.

—adapted from Thompson and Hickey, *Society in Focus*, p. 364

Sentences: 1. _____ 2. _____ 3. _____ 4. _____ 5. _____

7b   WHAT IS THE AUTHOR'S PURPOSE?

LEARNING OBJECTIVE 2
Identify the author's purpose

MyReadingLab

To practice identifying author's purpose, go to

▼ Study Plan
  ▼ Reading Skills
    ▼ Purpose and
       Tone

Writers have many different reasons or purposes for writing. Read the following statements and try to decide why each was written:

1. About 14,000 ocean-going ships pass through the Panama Canal each year. This averages to about three ships per day.
2. *New Unsalted Dry Roasted Almonds.* Finally, a snack with a natural flavor and without salt. We simply shell the nuts and dry-roast them until they're crispy and crunchy. Try a jar this week.
3. Man is the only animal that blushes. Or needs to. (Mark Twain)
4. If a choking person has fallen down, first turn him or her face up. Then knit together the fingers of both your hands and apply pressure with the heel of your bottom hand to the victim's abdomen.
5. If your boat capsizes, it is usually safer to cling to the boat than to try to swim ashore.

Statement 1 was written to give information, 2 to persuade you to buy almonds, 3 to amuse you and make a comment on human behavior, 4 to explain, and 5 to give advice.

In each of the examples, the writer's purpose is fairly clear, as it is in most textbooks (to present information), newspaper articles (to communicate daily events), and reference books (to compile facts). However, in many other types of writing, authors have varied, sometimes less obvious, purposes. In these cases, an author's purpose must be inferred.

Often a writer's purpose is to express an opinion indirectly. The writer may also want to encourage the reader to think about a particular issue or problem. Writers achieve their purposes by manipulating and controlling what they say and how they say it.

Writers may vary their styles to suit their intended audiences. A writer may write for a general-interest audience (anyone who is interested in the subject but is not considered an expert). Most newspapers and periodicals, such as *Time* and *Newsweek,* appeal to a general-interest audience. The article "Treating Wounded Soldiers: Polytrauma," seems to be written for the general public. It does not assume that readers have a special knowledge of polytrauma or its treatment.

On the other hand, a writer may have a particular interest group in mind. A writer may write for medical doctors in the *Journal of American Medicine,* for skiing enthusiasts in *Skiing Today,* or for antique collectors in *The World of Antiques.* A writer may also target his or her writing to an audience with particular political, moral, or religious attitudes. Articles in the *New Republic* often appeal to those interested in a particular political viewpoint, whereas articles in the *Catholic Digest* appeal to a specific religious group.

Depending on the group of people for whom the author is writing, he or she will change the level of language, choice of words, and method of presentation. One step toward identifying an author's purpose, then, is to ask yourself the question: Who is the intended audience? Your response will be your first clue to determining why the author wrote the article.

EXERCISE 7-3 . . . IDENTIFYING THE AUTHOR'S PURPOSE 1

Read each of the following statements. Then find the author's purpose for each statement in the box below and write it in the space provided.

to persuade	to entertain	to inform
to advise	to criticize	

_____ 1. If you are looking for specialized information on the Internet, the best approach is to use a metasearch engine such as ProFusion.

_____ 2. Good judgment comes from experience, and a lot of that comes from bad judgment. (Will Rogers)

_____ 3. The Constitution of the United States prescribes a separation of powers among the executive, legislative, and judicial branches of government.

_____ 4. Members of the art gallery enjoy benefits such as free admission and discounts on special gallery exhibits.

_____ 5. The governor's ill-advised plan to attach a "sin tax" to sales of tobacco and alcohol can only have a negative effect on tourism in our state.

EXERCISE 7-4 . . . IDENTIFYING THE AUTHOR'S PURPOSE 2

Read each of the following statements and identify the author's purpose. Write a sentence that describes the intended audience.

1. Chances are you're going to be putting money away over the next five years or so. You are hoping for the right things in life. Right now, a smart place to put your money is in mutual funds or bonds.

   _____

   _____

2. Think about all the places your drinking water has been before you drink another drop. Most likely it has been chemically treated to remove bacteria and chemical pollutants. Soon you may begin to feel the side effects of these treatments. Consider switching to filtered, distilled water today.

   _____

   _____

3. Introducing the new, high-powered Supertuner III, a sound system guaranteed to keep your mother out of your car.

   _____

   _____

4. Bright and White laundry detergent removes dirt and stains faster than any other brand.

   _____

   _____

5. As a driver, you're ahead if you can learn to spot car trouble before it's too late. If you can learn the difference between drips and squeaks that occur under normal conditions and those that mean that big trouble is just down the road, then you'll be ahead of expensive repair bills and won't find yourself stranded on a lonely road.

   _____

   _____

7c   WHAT IS THE TONE?

LEARNING OBJECTIVE 3
Evaluate tone

MyReadingLab

To practice recognizing tone, go to

▼ Study Plan
  ▼ Reading Skills
    ▼ Purpose and Tone

The tone of a speaker's voice helps you interpret what he or she is saying. If the following sentence were read aloud, the speaker's voice would tell you how to interpret it: "Would you mind closing the door?" In print you cannot tell whether the speaker is polite, insistent, or angry. In speech you could tell by whether the speaker emphasized the word *would, mind,* or *door.*

Just as a speaker's tone of voice tells how the speaker feels, a writer conveys a tone, or feeling, through his or her writing. **Tone** refers to the attitude or feeling a writer expresses about his or her subject. The tone of the article "Treating Wounded Soldiers: Polytrauma" is informative. The author presents facts, statistics, and other evidence to support the thesis.

A writer may adopt a sentimental tone, an angry tone, a humorous tone, a sympathetic tone, an instructive tone, a persuasive tone, and so forth. Here are a few examples of different tones. How does each make you feel?

- **Instructive**

When purchasing a piece of clothing, one must be concerned with quality as well as with price. Be certain to check for the following: double-stitched seams, matched patterns, and ample linings.

- **Sympathetic**

The forlorn, frightened-looking child wandered through the streets alone, searching for someone who would show an interest in helping her find her parents.

- **Persuasive**

Child abuse is a tragic occurrence in our society. Strong legislation is needed to control the abuse of innocent victims and to punish those who are insensitive to the rights and feelings of others.

- **Humorous**

Those people who study animal behavior professionally must dread those times when their cover is blown at a dinner party. The unfortunate souls are sure to be seated next to someone with animal stories. The conversation will invariably be about some pet that did this or that, and nonsense is the *polite* word for it. The worst stories are about cats. The proud owners like to talk about their ingenuity, what they are thinking, and how they "miss" them while they're at the party. Those cats would rub the leg of a burglar if he rattled the Friskies box. (Marge Thielman Hastreiter, "Not Every Mother Is Glad Kids Are Back in School." *Buffalo Evening News*)

■ **Nostalgic**

> Things change, times change, but when school starts, my little grand-daughter will run up the same wooden stairs that creaked for all of the previous generations and I will still hate it when the summer ends. (Hastreiter)

In the first example, the writer offers advice in a straightforward, informative style. In the second, the writer wants you to feel sorry for the child. This is accomplished through description. In the third example, the writer tries to convince the reader that action must be taken to prevent child abuse. The use of such words as *tragic, innocent,* and *insensitive* establish this tone. In the fourth example, the writer pokes fun at cat owners, and in the fifth example, the writer fondly reminisces about the start of school in the fall.

To identify an author's tone, pay particular attention to descriptive language and shades of meaning. Ask yourself: "How does the author feel about his or her subject and how are these feelings revealed?" It is sometimes difficult to find the right word to describe the author's tone. Table 7.1 on page 180 lists words that are often used to describe the tone of a piece of writing. Use this list to provoke your thinking when identifying tone. If any of these words are unfamiliar, be sure to check their meanings in a dictionary.

EXERCISE 7-5 . . . RECOGNIZING TONE 1

Read each of the following statements. Then choose a word from the box that describes the tone it illustrates, and write it in the space provided.

optimistic	angry	admiring	cynical/bitter
excited	humorous	nostalgic	disapproving
formal	informative	sarcastic	

_____ 1. Taking a young child to a PG-13 movie is inappropriate and shows poor judgment on the part of the parents.

_____ 2. The brown recluse spider has a dark, violin-shaped marking on the upper section of its body.

_____ 3. The dedication and determination of the young men and women participating in the Special Olympics were an inspiration to everyone there.

_____ 4. The first tomato of the summer always makes me think fondly of my grandfather's garden.

_____ 5. Nobody is ever a complete failure; he or she can always serve as a bad example.

_____ 6. The councilman once again demonstrated his sensitivity toward the environment when he voted to allow commercial development in an area set aside as a nature preserve.

_____ 7. The success of the company's youth mentoring program will inspire other business groups to establish similar programs.

_____ 8. Professional athletes have no loyalty toward their teams or their fans anymore, just their own wallets.

_____ 9. We were thrilled to learn that next year's convention will be held in San Antonio—we've always wanted to see the Alamo!

_____ 10. To be considered for the president's student-of-the-year award, an individual must demonstrate academic excellence as well as outstanding community service, and the individual must furnish no fewer than four letters of reference from faculty members.

EXERCISE 7-6 . . . RECOGNIZING TONE 2

Read each of the following statements, paying particular attention to the tone. Then write a sentence that describes the tone. Prove your point by listing some of the words that reveal the author's feelings.

1. No one says that nuclear power is risk-free. There are risks involved in all methods of producing energy. However, the scientific evidence is clear and obvious. Nuclear power is at least as safe as any other means used to generate electricity.

    _____

    _____

    _____

2. The condition of our city streets is outrageous. The sidewalks are littered with paper and other garbage—you could trip while walking to the store. The streets themselves are in even worse condition. Deep potholes and crumbling curbs make it unsafe to drive. Where are our city tax dollars going if not to correct these problems?

    _____

    _____

    _____

3. I am a tired American. I am tired of watching criminals walk free while they wait for their day in court. I'm tired of hearing about victims getting hassled as much or more than criminals. I'm tired of reading about courts of law that accept lawsuits in which criminals sue their intended victims.

    _____

    _____

    _____

4. Cross-country skis have heel plates of different shapes and materials. They may be made of metal, plastic, or rubber. Be sure that they are tacked

on the ski right where the heel of your boot will fall. They will keep snow from collecting under your foot and offer some stability.

_____

_____

_____

5.   My daughter, Lucy, was born with an underdeveloped brain. She was a beautiful little girl—at least to me and my husband—but her disabilities were severe. By the time she was two weeks old we knew that she would never walk, talk, feed herself, or even understand the concept of mother and father. It's impossible to describe the effect that her five-and-a-half-month life had on us; suffice it to say that she was the purest experience of love and pain that we will ever have, that she changed us forever, and that we will never cease to mourn her death, even though we know that for her it was a triumphant passing.

—Armstrong, "The Choices We Made," p. 165

_____

_____

_____

TABLE 7.1 WORDS FREQUENTLY USED TO DESCRIBE TONE

abstract	condemning	formal	joyful	reverent
absurd	condescending	frustrated	loving	righteous
amused	cynical	gentle	malicious	sarcastic
angry	depressing	grim	melancholic	satiric
apathetic	detached	hateful	mocking	sensational
arrogant	disapproving	humorous	nostalgic	serious
assertive	distressed	impassioned	objective	solemn
awestruck	docile	incredulous	obsequious	sympathetic
bitter	earnest	indignant	optimistic	tragic
caustic	excited	indirect	outraged	uncomfortable
celebratory	fanciful	informative	pathetic	vindictive
cheerful	farcical	intimate	persuasive	worried
comic	flippant	ironic	pessimistic	
compassionate	forgiving	irreverent	playful	

7d   IS THE AUTHOR BIASED?

LEARNING OBJECTIVE 4
Identify bias

Bias refers to an author's partiality, inclination toward a particular viewpoint, or prejudice. A writer is biased if he or she takes one side of a controversial issue and does not recognize opposing viewpoints. Perhaps the best example of bias is in advertising. A magazine advertisement for a new car model, for instance, describes only positive, marketable features—the ad does not recognize the car's limitations or faults. In some material the writer might be direct and forthright in expressing his or her bias; other times a writer's bias might be hidden and discovered only through careful analysis.

Read the following description of the environmental protection group Greenpeace. The author expresses a favorable attitude toward the organization and a negative one toward whale hunters. Notice, in particular, the underlined words and phrases.

> Greenpeace is an organization dedicated to the preservation of the sea and its great mammals, notably whales, dolphins, and seals. Its ethic is nonviolent but its aggressiveness in protecting our oceans and the life in them is becoming legendary. In their roving ship, the *Rainbow Warrior*, Greenpeace volunteers have relentlessly hounded the profiteering ships of any nation harming the resources Greenpeace deems to be the property of the world community. Whales, they believe, belong to us all and have a right to exist no matter what the demand for shoe-horns, cosmetics, and machine oil.
>
> —Wallace, *Biology: The World of Life*, p. 518

To identify bias, use the following suggestions:

1. **Analyze connotative meanings.** Do you encounter a large number of positive or negative terms used to describe the subject?
2. **Notice descriptive language.** What impression is created?
3. **Analyze the tone.** The author's tone often provides important clues.
4. **Look for opposing viewpoints.**

EXERCISE 7-7 . . . DETECTING BIAS 1

Read each of the following statements and place a check mark in front of each one that reveals bias.

_____ 1. Testing the harmful effects of cosmetics on innocent animals is an outrage.

_____ 2. Judaism, Christianity, and Islam share a common belief in an all-powerful creator.

_____ 3. One of Shakespeare's wittiest and most delightful romantic comedies is *The Taming of the Shrew*.

_____ 4. Each fall, thousands of greater sandhill cranes leave their nesting grounds in Idaho and fly south to the Rio Grande.

_____ 5. A laissez-faire policy asserts that businesses should be able to charge whatever they want for their goods and services without interference from the government.

_____ 6. Campaign finance reform is essential to restoring both the integrity of the election process and the faith of Americans in our political system.

_____ 7. The longest siege of the Civil War took place in Petersburg, Virginia, when Union troops blocked Confederate supply lines from June 1864 to April 1865.

_____ 8. Students should not waste their time joining fraternities and sororities; they should concentrate on their academic coursework.

_____ 9. Bicycling is the only way to fully experience the beautiful scenery of southern France.

_____ 10. The hardware in a computer system includes the physical system itself, which may consist of a keyboard, a monitor, a central processing unit (CPU), and a printer.

EXERCISE 7–8 . . . DETECTING BIAS 2

Read the following passage and underline words and phrases that reveal the author's bias.

Not unlike drugs or alcohol, the television experience allows the participant to blot out the real world and enter into a pleasurable and passive mental state. The worries and anxieties of reality are as effectively deferred by becoming absorbed in a television program as by going on a "trip" induced by drugs or alcohol. And just as alcoholics are only inchoately aware of their addiction, feeling that they control their drinking more than they really do ("I can cut it out any time I want—I just like to have three or four drinks before dinner"), people similarly overestimate their control over television watching. Even as they put off other activities to spend hour after hour watching television, they feel they could easily resume living in a different, less passive style. But somehow or other while the television set is present in their homes, the click doesn't sound. With television pleasures available, those other experiences seem less attractive, more difficult somehow.

—Winn, *The Plug-In Drug*

7e   HOW STRONG ARE THE DATA AND EVIDENCE?

LEARNING OBJECTIVE 5
Evaluate data and evidence

Many writers who express their opinions or state viewpoints provide the reader with data or evidence to support their ideas. Your task as a critical reader is to weigh and evaluate the quality of this evidence. You must examine the evidence and assess its adequacy. You should be concerned with two factors: the type of evidence being presented, and the relevance of that evidence. Various types of evidence include:

- personal experience or observation
- expert opinion
- research citation
- statistical data
- examples, descriptions of particular events, or illustrative situations
- analogies (comparisons with similar situations)
- historical documentation
- quotations
- description

Each type of evidence must be weighed in relation to the statement it supports. Acceptable evidence should directly, clearly, and indisputably support the case or issue in question.

EXERCISE 7-9 . . . EVALUATING DATA AND EVIDENCE

Refer to the article "Treating Wounded Soldiers: Polytrauma," on page 40. For each of the following paragraphs, identify the type(s) of evidence the author provides.

1. Paragraph 1 _____

2. Paragraph 4 _____

3. Paragraph 5 _____

4. Paragraph 7 _____

7f   HOW IS CONNOTATIVE LANGUAGE USED?

LEARNING OBJECTIVE 6
Understand connotative language

Which of the following would you like to be a part of: a crowd, mob, gang, audience, congregation, or class? Each of these words has the same basic meaning: "an assembled group of people." But each has a different *shade* of meaning. *Crowd* suggests a large, disorganized group. *Audience,* on the other hand, suggests a quiet, controlled group. Try to decide what meaning each of the other words in the list suggests.

This example shows that words have two levels of meanings—a literal meaning and an additional shade of meaning. These two levels of meaning are called denotative and connotative. A word's **denotative meaning** is the meaning stated in the dictionary—its literal meaning. A word's **connotative meaning** is the additional implied meanings, or nuances, that a word may take on. Often the connotative meaning carries either a positive or negative, favorable or unfavorable impression. The words *mob* and *gang* have a negative connotation because they imply a disorderly, disorganized group. *Congregation, audience,* and *class* have a positive connotation because they suggest an orderly, organized group.

Here are a few more examples. Would you prefer to be described as "slim" or "skinny"? As "intelligent" or "brainy"? As "heavy" or "fat"? As "particular" or "picky"? Notice that each pair of words has a similar literal meaning, but that each word within the pair has a different connotation.

Depending on the words they choose, writers can suggest favorable or unfavorable impressions of the person, object, or event they are describing. For example, through the writer's choice of words, the two sentences below create two entirely different impressions. As you read them, notice the underlined words that have a positive or negative connotation.

> The <u>unruly</u> crowd <u>forced</u> its way through the restraint barriers and <u>ruthlessly attacked</u> the rock star.
>
> The <u>enthusiastic</u> group of fans <u>burst</u> through the fence and <u>rushed</u> toward the rock star.

When reading any type of informative or persuasive material, pay attention to the writer's choice of words. Often a writer may communicate subtle or hidden messages, or he or she may encourage the reader to have positive or negative feelings toward the subject.

EXERCISE 7-10 . . . USING CONNOTATIVE LANGUAGE 1

For each of the following pairs of words, underline the word with the more positive connotation.

1. request   demand
2. overlook   neglect
3. ridicule   tease
4. display   expose
5. garment   gown
6. gaudy   showy
7. artificial   fake
8. costly   extravagant
9. choosy   picky
10. sieze   take

EXERCISE 7-11 . . . USING CONNOTATIVE LANGUAGE 2

For each of the following sentences, underline the word in parentheses that has the more appropriate connotative meaning. Consult a dictionary, if necessary.

1. The new superintendent spoke (extensively / enormously) about the issues facing the school system.

2. The day after we hiked ten miles, my legs felt extremely (rigid / stiff).

3. Carlos thought that he could be more (productive / fruitful) if he had a home office.

4. The (stubborn / persistent) ringing of the telephone finally woke me up.

5. The investment seemed too (perilous / risky) so we decided against it.

7g HOW IS FIGURATIVE LANGUAGE USED?

LEARNING OBJECTIVE 7
Interpret figurative language

Figurative language is a way of describing something that makes sense on an imaginative level but not on a literal or factual level. Many common expressions are figurative:

> The exam was a piece of cake.
> Sam eats like a horse.
> He walks like a gazelle.

In each of these expressions, two unlike objects are compared on the basis of some quality they have in common. Take, for example, Hamlet's statement "I will speak daggers to her, but use none." Here the poet is comparing the features of daggers (sharp, pointed, dangerous, harmful) with something that can be used like daggers—words.

Figurative language is striking, often surprising, even shocking. This reaction is created by the unlikeness of the two objects being compared. To find the similarity and understand the figurative expression, focus on connotative meanings rather than literal meanings. For example, in reading the lines

> A sea
> Harsher than granite

from an Ezra Pound poem, you must think not only of rock or stone but also of the characteristics of granite: hardness, toughness, impermeability. Then you can see that the lines mean that the sea is rough and resistant. Figurative words, which are also called figures of speech, are used to communicate and emphasize relationships that cannot be communicated through literal meaning. For example, the statement by Jonathan Swift, "She wears her clothes as if they were thrown on by a pitchfork," creates a stronger image and conveys a more meaningful description than saying "She dressed sloppily."

The three most common types of figurative expressions are similes, metaphors, and symbols. Similes make the comparison explicit by using the word *like* or *as*. Metaphors, on the other hand, directly equate the two objects. Here are several examples of each.

- **Similes**

> We lie back to back. Curtains
> lift and fall,
> like the chest of someone sleeping.
>
> —Kenyon

> Life, like a dome of many-colored glass,
> stains the white radiance of Eternity.
>
> —Shelley

- **Metaphors**

> My Life had stood—a Loaded Gun—
> In Corners—till a Day
> The Owner passed—identified—
> And carried Me away—
>
> —Emily Dickinson*

> . . . his hair lengthened into sunbeams . . .
>
> —Gustave Flaubert

EXERCISE 7-12 . . . USING FIGURATIVE LANGUAGE 1

Each of the following sentences uses figurative language. For each figurative expression, write the letter of the choice that best explains its meaning.

*Emily Dickinson, "My life had stood a loaded gun" (lines 1-4). Reprinted by permission of the publishers and the Trustees of Amherst College from THE POEMS OF EMILY DICKINSON, Thomas H. Johnson, ed., Cambridge, Mass.: The Belknap Press of Harvard University Press, Copyright © 1951, 1955, 1979, 1983 by the President and Fellows of Harvard College.

_____ 1. Craig looked <u>like a deer caught by headlights</u> when I found him eating the last piece of pie.

    a. startled into immobility

    b. worried he would be injured

    c. comfortable in the spotlight

    d. ready to be admired

_____ 2. Rosa was <u>walking on air</u> after she learned that she had made the dean's list.

    a. hurrying

    b. happy and lighthearted

    c. unable to get her footing

    d. numb

_____ 3. Throughout my grandmother's life, her church has been her <u>rock</u>.

    a. hard

    b. unfeeling

    c. source of strength

    d. heavy weight

_____ 4. Our computer is a <u>dinosaur</u>.

    a. very large

    b. frightening

    c. unique

    d. outdated

_____ 5. The food at the sales meeting tasted <u>like cardboard</u>.

    a. artificial

    b. tasteless

    c. stiff

    d. sturdy

EXERCISE 7-13 . . . USING FIGURATIVE LANGUAGE 2

Study the figurative expression in each of the following statements. Then, in the space provided, explain the meaning of each.

1. Hope is like a feather, ready to blow away.

_____

_____

_____

2. Once Alma realized she had made an embarrassing error, the blush spread across her face like spilled paint.

_____

_____

_____

3. A powerboat, or any other sports vehicle, is a hungry animal that devours money.

_____

_____

_____

4. Sally's skin was like a smooth, highly polished apple.

_____

_____

5. Upon hearing the news, I took shears and shredded my dreams.

_____

_____

_____

SUMMING IT UP

CRITICAL-READING QUESTIONS	BENEFITS
Is the material fact or opinion?	Facts are verifiable statements; you can determine whether they are true or false. Opinions express attitudes, feelings, or personal beliefs. By distinguishing statements of fact from opinions you will know what ideas to accept or verify and which to question.
What is the author's purpose?	Authors usually address specific audiences. Depending on their purpose, authors adjust content, language, and method of presentation to suit their audience. Recognizing the author's purpose will help you to grasp meaning more quickly and evaluate the author's work.
What is the tone?	Tone refers to the attitude or feeling an author expresses about his or her subject. Recognizing tone will help you evaluate what the writer is attempting to accomplish through his or her writing.

(continued on next page)

(continued from preceding page)

CRITICAL-READING QUESTIONS	BENEFITS
Is the author biased?	Bias refers to an author's partiality toward a particular viewpoint. Recognizing tone will help you evaluate whether the author is providing objective, complete information or selectively presenting information that furthers his or her purpose.
How strong are the data and evidence?	Data and evidence are used to support statements, opinions, and viewpoints. By evaluating the data and evidence, you will be able to decide whether to accept a writer's position.
How is connotative language used?	Connotative language refers to a word's implied meanings or nuances. By analyzing connotative language you will uncover writers' efforts to create favorable or unfavorable impressions of their subjects.
How is figurative language used?	Figurative language is a way of describing something that makes sense on an imaginative level but not on a literal level. It compares two unlike things that have some quality in common. By understanding figurative language you will more fully appreciate the writer's use of language and gain a fuller understanding of how the writer views his or her subject.

MyReadingLab

For Further Practice

For support in meeting this chapter's learning objectives, log in to http://www.myreadinglab.com, go to the Study Plan tab, click on **Reading Skills** and choose **Critical Thinking** from the list of subtopics. Read and view the videos and resources in the Review Materials section, and then complete the Recall, Practice, and Test exercises in the Activities section. You can check your scores and overall progress by using the Gradebook.

8 Organizing Ideas

LEARNING OBJECTIVES

In this chapter, you will learn how to

1 Highlight effectively

2 Use annotation to record your thinking

3 Paraphrase ideas

4 Outline text

5 Draw maps to show relationships

6 Summarize text

Have you ever wondered how you will learn all the facts and ideas from your textbooks and instructors? The key to handling the volume of information presented in each course is a two-step process. First, you must reduce the amount to be learned by deciding what is most important, less important, and unimportant to learn. Then you must organize the information to make it more meaningful and easier to learn. This section describes three strategies for reducing the information—textbook highlighting, annotating, and paraphrasing—and three means of organizing the information—outlining, mapping, and summarizing.

8a HIGHLIGHTING

LEARNING OBJECTIVE 1
Highlight effectively

MyReadingLab

To practice highlighting, go to

▼ Study Plan
  ▼ Reading Skills
    ▼ Notetaking and Highlighting

Highlighting is an excellent way to improve your comprehension and recall of textbook assignments. Highlighting forces you to decide what is important and sort the key information from less important material. Sorting ideas this way improves both comprehension and recall. To decide what to highlight, you must think about and evaluate the relative importance of each idea. To highlight most effectively, use these guidelines.

1. **Analyze the assignment.** Preview the assignment and define what type of learning is required. This will help you determine how much and what type of information you need to highlight.

2. **Assess your familiarity with the subject.** Depending on your background knowledge, you may need to highlight only a little or a great deal. Do not waste time highlighting what you already know.

190

3. **Read first, then highlight.** Finish a paragraph or self-contained section before you highlight. As you read, look for signals to organizational patterns (see Chapter 4). Each idea may seem important as you first encounter it, but you must see how it fits in with the others before you can judge its relative importance.

4. **Use the boldfaced headings.** Headings are labels that indicate the overall topic of a section. These headings serve as indicators of what is important to highlight.

5. **Highlight main ideas and only key supporting details.** Avoid highlighting examples and secondary details.

6. **Avoid highlighting complete sentences.** Highlight only enough so that your highlighting makes sense when you reread it. In the following selection, note that only key words and phrases are highlighted. Now read only the highlighted words. Can you grasp the key idea of the passage?

Biomes

By using imagination, we can divide the earth's land into several kinds of regions called biomes, areas of the earth that support specific assemblages of plants. As would be expected, certain kinds of animals occupy each type of biome, since different species of animals are dependent on different sorts of plant communities for food, shelter, building materials, and hiding places. . . .

Tropical rain forests are found mainly in the Amazon and Congo Basins and in Southeast Asia. The temperature in this biome doesn't vary much throughout the year. Instead, the seasons are marked by variation in the amount of rainfall throughout the year. In some areas, there may be pronounced rainy seasons. These forests support many species of plants. Trees grow throughout the year and reach tremendous heights, with their branches forming a massive canopy overhead. The forest floor, which can be quite open and easy to travel over, may be dark and steamy. Forests literally swarm with insects and birds. Animals may breed throughout the year as a result of the continual availability of food. Competition is generally considered to be very keen in such areas because of the abundance of species.

—Wallace, *Biology*, pp. 708, 710

7. **Move quickly through the document as you highlight.** If you have understood a paragraph or section, then your highlighting should be fast and efficient.

8. **Develop a consistent system of highlighting.** Decide, for example, how you will mark main ideas, how you will distinguish main ideas from details, and how you will highlight new terminology. Some students use a system of single and double highlighting, brackets, asterisks, and circles to distinguish various types of information; others use different colors of ink or combinations of pens and pencils.

9. **Use the 15–25 percent rule of thumb.** Although the amount you will highlight will vary from course to course, try to highlight no more than 15 to 25 percent of any given page. If you exceed this figure, it often means that you are not sorting ideas as efficiently as possible. Other times, it may mean that you should choose a different strategy for reviewing the material.

Remember, the more you highlight, the smaller your time-saving dividends will be as you review. The following excerpt provides an example of effective highlighting.

Temperate deciduous forests once covered most of the eastern United States and all of Central Europe. The dominant trees in these forests are hardwoods. The areas characterized by such plants are subject to harsh winters, times when the trees shed their leaves, and warm summers that mark periods of rapid growth and rejuvenation. Before the new leaves begin to shade the forest floor in the spring, a variety of herbaceous (nonwoody) flowering plants may appear. These wildflowers are usually perennials, plants that live and produce flowers year after year. In the early spring, they don't have time to manufacture the food needed to grow and bloom suddenly. Instead, they draw on food produced and stored in underground parts during the previous year. Rainfall may average 75 to 130 centimeters or more each year in these forests and is rather evenly distributed through out the year.

—Wallace, *Biology,* pp. 712–713

EXERCISE 8-1 . . . HIGHLIGHTING 1

Read the following pairs of paragraphs, which have been highlighted in two different ways. Look at each highlighted version, and then write your answers to the questions that follow in the spaces provided.

Example A

Murders, especially mass murders and serial murders, fascinate the public and criminologists. Murder is the least committed crime but receives the most attention. Murder trials often capture the attention of the entire nation. The O. J. Simpson murder trial was one of the most watched television programs in the history of network Nielson ratings.

—Fagin, *Criminal Justice,* p. 89

Example B

Murders, especially mass murders and serial murders, fascinate the public and criminologists. Murder is the least committed crime but receives the most attention. Murder trials often capture the attention of the entire nation. The O. J. Simpson murder trial was one of the most watched television programs in the history of network Nielson ratings.

1. Is Example A or Example B the better example of effective highlighting? _____

2. Why isn't the highlighting in the other example effective?

   _____

   _____

Example C

Air pollution results when several factors combine to lower air quality. Carbon monoxide emitted by automobiles contributes to air pollution, as do smoke and other chemicals from manufacturing plants. Air quality is usually worst in certain geographic locations, such as the Denver area and the Los Angeles basin, where pollutants tend to get trapped in the atmosphere. For this very reason, the air around Mexico City is generally considered to be the most polluted in the entire world.

—Ebert and Griffin, *Business Essentials,* p. 71

Example D

Air pollution results when several factors combine to lower air quality. Carbon monoxide emitted by automobiles contributes to air pollution, as do smoke and other chemicals from manufacturing plants. Air quality is usually worst in certain geographic locations, such as the Denver area and the Los Angeles basin, where pollutants tend to get trapped in the atmosphere. For this very reason, the air around Mexico City is generally considered to be the most polluted in the entire world.

3. Is Example C or Example D the better example of effective highlighting? _____

4. Why isn't the highlighting in the other example effective?

_____

_____

_____

EXERCISE 8-2 . . . HIGHLIGHTING 2

Highlight the following article, "What is Crime?"

Textbook
Excerpt

What is Crime?

Deviance vs. Crime

1   Most prisoners are incarcerated because they've broken a law. But how do we determine which behaviors are criminal? **Deviance** is the violation of norms that a society agrees upon. For example, teens who dye their hair in neon colors would be considered deviant in most parts of society. However, some acts that may be considered socially deviant, like refusing to bathe, for instance, aren't necessarily illegal, no matter how much you might wish they were. For something to be considered a **crime,** it has to be a violation of norms that have been written into law. Going above the speed limit is an example of a crime. Sociologists who specialize in **criminology** scientifically study crime, deviance, and social policies that the criminal justice system applies.

What is Deviance?

2   If deviance refers to violating socially agreed upon norms, then how do we determine what is and what isn't considered deviant? There are four specific characteristics that sociologists use to define deviance:

1. **Deviance is linked to time.** History changes the definition of deviance, so what is considered deviant today may not be deviant tomorrow. One hundred years ago, it was considered deviant for women to wear trousers. Today, it's normal for women to dress in trousers.
2. **Deviance is linked to cultural values.** How we label an issue determines our moral point of view. Cultural values come from religious, political, economic, or philosophical principles. For example, in Holland, active euthanasia for the terminally ill, or "mercy killing," is legal within some circumstances. In the United States, euthanasia is considered murder and is punished accordingly. Each culture defines euthanasia differently.
3. **Deviance is a cultural universal.** You can find deviants in every culture on the planet. Regardless of what norms a society establishes, you can always find a small number of nonconformists who will break those rules.
4. **Deviance is a social construct.** Each society views actions differently. If society tolerates a behavior, it is no longer deviant. For example, Prohibition in the 1920s and early 30s made drinking alcohol illegal in the United States, but today it's normal.

Street Crime

3   Although there are many different types of crime, when most people talk about "crime," they're likely talking about **street crime**, which refers to many different types of criminal acts, such as burglary, rape, and assault. Street crime has been the focus of most criminological research, but you may wonder how much street crime actually exists. The next section will discuss street crime and how it is measured.

Crime Statistics

4   After spending an hour watching a show like *CSI*, you'd think the police are able to solve crimes like they do on TV. Unfortunately, real life isn't as convenient as television. For example, when someone stole the tires off my car, I asked the police officer when I might get my wheels back. He said, "Probably never. These kinds of crimes are difficult to solve."

Uniform Crime Reports and the National Crime Victimization Survey

5   Another aspect of detective work often omitted from television is the paperwork that officers must file. The information in those files is vital to understand crime statistics. Criminologists use two primary sources of data to measure the amount of street crime: the UCRs and the NCVS. The Federal Bureau of Investigation (FBI) collects **Uniform Crime Reports (UCRs)**, the official police statistics of reported crimes. **The National Crime Victimization Survey (NCVS)** measures crime victimization by contacting a representative sample of over 70,000 households in the United States.

6   UCRs only contain data on reported crimes, so when a car is reported as stolen, it becomes a UCR statistic. This report also lists the **crime index**, which consists of eight offenses used to measure crime. These include four violent offenses: homicide, rape, robbery, and aggravated assault, as well as four property crimes: burglary, larceny-theft, motor vehicle theft, and arson.

7   Criminologists understand that many crimes go unreported, so they also refer to the NCVS statistics. NCVS data always account for more crime than UCR data. For example, in 2002 UCR reported fewer than 12 million offenses, whereas NCVS showed approximately 23 million crimes. This supports the criminologist's rule of thumb—about half the crimes committed go unreported.

Crime Trends

8   UCR and NCVS data are also used to determine crime trends, and the trend that seems most constant is that the crime rates change over time. The vast majority of crime in the United States is property crime. In 2006, property crimes made up 88 percent of all reported crimes, whereas violent crimes constituted less than 12 percent. These trends are in stark contrast to the media's portrayal of crime.

Gender and Crime

9   Throughout history, men have traditionally committed more crime than women. The demographic characteristics of street criminals in the United States have not changed much over time. In fact, 77 percent of people arrested are men. This is a significant statistic because men make up less than 50 percent of the population. However, several other factors also figure in crime trends.

Race and Crime

10   Although the gender differences in crime statistics are fairly easy to distinguish, discussing a link between race and crime is controversial. The major problem is the long history of racism in the United States. African Americans make up about 12 percent of the population, but they represent 27 percent of those arrested in the United States. Does this disproportionate representation suggest African Americans commit more crimes, or does the criminal justice system unfairly pursue them?

11   Some argue that the police's different enforcement practices are responsible for these data. Racial profiling is a controversial police practice of targeting criminals based on their race. Cole shows that traffic police disproportionately stop people of color. Jeffrey Reiman suggests that the police seek out the poor for arrest because the poor are easier to catch and easier to convict of crimes. Wealthy people can hire expensive lawyers; poor people must use the public defender system. This increases the odds that official statistics have an inherent racial bias because racial minorities disproportionately represent the poor in the United States.

Social Class and Crime

12   Although crime rates are higher in poorer neighborhoods, that doesn't necessarily mean people in lower classes actually commit more crime. This makes data on the link between social class and crime difficult to interpret. A number of studies have shown that poorer people are arrested at higher rates, but that doesn't mean everyone who lives in poor neighborhoods breaks the law or is more likely to break the law.

13   On the other side of the spectrum, Reiman shows that the upper classes' crimes are not prosecuted at the same rates. For example, in all 50 states, getting caught with five grams of crack cocaine can earn you up to five years in prison. However, a person

would have to possess 500 grams of cocaine powder to receive the same sentence. So what's the difference? People convicted of crack possession tend to be poor, while people caught with cocaine powder are usually wealthy.

14   **Reiman believes that social class makes a huge difference in who gets caught and who goes to prison.** He argues that laws are applied differently and that dangerous activities performed by the "elite" are not even considered crimes.

15   For example, doctors who accidentally kill a patient during an unnecessary surgery are not accused of manslaughter. Similarly, Reiman suggests that white-collar crimes are not reported because people want to avoid a scandal. Furthermore, we do not keep official records of white-collar crimes, so there is no way of knowing exactly how much of this occurs.

Age and Crime

16   Essentially, crime is a young person's game. This idea is supported by the relationship between age and crime. It indicates that the majority of arrests peak between the ages of 15 to 25. After that point, they follow a slow but steady decrease throughout life. Arrest data from other cultures and times in history also support this claim.

17   The link between age and crime is very clear in criminology. According to Steffensmeier and Harer, a 60 percent decrease in crime rates in the 1980s is attributable to a decrease in the total number of 15- to 24-year-olds. Clearly, age matters when discussing crime.

International Comparisons of Street Crime

18   In order to gain a better perspective on crime in the United States, sociologists often make international comparisons. However, making international comparisons of crime data creates certain problems for the researcher. Therefore, for this text I selected countries that are similar to the United States in a number of ways: they are all generally wealthy, and all keep good crime data. Here is a list of potentially complicating factors:

1. Crime numbers may or may not be accurate. Some countries deliberately skew their data to show lower crime rates in order to keep tourism high.
2. Legal definitions of crimes differ among nations. Some nations do not recognize marital rape as a crime; others have legalized drugs that are illegal in the United States.
3. Different methods of collecting data can result in differences in reported crimes. Some nations have extraordinarily reliable data collection systems, while others do not.
4. Cultures vary, as do programs to prevent, punish, and curb crime.

United States: Number One with a Bullet

19   Why does the United States have the highest murder rate in the industrialized world? Some blame easy access to guns, and others claim it's our violent history as a nation. Still others argue that it is the level of inequality in our country. Whatever the reasons, one thing is clear: U.S. citizens are three times more likely to be murdered compared to people in other developed nations.

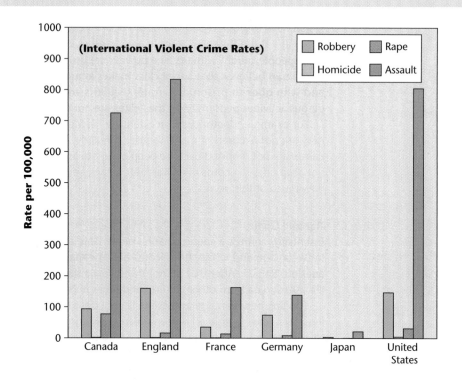

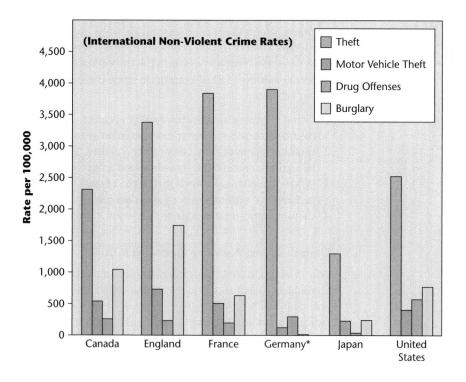

20   However, the graphs on page 198 present a somewhat different picture of violence with regard to international rates of rape and robbery. The countries selected are similar to the United States and give you a quick way to compare crime in the United States to that of other countries. As you can see from these data, England leads these nations in robbery, and Canada has the highest rate of rape. The United States has high rates of both crimes, but clearly is not the worst.

21   Property crimes present a different picture. The second graph provides data on four nonviolent crimes: theft, motor vehicle theft, drug offenses, and burglary. Generally speaking, occurrences of property crime are higher in other industrialized nations than in the United States.

22   These data leave a mixed picture for the international comparison of crime. Living in the United States increases the odds that one might be murdered, but it also decreases the chance of being a victim of most property crimes.

23   Comparing international crime rates shows that crime is common to all industrial societies. Some suggest this occurs because industrial societies have more high-value, lightweight items—such as iPods or laptops—that are easily stolen and sold.

8b   ANNOTATING

LEARNING OBJECTIVE 2
Use annotation to record your thinking

In many situations, highlighting alone is not a sufficient means of identifying what to learn. It does not give you any opportunity to comment on or react to the material. For this, you might want to use annotation. Annotating is an active reading process. It forces you to keep track of your comprehension as well as react to ideas. The chart on page 000 suggests various types of annotation used in marking a political science textbook chapter.

EXERCISE 8-3 . . . ANNOTATING 1

Review the chart on p. 200 and then add annotations to the reading "What is Crime?" on page 193.

EXERCISE 8-4 . . . ANNOTATING 2

Add annotations to the reading "Economic Change, Ideology, and Private Life" on page 171.

8c   PARAPHRASING

LEARNING OBJECTIVE 3
Paraphrase ideas

A **paraphrase** is a restatement of a passage's ideas in your own words. The author's meaning is retained, but your wording, *not* the author's, is used. We use paraphrasing frequently in everyday speech. For example, when you relay a message from one person to another you convey the meaning but do not use the person's exact wording. A paraphrase can be used to make a passage's meaning clearer and often more concise. Paraphrasing is also an effective learning and review strategy in several situations.

First, paraphrasing is useful for portions of a text for which exact, detailed comprehension is required. For example, you might paraphrase the steps in solving a math problem, the process by which a blood transfusion is administered, or the levels of jurisdiction of the Supreme Court.

Paraphrasing is also a useful way to be certain you understand difficult or complicated material. If you can express the author's ideas in your own words, you can be certain you understand it, and if you find yourself at a loss for words—except for those of the author—you will know your understanding is incomplete.

MARGINAL ANNOTATION

TYPES OF ANNOTATION		EXAMPLE
Circling unknown words		. . . redressing the apparent (asymmetry) of their relationship
Marking definitions	def	To say that the balance of power favors one party over another is to introduce a disequilibrium.
Marking examples	ex	. . . concessions may include negative sanctions, trade agreements . . .
Numbering lists of ideas, causes, reasons, or events		components of power include ① self-image, ② population, natural resources, and geography ③ ④
Placing asterisks next to important passages	*	Power comes from three primary sources . . .
Putting question marks next to confusing passages	? ⟶	war prevention occurs through institutionalization of mediation . . .
Making notes to yourself	Check def in soc text	power is the ability of an actor on the international stage to . . .
Marking possible test items	T	There are several key features in the relationship . . .
Drawing arrows to show relationships		. . . natural resources . . . , . . . control of industrial manufacture capacity
Writing comments, noting disagreements and similarities	Can terrorism be prevented through similar balance?	war prevention through balance of power is . . .
Marking summary statements	Sum	the greater the degree of conflict, the more intricate will be . . .

Paraphrasing is also a useful strategy when working with material that is stylistically complex, poorly written, or overly formal, awkward, or biased. Below is a paraphrase of a paragraph from "What is Crime?"

A SAMPLE PARAPHRASE

PARAGRAPH	PARAPHRASE
Essentially, crime is a young person's game. This idea is supported by the relationship between age and crime. It indicates that the majority of arrests peak between the ages of 15 and 25. After that point, they follow a slow but steady decrease throughout life. Arrest data from other cultures and times in history also support this claim.	Age and likelihood to commit a crime are related. Crime is mostly committed by young people. Most arrests are made for people between 15 and 25 years old. After that, as age increases, there is a steady decrease in arrests. This pattern is consistent with data from other cultures and other historical periods.

Use the following suggestions to paraphrase effectively.

1. **Read slowly and carefully.**
2. **Read the material through entirely before writing anything.**
3. **As you read, pay attention to exact meanings and relationships among ideas.**
4. **Paraphrase sentence by sentence.**
5. **Read each sentence and express the key idea in your own words.** Reread the original sentence; then look away and write your own sentence. Then reread the original and add anything you missed.
6. **Don't try to paraphrase word by word. Instead, work with ideas.**
7. **For words or phrases you are unsure of** or that are not words you feel comfortable using, check a dictionary to locate a more familiar meaning.
8. **You may combine several original sentences into a more concise paraphrase.**

EXERCISE 8-5 ... PARAPHRASING 1

Read each paragraph and the paraphrases following them. Answer the questions about the paraphrases.

Paragraph A

The use of silence can be an effective form of communication, but its messages and implications differ cross culturally. In Siberian households, the lowest status person is the in-marrying daughter, and she tends to speak very little. However, silence does not always indicate powerlessness. In American courts, comparison of speaking frequency between the judge, jury, and lawyers shows that lawyers, who have the least power, speak most, while the silent jury holds the most power.

—Miller, *Cultural Anthropology*, p. 302

Paraphrase 1

Silence carries a message as well as serves as a form of communication. Young married Siberian women speak very little, lawyers (who are powerless) speak a great deal, and the jury (which is most powerful) is silent.

Paraphrase 2

Silence is a way to communicate, but its meaning varies from culture to culture. In Siberia, women have low status in their husband's family and speak very little. In American courts, however, the most powerful group, the jury, is silent, while the least powerful—attorneys—speak the most.

Paraphrase 3

Silence has many meanings. Siberian women speak very little, indicating their low status. Lawyers speak a great deal, while a jury is silent.

1. Which is the best paraphrase of the paragraph? _____

2. Why are the other paraphrases less good?

_____

_____

_____

_____

_____

Paragraph B

Today, the dominant family form in the United States is the child-free family, where a couple resides together and there are no children present in the household. With the aging of the baby boomer cohort, this family type is expected to increase steadily over time. If current trends continue, nearly three out of four U.S. households will be childless in another decade or so.

—Thompson and Hickey, *Society in Focus*, p. 355

Paraphrase 1

A child-free family is one where two adults live together and have no children. It is the dominant family form.

Paraphrase 2

The child-free family is dominant in the U.S. Baby boomers are having fewer children. Three out of four homes do not have children in them.

Paraphrase 3

The child-free family is dominant in the U.S. As baby boomers get older, there will be even more of these families. Three-quarters of all U.S. homes will be child-less ten years from now.

3. Which is the best paraphrase of the paragraph?_____

4. Why are the other paraphrases less good?

_____

_____

_____

_____

_____

EXERCISE 8-6 . . . PARAPHRASING 2

Write a paraphrase of paragraph 11 in the reading "What is Crime" on page 196.

8d   OUTLINING TO ORGANIZE IDEAS

LEARNING OBJECTIVE 4
Outline text

MyReadingLab

To practice outlining, go to

▼ Study Plan
  ▼ Reading Skills
    ▼ Outlining and Summarizing

Outlining is a writing strategy that can assist you in organizing information and pulling ideas together. It is also an effective way to pull together information from two or more sources—your textbook and class lectures, for example. Finally, outlining is a way to assess your comprehension and strengthen your recall. Use the following tips to write an effective outline.

1. **Read an entire section and then jot down notes.** Do not try to outline while you are reading the material for the first time.

2. **As you read, be alert for organizational patterns** (see Chapter 4). These patterns will help you organize your notes.

3. **Record all the most important ideas in the briefest possible form.**

4. **Think of your outline as a list of the main ideas and supporting details of a selection.** Organize it to show how the ideas are related or to reflect the organization of the material.

5. **Write in your own words; do not copy sentences or parts of sentences from the selection.** Use words and short phrases to summarize ideas. Do not write in complete sentences.

6. **Use a system of indentation to separate main ideas and details.** As a general rule, the greater the importance of an idea, the closer it is placed to the left margin. Ideas of lesser importance are indented and appear closer to the center of the page. Your notes might follow a format like that shown on the following page:

**OUTLINE
FORMAT**

> TOPIC
> Main Idea
>> Supporting detail
>>> fact
>>> fact
>> Supporting detail
> Main Idea
>> Supporting detail
>> Supporting detail
>>> fact
>>> fact

To further illustrate the techniques of outlining, study the notes shown in the sample outline below. They are based on a portion (paragraph 1 and the table included in the reading) of the textbook excerpt "Ending a Relationship" on page 37.

**A SAMPLE
OUTLINE**

I. Ending a Relationship

   A. How to Break Up (Disengage)

      1. Five Strategies

         a) use a positive tone and express positive feelings

         b) blame the other person (negative identity management)

         c) give reasons for breakup (justification)

         d) reduce the strength of the relationship by avoiding the person or spending less time with him or her (behavioral de-escalation)

         e) reduce exclusivity (de-escalation)

      2. Strategy used depends on a person's goal

EXERCISE 8-7 . . . OUTLINING 1

Read the following passage and complete the outline.

Gender Characteristics

Masculinity refers to attributes considered appropriate for males. In American society, these traditionally include being aggressive, athletic, physically active, logical, and dominant in social relationships with females. Conversely, femininity refers to attributes associated with appropriate behavior for females, which in America include passivity, docility, fragility, emotionality, and subordination to males. Research conducted by Carol Gilligan and her students at Harvard's Gender Studies Department indicate that children are acutely aware of and feel pressure to conform to these powerful gender traits by the age of 4. Some people insist that gender traits such as male aggressiveness are innate characteristics linked to sex and do not depend on cultural definitions. However, the preponderance of research indicates that females and males can be equally aggressive under different social and cultural conditions and that levels of aggression vary as widely within the sexes as between them.

—adapted from Thompson and Hickey, *Society in Focus,* p. 285

Gender Characteristics

A. Masculinity

   1. attributes society believes appropriate for males

   2. include _____

      _____

B. Femininity

   1. _____

   2. include _____

     and subordination to males

C. _____ are aware of and feel pressure to conform to gender

   expectations by _____

D. Link to Sex

   1. some people believe linked to sex

   2. research shows both sexes can be equally aggressive and levels of

     _____

     _____

EXERCISE 8-8 . . . OUTLINING 2

Finish outlining the textbook excerpt "Ending a Relationship" on page 37.

8e   MAPPING TO SHOW RELATIONSHIPS

LEARNING OBJECTIVE 5
Draw maps to show relationships

Mapping is a way of drawing a diagram to describe how a topic and its related ideas are connected. Mapping is a visual means of learning by writing; it organizes and consolidates information.

   This section discusses four types of maps: conceptual maps, process diagrams, part and function diagrams, and time lines.

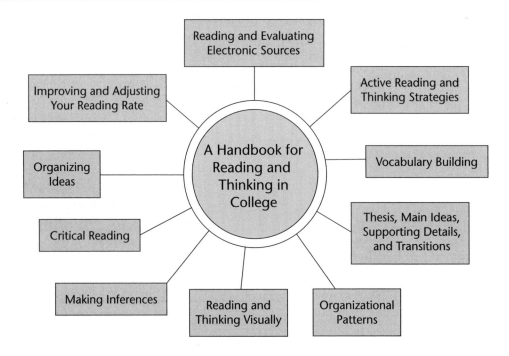

Conceptual Maps

A conceptual map is a diagram that presents ideas spatially rather than in list form. It is a "picture" of how ideas are related. Use the following steps in constructing a conceptual map.

1. **Identify the topic and write it in the center of the page.**
2. **Identify ideas, aspects, parts, and definitions that are related to the topic.** Draw each one on a line radiating from the topic.
3. **As you discover details that further explain an idea already recorded, draw new lines branching from the idea that the details explain.**

A conceptual map of Part One of this book is shown above. This map shows only the major topics included in Part One. Maps can be much more detailed and include more information than the one shown, depending on the purpose for drawing it.

EXERCISE 8-9 . . . DRAWING A CONCEPTUAL MAP 1

Read the following paragraph about social institutions. Complete the conceptual map that presents the ideas contained in this paragraph.

Society cannot survive without social institutions. A social institution is a set of widely shared beliefs, norms and procedures necessary for meeting the basic needs of society. The most important institutions are family, education, religion, economy, and politics. They have stood the test of time, serving society well. The family institution leads countless people to produce and raise children to ensure that they can eventually take over from the older generation the task of keeping society going. The educational institution teaches the young to become effective contributors to the welfare—such as the order, stability, or prosperity—of society. The religious institution fulfills spiritual needs, making earthly lives seem more meaningful and therefore more bearable or satisfying. The economic institution provides food, clothing, shelter, employment, banking, and other goods and services that we need to live. The political institution makes and enforces laws to prevent criminals and other similar forces from destabilizing society.

—Thio, *Sociology*, pp. 35–36

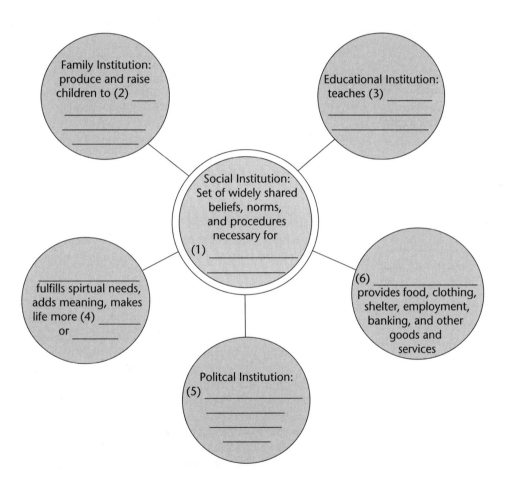

Family Institution: produce and raise children to (2) _____ _____ _____

Educational Institution: teaches (3) _____ _____ _____

Social Institution: Set of widely shared beliefs, norms, and procedures necessary for (1) _____ _____

fulfills spirtual needs, adds meaning, makes life more (4) _____ or _____

(6) _____ provides food, clothing, shelter, employment, banking, and other goods and services

Politcal Institution: (5) _____ _____ _____ _____

EXERCISE 8-10 . . . DRAWING A CONCEPTUAL MAP 2

Draw a conceptual map for the textbook excerpt "Ending a Relationship" on page 37.

Process Diagrams

In the technologies and the natural sciences, as well as in many other courses, *processes* are an important part of the course content. A diagram that visually describes the steps, variables, or parts of a process will make learning easier. For example, the diagram below visually describes the steps in the process of conducting research.

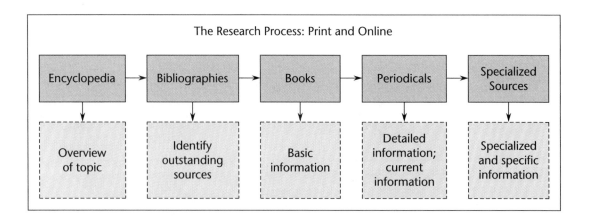

The Research Process: Print and Online

Encyclopedia	Bibliographies	Books	Periodicals	Specialized Sources
Overview of topic	Identify outstanding sources	Basic information	Detailed information; current information	Specialized and specific information

EXERCISE 8-11 . . . DRAWING A PROCESS DIAGRAM 1

The following paragraph describes how a bill becomes a law. Read the paragraph and then complete the process diagram that illustrates this procedure.

Federal criminal laws must originate in the House of Representatives or the U.S. Senate. A senator or representative introduces a proposal (known as a bill) to create a new law or modify an existing law. The merits of the bill are debated in the House or Senate and a vote is taken. If the bill receives a majority vote, it is passed on to the other house of Congress where it is again debated and put to a vote. If any changes are made, the amended bill must be returned to the house of Congress where it originated and voted on again. This process continues until the House and Senate agree on a single version of the bill. The bill is then forwarded to the president, who can sign the bill into law, veto it or take no action, in which case the bill dies automatically when Congress adjourns. If the president vetoes a bill, Congress can pass the law over the president's veto by a two-thirds vote of both houses. Whether approved by the president and the Congress or by the Congress alone, a bill becomes a law when it is published in the *U.S. Criminal Codes.*

—Fagin, *Criminal Justice*, p. 107

Drawing a Process Diagram

The Making of Federal Criminal Laws

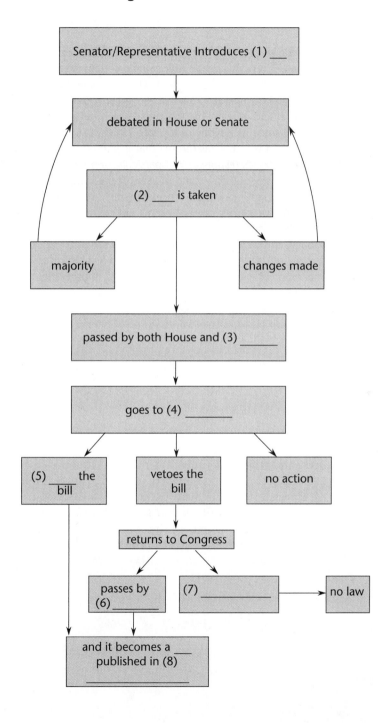

EXERCISE 8-12 . . . DRAWING A PROCESS DIAGRAM 2

The following paragraph describes the sequential effects of taking the psychedelic drug LSD. Read the paragraph and then draw a process diagram that describes this response sequence. Compare your diagram with those of several other students.

Psychedelics are . . . a group of drugs that produce hallucinations and various other phenomena that very closely mimic certain mental disorders. These drugs include lysergic acid diethylamide (LSD), mescaline, peyote, psilocybin, and various commercial preparations such as Sernyl and Ditran.

Of these, LSD is probably the best known, although its use has apparently diminished since its heyday in the late 1960s. LSD is synthesized from lysergic acid produced by a fungus (ergot) that is parasitic on cereal grains such as rye. It usually produces responses in a particular sequence. The initial reactions may include weakness, dizziness and nausea. These symptoms are followed by a distortion of time and space. The senses may become intensified and strangely intertwined—that is, sounds can be "seen" and colors "heard." Finally, there may be changes in mood, a feeling of separation of the self from the framework of time and space, and changes in the perception of the self. The sensations experienced under the influence of psychedelics are unlike anything encountered within the normal range of experiences. The descriptions of users therefore can only be puzzling to nonusers. Some users experience bad trips or "bummers," which have been known to produce long-term effects. Bad trips can be terrifying experiences and can occur in experienced users for no apparent reason.

—Donatelle, *Health*, p. 179

Time Lines

When you are studying a topic in which the sequence or order of events is a central focus, a time line is a helpful way to organize the information. Time lines are especially useful in history courses. To map a sequence of events, draw a single line and mark it off in year intervals, just as a ruler is marked off in inches. Then write events next to the correct year. For example, the following time line displays major events during the presidency of Franklin D. Roosevelt. The time line shows the sequence of events and helps you to visualize them clearly.

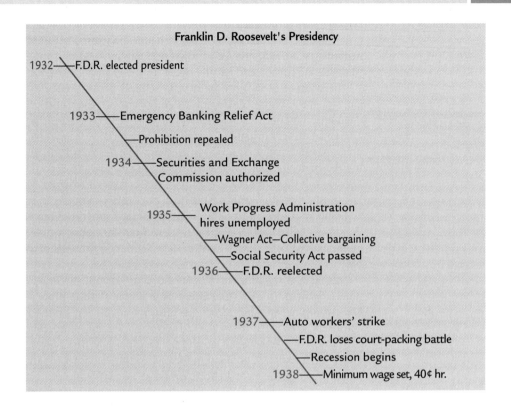

Franklin D. Roosevelt's Presidency

1932 — F.D.R. elected president

1933 — Emergency Banking Relief Act
     — Prohibition repealed

1934 — Securities and Exchange
       Commission authorized

1935 — Work Progress Administration
       hires unemployed
     — Wagner Act—Collective bargaining
     — Social Security Act passed

1936 — F.D.R. reelected

1937 — Auto workers' strike
     — F.D.R. loses court-packing battle
     — Recession begins

1938 — Minimum wage set, 40¢ hr.

EXERCISE 8-13 . . . DRAWING A TIME LINE

The following passage reviews the chronology of events in public school desegregation. Read the selection and then draw a time line that will help you to visualize these historical events.

Desegregating the Schools

The nation's schools soon became the primary target of civil-rights advocates. The NAACP concentrated first on universities, successfully waging an intensive legal battle to win admission for qualified blacks to graduate and professional schools. Led by Thurgood Marshall, NAACP lawyers then took on the broader issue of segregation in the country's public schools. Challenging the 1896 Supreme Court decision (*Plessy v. Ferguson*) which upheld the constitutionality of separate but equal public facilities, Marshall argued that even substantially equal but separate schools did profound psychological damage to black children and thus violated the Fourteenth Amendment.

A unanimous Supreme Court agreed in its 1954 decision in the case of *Brown v. Board of Education of Topeka*. Chief Justice Earl Warren, recently appointed by President Eisenhower, wrote the landmark opinion which flatly declared that "separate educational facilities are inherently unequal." To divide grade-school children "solely because of their race," Warren argued, "generates a feeling of inferiority as to their status in the community that may affect their hearts and minds in a way unlikely ever to be undone." Despite this sweeping language, Warren realized that it would be difficult to change historic patterns of segregation quickly. Accordingly, in 1955 the Court ruled that implementation should proceed "with all deliberate speed" and left the details to the lower federal courts.

The process of desegregating the schools proved to be agonizingly slow. Officials in the border states quickly complied with the Court's ruling, but states deeper in the South responded with a policy of massive resistance. Local White Citizen's Councils organized to fight for retention of racial separation; 101 congressmen and senators signed a Southern Manifesto in 1956 which denounced the *Brown* decision as "a clear abuse of judicial power." School boards, encouraged by this show of defiance, found a variety of ways to evade the Court's ruling. The most successful was the passage of pupil-placement laws. . . .

Southern leaders mistook Ike's silence for tacit support of segregation. In 1957, Governor Orville Faubus of Arkansas called out the national guard to prevent the integration of Little Rock's Central High School on grounds of a threat to public order. . . .

Despite the snail's pace of school desegregation, the *Brown* decision led to other advances. In 1957, the Eisenhower administration proposed the first general civil-rights legislation since Reconstruction. Strong southern resistance and compromise by both the administration and Senate Democratic leader Lyndon B. Johnson of Texas weakened the bill considerably. The final act, however, did create a permanent Commission for Civil Rights, one of Truman's original goals. It also provided for federal efforts aimed at "securing and protecting the right to vote." A second civil-rights act in 1960 slightly strengthened the voting-rights section.

—Divine, *America Past and Present,* pp. 890–891

Part and Function Diagrams

In courses that deal with the use and description or classification of physical objects, labeled drawings are an important learning tool. In a human anatomy and physiology course, for example, the easiest way to learn the parts and functions of the brain is to draw it. To study it, you would sketch the brain and test your recall of each part and its function.

EXERCISE 8-14 . . . DRAWING A PART AND FUNCTION DIAGRAM

The following paragraph describes the layers of the Earth. Read the paragraph and then draw a diagram that will help you to visualize how the Earth is structured.

Outer Layers of the Earth

The Earth's crust and the uppermost part of the mantle are known as the *lithosphere.* This is a fairly rigid zone that extends about 100 km below the Earth's surface. The crust extends some 60 km or so under continents, but only about

10 km below the ocean floor. The continental crust has a lower density than the oceanic crust. It is primarily a light granitic rock rich in the silicates of aluminum, iron, and magnesium. In a simplified view, the continental crust can be thought of as layered: On top of a layer of igneous rock (molten rock that has hardened, such as granite) lies a thin layer of sedimentary rocks (rocks formed by sediment and fragments that water deposited, such as limestone and sandstone); there is also a soil layer deposited during past ages in the parts of continents that have had no recent volcanic activity or mountain building.

Sandwiched between the lithosphere and the lower mantle is the partially molten material known as the *asthenosphere,* about 150 km thick. It consists primarily of iron and magnesium silicates that readily deform and flow under pressure.

—Berman and Evans, *Exploring the Cosmos,* p. 145

8f SUMMARIZING TO CONDENSE IDEAS

LEARNING OBJECTIVE 6
Summarize text

MyReadingLab

To practice summarizing, go to

▼ Study Plan
  ▼ Reading Skills
    ▼ Outlining and
        Summarizing

Like outlining, summarizing is an excellent way to learn from your reading and to increase recall. A **summary** is a brief statement that reviews the key points of what you have read. It condenses an author's ideas or arguments into sentences written in your own words. A summary contains only the gist of the text, with limited explanation, background information, or supporting detail. Writing a summary is a step beyond recording the author's ideas; a summary must pull together the writer's ideas by condensing and grouping them. Before writing a summary, be sure you understand the material and have identified the writer's major points. Then use the following suggestions:

1. **As a first step, highlight or write brief notes on the material.**
2. **Write one sentence that states the writer's overall concern or most important idea.** To do this, ask yourself what one topic the material is about. Then ask what point the writer is trying to make about that topic. This sentence will be the topic sentence of your summary.
3. **Be sure to paraphrase, using your own words rather than those of the author.**
4. **Review the major supporting information that the author gives to explain the major idea.**
5. **The amount of detail you include, if any, depends on your purpose for writing the summary.** For example, if you are writing a summary of a television documentary for a research paper, it might be more detailed than if you were writing it to jog your memory for a class discussion.
6. **Normally, present ideas in the summary in the same order in which they appeared in the original material.**
7. **If the writer presents a clear opinion or expresses an attitude toward the subject matter, include it in your summary.**
8. **If the summary is for your own use only and is not to be submitted as an assignment, do not worry about sentence structure.** Some students prefer to write summaries using words and phrases rather than complete sentences.

A sample summary of the article "Ending a Relationship," which appears on page 37, is shown below.

**A SAMPLE
SUMMARY**

> It is inevitable that some relationships do end. As a relationship ends, there are two concerns: how to end it and how to deal with the breakup. There are five ways to end a relationship, called disengagement strategies. They are: use a positive tone, blame the other person, give reasons for the breakup, reduce the intensity of the relationship, and reduce the exclusivity of the relationship. Breakups always cause stress. Six ways to deal with a breakup are to avoid loneliness and depression, avoid jumping into a new relationship, build self-esteem, get rid of hurtful reminders, seek help and support from family and friends, and avoid repeating the same mistakes.

EXERCISE 8-15 . . . SUMMARIZING 1

Complete this summary of the passage about psychedelic drugs on page 210.

Psychedelic drugs cause _____ and can cause reactions mimicking _____. Examples of these drugs include _____. LSD is the best known and was most popular in _____. It is created from _____, which comes from a _____. Initially, it causes weakness, _____, and _____ and later a distortion of time and space. It causes senses to be _____. The drug affects _____, creates a feeling of distance, and creates changes in _____. The sensations resulting are outside _____. _____ can have _____ consequences and the reason for them is not understood.

—Donatelle, *Health: The Basics,* p. 179

EXERCISE 8-16 . . . SUMMARIZING 2

Write a summary of the section titled "Social Class and Crime?" (paragraphs 12–15) of the article "What is Crime?" on page 196–97.

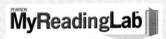

For Further Practice

For support in meeting this chapter's learning objectives, log in to http://www.myreadinglab.com, go to the Study Plan tab, click on **Reading Skills** and choose **Outlining and Mapping** and **Summarizing and Paraphrasing** from the list of subtopics. Read and view the videos and resources in the Review Materials section, and then complete the Recall, Practice, and Test exercises in the Activities section. You can check your scores and overall progress by using the Gradebook.

9 Improving and Adjusting Your Reading Rate

> **LEARNING OBJECTIVES**
>
> In this chapter, you will learn how to
>
> 1 Improve your reading rate
> 2 Adjust your reading rate

The speed at which you read, called your reading rate, is measured in words per minute (WPM). What should your reading rate be? Is it better to be a fast or slow reader? You should be able to read at 100, 200, 300, and even 400 words per minute, depending on what you are reading and why you are reading it. You should be both a slow and a fast reader; when you are reading difficult, complicated material, you should read slowly. When reading easy material or material that you do not have to remember for a test, you can afford to read faster. This section will offer some suggestions for improving your reading rate and explain how to adjust your reading rate.

9a IMPROVING YOUR READING RATE

LEARNING OBJECTIVE 1
Improve your reading rate

Here are a few suggestions for improving your overall reading rate.

1. **Try to read a little faster.** Sometimes by just being conscious of your reading rate, you can improve it slightly.
2. **Be sure to preview** (see Chapter 1, Section 1b). Previewing familiarizes you with the material and allows you to understand what you are reading more easily, thereby enabling you to read slightly faster.
3. **Improve your concentration.** If your mind wanders while you are reading, it will cost you time. Eliminate distractions, read in a place conducive to study, use writing to keep you mentally and physically alert, and alternate between different types of reading assignments.
4. **Set time goals.** Before you begin an assignment, decide approximately how much time it should take. Without a time goal, it is easy to drift and wander through an assignment rather than working straight through it efficiently.

9b   ADJUSTING YOUR RATE TO MEET COMPREHENSION DEMANDS

LEARNING OBJECTIVE 2
Adjust your reading rate

Do you read the newspaper in the same way and at the same speed at which you read a biology textbook? Do you read an essay for your English class in the same way and at the same speed at which you read a mystery novel? Surprisingly, many people do.

If you are an efficient reader, however, you read the newspaper more quickly and in a different way than you read a biology textbook. The newspaper is usually easier to read, and you have a different purpose for reading it. Efficient readers adapt their speed and comprehension levels to suit the material.

Rate and comprehension are the two main factors that you must keep in balance; as your reading rate increases, your comprehension may decrease. Your goal is to achieve a balance that suits the nature of the material and your purpose for reading it. The following steps will help you learn to vary your reading rate.

1. **Assess how difficult the assignment is.** Factors such as the difficulty of the vocabulary, length, and organization all affect text difficulty. Usually, longer or poorly-organized material is more difficult to read than shorter or well-organized material. Numerous typographical aids (italics, headings, etc.) can make material easier to read. As you preview an assignment, notice these features and estimate how difficult the material will be to read. There is no rule to use when adjusting your speed to compensate for differing degrees of difficulty. Instead, use your judgment to adjust your reading rate and style to the material.

2. **Assess your familiarity with and interest in the subject.** Your knowledge of and interest in a subject influence how fast you can read it. Material you are interested in or that you know something about will be easier for you to read, and you can increase your speed.

3. **Define your purpose.** The reason you are reading an assignment should influence how you read it. Different situations demand different levels of comprehension and recall. For example, you can read an article in *Time* magazine assigned as a supplementary reading in your sociology class faster than you can read your sociology text, because the magazine assignment does not require as high a level of recall and analysis.

4. **Decide what, if any, follow-up activity is required.** Will you have to pass a multiple-choice exam on the content? Will you be participating in a class discussion? Will you summarize the information in a short paper? The activities that follow your reading determine, in part, the level of comprehension that is required. Passing an exam requires a very high level of reading comprehension, whereas preparing for a class discussion requires a more moderate level of comprehension or retention.

Table 9.1 on page 218 shows the level of comprehension required for various types of material and gives approximate reading rates that are appropriate for each level.

TABLE 9.1 LEVELS OF COMPREHENSION

DESIRED LEVEL OF COMPREHENSION	TYPE OF MATERIAL	PURPOSE IN READING	RANGE OF READING RATES
Complete, 100%	Poetry, legal documents, argumentative writing	Analysis, criticism, evaluation	Less than 200 WPM
High, 80–100%	Textbooks, manuals, research documents	High comprehension, recall for exams, writing research reports, following directions	200–300 WPM
Moderate, 60–80%	Novels, paperbacks, newspapers, magazines	Entertainment, enjoyment, general information	300–500 WPM

EXERCISE 9-1 . . . ADJUSTING YOUR READING RATE

For each of the following situations, define your purpose and indicate the level of comprehension that seems appropriate.

1. Reading a credit card agreement or an insurance policy before signing it.

   Purpose: _____

   _____

   Comprehension level: _____

2. Reading a critical essay that analyzes a Shakespearean sonnet you are studying in a literature class.

   Purpose: _____

   _____

   Comprehension level: _____

3. Reading an online encyclopedia entry on poverty to narrow down a term paper assignment to a manageable topic.

   Purpose: _____

   _____

   Comprehension level: _____

4. Reading a newspaper article on a recent incident in the Middle East for your political science class.

Purpose: _____

_____

Comprehension level: _____

5. Reading an excerpt from a historical novel set in the Civil War period for your American history class.

Purpose: _____

_____

Comprehension level: _____

For support in meeting this chapter's learning objectives, log in to www.myreadinglab.com, go to the Study Plan tab, click on **Reading Skills** and choose **Reading Rate** from the list of subtopics. Read and view the videos and resources in the Review Materials section, and then complete the Recall, Practice, and Test exercises in the Activities section. You can check your scores and overall progress by using the Gradebook.

10 Reading and Evaluating Electronic Sources

Most of today's college students and teachers learned to read using print text. We have been reading print text much longer than electronic text; consequently our brains have developed numerous strategies or "work orders" for reading traditional printed material.

Electronic text has a wider variety of formats and presents us with more variables than traditional text. Because electronic text is a relatively new form of text, our brains need to develop new strategies in order to understand Web sites. And because Web sites vary widely in both purpose and reliability, it is important that your reading be critical.

10a READING ELECTRONIC TEXT EFFECTIVELY

LEARNING OBJECTIVE 1
Read electronic sources effectively

The first step in reading electronic text easily and effectively is to understand how it is different from print text. A print source is linear—it goes in a straight line from idea to idea. Electronic sources, in contrast, tend to be multidirectional. Using links, you can skip around easily. (See the accompanying figure.) Therefore, reading electronic sources demands a different type of thinking from reading print sources.

Using electronic text also requires new reading strategies. You need to change and adapt how you read. To do this, focus on your purpose, pay attention to how information is organized, and use links to find the information you need.

Focus on Your Purpose

Focus clearly on your purpose for visiting the site. What information do you need? Because you must create your own path through the site, fix in your mind what you are looking for. If you don't, you may wander aimlessly, waste valuable time, or even become lost, following numerous links that lead you farther and farther away from the site at which you began.

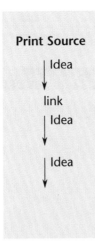

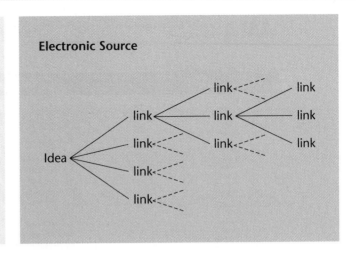

Pay Attention to How Information Is Organized

Because you can navigate through a Web site in many different ways, it is important to have the right expectations and to make several decisions before you begin. Some Web sites are much better organized than others. Some have clear headings and labels that make it easy to discover how to proceed; others do not and will require more thought before you begin. For example, if you are reading an article with as many as 10 or 15 underlined words (links), there is no prescribed order to follow and these links are not categorized in any way. Below are some suggestions on how to stay organized when using a Web site.

1. **Use the site map, if provided, to discover what information is available and how it is organized.** A sample site map for the American Management Association Web site is shown on the following page. Notice that the links are categorized according to the types of information (seminars, books, membership) a user may need.
2. **Consider the order in which you want to take in information.** Choose an order in which to explore links; avoid randomly clicking on link buttons. Doing so is somewhat like randomly choosing pages to read out of a reference book. Do you need definitions first? Do you want historical background first? Your decision will be partly influenced by your learning style.
3. **Consider writing brief notes to yourself as you explore a complicated Web site.** Alternatively, you could print the home page and jot notes on it. You can also save Web pages on to a disk or save them on your computer as a text file.
4. **Expect shorter, less detailed sentences and paragraphs.** Much online communication tends to be briefer and more concise than in traditional sources. As a result, you may have to mentally fill in transitions and make inferences about the relationships among ideas. For example, you may have to infer similarities and differences or recognize cause-and-effect connections on your own.

Use Links to Find the Information You Need

Links are unique to electronic text. The suggestions below will help you use links to find the information you need.

1. **Plan on exploring links to find complete and detailed information.** Both remote links (those that take you to another site) and related links (within a site) are intended to provide more detailed information on topics introduced on the home page.

2. **As you follow links, be sure to bookmark your original site and other useful sites you come across so you can find them again.** Bookmarking is a feature of your Internet browser that allows you to record Web site addresses and access them later by simply clicking on the site name. Different Web browsers use different terms for this function. Firefox and Safari use the term *Bookmarks;* Microsoft Explorer calls it *Favorites.* In addition, the browsers have a *History* or "Back" feature that allows a user to retrace the steps of the current search.

3. **If you use a site or a link that provides many pages of continuous paragraphs, print the material and read it offline.**

4. **If you find you are lacking background on a topic, use links to help fill in the gaps, or search for a different, less technical Web site on the same topic.**

EXERCISE 10-1 . . . NEW WAYS OF THINKING AND READING 1

Visit one of the following Web sites. Locate the information needed and take brief notes to record what you find.

URL | **Information to Locate**

1. **http://www.ftc.gov/bcp/edu/
pubs/consumer/autos/aut03.shtm**

List three tips for buying a used car.

_____

_____

_____

_____

2. **http://www.bls.gov/oco**

What is the job outlook for CAD operators?

_____

3. **http://thomas.loc.gov/
home/lawsmade.toc.html**

Why are lights and ringing bells used in parts of the Capitol building and U.S. House and Senate office buildings?

_____

_____

_____

_____

EXERCISE 10-2 . . . NEW WAYS OF THINKING AND READING 2

For one of the Web sites you visited above or a new site of your choice, follow at least three links and then answer the following questions.

1. What type of information did each contain?

_____

2. Was each source reliable? How do you know?

_____

3. Which was the easiest to read and follow? Why?

_____

10b   DISCOVERING THE PURPOSE OF WEB SITES

LEARNING OBJECTIVE 2
Discover the purpose of Web sites

There are millions of Web sites and they vary widely in purpose. Table 10.1 below summarizes five primary types of Web sites.

TABLE 10.1 TYPES OF WEB SITES

TYPE	PURPOSE	DESCRIPTION	URL EXTENSION
Informational	To present facts, information, and research data	May contain reports, statistical data, results of research studies, and reference materials	.edu or .gov
News	To provide current information on local, national, and international news	Often supplements print newspapers, periodicals, and television news programs	.com
Advocacy	To promote a particular cause or point of view	Usually concerned with a controversial issue; often sponsored by nonprofit groups	.org
Personal	To provide information about an individual and his or her interests and accomplishments	May list publications or include the individual's résumé	URL will vary; may contain .com or .org or may contain a tilde (˜)
Commercial	To promote goods or services	May provide news and information related to their products	.com

10c   EVALUATING WEB SITES

LEARNING OBJECTIVE 3
Evaluate Web sites

Once you have become familiar with the organization of a Web site and determined its purpose, you should evaluate it. To do this, consider its content, accuracy, authority, timeliness, objectivity, and usability.

Evaluate the Content of a Web Site

When evaluating the content of a Web site, evaluate its appropriateness, its level of technical detail, its completeness, and its links.

Evaluate appropriateness. To be worthwhile a Web site should contain the information you need. It should answer one or more of your search questions. If the site only touches upon answers to your questions but does not address them in detail, check the links on the site to see if they will lead you to more detailed information. If they do not, search for a more useful site.

Evaluate the level of technical detail. A Web site should contain a level of technical detail that is suited to your purpose. Some sites may provide information that is too sketchy for your search purposes; others assume a level of background knowledge or technical sophistication that you lack. For example, if you are writing a short, introductory-level paper on threats to the survival of marine animals, information on the Web site of the Scripps Institution of Oceanography (**http://www.sio.ucsd.edu**) may be too technical and contain more information than you need. Unless you already have some background knowledge in that field, you may want to search for a different Web site.

Evaluate completeness. Determine whether the site provides complete information on its topic. Does it address all aspects of the topic that you feel it should? For example, if a Web site on important twentieth-century American poets does not mention Robert Frost, then the site is incomplete. If you discover that a site is incomplete, search for sites that provide a more thorough treatment of the topic.

Evaluate the links. Many reputable sites supply links to other related sites. Make sure that the links work and are current. Also check to see if the sites to which you were sent are reliable sources of information. If the links do not work or the sources appear unreliable, you should question the reliability of the site itself. Also determine whether the links provided are comprehensive or only present a representative sample. Either is acceptable, but the site should make clear the nature of the links it is providing.

EXERCISE 10-3 . . . EVALUATING CONTENT

Evaluate the content of two of the following sites. Explain why you would either trust or distrust the site for reliable content.

1. **http://www.rainforestplace.com/index.htm**

_____

_____

_____

_____

_____

2. http://www1.umn.edu/ohr/careerdev/resources/resume/index.html

_____

_____

_____

3. http://www.idausa.org/facts/pg.html

_____

_____

_____

Evaluate the Accuracy of a Web Site

When using information on a Web site for an academic paper, it is important to be sure that you have found accurate information. The site itself will also provide clues about the accuracy of the information it contains, so ask the following questions:

1. **Is the information presented on the site verifiable?** Compare it with other online sources or with print sources (periodicals and books) on the same topic. If you find a discrepancy between the Web site and other sources, do not trust the site.
2. **Is the information complete or in summary form?** If it is a summary, use the site to locate the original source. Original information is less likely to contain errors and is usually preferred in academic papers.
3. **Could the site be a spoof?** Some sites that appear serious are actually spoofs, hoaxes, or satires designed to poke fun at topics and issues. An example is **http://www.theonion.com.** This site appears to offer legitimate information but actually provides political and social commentary through made-up stories.
4. **Does the site contain current links to other sources?** Accurate sites often provide links where additional information can be found on the Internet.
5. **Does the site provide a list of works cited?** As with any form of research, the sources of information used on the Web site must be documented. If sources are not credited, you should question the accuracy of the site.

EXERCISE 10-4 . . . EVALUATING ACCURACY

Evaluate the accuracy of two of the following Web sites.

1. **http://gunscholar.com/**

_____

_____

_____

2. **http://freeyourmindonline.net/victorytax.html**

_____

_____

_____

_____

_____

3. **http://www.bodyecology.com/autism.php**

_____

_____

_____

Evaluate the Authority of a Web Site

Before using information on a Web site, use the following questions to evaluate the authority of the person or group presenting the information.

1. **Who is the site's sponsor?** Is the sponsor a private individual, an institution, a corporation, a government agency, or a nonprofit organization? Who a site is sponsored by often suggests its purpose. For example, a Web site sponsored by Nike is designed to promote its products, while a site sponsored by a university library is designed to help students learn to use its resources more effectively. Often, the ending of the URL can help you identify the sponsor. The copyright indicates the owner of the site. Another way to check the ownership of a site is to locate the site's home page. You can do this by using only the first part(s) of its URL. For example, suppose you found a paper about Berlin during World War II on the Internet and you wanted to track its source. Its URL is **http://hti.math. uh.edu/curriculum/units/2004/01/04.01.09.php.** If you shorten it to **http://hti.math.uh.edu/,** this URL takes you to the University of Houston Teachers Institute, where this paper was submitted as a curriculum unit. In general, if the individual, business, or agency sponsor is not identified, the site lacks authority.

2. **Who authored the site?** Is the author's name given, or only the Webmaster's name? (The Webmaster handles the technical details of the site but is not responsible for, and does not create, content.) If the author's name is not given, the site lacks authority. If the author's name is given, is the author an expert in his or her field? If not, the information may not be trustworthy.

3. **Is contact information provided for the author?** Often an e-mail address or other contact information is provided. If it is not, again, this is evidence that the source may not be reliable.

EXERCISE 10-5 . . . EVALUATING AUTHORITY

Evaluate the authority of two of the following Web sites.

1. http://www.angelfire.com/apes/howard/shakespeare.html

   _____

   _____

   _____

   _____

   _____

   _____

2. http://www.youmeworks.com/funny.html

   _____

   _____

   _____

   _____

   _____

   _____

3. http://www.theharryrowellfamily.org/rodeofacts.htm

   _____

   _____

   _____

   _____

   _____

   _____

Evaluate the Timeliness of a Web Site

Although the Web is well known for providing up-to-the-minute information, not all Web sites are current. Evaluate a site's timeliness by checking:

- the date on which the Web site was posted (put on the Web).
- the date when the document you are using was added.

- the date when the site was last revised or updated.
- the date when the links were last checked.

This information is usually provided at the end of the site's home page or at the end of the document you are using.

Evaluate the timeliness of two of the following Web sites, using the directions given for each site.

1. **http://www.hwg.org/resources/?cid=30**
   See when these links were last checked. Find out what the consequences of this are by checking the links yourself.

   _____

   _____

2. **http://www.unicef.org/sowc99/facts.htm**
   Evaluate whether this site provides current information on illiteracy in the world. How could you find up-to-date information?

   _____

   _____

   _____

3. **http://www.benbest.com/computer/y2kdec.html**
   What is your reaction to this article? Explore the site for a more recent update. How does this add to the earlier pages?

   _____

   _____

Evaluate the Objectivity of a Web Site

When using a Web site to obtain information, be sure that the site is objective—that is, it treats the subject in a fair, unbiased manner. (See Chapter 7, Section 7d, p. 181 for more about bias.) Here are a few questions to ask:

1. **What is the goal of the Web site?** Is it to present information or to persuade you to accept a particular point of view or to take a specific action? If it is not to present information, you should question the site's objectivity.
2. **Is the site a mask for advertising?** Be cautious of sites that present information to persuade you to purchase a product or service. If a site resembles an infomercial you might see on television, be just as suspicious of it as you would be of an infomercial.

3. **Does the site present detailed information or focus on generalities?** If the site tends to focus on generalities, then you might suspect that its primary purpose is not to present information and it will not be useful as an in-depth information source.

4. **Are opinions clearly identified?** An author is free to express opinions, but they should be clearly identified as such. Look for words and phrases that identify ideas as opinions. (See Chapter 7, Section 7a, p. 170 for a list of these words and phrases.) If a site presents opinions as facts or does not distinguish between facts and opinions, it is an indication that the site is unreliable.

EXERCISE 10-7 . . . EVALUATING OBJECTIVITY

Evaluate the objectivity of two of the following Web sites.

1. **http://www.peacenow.org/**

   _____

   _____

   _____

2. **http://kidshealth.org/parent/pregnancy_center/your_pregnancy/ eating_pregnancy.html**

   _____

   _____

   _____

3. **http://www.legitgov.org/**

   _____

   _____

   _____

   _____

   _____

Evaluate the Usability of a Web Site

The design and ease of use of a site often provide clues to the care with which it was constructed. Be suspicious of carelessly put together sites. You might consider the following factors:

- **Navigability.** Is it easy to move around the site?
- **Links.** Do the links work?

- **Format.** Are the pages clear and easy to read or are they cluttered and disorganized?
- **Design.** Do the graphics, art, and buttons support the site's purpose?
- **Correctness.** Are there errors in spelling, grammar, or punctuation?

EXERCISE 10-8 . . . EVALUATING USABILITY

Evaluate the usability of two of the following Web sites.

1. **http://www.vietnamesecommunity.com/Education/edu/m-f.htm**

   _____

   _____

   _____

2. **http://www.vietnamesecommunity.com/Education/edu/m-f.htm**

   _____

3. **http://www.artbabble.org/**

   _____

   _____

   _____

   _____

   _____

   _____

   _____

EXERCISE 10-9 . . . EVALUATING WEB SITES

Assume you are taking a sociology class and you have been given the following assignment:

Write a five-page research paper comparing and contrasting men's and women's styles of communication. Use both online and print sources.

You have identified the following online sources. Which ones would be appropriate to use in your paper? Which ones would you question, and why? Be sure to evaluate each site for content, accuracy, authority, objectivity, timeliness, and usability.

http://ohioline.osu.edu/flm02/fs04.html

http://www.cla.purdue.edu/academic/comm/newsletter/Spring2004/ sexroles.html

http://knowledge.emory.edu/article.cfm?articleid=1103

http://www.cbmw.org/Resources/Articles/
Communication-between-Men-and-Women

http://www.crosswalk.com/spirituallife/women/1381415/

http://www.onlinedatingmagazine.com/columns/connect/
02-menwomencommunication.html

http://janesanders.com/articles/article_biology.html

http://raysweb.net/poems/articles/tannen.html

http://www.au.af.mil/au/awc/awcgate/uscg/gender_communication.htm

http://www.negotiations.com/articles/gender-bender/

http://www.npr.org/templates/story/story.php?storyId=12633456

 For support in meeting this chapter's learning objectives, log in to www.myreadinglab.com, go to the Study Plan tab, click on **Reading Skills** and choose **Critical Thinking** from the list of subtopics. Read and view the videos and resources in the Review Materials section, and then complete the Recall, Practice, and Test exercises in the Activities section. You can check your scores and overall progress by using the Gradebook.

PART TWO

Readings for Academic Disciplines

Introduction: Reading Across the Disciplines

Brian was a first-year student taking a full-time course load: Introductory Psychology, College Writing, Biology, and World History. He had received good grades in high school and was confident he would do well at a community college where he was majoring in pre-elementary education. After about the fourth week of the term, Brian realized he was not doing as well as he expected to do in his courses. He spent approximately 30 hours per week studying but was not earning top grades. He got C's on three biology labs, a B minus on a response essay for his writing class, a 70 on his first history exam, and 65, 75, and 70 on the first three psychology quizzes. Brian knew he would probably pass all of his courses, but his goal was to earn grades that would ensure his transfer to a four-year college of his choice.

Brian visited the campus Academic Skills Center and requested tutors for three of his courses. After the first few tutoring sessions he realized that his tutors used a unique approach to each of the disciplines. Specifically, they seemed to read, study, and think differently in each. Brian learned to vary his approach to the material he was studying in different courses. Before, he had studied each course the same way; now he has realized that different disciplines require specialized thinking skills.

Brian's realization is confirmed by a national research study titled "Understanding University Success"; it identified the critical thinking skills essential to success in various disciplines. The table on p. 35 demonstrates that different disciplines require different types of thinking and includes many of the skills identified in the research study. Study the table to get an idea of the types of thinking skills involved in each disciplinary grouping.

READINGS FOR ACADEMIC DISCIPLINES

Each college course you take will be different; in each you will be asked to master a unique set of information, learn new terminology, and demonstrate what you have learned. This section of the text provides you with opportunities to practice reading material from a wide range of disciplines, learn new terminology, and demonstrate your mastery of content through a variety of test-taking methods.

ADAPTING YOUR THINKING TO ACADEMIC DISCIPLINES

DISCIPLINE	SPECIALIZED TYPES OF THINKING REQUIRED	EXAMPLES
Social Sciences (sociology, psychology, anthropology, economics)	Evaluate ideas, make generalizations, be aware of bias, follow and evaluate arguments	Studying patterns of child development, examining causes of age discrimination, comparing cultures
Mathematics	Think sequentially, reason logically, evaluate solutions	Solving word problems, understanding theorems
Natural and Life Sciences (biology, chemistry, physiology, physics, astronomy, earth science)	Grasp relationships, ask questions, understand processes, evaluate evidence	Studying the theory of evolution, examining the question of life in outer space
Arts (literature, music, painting, sculpture)	Evaluate the work of others, express your own ideas, critique your own work	Evaluating a sculpture, revising a musical score
Applied Fields (career fields, technology, business)	Follow processes and procedures, make applications, make and evaluate decisions	Evaluating a patient (nursing), finding a bug in a computer program (computer technology)

Part Two contains 33 readings, three readings for each of the following disciplines: social sciences, communication/speech, arts/humanities/literature, political science/government/history, business/advertising/economics, technology/computers, health-related fields, life sciences, physical sciences/mathematics, career fields, and workplace issues.

When taking courses in these fields, you will read textbooks, but you will also read a variety of print and online sources, as well. To give you practice reading a wide range of sources, most chapters in Part Two contain one textbook reading and two non-textbook readings. The readings are preceded by information, tips, and questions intended to guide your reading. They are followed by questions that will help you evaluate your reading and practice with different test-taking formats. The types of questions and activities are intended to prepare you for future work in the different disciplines. They are in different formats so as to familiarize you with the variety of testing and evaluation methods used in these disciplines. Included are multiple-choice, fill-in-the-blank, true/false, and matching tests, as well as open-ended questions and brief writing assignments. Here is a review of the types of questions and activities you will work with.

- **Understanding the Thesis and Other Main Ideas.** These questions help you identify the most important information in each reading.
- **Identifying Details.** These questions help you discover the relationship between main ideas and details and distinguish between more and less important details.

- **Recognizing Methods of Organization and Transitions.** This activity guides you in discovering organizational patterns and using transitions.
- **Reviewing and Organizing Ideas.** This activity shows you how to learn the material in a reading. You will learn and practice a number of different review and study strategies, including mapping, summarizing, outlining, and paraphrasing.
- **Reading and Thinking Visually.** These questions help you examine graphic elements and integrate them with the rest of your reading.
- **Figuring Out Implied Meanings and Thinking Critically.** These two sections demonstrate the types of thinking and reasoning that are expected in college courses. The questions take you beyond the literal (factual) content of the selection and guide you in applying many of the critical thinking skills you learned in Part One.
- **Building Vocabulary.** This section gives you practice in learning the terminology that is an essential part of each new academic discipline. You will learn how to use both context and word parts to master new terminology.
- **Selecting a Learning/Study Strategy.** Choosing appropriate learning and study methods is important in every discipline. This activity guides you in identifying appropriate ways to learn and study the material in a selection.
- **Exploring Ideas Through Discussion and Writing.** Because class participation is an important part of many college courses, this activity provides topics that can be used for class discussion. As many college courses involve writing papers and research reports and taking written exams, this activity also provides an opportunity for you to begin to apply your writing skills to various disciplines.
- **Beyond the Classroom to the Web.** Many instructors expect their students to extend and apply their learning to situations outside the classroom. This activity extends your learning beyond the reading selection and provides ways you can use or apply new information.

11 Social Sciences

The **social sciences** are concerned with the study of people, their history and development, and how they interact and function together. These disciplines deal with the political, economic, social, cultural, and behavioral aspects of people. Social scientists study how we live, how we act, how we dress, how we get along with others, and how our culture is similar to and different from other cultures. By reading in the social sciences, you will learn a great deal about yourself and those around you. In "A Surveillance Society" you will read about how surveillance cameras make our daily activities more public. "The New Flirting Game" examines a much more personal form of human interaction—flirtation. "Coming Into My Own" considers a social problem—racial discrimination—and shows how an African American neurosurgeon dealt with it. Use the following tips when reading in the social sciences.

TIPS FOR READING IN THE SOCIAL SCIENCES

- **Pay attention to terminology.** The social sciences use precise terminology to describe their subject matter. Learn terms that describe behavior, name stages and processes, and label principles, theories, and models. Also learn the names of important researchers and theorists. As you read, highlight new terms. You can transfer them later to index cards or a vocabulary log for that course.

- **Understand explanations and theories.** The social sciences are devoted, in part, to explaining how people behave as they do. In this chapter you will read an explanation of how people flirt, for example. As you read theories and explanations, ask these questions: What behavior is being explained? What evidence is offered that it is correct? Of what use is the explanation?

- **Look for supporting evidence.** As you read, look for details, examples, anecdotes, or research evidence that demonstrates that the writer's explanations are reasonable or correct. When reading "The New Flirting Game," look for the author's examples of women's flirting behaviors, for instance. Often, too, in the social sciences, the examples and applications are highly interesting and will help you remember the theories they illustrate.

- **Make comparisons and connections.** Try to see relationships and make comparisons. Draw connections between topics. Sketch charts or maps that compare different explanations, for example.

- **Make practical applications.** As you read, consider how the information is useful to you in real-life situations. Make marginal notes of situations that illustrate what you are reading about. Write comments, for example, about what you have observed about flirting or about instances of racial discrimination.

237

SELECTION 1

A Surveillance Society

William E. Thompson and Joseph V. Hickey

Textbook Excerpt
Contemporary
Issues Reading

This reading selection from a textbook titled *Society in Focus* describes the increasing use of surveillance systems in public places. Read the selection to discover the benefits and risks of high-tech surveillance.

PREVIEWING THE READING

Using the steps listed on page 36, preview the reading selection. When you have finished, complete the following items.

1. What is the subject of this selection? _____

2. List four questions you expect to be able to answer after reading this selection.

   a. _____

   b. _____

   c. _____

   d. _____

 MAKING CONNECTIONS

Think about public places in which you have noticed security cameras. Do these cameras make you feel safer? Why or why not?

READING TIP

As you read, look for and highlight the risks and benefits of surveillance systems.

A Surveillance Society

1   The cameras are familiar to most people, perhaps even comforting to some. They are perched high atop almost every lamppost, rooftop, and streetlight. Elsewhere, they are undetectable, except to the authorities. Video cameras are never turned off. They pan up and down, left and right, surveying traffic, pedestrians, and everything else in public view, day and night.

Here, a surveillance camera is disguised as a light.

Growing Trends

2   You might be thinking that this scene offers a glimpse of the future. Perhaps it is a dark, futuristic vision, much like George Orwell's nightmare of *Big Brother* monitoring and controlling people's lives down to the smallest details. But by now you are aware that *things are not necessarily what they seem.*

Big Brother
a fictional character from George Orwell's futuristic novel *Nineteen Eighty-Four*

3   This is not some grim, dystopian vision of the future, but a growing trend almost everywhere in the world–including most shopping malls and stores, almost all government and corporate offices, and many other social arenas. In the name of public security, the British have been most active of all nations in installing surveillance monitoring systems. In the beginning, they were tried in a handful of "trouble spots." Now more than 4.2 million cameras have been installed throughout Britain, and the average Londoner can expect his or her picture to be taken hundreds of times each day. Alarmed at the amount of surveillance and the astonishing amount of personal data that is hoarded by the state and by commercial organizations, Ross Clark asks whom should we fear most: the government agencies that are spying on us or the criminals who seem to prosper in the swirling fog of excessive data collection?

4   Since the 9/11 terrorist attacks, the United States has been trying to catch up. Times Square in New York and the nation's capital have seen a proliferation of surveillance cameras installed in public places. Experiments in face-recognition technology have been expanded, and "photo radar" that uses cameras and computers to photograph license plates, identify traffic violators, and issue citations is catching on as well. And in all cases, the technology has also grown more sophisticated. The USA PATRIOT Act, passed after 9/11 and renewed in 2006, expanded the government's authority to "spy" on private citizens.

5   In the private sector, cameras and computers are abundant and socially accepted. Today, there are millions of tiny private security cameras at hotels, malls, parking lots—everywhere businesses and shoppers can be found. The new digital surveillance systems are more sophisticated than those from just a few years ago. Today's technology not only can scan businesses and malls, but also analyze what it is watching and recording and, if something is unusual, alert security. Likewise, digital security systems can now record, store, and index images, making it possible for security personnel to "instantly retrieve images of every person who passed through a door on any given day."

Surveillance Technologies

6   High-tech surveillance devices are becoming more common across the urban landscape. Although many people may be wary of these devices, few are aware that they are but a small part of surveillance technologies that now routinely monitor all of our personal histories, daily routines, and tastes. And 9/11 and global terrorist threats have increased public willingness for added security and new surveillance technologies.

7   Police and military surveillance is impressive—with video scanners, electronic ankle monitors, night-vision goggles, and pilotless airborne spy vehicles, to name just a few. But high-tech surveillance has expanded well beyond the police and military to thousands of corporations, government agencies, and even individuals who routinely monitor the workplace, marketplace, and almost all other social arenas. As one sociologist noted, "Being able to hide and remain anonymous has become more difficult . . . we are moving toward a glass village in which everyone is available for view online."

Information Sharing

8   Today, corporations and government agencies routinely share databases. In "computer matching," organizations swap back and forth personal information on different kinds of populations and combine them to suit their own needs. The Pentagon's "Total Information Awareness Program" is one of the most ambitious plans to combine computer databases. The Pentagon maintains that it relies mainly on information from government, law enforcement, and intelligence databases to "forestall terrorism," but its use of other kinds of data—like personal financial and health records—remains unresolved. Critics argue that because such a system could (and some say already has) tap into e-mail, culling records, and credit card and banking transactions as well as travel documents, it poses a direct threat to civil liberties.

9   Similar arguments were made after the passage of the USA PATRIOT Act in 2001, which gave the government the right to "search suspected terrorists' library records—and add them to government databases—without the patron ever knowing." By early 2002, one study found that over 85 libraries had already been asked for information on patrons in connection with the 9/11 investigation.

10   Post-9/11 surveillance surfaced as a controversial political issue in 2006 when it was discovered that after the 9/11 attacks the government gave approval to the highly secretive National Security Agency (NSA) to solicit phone records of private citizens from the nation's largest phone companies. Only weeks later it was revealed that the government also had begun monitoring the banking habits of private

citizens in an effort to thwart terrorist activities. Open debates developed over how much personal privacy Americans were willing to relinquish for the promise of safety from terrorism. Nevertheless, the act was renewed in 2006.

apparatus 11
structure or system

The government is not the only one in the spying business. Some of the most sophisticated surveillance devices are available to the public and can be ordered from retail catalogues. For example, night-vision goggles can be had for the price of a good video camera. High-tech scanners are available that can trace ink patterns and read the content of letters "without ever breaking the seal." Brin believes that there is a good possibility that as cameras get smaller and more mobile we should expect "mosquito-scale drones" that fly in and out of office and home windows, making privacy difficult or impossible. Of course, cell phones and other mobile devices with digital cameras have proliferated, as have pinhole cameras, microvideo systems, and wireless video that potentially could make everyone part of the security apparatus.

The Impact of Surveillance

12

Journalists have largely focused their attention on how surveillance relates to political citizenship and "privacy" issues, but much more is involved. According to sociologist David Lyon, new surveillance systems have expanded to the point at which they have become a major social institution that affects all social relationships, as well as people's very identities, personal space, freedom, and dignity. Increasingly, data images—computer-integrated profiles of each individual's finances, health, consumer preferences, ethnicity, neighborhood, education, criminal record, and other "significant" characteristics—are the "looking-glass" that provides social judgments about "who we are" and our life changes. Using the old South Africa as his guide, Lyon asks, will the new "non-persons," segregated by surveillance systems, be bankrupt individuals or perhaps non consumers?

fatalism 13
the belief that events are determined by fate and cannot be changed by human actions

Many people see the benefits of new surveillance as far outweighing the risks and argue that only criminals and terrorists should be concerned about the intensification of surveillance. They assert, "Why should I worry about privacy? I have nothing to hide." Lyon himself makes the point that dark visions about corporate and government Big Brothers may be counter productive in that they may produce nothing more than paranoia, fatalism, and inaction. New surveillance, in fact, both constrains and enables. Although it is unequally distributed, with large organizations controlling most information technologies, these same technologies have given ordinary people access to many new channels of participation and protest, not only nationally but globally. However, today's increases in identity theft, spying, selling of personal information, and other technological invasions of privacy prompted one sociologist to conclude that "public access to private information has taken on even more ominous tones."

A. UNDERSTANDING THE THESIS AND OTHER MAIN IDEAS

Select the best answer.

_____ 1. The authors' primary purpose in this selection is to

      a. promote the use of high-tech surveillance systems for public security.

b. criticize the government's widespread use of surveillance technologies.

c. describe the growing use of surveillance systems in public places.

d. compare and contrast surveillance techniques in other countries.

_____ 2. The main focus of paragraph 4 is on

a. where surveillance cameras have been installed.

b. how face-recognition technology is expanding.

c. when photo radar is used most effectively.

d. how the United States has increased surveillance since 9/11.

_____ 3. The statement that best expresses the main idea of paragraph 7 is

a. "Police and military surveillance is impressive."

b. "High-tech surveillance has expanded beyond the police and military to corporations, government agencies, and individuals."

c. "Individuals routinely monitor the workplace, marketplace, and almost all other social arenas."

d. "Police and the military use video scanners, electronic ankle monitors, night-vision goggles, and airborne spy vehicles."

_____ 4. According to the selection, data images are computer-integrated profiles that include information about an individual's

a. health and finances.

b. consumer preferences.

c. criminal record.

d. all of the above.

_____ 5. The topic of paragraph 11 is

a. the government.

b. spies.

c. surveillance devices.

d. privacy.

B. IDENTIFYING DETAILS

Complete each of the following statements by underlining the word in parentheses that makes the statement true.

1. The USA PATRIOT Act was originally passed (before/after) the terrorist attacks of 9/11.

2. The USA PATRIOT Act (was/was not) renewed in 2006.

3. The USA PATRIOT Act authorized the government to search suspected terrorists' library records (with/without) their knowledge.

4. After 9/11, the NSA solicited the phone records of private citizens (with/without) government approval.

5. The government's post-9/11 antiterrorism efforts (did/did not) include monitoring the banking habits of private citizens.

C. RECOGNIZING METHODS OF ORGANIZATION AND TRANSITIONS

Complete the following statements by filling in the blanks.

1. In paragraph 5, the transition word that points out a similarity between digital surveillance and security systems is _____.

2. In paragraph 10, two transitions that indicate the chronological order of events are _____ and _____. A contrasting idea is also indicated in this paragraph by the transition _____.

3. In paragraph 11, the authors use the generalization and example organizational pattern to explain that the government is not alone in the spying business. A transitional phrase that indicates this pattern is _____.

D. REVIEWING AND ORGANIZING IDEAS: MAPPING

Complete the following map of paragraphs 3–5 by filling in the blanks.

Government

Britain is the most active nation in _____ _____

- There are _____ million cameras throughout the country
- The average Londoner is _____ hundreds of times each day

The United States has been trying to catch up since _____

- More cameras installed in public spaces
- _____ technology experiments expanded
- Photo radar used for _____
- Government's authority to "spy" on private citizens expanded by _____

Private Sector

Cameras and computers are _____ and socially accepted

Digital surveillance systems are more _____

- Systems scan, analyze, and _____ _____ if necessary
- Images are recorded, stored, and _____ for instant retrieval

E. READING AND THINKING VISUALLY

Answer each of the following questions.

1. What concepts in the selection are illustrated by the photograph?

   _____

2. What can you tell about the people shown in the photograph?

   _____

F. FIGURING OUT IMPLIED MEANINGS

Indicate whether each statement is true (T) or false (F).

_____ 1. In the opening paragraphs, the authors acknowledge that people respond differently to surveillance cameras in public places.

_____ 2. Ross Clark's question in paragraph 3 indicates that he supports increased surveillance and the collection of personal data.

_____ 3. The public became more willing to tolerate increased surveillance after the terrorist attacks of 9/11.

_____ 4. The sociologist's comment about a "glass village" in paragraph 7 refers to the increased transparency of government actions and policies.

_____ 5. The authors believe that the Pentagon's "Total Information Awareness Program" poses a direct threat to civil liberties.

G. THINKING CRITICALLY

Select the best answer.

_____ 1. The tone of this selection can best be described as

    a. apathetic.

    b. informative.

    c. angry.

    d. amused.

_____ 2. The authors support their thesis with all of the following *except*

    a. facts.

    b. descriptions.

    c. personal experience.

    d. examples.

_____ 3. Of the following words in paragraphs 3, the only one with a positive connotation is

    a. grim.

    b. hoarded.

    c. prosper.

    d. excessive.

_____ 4. The most important point the authors make at the end of this selection is that new surveillance technologies

    a. should concern only those who are breaking the law.

    b. produce dark visions about corporations and government.

    c. have had outcomes that are negative as well as beneficial.

    d. increase identity theft and other invasions of privacy.

_____ 5. The intended audience for this selection is most likely to be

    a. government officials.

    b. surveillance professionals.

    c. sociology students.

    d. security consultants.

H. BUILDING VOCABULARY

Context

Using context and a dictionary, if necessary, determine the meaning of each word as it is used in the selection.

_____ 1. pan (paragraph 1)

    a. move

    b. criticize

    c. contain

    d. separate

_____ 2. proliferation (paragraph 4)

    a. clear decline

    b. major alteration

    c. excessive increase

    d. preservation

_____ 3. abundant (paragraph 5)

    a. unusual

    b. plentiful

    c. expensive

    d. simple

_____ 4. wary (paragraph 6)

    a. upset

    b. indifferent

    c. comfortable

    d. cautious

_____ 5. ominous (paragraph 13)

    a. risky

    b. threatening

    c. illegal

    d. weak

Word Parts

A REVIEW OF PREFIXES

UN- means *not*

DYS- means *bad or difficult*

COUNTER- means *against or opposite*

IN- means *not*

Use your knowledge of word parts and the review above to fill in the blanks in the following sentences.

1. Something that is *undetectable* (paragraph 1) is _____ visible.

2. If the term *utopia* refers to a perfect or ideal state, then a *dystopian* (paragraph 3) vision of the future is one that is _____.

3. When a problem or issue is *unresolved* (paragraph 8), it has _____ been settled or decided.

4. Ideas that are *counterproductive* (paragraph 13) tend to produce the _____ of the desired effect.

5. A belief that leads to *inaction* (paragraph 13) results in _____ action.

I. SELECTING A LEARNING/STUDY STRATEGY

Assume you will be tested on this selection on an upcoming exam. Evaluate the usefulness of the map you completed on page 243 as a study tool. Which other paragraphs would be useful to map?

J. EXPLORING IDEAS THROUGH DISCUSSION AND WRITING

1. Evaluate this selection's introduction. How effective was it in capturing your attention?

2. Over the course of a week, keep a list of the public places you go, and observe which places have installed security cameras. At the end of the week, write a paragraph describing the different types of public places you visited that are under surveillance.

3. Do you agree with those who say that only criminals and terrorists should be concerned about the intensification of surveillance? Why or why not?

K. BEYOND THE CLASSROOM TO THE WEB

Explore the site for the Electronic Privacy Information Center (EPIC) at **http://epic. org/.** *Choose one of the "Hot Policy Issues," and write a paragraph summarizing the issue and describing your response to it.*

TRACKING YOUR PROGRESS

Selection 1

Section	Number Correct		Score
A. Thesis and Main Ideas (5 items)	_____	× 4	_____
B. Details (5 items)	_____	× 2	_____
C. Organization and Transitions (5 items)	_____	× 2	_____
F. Implied Meanings (5 items)	_____	× 4	_____
G. Thinking Critically (5 items)	_____	× 4	_____
H. Vocabulary			
Context (5 items)	_____	× 2	_____
Word Parts (5 items)	_____	× 2	_____
		TOTAL SCORE	_____%

SELECTION 2

The New Flirting Game

Deborah A. Lott

This article first appeared in *Psychology Today*. Read it to discover how psychologists study the age-old custom of flirtation.

PREVIEWING THE READING

Using the steps listed on page 36, preview the reading selection. When you have finished, complete the following items.

1. The subject of this reading is _____.

2. List at least three questions you expect to be able to answer after reading the article.

   a. _____

   b. _____

   c. _____

 ### MAKING CONNECTIONS

How do you know when someone is flirting with you? What do they say and do? Are the signals obvious, subtle, or a combination of both?

READING TIP

As you read, look for and highlight the qualities and characteristics of flirting. Highlighting will make it easier to review the reading and find information you need.

The New Flirting Game

social psychologist
a person who
studies how groups
behave and how
individuals are
affected by the group

1   We flirt with the intent of assessing potential lifetime partners, we flirt to have easy, no-strings-attached sex, and we flirt when we are not looking for either. We flirt because, most simply, flirtation can be a liberating form of play, a game with suspense and ambiguities that brings joys of its own. As Philadelphia-based **social psychologist** Tim Perper says, "Some flirters appear to want to prolong the interaction because it's pleasurable and erotic in its own right, regardless of where it might lead."

2   Here are some of the ways the game is currently being played.

Are these people flirting with each other? How can you tell?

Taking the Lead

3   When it comes to flirting today, women aren't waiting around for men to make the advances. They're taking the lead. Psychologist Monica Moore, Ph.D., of Webster University in St. Louis, Missouri, has spent more than 2000 hours observing women's flirting maneuvers in restaurants, singles bars and at parties. According to her findings, women give nonverbal cues that get a flirtation rolling fully two-thirds of the time. A man may think he's making the first move because he is the one to literally move from wherever he is to the woman's side, but usually he has been summoned.

evolutionary psychologists
people who track how human behavior and psychological traits have developed and changed over the course of history

4   By the standards set out by **evolutionary psychologists**, the women who attract the most men would most likely be those with the most symmetrical features or the best hip-to-waist ratios. Not so, says Moore. In her studies, the women who draw the most response are the ones who send the most signals. "Those who performed more than 35 displays per hour elicited greater than four approaches per hour," she notes, "and the more variety the woman used in her techniques, the more likely she was to be successful."

Sexual Semaphores

semaphores
visual, nonverbal systems for sending information or signals

5   Moore tallied a total of 52 different nonverbal courtship behaviors used by women, including glancing, gazing (short and sustained), primping, preening, smiling, lip licking, pouting, giggling, laughing and nodding, as if to nonverbally indicate, "Yes! yes!" A woman would often begin with a room-encompassing glance, in actuality a casing-the-joint scan to seek out prospects. When she'd zeroed in on a target she'd exhibit the short darting glance—looking at a man, quickly looking away, looking back and then away again. There was something shy and indirect in this initial eye contact.

6   But women countered their shy moves with other, more aggressive and overt tactics. Those who liked to live dangerously took a round robin approach, alternately flirting with several different men at once until one responded in an unequivocal fashion. A few women hiked their skirts up to bring more leg into a particular man's field of vision. When they inadvertently drew the attention of other admirers, they quickly pulled their skirts down. If a man failed to get the message, a woman might parade, walking across the room towards him, hips swaying, breasts pushed out, head held high.

Who's Submissive?

ethologists
people who study
behavior patterns

7   Moore observed some of the same nonverbal behaviors that Eibl Eibesfeldt and other **ethologists** had deemed universal among women: the eyebrow flash (an exaggerated raising of the eyebrows of both eyes, followed by a rapid lowering), the coy smile (a tilting of the head downward, with partial averting of the eyes and, at the end, covering of the mouth), and the exposed neck (turning the head so that the side of the neck is bared.

8   But while many ethologists interpret these signs as conveying female submissiveness, Moore has an altogether different take. "If these behaviors serve to orchestrate courtship, which they do, then how can they be anything but powerful?" she observes. "Who determined that to cover your mouth is a submissive gesture? Baring the neck may have a lot more to do with the neck being an erogenous zone than its being a submissive posture." Though women in Moore's sample used the coy smile, they also maintained direct eye contact for long periods and smiled fully and unabashedly.

9   Like Moore, Perper believes that ethologists have overemphasized certain behaviors and misinterpreted them as signifying either dominance or submission. For instance, says Perper, among flirting American heterosexual men and women as well as homosexual men, the coy smile is less frequent than direct eye contact and sustained smiling. He suggests that some cultures may use the coy smile more than others, and that it is not always a sign of deference.

10   In watching a flirtatious couple, Perper finds that a male will perform gestures and movements that an ethologist might consider dominant, such as sticking out his chest and strutting around, but he'll also give signs that could be read as submissive, such as bowing his head lower than the woman's. The woman may also do both. "She may drop her head, turn slightly, bare her neck, but then she'll lift her eyes and lean forward with her breasts held out, and that doesn't look submissive at all," Perper notes.

synchronization
happening at the
same time

11   Men involved in these encounters, says Perper, don't describe themselves as "feeling powerful." In fact, he and Moore agree, neither party wholly dominates in a flirtation. Instead, there is a subtle, rhythmical and playful back and forth that culminates in a kind of physical **synchronization** between two people. She turns, he turns; she picks up her drink, he picks up his drink.

12   Still, by escalating and de-escalating the flirtation's progression, the woman controls the pace. To slow down a flirtation, a woman might orient her body away slightly or cross her arms across her chest, or avoid meeting the man's eyes. To stop the dance in its tracks, she can yawn, frown, sneer, shake her head from side to side as if to say "No," pocket her hands, hold her trunk rigidly, avoid the man's gaze, stare over his head, or resume flirting with other men. If a man is really dense, she might hold a strand of hair up to her eyes as if to examine her split ends or even pick her teeth.

Learning the Steps

13   If flirting today is often a conscious activity, it is also a learned one. Women pick up the moves early. In observations of 100 girls between the ages of 13 and 16 at shopping malls, ice skating rinks and other places adolescents congregate, Moore found the teens exhibiting 31 of the 52 courtship signals deployed by adult women. (The only signals missing were those at the more overt end of the spectrum, such as actual caressing.) Overall, the teens' gestures looked less natural than ones made by mature females: they laughed more boisterously and preened more obviously, and their moves were broader and rougher.

alpha female
the "first" female
in a group, the
leader whose
behavior is
copied by the
others in the
group

14   The girls clearly modeled their behavior on the leader of the pack. When the **alpha female** stroked her hair or swayed her hips, her companions copied quickly. "You never see this in adult women," says Moore, "Indeed, women go to great lengths to stand out from their female companions."

15   Compared with adults, the teens signaled less frequently—7.6 signs per hour per girl, as opposed to 44.6 per woman—but their maneuvers, though clumsy, were equally effective at attracting the objects of their desire, in this case, teen boys.

16   Some of the exhilaration of flirting, of course, lies in what is hidden, the tension between what is felt and what is revealed. Flirting pairs volley back and forth, putting out ambiguous signals, neither willing to disclose more than the other, neither wanting to appear more desirous to the other.

17   To observers like Moore and Perper, flirtation often seems to most resemble the antics of children on the playground or even perhaps the ritual peek-a-boo that babies play with their caregivers. Flirters jostle, tease and tickle, even sometimes stick out a tongue at their partner or reach around from behind to cover up their eyes. As Daniel Stern, researcher, psychiatrist, and author of *The Interpersonal World of the Infant,* has pointed out, the two groups in our culture that engage in the most sustained eye contact are mothers and infants, and lovers.

18   And thus in a way, the cycle of flirting takes us full circle. If flirting sets us off on the road to producing babies, it also whisks us back to the pleasures of infancy.

A. UNDERSTANDING THE THESIS AND OTHER MAIN IDEAS

Select the best answer.

_____ 1. The author's primary purpose in "The New Flirting Game" is to
  a. expose the shallowness and superficiality of flirting behavior.
  b. teach women and men the modern methods of flirting.
  c. compare flirting behaviors of today with those of previous generations.
  d. describe how and why women and men flirt.

_____ 2. The main idea of paragraph 1 is that women and men flirt
  a. to find lifetime partners.
  b. to have uncomplicated sex.
  c. as a game.
  d. for many different reasons.

_____ 3. The main idea of paragraph 3 is expressed in the
  a. first sentence.
  b. third sentence.
  c. fourth sentence.
  d. last sentence.

_____ 4. The topic of paragraph 6 is
  a. risky behavior.
  b. male responses.
  c. flirting tactics.
  d. flirting mistakes.

_____ 5. The main idea of paragraph 8 is that
  a. nonverbal flirting behaviors convey female submissiveness.
  b. women use both a smile and eye contact when flirting.
  c. the neck is an erogenous zone.
  d. nonverbal flirting behaviors are often powerful rather than submissive.

_____ 6. The statement that best expresses the main idea of paragraph 13 is
  a. "If flirting today is often a conscious activity, it is also a learned one."
  b. "Women pick up the moves early."
  c. "The only signals missing were those at the more overt end of the spectrum."
  d. "Overall, the teens' gestures looked less natural than ones made by mature females."

_____ 7. The main idea of paragraph 17 is that
   a. flirters are immature.
   b. flirtation resembles play.
   c. eye contact is important to mothers and infants.
   d. the eye contact between lovers is like that between mothers and infants.

B. IDENTIFYING DETAILS

Select the best answer.

_____ 1. According to Dr. Moore's research, the women who attract the most men are those
   a. with the most symmetrical features.
   b. with the best hip-to-waist ratios.
   c. who send the most signals.
   d. who are least interested in attracting men.

_____ 2. All of the following courtship behaviors are considered "sexual semaphores" *except*
   a. glancing and gazing.
   b. using suggestive language.
   c. primping and preening.
   d. smiling and laughing.

_____ 3. As described in the reading, one way that a woman can slow the pace of a flirtation is by
   a. staring directly into the man's eyes.
   b. nodding as if in agreement.
   c. orienting her body toward him.
   d. crossing her arms across her chest.

_____ 4. Nonverbal flirting behaviors that are considered universal among women include all of the following *except* the
   a. eyebrow flash.
   b. coy smile.
   c. wink.
   d. exposed neck.

_____ 5. As compared to the flirting behavior of adult women, the adolescent girls observed by Dr. Moore did all of the following *except*
   a. exhibit many of the same courtship signals.
   b. look less natural in their gestures.

    c. go to greater lengths to stand out from their female companions.

    d. signal less frequently.

_____ 6. According to Dr. Moore's findings, women give nonverbal cues that begin a flirtation

    a. one-third of the time.

    b. one-half of the time.

    c. two-thirds of the time.

    d. three-fourths of the time.

C. RECOGNIZING METHODS OF ORGANIZATION AND TRANSITIONS

Complete the following item.

1. Locate a phrase in paragraph 9 that indicates an example is to follow.

_____

Complete the following statements by filling in the blanks.

2. In paragraphs 13–15, Dr. Moore's observations of adult women and adolescent girls are discussed using an organizational pattern called _____. A transitional phrase that helps identify the organizational pattern in this section is _____.

D. REVIEWING AND ORGANIZING IDEAS: PARAPHRASING

Complete the following paraphrase of paragraph 8 by filling in the blanks with the correct words or phrases.

Although many _____ believe these _____ convey female _____, Dr. Moore disagrees. She says that since these _____ seem to promote _____, they must be _____. She also disagrees that _____ is a _____ gesture and states that _____ may have more to do with it being an _____ than to it being a _____ posture. Women in Moore's _____ used the _____ but they also maintained _____ for extended periods and _____ fully and openly.

E. READING AND THINKING VISUALLY

Select the best answer.

_____ 1. The author likely included the photo in this selection in order to
   a. emphasize the fact that women flirt more than men do.
   b. provide a visual illustration of flirting behaviors.
   c. imply that most flirting takes place at restaurants and other eating establishments.
   d. illustrate a situation in which men are dominant and women are submissive.

_____ 2. In the photo, all of the following "flirtation signals" are apparent *except for*
   a. smiles.
   b. eye contact.
   c. covering of the mouth.
   d. raised eyebrows.

F. FIGURING OUT IMPLIED MEANINGS

Indicate whether each statement is true (T) or false (F).

_____ 1. Some people enjoy flirting simply for the fun of it.
_____ 2. The people in the studies mentioned in the reading knew they were being observed.
_____ 3. Evolutionary psychology and social psychology are the same thing.
_____ 4. Flirting behaviors are the same in all cultures.
_____ 5. Teenage girls learn most of their flirting behaviors from watching adult women.

G. THINKING CRITICALLY

Select the best answer.

_____ 1. The author supports the thesis of "The New Flirting Game" primarily with
   a. cause-and-effect relationships.
   b. research evidence.
   c. personal experience.
   d. statistics.

_____ 2. The author's tone throughout the article can best be described as
   a. serious and concerned.
   b. judgmental and opinionated.
   c. pessimistic and depressing.
   d. light and factual.

_____ 3. Another appropriate title for this reading would be
   a. "The Modern Moral Decline."
   b. "Commitment in the Twenty-First Century."
   c. "The Art and Science of Flirting."
   d. "Nonverbal Communication Between Women and Men."

_____ 4. In paragraph 3, the phrase "but usually he has been summoned" means that the man
   a. is usually the one who makes the first move.
   b. is expected to move from his location to the woman's.
   c. has been waved at from across the room.
   d. doesn't realize that he is responding to the woman's nonverbal invitation.

_____ 5. The author ends the reading with
   a. a pleasing comparison.
   b. a warning.
   c. an appeal to action.
   d. a sympathetic note.

H. BUILDING VOCABULARY

Context

Using context and a dictionary, if necessary, determine the meaning of each word as it is used in the selection.

_____ 1. elicited (paragraph 4)
   a. expected from
   b. brought forth
   c. directed at
   d. returned to

_____ 2. encompassing (paragraph 5)
   a. avoiding
   b. emptying

c. filling

d. including

_____ 3. overt (paragraph 6)

   a. obvious

   b. secret

   c. friendly

   d. private

_____ 4. dominance (paragraph 9)

   a. control

   b. stubbornness

   c. friendliness

   d. extroversion

_____ 5. culminates (paragraph 11)

   a. fears

   b. concludes

   c. recovers

   d. begins

_____ 6. congregate (paragraph 13)

   a. depart

   b. arrange

   c. plan

   d. gather

Word Parts

A REVIEW OF PREFIXES MEANING "NOT"

Each of the following prefixes means "not".

DE-

IN-

MIS-

NON-

UN-

Match each word in Column A with its meaning in Column B. Write your answers in the spaces provided.

Column A
Prefix + Root

Column B
Meaning

_____ 1. nonverbal

a. not on purpose

_____ 2. indirect

b. not understood correctly

_____ 3. unequivocal

c. without embarrassment

_____ 4. inadvertently

d. not spoken

_____ 5. unabashedly

e. not obvious

_____ 6. misinterpreted

f. without doubt or misunderstanding

Unusual Words/Understanding Idioms

Indicate whether each statement is true (T) or false (F).

_____ 1. In paragraph 1, the phrase **no-strings-attached** sex means sex that is uncomplicated by expectations of commitment.

_____ 2. In paragraph 12, the phrase **to stop the dance in its tracks** means to bring an end to the flirtation.

I. SELECTING A LEARNING/STUDY STRATEGY

Discuss how visualization might help you learn the characteristics of flirting presented in this article.

J. EXPLORING IDEAS THROUGH DISCUSSION AND WRITING

1. The author uses terms that imply games or sports, such as the phrases "a round robin approach" (paragraph 6) and "volley back and forth" (paragraph 16). How do these phrases support her central thesis?

2. What images do the words *maneuvers* (paragraph 3) and *deployed* (paragraph 13) bring to mind?

3. Why is the reading called "The *New* Flirting Game"? What do you think the old flirting game consisted of?

K. BEYOND THE CLASSROOM TO THE WEB

Visit "How to Flirt" at http://www.wikihow.com/flirt.

Read the tips provided on this Web site. Compare the reliability of this Web site with Lott's article. Which is more likely to provide helpful information on dating and relationships? Why?

TRACKING YOUR PROGRESS

Selection 2

Section	Number Correct		Score
A. Thesis and Main Ideas (7 items)	_____	× 4	_____
B. Details (6 items)	_____	× 2	_____
C. Organization and Transitions (3 items)	_____	× 2	_____
E. Reading and Thinking Visually (2 items)	_____	× 3	_____
F. Implied Meanings (5 items)	_____	× 3	_____
G. Thinking Critically (5 items)	_____	× 3	_____
H. Vocabulary			
Context (6 items)	_____	× 2	_____
Word Parts (6 items)	_____	× 1	_____
		TOTAL SCORE	_____ %

Coming Into My Own

Ben Carson

This reading was taken from an autobiography titled *Gifted Hands: The Ben Carson Story*. In his book, Carson, a well-known neurosurgeon, describes his journey from his childhood in inner-city Detroit to a position as director of pediatric neurosurgery at Johns Hopkins Hospital.

PREVIEWING THE READING

Using the steps listed on page 36, preview the reading selection. When you have finished, answer the following questions.

1. What is the setting of the first half of the reading?

   _____

2. What is the subject's profession in this reading?

   _____

MAKING CONNECTIONS

The reading discusses how an African American doctor struggled to overcome prejudice and discrimination. What types of prejudice and/or discrimination do you witness? What specific behaviors do you see?

READING TIP

As you read, notice situations that reveal racial discrimination or prejudice and how the author responded to them.

Coming Into My Own

1   The nurse looked at me with disinterest as I walked toward her station. "Yes?" she asked, pausing with a pencil in her hand. "Who did you come to pick up?" From the tone of her voice I immediately knew that she thought I was an **orderly**. I was wearing my green scrubs, nothing to indicate I was a doctor.

orderly
an attendant who does routine, nonmedical work in a hospital

2   "I didn't come to pick up anyone." I looked at her and smiled, realizing that the only Black people she had seen on the floor had been orderlies. Why should she think anything else? "I'm the new **intern**."

3   "New intern? But you can't—I mean—I didn't mean to" the nurse stuttered, trying to apologize without sounding prejudiced.

4   "That's OK," I said, letting her off the hook. It was a natural mistake. "I'm new, so why should you know who I am?"

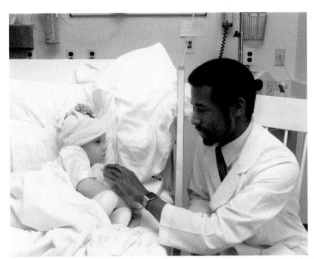

Dr. Benjamin Carson at Johns Hopkins Hospital. What do you suppose Dr. Carson is doing in this photo?

intern
a recent medical
school graduate
undergoing
supervised
practical
training

Intensive Care
Unit
a specialized
section of a
hospital
containing the
equipment,
medical and
nursing staff,
and monitoring
devices necessary
to provide care
to extremely ill
patients

5

6

7

8

9

10

11

12

13

14

The first time I went into the Intensive Care Unit, I was wearing my whites (our monkey suits, as we interns called them), and a nurse signaled me. "You're here for Mr. Jordan?"

"No, ma'am, I'm not."

"You sure?" she asked as a frown covered her forehead. "He's the only one who's scheduled for respiratory therapy today."

By then I had come closer and she could read my name badge and the word *intern* under my name.

"Oh, I'm so very sorry," she said, and I could tell she was.

Although I didn't say it, I would like to have told her, "It's all right because I realize most people do things based on their past experiences. You've never encountered a Black intern before, so you assumed I was the only kind of Black male you'd seen wearing whites, a respiratory therapist." I smiled again and went on.

It was inevitable that a few White patients didn't want a Black doctor, and they protested to Dr. Long. One woman said, "I'm sorry, but I do not want a Black physician in on my case."

Dr. Long had a standard answer, given in a calm but firm voice. "There's the door. You're welcome to walk through it. But if you stay here, Dr. Carson will handle your case."

At the time people were making these objections, I didn't know about them. Only much later did Dr. Long tell me as he laughed about the prejudices of some patients. But there was no humor in his voice when he defined his position. He was adamant about his stance, allowing no prejudice because of color or ethnic background.

Of course, I knew how some individuals felt. I would have had to be pretty insensitive not to know. The way they behaved, their coldness, even without saying anything, made their feelings clear. Each time, however, I was able to remind myself they were individuals speaking for themselves and not representative of all Whites. No matter how strongly a patient felt, as soon as he voiced his objection he learned that Dr. Long would dismiss him on the spot if he said anything more. So far as I know, none of the patients ever left!

15   I honestly felt no great pressures. When I did encounter prejudice, I could hear Mother's voice in the back of my head saying things like, "Some people are ignorant and you have to educate them."

16   The only pressure I felt during my internship, and in the years since, has been a self-imposed obligation to act as a role model for Black youngsters. These young folks need to know that the way to escape their often dismal situations is contained within them-selves. They can't expect other people to do it for them. Perhaps I can't do much, but I can provide one living example of someone who made it and who came from what we now call a disadvantaged background. Basically I'm no different than many of them.

17   As I think of Black youth, I also want to say I believe that many of our pressing ra-cial problems will be taken care of when we who are among the minorities will stand on our own feet and refuse to look to anybody else to save us from our situations. The culture in which we live stresses looking out for number one. Without adopting such a self-centered value system, we can demand the best of ourselves while we are extending our hands to help others.

18   I see glimmers of hope. For example, I noticed that when the Vietnamese came to the United States they often faced prejudice from everyone—White, Black, and Hispanics. But they didn't beg for handouts and often took the lowest jobs offered. Even well-educated individuals didn't mind sweeping floors if it was a paying job.

entrepreneurs
people who start
and successfully
manage businesses
after taking some
risks to do so

19   Today many of these same Vietnamese are property owners and **entrepreneurs**. That's the message I try to get across to the young people. The same opportunities are there, but we can't start out as vice president of the company. Even if we landed such a position, it wouldn't do us any good anyway because we wouldn't know how to do our work. It's better to start where we can fit in and then work our way up.

A. UNDERSTANDING THE THESIS AND OTHER MAIN IDEAS

Select the best answer.

_____ 1. The writer of "Coming Into My Own" can best be described as
   a. a black respiratory therapist.
   b. a white female nurse.
   c. a black male doctor.
   d. the white patient of a black doctor.

_____ 2. The statement from the reading that best supports the writer's pri-mary thesis is
   a. "From the tone of her voice I immediately knew that she thought I was an orderly." (paragraph 1)
   b. "It was inevitable that a few White patients didn't want a Black doctor." (paragraph 11)
   c. "I can provide one living example of someone who made it and who came from what we now call a disadvantaged background." (paragraph 16)
   d. "I see glimmers of hope." (paragraph 18)

_____ 3. According to the writer, the only pressure he felt during and after his internship has been from

    a. himself as he strives to be a role model for black youngsters.

    b. white nurses and doctors who treat him as less than equal.

    c. his parents and other family members because of their high expectations for him.

    d. members of other ethnic groups who resent his success.

_____ 4. The statement that best expresses the main idea of paragraph 17 is

    a. People should look to themselves rather than others to improve their situations.

    b. Adopting a self-centered value system is the only way to succeed in our culture.

    c. The racial problems in our society are primarily caused by misunderstanding.

    d. Extending help to others is not as important as getting ahead.

_____ 5. The topic of paragraph 18 is

    a. low-paying jobs.

    b. Vietnamese immigrants.

    c. prejudice among ethnic groups.

    d. education levels of immigrants.

_____ 6. The main point of paragraph 19 is expressed in the

    a. first sentence.

    b. second sentence.

    c. fourth sentence.

    d. last sentence.

B. IDENTIFYING DETAILS

Indicate whether each statement is true (T) or false (F).

_____ 1. The writer/intern was mistaken for both an orderly and a respiratory therapist.

_____ 2. The white patients who were prejudiced were careful to hide their feelings.

_____ 3. Many patients left the hospital immediately rather than be treated by a black doctor.

_____ 4. The writer came from a privileged background.

_____ 5. Many Vietnamese immigrants who started in low-paying jobs now own property.

C. RECOGNIZING METHODS OF ORGANIZATION AND TRANSITIONS

Select the best answer.

_____ 1. In paragraphs 1–10, the writer describes the prejudice he has faced. The organizational pattern used in these paragraphs is

    a. cause and effect.

    b. time sequence.

    c. enumeration.

    d. comparison and contrast.

_____ 2. A phrase in paragraph 18 that indicates that the writer will illustrate his ideas is

    a. But.   c. For example.

    b. Even.   d. if.

D. REVIEWING AND ORGANIZING IDEAS: SUMMARIZING

Complete the following summaries of paragraphs 5–10 and 11–13 by filling in the missing words and phrases.

Paragraphs 5–10: The nurse assumed that the writer was a _____ _____ , not a _____. The writer understood that the nurse's assumption was based on her _____.

Paragraphs 11–13: Some _____ patients did not want to be treated by a _____ doctor. When they _____ to Dr. Long, his response was that _____ _____. Dr.Long later _____ about the patients' _____ , but he also made it clear that he would not tolerate _____.

E. READING AND THINKING VISUALLY

Select the best answer.

_____ 1. Photos often require inference skills. Look closely at the photo that accompanies the reading. Where was the photo taken?

    a. in Dr. Carson's office

    b. in an inner-city clinic

    c. in a sealed environment

    d. in a hospital

_____ 2. Just like text, photos can offer comparisons and contrasts. Which contrast is not shown in the photo?

   a. rich and poor

   b. older and younger

   c. black and white

   d. male and female

F. FIGURING OUT IMPLIED MEANINGS

Indicate whether each statement is true (T) or false (F).

_____ 1. From the situation described in paragraphs 1–4, it can be inferred that all orderlies are black males.

_____ 2. From the description of the writer's mother, it can be inferred that she believed that her son could change people's attitudes toward blacks.

_____ 3. From paragraphs 18–19, it can be inferred that the writer believes that immigrants are taking jobs away from blacks.

G. THINKING CRITICALLY

Select the best answer.

_____ 1. The writer's primary purpose in writing this article is to

   a. expose prejudice in the medical profession.

   b. persuade others, especially black youth, that it is possible to succeed in spite of prejudice and a disadvantaged background.

   c. discourage black males from becoming doctors.

   d. argue against affirmative action programs that offer "handouts" to minorities.

_____ 2. The writer supports his ideas primarily by

   a. describing his personal experience.

   b. reporting statistics.

   c. defining terms.

   d. citing facts.

_____ 3. By stating in paragraph 2 that he looked at the nurse "and smiled," the writer indicates that he

   a. was being sarcastic.

   b. understood the nurse's error and forgave her.

   c. was incredulous at being treated that way.

   d. thought the nurse was joking.

_____ 4. The writer's tone throughout the article can best be described as

    a. bitter.

    b. angry.

    c. encouraging.

    d. grateful.

H. BUILDING VOCABULARY

Context

Using context and a dictionary, if necessary, determine the meaning of each word as it is used in the selection.

_____ 1. prejudiced (paragraph 3)

    a. confused   c. inconsiderate

    b. biased   d. distracted

_____ 2. inevitable (paragraph 11)

    a. unfortunate   c. unavoidable

    b. disappointing   d. unexpected

_____ 3. adamant (paragraph 13)

    a. uncompromising   c. easygoing

    b. angry   d. humorous

_____ 4. pressing (paragraph 17)

    a. pushy   c. unnecessary

    b. urgent   d. minor

Word Parts

> **A REVIEW OF PREFIXES**
>
> **DIS-** means *not*
> **IN-** means *not*

*Use your knowledge of word parts and the review above to choose the answer that best defines the **boldfaced** word in each sentence.*

_____ 1. "The nurse looked at me with **disinterest** as I walked toward her station." (paragraph 1)

    a. fascination   c. fear

    b. approval   d. indifference

_____ 2. "I would have had to be pretty **insensitive** not to know."
(paragraph 14)

    a. concerned   c. unhappy

    b. not aware   d. emotional

_____ 3. "... I can provide one living example of someone who made it and
who came from what we now call a **disadvantaged** background."
(paragraph 16)

    a. wealthy   c. poor

    b. privileged   d. unlimited

Unusual Words/Understanding Idioms

_Use the meanings given below to write a sentence using the **boldfaced**
phrase._

1. The expression **letting someone off the hook** (paragraph 4) means to
release someone from an embarrassing situation or to forgive someone for
an embarrassing mistake.

    Your sentence: _____

    _____

2. The phrase **looking out for number one** (paragraph 17) means to be
concerned only with yourself or your own wants and needs.

    Your sentence: _____

    _____

I. SELECTING A LEARNING/STUDY STRATEGY

Assume you will be tested on this reading on an upcoming exam. Evaluate the usefulness of the summaries you completed above. Which other paragraphs would be useful to summarize?

J. EXPLORING IDEAS THROUGH DISCUSSION AND WRITING

1. Do you think the writer's response to prejudice was typical? How do you
think you would react in a similar situation?

2. Have you observed or experienced situations in which someone revealed
prejudice? How did you or the person handle the situation?

K. BEYOND THE CLASSROOM TO THE WEB

Vist the Academy of Achievement Gallery's site for Ben Carson at **http://www. achievement.org/autodoc/page/car1int-1**.

Read his profile and his biography. Read or watch the interview and explore the photo gallery. After reviewing all this additional information, how does your view of Ben Carson change, if at all?

TRACKING YOUR PROGRESS

Selection 3

Section	Number Correct		Score
A. Thesis and Main Ideas (6 items)	_____	× 5	_____
B. Details (5 items)	_____	× 4	_____
C. Organization and Transitions (2 items)	_____	× 2	_____
E. Reading and Thinking Visually (2 items)	_____	× 4	_____
F. Implied Meanings (3 items)	_____	× 4	_____
G. Thinking Critically (4 items)	_____	× 3	_____
H. Vocabulary			
Context (4 items)	_____	× 2	_____
Word Parts (3 items)	_____	× 2	_____
	TOTAL SCORE		_____ %

12 Communication/Speech

The field of **communication** is concerned with the exchange of information between individuals and groups through speaking, writing, or nonverbal communication (body language, such as gestures). Communication may be interpersonal, such as that between two persons; may occur within a small group, such as in a group of friends or in a class discussion; and may also be public, in which a speaker addresses an audience. Communication skills are important for success in college, for finding and keeping a rewarding job, and for building and maintaining healthy, strong relationships with family, friends, and co-workers.

By studying communication, you will come to understand those around you and exchange ideas with them more effectively. "Teen Slang" explores slang as a feature of popular culture. "Citizen-Powered Journalism Fills a Void" presents a new form of journalism. In "Relationships and Technology" you will read about online dating and discover its advantages and disadvantages. Use the following tips when reading in the communication field.

TIPS FOR READINGS IN COMMUNICA- TION SPEECH	■ **Pay attention to processes.** In "Teen Slang," pay attention to the process by which new words enter our language. ■ **Pay attention to principles—rules that govern how communication works.** When reading "Teen Slang" look for the principles on which teen slang is based. ■ **Notice theories (explanations that attempt to describe how or why something happens).** In "Relationships and Technology" the author explains **how** online dating Web sites affect relationships. ■ **Be alert for cultural differences.** Not all cultures and ethnic groups follow the same conventions and theories. Do you think the online matchmaking described in "Relationships and Technology" would be considered appropriate in all cultures? ■ **Pay attention to language and terminology.** "Teen Slang" explores the uses of slang and discusses the online dictionary Urbandictionary.com. ■ **Think critically.** As you read theories, ask challenging questions, such as "Does this information fit with what I already know and have experienced?" For example, when reading "Citizen-Powered Journalism Fills a Void," you might question the accuracy and reliability of news contributions from private citizens.

Teen Slang

Denise Ryan

This selection, which first appeared in *The Vancouver Sun*, discusses slang vocabulary. Read the selection to find out how slang is defined, who uses it, and why.

PREVIEWING THE READING

Using the steps listed on page 36, preview the reading selection. When you have finished, complete the following items.

1. The subject of this selection is _____.

2. List at least four slang terms mentioned in the selection.

   a. _____

   b. _____

   c. _____

   d. _____

MAKING CONNECTIONS

What slang terms do you use in conversation? Can you remember where you first heard the terms you use?

READING TIP

As you read, highlight the definition of slang, information on how it develops, and the reasons people use it to communicate.

Teen Slang

scat singers
jazz vocalists who
improvise melodies
and rhythms using
sounds in place of
words in a song

1   Enter at your own risk. Best to hold your tongue or risk sounding utterly 'ridonkulous' if you're older than 30. If your kids are slangin' with as much delight as **scat singers** running up and down a new vocabulary of sounds, don't even think of joining in. It blows chunks when parents try to talk like kids, and there's a good reason for that. We're too old. Slang vocabulary, like musical tastes, or physical height, may be one of those things that is more or less fully formed before we exit our teens.

"That's like, so random!"

2   Last week, when I asked my eight-year-old son how his last day at summer camp went, he casually dropped the word "random" into his reply—as in "Mommy, that question was so random." There were more random acts of vocabulary to come. Summer camp had apparently involved a lot of time within earshot of some very sick teenage counselors. That's sick as in cool, dope, sweet or bomb.

3   Suddenly things my son didn't want to do were "lame." Things that made him happy were "sweet" or "fresh." He had also mastered an accomplished new lexicon of swear words. (Which he's filed away, no doubt for later use.) Learning teen slang—not to mention the so-called "bad" words—this summer was like getting the keys to a

linguistic
related to
language

secret kingdom. I could tell he was pleased with himself. With each new word, the door of understanding, both social and **linguistic**, cracked opened a little more.

4   Pamela Munro, a linguist and editor of U.C.L.A. Slang 6, defines slang as "language whose use serves to mark the user as belonging to some distinct group within society." In other words, when your kid is slangin,' he's really saying he is different than you—and he likes it that way. "Anthropologically, kids form themselves," said Munro. "Slang is a kind of code or password if people are trying to show that they are a member of your group."

5   "Most people start using active slang when they are in junior high," said Munro. By the age of 17 or 18, they have a fully developed slang vocabulary that is particular to their unique **demographic**. Adults rarely add much that's new to the slang vocabulary, said Munro. "You just can't do it if you're over 40. Even 30 is too late," she said.

demographic
a section of the
population that
shares common
characteristics,
such as age, sex,
or class

6   It is in high school and college that people formulate the vocabulary they will use for the rest of their lives. "We will always feel those words are absolutely right and appropriate for a given situation even as younger groups coin their own terms," said Munro. The way we use slang therefore becomes a dead giveaway to our age. We may dye our hair, have babies later in life, and keep our bodies intact but if we try and talk like someone 20 years younger, we won't be able to pull it off. It won't feel right, it won't sound right, and it will be clear we're just TTH. (Trying too hard.)

Adults can't pull it off

7   Jasmine Lattimore, a 17-year-old Richmond student going into Grade 12, said it backfires when adults try to "be hip."

8   "My Spanish teacher used to say pwn, as in owning somebody. People laughed out of courtesy, but it was painful to hear. She was fortysomething." (Pwn, pronounced "pown" according to urbandictionary.com, is an act of dominating an opponent . . . as in "I pwn these guys on Battle.net.") The fortysomething teacher probably should have stuck to, say, "I totally rocked it."

9   Anna Ward, 18, who recently graduated from Vancouver's Lord Byng high school, said she'd laugh if her parents used her age group's slang. Ward feels slang is good harmless fun. "I'd curb it if I went to a job interview, or in certain situations. Mostly we just mock our own age group and mock ourselves." Ward said abbreviating is common—Obvs for obvious, for example, vis for visit. "We add "skis" to the back of anything," she said. Whatevskis for whatever, whenskis for when, drinkskis for drink.

10   Munro said slang comes from sources that include standard words, abbreviations, "acronymy" (DILF and MILF), initialism (LOL, OMG, WTF) and African American culture. According to Munro, swear words are less taboo among her students than they have been for previous generations. "I didn't even know of the existence of certain words until I was in my 20s," said Munro. Among her students now, swear words are used almost **colloquially**. Slang phrases may have helped the expletives devolve in power. While not technically slang words, they are a common part of many slang expressions.

colloquially
informally, as
part of ordinary
or familiar
conversation

11   "I swear like a sailor," said Lattimore. "You get used to it and it loses meaning." When Lattimore and her friends go out, it could just be for "shits and nipples," for

example, which means to have a good time. (While they're at it they might hook up with some pimp guys, rickroll a buddy, ditch the crunk hoodrats, and stay out troubs with the po-po.)

12   Lattimore likes to keep up with what's in and what's out (lame, for example, is out). If she hears new slang, she won't ask what it means—that might expose her as being out of the loop. She jumps online and looks it up on Urbandictionary.com. The website has become the go-to decoder for both kids and parents. But is a word still cool if everyone knows what it means, including grown-ups? Linguist Robert Leonard recently argued in *The New York Times* that the Internet is stripping slang of its "exclusionary power."

13   Munro rejects the notion that accessibility lessens slang's cool factor. "The Internet can't make control of slang available to all groups . . . your grandmother won't be talking like **L'il Wayne** even if she knows the words."

L'il Wayne
an American
rapper

14   Aaron Peckham, the founder of Urbandictionary.com, said his website is really just about "helping people understand each other better." Urbandictionary.com, where words both "fularious" and "ridonkulous" are explained, draws 15.5 million unique visitors a month. Anyone can submit words and phrases, contribute to and vote on definitions.

15   Peckham doesn't believe that a posting on his website automatically robs a slang word of its **street cred**. "It is interesting," Peckham said, "that something that is exclusionary, people also like to share." Peckham, 28, started Urbandictionary.com as a lark when he was a college student in 1999. He recently left his job as Google software engineer to run his website full-time.

street cred
acceptability,
especially among
young people in
urban areas

16   Eighty percent of Urbandictionary.com's users are under 25. The other 20 percent Peckham figures includes parents trying to decode what their kids are saying, texting and coining. Staying current isn't easy simply because language among the under-20 set morphs so rapidly. Peckham and a group of volunteers sort through about 1,000 submissions a day, and discard about 50 percent of them. "My editors reject words that don't make sense, and especially words that refer to anything that's really violent," said Peckham.

Site 'of value' to kids

17   The site gained notoriety as part of the ACLU's successful 2006 fight against the American Child Online Protection Act—COPA would have effectively put Urban Dictionary out of business by requiring filters to keep minors off the site. When Peckham was asked on the witness stand whether his site offered sexually explicit words, he admitted that 18 of the top 20 most popular words on the site were sexually explicit in nature. But he argued that the site provided a service that was of value, even to minors. Peckham said, "I remember being a third-grader . . . there was a vocabulary I wanted to understand but the dictionary simply denied the word existed."

18   When the prosecutor asked for a clarification of the website's definition system, he brandished a list of sexually explicit slang culled from the site and insisted Peckham explain, using the word "teabagging." (I'd explain the word here but it is NSFW: Not Safe For Work.) Peckham managed a modest explanation, and the ACLU won the case. The website stayed up, and teabagging stayed on it.

SUMMING IT UP

THE NEW SLANG

IN	OUT	POPULAR ACRONYMS
Crunk (Crazy plus Drunk)	Fo' Shizzle	IDK (I don't know)
Fiending (Want it bad)	Fierce	IMAO (In my arrogant opinion)
Sweet (Cool)	Boss	
Emo (angsty teen)	Dawg	FTW (For the wind . . . used to add positive emphasis)
Scene (hip alt music type)	Uber	
Po Po (Cops)	Noob	ASDF (Figure it out)
420 (Marijuana)	Off the heezie	FML (F—my life)

pundits
commentators

19   In an ironic twist that perfectly demonstrates just why a site like Urbandictionary.com is of sociolinguistic importance, the term "teabagging" made headlines again recently when U.S. conservatives used it as part of a populist tax protest. Citizens were urged to send teabags to the White House in an apparent reference to the Boston Tea Party tax protest of 1773. "Teabagging" events were enthusiastically promoted by Republicans, conservative **pundits**, and the FOX network. What the tax teabaggers didn't know was that the term has some very unique—and overtly sexual—connotations in contemporary pop culture. Had the Republicans looked up "teabagging" on Urbandictionary.com, they might have avoided the gleeful public skewering that followed in the media.

20   For those who do want to keep up, Urbandictionary.com also picks a word of the day. A recent one was "after clap." It means "That last person/people who keep[s] clapping after everyone else has stopped. Normally, parents." So, even if you are an after-clapper (or simply over 30), the teabagging incident is a good example of why it's so important to keep up with pop culture by learning its lingo, even if your kids don't want you to use it.

A. UNDERSTANDING THE THESIS AND OTHER MAIN IDEAS

Select the best answer.

_____ 1. The central thesis of this selection is that

    a. young children should not be allowed to use slang.

    b. filters should be required on Web sites that contain explicit language.

    c. swear words are a common part of many slang expressions.

    d. each generation develops a unique slang vocabulary during its youth.

_____ 2. The author's primary purpose is to

    a. introduce readers to a variety of slang.

    b. describe the development and use of slang.

    c. persuade adults to try using slang in conversation.

    d. discuss how the Internet has promoted the use of slang.

_____ 3. The main idea of paragraph 6 is expressed in the

    a. first sentence.

    b. second sentence.

    c. fourth sentence.

    d. last sentence.

_____ 4. The purpose of paragraph 10 is to

    a. list examples of acronymy and initialism.

    b. discuss sources and types of slang.

    c. change how swear words are viewed.

    d. compare current students with previous generations.

_____ 5. The author included the story about "teabagging" in paragraph 19 to demonstrate

    a. how words and definitions have changed since the Boston Tea Party.

    b. why filters are necessary to protect minors online.

    c. how teens are typically less offended than adults by explicit language.

    d. why it is important to be aware of slang as a part of popular culture.

B. IDENTIFYING DETAILS

Indicate whether each statement is true (T) or false (F).

_____ 1. Urbandictionary.com was created by a linguist named Robert Leonard.

_____ 2. Only teenagers are allowed to submit entries and vote on the definitions of slang terms on Urbandictionary.com.

_____ 3. The majority of Urbandictionary.com's users are under 25 years old.

_____ 4. The ACLU won its 2006 case against the American Child Online Protection Act.

_____ 5. Urbandictionary.com does not allow sexually explicit terms on its site.

C. RECOGNIZING METHODS OF ORGANIZATION AND TRANSITIONS

Complete the sentences by filling in the blanks.

1. In paragraph 4 the author uses the _____ organizational pattern to explain the term *slang*.

2. The transition that indicates a cause-and-effect relationship in paragraph 6 is _____.

3. The transition that signals an example in paragraph 9 is _____.

D. REVIEWING AND ORGANIZING IDEAS: SUMMARIZING

Complete the following summary of paragraphs 1–6 by filling in the missing words or phrases.

Our _____ is formed during our teens. Slang is defined as _____ whose use serves to mark _____ as belonging to _____ within society. Most people start using slang in _____ and have a fully developed _____ unique to their age group by age _____. Adults use the vocabulary they formed in _____ for the rest of their lives. The way we use _____ reveals our _____.

E. READING AND THINKING VISUALLY

Complete each of the following sentences.

1. The purpose of the box titled "The New Slang" is to _____
   _____.

2. The Web site that is referred to in the heading "Site 'of value' to kids" is
   _____.

3. The purpose of the cartoon that accompanies this reading is to _____
   _____.

F. FIGURING OUT IMPLIED MEANINGS

Indicate whether each statement is true (T) or false (F).

_____ 1. The writer's son described his camp counselors as "sick" because they were actually very ill.

_____ 2. Pamela Munro can be considered an expert on language and teen slang.

_____ 3. The teenagers quoted in the article like it when their parents and teachers use teen slang.

_____ 4. The use of swear words among young people today is more common and casual than in past generations.

_____ 5. People of all ages use the Internet to find out the meanings of slang words.

_____ 6. The founder of Urbandictionary.com testified in favor of the American Child Online Protection Act.

G. THINKING CRITICALLY

Select the best answer.

_____ 1. The author supports her central thesis with
   a. personal experience.
   b. expert opinions.
   c. facts and statistics.
   d. all of the above.

_____ 2. The tone of this selection can best be described as
   a. judgmental and disapproving.
   b. casual and playful.
   c. formal and serious.
   d. pessimistic and negative.

_____ 3. The primary reason the author wrote about her son in paragraphs 2–3 was to illustrate
   a. her admiration and respect for teenagers.
   b. his pleasure at discovering teen slang.
   c. her disapproval of his new vocabulary.
   d. her willingness to learn new words.

_____ 4. When the author describes Urbandictionary.com as the "go-to decoder" in paragraph 12, she means that the site
   a. is written in a code that is difficult for most people to understand.
   b. offers technical assistance to people having trouble understanding the Internet.
   c. is considered the most useful tool for finding out what specific slang terms mean.
   d. tries to eliminate words from our vocabulary that are violent or don't make sense.

_____ 5. In paragraph 18, the word that reveals the prosecutor's negative attitude toward Urbandictionary.com is

a. clarification.

b. system.

c. brandished.

d. modest.

H. BUILDING VOCABULARY

Context

Using context and a dictionary, if necessary, determine the meaning of each word as it is used in the selection.

_____ 1. lexicon (paragraph 3)

a. vocabulary

b. puzzle

c. criticism

d. disagreement

_____ 2. devolve (paragraph 10)

a. grow

b. develop

c. decrease

d. revive

_____ 3. morphs (paragraph 16)

a. allows

b. prevents

c. changes

d. declines

_____ 4. notoriety (paragraph 17)

a. fame/attention

b. disregard

c. secrecy

d. punishment

_____ 5. culled (paragraph 18)

a. avoided

b. stolen

c. added

d. selected

_____ 6. overtly (paragraph 19)

  a. mistakenly

  b. openly

  c. indirectly

  d. secretly

Word Parts

> ### A REVIEW OF PREFIXES AND ROOTS
>
> **ANTHROPO** means *human being*
> **LOG** means *study, thought*
> **EX-** means *from, out of, former*

Use your knowledge of word parts and the review above to fill in the blanks in the following sentences.

1. The term *anthropologically* (paragraph 4) refers to the _____ of

_____ .

2. Something with *exclusionary* (paragraph 12) power has the ability to keep

others _____ being included.

Unusual Words/Understanding Idioms

*Use the meanings given below to write a sentence using the **boldfaced** word or phrase.*

1. A **dead giveaway** (paragraph 6) is a sign that reveals or exposes something in an obvious manner.

   Your sentence: _____

   _____

2. Someone who is considered to be **out of the loop** (paragraph 12) is uninformed or not up-to-date with information.

   Your sentence: _____

   _____

3. A person who does something **as a lark** (paragraph 15) is doing it for fun.

   Your sentence: _____

   _____

4. To experience a **skewering** (paragraph 19) is to be sharply criticized or ridiculed.

   Your sentence: _____

   _____

I. SELECTING A LEARNING/STUDY STRATEGY

Assume you will be tested on this article on an upcoming exam. Evaluate your highlighting as well as the summary you completed. How else might you prepare for a test on this material?

J. EXPLORING IDEAS THROUGH DISCUSSION AND WRITING

1. Discuss the different types of teen slang. Which words or phrases have you heard before? Which ones do you use?

2. Write your own brief definition of each term listed as "Out" in the box that accompanies the reading. Can you think of five more "Popular Acronyms" to add to the list in the box?

3. Discuss some of the comments of the teenagers quoted in this article. For example, do you agree that it "backfires" when adults use slang that belongs to your age group? In what situations do you curb your use of slang?

K. BEYOND THE CLASSROOM TO THE WEB

Visit the Web site **http://www.urbandictionary.com/** *and explore the "Word of the Day" section. Choose five words or phrases that you find interesting and explain how each term reflects popular culture or current events. Do these terms belong to your demographic? Discuss why or why not.*

TRACKING YOUR PROGRESS

Selection 4

Section	Number Correct		Score
A. Thesis and Main Ideas (5 items)	_____	×4	_____
B. Details (5 items)	_____	×3	_____
C. Organization and Transitions (3 items)	_____	×4	_____
F. Implied Meanings (6 items)	_____	×3	_____
G. Thinking Critically (5 items)	_____	×4	_____
H. Vocabulary			
Context (6 items)	_____	×2	_____
Word Parts (3 items)	_____	×1	_____
		TOTAL SCORE	_____%

SELECTION 5

Citizen-Powered Journalism Fills a Void

Angelo Fernando

Contemporary
Issues Reading
The following article appeared in *Communication World,* a bimonthly magazine published by the IABC (International Association of Business Communicators). Read it to discover how the average "person on the street" is helping to change journalism.

PREVIEWING THE READING

Using the steps listed on page 36, preview the reading selection. When you have finished, complete the following items.

1. This selection is about _____

_____

2. List at least two countries discussed in the selection. _____

_____

MAKING CONNECTIONS

Have you ever uploaded photos to Facebook or another social media site? If so, what types of photos have you shared? For example, did you take photos at a concert, parade, or sporting event and share them?

READING TIP

Because this reading selection is intended for a specialized group of people (journalists and professional communicators), it contains several terms that may be familiar only to them. For example, you may not know that Flickr (paragraph 2) is a Web site that allows people to share photos. As you read, note terms with which you are not familiar, and then conduct a Google search to learn more about them.

Citizen-Powered Journalism Fills a Void

With blogs, camera phones and more, ordinary people are sharing the events in their world in near real time

1   The prerequisite for Journalism 1.0 was a deep sense of curiosity and some comfort with risk. Journalism 2.0 still needs those two ingredients, plus some comfort with technology. With an accelerated news cycle and so many disasters and global events to cover, a new type of open-source reporting, citizen journalism, has stepped in to fill the breach. Before you think citizen journalism involves a maverick muckraker with a laptop, consider the traditional media's response. Many "CitJos," as they are called, work alongside old hands in the newsrooms. In fact, many of the stories you read, listen to, or watch in the mainstream media could be coming from them.

2   In Myanmar in September, when the military killed several protesters, citizen reporters leapt into action to fill the traditional role of local and international media, which were heavily censored by the ruling **junta**. When Japanese journalist Kenji Nagai was killed in the line of duty, the first images of the event seeped out through an invisible news "bureau"—a combination of blogs, Flickr photos, videos on YouTube, and even e-mail. Blogs such as the Burma Underground were filled with reports filed by CitJos.

junta
a military group that rules a country after taking power by force

3   When did this shift take place? Citizens have been participating in their news for decades, but their input was limited to letters and call-ins. There were technical limitations with regard to the timeliness of citizen input too. Camera phones and blogs became commercially viable only after 2002; blogs arguably started gaining critical mass around the same time. Two years prior, a real push toward citizen journalism came from the east, when South Korean entrepreneur Oh Yeon-ho started OhmyNews, with 727 citizen reporters. It wasn't on many people's radar until it became a major force in South Korea's presidential elections in 2002. OhmyNews is now one of the world's largest citizen journalism enterprises, with 1,900 citizen journalists, not counting 65 full-time staff reporters.

Adapting to the Model

4   Technology has been a big driver of the adoption of citizen journalism, equipping it well for speed, collaboration, and delivery. Without needing to invest in expensive GPS phones or briefcase satellites, CitJos are filing stories via text messages, grainy pictures on camera phones, cyber cafés and, when necessary, **proxy servers** to cover their tracks.

proxy servers
Internet sites
that allow
users to hide
their locations

5   So it is not surprising that mainstream journalism has bolted citizen-powered journalism onto its business practice. Reuters, for instance, has partnered with Global Voices to integrate feeds into its country pages and special reports. The Associated Press wire service just partnered with the Vancouver, British Columbia–based NowPublic citizen journalist site (tag line: "Crowd powered media"), which has thousands of contributors in 140 countries. To give you some sense of scale, NowPublic's footprint dwarfs that of AP, which has bureaus in just 97 countries. Soon after the Minneapolis, Minnesota, bridge collapse in August, AP began using images obtained through Flickr and Facebook. "Grab your camera and start weaving your tale," urges CNN on a portion of its site dedicated to getting readers to be its eyes and ears. "We're not looking for press releases; we want to see your full-fledged storytelling."

Different Folks, Different Strokes

6   Lest this all seems like working off the same "freelance" template, consider this: The Poynter Institute has attempted to identify 11 stages for news sites to engage citizen journalists, ranging from pure open-source, unedited formats, to those that are moderated and edited, to those that combine amateur and professional journalists. Those stages are:

1. Opening a news Website to public comment.

2. The citizen add-on reporter—allowing citizens to comment on specific articles.

3. Open-source reporting—a professional journalist collaborates with citizens as sources. Citizens sometimes contribute some of the reporting for the journalist's story.

4. The citizen bloghouse—inviting citizens to blog regularly on the site.

5. Newsroom "transparency" blogs—for citizens to post complaints or praise about the news organization's work.

6. Stand-alone citizen journalism sites (edited)—establishing a news-oriented Website that is made up entirely or nearly entirely of contributions from the community.

7. Stand-alone citizen journalism sites (unedited).

8. Adding a print version—producing a print version of a standalone citizen journalist site.

9. The hybrid—professional and citizen journalism.

10. Integrating professional and citizen journalism under one roof—content by citizen journalists is presented alongside content by professional journalists.

11. **Wiki** journalism—where citizens are editors.

wiki
refers to any technology 7 that allows anyone to contribute or edit materials

cadre
a small group of people trained for a specific purpose 8 or profession

It appears that the hybrid model sits well with newspapers that continue to add bloggers to their **cadre** of reporters, turn old-school journalists into MoJos—mobile journalists—and actively solicit reader submissions. The *News & Observer*, a North Carolina newspaper, is doing it. In radio, the Brian Lehrer Show on New York City's WNYC did a story in October on price gouging, putting out a call to people to "report" back on the price of three simple items at the grocery store: milk, beer and lettuce. Responses came in from 357 listeners. Back in Myanmar, the story continues to be covered by ordinary people filing reports that are picked up by major networks.

Call it what you will, this new form of hybrid, grassroots, open-source, participatory reporting has left its mark on the business of news. *Newsvine* has called it the new "ecosystem" of journalism. And it's here to stay.

A. UNDERSTANDING THE THESIS AND OTHER MAIN IDEAS

Select the best answer.

_____ 1. The central thesis of the selection is that

    a. new technologies are allowing the mainstream media to use the contributions of citizen journalists.

    b. government repression of professional journalism in foreign countries has led to an increase in citizen journalism.

    c. professional journalists are uncomfortable with the idea of using the contributions of nonprofessional journalists.

    d. across the globe, blogs have become a dominant form of sharing news, photos, and political commentary.

_____ 2. The author's primary purpose is to

    a. suggest that citizens take at least one course in journalism before submitting their work to the mainstream media.

    b. explain how new electronic technologies are allowing traditional journalists to work with citizens in a fast-paced world.

      c. compare and contrast the news media in the United States with the news media in other countries, such as Myanmar.

      d. outline the reasons that citizen journalism is not as trustworthy as the reporting by trained professionals.

_____ 3. The topic of paragraph 1 is

      a. Journalism 1.0.

      b. muckrakers.

      c. citizen journalism.

      d. the mainstream media.

_____ 4. The main idea of paragraph 5 is found in the

      a. first sentence.

      b. second sentence.

      c. fourth sentence.

      d. last sentence.

_____ 5. The term "CitJos" refers to

      a. bloggers.

      b. political prisoners.

      c. citizen journalists.

      d. technology "geeks."

_____ 6. The "hybrid model" mentioned in paragraph 7 refers to

      a. newspaper offices that make use of energy-saving technologies.

      b. a type of journalism that mixes the work of professionals with the contributions of citizens.

      c. journalistic reporting that is published on the Web rather than in print.

      d. the ability of today's readers to keep up with world events through Facebook and blogs.

B. IDENTIFYING DETAILS

Select the best answer.

_____ 1. Which of the following is not a prerequisite for Journalism 2.0?

      a. a strong sense of curiosity

      b. comfort with technology

      c. a willingness to take risks

      d. the ability to speak two languages

_____ 2. According to the reading, the technological advances that spurred citizen participation in journalism reached critical mass in

a. 1996.   c. 2002.

b. 2000.   d. 2008.

_____ 3. All of the following are synonyms for citizen journalism *except*

a. MoJo reporting.

b. grassroots reporting.

c. open-source reporting.

d. participatory reporting.

_____ 4. The Burma Underground is a

a. blog.

b. newspaper.

c. Web site.

d. magazine.

_____ 5. Which of the following is *not* run primarily by citizen journalists?

a. NowPublic

b. OhmyNews

c. the Burma Underground

d. The *News & Observer*

_____ 6. Wiki journalism refers to a type of journalism in which

a. citizens are allowed to comment on specific articles.

b. a professional journalist collaborates with citizens as sources.

c. citizens serve as editors.

d. citizen contributions are printed in a standalone publication.

_____ 7. The article discusses all of the following news events *except*

a. the collapse of a bridge in Minneapolis, Minnesota.

b. the South Korean presidential election of 2002.

c. the assassination of a political activist in Vancouver, British Columbia.

d. the death of a Japanese journalist in Myanmar.

_____ 8. Brian Lehrer's radio show focused on the prices of which three consumer goods?

a. lettuce, milk, and beer

b. cigarettes, wine, and bread

c. utilities, gasoline, and houses

d. napkins, butter, and bottled water

C. RECOGNIZING METHODS OF ORGANIZATION AND TRANSITIONS

Select the best answer.

_____ 1. The organizational pattern of paragraph 2 is
   a. narration.
   b. comparison and contrast.
   c. generalization and example.
   d. process.

_____ 2. The organizational pattern of paragraph 5 is
   a. chronological order.
   b. generalization and example.
   c. classification.
   d. definition.

_____ 3. The transitional word or phrase in paragraph 5 that indicates that
        the author is going to illustrate his idea is
   a. business practice.   c. sense of scale.
   b. for instance.   d. eyes and ears.

_____ 4. Which organizational pattern does paragraph 6 utilize?
   a. spatial order
   b. cause and effect
   c. comparison and contrast
   d. listing

_____ 5. The pattern of organization of paragraph 7 is
   a. generalization and example.
   b. order of importance.
   c. classification.
   d. narration.

D. REVIEWING AND ORGANIZING IDEAS: PARAPHRASING

Complete the following paraphrases with the correct word, phrase, or number.

Paragraph 5

Mainstream journalism has made _____ journalism part of its
everyday business _____. Reuters has partnered with _____,
and the Associated Press has partnered with _____, a huge organization with thousands of contributors in _____ countries. Even news stations like _____ are asking citizens to take part in journalistic efforts.

Paragraph 7

Many newspapers, such as North Carolina's _____, are using a hybrid model that combines the work of trained _____ with submissions from _____. In radio, a NYC-based show used listeners as part of a story on _____. In Myanmar, ordinary people file reports that are picked up by major _____.

E. READING AND THINKING VISUALLY

Select the best answer.

_____ 1. The author chose to include the photo on page 282 in order to

    a. encourage readers to take photography courses to improve their journalistic skills.

    b. demonstrate how people can use a common technology to capture newsworthy events as they are happening.

    c. illustrate the way professional journalists are making use of cell phones to do their investigative reporting.

    d. emphasize that photos and videos from cell phones are more valuable journalistic tools than blogs or other word-based media.

_____ 2. Suppose the author of this selection wanted to help the reader become acquainted with Myanmar, a country that many people have never heard of. Which visual aid would best accomplish this goal?

    a. a photo of Rangoon, Myanmar's largest city

    b. a line graph showing how the population of Myanmar has changed over the last 20 years

    c. a map of the globe showing Myanmar's location

    d. a table showing the number of homes with electricity in different parts of Myanmar

F. FIGURING OUT IMPLIED MEANINGS

Indicate whether each statement is true (T) or false (F).

_____ 1. The author implies that citizens should be equipped with more sophisticated technologies, such as briefcase satellites, if they wish to become reporters.

_____ 2. In Journalism 1.0, citizen journalism was usually limited to letters and call-ins.

_____ 3. Myanmar and Burma are the same country.

_____ 4. The Associated Press is a much larger organization than NowPublic.

_____ 5. OhmyNews had a significant effect on the results of South Korea's presidential election in 2002.

_____ 6. The author suggests that professional journalists resent the way citizens are involving themselves in journalistic activities.

_____ 7. The article implies that citizens have as much power as journalists when they serve as editors.

G. THINKING CRITICALLY

Select the best answer.

_____ 1. The tone of the selection can best be described as

    a. arrogant.   c. solemn.

    b. informative.   d. pessimistic.

_____ 2. The central thesis of the selection is supported primarily by

    a. personal experience.

    b. analogies.

    c. examples.

    d. research citations.

_____ 3. The phrase "maverick muckraker" in paragraph 1 means

    a. a citizen journalist who makes use of cell phones and YouTube videos.

    b. a journalism professor at a respected university.

    c. a criminal who steals passwords and hacks Web sites.

    d. an investigative journalist who uncovers scandalous information.

_____ 4. A *rhetorical question* is a device that writers use to gain the reader's interest. The writer asks a question and then answers it. Which paragraph makes use of this device?

    a. paragraph 2   c. paragraph 5

    b. paragraph 3   d. paragraph 7

_____ 5. A *neologism* is a new word that is coined to describe a new phenomenon, and it is usually not found in a dictionary. Which of the following words used in the selection is a neologism?

    a. CitJo (paragraph 1)

    b. junta (paragraph 2)

    c. freelance (paragraph 6)

    d. cadre (paragraph 7)

_____ 6. The author puts the word "report" in quotation marks in paragraph 7 to

    a. signify that it is an important vocabulary word that readers should commit to memory.

    b. suggest that the radio show's host should not have asked listeners, who are not trained journalists, to call in the information.

    c. imply that this type of information is not truly reporting as the term is generally understood by professional journalists.

    d. point to the fact that information provided by phone is very different from information provided in written format.

_____ 7. The selection closes (in paragraph 8) with a

    a. research citation.

    b. summary statement.

    c. statistic.

    d. comparison-and-contrast statement.

_____ 8. In paragraph 8, the author uses the phrase "ecosystem of journalism" to imply that

    a. the best news stories are those covering environmental topics, such as global warming.

    b. journalism makes the greatest contribution when it is integrated with the economics of newspaper publishing and TV news reporting.

    c. *Newsvine* is the most important source of any and all citizen-provided information in both the United States and foreign countries.

    d. the world of journalism has expanded permanently to include average citizens and commonplace technology.

H. BUILDING VOCABULARY

Context

Using context and a dictionary, if necessary, determine the meaning of each word as it is used in the selection.

_____ 1. accelerated (paragraph 1)

    a. new

    b. speeded up

    c. open

    d. Web-based

_____ 2. breach (paragraph 1)

    a. gap   c. shore

    b. need   d. grasp

_____ 3. seeped (paragraph 2)

    a. made obsolete

    b. publicized

    c. trickled

    d. overflowed

_____ 4. viable (paragraph 3)

    a. inexpensive

    b. unsuccessful

    c. new

    d. possible

_____ 5. full-fledged (paragraph 5)

    a. complete

    b. media-based

    c. amateur

    d. nonfiction

_____ 6. solicit (paragraph 7)

    a. make illegal   c. isolate

    b. ask for   d. support

Word Parts

A REVIEW OF PREFIXES
PRE- means *before* **COL-** means *with* or *together* **UN-** means *not*

Use your knowledge of word parts and the review above to fill in the blanks in the following sentences.

1. A *prerequisite* for Journalism 1.0 (paragraph 1) is something that is required

    _____ you can be successful at Journalism 2.0.

2. Technology that supports *collaboration* (paragraph 4) helps people work

    _____ .

3. *Unedited* news formats (paragraph 6) have _____ been edited by professional editors.

Unusual Words/Understanding Idioms

*Use the meanings given below to write a sentence using the **boldfaced** word or phrase.*

1. **Open-source** reporting (paragraph 1) is a type of reporting that relies on information provided by multiple sources, not just the career journalists who research and report the news.

   Your sentence: _____

   _____

2. A person described as an **old hand** (paragraph 1) is an experienced person who has been doing his or her job for a long time.

   Your sentence: _____

   _____

3. A new technology gains **critical mass** (paragraph 3) when enough people own it or have access to it for it to become an accepted part of everyday life.

   Your sentence: _____

   _____

4. When Organization A **dwarfs** (paragraph 5) Organization B, Organization A is much, much larger than Organization B.

   Your sentence: _____

   _____

5. A member of the **old school** (paragraph 7) thinks and behaves in ways that are considered traditional. Often, old school has a connotation of *old-fashioned* or *antitechnology*.

   Your sentence: _____

   _____

I. SELECTING A LEARNING/STUDY STRATEGY

Select the best answer.

_____ 1. Assume you will be tested on the 11 stages in paragraph 6. What is the best method of studying for this exam?

   a. writing a paraphrase of the 11 stages

   b. researching a real-world example of each of the 11 stages

   c. creating a summary table of the 11 stages

   d. drawing a line graph to illustrate the 11 stages

J. EXPLORING IDEAS THROUGH DISCUSSION AND WRITING

1. You have probably watched "viral" videos on the Web—that is, videos that have become unexpectedly popular. How do these videos compare to the professional videography you see on the nightly news? How are they similar? How are they different?

2. What do you see as the benefits of allowing average citizens to take part in reporting the news? What are the possible drawbacks?

K. BEYOND THE CLASSROOM TO THE WEB

*Visit YouTube (**http://www.youtube.com**) and search for videos about something that is currently in the news—for example, a local election or other news item. Watch several of the videos. Which were produced professionally? Which were produced by amateurs? How can you tell the difference? What, if anything, did you learn from the comments on each video? Try to come up with different classifications for at least five videos you see, for example, a professional video shot by a TV station or an amateur video shot by a bystander at an event.*

1. _____

   _____

2. _____

3. _____

4. _____

5. _____

TRACKING
YOUR
PROGRESS

Selection 5

Section	Number Correct		Score
A. Thesis and Main Ideas (6 items)	_____	×3	_____
B. Details (8 items)	_____	×2	_____
C. Organization and Transitions (5 items)	_____	×2	_____
E. Reading and Thinking Visually (2 items)	_____	×4	_____
F. Implied Meanings (7 items)	_____	×2	_____
G. Thinking Critically (8 items)	_____	×2	_____
H. Vocabulary	_____		_____
Context (6 items)	_____	×2	_____
Word Parts (3 items)	_____	×2	_____
		TOTAL SCORE	_____ %

SELECTION 6

Relationships and Technology

Joseph A. DeVito

Textbook Excerpt
Contemporary
Issues Reading

Taken from a textbook titled *Interpersonal Messages: Communication and Relationship Skills,* this reading selection discusses the influence of technology on interpersonal relationships.

PREVIEWING THE READING

Using the steps listed on page 36, preview the reading selection. When you have finished, complete the following items.

1. The subject of this selection is _____.

2. List two questions you expect to be able to answer after reading this selection:

   a. _____

   b. _____

 MAKING CONNECTIONS

How do you typically use the Internet? Estimate what percentage of the total amount of time you spend on the Internet is spent in each of the following categories: social, work, school, entertainment, and news.

READING TIP

As you read, be sure to highlight the advantages and disadvantages of online relationships.

Relationships and Technology

1   Perhaps even more obvious than culture is the influence of technology on interpersonal relationships. Clearly, online interpersonal relationships are on the increase. The number of Internet users is rapidly increasing, and commercial websites devoted to helping people meet other people are proliferating, making it especially easy to develop online relationships. Such websites as spark.com (www.spark.com), Friend

Finder (www.friendfinder.com), Date (www.date.com), Match (www.match.com), Lavalife (www.lavalife.com), and Where Singles Meet (www.wheresinglesmeet.com) number their members in the millions, making it especially likely that you'll find someone you'd enjoy dating.

2   And not surprisingly, there are websites (for example, www.comparedatingweb-sites.com and www.homeandfamilyreview.com/dating.htm) that offer comparisons of the various dating websites, distinguishing between those that are best for seri-ous daters who are looking for lifetime commitment from those that are for people who want to find someone for casual dating. Lavalife, for example, has a pull down menu where you can indicate whether you want a casual date, a relationship, or an intimate encounter. And of course there are dating websites for different **affectional orientations** and different religious preferences.

affectional orientation
an alternative term for sexual or romantic orientation

3   Some dating websites—eharmony.com and perfectmatch.com are perhaps the most notable—have members complete extensive scientific questionnaires about their preferences and personalities which helps further in successfully matching people.

4   Some of these websites, for example, Friend Finder, give free trials so you can test the systems before registering or subscribing. And, to make these websites even more inviting, many of them offer chat rooms, dating and relationship advice, news-letters, and self-tests about love, relationships and dating.

5   Clearly, many people are turning to the Internet to find a friend or romantic part-ner. And, as you probably know, college students are making the most of sites such as Facebook.com and MySpace.com to meet other students on their own campus. In one study of MOOs (online role-playing games), 93.6 percent of the users formed ongoing friendships and romantic relationships. Some people use the Internet as their only means of interaction; others use it as a way of begining a relationship and intend to supplement computer talk later with photographs, phone calls, and face-to-face meetings. Interestingly, a *New York Times* survey found that by 2003 online dating was losing its earlier stigma as a last resort for losers.

6   Note that the importance of physical attractiveness enters the face-to-face rela-tionship through nonverbal cues—you see the person's eyes, face, body—and you perceive such attractiveness immediately. In online relationships, just a few years ago, physical attractiveness could have only been signaled through words and descrip-tions. And in this situation the face-to-face encounter favored those who were physi-cally attractive, whereas the online encounter favored those who were verbally adept at self-presentation. Today, with the numerous social networks such as MySpace, you can post your photo and reveal your attractiveness. Many of the online dating services (such as Friend Finder) now provide you with opportunities to not only post your photograph but also a voice introduction. Of course you still reveal more of yourself in face-to-face encounters, but the differences are clearly diminishing. Table A (p. 296) provides one example of the stages of Internet relationships.

7   Other research on Internet use finds that a large majority of users form new acquaintances, friendships, and romantic partnerships through the Internet. One study, published in 1996 found that almost two-thirds of newsgroup users had formed new relationships with someone they met online. Almost one-third said

TABLE A ONLINE RELATIONSHIP STAGES

This table represents one attempt to identify the stages that people go through in Internet relationships. As you read down the table, consider how accurately this represents what you know of online relationships. How would you describe the way Internet relationships develop?

STAGE	BEHAVIOR
1. Curiosity	You explore and search for individuals through chat rooms and other online sources.
2. Investigation	You find out information about the individual.
3. Testing	You introduce various topics, looking for common ground.
4. Increasing frequency of contact	You increase the breadth and depth of your relationship.
5. Anticipation	You anticipate face-to-face interaction and wonder what that will bring.
6. Fantasy integration	You create a fantasy of what the person looks like and how the person behaves.
7. Face-to-face meeting	You meet face-to-face, and reality and fantasy meet.
8. Reconfiguration	You adjust the fantasy to the reality and may decide to end the relationship or to pursue it more vigorously.
9. Already separated	If you decide to maintain the relationship, you explore ways you can accomplish this.
10. Long-term relationship	You negotiate the new relationship, whether it will be maintained in its online form or in a new face-to-face form.

Source: This table is adapted from Leonard J. Shedletsky and Joan E. Aitken, *Human Communication on the Internet.* Published by Allyn and Bacon, Boston, MA. Copyright © by Pearson Education. By permission of the publisher. Adapted by permission of the publisher.

that they communicated with their partner at least three or four times a week; more than half communicated on a weekly basis. And, a study published in 2006 found that 74 percent of Internet users who identify themselves as single and looking for romantic partners used the Internet for this purpose.

8   Women, it seems, are more likely to form relationships on the Internet than men. An early study showed that about 72 percent of women and 55 percent of men had formed personal relationships online. And women are more likely to use the Internet to deepen their interpersonal relationships.

9   As relationships develop on the Internet, network convergence occurs; that is, as a relationship between two people develops, they begin to share their network of other communicators with each other. This, of course, is similar to relationships formed through face-to-face contact. Online work groups also are on the increase and have been found to be more task oriented and more efficient than face-to-face groups. Online groups also provide a sense of belonging that may once have been thought possible only through face-to-face interactions.

Advantages of Online Relationships

10   There are many advantages to establishing relationships online. For example, online relationships are safe in terms of avoiding the potential for physical violence or sexually transmitted diseases. Unlike relationships established in face-to-face encounters, in which physical appearance tends to outweigh personality, relationships formed through Internet communication focus on your inner qualities first. Rapport and mutual self-disclosure become more important than physical attractiveness in promoting intimacy. And, contrary to some popular opinions, online relationships rely just as heavily on the ideals of trust, honesty, and commitment as do face-to-face relationships. Friendship and romantic interaction on the Internet are a natural boon to shut-ins and extremely shy people, for whom traditional ways of meeting someone are often difficult. Computer talk is empowering for those with "physical disabilities or disfigurements," for whom face-to-face interactions often are superficial and often end with withdrawal. By eliminating the physical cues, computer talk equalizes the interaction and doesn't put the disfigured person, for example, at an immediate disadvantage in a society in which physical attractiveness is so highly valued. On the Internet you're free to reveal as much or as little about your physical self as you wish, when you wish.

11   Another obvious advantage is that the number of people you can reach is so vast that it's relatively easy to find someone who matches what you're looking for. The situation is like finding a book that covers just what you need from a library of millions of volumes rather than from a collection holding only several thousand.

Disadvantages of Online Relationships

12   Of course, online relationships also have their disadvantages. For one thing, in many situations you can't see the other person. Unless you use a service that enables

"People are more frightened of being lonely than of being hungry, or being deprived of sleep, or having their sexual needs unfulfilled."—Fried Fromm Reichman

you to include photos or exchange photos or meet face-to-face, you won't know what the person looks like. Even if photos are posted or exchanged, how certain can you be that the photos are of the person or that they were taken recently? In addition, in most situations you can't hear the person's voice and this too hinders you as you seek to develop a total picture of the other person. Of course, you can always add an occasional phone call to give you this added information.

13   Online, people can present a false self with little chance of detection. For example, minors may present themselves as adults, and adults may present themselves as children in order to conduct illicit and illegal sexual communications and, perhaps, arrange meetings. Similarly, people can present themselves as poor when they're rich, as mature when they're immature, as serious and committed when they're just enjoying the online experience. Although people can also misrepresent themselves in face-to-face relationships, the fact that it's easier to do online probably accounts for greater frequency of misrepresentation in computer relationships.

14   Another potential disadvantage—though some might argue it is actually an advantage—is that computer interactions may become all-consuming and may substitute for face-to-face interpersonal relationships in a person's life.

15   Perhaps the clearest finding that emerges from all the research on face-to-face and online relationships is that people will seek out and find the relationship that works best for them at a given stage in their lives. For some that relationship will be online, for others face-to-face, for still others a combination. And just as people change, their relationship needs and wants also change, what works now may not work two years from now, and what doesn't work now may be exactly right in a few years.

Source: From DeVito, Joseph A. *Interpersonal Messages: Communication and Relationship Skills,* 1e. Published by Allyn and Bacon, Boston, MA. Copyright © 2008 by Pearson Education. Reprinted by permission of the publisher.

A. UNDERSTANDING THE THESIS AND OTHER MAIN IDEAS

Select the best answer.

_____ 1. The author's primary purpose in this selection is to

   a. caution people to stay away from online relationships.

   b. promote specific Web sites for online relationships.

   c. describe how technology affects interpersonal relationships.

   d. identify cultural factors that influence interpersonal relationships.

_____ 2. The main idea of paragraph 1 is that

   a. culture has a major impact on interpersonal relationships.

   b. the number of Internet users is rapidly increasing.

   c. some Web sites are especially good at helping people meet.

   d. online interpersonal relationships are on the increase.

_____ 3. The main idea of paragraph 5 is expressed in the
   a. first sentence.
   b. second sentence.
   c. third sentence.
   d. last sentence.

_____ 4. The topic of paragraph 10 is
   a. online relationships.
   b. physical appearance.
   c. face-to-face interactions.
   d. self-disclosure.

_____ 5. The main idea of paragraph 12 is that online it is easy for people to
   a. establish meaningful relationships.
   b. detect misinformation about others.
   c. find someone who matches their needs.
   d. misrepresent themselves.

_____ 6. According to the selection, "network convergence" takes place when two people in an online relationship begin to
   a. look for common ground on a variety of topics.
   b. make plans to meet in person.
   c. share their network of other communicators.
   d. decide whether to continue the relationship.

B. IDENTIFYING DETAILS

Select the best answer.

_____ 1. According to the selection, the term MOOs refers to online
   a. newsgroups.
   b. dating services.
   c. role-playing games.
   d. chat rooms.

_____ 2. All of the following statements about online relationships are true *except*
   a. Men are more likely than women to form online relationships.
   b. Women are more likely than men to use the Internet to deepen their interpersonal relationships.
   c. Online work groups are more task oriented and more efficient than face-to-face groups.
   d. Online groups provide a sense of belonging for their members.

Based on the examples given in the selection, match each Web site in Column A with the description that corresponds to it in Column B.

Column A	Column B
_____ 3. friendfinder.com	a. provides comparisons of the various dating Web sites
_____ 4. lavalife.com	b. has a pull-down menu so users can indicate the type of relationship they seek
_____ 5. eharmony.com	c. allows users to post photographs and voice introductions
_____ 6. homeandfamilyreview .com	d. has members complete scientific questionnaires about their preferences and personalities

C. RECOGNIZING METHODS OF ORGANIZATION AND TRANSITIONS

Complete the following statements by filling in the blanks.

In paragraph 6, the author uses the _____ organizational pattern to discuss the importance of physical appearance in face-to-face encounters versus online relationships. A transitional word that signals this pattern is _____.

D. REVIEWING AND ORGANIZING IDEAS: MAPPING

Complete the following map of paragraphs 10–14 by filling in the blanks.

ONLINE RELATIONSHIPS

ADVANTAGES

1. The potential for _____ _____ or sexually transmitted diseases is avoided.

2. The focus is on _____ rather than physical appearance.

3. Computer talk empowers those for whom traditional ways of meeting are difficult (for example, _____ _____).

4. Because such a huge number of people can be reached, it is relatively easy to find a match.

DISADVANTAGES

1. Many times you will not be able to see what the person looks like.

2. It is hard to form a total picture of someone without seeing or hearing him or her.

3. People may _____ _____ (for example, minors posing as adults or adults posing as children).

4. Computer interactions may become _____ and replace _____.

E. READING AND THINKING VISUALLY

Select the best answer.

_____ 1. Review the photo and caption included with the reading. By including this photo, the author implies that _____ is one of the most common reasons people seek online relationships.

    a. too much free time

    b. loneliness

    c. the desire to get married

    d. boredom

_____ 2. Review Table A, "Online Relationship Stages." In which state do two people adjust their expectations of the other person in the relationship and determine whether or not to continue it?

    a. anticipation

    b. testing

    c. reconfiguration

    d. fantasy integration

F. FIGURING OUT IMPLIED MEANINGS

Indicate whether each statement is true (T) or false (F).

_____ 1. Dating Web sites are designed for people who want a casual relationship only.

_____ 2. Many single Internet users look online for romantic partners.

_____ 3. For many people, online relationships are preferable to face-to-face interactions.

_____ 4. It can be inferred that most people looking for an online relationship are unconcerned about physical appearance.

G. THINKING CRITICALLY

Select the best answer.

_____ 1. The author's tone can best be described as

    a. judgmental.

    b. lighthearted.

    c. concerned.

    d. objective.

_____ 2. The primary purpose of Table A is to
   a. compare the progression of online relationships with relationships based on traditional ways of meeting.
   b. recommend a series of steps for people who are thinking about entering an online relationship.
   c. identify the stages that people often go through in online relationships.
   d. describe acceptable and unacceptable behaviors for online dating.

_____ 3. Which one of the following words has a negative connotation?
   a. self-disclosure
   b. task oriented
   c. interactions
   d. disfigurements

_____ 4. The author supports his thesis by doing all of the following *except*
   a. giving examples and illustrations.
   b. describing his personal experience.
   c. citing research evidence.
   d. providing statistical support.

_____ 5. When the author states that "computer talk equalizes the interaction" (paragraph 10), he means that
   a. even people with limited technological skill can meet others online.
   b. people are more likely to be honest with each other online.
   c. people with physical issues are not at a disadvantage online.
   d. geographic distances do not matter in online relationships.

H. BUILDING VOCABULARY

Context

Using context and a dictionary, if necessary, determine the meaning of each word as it is used in the selection.

_____ 1. proliferating (paragraph 1)
   a. ending
   b. multiplying
   c. altering
   d. continuing

_____ 2. stigma (paragraph 5)

    a. shame

    b. acceptance

    c. positive sign

    d. substitute

_____ 3. adept (paragraph 6)

    a. useless

    b. obvious

    c. skillful

    d. selfish

_____ 4. rapport (paragraph 10)

    a. information

    b. connection

    c. privacy

    d. safety

_____ 5. boon (paragraph 10)

    a. sound

    b. mistake

    c. emotion

    d. benefit

_____ 6. hinders (paragraph 12)

    a. invites in

    b. gets in the way

    c. pushes out

    d. delivers to

Word Parts

> ### A REVIEW OF PREFIXES
> **NON-** means *not*
> **IL-** means *not*
> **SUPER-** means *above*
> **MIS-** means *wrongly*

Match each word in Column A with its meaning in Column B. Write your answers in the spaces provided.

Column A

_____ 1. nonverbal

_____ 2. superficial

_____ 3. illicit

_____ 4. misrepresent

Column B

a. on the surface

b. give wrong or misleading information

c. not spoken

d. not permitted

I. SELECTING A LEARNING/STUDY STRATEGY

Evaluate the effectiveness of the map you completed showing the advantages and disadvantages of online relationships. How else might you organize the material in this selection to study for an exam?

J. EXPLORING IDEAS THROUGH DISCUSSION AND WRITING

1. What do you think of online relationships? If you have met people online, either for friendship or a romantic relationship, has your experience generally been positive or negative? Explain your answer.

2. Make a prediction about the future of online dating. Do you think the current trend will continue? Why or why not?

3. Reread Table A. Discuss whether the table accurately represents what you know about online relationships, and answer the question posed by the author in the table's caption: How would you describe the way Internet relationships develop?

4. Discuss the perception of online dating as "a last resort for losers" (paragraph 5). Do you agree with the 2003 *New York Times* survey that the stigma is disappearing?

K. BEYOND THE CLASSROOM TO THE WEB

Read these online dating tips from a university counseling center: **http://www.uwec.edu/counsel/pubs/datingonline.htm.** *Prepare a speech for new students at your school about online dating using this page, the reading, and other information from your own experience.*

TRACKING
YOUR
PROGRESS

Selection 6

Section	Number Correct	Score
A. Thesis and Main Ideas (6 items)	_____ ×4	_____
B. Details (6 items)	_____ ×3	_____
C. Organization and Transitions (2 items)	_____ ×2	_____
E. Reading and Thinking Visually (2 items)	_____ ×1	_____
F. Implied Meanings (4 items)	_____ ×3	_____
G. Thinking Critically (5 items)	_____ ×4	_____
H. Vocabulary		
Context (6 items)	_____ ×2	_____
Word Parts (4 items)	_____ ×2	_____
	TOTAL SCORE	_____ %

13 Arts/Humanities/Literature

The **humanities and arts** are areas of knowledge concerned with human thoughts and ideas and their creative expression in written, visual, or auditory form. They deal with large, global issues such as "What is worthwhile in life?" "What is beautiful?" and "What is the meaning of human existence?" Works of art and literature are creative records of the thoughts, feelings, emotions, or experiences of other people. By studying art and reading literature you can learn about yourself and understand both joyful and painful experiences without going through them yourself. "Issue-Oriented and Street Art" focuses on two forms of modern art. In the short story "The Hockey Sweater" a young Canadian boy who loves hockey is forced to wear a rival team's jersey. In the poem "Picnic, Lightning" you share the experience of a woman exploring issues of life and death.

Use the following tips when reading and studying in the arts, humanities, and literature.

TIPS FOR READING IN THE ARTS/ HUMANITIES/ LITERATURE

- **Focus on values.** Ask yourself why the work or piece is valuable and important. In "Issue-Oriented and Street Art" you will explore new art forms and their contributions to the world of art.

- **Pay attention to the medium.** Words, sound, music, canvas, and clay are all means through which artistic expression occurs. Readings in this chapter are concerned with words and art. Three different vehicles are used in this chapter to express meaning through words: a textbook excerpt, a short story, and a poem.

- **Look for a message or an interpretation.** Works of art and literature express meaning or create a feeling or impression. "Picnic, Lightning" examines important issues surrounding life and death. As you read "The Hockey Sweater" try to discover what Carrier is saying about childhood issues and the importance of sports.

- **Read literature slowly and carefully.** Rereading may be necessary. Pay attention to the writer's choice of words, descriptions, comparisons, and arrangement of ideas. You should definitely read poetry several times.

SELECTION 7 | Issue-Oriented and Street Art
Patrick Frank

Textbook
Excerpt

Taken from a textbook titled *Prebles' Artforms: An Introduction to the Visual Arts*, this reading selection describes two movements of the present generation of modern artists.

PREVIEWING THE READING

Using the steps listed on page 36, preview the reading selection. When you have finished, complete the following items.

1. The topic of this selection is _____.

2. The two categories of modern art that are discussed in this selection are:

   a. _____

   b. _____

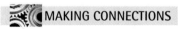

MAKING CONNECTIONS

Think about how you define art. Then consider street art and graffiti that you have seen. Would you consider them art?

READING TIP

Take time to examine the different works of modern art included in this selection as you read about the artists who created them.

Issue-Oriented and Street Art

1   Today the public accepts most modern art. Exhibitions of work by such former rule-breaking radicals as Henri Matisse, Paul Gauguin, Paul Cézanne, and Claude Monet fill museums with visitors. Nine of the ten most expensive paintings ever sold at auction are modern works (three each by Picasso and van Gogh; one each by Cézanne, Renoir, and Jackson Pollock). The modern-style Vietnam Veterans Memorial is a national shrine. Modern art is no longer controversial.

2   The impact of this situation is not yet clear. Art of our own time is always the most difficult to evaluate. In general, most artists of the present generation do not appear intent on perfecting form, creating beauty, or fine-tuning their sense of sight. They mostly want to comment on life in all of its aspects. They want to create work that illuminates the relationships between what we see and how we think. Rather than being objects of timeless beauty, most art since the 1980s consists of objects laden with information about the period in which we live. This article will present two movements of the present generation.

Issue-Oriented Art

aesthetic concerned with what is beautiful or pleasing in appearance

3   Many artists in the past twenty years have sought to link their art to current social questions. Issue-oriented artists believe that if they limit their art to **aesthetic** matters, then their work will be only a distraction from pressing problems. Furthermore, they recognize that what we see influences how we think, and they do not want to miss an opportunity to influence both.

4   Photographer Richard Misrach presents new kinds of landscape in new ways. His photograph SUBMERGED LAMPPOST, SALTON SEA captures the silent yet ironic beauty of a small town in California that was flooded by a misguided irrigation system. In other works he has documented in chilling detail the bloated carcasses of animals killed on military proving grounds in Nevada. His brand of nature photography is the opposite of the common calendars that include soothing views of pristine landscapes. He wants us to know that such scenes are fast disappearing.

5   Barbara Kruger was trained as a magazine designer, and this profession shows in her piece UNTITLED (I SHOP THEREFORE I AM). She invented the slogan, which sounds as though it came from advertising. The position of the hand, too, looks like it came from an ad for aspirin or sleeping medication. Do our products define us? Are we what we shop for? Often we buy a product because of what it will say about us and not for the thing itself.

Barbara Kruger. *Untitled (I Shop Therefore I Am)*. 1987. Photographic silkscreen/vinyl. 111" × 113". Courtesy Mary Boone Gallery, New York.

silkscreened
printed using a   6
special stencil
process

installation
a work of art made
up of multiple
components, often
in different media,
and exhibited in
an arrangement
specified by the
artist

7

These are some of the messages present in this simple yet fascinating work. Perhaps its ultimate irony is that the artist had it **silkscreened** onto a shopping bag.

Artists who create works about racism and class bias show how common practices of museum display contribute to such problems. In 1992, the Maryland Historical Society invited African-American artist Fred Wilson to rearrange the exhibits on one floor to create an **installation** called MINING THE MUSEUM. He spent a year preparing for the show, rummaging through the Society's holdings and documentary records; the results were surprising. He found no portraits, for example, of noted African-American Marylanders Benjamin Banneker (who laid out the boundaries of the District of Columbia), Frederick Douglass (noted abolitionist and journalist), or Harriet Tubman (founder of the Underground Railroad). He found instead busts of Henry Clay, Andrew Jackson, and Napoleon Bonaparte, none of whom ever lived in Maryland. He exhibited those three busts next to three empty pedestals to symbolize the missing African Americans. He set out a display of Colonial Maryland silverware and tea utensils, and included a pair of slave shackles. This lesser-known form of metalwork was perhaps equally vital to the functioning of nineteenth-century Maryland. He dusted off the Society's collection of wooden cigar-store Indians and stood them, backs to viewers, facing photographs of real Native Americans who lived in Maryland. In an accompanying exhibition brochure he wrote that a museum should be a place that can make you think. When MINING THE MUSEUM went on display, attendance records soared.

The Swiss-born Thomas Hirschhorn took up the issue of the Iraq war, but only indirectly, in the context of today's media-saturated society. His 2006 installation

Fred Wilson. *Mining the Museum.* 1992. Installation. Cigar-store Indians facing photographs of Native American Marylanders. Museum and Library of History. Photograph: Jeff D. Goldblum.

SUPERFICIAL ENGAGEMENT filled the entire gallery space with a dizzying array of objects that resembled a parade float on drugs, or a cross between an insane asylum and a grocery store. Photos of mangled war dead competed for space with coffins, nail-studded mannequins, blaring headlines, and reproductions of abstract artworks. The nailed bodies refer to traditional African magic sculptures, and the abstract art was mostly copied from the Austrian mystic Emma Kunz in what the artist called "friendly piracy." The headlines shout the aimless alarmism of cable news channels: "Decision Time Approaches," "Broken Borders," "An Assault on Hypocrisy," "The Real Crisis." The artist used only cheap materials (cardboard, plastic, plywood, package tape) in an effort to avoid art-world pretense and make it more accessible. He said of his brash style, "Art is a tool, a tool to encounter the world, to confront the reality and the time I am living in." The shrill volume of this exhibition only paralleled the strident intensity of today's news, where a disaster might follow a fashion show. At the opening reception, the artist provided hammers and screwdrivers, and the crowd joined in attaching nails and screws, thus finishing the piece.

Street Art

8   In the late 1990s, many galleries in various cities began to exhibit work by artists who had previously made illegal graffiti. Many of these "street artists" were based in the culture of skateboards and Punk music, and they used materials bought at the hardware store rather than the art supply house. Their creations were only rarely related to gang-oriented graffiti, which usually marks out territories of influence. Nor were they autobiographical or personal. Rather, the street artists made much

Shepard Fairey. *Revolution Girl.* 2006. Screenprinted temporary mural. 16' × 19'. Outdoor location, Los Angeles, Obey Giant Art, CA.

broader statements about themselves and the world in a language that was widely understandable. The ancestors of the movement in the 1980s were Keith Haring and Jean-Michel Basquiat, both of whom worked illegally for years before exhibiting in galleries. By the turn of the twenty-first century, Street Art was a recognized movement, and most of its main practitioners work both indoors and out.

9   The career of Shepard Fairey is exemplary. He studied at the Rhode Island School of Design, but was never satisfied in the art world, which seemed to him closed-off and elitist. He began working outdoors, and quickly acquired notoriety for posting dozens of signs and stickers with the single word "Obey" below the ominous-looking face of wrestler Andre the Giant. His vocabulary soon expanded to include advertising symbols, propaganda posters, and currency, even as the scale of his work increased to billboard size.

10   His 2006 work REVOLUTION GIRL is an anti-war mural created on a legal wall for a three-month show in West Hollywood. The dominant motif is a huge female Communist soldier from the Vietnam War that the artist borrowed from Chinese propaganda, but her rifle has a flower protruding; her weapon has become an elaborate vase. Other motifs from Chinese propaganda decorate the center right, repurposed for a peace campaign. In the lower corner, posters of a female face with flowery hair symbolize nurturing. The message of the mural is anti-war, but the artist made the statement positive rather than negative, expressing the hope that we can convert our weapons into flower holders. His friend and fellow street artist Blake Marquis provided the vivid leafy patterns at the left. We see the artist himself in the foreground.

11   Some of today's most skillful street art is created by Swoon, a woman who uses the pseudonym to avoid prosecution. She carves large linoleum blocks and makes life-sized relief prints from them, usually portraits of everyday people. She prints them on large sheets of cheap (usually recycled) newsprint and pastes them on urban walls, beginning on the Lower East Side of Manhattan but now in cities on every continent. Her UNTITLED installation at Deitch Projects was a recent indoor work. Against objections that her work is mostly illegal, she replies that her creations are far easier to look at than advertising, that they lack any persuasive agenda, and that they glorify common people. Moreover, the newsprint that she uses decays over time so that her work is impermanent. Although she works mostly outdoors, she sometimes shows in galleries because, she admits, "I have to make a living," but she charges far less for her work than most other artists of wide repute.

12   Probably the most famous street artist is Banksy (who also uses a pseudonym). He placed his own art in the collections of several major museums in 2005 by merely entering the galleries and sticking his pieces to the wall. His street graffiti is generally witty, as we see in his GRAFFITI REMOVAL HOTLINE, PENTONVILLE ROAD. There is no such thing as a graffiti removal hotline; the artist stenciled the words and then created the youth who seems to paint out the phone number. Banksy is currently one of the most popular artists in England, and many of his outdoor works have been preserved. When a prominent work of his was recently defaced by another graffiti artist, protests ensued and the defacer was arrested for vandalism! Thus street artists often blur the line between legal and illegal.

Swoon. *Untitled.* 2005.
Linoleum cut,
newsprint, ink, and wheat
paste. Variable dimensions.
Deitch Projects, New York.

A. UNDERSTANDING THE THESIS AND OTHER MAIN IDEAS

Select the best answer.

_____ 1. The author's primary purpose in this selection is to

    a. compare and contrast modern and traditional art.

    b. discuss historical events that made an impact on modern art.

    c. explore the effects of culture on art in different parts of the world.

    d. describe two types of modern art and the artists who represent each.

_____ 2. The main idea of paragraph 1 is that

    a. modern art will always be controversial.

    b. modern artists are as popular as traditional masters.

    c. most modern art has become acceptable to the public.

    d. the most expensive paintings sold at auction are modern works.

_____ 3. The main idea of paragraph 6 is expressed in the

    a. first sentence only.

    b. first and last sentences.

    c. second sentence.

    d. third sentence.

_____ 4. The topic of paragraph 7 is

    a. the Iraq war.

    b. modern media.

    c. Thomas Hirschhorn's art.

    d. the Austrian mystic Emma Kunz.

_____ 5. The main idea of paragraph 8 is that street art became an acceptable form because

    a. the artists used high-quality materials from renowned art supply stores.

    b. gangs stopped using street art to mark out their territories of influence.

    c. most street artists began working primarily indoors rather than outdoors.

    d. the art consisted of broad statements about the artists and about the world.

B. IDENTIFYING DETAILS

Select the best answer.

_____ 1. According to the selection, most artists of the present generation are intent on

    a. perfecting form.

    b. creating objects of beauty.

    c. fine-tuning their sense of sight.

    d. commenting on life in all of its aspects.

_____ 2. Issue-oriented artists link their art to

    a. current social questions.

    b. soothing views of nature.

    c. autobiographical statements.

    d. the culture of skateboards and punk music.

_____ 3. To illustrate racism, artist Fred Wilson did all of the following in his installation _Mining the Museum except_

    a. exhibit busts of white non-Marylanders next to empty pedestals symbolizing famous African American Marylanders.

    b. include a pair of slave shackles along with silverware and tea utensils in a display of Colonial Maryland metalwork.

    c. provide hammers and screwdrivers to museum visitors so they could join in completing the installation.

    d. place a collection of wooden cigar-store Indians facing photographs of Native American Marylanders.

_____ 4. The two pieces of antiwar art in the selection were created by the artists

    a. Misrach and Kruger.

    b. Wilson and Hirschhorn.

    c. Hirschhorn and Fairey.

    d. Haring and Basquiat.

_____ 5. The street artist who placed his own work in major museums by walking in and sticking his pieces to the gallery walls is

a. Banksy.

b. Swoon.

c. Shepard Fairey.

d. Jackson Pollock.

C. RECOGNIZING METHODS OF ORGANIZATION AND TRANSITIONS

Select the best answer.

_____ 1. In paragraph 6, the organizational pattern that is used to show the different elements of Fred Wilson's installation at the Maryland Historical Society is

a. comparison and contrast.   c. chronological order.

b. definition.   d. cause and effect.

_____ 2. A word or phrase in paragraph 6 that signals the organizational pattern is

a. In 1992.   c. instead.

b. the results.   d. next.

D. REVIEWING AND ORGANIZING IDEAS: MAPPING

Complete the following map of paragraphs 3–7 by filling in the blanks.

Issue-Oriented Art		
Artist	**Work**	**Purpose/Focus**
_____	Nature photography: *Submerged Lamppost, Salton Sea*	How humans affect _____, in the form of disappearing landscapes
Barbara Kruger	Photographic silk-screen: _____ _____	How we define ourselves and what our purchases say about us
Fred Wilson	Installation: _____	How museum displays contribute to _____
_____	Installation: _____ _____	Antiwar in the context of a modern society dominated by news and media

E. READING AND THINKING VISUALLY

Select the best answer.

_____ 1. Review the photo of *Mining the Museum* on page 309. By positioning the backs of the Native Americans facing viewers, the artist implies that

  a. their feathered headdresses were not an essential part of their culture.

  b. Maryland was not home to a significant number of Native Americans.

  c. the contributions of Native Americans are largely ignored or dismissed.

  d. tobacco companies should compensate Native Americans for the use of their images in advertising.

_____ 2. All of the following visual elements are common to both Swoon's *Untitled* and Banksey's *Graffiti Removal Hotline except*

  a. graffiti.

  b. children.

  c. a single bold color among other muted colors.

  d. birds.

_____ 3. Based on the author's inclusion of *Revolution Girl* and *Graffiti Removal Hotline* with the reading, it is safe to assume that the author is a fan of

  a. female artists.

  b. outdoor art.

  c. small-scale art.

  d. abstract art.

F. FIGURING OUT IMPLIED MEANINGS

Each of the following boldfaced words has a strong positive or negative connotation (shade of meaning). Make inferences by indicating whether the word creates a positive (P) or negative (N) image for the reader.

_____ 1. "Rather than being objects of timeless **beauty** . . ." (paragraph 2)

_____ 2. ". . . he has documented in **chilling** detail" (paragraph 4)

_____ 3. ". . . calendars that include **soothing** views" (paragraph 4)

_____ 4. ". . . a **dizzying** array of objects" (paragraph 7)

_____ 5. "The **shrill** volume of this exhibition . . ." (paragraph 7)

G. THINKING CRITICALLY

Select the best answer.

_____ 1. The tone of the reading can best be described as
   a. critical.
   b. informative.
   c. amused.
   d. distressed.

_____ 2. The central thesis is supported primarily by
   a. research evidence.
   b. cause and effect relationships.
   c. descriptions and examples.
   d. personal experience.

_____ 3. Of the following statements from paragraph 5, the only one that does not contain an opinion is
   a. "Barbara Kruger was trained as a magazine designer . . ."
   b. "The position of the hand, too, looks like it came from an ad for aspirin or sleeping medication."
   c. "Often we buy a product because of what it will say about us and not for the thing itself."
   d. "These are some of the messages present in this simple yet fascinating work."

_____ 4. Of the following statements from paragraph 7, the only one that does not contain an opinion is
   a. "His 2006 installation . . . filled the entire gallery space with a dizzying array of objects that resembled a parade float on drugs, or a cross between an insane asylum and a grocery store."
   b. "The headlines shout the aimless alarmism of cable news channels . . ."
   c. "The shrill volume of this exhibition only paralleled the strident intensity of today's news, where a disaster might follow a fashion show."
   d. "At the opening reception, the artist provided hammers and screw drivers, and the crowd joined in attaching nails and screws . . ."

_____ 5. In paragraph 7, the artist Thomas Hirschhorn uses the term "friendly piracy" to refer to the
   a. common theme of theft in his art.
   b. use of another person's ideas in his art.

c. high prices charged in some art galleries.

d. practice of using stolen materials to create art.

_____ 6. What do Kruger's *Untitled* and Fairey's *Revolution Girl* have in common?

a. Both make a political statement.

b. Both use words to help convey their message.

c. Both are displayed indoors.

d. Both rely on muted colors.

_____ 7. In Fairey's *Revolution Girl* the element that is out of place with the rest of the scene is

a. the woman's hat

b. the man in the background

c. the background pictures of other soldiers

d. the rose in the gun barrel.

H. BUILDING VOCABULARY

Context

Using context and a dictionary, if necessary, determine the meaning of each word as it is used in the selection.

_____ 1. pristine (paragraph 4)

a. private

b. untouched

c. valuable

d. useful

_____ 2. pretense (paragraph 7)

a. falseness

b. concern

c. excuse

d. function

_____ 3. brash (paragraph 7)

a. sharp

b. easy

c. daring

d. cheap

_____ 4. strident (paragraph 7)

    a. pleasant

    b. harsh

    c. obvious

    d. mild

_____ 5. motif (paragraph 10)

    a. memorable tune

    b. dominant theme

    c. strong argument

    d. logical evidence

_____ 6. repute (paragraph 11)

    a. fame

    b. similarity

    c. arrangement

    d. declaration

_____ 7. defaced (paragraph 12)

    a. added

    b. lost

    c. damaged

    d. created

Word Parts

A REVIEW OF PREFIXES AND SUFFIXES

MIS- means *wrongly*

IM- means *not*

PSEUDO- means *false*

-IST means *one who*

-ER means *one who*

-ARY means *pertaining to* or *referring to*

Match each word in Column A with its meaning in Column B. Write your answers in the spaces provided.

Column A	Column B
_____ 1. misguided	a. referring to a typical example
_____ 2. practitioner	b. false name
_____ 3. exemplary	c. wrongly or mistakenly undertaken
_____ 4. elitist	d. temporary; not permanent
_____ 5. pseudonym	e. one who practices an art or profession
_____ 6. impermanent	f. one who believes he or she is part of a superior or elite group

Unusual Words/Understanding Idioms

*Use the meaning given below to write a sentence using the **boldfaced** phrase.*

To **blur the line** (paragraph 12) between two separate things is to make it difficult to see the difference between the two.

Your sentence: _____

_____

I. SELECTING A LEARNING/STUDY STRATEGY

Using the map you completed for issue-oriented artists as a model, create a map based on the street artists described in paragraphs 8–12.

J. EXPLORING IDEAS THROUGH DISCUSSION AND WRITING

1. Evaluate the introduction to this selection. Did it capture your attention?

2. Write your own definition of art. Does it include modern art forms such as issue-oriented art and street art? Why or why not?

3. Choose one of the pieces of art included with the selection and write a paragraph about it. Begin with a description of the piece, followed by your own interpretation of what the artist was trying to say through that particular work. End the paragraph with your response to the piece of art, explaining whether it was positive or negative and why.

4. Did this selection make you curious about other types of modern art? Discuss the types of art that you find most (and least) appealing.

K. BEYOND THE CLASSROOM TO THE WEB

Explore the site for the Street Art exhibition at the Tate Modern in London: **http://www.tate.org.uk/modern/exhibitions/streetart/default.shtm.** *Write down the words that come into your head when you view the art. What is your opinion of street art? What is your opinion of a museum-sponsored street art exhibition? Write an editorial expressing these opinions.*

TRACKING YOUR PROGRESS

Selection 7

Section	Number Correct		Score
A. Thesis and Main Ideas (5 items)	_____	× 3	_____
B. Details (5 items)	_____	× 3	_____
C. Organization and Transitions (2 items)	_____	× 2	_____
E. Reading and Thinking Visually (3 items)	_____	× 1	_____
F. Implied Meanings (5 items)	_____	× 3	_____
G. Thinking Critically (7 items)	_____	× 3	_____
H. Vocabulary			
Context (7 items)	_____	× 3	_____
Word Parts (6 items)	_____	× 1	_____
	TOTAL SCORE		_____ %

SELECTION
8

The Hockey Sweater

Roch Carrier

Roch Carrier, the author of this short story, is a native of the Canadian province of Quebec. Although much of Canada uses English as its native language, French is the preferred language in Quebec, which has tried (unsuccessfully) to secede from Canada and become an independent country. The story describes hockey's influence on the lives of Canadian boys and what happens when the narrator's mother forces him to wear a rival team's jersey.

PREVIEWING THE READING

Short stories are not previewed in the same way as textbooks. For that reason, the headnote above gives you an overview of the plot. Based on the information in the headnote, write at least three questions you expect the story to answer.

a. _____

b. _____

c. _____

 ### MAKING CONNECTIONS

What role did sports play in your life when you were younger? What role do they play now? Were you ever fanatically devoted to one particular team or player?

READING TIP

As you read, notice that the author (an adult) is looking back on an experience from his boyhood. What does the adult see that the boy does not?

The Hockey Sweater

1   The winters of my childhood were long, long seasons. We lived in three places—the school, the church and the skating-rink—but our real life was on the skating-rink. Real battles were won on the skating-rink. Real strength appeared on the skating-rink. The real leaders showed themselves on the skating-rink. School was a sort of punishment. Parents always want to punish children and school is their most natural way of punishing us. However, school was also a quiet place where we could prepare

for the next hockey game, lay out our next strategies. As for church, we found there the tranquility of God: there we forgot school and dreamed about the next hockey game. Through our daydreams it might happen that we would recite a prayer: we would ask God to help us play as well as Maurice Richard.

2   We all wore the same uniform as he, the red, white and blue uniform of the Montreal Canadiens, the best hockey team in the world; we all combed our hair in the same style as Maurice Richard, and to keep it in place we used a sort of glue—a great deal of glue. We laced our skates like Maurice Richard, we taped our sticks like Maurice Richard. We cut all his pictures out of the papers. Truly, we knew everything about him.

3   On the ice, when the referee blew his whistle the two teams would rush at the puck; we were five Maurice Richards taking it away from five other Maurice Richards; we were ten players, all of us wearing with the same blazing enthusiasm the uniform of the Montreal Canadiens. On our backs, we all wore the famous number 9.

4   One day, my Montreal Canadiens sweater had become too small; then it got torn and had holes in it. My mother said: "If you wear that old sweater people are going to think we're poor!" Then she did what she did whenever we needed new clothes. She started to leaf through the catalogue the Eaton company sent us in the mail every year. My mother was proud. She didn't want to buy our clothes at the general store; the only things that were good enough for us were the latest styles from Eaton's catalogue. My mother didn't like the order forms included with the catalogue; they were written in English and she didn't understand a word of it. To order my hockey sweater, she did as she usually did; she took out her writing paper and wrote in her gentle schoolteacher's hand: "Cher **Monsieur** Eaton, Would you be kind enough to send me a Canadiens' sweater for my son who is ten years old and a little too tall for his age and **Docteur** Robitaille thinks he's a little too thin? I'm sending you three dollars and please send me what's left if there's anything left. I hope your wrapping will be better than last time."

Monsieur
Mister (French)

Docteur
Doctor (French)

5   Monsieur Eaton was quick to answer my mother's letter. Two weeks later we received the sweater. That day I had one of the greatest disappointments of my life! I would even

Roch Carrier as a boy in Quebec.

say that on that day I experienced a very great sorrow. Instead of the red, white and blue Montreal Canadiens sweater, Monsieur Eaton had sent us a blue and white sweater with a maple leaf on the front—the sweater of the Toronto Maple Leafs. I'd always worn the red, white and blue Montreal Canadiens sweater; all my friends wore the red, white and blue sweater; never had anyone in my village ever worn the Toronto sweater, never had we even seen a Toronto Maple Leafs sweater. Besides, the Toronto team was regularly trounced by the triumphant Canadiens. With tears in my eyes, I found the strength to say:

6   "I'll never wear that uniform."

7   "My boy, first you're going to try it on! If you make up your mind about things before you try, my boy, you won't go very far in this life."

8   My mother had pulled the blue and white Toronto Maple Leafs sweater over my shoulders and already my arms were inside the sleeves. She pulled the sweater down and carefully smoothed all the creases in the abominable maple leaf on which, right in the middle of my chest, were written the words "Toronto Maple Leafs." I wept.

9   "I'll never wear it."

10   "Why not? This sweater fits you . . . like a glove."

11   "Maurice Richard would never put it on his back."

12   "You aren't Maurice Richard. Anyway, it isn't what's on your back that counts, it's what you've got inside your head."

13   "You'll never put it in my head to wear a Toronto Maple Leafs sweater."

14   My mother sighed in despair and explained to me:

15   "If you don't keep this sweater which fits you perfectly I'll have to write to Monsieur Eaton and explain that you don't want to wear the Toronto sweater. Monsieur Eaton's an *Anglais*. He'll be insulted because he likes the Maple Leafs. And if he's insulted do you think he'll be in a hurry to answer us? Spring will be here and you won't have played a single game, just because you didn't want to wear that perfectly nice blue sweater."

Anglais
Englishman

16   So I was obliged to wear the Maple Leafs sweater. When I arrived on the rink, all the Maurice Richards in red, white and blue came up, one by one, to take a look. When the referee blew his whistle I went to take my usual position. The captain came and warned me I'd be better to stay on the forward line. A few minutes later the second line was called; I jumped onto the ice. The Maple Leafs sweater weighed on my shoulders like a mountain. The captain came and told me to wait; he'd need me later, on defense. By the third period I still hadn't played; one of the defensemen was hit in the nose with a stick and it was bleeding. I jumped on the ice: my moment had come! The referee blew his whistle; he gave me a penalty. He claimed I'd jumped on the ice when there were already five players. That was too much! It was unfair! It was persecution! It was because of my blue sweater! I struck my stick against the ice so hard it broke. Relieved, I bent down to pick up the debris. As I straightened up I saw the young vicar, on skates, before me.

17   "My child," he said, "just because you're wearing a new Toronto Maple Leafs sweater unlike the others, it doesn't mean you're going to make the laws around here. A proper young man doesn't lose his temper. Now take off your skates and go to the church and ask God to forgive you."

18   Wearing my Maple Leafs sweater I went to the church, where I prayed to God; I asked Him to send, as quickly as possible, moths that would eat up my Toronto Maple Leafs sweater.

A. UNDERSTANDING THE THESIS AND OTHER MAIN IDEAS

Select the best answer.

_____ 1. The central theme of "The Hockey Sweater" is that

    a. children must do everything in their power to resist peer pressure.

    b. parents must be careful not to force their children into doing things the children do not want to do.

    c. adults face a difficult challenge when they try to understand the way children think and behave.

    d. children are often single-minded, fixating on a single goal.

_____ 2. The author's primary purpose is to

    a. encourage children to obey their parents even when doing so will make them unpopular.

    b. provide a critical look at Canadian society and its obsession with hockey.

    c. recount a story from childhood that illustrates a characteristic of youth.

    d. give readers insight into the rivalry between the Canadiens and the Maple Leafs.

B. IDENTIFYING DETAILS

Select the best answer.

_____ 1. For the children in the story, the only place that really matters is

    a. their home.

    b. school.

    c. the hockey rink.

    d. church.

_____ 2. Which two colors make up the Maple Leafs' hockey uniform?

    a. white and blue

    b. green and yellow

    c. black and white

    d. red and white

_____ 3. In paragraph 15, the author's mother gets her son to wear the new hockey sweater by

    a. threatening to withhold his allowance.

     b. implying that failure to do so means he won't be able to play hockey the entire winter.

     c. suggesting that the boy's father will be very angry if the boy doesn't wear the sweater.

     d. telling him that she does not have the money to buy him a different hockey sweater.

_____ 4. According to the author, a parent's most natural form of punishing children is

     a. spanking them.

     b. sending them to live with relatives.

     c. making them go to school.

     d. refusing to speak with them.

_____ 5. The name of the author's doctor is

     a. Eaton.

     b. Maurice.

     c. Richard.

     d. Robitaille.

_____ 6. The hometown of the Canadiens is _____, while the hometown of the Maple Leafs is _____.

     a. Quebec, Alberta

     b. Montreal, Toronto

     c. Vancouver, Banff

     d. Edmonton, Ottawa

C. RECOGNIZING METHODS OF ORGANIZATION AND TRANSITIONS

Select the best answer.

_____ 1. What organizational pattern is used throughout the story?

     a. comparison and contrast

     b. chronological order

     c. classification

     d. cause and effect

_____ 2. The organizational pattern used in paragraph 15 is

     a. comparison and contrast

     b. classification

     c. cause and effect

     d. spatial order

List one transitional word that is used in each of the following paragraphs.

3. paragraph 1: _____

4. paragraph 4: _____

D. REVIEWING AND ORGANIZING IDEAS: SUMMARIZING

Use the following words and phrases to complete the summary of the story.

Canadiens	captain	catalogue	hockey stick	ice rink
Maple Leafs	Maurice Richard	moths	narrator	vicar

The story opens with the _____ talking about the role that hockey played in his life as a boy. All the boys wore the uniform of the Montreal _____, and they all idolized _____. Then, one day, the narrator's mother ordered a new sweater for him from a _____. He was horrified that the new sweater featured the logo and colors of the Toronto _____! At first he refused to wear it, but his mother made him try it on, and it fit him well. When he showed up at the _____, he believed that his _____ would not let him play because he was wearing the wrong sweater. In frustration, the narrator broke his _____ on the ice. The _____, who had witnessed the act, sent the narrator to church, where he prayed that _____ would eat up the detested sweater.

E. READING AND THINKING VISUALLY

Select the best answer.

_____   The photo included with the story on page 322 is in black and white. If the photo were in color, the colors of the boy's sweater would likely be:

a. light blue, black, and white

b. yellow, green, and black

c. red, orange, and yellow

d. blue, white, and red

F. FIGURING OUT IMPLIED MEANINGS

Indicate whether each statement is true (T) or false (F).

_____ 1. The number on Maurice Richard's hockey uniform was 5.

_____ 2. The author implies that the boys in the story greatly prefer the Canadiens over the Maple Leafs because the Canadiens won many more games.

_____ 3. The author believes that his hockey captain and teammates will not let him play because he is wearing an unacceptable hockey sweater.

_____ 4. The author speaks English, but his mother does not.

_____ 5. The author's mother makes him wear the Maple Leafs sweater even though it does not fit him very well.

_____ 6. Monsieur Eaton disregarded the mother's request and sent the wrong jersey.

_____ 7. By asking Monsieur Eaton to "send me what's left if there's anything left" in paragraph 4, the author's mother is implying that she'll accept any hockey sweater from the remaining inventory.

G. THINKING CRITICALLY

Select the best answer.

_____ 1. The overall tone of "The Hockey Sweater" is best described as:

a. critical.

b. nostalgic.

c. angry.

d. embarrassed.

_____ 2. In paragraph 4, the author writes, "One day, my Montreal Canadiens sweater had become too small; then it got torn and had holes in it." The author means that

a. he has outgrown his current hockey sweater.

b. he has not taken very good care of his hockey sweater.

c. he has gotten into fights with the boys on a rival team, who have torn his sweater.

d. his family was too poor to afford a better-fitting hockey sweater.

_____ 3. Based on the author's description of his mother and the letter she writes in paragraph 4, we can accurately describe her as all of the following, *except*

a. stubborn.

b. frugal.

c. foolish.

d. proud.

_____ 4. In general, the adults in the story are portrayed as

    a. cruel.

    b. authority figures.

    c. religious.

    d. sympathetic.

_____ 5. In paragraph 5, the author uses humorous _____ to describe how terrible the new hockey sweater made him feel.

    a. puns

    b. irony

    c. similes

    d. exaggeration

_____ 6. The phrase "weighed on my shoulders like a mountain" in paragraph 16 is an example of

    a. an expert opinion.

    b. a positive connotation.

    c. a cause-and-effect statement.

    d. a simile.

_____ 7. Although "The Hockey Sweater" is in many ways a tale of childhood, in some ways it is symbolic. The Montreal Canadiens uniform in this story can be considered a symbol of

    a. the huge amount of money that changes hands in professional sports.

    b. French-Canadian unity.

    c. the importance of teamwork and team solidarity.

    d. Canada's victory over the bitterly cold weather it experiences every winter.

H. BUILDING VOCABULARY

Context

Using context and a dictionary, if necessary, determine the meaning of each word as it is used in the selection.

_____ 1. tranquility (paragraph 1)

    a. strength

    b. peace

    c. isolation

    d. meaning

_____ 2. triumphant (paragraph 5)

     a. rich

     b. native

     c. handsome

     d. victorious

_____ 3. abominable (paragraph 8)

     a. huge

     b. blue

     c. hateful

     d. inappropriate

_____ 4. persecution (paragraph 16)

     a. unfairness

     b. against the rules

     c. untimely

     d. mistreatment

_____ 5. vicar (paragraph 16)

     a. clergyman

     b. janitor

     c. coach

     d. teacher

Word Parts

> **A REVIEW OF PREFIXES**
>
> **UNI-** means *one*

Use your knowledge of word parts and the review above to fill in the blank in the following sentence.

A *uniform* (paragraph 2) is _____ suit worn by all the people on a team.

I. SELECTING A LEARNING/STUDY STRATEGY

In preparation for a class discussion in a literature class, write a brief statement outlining the theme(s) of "The Hockey Sweater."

J. EXPLORING IDEAS THROUGH DISCUSSION AND WRITING

1. One of the themes running through the story is the way boys worship sports stars—in this case, the Canadian hockey player Maurice Richard. Who are today's sports heroes? What makes young people idolize them?

2. Athletes are not the only people whom children seek to emulate. Actors, singers, and TV personalities can also be role models. How would you define *role model?* What makes someone a good role model? What qualities would make someone a bad role model?

3. In the story, the adults tend to speak very wisely. Locate and discuss at least two lines (spoken by adults) that indicate their wisdom.

K. BEYOND THE CLASSROOM TO THE WEB

One way to approach literature is to learn more about its author. Often, biographical information about a writer can provide insight into his or her work and themes. Conduct a Web search for information about Roch Carrier and share at least two interesting facts about him with your classmates. For example, you may be interested to know that Maurice Richard himself read this story and was so touched by it that he gave the adult Roch Carrier one of his old hockey sweaters as a gift! (You may also choose to research another writer in whom you are interested.)

TRACKING
YOUR
PROGRESS

Selection 8

Section	Number Correct		Score
A. Thesis and Main Ideas (2 items)	_____	× 4	_____
B. Details (6 items)	_____	× 4	_____
C. Organization and Transitions (4 items)	_____	× 3	_____
E. Reading and Thinking Visually (1 item)	_____	× 2	_____
F. Implied Meanings (7 items)	_____	× 3	_____
G. Thinking Critically (7 items)	_____	× 3	_____
H. Vocabulary			
Context (5 items)	_____	× 2	_____
Word Parts (1 item)	_____	× 2	_____
		TOTAL SCORE	_____ %

SELECTION 9

Picnic, Lightning

Billy Collins

Billy Collins, a native of New York City, was Poet Laureate of the United States from 2001 to 2003 and New York State Poet from 2004 to 2006. He is a professor at Lehman College and was called "the most popular poet in America" by *The New York Times*.

PREVIEWING THE READING

Previewing, as described on page 36, does not work well for poetry. Instead of previewing the poem, read it through once to determine its literal content—who is doing what, when, and where? When you have finished, answer the following questions.

1. What is the location of this poem? That is, where is the poet speaking from?

   _____

2. What living things appear in the poem?

   _____

 MAKING CONNECTIONS

Think about the changing of the seasons and the passing of time. How does your mood change as fall turns into winter, or as winter turns into spring? How is the cycle of life related to the seasons and the sun?

READING TIP

"Picnic, Lightning" is a poem of contrasts. As you read the poem, trace the change in the poet's thoughts and mood. What is the poet thinking about at the beginning of the poem? At the end of the poem? How has his mood changed? What contrasts does the poet make in the poem?

Picnic, Lightning

Lolita
A 1958 novel

My very photogenic mother died in a freak accident
(picnic, lightning) when I was three.

—*Lolita*, by Vladimir Nabokov

1   It is possible to be struck by a meteor
or a single-engine plane
while reading in a chair at home.
Safes drop from rooftops
5   and flatten the odd pedestrian
mostly within the panels of the comics,
But still, we know it is possible,
as well as the flash of summer lightning,
the thermos toppling over,
10   spilling out on the grass.

And we know the message
can be delivered from within.
The heart, no valentine,
decides to quit after lunch,
15   the power shut off like a switch,
or a tiny dark ship is unmoored
into the flow of the body's rivers,
the brain a monastery,
defenseless on the shore.

20   This is what I think about
when I shovel compost
into a wheelbarrow,
and when I fill the long flower boxes,
then press into rows

impatiens
a flowering plant

25   the limp roots of red **impatiens**—
the instant hand of Death
always ready to burst forth
from the sleeve of his voluminous cloak.

Then the soil is full of marvels,

fresco
painting done
on wet plaster

30   bits of leaf like flakes off a **fresco**,
red-brown pine needles, a beetle quick
to burrow back under the **loam**.

loam
fertile soil

Then the wheelbarrow is a wilder blue,
the clouds a brighter white,

35 and all I hear is the rasp of the steel edge
against a round stone,
the small plants singing
with lifted faces, and the click
of the sundial
40 as one hour sweeps into the next.

A. UNDERSTANDING THE THESIS AND OTHER MAIN IDEAS

Select the best answer.

_____ 1. The central theme of "Picnic, Lightning" focuses on
   a. gardening.
   b. sickness and health.
   c. life and death.
   d. the changing colors of the seasons.

_____ 2. The first stanza lists sudden deaths that can best
       be described as
   a. dramatic and unlikely.
   b. common and expected.
   c. impossible.
   d. humorous and ironic.

_____ 3. The second stanza talks about deaths that are the result of
   a. unexpected accidents.
   b. old age.

          c. murder.

          d. the failure of internal organs.

_____ 4. All of the following are clues to the poem's location *except*

          a. wheelbarrow.

          b. soil.

          c. cloak.

          d. sundial.

_____ 5. In line 35, the "rasp of the steel edge" is the sound of

          a. the shovel hitting a rock.

          b. the wheelbarrow's squeaky wheels.

          c. the small plants singing.

          d. the pine needles falling from the trees.

B. IDENTIFYING DETAILS

Select the best answer.

_____ 1. Which of the following bright colors does the poet *not* use to paint a picture of bright sunshine and life?

          a. red

          b. pink

          c. blue

          d. white

_____ 2. The poet notices the passing of time in the poem by looking at

          a. his watch.

          b. the direction in which the clouds are blowing.

          c. the sundial.

          d. the falling leaves.

_____ 3. The type of death referred to in the quote that precedes the poem ("My very photogenic mother died in a freak accident/(picnic, lightning) when I was three") is most similar to the deaths described in the

          a. first stanza.

          b. second stanza.

          c. third stanza.

          d. fourth stanza.

_____ 4. Which of the following details does the poet *not* use to convey a sense of life?

    a. plants singing

    b. the clouds looking brighter and whiter

    c. a tiny ship flowing on a river

    d. a burrowing beetle

C. RECOGNIZING METHODS OF ORGANIZATION AND TRANSITIONS

Complete the sentences by filling in the blanks.

1. Two patterns are used in "Picnic, Lightning." The poet uses _____ to explore the differences between death and life. Because he provides many examples in no particular order, the poem also uses a _____ pattern.

2. In the fourth stanza, the poet uses the same transitional word twice to show the passing of time. This word is _____.

D. REVIEWING AND ORGANIZING IDEAS: MAPPING

Complete the following map by adding the actions that occur in the first three stanzas, the images in the fourth stanza, and the sounds in the fifth stanza. The first stanza has been completed for you.

1st Stanza Actions	2nd Stanza Actions	3rd Stanza Actions	4th Stanza Images	5th Stanza Sounds
Meteor or single-engine plane strikes	_____	_____	_____	_____
Safes drop	_____	_____	_____	_____
Lightning flashes	_____	_____	_____	_____
Thermos topples	_____	_____	_____	_____

E. READING AND THINKING VISUALLY

Select the best answer.

_____ 1. How does the image provided with the poem reflect the poem's theme?

   a. It shows a tiny new life sprouting from what appears to be life-less earth.

   b. It reflects the poet's love of plants and flowers.

   c. It portrays a plant struggling for life when everything else around it has been killed.

   d. It implies that, like plants, humans start out small but can end up quite large and powerful.

_____ 2. All of the following images would be appropriate to illustrate the poem's theme *except*

   a. a sundial.

   b. a beetle.

   c. a dying old man.

   d. a wheelbarrow full of dirt.

F. FIGURING OUT IMPLIED MEANINGS

Indicate whether each statement is true (T) or false (F).

_____ 1. In the first stanza, the author implies that death by meteor is possible but not very common.

_____ 2. The poem takes place at night.

_____ 3. The flowers in the third stanza are dead.

_____ 4. The poet implies that life is a lot like comic books.

_____ 5. The quote that precedes the poem describes a common occurrence.

_____ 6. In the poem, red and blue are colors of life.

_____ 7. The last two stanzas imply that life is always renewing itself and that we should not dwell on death.

G. THINKING CRITICALLY

Select the best answer.

_____ 1. The tone of the poem can best be described as

   a. humorous.

   b. pessimistic.

    c. depressing.

    d. life-affirming.

_____ 2. An example of a *metaphor* (a literary device in which something is equated with something else that may seem quite different) can be found in

    a. line 4.

    b. line 18.

    c. line 21.

    d. line 34.

_____ 3. An example of a *simile* (comparison) in this poem can be found in

    a. line 1.

    b. line 9.

    c. line 27.

    d. line 30.

_____ 4. In literature, *personification* occurs when an abstract concept is given human form. In this poem, personification occurs in

    a. line 4.

    b. line 11.

    c. line 26.

    d. line 35.

_____ 5. When the poet says that the heart is "no valentine" in line 13, he means that

    a. the heart can be a source of physical illness as well as romance.

    b. gardens should be planted only in spring or summer, not in fall or winter.

    c. messages from loved ones are sometimes difficult to understand.

    d. love can be a source of unhappiness.

_____ 6. Considering the overall theme of the poem, the word "Picnic" in the title represents

    a. an outing where lightning often strikes people.

    b. a common occurrence that brings pleasure and happiness.

    c. an outdoor event at which many people die.

    d. the poet's mother.

_____ 7. The phrase "freak accident" in the opening quote is referenced in

    a. the deaths in the poem's first stanza.

    b. the deaths in the poem's second stanza.

    c. the types of fertilizers in the third stanza.

    d. the sounds of nature in the fifth stanza.

_____ 8. The poet's purpose is to

    a. fool himself into thinking that he will not die.

    b. convince the reader to accept unexpected accidental deaths when they happen to loved ones.

    c. show the reader that life is abundant even when thoughts of death are present.

    d. write a poem in memory of his mother.

H. BUILDING VOCABULARY

Context

Using context and a dictionary, if necessary, determine the meaning of each word as it is used in the poem.

_____ 1. unmoored (line 16)

    a. insane

    b. darkened

    c. detached

    d. emotionless

_____ 2. compost (line 21)

    a. dirt

    b. weeds

    c. fertilizer

    d. seeds

_____ 3. voluminous (line 28)

    a. loud

    b. loose and ample

    c. sneaky and unexpected

    d. long-winded and boring

_____ 4. burrow (line 32)

    a. dig

    b. scream

    c. donkey

    d. hide

Word Parts

> ## A REVIEW OF ROOTS AND PREFIXES
>
> **PED** means *foot*
>
> **MON-** or **MONO-** means *one*

Use your knowledge of word parts and the review above to select the best answer.

_____ 1. A *pedestrian* (line 5) is someone who is

    a. sitting.

    b. swimming.

    c. sleeping.

    d. walking.

_____ 2. A *monastery* (line 18) is place where monks or nuns go to live

    a. forgiven.

    b. outdoors.

    c. alone.

    d. in a city.

Unusual Words/Understanding Idioms

Answer the question below.

Quick means "fast," but it also can mean "alive." How does the poem make use of this double meaning in line 31?

_____

_____

I. SELECTING A LEARNING/STUDY STRATEGY

How would you prepare for a class discussion of this poem?

J. EXPLORING IDEAS THROUGH DISCUSSION AND WRITING

1. What kind of mood does the poet create in "Picnic, Lightning"? How does he accomplish this?

2. Discuss how you feel about the writing, reading, and study of poetry. How relevant is it to your life?

3. How often, if ever, do you think about death—either your own or that of other people? What types of emotions did this poem evoke in you? Do you have any additional perspective on death after reading the poem?

4. The poet in "Picnic, Lightning" is thinking about serious issues while he engages in a fairly routine activity (gardening). Write a paragraph in which you discuss what you think about when you have time to yourself or when you are doing chores.

K. BEYOND THE CLASSROOM TO THE WEB

Some people believe Billy Collins is popular because his poetry is easy to under-stand and speaks to so many people. Do a Google search to locate other poems by Billy Collins available on the Internet. Choose one and compare and contrast it with "Picnic, Lightning." How are the two poems similar? How are they different?

TRACKING YOUR PROGRESS

Selection 9

Section	Number Correct		Score
A. Thesis and Main Ideas (5 items)	_____	× 4	_____
B. Details (4 items)	_____	× 3	_____
C. Organization and Transitions (3 items)	_____	× 1	_____
E. Reading and Thinking Visually (2 items)	_____	× 4	_____
F. Implied Meanings (7 items)	_____	× 3	_____
G. Thinking Critically (8 items)	_____	× 3	_____
H. Vocabulary			
Context (4 items)	_____	× 2	_____
Word Parts (2 items)	_____	× 2	_____
	TOTAL SCORE		_____%

Political Science/Government/ History

We live in a political world shaped by history and current events. The economy, the job market, and even television sitcoms are influenced by national and international events. To study political science, government, and history is to understand factors that influence your daily life. Readings in this chapter demonstrate the relevance of these disciplines. In "Combat High" you will read about the plight of American soldiers deployed to Afghanistan. "Camping for Their Lives" addresses the issue of homelessness through a discussion of tent cities. "Whether to Vote: A Citizen's First Choice" examines reasons for voting and explores possible innovations in registering and voting.

Use the following suggestions when reading in the fields of political science, government, and history.

TIPS FOR READING IN POLITICAL SCIENCE/ GOVERNMENT/ HISTORY

- **Focus on the significance of events, both current and historical.** What immediate and long-range effects will or did a particular event, situation, or action have? As you read "Combat High," consider the impact of daily contact with death and violence on the lives of soldiers.

- **Analyze motivations.** What causes people and groups to take action? As you read "Combat High," consider what factors motivate people to join the military.

- **Consider political organizations.** How and why do people organize themselves into political groups and parties? Observe how political power is distributed and who makes important political decisions. As you read "Camping for Their Lives," you will learn about efforts to organize and control those living in tent cities.

- **Be alert for bias and partisanship** (support of a viewpoint or position because it is held by one's political party). As you read "Camping for Their Lives," look for disparate viewpoints on the future of tent cities.

- **Sort facts from opinions.** Opinions and historical interpretation are worthwhile but need to be evaluated. As you read "Whether to Vote: A Citizen's First Choice," observe how the authors provide evidence to support statements of opinion.

SELECTION
10

Combat High

Sebastian Junger

Contemporary
Issues Reading

In 2007 and 2008, journalist Sebastian Junger spent 14 months with U.S. troops in Afghanistan, patrolling with them and living among them at their main base, known as KOP (for Korengal Outpost), and at Outpost Restrepo nearby, named for Juan Restrepo, an Army medic who was fatally wounded there. What the place was like and what it did to the young Americans who fought there are described vividly in this adaptation from Junger's book *War*.

PREVIEWING THE READING

Using the steps listed on page 36, preview the reading selection. When you have finished, complete the following items.

1. This selection is about _____

   _____

2. List at least three questions you might be able to answer after reading the selection:

   a. _____

   b. _____

   c. _____

MAKING CONNECTIONS

People in stressful or unfamiliar surroundings must adapt to their situation in order to survive. This reading describes some of the ways soldiers have adapted to fighting a violent war in a foreign country. What new situations in your life have you needed to adapt to, and how did you cope? For example, have you moved from one country to another, had a child, or dealt with the loss of a parent?

READING TIP

As you read, you may encounter unfamiliar military vocabulary. Use context to discover the meanings of the words. Focus on the main ideas of the reading, and do a Google search for some photos of Afghanistan to get a sense of the desert conditions in which the soldiers are fighting.

Combat High

For one platoon, the challenge isn't surviving the war. It's surviving the peace.

eavesdropping
listening secretly to
a conversation

.50 cal
a type of machine
gun

ammo hooch
storage shelter for
ammunition

1   Most of the fighting was at four or five hundred yards, so no one ever got to see—or had to deal with—the effects of all that firepower on the human body. There were exceptions, though. One day Prophet (as the American **eavesdropping** operation was known) called in saying they'd overheard enemy fighters discussing how they wouldn't shoot at the Americans unless a patrol crossed to the east side of the valley. Soon afterward, Afghan soldiers spotted armed men in the riverbed and started shooting at them. The men fled up the flanks of the Abas Ghar ridge, and Second Platoon sent a patrol out of the KOP (the main base in the valley) to give chase. They took contact as soon as they crossed the river and found themselves badly pinned down behind a rock wall. Within seconds every American position in the valley opened up. The enemy was caught in the open without much cover, and the valley essentially turned into one enormous shooting gallery. The KOP started dropping mortars on them, and Observation Post 3 engaged them with a **.50 cal** and a Barrett sniper rifle, and the trucks opened up from above Babiyal, and Outpost Restrepo swung its 240s around and poured gunfire across the valley for almost an hour.

2   It was a hot day and there hadn't been much fighting lately, so when the men jumped on the guns most of them were wearing only flip-flops and shorts. They joked and laughed and called for cigarettes between bursts. Once in a while a round would crack past us, but mostly it was just a turkey shoot at a wide-open mountainside where the enemy had nowhere to hide. Hot brass was filling up the fighting positions, and more was cascading down out of the weapons every second. At one point I watched a shell drop into Pemble's untied shoe, and he slipped it off, wiggled the shell out, and then slipped his shoe back on without ever stopping firing. The lieutenant was shirtless on the **ammo hooch**, calling coordinates into the KOP, and some of the Afghans were firing from the hip even though they didn't stand a chance of hitting anything that way, and Jackson was up on the guard position unloading one of the machine guns. Restrepo alone had to be putting out a thousand rounds a minute, and the Abas Ghar was sparkling with bullet-strikes even though it was broad daylight. Finally Hog showed up—Hog was the radio call-sign for the A-10s—and dropped a couple of bombs on the mountain for good measure.

3   At some point a call came in over the radio that the Scouts were watching a guy crawl around on the mountainside without a leg. They watched until he stopped moving, and then they called in that he'd died. Everyone at Restrepo cheered. That night I couldn't sleep, and I crept out of my bunk and went and sat on the roof of the ammo hooch. It was a nice place to watch the heat lightning out along the Pech river or to lie back on the sandbags and look up at the stars. I couldn't stop thinking about that cheer; in some ways it was more troubling than all the killing that was going on. Stripped of all politics, the fact of the matter was that the man had died alone on a mountainside trying to find his leg. He must have been crazed with thirst and bewildered by the sheer amount of gunfire stitching back and forth across the ground looking for him. At one point or another every man in the platoon had been pinned down long enough to think they were going to die—bullets hitting around them, bodies

Personal messages on a belt of grenades.

braced for impact—and that's with just one or two guns. Imagine a whole company's worth of firepower directed at you. I got the necessity for that kind of overkill, but I didn't get the joy. It seemed like I either had to radically re-understand the men on this hilltop, or I had to acknowledge the power of a place like this to change them.

4   "You're thinking that this guy could have murdered my friend," Steiner explained to me later. "The cheering comes from knowing that that's someone we'll never have to fight again. Fighting another human being is not as hard as you think when they're trying to kill you. People think we were cheering because we just shot someone, but we were cheering because we just stopped someone from killing us. That person will no longer shoot at us anymore. That's where the **fiesta** comes in."

5   Combat was a game that the United States had asked Second Platoon to become very good at, and once they had, the United States had put them on a hilltop without women, hot food, running water, communication with the outside world or any kind of entertainment for more than a year. Not that the men were complaining, but that sort of thing has consequences. Society can give its young men almost any job, and they'll figure out how to do it. They'll suffer for it and die for it and watch their friends die for it, but in the end it will get done. That means only that society should be careful about what it asks for. In a very **crude** sense the job of young men is to undertake the work that their fathers are too old for, and the current generation of American fathers has decided that a certain six-mile-long valley in Kunar province needs to be brought under military control. Nearly 50 American soldiers have died carrying out those orders. I'm not saying that's a lot or a little, but the cost does need to be acknowledged. Soldiers themselves are reluctant to evaluate the costs of war (for some reason, the closer you are to combat the less inclined you are to question it), but someone must. That evaluation, ongoing and unadulterated by politics, may be the one thing a country absolutely owes the soldiers who defend its borders.

fiesta
Spanish for *party*

crude
basic

A U.S. soldier checks a thermal-imaging machine used to detect the enemy after dark.

6   There are other costs to war as well—vaguer ones that don't lend themselves to conventional math. One American soldier has died for every hundred yards of forward progress in the valley, but what about the survivors? Is that territory worth the psychological cost of learning to cheer someone's death? It's an impossible question to answer but one that should keep getting asked. Ultimately, the problem is that they're normal young men with normal emotional needs that have to be met within the very narrow options available on that hilltop. Young men need **mentors**, and mentors are usually a generation or so older. That isn't possible at Restrepo, so a 22-year-old team leader effectively becomes a father figure for a 19-year-old private. Up at Restrepo a 27-year-old is considered an old man, an effeminate Afghan soldier is seen as a woman, and new privates are called "cherries" and thought of as children. Men form friendships that are not at all sexual but contain much of the devotion and intensity of a romance. Almost every relationship that occurs in open society exists in some compressed form at Restrepo, and almost every human need from back home gets fulfilled in some truncated, jury-rigged way. The men are good at constructing what they need from what they have. They are experts at making do.

mentor
an experienced, trusted advisor

7   As for a sense of purpose, combat is it—the only game in town. Almost none of the things that make life feel worth living back home are present at Restrepo, so the entire range of a young man's self-worth has to be found within the ragged choreography of a firefight. The men talk about it and dream about it and rehearse for it and analyze it afterward but never plumb its depths enough to lose interest. It's the ultimate test, and some of the men worry they'll never again be satisfied with a "normal life"—whatever that is—after the amount of combat they've been in. They worry that they may have been ruined for anything else.

8   War is a lot of things, and it's useless to pretend that exciting isn't one of them. It's insanely exciting. The machinery of war and the sound it makes and the urgency of its use and the consequences of almost everything about it are the most exciting

things anyone engaged in war will ever know. Soldiers discuss that fact with each other and eventually with their chaplains and their shrinks and maybe even their spouses, but the public will never hear about it. It's just not something that many people want acknowledged. War is supposed to feel bad because undeniably bad things happen in it, but for a 19-year-old at the working end of a .50 cal during a firefight that everyone comes out of OK, war is life multiplied by some number that no one has ever heard of. In some ways 20 minutes of combat is more life than you could scrape together in a lifetime of doing something else. Combat isn't where you might die—though that does happen—it's where you find out whether you get to keep on living. Don't underestimate the power of that revelation. Don't underestimate the things young men will wager in order to play that game one more time.

9   "I like the firefights," O'Byrne admitted to me once. We'd been talking about going home and whether he was going to get bored. "I know," he added, probably realizing how that sounded. "Saddest thing in the world."

A. UNDERSTANDING THE THESIS AND OTHER MAIN IDEAS

Select the best answer.

_____ 1. The central thesis of the selection is that
   a. soldiers form strong bonds with one another during a war and even end up enjoying the dangerous situations in which they find themselves.
   b. Afghani soldiers are less prepared for war than American soldiers.
   c. the U.S. government is not providing properly for overseas soldiers, but Congress is unwilling to increase war spending.
   d. soldiers on the ground are not good at calculating the costs of war because they are too young and inexperienced to see the big picture.

_____ 2. The author's primary purpose in "Combat High" is to
   a. describe the latest weapons of war.
   b. make the reader aware of Afghanistan's desert-like qualities.
   c. create sympathy for the Afghani soldier whose death is watched by U.S. soldiers.
   d. explain how war affects the young U.S. soldiers who take part in combat.

_____ 3. The American soldiers cheer the death of the Afghani soldier because
   a. their goal is to kill as many Afghanis as possible.
   b. they lack human feeling.
   c. they know the dead man will not be able to kill them.
   d. they experience a disconnect between war and reality.

4. The main idea of paragraph 6 is found in the
   a. first sentence.
   b. second sentence.
   c. second to the last sentence.
   d. last sentence.

5. The topic of paragraph 7 is
   a. combat.
   b. self-worth.
   c. Outpost Restrepo.
   d. young men.

6. The main idea of paragraph 8 is that
   a. war causes emotional problems for the people who fight in it.
   b. war affects young people less than it affects the elderly.
   c. the public has no idea what happens "behind the scenes" on a battleground.
   d. war is exciting to young soldiers.

B. IDENTIFYING DETAILS

Select the best answer.

1. How many American soldiers have died for every 100 yards of forward progress in the valley?
   a. one
   b. five
   c. ten
   d. one hundred

2. The American eavesdropping operation in Afghanistan is known as
   a. Restrepo.
   b. Hog.
   c. Prophet.
   d. Abas Ghar.

3. For more than a year, the men of the Second Platoon existed without all of the following *except*
   a. hot food.
   b. running water.
   c. communication with the outside world.
   d. cigarettes.

_____ 4. All of the following parts of Afghanistan are mentioned in the reading *except*

    a. the Abas Ghar ridge.

    b. the Pech river.

    c. the city of Kabul.

    d. Kunar province.

_____ 5. Which of the following soldiers is not discussed in the reading?

    a. Steiner

    b. O'Byrne

    c. Pemble

    d. Thompson

_____ 6. Which body part was missing on the dying Afghani soldier?

    a. hand

    b. arm

    c. leg

    d. foot

_____ 7. According to paragraph 5, the men of the Second Platoon see war as:

    a. their job.

    b. a battle between good and evil.

    c. politically motivated.

    d. an enormous cost to society.

_____ 8. Which term does the reading use as the opposite of "combat"?

    a. "normal life"

    b. "marriage"

    c. "strategic ops"

    d. "firefight"

C. RECOGNIZING METHODS OF ORGANIZATION AND TRANSITIONS

Select the best answer.

_____ 1. The organizational pattern used by the author in paragraphs 1–4 is

    a. comparison and contrast.

    b. chronological order.

    c. classification.

    d. definition.

_____ 2. The organizational pattern of paragraph 6 is
   a. definition.
   b. cause and effect.
   c. comparison and contrast.
   d. classification.

The reading and introduction define many key military terms. Match each term with its definition.

_____ 3. KOP	a. radio call-in sign for A-10 bombers
_____ 4. Hog	b. an army outpost named for a fallen medic
_____ 5. 240	c. the main base in the valley
_____ 6. Restrepo	d. a combat weapon

D. REVIEWING AND ORGANIZING IDEAS: SUMMARIZING

Use the following words to complete the summary of paragraphs 6–9.

calculate	children	combat	emotional
excitement	friendships	mentors	older

It can be hard to _____ all the costs of war. Combat soldiers have _____ needs that must be met. For example, younger men need _____, but in combat situations there are relatively few _____ men to serve that role. In a combat unit with men in their mid-twenties, new privates are considered _____. As a result of their intense experiences together, the men form very close _____, and _____ gives them their sense of purpose. Some soldiers believe they'll never be satisfied with a normal life after they've taken part in the _____ of war.

E. READING AND THINKING VISUALLY

Select the best answer.

_____ 1. The author chose to include the photo of the grenades in order to
   a. emphasize that the soldiers, while loving their families, are still violent men who enjoy killing.
   b. point out that modern war may appear to be high-tech, but it actually relies on many old-fashioned technologies and weapons.

    c. make the reader feel sympathy for the innocent Afghanis who will be killed by these grenades.

    d. show how the soldiers try to make the outpost reflect the people and things they care about.

_____ 2. Why did the author choose to include the photo of the soldier checking the thermal-imaging machine?

    a. to present an image of a lonely soldier who has been rejected by his platoon

    b. to draw a contrast between the beauty of the surroundings and the ugly reality of war

    c. to emphasize the high-tech nature of modern warfare

    d. to show how U.S. soldiers in Afghanistan must cope with poor materials and makeshift tents

F. FIGURING OUT IMPLIED MEANINGS

Indicate whether each statement is true (T) or false (F).

_____ 1. The author implies that the soldiers of the Second Platoon spend a great deal of their time complaining.

_____ 2. The American soldiers described in "Combat High" are mostly young men.

_____ 3. The author implies that soldiers never get tired of talking about combat.

_____ 4. The "father figures" for the men of the Second Platoon are usually much older than the soldiers they are mentoring.

_____ 5. The author implies that soldiers taking part in combat usually do not think about the costs of war because they are too busy trying to stay alive.

_____ 6. The author implies that the men of the Second Platoon engage in homosexual behavior.

G. THINKING CRITICALLY

Select the best answer.

_____ 1. The author's tone can be described as all of the following *except*

    a. concerned.

    b. sympathetic.

    c. excited.

    d. compassionate.

_____ 2. The author got his information about the soldiers' experiences primarily through

    a. reading the soldiers' diaries.

    b. talking to their commanding officers.

    c. spending time with them in a combat situation.

    d. reading army Web sites.

_____ 3. The author's purpose in paragraphs 1–4 is to

    a. describe combat and a war zone for readers who likely have never experienced combat.

    b. describe the advanced technologies used in modern warfare.

    c. describe the country of Afghanistan and what makes it such a difficult place for American soldiers to live in.

    d. describe the brutal experience of the Afghani soldier who died on the mountainside.

_____ 4. For what type of reader is the author writing?

    a. soldiers

    b. civilians (non-soldiers)

    c. military officers

    d. government policy makers

_____ 5. When the author describes the gunfire as a "turkey shoot" (paragraph 2), he means that

    a. wild turkeys interfere with the combat.

    b. the soldiers have run out of ammunition.

    c. the enemy is at a serious disadvantage in this situation.

    d. the scorching sun is so hot that it is baking the soldiers like turkeys.

_____ 6. Which statement best summarizes the author's feelings toward the futures of the soldiers he writes about?

    a. He believes that the soldiers will become high-ranking military officers as a result of the sacrifices they have made.

    b. He believes that at least some of the soldiers will become traitors who will begin fighting for the enemy.

    c. He is delighted that these young men, who have little or no formal education, have found a job that excites them and to which they feel dedicated.

    d. He is concerned that war will be the high point of these soldiers' lives and that anything they do when they return home will not be as exciting as the battlefield.

_____ 7. Which statement is a mixture of fact and opinion?

    a. It was a hot day and there hadn't been much fighting lately, so when the men jumped on the guns most of them were wearing only flip-flops and shorts. (paragraph 2)

    b. I got the necessity for that kind of overkill, but I didn't get the joy. (paragraph 3)

    c. Nearly 50 American soldiers have died carrying out those orders. (paragraph 5)

    d. It's an impossible question to answer but one that should keep getting asked. (paragraph 6)

_____ 8. The last line of the reading, "Saddest thing in the world," refers to

    a. the death of American soldiers.

    b. the long and drawn-out nature of warfare.

    c. the soldiers' pleasure in combat.

    d. the death of the Afghani man on the mountainside.

_____ 9. "Combat isn't where you might die—though that does happen—it's where you find out whether you get to keep on living." This statement from paragraph 8 most closely reflects the _____ perspective.

    a. soldiers'

    b. author's

    c. chaplain's (priest's)

    d. typical American citizen's

_____ 10. The title, "Combat High," refers to

    a. the mountainous territory in which the soldiers are fighting.

    b. the tendency for soldiers to become addicted to dangerous drugs like opium.

    c. the high number of American deaths in Afghanistan.

    d. the sense of excitement that soldiers feel during combat.

H. BUILDING VOCABULARY

Context

Using context and a dictionary, if necessary, determine the meaning of each word as it is used in the selection.

_____ 1. flanks (paragraph 1)

    a. rivers

    b. mountains

    c. sides

    d. valleys

_____ 2. mortars (paragraph 1)

    a. surprises

    b. uniforms

    c. bombs

    d. ammunition

_____ 3. inclined (paragraph 5)

    a. willing

    b. slanted

    c. angry

    d. insulted

_____ 4. truncated (paragraph 6)

    a. elephant-like

    b. related to trees

    c. shortened

    d. artificial

_____ 5. plumb (paragraph 7)

    a. mention

    b. discuss

    c. explore

    d. drown

Word Parts

> **A REVIEW OF PREFIXES AND ROOTS**
>
> **UN-** and **IM-** mean *not*
> **RE-** means *again*
> **FEM** means *female*

Use your knowledge of word parts and the review above to indicate whether each statement is true (T) or false (F).

_____ 1. Making an effort to *re-understand* someone (paragraph 3) implies that you are making this effort for the first time.

_____ 2. A substance that is *unadulterated* (paragraph 5) is not contaminated.

_____ 3. Something *impossible* (paragraph 6) is not possible.

_____ 4. An *effeminate* man (paragraph 6) acts or looks like a child.

Unusual Words/Understanding Idioms

Use the meanings given below to write a sentence using the boldfaced word.

1. Something that is **jury-rigged** (paragraph 6) is makeshift, temporary, or thrown together using what's available (rather than what is required for the job).

   _____

   _____

2. **Choreography** (paragraph 7) generally refers to the steps in a dance routine, but metaphorically it can refer to any elaborate process with many steps.

   _____

   _____

I. SELECTING A LEARNING/STUDY STRATEGY

Suppose you are planning to participate in a class discussion on the experience of young soldiers in Afghanistan. How could you use this reading to prepare for the discussion?

_____

_____

_____

J. EXPLORING IDEAS THROUGH DISCUSSION AND WRITING

1. Do you serve in the military, or do you know anyone who does? If so, have you or they seen active duty? List at least three ways in which military life is different from civilian life.

2. This reading can be divided into two parts. Where would you begin the first part, and where would you begin the second part? Write a heading for each part.

3. How do you think this reading might apply to the desire of many young males to play video games?

4. Suppose you wanted to put together a care package to send to the men of the Second Platoon. What would you include in the package, and why?

K. BEYOND THE CLASSROOM TO THE WEB

In "Combat High," Sebastian Junger implies that soldiers who return home from the war in Afghanistan may face unexpected emotional issues or problems.

One common problem that faces war veterans is post-traumatic stress disorder, or PTSD. To read more about PTSD and the other emotional difficulties faced by ex-soldiers, visit **http://www.vietnam-war.info/veterans/**.

Choose four of the problems listed on this site and try to explain what might cause each problem for an ex-soldier. For example, anxiety might be the result of living in a situation where bombs can be dropped on you at any moment.

TRACKING YOUR PROGRESS

Selection 10

Section	Number Correct		Score
A. Thesis and Main Ideas (6 items)	_____	× 3	_____
B. Details (8 items)	_____	× 2	_____
C. Organization and Transitions (6 items)	_____	× 1	_____
E. Reading and Thinking Visually (2 items)	_____	× 2	_____
F. Implied Meanings (6 items)	_____	× 3	_____
G. Thinking Critically (10 items)	_____	× 2	_____
H. Vocabulary			
Context (5 items)	_____	× 2	_____
Word Parts (4 items)	_____	× 2	_____
	TOTAL SCORE		_____%

SELECTION 11

Camping for Their Lives
Scott Bransford

Contemporary
Issues Reading  In this selection, the author describes how tent cities for homeless people have emerged throughout the American West. Read the selection to find out what life is like in a tent city.

PREVIEWING THE READING

Using the steps listed on page 36, preview the reading selection. When you have finished, complete the following items.

1. This selection is about _____.

2. The tent city that is the primary focus of this article is located in

_____.

 ### MAKING CONNECTIONS

Where would you live if you could not afford to pay for housing?

READING TIP

As you read, underline factors that have led to the development of tent cities and highlight words that are used to describe tent cities.

Camping for Their Lives

Call them squatter villages, tent cities, or informal urbanism— more people are calling them home.

1   Marie and Francisco Caro needed a home after they got married, but like many people in California's Central Valley, they didn't have enough money to sign a lease or take out a mortgage. They were tired of sleeping on separate beds in crowded shelters, so they found a slice of land alongside the Union Pacific Railroad tracks in downtown Fresno. The soil was sandy and dry, prone to rising up into clouds when the autumn winds came. All around, farm equipment factories and warehouses loomed out of the dust, their walls coarse and sun-bleached like desert mountainsides. Even a strong person could wither in a place like this, but if they wanted to build a home, nobody was likely to stop them. So Marie and Francisco gathered scrap wood and took their chances. They raised their tarp roof high like a steeple, then walled off the world with office cubicle dividers. Thieves stayed outside and so did the wind, and the sound of the passing freight trains softened.

A tent city in Sacramento, California, in March 2009.

2   When I visited the Caros in January, a fire burned in a repurposed oil barrel, warming the cool air, and fresh-cut Christmas tree boughs hung on the walls for decoration. While Francisco chopped wood, Marie confided that she wants to live somewhere else. All she needs is a modest place with a sink and a gas stove, she said, maybe even a television. But until times change, she said, she'll be happy in her self-made abode, cooking on top of the oil barrel, making meals with whatever food God brings. "He gives us bread," said Marie, a Fresno native who quit school in the 10th grade, ashamed of a learning disability that got in the way of her reading. "I'm just waiting for my home."

3   From the well-kept interior of the Caros' place, one can hardly see the jagged rows of tents and shanties on the vacant land around them. About 200 people— primarily poor whites and migrant workers from Mexico—have built informal habitats along the railroad tracks. There are many names for this fledgling city, where **Old Glory** flies from improvised flagpoles and trash heaps rise and fall with the wavering population. To some it's Little Tijuana, but most people call it Taco Flat. Just to the south, under a freeway overpass, there's another camp of roughly equal size called New Jack City where most of the residents are black. Even more makeshift dwellings are scattered throughout the neighborhood nearby. Fresno, which the Brookings Institution ranked in 2005 as the American city with the greatest concentration of poverty, is far from the only place where people are resorting to life

Old Glory
the American flag

in makeshift abodes. Similar encampments are proliferating throughout the West, everywhere from the industrial hub of Ontario, California, to the struggling casino district of Reno, Nevada, and the upscale suburbs of Washington state.

4   In any other country, these threadbare villages would be called slums, but in the United States, the preferred term is *tent city,* a label that implies that they are just a temporary phenomenon. Many journalists, eager to prove that the country is entering the next Great Depression, blame the emergence of these shantytowns on the economic downturn, calling them products of foreclosures and layoffs. While there's some truth to this notion, the fact is that these roving, ramshackle neighborhoods were part of the American cityscape long before the stock market nosedived, and they are unlikely to disappear when prosperity returns. The recent decades of real estate speculation and tough-love social policies have cut thousands of people out of the mainstream markets for work and housing, and the existing network of shelters for the homeless is overburdened and outdated.

vanguard
the forefront or
leading position

5   People such as the Caros are part of a **vanguard** that has been in crisis for years, building squatter settlements as a do-or-die alternative to the places that rejected them. This parallel nation, with a population now numbering at least 2,000 in Fresno alone, was born during the boom times, and it is bound to flourish as the economy falters. "The chickens are coming home to roost," says Larry Haynes, executive director of Mercy House, an organization based in Southern California that serves homeless people. "What this speaks of is an absolute crisis of affordability and accessibility."

6   Against a backdrop of faded industrial buildings and rusty water towers, Taco Flat looks like a relic of a bygone era. These rough-and-ready dwellings, untouched by the luxuries of electricity, sewage lines, and cable connections, seem like an aberration in a country that has grown accustomed to newness. Much of the shock value of tent cities comes from the fact that they force one to do a bit of time travel, revisiting an atmosphere of social disorder that seems more fitting to a Gold Rush–era squatter camp, and a level of destitution that recalls the **Hoovervilles** of the 1930s. Even tent city residents themselves feel trapped in circular trajectories of history, doomed to lives shaped by the threat of lawlessness and the ever-looming peril of relocation.

Hoovervilles
homeless camps
that arose during
the Depression
and were so
named to
cast blame
on President
Herbert Hoover

7   Frankie Lynch, one of the self-proclaimed mayors of Taco Flat, has ancestors who fled Oklahoma during the Dust Bowl years, only to discover a new kind of poverty in the farmworker camps of California's Central Valley. Now he's drifting, too, unable to find the construction work that used to pay his bills. "It's just going back to the same thing," says Lynch, 50. "I remember my grandparents and my dad talking about labor camps, and going town to town to work."

incarcerated
put in jail

8   Crime is a concern here—according to county estimates, 41 percent of the homeless population has been **incarcerated** at some point—but the greatest fear for most Taco Flat residents is that they've lost their place in mainstream society, whether as a result of mental or physical illness, of past mistakes, or of the whims of global capitalism. In better times, they might have weathered their troubles, getting by with work in factories, call centers, or construction sites. But those jobs are gone, and many people wonder if they will ever come back.

9   Tent cities have much in common with the squatter camps of the Great Depression, but to simply call them Hoovervilles is to ignore their complexity. To truly

understand them, one must look at current trends in the developing world, where informal urbanism—a form of "slum" development that takes place outside the conventions of city planning—is now the predominant mode of city-making. Informal urbanism, characterized by unauthorized occupation of land, makeshift construction, and lack of public utilities, is how many burgeoning nations meet their housing needs. It thrives in places like Fresno, where poverty is **endemic** and there is a wide gap between rich and poor.

endemic
common in a
particular area

10   Rahul Mehrotra, an associate professor in the urban studies and planning department at the Massachusetts Institute of Technology, says there's a kinship between Taco Flat and the squatter settlements of Mumbai, India, where he runs an architectural firm. "It's really a reflection of the government's inability to provide housing affordably across society," Mehrotra says. Informal urbanism also thrives wherever people face exclusion from the mainstream markets for work and shelter, he adds, whether they are excluded for ethnic, economic, or political reasons.

11   This can be seen in Taco Flat's large contingent of undocumented workers, who left their homes in Latin America to find work on the Central Valley's farms and construction sites. As borders tighten and the threat of immigration raids lingers, the act of signing a lease has become more risky, prompting many to forgo formal housing altogether. Undocumented workers are also plagued by low wages, which aren't keeping pace with the rising costs of housing. This hardship has only been exacerbated by jobs disappearing in the Central Valley, where an ongoing drought is turning some of the world's most fertile farmland into a desert. The situation has left Mexican workers like Juan Garcia, 21, suspended between two countries. In neither country is there a guarantee of a livelihood and home is all too often an abstraction. At least in Garcia's native state of Colima, there are always the comforts of family. "It's better in Mexico," Garcia says. "I'm going back."

12   In Fresno and other struggling cities, which perpetually strive to boost tax revenues with development, tent cities are often seen as symbols of criminality and dereliction, glaring setbacks to neighborhood revitalization efforts. That perception is common wherever informal urbanism exists, Mehrotra says, and it often leaves squatter camps on the brink of ruin. "You are always on the edge of demolition," he says. This hit home in Fresno a few years ago, when workers began raiding encampments throughout the city, tearing down makeshift homes and destroying personal property. The city of Fresno and the California Department of Transportation conducted these sweeps in the name of public health, citing citizen complaints about open-air defecation. Yet the raids did nothing to stop tent cities from forming, and they ultimately led to lawsuits. In October 2006, residents who lost their homes in the raids filed a class-action suit against the city of Fresno and the state of California. A U.S. district judge ordered the defendants to pay $2.3 million in damages.

13   Two hundred miles south of Fresno, there's also been a battle over tent cities in the Inland Empire, an industrial stronghold that stretches out into the deserts east of Los Angeles. Flying into Ontario International Airport, one can see the nucleus of this struggle, in a neighborhood less than a mile from the tarmac. There, on a stretch of vacant land surrounded by aging homes and abandoned orchards, tents are arranged in neat rows. This used to be one of Southern California's largest squatter settlements, an unruly village of tarp and scrap wood that grew until some 400 residents called it

home. People moved here from as far away as Florida, recalls Brent Schultz, Ontario's director of housing and neighborhood revitalization.

14   Local officials were disturbed to find out that Ontario was becoming a magnet for the dispossessed, Schultz says. Rather than simply bulldoze the makeshift neighborhood, Ontario officials embarked on a $100,000 campaign to discipline and punish squatters, setting up a formal camp where tarp dwellings became symbols of order. In the spring of last year, police and code enforcement officers issued color-coded bracelets to distinguish Ontario residents from newcomers, then gradually banished the out-of-towners. Then they demolished the shanties and set up an official camp with a chain-link fence and guard shack. Residents were issued IDs and a strict set of rules: no coming and going after 10 p.m., no pets, no children or visitors, no drugs, and no alcohol. About 120 people stuck around, but many left to escape the regimentation. As of July, the population was about 60.

15   "It's like a prison," says Melody Woolsey, 40, who has lived in both versions of the encampment. Schultz, on the other hand, considers the camp one of Ontario's greatest success stories. Some of the camp's residents agree: They say it's a bit like a gated community on a modest scale, a rare haven where one can live affordably without fear of robbery or violence.

16   "Some people come up here and say it looks like a concentration camp, but they don't live here," says Robert, 51, an unemployed factory technician. "They're only looking at it from the outside. I look at it that it's a secure community." Yet the neighborhood is filled with angry people who were excluded from the camp and left to take shelter in cars or in other vacant lots, often under threat of police citations. Many of these outcasts see the camp as a symbol of injustice, a cynical and inauthentic gesture of compassion.

17   For people throughout the American West, the very concept of home is changing, adjusting downward to a reality in which buying cheap land, picking out a subdivision lot, or even renting an apartment has become nothing more than a fancy daydream. That's a painful realization for a region steeped in myths of plenty. But in these hard times, tent cities increasingly are the last province of hope for having a place of one's own. Tent cities like Taco Flat are communities like any other, and if they are neglected, they will be lost to crime, addiction, and illness. Yet whenever officials act to destroy or stifle them with punitive regulations, they not only wipe out the pride of residents struggling to survive, they also jettison a spirit of self-reliance and innovation that could be harnessed to help meet the housing needs of the future.

18   The promise of tent cities begins with their architecture. Makeshift dwellings may not be the dream homes of yesteryear, but they are simple, affordable, and sustainable in their use of salvaged materials. With imaginative designers, they could help solve the present housing crisis, a faster alternative to the process of building shelters and low-income apartment complexes. That possibility is already taking shape in Portland, Oregon, where activists have carved out a space for improvised dwellings in Dignity Village, a community that can house up to 60 people. Founded in 2000 and now approved by the city, it's considered a model by housing advocates worldwide.

19   Beyond the check-in desk in the village's security post, residents find a balance between the human needs for safety and personal freedom. Most are required to do

at least 10 hours of community service a week—helping build or remodel homes, for example—but otherwise they set their own schedules. "This isn't a flophouse," says Joe Palinkas, 55. "This is a community place. You support the village by taking care of yourself as if you were on your own." Tent cities also could become a locus for action and dialogue, a place where outreach workers, social service agencies, and everyday citizens can reach out to society's most vulnerable members.

20   Leaders in California's Central Valley might do well to take inspiration from Dignity Village. Instead, planners still see tent cities as obstacles to revitalization. Fresno and Madera counties recently adopted a 10-year plan to end homelessness, and Gregory Barfield, the area's newly appointed homelessness czar, says tent cities aren't part of the picture. "A Dignity Village for us is not the best course of action," says Barfield. "We've got to find out a way to move forward with housing people."

21   But such talk means little to Taco Flat residents like Arthur Barela, 45, who lost his job when the Central Valley's farms began to dry out. For him, the only real home is the one he has made with his blankets, his tent, and his tarp. He still has the strength to keep his place clean, but his frame is nearly skeletal. "Hopefully, things don't get chaotic and things don't get out of hand," says Barela, kneeling before his tent as if in prayer. "Sometimes hunger can make a person do crazy things."

A. UNDERSTANDING THE THESIS AND OTHER MAIN IDEAS

Select the best answer.

_____ 1. The author's primary purpose in this selection is to
  a. argue for better social programs on behalf of the homeless population.
  b. describe the development of tent cities and the people who live in them.
  c. compare modern-day tent cities with the squatter camps of the Depression.
  d. criticize people who live in tent cities for not finding jobs and better housing.

_____ 2. The tent city that is the main focus of this article is called
  a. New Jack City.
  b. Hooverville.
  c. the Inland Empire.
  d. Taco Flat.

_____ 3. The topic of paragraph 9 is
  a. squatter camps.
  b. the Great Depression.
  c. informal urbanism.
  d. Hoovervilles.

_____ 4. The main idea of paragraph 17 is that

    a. people in the American West are having to adjust their concept of home.

    b. many people move to the West as their last hope for a place of their own.

    c. tent cities can be destroyed by crime, addiction, illness, or neglect.

    d. officials ruin tent cities whenever they try to impose regulations.

_____ 5. The model community called Dignity Village is located in

    a. Ontario, Canada.

    b. Fresno, California.

    c. Portland, Oregon.

    d. Mumbai, India.

B. IDENTIFYING DETAILS

Indicate whether each statement is true (T) or false (F).

_____ 1. Marie and Francisco Caro live in an abandoned trailer.

_____ 2. The population of Taco Flat is about 200.

_____ 3. In 2005, Fresno was ranked as the American city with the highest concentration of poverty.

_____ 4. The tents and shanties in Taco Flat are equipped with electricity and sewage lines.

_____ 5. According to Fresno county estimates, 41 percent of the homeless population has spent time in jail.

C. RECOGNIZING METHODS OF ORGANIZATION AND TRANSITIONS

Complete the following statements by filling in the blanks.

1. In paragraphs 1–2, the author uses the cause and effect pattern to describe how Marie and Francisco Caro came to live in a tent city. In their case, the *cause* was their inability to _____ housing and the *effect* was _____ a tent city.

2. In paragraph 9, the author uses the _____ pattern to explain the meaning of the term *informal urbanism.*

3. In paragraphs 15–16, two transitions that indicate the contrast organizational pattern are _____ and _____.

D. REVIEWING AND ORGANIZING IDEAS: MAPPING

Using the descriptions in paragraphs 13–14, determine the chronological order of the events below and put them in the correct order on the time line by writing the letters that correspond to the events in the blanks. Some have been done for you.

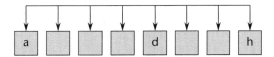

a. The population of a squatter village in Ontario includes 400 residents.

b. Out-of-towners are gradually banished and shanties are demolished.

c. Many decide to leave because of strict rules.

d. Official camp is established with fence and guard shack.

e. Color-coded bracelets are issued to distinguish Ontario residents from newcomers.

f. Residents are issued IDs and are subject to new rules.

g. Officials begin $100,000 campaign to discipline squatters and create a formal camp.

h. The population declines to about 60 residents.

E. READING AND THINKING VISUALLY

Answer each of the following questions.

1. What details do you notice in the photograph of the tent city in Sacramento?

_____

2. How does the tent city in the photograph correspond to the descriptions of different tent cities discussed in the selection?

_____

_____

F. FIGURING OUT IMPLIED MEANINGS

For each of the following quotes from the selection, determine whether the bold-faced word has a positive (P) or negative (N) connotation.

_____ 1. "Even a strong person could **wither** in a place like this" (paragraph 1)

_____ 2. "**fresh-cut** Christmas tree boughs hung on the walls for decoration" (paragraph 2)

_____ 3. "these roving, **ramshackle** neighborhoods" (paragraph 4)

_____ 4. "**doomed** to lives shaped by the threat of lawlessness" (paragraph 6)

_____ 5. "symbols of **criminality** and dereliction" (paragraph 12)

_____ 6. "a rare **haven** where one can live affordably" (paragarph 15)

_____ 7. "whenever officials act to destroy or **stifle** them" (paragraph 17)

_____ 8. "The **promise** of tent cities begins with their architecture" (paragraph 18)

_____ 9. "a balance between the human needs for safety and personal **freedom**" (paragraph 19)

_____ 10. "his frame is nearly **skeletal**" (paragraph 21)

G. THINKING CRITICALLY

Select the best answer.

_____ 1. The title "Camping for Their Lives" indicates that most people in tent cities

    a. are having the time of their lives.

    b. have no other options for housing.

    c. are only visiting and are not residents.

    d. prefer the camping lifestyle.

_____ 2. The author supports his thesis with

    a. facts and statistics.

    b. descriptions and examples.

    c. expert opinions.

    d. all of the above.

_____ 3. The author attributes the emergence of tent cities to all of the following _except_

    a. real estate speculation.

    b. tough-love social policies.

    c. the most recent drop in the stock market.

    d. an overloaded and outdated network of homeless shelters.

_____ 4. The author includes the description of Dignity Village in order to

    a. recommend it as a model for affordable communities.

    b. compare and contrast it with the other tent cities in the article.

    c. emphasize the community potential of tent cities.

    d. do all of the above.

_____ 5. The author's overall tone can best be described as

    a. judgmental.

    b. sympathetic.

    c. indifferent.

    d. sarcastic.

H. BUILDING VOCABULARY

Context

Using context and a dictionary, if necessary, determine the meaning of each word as it is used in the selection.

_____ 1. fledgling (paragraph 3)

    a. birdlike

    b. new or beginning

    c. expensive

    d. established

_____ 2. aberration (paragraph 6)

    a. abnormality

    b. observation

    c. recommendation

    d. improvement

_____ 3. destitution (paragraph 6)

    a. structure

    b. comfort

    c. application

    d. poverty

_____ 4. trajectories (paragraph 6)

    a. laws

    b. paths

    c. surfaces

    d. forces

_____ 5. burgeoning (paragraph 9)

    a. allowing

    b. stalling

    c. growing

    d. departing

_____ 6. contingent (paragraph 11)

    a. commitment

    b. group

    c. independent

    d. arrangement

_____ 7. exacerbated (paragraph 11)

    a. made worse

    b. relinquished

    c. suspended

    d. enhanced

_____ 8. regimentation (paragraph 14)

    a. appearance

    b. informality

    c. strict discipline

    d. inconsistency

_____ 9. jettison (paragraph 17)

    a. join

    b. throw away

    c. strain

    d. apply

_____ 10. locus (paragraph 19)

    a. center

    b. dispute

    c. distance

    d. view

Word Parts

A REVIEW OF PREFIXES

RE- means *again*

DIS- means *apart, away, not*

IN- means *not*

UN- means *not*

Use your knowledge of word parts and the review above to fill in the blanks in the following sentences.

1. When an object has been *repurposed* (paragraph 2), it has been adapted so that it can be used _____ for another purpose.

2. To describe workers as *undocumented* (paragraph 11) is to say that they do _____ have the appropriate legal documents, such as immigration or working papers.

3. People who are described as *dispossessed* (paragraph 14) are those who do _____ have homes, property, or possessions.

4. A symbol of *injustice* (paragraph 16) is something that represents an action or treatment that is _____ just or fair.

5. When someone describes a gesture as *inauthentic* (paragraph 16), he or she perceives that it is _____ genuine or sincere.

Unusual Words/Understanding Idioms

Use the meanings given below to write a sentence using the boldfaced word or phrase.

1. Something described as **makeshift** (paragraph 3) is considered a crude and temporary solution made up from whatever is available.

   Your sentence: _____

   _____

2. Someone who says that **the chickens are coming home to roost** (paragraph 5) means that consequences are occurring because of certain actions or mistakes in the past.

   Your sentence: _____

   _____

I. SELECTING A LEARNING/STUDY STRATEGY

Suppose you read this article in preparation for a class discussion on whether or not tent cities are obstacles to revitalization. What techniques would you use to organize the information in the article to support your position?

J. EXPLORING IDEAS THROUGH DISCUSSION AND WRITING

1. Do you detect any bias in this selection? Consider the author's tone, his language, and the evidence he uses to support his position. Does he include opposing viewpoints?

2. According to the selection, leaders in California's Central Valley rejected the idea of a Dignity Village–type tent city (paragraph 20). Why do you think they rejected it?

3. The author quotes a variety of people in the selection, from tent city residents to an urban studies professor to a homelessness czar. Whose opinions did you find most persuasive and why?

4. Compare the introductory paragraphs about the Caros to the last paragraph, about Arthur Barela. Why do you think the author chose to begin and end the article this way?

K. BEYOND THE CLASSROOM TO THE WEB

Visit the Dignity Village Web site at **http://www.dignityvillage.org/.** *After you have explored the site, write a paragraph describing the aspects of this tent city that sound like your own community, as well as those characteristics that set it apart.*

TRACKING YOUR PROGRESS

Selection 11

Section	Number Correct		Score
A. Thesis and Main Ideas (5 items)	_____	× 4	_____
B. Details (5 items)	_____	× 2	_____
C. Organization and Transitions (5 items)	_____	× 2	_____
F. Implied Meanings (10 items)	_____	× 2	_____
G. Thinking Critically (5 items)	_____	× 4	_____
H. Vocabulary			
Context (10 items)	_____	× 1	_____
Word Parts (5 items)	_____	× 2	_____
		TOTAL SCORE	_____%

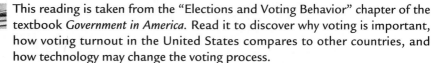

SELECTION 12

Whether to Vote: A Citizen's First Choice

George C. Edwards III, Martin P. Wattenberg, and Robert L. Lineberry

Textbook Excerpt
Contemporary
Issues Reading

This reading is taken from the "Elections and Voting Behavior" chapter of the textbook *Government in America*. Read it to discover why voting is important, how voting turnout in the United States compares to other countries, and how technology may change the voting process.

PREVIEWING THE READING

Using the steps listed on page 36, preview the reading selection. When you have finished, complete the following items.

1. What is the topic of this selection? _____

2. Why might citizens vote? List two reasons.

   a. _____

   b. _____

 MAKING CONNECTIONS

Do you vote? Why or why not? Explain your reasons.

READING TIP

suffrage
the legal right to
vote, extended
to African-
Americans by
the Fifteenth
Amendment,
to women by
the Nineteenth
Amendment, and to
people over the age
of 18 by the Twenty-
sixth Amendment

As you read, keep track of the dates and statistics that are provided.

Whether to Vote: A Citizen's First Choice

1   Two centuries of American electoral history include greatly expanded **suffrage**—the right to vote. In the election of 1800, only property-owning White males over the age of 21 were typically allowed to vote. Now virtually everyone over the age of 18—male or female, White or non-White, rich or poor—has the right to vote. The two major exceptions concern noncitizens and convicted criminals. No state currently permits residents who are not citizens to vote. Some immigrant groups feel that this ought to at least be changed at the local level. State law varies widely when it comes to crime and voting: 46 states deny prisoners the right to vote, 32 states

extend the ban to people on parole, and 10 states impose a lifetime ban on con-victed felons.

2   Interestingly, as the right to vote has been extended, proportionately fewer of those eligible have chosen to exercise that right. In the past 115 years, the 80 per-cent turnout in the 1896 election was the high point of electoral participation. In 2004, only 55 percent of the adult population voted in the presidential election (see Figure A).

Deciding Whether to Vote

3   Realistically, when over 100 million people vote in a presidential election, as they did in 2004, the chance of one vote affecting the outcome is very, very slight. Once in a while, of course, an election is decided by a small number of votes, as occurred in Florida in 2000. It is more likely, however, that you will be struck by lightning dur-ing your lifetime than participate in an election decided by a single vote.

4   Not only does your vote probably not make much difference to the outcome, but voting is somewhat costly. You have to spend some of your valuable time becoming informed, making up your mind, and getting to the polls. If you carefully calculate your time and energy, you might rationally decide that the costs of voting outweigh

FIGURE A   THE DECLINE OF TURNOUT 1892–2004

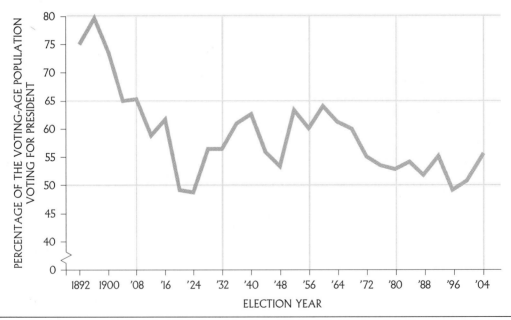

Sources: For data up to 1968, Historical Statistics of the United States (Washington, D.C.: Government Printing Office, 1975), part 2, 1071. For 1972–1988, *Statistical Abstract of the United States, 1990* (Washington, D.C.: Government Printing Office, 1990), 264. Subsequent years from census reports and authors' calculations.

the benefits. Indeed, the most frequent response given by nonvoters in the 2000 Census Bureau survey on turnout was that they could not take time off from work or school that day. Some scholars have therefore proposed that one of the easiest ways to increase American turnout levels would be to move election day to Saturday or make it a holiday.

5   Economist Anthony Downs, in his model of democracy, tries to explain why a rational person would ever bother to vote. He argues that rational people vote if they believe that the policies of one party will bring more benefits than the policies of the other party. Thus people who see policy differences between the parties are more likely to join the ranks of voters. If you are an environmentalist and you expect the Democrats to pass more environmental legislation than the Republicans, then you have an additional incentive to go to the polls. On the other hand, if you are truly indifferent—that is, if you see no difference whatsoever between the two parties—you may rationally decide to abstain.

6   Another reason why many people vote is that they have a high sense of **political efficacy**—the belief that ordinary people can influence the government. Efficacy is measured by asking people to agree or disagree with statements such as "I don't think public officials care much what people like me think." Those who lack strong feelings of efficacy are being quite rational in staying home on Election Day because they don't think they can make a difference. Yet even some of these people will vote anyway, simply to support democratic government. In this case, people are impelled to vote by a sense of **civic duty**. The benefit from doing one's duty is the long term contribution made toward preserving democracy.

political efficacy
the belief that one's political participation really matters—that one's vote can actually make a difference

civic duty
the belief that in order to support democratic government, a citizen should always vote

Young people have one of the lowest rates of election turnout. Music stars like P. Diddy have tried to change this by actively participating in events that encourage young people to vote.

Why Turnout in the United States Is So Low Compared to Other Countries*

7   Despite living in a culture that encourages participation, Americans have a woefully low turnout rate compared to other democracies. There are several reasons given for Americans' abysmally low turnout rate. Probably the reason most often cited is the American requirement of voter registration. The governments of many, but not all, other democracies take the responsibility of seeing to it that all their eligible citizens are on the voting lists. In America, the responsibility for registration lies solely with the individual. If we were to be like the Scandinavian countries and have the government take care of registering every eligible citizen, no doubt our turnout rate would be higher.

8   A second difference between the United States and other countries is that the American government asks citizens to vote far more often. Whereas the typical European voter may be called upon to cast two or three ballots in a four-year period, many Americans are faced with a dozen or more separate elections in the space of four years. Furthermore, Americans are expected to vote for a much wider range of political offices. With one elected official for every 442 citizens and elections held somewhere virtually every week, it is no wonder that it is so difficult to get Americans to the polls. It is probably no coincidence that the one European country that has a lower turnout rate—Switzerland—has also overwhelmed its citizens with voting opportunities, typically asking people to vote three times every year.

9   Finally, the stimulus to vote is low in the United States because the choices offered Americans are not as stark as in other countries. This is because the United States is quite unusual in that it has always lacked a major left-wing socialist party. When European voters go to the polls, they are deciding on whether their country will be run by parties with socialist goals or by conservative (and in some cases religious) parties. The consequences of their vote for redistribution of income and the scope of government are far greater than the ordinary American voter can imagine.

Registering and Voting by E-mail?

10   Future reform designed to increase turnout may well focus on conducting elections through e-mail. Although modern technology is widely available, Americans have not harnessed much of it to improve democracy. Though many precincts now use computer touch screens to record votes, the high-tech age has not yet made much of an impact on the voting process. There is good reason to expect that this will change in the twenty-first century.

11   The development of the personal computer and the World Wide Web are likely to facilitate the process of voter registration. Already, one can go to the website of the Federal Election Commission (**http://www.fec.gov/votregis/vr.htm**) and download the "National Mail Voter Registration Form." Twenty-two states currently accept copies of this application printed from the computer image, signed by the applicant, and mailed in the old-fashioned way. As e-mail becomes ever more popular and "snail mail" fades into a method reserved for packages, the entire voter registration process may someday be conducted mostly through electronic means. In an

---

*Reprinted by permission of the publisher from *Where Have All the Voters Gone?* by Martin P. Wattenberg, p. 15, Cambridge, Mass.: Harvard University Press, Copyright © 2002 by the President and Fellows of Harvard College.

age where personal computers in the home are nearly as common as television sets are today, this technology would clearly make registering to vote more user-friendly.

12   If people can register by computer, the next step is voting by e-mail. A growing trend in the Pacific Coast states has been voting by mail. In 1998, Oregon voters approved a **referendum** to eliminate traditional polling places and conduct all future elections by mail. In California, approximately 25 percent of the votes cast currently come in via the post office. Again, as e-mail takes the place of regular mail, why not have people cast their votes through cyberspace?

referendum
a vote on a specific
question or issue

13   Voting through the Internet would be less costly for the state, as well as easier for the average citizen—assuming that computer literacy reaches near-universal proportions sometime in the future. The major concerns, of course, would be ensuring that no one votes more than once and preserving the confidentiality of the vote. These security concerns are currently being addressed by some of the world's top computer programmers, as commercial enterprises look toward using the Internet to conduct business. If the technology can be perfected to allow trillions of dollars of business to be conducted via the Internet, then it seems reasonable that similar problems can be overcome with regard to the voting process.

14   Whether these possible developments will improve democracy in America is debatable. Making voting more user-friendly should encourage turnout, but people will still have to be interested enough in the elections of the future to send in their e-mail ballots. If old-style polling places are relegated to the history books and everyone votes electronically in the convenience of their own homes, the sense of community on Election Day may be lost. This loss could lead to even lower turnout. You be the policymaker: Do the benefits of voting by e-mail outweigh the potential costs?

A. UNDERSTANDING THE THESIS AND OTHER MAIN IDEAS

Select the best answer.

_____ 1. The central thesis of this selection is that

  a. computer voting will increase turnout.

  b. voter turnout in the United States is low.

  c. people in other countries are more inclined to vote.

  d. voting is a right that not everyone chooses to exercise.

_____ 2. The authors' primary purpose is to

  a. present information on voting history, statistics, and innovations.

  b. persuade readers to exercise their right to vote.

  c. explain why voter turnout is lower in the United States than in Europe.

  d. argue that today's citizens do not deserve the right to vote.

_____ 3. The first paragraph

  a. grabs the reader's attention with interesting trivia.

  b. provides important background information on voting rights.

c. explains how women and African-Americans struggled for the right to vote.

d. introduces the issues surrounding low voter turnout.

_____ 4. The main idea of paragraph 4 is that

    a. election day should be a national holiday.

    b. not everyone can take time off from work to vote.

    c. elections decided by one vote are very rare.

    d. reasons people offer for not voting include lack of time and energy.

_____ 5. In paragraph 7, the authors focus on

    a. the way in which Scandinavian countries register their citizens to vote.

    b. the main reasons for poor voter turnout.

    c. the voter registration process.

    d. voter turnout statistics.

_____ 6. In the last paragraph, the authors

    a. doubt that we will ever raise voter turnout.

    b. conclude that people will be more interested in voting if we use e-mail ballots.

    c. lament the possible loss of community if we go to computer-based voting.

    d. offer a solution to the lack of voter motivation and interest.

B. IDENTIFYING DETAILS

Select the best answer.

_____ 1. Which group cannot vote in any state?

    a. convicted felons

    b. prisoners

    c. noncitizens

    d. people on parole

_____ 2. As more types of people have been given the right to vote, the voter turnout has

    a. increased.

    b. decreased.

    c. stayed the same.

    d. varied considerably.

_____ 3. The Florida 2000 election (paragraph 3) was a
   a. presidential election.
   b. gubernatorial election.
   c. senatorial election.
   d. judicial election.

_____ 4. According to economist Anthony Downs,
   a. the voter registration process is too complicated for the average citizen.
   b. environmentalists vote more than other groups.
   c. voters only consider issues that are important to them.
   d. people vote if they perceive a difference between parties.

_____ 5. One reason people vote that is not included in the reading is
   a. civic duty.
   b. political efficacy.
   c. peer pressure.
   d. support of democratic process.

_____ 6. A difference between U.S. and European elections _not_ mentioned in the selection is
   a. American voters are more apathetic than Europeans.
   b. the voter registration process is more difficult in the United States.
   c. voters in the United States are overwhelmed by the number of elections in which they are expected to participate.
   d. Europeans have more distinct choices with more significant consequences.

_____ 7. What technologies do the authors mention are used or could be used in the election process?
   a. touch-screen recording, Internet registration, and e-mail voting
   b. touch-screen voting and voting by instant message
   c. Internet registration, e-mail voting, and voting by text message
   d. Internet registration, touch-screen voting, and RFID tracking of absentee ballots

_____ 8. Electronic voting is
   a. a sure way to increase voter turnout.
   b. unconstitutional.
   c. a potential security concern.
   d. impossible to implement.

C. RECOGNIZING METHODS OF ORGANIZATION AND TRANSITIONS

Select the best answer.

_____ 1. What is the organizational pattern used to discuss the reasons why Americans choose to vote?

    a. listing

    b. time sequence

    c. cause and effect

    d. comparison and contrast

_____ 2. What pattern is used to organize the information in paragraphs 7 through 10?

    a. listing

    b. time sequence

    c. definition

    d. comparison and contrast

D. REVIEWING AND ORGANIZING IDEAS: SUMMARIZING

Complete the time line of significant voting events described in the selection.

DATE	EVENT
1800	Only _____ over the age of _____ were allowed to vote.
1896	The voter turnout was _____, representing the _____ of electoral participation ever.
1998	In the state of _____, voters decided to conduct future elections by _____.
2000	Census information indicates that people who cannot take off from _____ are _____ to vote.
2000	The presidential election in the state of _____ is decided by a _____ of votes.
2004	Over _____ people voted in the presidential election.

E. READING AND THINKING VISUALLY

Select the best answer.

_____ 1. According to Figure A, the second-highest point of electoral participation in the United States took place in
   a. 1892.
   b. 1900.
   c. 1904.
   d. 1908.

_____ 2. The author likely chose to include the photo of P. Diddy (page 371) with the reading for all of the following reasons *except*
   a. to grab the interest of the college students who are reading the textbook from which the reading was taken.
   b. to explain why voter turnout is often quite low in inner-city communities.
   c. to provide an example of one effective method of getting younger people to cast their votes.
   d. to emphasize the positive consequences of voting and the negative consequences of not voting.

F. FIGURING OUT IMPLIED MEANINGS

Indicate whether each statement is true (T) or false (F).

_____ 1. American women could not vote before 1800.

_____ 2. The election results in Florida in 2000 were unusual.

_____ 3. Republicans do not pass environmental legislation.

_____ 4. European countries do not elect as many officials as the United States.

_____ 5. In the future Americans might vote via the Internet.

G. THINKING CRITICALLY

Select the best answer.

_____ 1. The authors support the central thesis of "Whether to Vote" primarily by
   a. citing authorities.
   b. citing personal experience.
   c. making comparisons.
   d. reporting facts and statistics.

_____ 2. The tone of the selection can best be described as

    a. bitter.

    b. excited.

    c. informative.

    d. sympathetic.

_____ 3. Of the following statements from the reading, which is an opinion?

    a. "State law varies widely when it comes to crime and voting." (paragraph 1)

    b. "Interestingly, as the right to vote has been extended, proportionally fewer of those eligible have chosen to exercise that right." (paragraph 2)

    c. "Some scholars have therefore proposed that one of the easiest ways to increase American turnout levels would be to move election day to Saturday or make it a holiday." (paragraph 4)

    d. "If we were to be like the Scandinavian countries and have the government take care of registering every eligible citizen, no doubt our turnout rate would be higher." (paragraph 7)

_____ 4. The authors include statistics in the reading in order to

    a. provide supporting evidence.

    b. impress the reader with startling facts.

    c. show how misleading statistics can be.

    d. relate the most important information that someone should know about voting behavior.

_____ 5. The authors compare the United States with other countries

    a. to embarrass American voters.

    b. to explain why American voter turnout might be so low.

    c. to describe places to which civic-minded Americans might want to move.

    d. to prove that no country is perfect when it comes to voter turnout.

_____ 6. Overall, the authors' attitude toward voter turnout in the United States seems to be

    a. indifferent.

    b. hopeful.

    c. concerned.

    d. amused.

H. BUILDING VOCABULARY

Context

Using context and a dictionary, if necessary, determine the meaning of each word as it is used in the selection.

_____ 1. rationally (paragraph 4)
    a. simply   c. mindlessly
    b. practically   d. reasonably

_____ 2. woefully (paragraph 7)
    a. distressingly   c. dangerously
    b. carelessly   d. recklessly

_____ 3. abysmally (paragraph 7)
    a. secretly   c. incomprehensibly
    b. profoundly   d. superficially

_____ 4. harnessed (paragraph 10)
    a. powered   c. benefited from
    b. tried   d. made use of

_____ 5. facilitate (paragraph 11)
    a. increase   c. make easier
    b. speed up   d. resolve

_____ 6. relegated (paragraph 14)
    a. banished   c. elected
    b. chosen for   d. dedicated

Word Parts

> **A REVIEW OF PREFIXES AND ROOTS**
>
> **IN-, IM-** means *into*
>
> **CYBER-** refers to *computers*
>
> **PELL** means *drive, move*

Use your knowledge of word parts and the review above to fill in the blanks in the following sentences.

1. *Immigrants* (paragraph 1) are people who have moved _____ a new country.

2. Some citizens are *impelled* (paragraph 6) by civic duty to _____ action and vote.

3. *Cyberspace* (paragraph 12) is the medium in which electronic data from _____ exists or is exchanged.

Unusual Words/Understanding Idioms

Use the meanings given below to write a sentence using the boldfaced word or phrase.

1. If you have recently **joined the ranks** (paragraph 5) of new college students you are in a new group of people all doing the same thing.

   Your sentence: _____

   _____

2. **Snail mail** (paragraph 11) is a term used to refer to regular paper mail sent through the U.S. Postal Service.

   Your sentence: _____

   _____

I. SELECTING A LEARNING/STUDY STRATEGY

Select the best answer.

_____   This reading contains many facts about voting behavior. What would be the best way to learn these facts?

a. visualize the scene at a polling place on election day

b. record the facts on a study sheet

c. read the facts over and over

d. summarize the reading

J. EXPLORING IDEAS THROUGH DISCUSSION AND WRITING

1. Discuss the situation of low voter turnout. Why do you think more eligible Americans do not vote? What do you think would boost voter turnout?

2. Pick a target group. Discuss strategies that would encourage that group to vote.

3. Interview someone from another country about voting behavior. Summarize your findings.

K. BEYOND THE CLASSROOM TO THE WEB

Visit the site for Community Voters Project, an organization that seeks to register minority voters at **http://www.progressivefuture.org/ed/edfund/cvp.** *Review the information on this website and then write a brief description of the organization and its activities.*

TRACKING
YOUR
PROGRESS

Selection 12

Section	Number Correct		Score
A. Thesis and Main Ideas (6 items)	_____	× 3	_____
B. Details (8 items)	_____	× 3	_____
C. Organization and Transitions (2 items)	_____	× 2	_____
E. Reading and Thinking Visually (2 items)	_____	× 3	_____
F. Implied Meanings (5 items)	_____	× 3	_____
G. Thinking Critically (6 items)	_____	× 3	_____
H. Vocabulary			
Context (6 items)	_____	× 2	_____
Word Parts (3 items)	_____	× 1	_____
		TOTAL SCORE	_____%

15 Business/Advertising/Economics

Business is a diverse field that includes business management, marketing, finance, statistics, retailing, information systems, and organizational behavior. In general, **business** is concerned with the production and sale of goods and services. All of us are in contact with businesses on a daily basis. When you stop for gas, buy a sandwich, or pick up the telephone, you are involved in a business transaction. In "The Super Bowl: The Mother of All Advertising Events—But Is It Worth It?" you will how advertising, particularly for the Super Bowl, plays an important role in selling products and services. Studying business can also make you a savvy, better-informed consumer. When you read "McDonald's Makes a Lot of People Angry for a Lot of Different Reasons," you will learn how McDonald's, a popular fast food chain, has not acted as a responsible business leader in the opinion of the authors. Business courses can help you make career decisions and discover a wide range of employment opportunities. Business courses also examine the issue of ethnic and cultural diversity since today's workforce consists of individuals from a variety of cultural and ethnic groups. As you read "Product Placement and Advergaming," you will see how product advertisement through placement seeps into popular culture.

Use the following techniques for reading in business.

TIPS FOR READING IN BUSINESS/ ADVERTISING/ ECONOMICS	■ **Focus on process.** Many courses in business examine how things work and how things get done. In "Product Placement and Advergaming" you will learn how specific products and brand names are used in movies, television, and other media. In "The Super Bowl: The Mother of All Advertising Events—But Is It Worth It?" you will discover how advertisers build interest in and excitement about their ads.
	■ **Focus on the theme of globalization.** Growing numbers of U.S. businesses are doing business with firms in other countries and are competing in foreign markets. In "McDonald's Makes a Lot of People Angry for a Lot of Different Reasons," you will see that McDonald's has become a global corporation.
	■ **Consider ethical decision making and social responsibility.** The application of moral standards to business activities and operations is of increasing importance in the field of business. Issues of honesty, fairness, environmental safety, and public health are often discussed in business courses. In "McDonald's Makes a Lot of People Angry for a Lot of Different Reasons," the authors suggest that McDonald's has acted irresponsibly in a number of different areas.

| SELECTION 13 | The Super Bowl: The Mother of All Advertising Events—But Is It Worth It? |

Philip Kotler and Gary Armstrong

Textbook
Excerpt

This reading was taken from the "Advertising and Public Relations" chapter of the textbook *Principles of Marketing*. Read it to learn about the costs and benefits of advertising during the Super Bowl.

PREVIEWING THE READING

Using the steps listed on page 36, preview the reading selection. When you have finished, complete the following items.

1. The subject of this selection is _____.

2. The main question you expect to be able to answer after reading this selection is:

_____

 MAKING CONNECTIONS

Do you typically watch the Super Bowl? If so, do you look forward to the commercials as part of your viewing experience or do you ignore them?

READING TIP

As you read, use two different colors of ink to highlight the pros and cons of advertising during the Super Bowl.

The Super Bowl: The Mother of All Advertising Events—But Is It Worth It?

1   The Super Bowl is the mother of all advertising events. Each year, dozens of blue chip advertisers showcase some of their best work to huge audiences around the world. But all this doesn't come cheap. Last year, major advertisers plunked down an average of $2.7 million per 30-second spot and will top $3 million in 2009. Over the past two decades, they've spent over $2 *billion* on just 11.5 hours of Super Bowl advertising time. But that's just for the air time. Throw in ad production costs—often

$1 million or more per showcase commercial—and running even a single Super Bowl ad becomes a super-expensive proposition. Anheuser-Busch ran *seven* spots last year.

2   So every year, as the Super Bowl season nears, up pops the BIG QUESTION: Is Super Bowl advertising worth all that money? Does it deliver a high advertising **ROI**? As it turns out, there's no easy answer to the question.

ROI
return on
investment

3   Advertiser and industry expert opinion varies widely. Super Bowl stalwarts such as Anheuser-Busch, FedEx, General Motors, CareerBuilder, and the Frito-Lay, Gatorade, and Pepsi-Cola divisions of PepsiCo must think it's a good investment—they come back year after year. But what about savvy marketers such as Unilever, who opted out last year? In a survey of board members of the National Sports Marketing Network, 31 percent said they would recommend Super Bowl ads. But 41 percent said no—Super Bowl ads just aren't worth the money.

4   The naysayers make some pretty good arguments. Super Bowl advertising is outrageously expensive. Advertisers pay 85 percent more per viewer than they'd pay using prime-time network programming. And that $2.7 million would buy a lot of alternative media—for example, 50 different product placements in movies, TV shows, and video games; or two massive billboards in New York's Times Square that would be seen by a million people each day for a year. Beyond the cost, the competition for attention during the Super Bowl is fierce. Every single ad represents the best efforts of a major marketer trying to design a knock-your-socks-off spectacular that will reap high ratings from both critics and consumers. Many advertisers feel they can get more for their advertising dollar in venues that aren't so crowded with bigger-than-life commercials.

5   Then there's the question of strategic fit. Whereas the Super Bowl might be a perfect advertising event for big-budget companies selling beer, snacks, soft drinks, or sporting goods, it simply doesn't fit the pocketbooks or creative strategies of many other companies and their brands. One media executive likens a Super Bowl ad to a trophy wife: "It makes sense if you are an advertiser with a huge budget," he says. "But if you're an advertiser with a modest budget, that would not be the best use of your money."

6   As for creative fit, consider Unilever's Dove. Three years ago, the company ran a sentimental 45-second commercial from the Dove "Campaign for Real Beauty." The ad was highly rated by consumers and it created considerable buzz—some 400 million impressions of the ad before and after its single appearance on the Super Bowl. But much of that buzz came from publicity surrounding the issue of girls' self-esteem rather than the product. And research showed that the ad produced low levels of involvement with the brand message.

7   Dove got almost equal exposure numbers and more engagement for a lot less money from an outdoor campaign that it ran that same year, and it got a much larger online response from its **viral** "Dove Evolution" and "Onslaught" films, which incurred no media cost at all. "The Super Bowl really isn't the right environment for Dove," says a Unilever executive. The past two years, instead, Dove opted to run consumer-generated ads during the more-female-oriented Academy Awards, an event where beauty brands thrive.

viral
made wildly
popular via
the Internet

8   Still, the Super Bowl has a lot to offer to the right advertisers. It's the most-watched TV event of the year. It plays to a huge and receptive audience—97.5 million viewers who put away their DVR remotes and watch it live, glued to their screens, ads and all. In fact, to many viewers, the Super Bowl ads are more important than what happens on the **gridiron**. Last year, the game itself drew an average 41.6 rating; the ads drew 41.22.

gridiron
football field

9   "There is no other platform quite like the Super Bowl," says the chief creative officer at Anheuser-Busch. "It's worth it. When you can touch that many households [with that kind of impact] in one sitting, it's actually efficient." In terms of dollars and cents, a study by one research firm found that consumer package-goods firms get a return of $1.25 to $2.74 for every dollar invested in Super Bowl advertising and one Super Bowl ad is as effective as 250 regular TV spots.

10   What's more, for most advertisers, the Super Bowl ad itself is only the centerpiece of something much bigger. Long after the game is over, ad critics, media pundits, and consumers are still reviewing, rehashing, and rating the commercials. It's one of the few sports-related events where "it ain't over when it's over." Thus, measuring the effectiveness of Super Bowl advertising involves a lot more than just measuring eyeballs and reach. "Those 30 seconds of fame are only the tip of the iceberg," says the analyst, "with online views, water-cooler chatter, blog buzz, and *USA Today's* ratings all below the surface."

11   The Super Bowl is the only media property where the advertising is as big a story as the content of the show," says Steven Schreibman, vice president of advertising and brand management for Nationwide Financial, "so you want to see how much you can leverage it." Schreibman is still agog over the response to Nationwide's Super Bowl spot two years ago that featured the hunk Fabio demonstrating that "life comes at you fast." Months afterward, consumers were

still visiting Web sites such as ifilm.com to watch the commercial. "We got 1.8 million downloads on [just] that one site," says Schreibman. "Fabio himself keeps me apprised of that."

12   Advertisers don't usually sit back and just hope that consumers will talk about their ads. They build events that help to boost the buzz. For example, year before last, leading up to the Super Bowl at least three advertisers—GM's Chevrolet Division, the NFL, and Doritos—held contests inviting consumers to create their own Super Bowl ads. Doritos' "Crash the Super Bowl Challenge" contest produced more than 1,000 quality entries, considerable media attention, and a bunch of online consumer interest. The winning ad topped the IAG Top 10 Best-Liked Super Bowl Ads list and came in fourth in the *USA Today* Ad Meter rankings.

13   The Super Bowl's largest advertiser, Anheuser-Busch, extends the festivities far beyond game day. It follows up with a postgame e-mail campaign to keep the fires burning. It also hosts a designated Web site where consumers can view all of the company's Super Bowl ads and vote for their favorites via the Web site or text messages.

14   So—back to the original question. Is the Super Bowl advertising really worth the huge investment? It seems that there's no definitive answer—for some advertisers it's "yes": for others, "no." The real trick is in trying to measure the returns. As the title of one recent article asserts, "Measuring Bowl Return? Good Luck!" The writer's conclusion; "For all the time, energy, and angst marketers spend crafting the perfect Super Bowl spot, [that's] a relative breeze compared to trying to prove its return on investment."

A. UNDERSTANDING THE THESIS AND OTHER MAIN IDEAS

Select the best answer.

_____ 1. The central question that the authors address in this selection is:
   a. How much do television ads cost during the Super Bowl?
   b. Do most viewers watch commercials during the Super Bowl?
   c. Is Super Bowl advertising worth the cost?
   d. What is the most popular Super Bowl ad?

_____ 2. The authors' primary purpose is to
   a. persuade companies to advertise during the Super Bowl.
   b. criticize networks for overcharging for Super Bowl ads.
   c. explain why Super Bowl ads cost so much to produce.
   d. discuss the benefits and costs of Super Bowl advertising.

_____ 3. The main point of paragraphs 6–7 is that Unilever's Dove ad during the Super Bowl was
   a. overly sentimental.
   b. too expensive.
   c. too female oriented.
   d. not a good fit creatively.

_____ 4. The statement that best expresses the main idea of paragraph 10 is
   a. "for most advertisers, the Super Bowl ad itself is only the center-piece of something much bigger."
   b. "ad critics, media pundits, and consumers are still reviewing, rehashing, and rating the commercials."
   c. "It's one of the few sports-related events where 'it ain't over when it's over.'"
   d. "Those 30 seconds of fame are only the tip of the iceberg."

_____ 5. The main idea of paragraph 12 is that advertisers
   a. hope that consumers will talk about their ads.
   b. create special events to increase the effect of their ads.
   c. hold contests inviting consumers to make their own Super Bowl ads.
   d. compete with each other for the highest Ad Meter rankings.

B. IDENTIFYING DETAILS

Complete each of the following statements by filling in the blank with the correct numerical amount.

1. Last year, major advertisers paid an average of $_____ per 30-second spot.

2. Over the past two decades, advertisers have spent more than $_____ on _____ hours of Super Bowl advertising time.

3. Production costs for a single showcase Super Bowl commercial are often $_____ or more.

4. In a survey of board members of the National Sports Marketing network, _____ percent would recommend Super Bowl ads and _____ percent would not.

5. Advertisers pay _____ percent more per viewer than they would pay using prime-time network programming.

6. Consumer package-goods firms get a return of $_____ to $_____ for every dollar invested in Super Bowl advertising.

7. One Super Bowl ad is as effective as _____ regular TV spots.

C. RECOGNIZING METHODS OF ORGANIZATION AND TRANSITIONS

Complete the statements by filling in the blanks.

1. In paragraph 3, the phrase that signals that examples will follow is _____.

2. In paragraph 5, the authors use the _____ organizational pattern to discuss how Super Bowl advertising may be a good strategic fit for some companies and not for others. Two transitions that indicate the authors' pattern are _____ and _____.

3. In paragraphs 6–7, the authors explain the importance of creative fit by contrasting different Dove ad campaigns. The transition that signals Dove's decision to change to a better environment for its product is _____.

D. REVIEWING AND ORGANIZING IDEAS: PARAPHRASING

Complete the following paraphrase of paragraph 8 by filling in the missing words and phrases.

The _____ is a good option for the right _____. More people watch it each year than _____. The Super Bowl's _____ of _____ million people watches the _____ and the _____ live. For many, what happens in the _____ is less important than the _____. Last year's _____ had an average rating of _____ compared to a rating of _____ for the ads.

E. READING AND THINKING VISUALLY

Answer the following questions.

1. What adjectives would you use to describe the people in the photograph that accompanies this reading?

_____

2. What ideas in the reading does this photograph explain or enhance?

_____

_____

F. FIGURING OUT IMPLIED MEANINGS

Indicate whether each statement is true (T) or false (F).

_____ 1. It can be inferred that Anheuser-Busch spent several million dollars on its Super Bowl ads last year.

_____ 2. Advertisers and industry experts are in complete agreement that Super Bowl advertising is worth the money.

_____ 3. Super Bowl advertising is more appropriate for certain types of products than others.

_____ 4. Super Bowl advertising is a good creative fit for beauty brands like Dove.

_____ 5. Anheuser-Busch believes that Super Bowl ads are worth the investment.

G. THINKING CRITICALLY

Select the best answer.

_____ 1. The authors support their thesis with all of the following *except*

    a. facts.

    b. statistics.

    c. examples.

    d. personal experience.

_____ 2. The title refers to the Super Bowl as "the mother of all advertising events" because it

    a. was the first television event to feature advertising.

    b. is the biggest and most important advertising event.

    c. has generated many other advertising events.

    d. has created a loyal and devoted following.

_____ 3. The authors include the story about Nationwide's Super Bowl ad in paragraph 11 to illustrate

    a. how popular Fabio is with football fans.

    b. how viewers use the Internet to watch commercials.

    c. why advertisers feature well-known celebrities in ads.

    d. how ads continue to generate attention after the Super Bowl.

_____ 4. The conclusion of the selection suggests that

    a. Super Bowl advertising is worth the investment.

    b. Super Bowl advertising is definitely *not* worth the investment.

    c. trying to prove a Super Bowl ad's return on investment is difficult.

    d. marketers spend too much time trying to craft the perfect Super Bowl ad.

_____ 5. The overall tone of this selection can best be described as

    a. disapproving.

    b. serious.

    c. informal.

    d. indignant.

H. BUILDING VOCABULARY

Context

Using context and a dictionary, if necessary, determine the meaning of each word as it is used in the selection.

_____ 1. stalwarts (paragraph 3)

    a. loyal participants

    b. detractors

    c. critics

    d. consumers

_____ 2. savvy (paragraph 3)

    a. difficult

    b. shrewd

    c. picky

    d. similar

_____ 3. massive (paragraph 4)

    a. complex

    b. essential

    c. huge

    d. dark

_____ 4. reap (paragraph 4)

    a. adjust

    b. introduce

    c. allow

    d. collect

_____ 5. incurred (paragraph 7)

    a. forced

    b. brought on

    c. repeated

    d. misplaced

_____ 6. leverage (paragraph 11)

    a. resist

    b. influence

    c. select

    d. disapprove

_____ 7. agog (paragraph 11)

    a. very excited

    b. very confused

    c. against

    d. upset

_____ 8. apprised (paragraph 11)

    a. promised

    b. complained

    c. informed

    d. trained

_____ 9. angst (paragraph 14)

    a. ease

    b. anxiety

    c. power

    d. enjoyment

Word Parts

Complete the following sentence by filling in the blank.

If you know that the prefix *post-* means *after*, then a **postgame** e-mail campaign (paragraph 13) is one that takes place _____ the game.

Unusual Words/Understanding Idioms

Use the meanings given below to write a sentence using the boldfaced word or phrase.

1. Something that is described as **blue chip** (paragraph 1) is of the highest quality.

    Your sentence: _____

    _____

2. The phrase **knock-your-socks-off** (paragraph 4) applies when something is astonishingly good.

    Your sentence: _____

    _____

3. Something that is described as **the tip of the iceberg** (paragraph 10) is just a small, observable part of something much larger.

    Your sentence: _____

    _____

I. SELECTING A LEARNING/STUDY STRATEGY

Evaluate your highlighting in this reading. How else might you organize information about the pros and cons of advertising during the Super Bowl?

J. EXPLORING IDEAS THROUGH DISCUSSION AND WRITING

1. If you watch the Super Bowl, do you care more about the game or the commercials? After watching a Super Bowl, do you ever rewatch the commercials online or discuss them with friends or co-workers?

2. Consider the different products you use or consume on a regular basis. Which ones do you think would be a good strategic or creative fit for the Super Bowl? Which would be better for the Academy Awards or some other advertising event? Write a paragraph explaining your answers.

3. Describe a commercial that was memorable to you. What features made the commercial appealing? Were you persuaded to buy the product being advertised?

K. BEYOND THE CLASSROOM TO THE WEB

Go to **http://www.nielsen.com/us/en/insights/top10s.html** *and explore the "Top Tens and Trends" section of the Web site for the Nielsen Company, a global marketing and advertising research company. Which trends did you find most surprising or interesting? What other parts of the Web site attracted your attention and why?*

TRACKING YOUR PROGRESS

Selection 13

Section	Number Correct		Score
A. Thesis and Main Ideas (5 items)	_____	×4	_____
B. Details (10 items)	_____	×2	_____
C. Organization and Transitions (5 items)	_____	×2	_____
F. Implied Meanings (5 items)	_____	×4	_____
G. Thinking Critically (5 items)	_____	×4	_____
H. Vocabulary			
Context (9 items)	_____	×1	_____
Word Parts (1 item)	_____	×1	_____
		TOTAL SCORE	_____ %

SELECTION 14

McDonald's Makes a Lot of People Angry for a Lot of Different Reasons

Contemporary Issues Reading

This article was written by the McInformation Network, a volunteer organization dedicated to collecting information and encouraging debate about the workings, policies, and practices of the McDonald's Corporation.

PREVIEWING THE READING

Using the steps listed on page 36, preview the reading selection. When you have finished, complete the following items.

1. What question do you expect the reading to answer?

   _____

2. List at least four issues addressed in the reading.

   a. _____

   b. _____

   c. _____

   d. _____

MAKING CONNECTIONS

How often do you eat fast food? Have you ever thought about fast food's effects on society, workers, and people's waistlines?

READING TIP

This reading uses emotional language to present information. Be sure to note whether the authors' statements are based on facts or opinions.

McDonald's Makes a Lot of People Angry for a Lot of Different Reasons

1   McDonald's makes a lot of people angry for a lot of different reasons.

Nutrition

nutritionists
experts in the
field of nutrition

2   **Nutritionists**, for example, argue that the type of high fat, low fiber diet promoted by McDonald's is linked to serious diseases such as cancer, heart disease, obesity, and diabetes—the sort of diseases that are now responsible for nearly three quarters of premature deaths in the western world. McDonald's responds that the scientific evidence is not conclusive and that its food can be a valuable part of a balanced diet.

3   Some people say McDonald's is entitled to sell junk food in exactly the same way that chocolate or cream cake manufacturers do: if people want to buy it, that's their decision. But should McDonald's be allowed to advertise its products as nutritious? Why does it sponsor sports events when it sells unhealthy products? And what on earth is McDonald's doing opening restaurants in hospitals?

Environment

conservationists
people who
advocate the
conservation
of natural
resources

4   **Conservationists** have often focused on McDonald's as an industry leader promoting business practices detrimental to the environment. And yet the company spends a fortune promoting itself as environmentally friendly. What's the story?

5   One of the most well-known and sensitive questions about McDonald's is: is McDonald's responsible for the destruction of tropical forests to make way for cattle ranching? McDonald's says no. Many people say yes. So McDonald's sues them. Not so many people say yes anymore, but does this mean McDonald's isn't responsible?

6   McDonald's annually produces over a million tons of packaging, used for just a few minutes before being discarded. What environmental effect does the production and disposal of all this have? Is its record on recycling and recycled products as green as it makes out? Is McDonald's responsible for litter on the streets, or is that the fault of the customer who drops it? Can any multinational company operating on McDonald's scale *not* contribute to global warming, ozone destruction, depletion of mineral resources, and the destruction of natural habitats?

Advertising

7   McDonald's spends over two billion dollars each year on advertising: the Golden Arches are now more recognized than the Christian cross. Using collectible toys, television ads, promotional schemes in schools, and figures such as Ronald McDonald, the company bombards its main target group: children. Many parents object strongly to the influence this has over their own children.

philanthropy
an activity or
institution intended
for the good of
humankind

8   McDonald's argues that its advertising is no worse than anyone else's and that it adheres to all the advertising codes in each country. But others argue it still amounts to cynical exploitation of children—some consumer organizations are calling for a ban on advertising to children. Why does McDonald's sponsor so many school events and learning programs? Is its Children's Charities genuine **philanthropy** or is there a more explicit publicity and profit motive?

Employment

9   The Corporation has pioneered a global, highly standardized and fast production-line system, geared to maximum turnover of products and profits. McDonald's now employs more than a million mostly young people around the world. Some say a million people might otherwise be out of work; others, however, consider that McDonald's is in fact a net destroyer of jobs by using low wages and the huge size of its business to undercut local food outlets and thereby force them out of business. Is McDonald's a great job opportunity or is it taking advantage of high unemployment to exploit the most vulnerable people in society, working them very hard for very little money? Complaints from employees range from discrimination and lack of rights, to understaffing, few breaks and illegal hours, to poor safety conditions and kitchens flooded with sewage, to the sale of food that has been dropped on the floor. This type of low-paid work has even been termed "McJobs."

trade unionists 10 members of a labor union, especially those in the same trade

10   **Trade unionists** don't like McDonald's either. The company is notorious for the vehemence with which it tries to crush any unionization attempt. McDonald's argues that all its workers are happy and that any problems can be worked out directly without the need for interference from a third party, but is McDonald's in fact just desperate to prevent any efforts by the workers to improve wages and conditions?

Animals

vegetarians 11 people who maintain a meat-free diet

11   **Vegetarians** and animal welfare campaigners aren't too keen on McDonald's—for obvious reasons. As the world's largest user of beef, McDonald's is responsible for the slaughter of hundreds of thousands of cows per year. In Europe alone McDonald's uses half a million chickens every week, all from windowless factory farms. All such animals suffer great cruelty during their unnatural, painful and short lives, many being kept inside with no access to fresh air and sunshine, and no freedom of movement—how can such cruelty be measured? Is it acceptable for the food industry to exploit animals at all? Again, McDonald's argues that it sticks to the letter of the law and if there are any problems it is a matter for government. McDonald's also claims to be concerned with animal welfare.

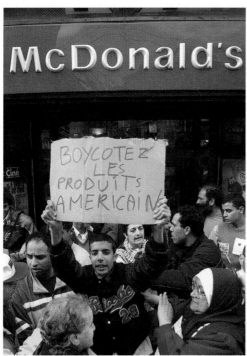

Expansion

12   In 1996 McDonald's opened in India for the first time: a country where the majority of the population is vegetarian and the cow is sacred. This is just one example of the inexorable spread of western multinationals into every corner of the globe, a spread which is creating a globalized system in which wealth is drained out of local economies into the hands of a very few, very rich elite. Can people challenge the undermining of long-lived and stable cultures and regional diversity? Self-sufficient and sustainable farming is replaced by cash crops and agribusiness under control of multinationals—but how are people fighting back?

capitalism
an economic system in which the means of production and distribution are privately or corporately owned

socialism
a social system in which the means of producing and distributing goods are owned collectively and political power is exercised by the whole community

anarchism
the theory or doctrine that all forms of government are oppressive and undesirable and should be abolished

Free Speech

13   So, it seems as though lots of people are opposed to the way McDonald's goes about its business. So there is a big global debate going on about them, right? Wrong. McDonald's knows full well how important its public image is and how damaging it would be if any of the allegations started becoming well-known among its customers. So McDonald's uses its financial clout to influence the media and legal powers to intimidate people into not speaking out, directly threatening free speech. The list of media organizations who have been sued in the past is daunting, and the number of publications suppressed or pulped is frightening. But what are the lessons of the successful and ever-growing anti-McDonald's campaign for those also determined to challenge those institutions which currently dominate society?

Capitalism

14   Nobody is arguing that the huge and growing global environmental and social crisis is entirely the fault of one high-profile burger chain, or even just the whole food industry. McDonald's is, of course, simply a particularly arrogant, shiny and self-important example of a system that values profits at the expense of anything else. Even if McDonald's were to close down tomorrow, someone else would simply slip straight into its position. There is a much more fundamental problem than Big Macs and French fries: **capitalism**. But what about anti-capitalist beliefs like **socialism** and **anarchism**? Is it possible to create a world run by ordinary people themselves, without multinationals and governments—a world based on sharing, freedom, and respect for all life?

A. UNDERSTANDING THE THESIS AND OTHER MAIN IDEAS

Select the best answer.

_____ 1. The central thesis of "McDonald's Makes a Lot of People Angry for a Lot of Different Reasons" is that
   a. many customers are unhappy with the service they get at McDonald's.
   b. competitors, such as Burger King and Hardee's, resent the success of McDonald's.
   c. McDonald's restaurants have been a target for robbery, vandalism, and other serious crimes.
   d. many different groups of people are disturbed by the global effects of McDonald's and other multinational corporations.

_____ 2. The authors' primary purpose in the article is to
   a. describe their efforts to bring about reform.
   b. compare McDonald's with more environmentally sensitive corporations.
   c. describe the harmful effects of McDonald's.
   d. persuade consumers to boycott McDonald's and other fast-food restaurants.

_____ 3. The topic of paragraph 6 is
   a. McDonald's environmental effects.
   b. consumers who litter.
   c. recycling.
   d. global warming.

_____ 4. The topic of paragraph 8 is
   a. children's charities.
   b. consumer organizations.
   c. philanthropy.
   d. advertising.

_____ 5. The main idea of paragraph 11 is expressed in the
   a. first sentence.
   b. second sentence.
   c. third sentence.
   d. last sentence.

_____ 6. The main idea of paragraph 13 is that
   a. there is currently a global debate about McDonald's practices.
   b. McDonald's uses its power to silence critics, thus threatening free speech.
   c. a lot of people are opposed to the way McDonald's conducts business.
   d. the anti-McDonald's campaign is successful and ever-growing.

_____ 7. The statement that best expresses the main idea of paragraph 14 is
   a. "Nobody is arguing that the huge and growing global environmental and social crisis is entirely the fault of one high-profile burger chain . . . "
   b. "McDonald's is, of course, simply a particularly arrogant . . . example . . . "
   c. "Even if McDonald's were to close down tomorrow, someone else would simply slip straight into its position."
   d. "There is a much more fundamental problem than Big Macs and French fries: capitalism."

B. IDENTIFYING DETAILS

Indicate whether each statement is true (T) or false (F).

_____ 1. The term "McJobs" has been used to describe a type of low-paid work.

_____ 2. McDonald's is not permitted to open restaurants in hospitals.

_____ 3. According to the authors, McDonald's annually spends more than two billion dollars on advertising.

_____ 4. McDonald's opened in India for the first time in 1996.

_____ 5. McDonald's employs more than a million people in America.

C. RECOGNIZING METHODS OF ORGANIZATION AND TRANSITIONS

Complete the following statements by filling in the blanks.

1. In paragraph 2, the authors report that nutritionists believe McDonald's food can be linked to serious diseases and that McDonald's disagrees. This organizational pattern is _____ because the authors present both points of view.

2. In paragraph 9, the authors use _____ to present opposing points of view about McDonald's employment.

3. The transitional phrase in paragraph 9 that indicates a contrast between two ideas is _____ .

D. REVIEWING AND ORGANIZING IDEAS: OUTLINING

Complete the following outline of the "Employment" section (paragraphs 9 and 10) by filling in the missing words.

I. McDonald's system

    A. Global _____

    B. Highly _____

    C. Fast _____

    D. Geared to _____ of products and _____

II. Employees

    A. More than _____ employees worldwide

       1. Great job opportunity for people who would otherwise be

         _____

       2. Net _____ of jobs

         a. Uses _____ wages

         b. Huge size forces _____ out of business

         c. Exploiting most _____ people in society

       3. _____

         a. Discrimination

         b. Lack of _____

    c. _____

    d. Few _____

    e. _____ hours

    f. Poor _____ conditions

    g. Kitchens flooded with _____

    h. Sale of food that has been _____

  4. Low-paid work called _____

III. _____

  A. Don't like McDonald's

  B. McDonald's prevents _____

    1. Argues that employees are _____

    2. _____ can be worked out without the need for _____ interference

    3. Desperate to prevent _____ from improving _____

E. READING AND THINKING VISUALLY

Select the best answer.

_____ 1. The author probably chose to include the photo shown on page 395 in order to

  a. illustrate the international reach of the McDonald's corporation.

  b. imply that most Indians are vegetarian and wish to outlaw companies that sell hamburgers.

  c. show that the residents of foreign countries sometimes resent the presence of American businesses.

  d. make the point that local McDonald's restaurants tend to have a negative effect on the communities in which they are located.

_____ 2. The sign in the photo reads "Boycott American Products" (translated from French). Which of the following reasons are boycotters *least* likely to give for boycotting American companies and products?

  a. They believe that American companies are unfair to their workers.

  b. They want people from their own country to start businesses rather than have American businesses take over their local economy.

  c. They believe that their own country produces products that are of higher quality than American ones.

  d. They want people to support the creation of jobs in their own country rather than in America.

F. FIGURING OUT IMPLIED MEANINGS

Make inferences by indicating whether each of the following boldfaced words creates a positive (P) or negative (N) image for the reader.

_____ 1. ". . . part of a **balanced** diet." (paragraph 2)

_____ 2. ". . . environmentally **friendly.**" (paragraph 4)

_____ 3. ". . . the company **bombards** its main target group . . ." (paragraph 7)

_____ 4. ". . . is McDonald's in fact just **desperate** . . ." (paragraph 10)

_____ 5. ". . . wealth is **drained** out of local economies . . ." (paragraph 12)

G. THINKING CRITICALLY

Select the best answer.

_____ 1. The authors' tone throughout the article can best be described as
  a. critical and concerned.
  b. sympathetic.
  c. realistic and honest.
  d. objective and unbiased.

_____ 2. When the authors ask questions throughout the reading, they are primarily trying to
  a. add humor to the article.
  b. emphasize how curious they are.
  c. provoke thought about the issues.
  d. show that they don't know the answers.

_____ 3. The authors refer to all of the following groups to support their thesis *except*
  a. nutritionists.
  b. politicians.
  c. conservationists.
  d. animal welfare campaigners.

_____ 4. According to the authors, McDonald's has responded to critics in environmental groups and the media by
  a. ignoring them.
  b. bribing them.
  c. suing them.
  d. amending its operations.

H. BUILDING VOCABULARY

Context

Using context and a dictionary, if necessary, determine the meaning of each word as it is used in the selection.

_____ 1. detrimental (paragraph 4)
   a. advantageous
   b. minor
   c. harmful
   d. intense

_____ 2. depletion (paragraph 6)
   a. discussion
   b. reduction
   c. replacement
   d. contribution

_____ 3. notorious (paragraph 10)
   a. having a common trait
   b. famous for something undesirable
   c. well respected
   d. strong and forceful

_____ 4. vehemence (paragraph 10)
   a. forcefulness
   b. professionalism
   c. sympathy
   d. calmness

_____ 5. diversity (paragraph 12)
   a. agreement
   b. similarity
   c. variety
   d. differences

_____ 6. daunting (paragraph 13)
   a. lengthening
   b. diminishing
   c. harmful
   d. intimidating

Word Parts

> **A REVIEW OF PREFIXES**
>
> **ANTI-** means *against*
>
> **IN-** means *not*
>
> **MULTI-** means *many*
>
> **PRE-** means *before*
>
> **UN-** means *not*

Match each word in Column A with its meaning in Column B. Write your answers in the spaces provided.

Column A	Column B
_____ 1. anticapitalist	a. lack of work
_____ 2. multinational	b. before the normal time
_____ 3. inexorable	c. against capitalism
_____ 4. premature	d. having operations or investments in more than two countries
_____ 5. unemployment	e. not preventable, relentless

Unusual Words/Understanding Idioms

Select the best answer.

_____ 1. When the authors ask if McDonald's has a record on recycling that is as "**green**" as it claims (paragraph 6), the word *green* refers to

a. the color green.

b. the environment.

c. money.

d. a lack of experience.

_____ 2. The word "**pulped**" (paragraph 13) means

a. inflated.

b. reduced.

c. crushed.

d. turned to paper.

I. SELECTING A LEARNING/STUDY STRATEGY

Suppose you have been asked to evaluate the evidence the authors provide to support their accusations against McDonald's. For each accusation, highlight the specific evidence the authors provide. For each statement you highlight, decide whether there is sufficient or insufficient evidence to support the claim.

J. EXPLORING IDEAS THROUGH DISCUSSION AND WRITING

1. The authors are biased against McDonald's. In what ways is this bias revealed?

2. What ethical or moral issues does this selection raise?

3. What is the opposing viewpoint not presented in this article? That is, in what ways does McDonald's benefit society?

K. BEYOND THE CLASSROOM TO THE WEB

Read this statement about Happy Meals on the Web site of Corporate Accountability International: **http://www.stopcorporateabuse.org/node/1421.**

Do you agree? Why or why not? Write a short response to this statement.

**TRACKING
YOUR
PROGRESS**

Selection 14

Section	Number Correct		Score
A. Thesis and Main Ideas (7 items)	_____	×3	_____
B. Details (5 items)	_____	×3	_____
C. Organization and Transitions (3 items)	_____	×3	_____
E. Reading and Thinking Visually (2 items)	_____	×3	_____
F. Implied Meanings (5 items)	_____	×3	_____
G. Thinking Critically (4 items)	_____	×3	_____
H. Vocabulary			
Context (6 items)	_____	×2	_____
Word Parts (5 items)	_____	×2	_____
		TOTAL SCORE	_____%

SELECTION 15

Product Placement and Advergaming

Michael Solomon

Textbook
Excerpt

Taken from a textbook titled *Consumer Behavior,* this reading selection describes how specific products and brand names are used in movies, television, and other media.

PREVIEWING THE READING

Using the steps listed on page 36, preview the reading selection. When you have finished, complete the following items.

1. The topic of this selection is _____.

2. List four questions you might be able to answer after reading this selection.

   a. _____

   b. _____

   c. _____

   d. _____

MAKING CONNECTIONS

Think about a movie or television show you have seen recently and try to recall whether you noticed the particular products or brands being shown.

READING TIP

This selection contains many examples of the "what"—in other words, the particular brands and products that appear in different types of media. As you read, be sure to notice the "why"—the reasons given for the use of product placement in each type of media.

Product Placement and Advergaming

Product Placement and Advergaming

1   Back in the day, TV networks demanded that producers "geek" (alter) brand names before they appeared in a show, as when *Melrose Place* changed a

aura
atmosphere

Nokia cell phone to a "Nokio." Today, real products pop up everywhere. Many are well-established brands that lend an **aura** of realism to the action, while others are upstarts that benefit tremendously from the exposure. For example, in the movie version of *Sex and the City* Carrie's assistant admits that she "borrows" her expensive pricey handbags from a rental Web site called Bag Borrow or Steal. The company's head of marketing commented, "It's like the *Good Housekeeping* Seal of Approval. It gives us instant credibility and recognition."

Product Placement

2   Bag Borrow or Steal got a free plug (oops, they got another one here!). In many cases, however, these "plugs" are no accident. Product placement is the insertion of real products in fictional movies, TV shows, books, and plays. Many types of products play starring (or at least supporting) roles in our culture; the most visible brands range from Coca-Cola and Nike apparel to the Chicago Bears football team and the Pussycat Dolls band. The TV shows that feature the most placements include *The Biggest Loser* (it showed about 4,000 brands in just a three-month period), *American Idol* (how subtle is that Coca-Cola glass each judge holds?), *The Apprentice, America's Next Top Model,* and *One Tree Hill.* This practice is so commonplace (and profitable) now that it's evolved into a new form of promotion we call branded entertainment, where advertisers showcase their products in longer-form narrative films instead of brief commercials. For example, *SportsCenter* on ESPN showed installments of "The Scout presented by Craftsman at Sears," a 6-minute story about a washed-up baseball scout who discovers a stunningly talented stadium groundskeeper.

A dining room influenced by the TV show *Dexter*, which features a serial killer.
Source: Photo by Adam Chinitz/Courtesy of AC Imaging, LLC.

3   Product placement is by no means a casual process: Marketers pay about $25 billion per year to plug their brands in TV and movies. Several firms specialize in arranging these appearances; if they're lucky they manage to do it on the cheap when they get a client's product noticed by prop masters who work on the shows. For example, in a cafeteria scene during an episode of *Grey's Anatomy* it was no coincidence that the character Izzie Stevens happened to drink a bottle of Izze Sparkling Pomegranate fruit beverage. The placement company that represents PepsiCo paid nothing to insert the prop in that case, but it probably didn't get off so easily when the new brand also showed up in HBO's *Entourage, Big Bang Theory,* and *The New Adventures of Old Christine* on CBS.

4   Today most major releases brim with real products, even though a majority of consumers believe the line between advertising and programming is becoming too fuzzy and distracting (though as we might expect, concerns about this blurring of boundaries are more pronounced among older people than younger). A study reported that consumers respond well to placements when the show's plot makes the product's benefit clear. Similarly, audiences had a favorable impression of when a retailer provided furniture, clothes, appliances, and other staples for struggling families who get help on ABC's *Extreme Makeover: Home Edition.*

5   Although we hear a lot of buzz today about product placement, in reality it's a long-standing cinematic tradition. The difference is that today the placements are more blatant and financially lucrative. In the heyday of the major Hollywood studios, brands such as Bell telephone, Buick, Chesterfield cigarettes, Coca-Cola, De Beers diamonds, and White Owl cigars regularly appeared in films. For example, in a scene in the classic *Double Indemnity* (1944) that takes place in a grocery store, the director Billy Wilder made some products such as Green Giant vegetables face the camera whereas others "mysteriously" were turned around to hide their labels. Indeed, the practice dates at least as far back as 1896, when an early movie shows a cart bearing the brand name Sunlight (a Lever Brothers brand) parked on a street. Perhaps the greatest product placement success story was Reese's Pieces; sales jumped by 65 percent after the candy appeared in the film *E.T.*

6   Some researchers claim that product placement aids consumer decision making because the familiarity of these props creates a sense of cultural belonging while they generate feelings of emotional security. Another study found that placements consistent with a show's plot do enhance brand attitudes, but incongruent placements that aren't consistent with the plot affect brand attitudes *negatively* because they seem out of place.

MARKETING PITFALL

The product placement industry has come under government scrutiny as pressure grows from consumer groups to let viewers know when companies pay to use their products as props. The Federal Communications Commission (FCC) is considering whether it should regulate this practice. Currently shows have to disclose this information but only at the end of the show and in small print. An FCC official says, "You shouldn't need a magnifying glass to know who's pitching you."

Advergaming

7   If you roar down the streets in the *Need for Speed Underground 2* video racing game, you'll pass a Best Buy store as well as billboards that hawk Old Spice and Burger King. *America's Army,* produced by the U.S. government as a recruitment tool, is one of the most successful advergames. Twenty-eight percent of those who visit the *America's Army* Web page click through to the recruitment page.

8   About three-quarters of American consumers now play video games, yet to many marketers the idea of integrating their brands with the stories that games tell is still a well-kept secret. Others including Axe, Mini Cooper, and Burger King have figured this out—they create game narratives that immerse players in the action. Orbitz offers playable banner-games that result in the highest **click-through rate** of any kind of advertising the online travel site does. Even though the game industry brings in more revenue than feature films or music sales, only about 10 percent of marketers execute any promotions in this space.

click-through rate
the percentage of people who click on an Internet link

9   Even so, it's likely that the future is bright for advergaming—where online games merge with interactive advertisements that let companies target specific types of consumers. These placements can be short exposures such as a billboard that appears around a racetrack, or they can take the form of branded entertainment and integrate the brand direcdy into the action. For example, a game that Dairy Queen helped to create called *DQ Tycoon* lets players run their own fast-food franchise. The game requires players to race against the clock to prepare Peanut-Buster Parfaits, take orders, restock the refrigerator, and dip cones.

mushrooming
rapidly increasing

10   The **mushrooming** popularity of user-generated videos on YouTube and other sites creates a growing market to link ads to these sources as well. This strategy is growing so rapidly that there's even a new (trademarked) term for it. Plinking™ is the act of embedding a product or service link in a video.

11   Why is this new medium so hot?

- Compared to a 30-second TV spot, advertisers can get viewers' attention for a much longer time. Players spend an average of 5 to 7 minutes on an advergame site.
- Physiological measures confirm that players are highly focused and stimulated when they play a game.
- Marketers can tailor the nature of the game and the products in it to the profiles of different users. They can direct strategy games to upscale, educated users, while they can gear action games to younger users.
- The format gives advertisers great flexibility because game makers now ship PC video games with blank spaces in them to insert virtual ads. This allows advertisers to change messages on the fly and pay only for the number of game players that actually see them. Sony Corp. now allows clients to directly insert online ads into PlayStation 3 videogames—the in-game ads change over time through a user's Internet connection.
- There's great potential to track usage and conduct marketing research. For example, an inaudible audio signal coded into Activision's *Tony Hawk's Underground 2* skating game on PCs alerts a Nielsen monitoring system each time the test game players view Jeep product placements within the game.

Mead's branded video game attracted over 10 million players.

Source: From www.miniclip.com. Used by permission of Miniclip (UK) Ltd.

A. UNDERSTANDING THE THESIS AND OTHER MAIN IDEAS

Select the best answer.

_____ 1. The author's primary purpose in this selection is to

    a. discuss the use of real products and brands in movies, television shows, and video games.

    b. compare and contrast product placement in movies and games with controversial advertising methods.

    c. explore the controversies surrounding product placements and advergaming.

    d. describe the latest advances in technology used for film and video game production.

_____ 2. The main idea of paragraph 1 is that

    a. brand names must be altered before they can be used on television.

    b. branded entertainment is taking the place of typical commercials.

    c. *Sex and the City* is the best modern example of product placement techniques.

    d. product placement has become common in our culture.

_____ 3. The topic of paragraph 3 is

    a. Hollywood.

    b. product placement.

c. popular brands.

d. popular films.

_____ 4. The main idea of paragraph 9 is found in the

a. first sentence.

b. second sentence.

c. third sentence.

d. last sentence.

_____ 5. The question answered in the set of bullet points in paragraph 11 is

a. How can businesses use video games to conduct market research?

b. Why is advergaming growing in popularity?

c. How much does product placement cost in comparison to traditional advertising?

d. How do "virtual advertisements" work?

B. IDENTIFYING DETAILS

Select the best answer.

_____ 1. The act of embedding a product or service link in a video is called

a. Advertorial.

b. Plinking.

c. Advergaming.

d. Nielsen Monitoring.

_____ 2. Which statement best summarizes consumers' attitude toward product placement?

a. Because consumers are bombarded with too much advertising, it is almost always unfavorable.

b. It is favorable when products are placed in movies, but unfavorable when products are placed in video games.

c. It is favorable if the plot or setting is related to the products being placed, but unfavorable if the products seem out of place.

d. It is favorable if the lead actor uses the product, but it is unfavorable if supporting actors or "extras" use the product.

_____ 3. According to the selection, advergaming has been used as a recruitment tool by

a. volunteer organizations.

b. colleges and universities.

c. the U.S. military.

d. children's toy manufacturers.

_____ 4. Which of the following is *not* true of advergaming?

    a. Advergaming is most successful when it is directed at teenage boys, who are the main purchasers of video games in the United States.

    b. Players are highly focused and stimulated when they are playing a game.

    c. Advergaming allows companies to target specific consumer segments, such as children or older adults.

    d. In some game systems that work with an Internet connection, ads can be changed over time.

Match each brand with the television show, movie, Web site, or video game in which it appeared, according to the selection.

TV Show, Movie, Web Site, or Video Game	Brand
_____ 5. *Double Indemnity*	a. Nokia
_____ 6. *American Idol*	b. Pepsi
_____ 7. *Need for Speed Underground 2*	c. Coca-Cola
_____ 8. *Entourage*	d. Green Giant vegetables
_____ 9. *Melrose Place*	e. Reese's Pieces
_____ 10. *E.T.*	f. Burger King
_____ 11. *Grey's Anatomy*	g. Sears
_____ 12. *ESPN Sports Center*	h. Izze Sparkling juice

C. RECOGNIZING METHODS OF ORGANIZATION AND TRANSITIONS

Select the best answer.

_____ 1. In paragraph 2, the author explains the meanings of *product placement* and *branded entertainment* using the organizational pattern called

    a. cause and effect.

    b. comparison and contrast.

    c. definition.

    d. process.

_____ 2. In paragraph 2, a word or phrase that signals that the author will illustrate the terms he has defined is

    a. oops.

    b. however.

    c. now.

    d. for example.

_____ 3. In paragraph 5, which organizational pattern does the author use to describe the difference between traditional and modern product placement?

    a. cause and effect

    b. comparison and contrast

    c. classification

    d. enumeration

_____ 4. The transitional word or phrase that signals paragraph 5's organizational pattern is

    a. although.

    b. difference.

    c. for example.

    d. perhaps.

_____ 5. The pattern of organization used in paragraph 11 is

    a. spatial order.

    b. comparison and contrast.

    c. definition.

    d. listing or enumeration.

D. REVIEWING AND ORGANIZING IDEAS: MAPPING

Complete the following maps by filling in the blanks.

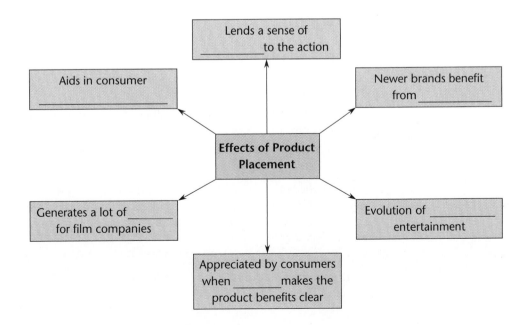

Lends a sense of _____ to the action

Aids in consumer _____

Newer brands benefit from _____

Effects of Product Placement

Generates a lot of _____ for film companies

Evolution of _____ entertainment

Appreciated by consumers when _____ makes the product benefits clear

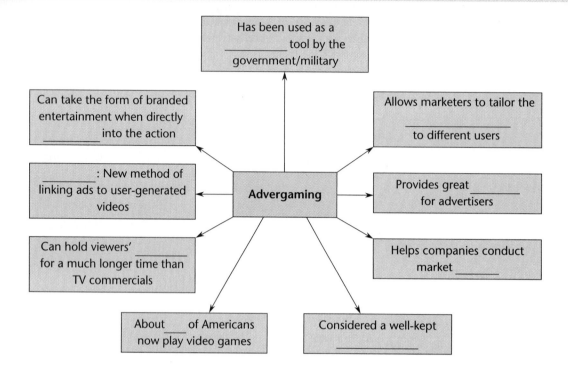

E. READING AND THINKING VISUALLY

Select the best answer.

_____ 1. The author included the photo shown on page 405 in order to

    a. emphasize that most product placements appeal to wealthy consumers.

    b. show the lengths to which people will go to mimic the TV shows they watch.

    c. imply that serious dramas use product placement more often than comedies.

    d. argue that product placement is the most profitable type of advertising.

_____ 2. Suppose the author wished to include another visual aid with this selection. Knowing that the author's intended audience is first-year college students, which of the following would you recommend the author include?

    a. a scene from *Double Indemnity*

    b. a screen capture from the original "Pong" video game

    c. a screen capture from a popular video game franchise, such as *Prince of Persia*

    d. a scene from an 1890s silent film

F. FIGURING OUT IMPLIED MEANINGS

Indicate whether each statement is true (T) or false (F).

_____ 1. Overall, young people seem more concerned about the blurring line between programming and advertising than older people do.

_____ 2. The most successful product placement of all time took place on *American Idol.*

_____ 3. Most, but not all, product placements are paid for.

_____ 4. In some video games, product placements aren't disguised; they are actually shown as advertisements in a setting (such as a football stadium) that would have advertisements in real life.

_____ 5. The author implies that only large corporations such as Pepsi and Burger King can afford to pay for product placements.

_____ 6. In the early days of television and movies, product placements tended to be more subtle.

_____ 7. American consumers would most likely resent a product placement for suntan lotion on a travel show focusing on island vacations.

_____ 8. Most of the people who play video games are young and fairly uneducated.

_____ 9. Product placement is the most profitable form of advertising.

G. THINKING CRITICALLY.

Select the best answer.

_____ 1. The tone of the reading can best be described as

    a. arrogant.

    b. informal.

    c. pessimistic.

    d. sympathetic.

_____ 2. The central thesis is supported by all of the following *except*

    a. examples.

    b. statistical data.

    c. descriptions.

    d. personal experience.

_____ 3. In paragraph 1, the author puts the word "geek" in quotation marks to
   a. show that it is a term used in the advertising business.
   b. imply that unpopular people are more likely to be affected by product placements.
   c. make it clear that he disagrees with the information he is presenting.
   d. create an ironic and sarcastic tone.

_____ 4. When the author says "oops, they got another one here!" in paragraph 2, he means that
   a. he has been paid to advertise the Bag Borrow or Steal Web site.
   b. simply by mentioning the Bag Borrow or Steal Web site, he has advertised it for free.
   c. he is a very strong advocate for product placement, advergaming, and other modern forms of advertising.
   d. he needs to provide a real-world example to have credibility as an author.

_____ 5. In paragraph 5, when the author says that the labels of some products were "mysteriously" hidden from the camera in _Double Indemnity,_ he means that
   a. no one is sure why they were turned around.
   b. the hidden product labels were intended to be a mystery to reflect the plot of the movie.
   c. the director intentionally obscured some product labels to draw attention to others, such as Green Giant.
   d. the director was experimenting with special effects during the filming of the movie.

_____ 6. It can be argued that the author is biased in favor of product placement because
   a. he cites many examples of successful product placements.
   b. he is a well-known businessman whose goal is to make as much money as possible.
   c. he understands that today's consumers are much more video oriented than earlier generations were.
   d. he does not offer any serious criticisms of product placement or the negative effects of embedding ads in video games.

H. BUILDING VOCABULARY

Context

Using context and a dictionary, if necessary, determine the meaning of each word as it is used in the selection.

_____ 1. evolved (paragraph 2)
    a. prevented
    b. grew
    c. allowed
    d. performed

_____ 2. brim (paragraph 4)
    a. remove
    b. substitute
    c. are full of
    d. cover up

_____ 3. staples (paragraph 4)
    a. necessities   c. obstructions
    b. problems   d. devices

_____ 4. blatant (paragraph 5)
    a. timely
    b. obvious
    c. offensive
    d. private

_____ 5. lucrative (paragraph 5)
    a. profitable   c. destructive
    b. similar   d. unnecessary

_____ 6. immerse (paragraph 8)
    a. become deeply involved in
    b. walk up a steep hill
    c. remove from
    d. serve as a creative force

_____ 7. physiological (paragraph 11)
    a. emotional   c. bodily
    b. mental   d. unrealistic

Word Parts

A REVIEW OF PREFIXES AND SUFFIXES

IN- means *not*
-IVE and **-IC** mean a *state, condition,* or *quality*

Use your knowledge of word parts and the review on the previous page to fill in the blanks in the following sentences.

1. If *narrate* means "tell a story," then a **narrative** film (paragraph 2) is one that tells a _____.

2. If the term *cinema* refers to films or movies, then a **cinematic** tradition (paragraph 5) is one having to do with _____.

3. If something is *congruent*, it is fitting or compatible with something else. Therefore, **incongruent** placements in films (paragraph 6) are ones that are _____ with other elements of the film.

4. If something *audible* can be heard, then an **inaudible** audio signal (paragraph 11) _____ be heard.

Unusual Words/Understanding Idioms

Use the meanings given below to write a sentence using the boldfaced word or phrase.

1. To **hawk** something (paragraph 7) is to sell it aggressively. It is an older use of the word and was applied to traveling salespeople who carried their goods around and offered them for sale by shouting on street corners.

   Your sentence: _____

   _____

2. A **banner-game** (paragraph 8) appears in a banner at the top of a Web page. It is usually fairly large and colorful, inviting players to click and play the game.

   Your sentence: _____

   _____

3. An **upscale** consumer (paragraph 11) is well-to-do and has money to spend.

   Your sentence: _____

   _____

4. Something done **on the fly** (paragraph 11) is done quickly and (often) easily.

   Your sentence: _____

   _____

I. SELECTING A LEARNING/STUDY STRATEGY

Predict an essay question about this selection that might be used on an exam.

J. EXPLORING IDEAS THROUGH DISCUSSION AND WRITING

1. Choose one or two television shows to watch for product placement in the next week. Make a list of the products or brands used during the show and indicate whether they were part of the storyline or simply used as props for the characters. If they were props, what do you think they were intended to reveal about the character or story? If they were part of the storyline, what did they add to the plot?

2. Discuss the pros and cons of product placement. For example, do you think using a product that is currently popular will make a movie or TV show seem outdated in a year or two?

3. Why do you think networks no longer require producers to alter brand names?

4. Do you think that product placement has had an effect on your own decisions as a consumer? Why or why not?

5. Do you play video games? If so, have you ever noticed product placements in them? If so, how much attention have you paid to them in comparison to other types of ads (such as TV or radio ads)? What makes you decide whether to pay attention to an ad or not?

K. BEYOND THE CLASSROOM TO THE WEB

One company that has been very successful at product placement is Apple, the creator of the iMac and MacBook personal computers, as well as the iPhone and the iPad. Do a Web search (perhaps using the "Images" option on Google) to find Apple product placements. (You can also use your own experience.) What do you notice about the types of people shown using Apple computers? What does this tell you about the company's marketing strategies and its customers?

TRACKING YOUR PROGRESS

Selection 15

Section	Number Correct		Score
A. Thesis and Main Ideas (5 items)	_____	×3	_____
B. Details (12 items)	_____	×2	_____
C. Organization and Transitions (5 items)	_____	×2	_____
E. Reading and Thinking Visually (2 items)	_____	×3	_____
F. Implied Meanings (9 items)	_____	×2	_____
G. Thinking Critically (6 items)	_____	×2	_____
H. Vocabulary			
Context (7 items)	_____	×1	_____
Word Parts (4 items)	_____	×2	_____
		TOTAL SCORE	_____%

16 Technology/Computers

Technology has become an important part of our daily lives. In some cases, technology directly controls our lives. For example, if your car does not start or the bus breaks down, you may miss class. People's lives have been saved by medical technology: for example, when a person's heart has stopped and been restarted by a machine. In other situations, technology influences the quality of our lives. Without technology we would lack many conveniences that we take for granted. For example, we would not have computers, elevators, automated teller machines, or microwave ovens. Technology affects our communication through radio, television, and the Internet; our comfort through furnaces, air conditioners, and plumbing systems; our health through vaccines, drugs, and medical research; and our jobs through computers, copiers, and fax machines. In fact, it is difficult to think of any aspect of our daily lives untouched by technology.

In this chapter you will explore the effects of technology and read about upcoming innovations. In "E-Waste Is Growing," you will discover the environmental effects of our society's increased use of and reliance upon technology. "Lost in Electronica" explores the psychological effects of our dependence on technology. As you read "DNA Fingerprinting: Cracking Our Genetic 'Barcode,'" you will learn how DNA fingerprinting works.

Use the following suggestions when reading technical material.

TIPS FOR READING IN TECHNOLOGY/ COMPUTERS	<ul><li>**Read slowly.** Technical material tends to be factually dense and requires careful, slow reading.</li><li>**Pay attention to technical vocabulary.** Both "E-Waste Is Growing" and "DNA Fingerprinting: Cracking Our Genetic 'Barcode,'" for example, include some specialized terminology.</li><li>**Focus on process.** Much technical writing focuses on how things work. "DNA Fingerprinting: Cracking Our Genetic 'Barcode,'" explains how DNA fingerprinting works.</li><li>**Use visualization.** Visualization is a process of creating mental pictures or images. As you read, try to picture in your mind the process or procedure that is being described. Visualization makes reading these descriptions easier and will improve your ability to recall details. As you read "E-Waste Is Growing," try to visualize landfills overflowing with e-waste.</li></ul>

SELECTION 16

"E-Waste" Is Growing

Jay Withgott and Scott Brennan

Contemporary
Issues Reading

Taken from a textbook titled *Environment: The Science Behind the Stories*, this reading selection examines the consequences of the growing amount of electronic waste in our world.

PREVIEWING THE READING

Using the steps listed on page 36, preview the reading selection. When you have finished, complete the following items.

1. The topic of this selection is _____.

2. List three questions you expect to be able to answer after reading this selection:

   a. _____

   b. _____

   c. _____

 MAKING CONNECTIONS

What kinds of things do you recycle? Describe what happens to your old cell phones and other electronic devices when you have finished using them.

READING TIP

As you read, underline statistics that show the impact of e-waste, and highlight descriptions of environmental damage and health risks associated with e-waste.

E-Waste Is Growing

1   Today's proliferation of computers, printers, cell phones, handheld devices, TVs, DVD players, fax machines, MP3 players, and other electronic technology has created a substantial new source of waste. These products have short lifetimes before people judge them obsolete, and most are discarded after only a few years. The amount of this **electronic waste**—often called **e-waste**—is growing rapidly, and now comprises 2% of the U.S. solid waste stream. Over 3 billion electronic devices have been sold in the United States since 1980. Of these, half have been disposed of, about 40% are still being used (or reused), and 10% are in storage. American households discard close to 400 million electronic devices per year—two-thirds of them still in working order.

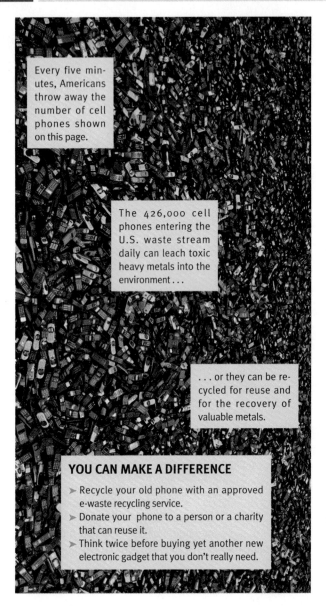

Every five minutes, Americans throw away the number of cell phones shown on this page.

The 426,000 cell phones entering the U.S. waste stream daily can leach toxic heavy metals into the environment...

...or they can be recycled for reuse and for the recovery of valuable metals.

YOU CAN MAKE A DIFFERENCE

➤ Recycle your old phone with an approved e-waste recycling service.
➤ Donate your phone to a person or a charity that can reuse it.
➤ Think twice before buying yet another new electronic gadget that you don't really need.

incinerators
furnaces designed to burn waste completely

EPA
Environmental Protection Agency

2   Of the electronic items we discard, roughly four of five go to landfills and **incinerators**, where they have traditionally been treated as conventional solid waste. However, most electronic products contain heavy metals and toxic flame retardants, and recent research suggests that e-waste should instead be treated as hazardous waste (see **THE SCIENCE BEHIND THE STORY**, p. 421). The **EPA** and a number of states are now taking steps to keep e-waste out of conventional sanitary landfills and incinerators and instead treat it as hazardous waste.

3   More and more e-waste today is being recycled. The devices are taken apart, and parts and materials are refurbished and reused in new products. According to EPA estimates, Americans were recycling 15% of e-waste in 1999, and this rose to 18% by 2007. However, so many more items have been manufactured each year that the amount of e-waste we sent to landfills and incinerators in that time period increased by a greater amount. Disposal has risen faster than recycling: In 2007 we recycled 45 million more tons of e-waste than in 1999, but we also disposed of 169 million more tons of e-waste in landfills and incinerators.

4   Besides keeping toxic substances out of our environment, e-waste recycling is beneficial because a number of trace metals used in electronics are globally rare, so they can be lucrative to recover. A typical cell phone contains close to a dollar's worth of precious metals. Every bit of metal we can recycle from a manufactured item is a bit of metal we don't need to mine from the ground, so "mining" e-waste for precious metals helps reduce the environmental impacts that mining exerts. By one estimate, 1 ton of computer scrap contains more gold than 16 tons of mined ore from a gold mine. In one of the more intriguing efforts to promote sustainability through such recycling, the 2010 Winter Olympic Games in Vancouver produced its stylish gold, silver, and bronze medals from metals recovered from recycled and processed e-waste!

5   There are serious concerns, however, about the health risks that recycling may pose to workers doing the disassembly. Wealthy nations ship much of their e-waste

to developing countries, where low-income workers disassemble the devices and handle toxic materials with minimal safety regulations. These environmental justice concerns need to be resolved, but if electronics recycling can be done responsibly, it seems likely to be the way of the future.

6   In many North American cities, used electronics are collected by businesses, nonprofit organizations, or municipal services, and are processed for reuse or recycling. So next time you upgrade to a new computer, TV, DVD player, cell phone, or handheld device, find out what opportunities exist in your area to recycle your old ones.

leach
leak or seep out

THE SCIENCE BEHIND THE STORY

TESTING THE TOXICITY OF "E-WASTE"

The EPA funded Timothy Townsend's lab at the University of Florida at Gainesville to determine whether e-waste is toxic enough to be classified as hazardous waste under the Resource Conservation and Recovery Act.

With students and colleagues, Townsend determined in 1999–2000 that cathode ray tubes (CRTs) from computer monitors and color televisions leach an average of 18.5 mg/L of lead, far above the regulatory threshold of 5 mg/L. Following this research, the EPA proposed classifying CRTs as hazardous waste, and several U.S. states banned these items from conventional landfills.

Then in 2004, Townsend's lab group completed experiments on 12 other types of electronic devices. To measure their toxicity, Townsend's group used the EPA's standard test, the Toxicity Characteristic Leaching Procedure (TCLP), designed to mimic the process by which chemicals leach out of solid waste in landfills.

The team's results are summarized in the accompanying bar chart. Lead was the only heavy metal found to exceed the EPA's regulatory threshold, but this threshold (5 mg/L) was exceeded in the majority of trials. Computer monitors leached the most lead (47.7 mg/L on average), as expected, because monitors include the cathode ray tubes already known to be a problem. However, laptops, color TVs, smoke detectors, cell phones, and computer mice also leached high levels of lead. Next came remote controls, VCRs, keyboards, and printers, all of which leached more lead on average than the EPA threshold, and did so in 50% or more of the trials. Whole CPUs and flat panel monitors were the only devices to leach less than 5 mg/L of lead on average, but even these exceeded the threshold more than one-quarter of the time.

The researchers found that items containing more ferrous metals (such as iron) tended to leach less lead. For instance, CPUs contain 68% ferrous metals (compared to only 7% in laptops), and laptops leached seven times as much lead as CPUs. Further experiments confirmed that ferrous metals were chemically reacting with lead and stopping it from leaching.

Townsend says the work suggests that many electronic devices have the potential to be classified as hazardous waste because they frequently surpass the toxicity criterion for lead. However, EPA scientists must decide how to judge results from the modified TCLP methods, and must evaluate other research, before determining whether to alter regulatory standards.

Furthermore, lab tests may or may not accurately reflect what actually happens in landfills. So Townsend's team is filling columns measuring 24 cm (2 ft) wide by 4.9 m (16 ft) long with e-waste and municipal solid waste, burying them in a Florida landfill, and then testing the leachate that results. The results from such research should help regulators decide how best to dispose of the e-waste that is not reused or recycled.

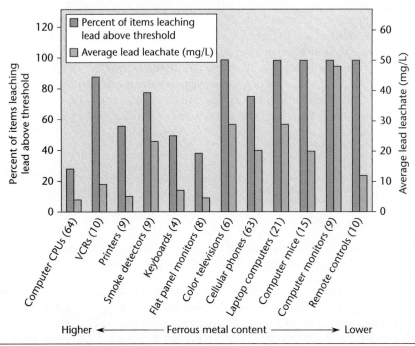

Some proportion of all 12 devices tested exceeded the EPA regulatory standard for lead leachate. Devices with higher ferrous metal content tended to leach less lead. Where both standard and modified Toxicity Characteristic Leaching Procedures (TCLPs) were used, results are averaged.

Source: Data from Townsend, T.G. et al. 2004. RCRA Toxicity Characterization of Computer CPUs and Other Disgarded Electronic Devices. July 15, 2004, report to the U.S. EPA.

A. UNDERSTANDING THE THESIS AND OTHER MAIN IDEAS

Select the best answer.

_____ 1. The central thesis of this selection is that the growing use of electronics has

a. raised public awareness of the importance of recycling.

b. generated new business opportunities for developing countries.

c. created a substantial and harmful new source of waste.

d. led to changes in regulatory standards for toxic waste.

_____ 2. The authors' primary purpose is to

a. present information on recycling.

b. explain the impact of e-waste.

c. address concerns about environmental justice.

d. argue for stricter EPA regulations.

_____ 3. The topic of paragraph 1 is
  a. new technology.   c. the U.S. solid waste stream.
  b. electronic devices.   d. electronic waste.

_____ 4. The main idea of paragraph 3 is expressed in the
  a. first sentence.   c. third sentence.
  b. second sentence.   d. last sentence.

_____ 5. According to the authors, e-waste recycling is beneficial because
  a. it keeps toxic substances out of the environment.
  b. recovering the rare metals used in electronics can be lucrative.
  c. it helps reduce the environmental impacts of mining for precious metals.
  d. all of the above.

B. IDENTIFYING DETAILS

In the space next to items 1–10, write the letter of the corresponding statistic from the box below.

A. 18%	F. Over 3 billion
B. Close to 400 million	G. Two-thirds
C. Four out of five	H. 50%
D. 40%	I. 10%
E. 169 million	J. 2%

_____ 1. The percentage of the United States solid waste stream that is e-waste

_____ 2. The number of electronic devices sold in the United States since 1980

_____ 3. Of the devices sold in the United States since 1980, the percentage disposed of

_____ 4. Of the devices sold in the United States since 1980, the percentage still being used

_____ 5. Of the devices sold in the United States since 1980, the percentage in storage

_____ 6. The number of electronic devices discarded by American households each year

_____ 7. Of the discarded electronic devices, the portion that still works

_____ 8. Of the discarded electronic devices, the portion that goes to landfills and incinerators

_____ 9. The percentage of e-waste that Americans recycled in 2007

_____ 10. The increase in tons of e-waste disposed of in 2007 compared to 1999

C. RECOGNIZING METHODS OF ORGANIZATION AND TRANSITIONS

Select the best answer.

_____ 1. In paragraphs 1–3 of "The Science Behind the Story," the authors use transitional phrases to indicate a progression of events after Dr. Townsend's lab was funded, including

    a. in 1999–2000.

    b. Following this research.

    c. Then in 2004.

    d. all of the above.

_____ 2. The organizational pattern signaled in paragraphs 1–3 is

    a. comparison and contrast.

    b. chronological order.

    c. classification.

    d. order of importance.

D. REVIEWING AND ORGANIZING IDEAS: MAPPING

Complete the following map of paragraphs 4–5 by filling in the blanks.

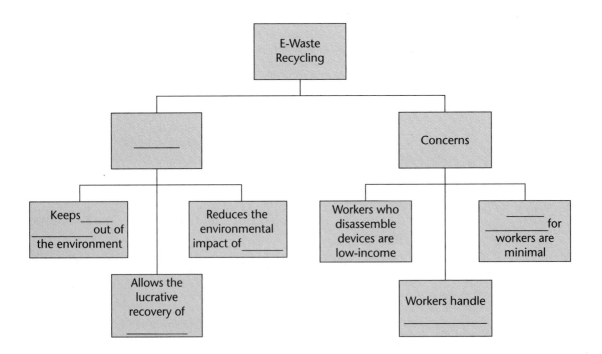

E. READING AND THINKING VISUALLY

Complete the following items.

1. The purpose of the photograph that accompanies the reading is to _____
   _____.

2. With the photo are three suggestions for how you can make a difference:
   recycle your old phone, donate your phone, and _____
   _____.

F. FIGURING OUT IMPLIED MEANINGS

Indicate whether each statement based on "The Science Behind the Story" is true (T) or false (F).

It can be inferred that

_____ 1. the EPA opposes Dr. Townsend's research into the toxicity of e-waste.

_____ 2. Townsend's research caused several states to ban CRTs from conventional landfills.

_____ 3. Townsend's lab group is made up of EPA scientists.

_____ 4. Townsend's research focuses primarily on whether gold is present in e-waste.

_____ 5. the EPA is responsible for evaluating research and determining regulatory standards.

G. THINKING CRITICALLY

Select the best answer.

_____ 1. The central thesis of the selection is supported primarily with
   a. facts and statistics.
   b. analogies.
   c. personal experience.
   d. examples and descriptions.

_____ 2. In paragraph 4, the statement that reveals the authors' positive attitude about recycling e-waste is
   a. "[A] number of trace metals used in electronics are globally rare."
   b. "A typical cell phone contains close to a dollar's worth of precious metals."
   c. "By one estimate, 1 ton of computer scrap contains more gold than 16 tons of mined ore from a gold mine."

       d. "[T]he 2010 Winter Olympic Games . . . produced its stylish gold, silver, and bronze medals from metals recovered from recycled and processed e-waste!"

_____ 3. The purpose of the bar chart in "The Science Behind the Story" (p. 422) is to

    a. summarize the results of e-waste toxicity tests.

    b. compare e-waste with other types of hazardous waste.

    c. suggest ways to reduce the effects of e-waste.

    d. explain the process of testing for e-waste toxicity.

_____ 4. The bar chart answers all of the following questions about different types of electronic devices *except*

    a. What is the average lead leachate for each type of electronic device?

    b. What percent of the items leach lead above the EPA's regulatory threshold?

    c. What is the ferrous metal content of each type of item?

    d. Which types of items contain the most and the least ferrous metal?

_____ 5. The overall tone of this selection can best be described as

    a. pessimistic.

    b. informative.

    c. lighthearted.

    d. indignant.

H. BUILDING VOCABULARY

Context

Using context and a dictionary, if necessary, determine the meaning of each word as it is used in the selection.

_____ 1. obsolete (paragraph 1)

    a. defective

    b. outdated

    c. expensive

    d. obvious

_____ 2. comprises (paragraph 1)

    a. makes up

    b. matches

    c. disappears

    d. improves

_____ 3. toxic (paragraph 2)

     a. complex

     b. useful

     c. poisonous

     d. solid

_____ 4. lucrative (paragraph 4)

     a. difficult

     b. ordinary

     c. risky

     d. profitable

_____ 5. exerts (paragraph 4)

     a. handles

     b. causes

     c. requests

     d. prevents

_____ 6. intriguing (paragraph 4)

     a. abnormal

     b. dishonest

     c. interesting

     d. mysterious

Word Parts

> ### A REVIEW OF PREFIXES AND ROOTS
>
> **DIS-** means *apart, away, not*
> **BENE-** means *good, well*

Use your knowledge of word parts and the review above to fill in the blanks in the following sentences.

1. Items that are *discarded* (paragraph 1) are thrown _____, usually because they are no longer considered useful.

2. Something that is *disposed* of (paragraph 1) has been done _____ with or destroyed.

3. An action that is *beneficial* (paragraph 4) has _____ or positive effects.

4. To assemble an item is to put it together, so the *disassembly* (paragraph 5) of an item involves taking it _____.

I. SELECTING A LEARNING/STUDY STRATEGY

How would you prepare if you knew you had to answer the following essay question? Describe the consequences of e-waste in terms of the environment and human health, and discuss the benefits of e-waste recycling.

J. EXPLORING IDEAS THROUGH DISCUSSION AND WRITING

1. Discuss the e-waste statistics cited in this selection. Were you surprised at the numbers? Talk about ways to persuade people to recycle or donate their old electronics.

2. Write an essay describing how you can reduce the amount of e-waste that you generate in your own life.

3. Did this article affect your opinion about donating or recycling your old electronics? Will it make you "think twice" before buying a new electronic gadget? Write a paragraph explaining your answers.

K. BEYOND THE CLASSROOM TO THE WEB

Visit the Web site for the U.S. Environmental Protection Agency at **http://www.epa.gov/** *and spend some time exploring the Popular Topics section. Learn about local environmental information in the MyEnvironment section and discover where you can donate or recycle electronic devices. Write a brief summary of what you found out.*

TRACKING YOUR PROGRESS

Selection 16

Section	Number Correct		Score
A. Thesis and Main Ideas (5 items)	_____	×4	_____
B. Details (10 items)	_____	×2	_____
C. Organization and Transitions (2 items)	_____	×5	_____
F. Implied Meanings (5 items)	_____	×3	_____
G. Thinking Critically (5 items)	_____	×3	_____
H. Vocabulary			
Context (6 items)	_____	×2	_____
Word Parts (4 items)	_____	×2	_____
	TOTAL SCORE		_____%

SELECTION 17

Lost in Electronica

George F. Will

Contemporary
Issues Reading

George F. Will is an influential newspaper and magazine journalist and columnist. He writes the back-page column for *Newsweek* magazine and is known for his conservative political views.

PREVIEWING THE READING

Using the steps listed on page 36, preview the reading selection. When you have finished, complete the following items.

1. The subject of the article is the effects of _____
   _____.

2. List three types of electronic stimulus that can preoccupy young people or adults.

   a. _____

   b. _____

   c. _____

MAKING CONNECTIONS

How well can you read, concentrate, or study when you receive text messages during your study time? Do you think interrupting your studies to read or answer text messages hurts or improves your grades? Do you ever use your cell phone or computer because you are bored?

READING TIP

As you read, highlight the results of being overstimulated by electronic media. These are the key points of the article. Do not let the vocabulary confuse you; use context to help you determine the meanings of any words with which you are unfamiliar.

Lost in Electronica

The Costs of "The Chaos of Constant Connection"

1   Can trout be bored? Can dolphins or apes? Are they neurologically complex enough to experience boredom? What might boredom mean to such creatures?

Humanity can boast that it is capable of boredom, but there may now be an unhealthy scarcity of that particular brain pain.

eons
very long
periods of time

2   Human beings evolved over dangerous **eons**. Brains formed in response to constant hazards may react with boredom when exposed to the safety of modern life. Perhaps flight from boredom prompts people today to take refuge in constant stimulation by visual and audio entertainments.

3   Adam J. Cox is a clinical psychologist worried about the effect of today's cornucopia of electronic stimuli on the cognition of young boys. Writing in *The New Atlantis,* he says human beings evolved in a world of nutritional scarcity and have responded to the sudden abundance of salt, sugar, and fat by creating an epidemic of obesity. And, he says, the mind, too, now craves junk nourishment: "Fifty years ago, the onset of boredom might have followed a two-hour stretch of nothing to do. In contrast, boys today can feel bored after thirty seconds with nothing specific to do."

4   The ubiquitous barrage of battery-powered stimuli delivered by phones, computers, and games makes "the chaos of constant connection" an addictive electronic narcotic. As continuous stimulation becomes the new normal, "gaps between moments of heightened stimulation" are disappearing; amusement "has squeezed the boredom out of life." For the hyperstimulated, "the **synaptic** mindscape of daily life" becomes all peaks and no valleys.

synaptic
referring to
areas of the
brain that
transmit signals
to one another

5   But valleys can be good for us. Cox believes that a more common occurrence of boredom in the young would be welcome evidence of "the presence of available resources for thought, reflection, and civil behavior." Cox notes that "being civil is rarely fun—it requires patience, forethought, and some willingness to tolerate tedium." So for the overstimulated, "civility feels like submission."

6   Cox worries about the deficits in the communication abilities of young males for whom a "womb of all-encompassing stimulation" induces "a pleasant trance from which they do not care to be awakened." Hence, perhaps, the "failure to launch" of many young males who, "preoccupied with self-amusement," struggle to make the transition from adolescence to adulthood. What Cox calls "the unbearable lightness of adolescence" is not new; what is new is an "excess of amusement" producing a deficient sense of gravity.

7   "Unlike reading and listening to stories," Cox warns, "the blitz of electronica doesn't build deeper listening skills or a greater range of emotional expression." Self-absorption, particularly among young males, may be the greatest danger of immersion in the bath of digital amusement: "Not only does withdrawal into electronica enable them to bypass the confusion and pain of trying to give their emotions some **coherence**, it also helps them avoid the realities of being a flawed, vulnerable, ordinary human being." So "the silent, sullen boy at the mall's game store may be next in line for an underemployed, lonely adulthood if we don't teach him how to maintain effective social contacts with others."

coherence
unity

advent
arrival

8   Cox doubts it is a mere coincidence that "the stratospheric increase in diagnosed learning and attention deficits" has correlated with "the **advent** of the electronic playground." When so many Americans meet the diagnostic criteria for attention-deficit/hyperactivity disorder, it "is arguably no longer a disorder at all—it's just the way we are."

insatiably
in a way that is
impossible to
satisfy

9   Yes, "we." Not just boys but adults of both sexes, too, seem **insatiably** hungry for handheld devices that deliver limitless distractions. Neuroscience demonstrates

impede
interfere with or prevent

myriad
a very high number

rue
regret

paragons
perfect examples

that the brain is not a finished product; neural networks can be rewired by intense and prolonged experiences. Some research suggests that the constant short-term stimulation of flitting to and fro among digital promptings can **impede** long-term memory on which important forms of intelligence depend.

10   We are in the midst of a sudden and vast social experiment involving **myriad** new means of keeping boredom at bay. And we may yet **rue** the day we surrendered to the insistent urge to do so. There are, however, **paragons** among whom boredom flourishes. Valerie Jarrett, one of Barack Obama's closest confidantes, says (as reported in David Remnick's *The Bridge*), "He knows exactly how smart he is . . . He's been bored to death his whole life. He's just too talented to do what ordinary people do." Even regarding boredom, he is a reproach to the rest of us.

A. UNDERSTANDING THE THESIS AND OTHER MAIN IDEAS

Select the best answer.

_____ 1. The article summarizes the research of
   a. George Will.
   b. David Remnick.
   c. Adam Cox.
   d. Valerie Jarrett.

_____ 2. The central thesis of this selection is that
   a. boys' needs for constant electronic stimulation is affecting their emotional and social development.
   b. electronic devices should be banned from the home.
   c. universities should invest more money in identifying the effects of video games on the brain.
   d. the brain develops in unexpected ways that are not well understood.

_____ 3. The author's primary purpose is to
   a. imply that today's parents are responsible for boys' refusal to be bored.
   b. make readers aware of the long-term effects of electronic stimuli.
   c. advocate for the use of video games as educational tools.
   d. provide insight into the personality of President Barack Obama.

_____ 4. The main idea of paragraph 4 is that electronic stimuli have led to the disappearance of
   a. excitement.
   b. boredom.
   c. adolescence.
   d. friendships.

_____ 5. The main idea in paragraph 9 can be found in the

    a. first sentence.

    b. second sentence.

    c. third sentence.

    d. fourth sentence.

B. IDENTIFYING DETAILS

Indicate whether each statement is true (T) or false (F).

_____ 1. The human response to an abundance of sugar and fat has been an increase in cancer.

_____ 2. An "excess of amusement" is a much more recent phenomenon than the "unbearable lightness of adolescence."

_____ 3. Reading and listening to stories builds deeper listening skills and a greater range of emotional expression.

_____ 4. Constant attention to the interruptions of text messages can have a negative effect on a person's long-term memory.

_____ 5. Adam Cox's research focuses on school-age boys and girls.

C. RECOGNIZING METHODS OF ORGANIZATION AND TRANSITIONS

Select the best answer.

_____ 1. The article uses a cause-and-effect pattern of organization. The cause is

    a. girls' lack of social skills.

    b. boys' cravings for salt, sugar, and fat.

    c. children's lack of emotional development.

    d. constant electronic connection.

_____ 2. Which of the following is not one of the effects discussed in the article?

    a. Young people become less introspective, less thoughtful, and less civil.

    b. Boys become preoccupied with keeping themselves constantly amused.

    c. Boys' friendships become centered around computers and technology rather than school or sports.

    d. Young people find it difficult to make a successful transition from adolescence to adulthood.

_____ 3. While the overall method of organization for the reading is cause and effect, paragraph 3 makes use of an additional pattern. Which transitional word or phrase signals that pattern?

    a. in contrast

    b. evolved

    c. responded

    d. craves

D. REVIEWING AND ORGANIZING IDEAS: PARAPHRASING

Complete the following paraphrase of the reading by filling in the missing words and phrases.

The human brain evolved in response to _____, which may explain why it becomes bored by the _____ of modern life. Perhaps as a way of fighting _____, boys' brains now seek constant _____, much of which is provided by _____. But the constant stimuli create a sort of _____ from which boys do not want to be awakened. They become preoccupied with _____, which prevents them from building _____ skills and developing a wider range of _____. Over the long term, the results of constant electronic communication may include lack of employment, _____, and decreased _____ memory.

E. READING AND THINKING VISUALLY

Select the best answer.

A

B

_____   Suppose the author wanted to select a photo to support his central thesis. Which photo should the author choose?

    a. Photo A, because the image features a young man; and young men are the focus of the article.

    b. Photo A, because it shows a young man who seems isolated and unhappy as a result of technology.

    c. Photo B, because it shows video games being played in a positive family atmosphere.

    d. Photo B, because it includes a woman, which will make women more likely to read the article.

F. FIGURING OUT IMPLIED MEANINGS

Indicate whether each statement is true (T) or false (F).

_____   1. The author implies that boredom can actually be healthy.

_____   2. It is likely that humans as a whole were thinner in the early days of human evolution.

_____   3. The author believes that being bored is necessary for thought and reflection.

_____   4. The author implies that boys who spend a lot of time playing video games will have an advantage when they become adults and start looking for employment.

_____   5. The author believes that the rise of the "electronic playground" has led to a huge increase in the number of students diagnosed with attention-deficit/hyperactivity disorder.

_____   6. The article implies that intelligent people are less likely to be bored than unintelligent people.

G. THINKING CRITICALLY

Select the best answer.

_____   1. The overall tone of this article is

    a. angry.

    b. satirical.

    c. concerned.

    d. excited.

_____   2. All of the following are facts *except*

    a. Human beings evolved over dangerous eons. (paragraph 2)

    b. Cox worries about the deficits in the communication abilities of young males. (paragraph 6)

     c. When so many Americans meet the diagnostic criteria for attention-deficit/hyperactivity disorder, "it is arguably no longer a disorder at all." (paragraph 8)

     d. Neuroscience demonstrates that the brain is not a finished product. (paragraph 9)

_____ 3. In paragraph 1, the author uses the term *brain pain* as a synonym for

     a. boredom.

     b. evolution.

     c. headaches.

     d. self-consciousness.

_____ 4. In paragraph 4, the author uses the word *narcotic* because of its connotation of

     a. painkiller.

     b. addiction.

     c. illegality.

     d. sleep-inducing qualities.

_____ 5. The phrase "failure to launch" in paragraph 6 refers to

     a. a rocket's inability to get enough propulsion to leave the stratosphere.

     b. the inability of post-adolescent males to find jobs and leave home.

     c. Adam Cox's inability to awaken men from their self-induced video-game trances.

     d. teenagers' inability to communicate with their elders.

_____ 6. The figurative phrase "immersion in the bath of digital amusement" in paragraph 7 means

     a. the high cost of electronic technology.

     b. the sense of drowning that comes with playing certain video games.

     c. the tendency for boys to become involved in electronic gaming at the expense of everything else.

     d. the very real possibility of electrocution if electronic games are played in or near the water.

H. BUILDING VOCABULARY

Context

Using context and a dictionary, if necessary, determine the meaning of each word as it is used in the selection.

_____ 1. cornucopia (paragraph 3)

    a. basket

    b. abundant supply

    c. confusion

    d. fuel

_____ 2. obesity (paragraph 3)

    a. diabetes

    b. disease

    c. cravings

    d. fatness

_____ 3. ubiquitous (paragraph 4)

    a. present everywhere

    b. expensive

    c. frustrating and difficult

    d. chaotic and unexpected

_____ 4. barrage (paragraph 4)

    a. bombardment

    b. banning

    c. war

    d. alcohol

_____ 5. tedium (paragraph 5)

    a. cleanliness

    b. darkness

    c. boredom

    d. solitary confinement

Word Parts

> ## A REVIEW OF PREFIXES AND ROOTS
>
> **HYPER-** means _over_ or _excessive_
> **NEURO** means _nerve_

Use your knowledge of word parts and the review above to fill in the blanks in the following sentences.

1. Someone having _neurological_ problems (paragraph 1) is having problems with his or her _____ system.

2. A child who is *hyperstimulated* (paragraph 4) is _____ stimulated, to the point of being irritable and unable to concentrate.

Unusual Words/Understanding Idioms

Use the meanings given below to write a sentence using the boldfaced word.

1. While **gravity** often refers to a law of physics that attracts things toward the center of the Earth, in paragraph 6 it means "seriousness."

   Your sentence: _____

   _____

2. While *stratosphere* refers to the upper levels of the atmosphere, **stratospheric** is an adjective that indicates a large increase in something.

   Your sentence: _____

   _____

I. SELECTING A LEARNING/STUDY STRATEGY

Select the best answer.

_____   If you were writing a research paper on the effects of electronic technology on children and wanted to use this article as one of your sources, the most useful strategy would be to

   a. highlight all the key terms in the article.

   b. outline the article.

   c. draw a concept map of the main ideas.

   d. paraphrase useful information.

J. EXPLORING IDEAS THROUGH DISCUSSION AND WRITING

1. Discuss your use of electronic technologies. How often do you use them (how many hours a day)? How much of that time is spent in "useful" or "productive" activities like studying or communicating for your job, and how much of that time is spent socializing or killing time?

2. What do you do when you feel bored? Suppose you could not watch TV, text on your cell phone, or play on your computer. What would you do instead?

3. Discuss with your classmates how you could find more information about the effects of video gaming and other electronic stimuli on children and teenagers. Conduct a Google search and print out an informative article on the topic. Write a paraphrase of that article and share it with the class.

K. BEYOND THE CLASSROOM TO THE WEB

A longtime controversy surrounding video games is the claim that violent games make children more likely to become violent themselves. The Web site **http:// videogames.procon.org/** *provides a wealth of articles addressing both sides of the argument.*

Which side do you take? In other words, do you believe that video games can make children more violent? Now choose an article from the Web site that takes the opposite side, and write a summary of it. Has reading that article influenced the way you think about the subject?

TRACKING
YOUR
PROGRESS

Selection 17

Section	Number Correct		Score
A. Thesis and Main Ideas (5 items)	_____	×4	_____
B. Details (5 items)	_____	×3	_____
C. Organization and Transitions (3 items)	_____	×4	_____
E. Reading and Thinking Visually (1 item)	_____	×3	_____
F. Implied Meanings (6 items)	_____	×3	_____
G. Thinking Critically (6 items)	_____	×3	_____
H. Vocabulary			
Context (5 items)	_____	×2	_____
Word Parts (2 items)	_____	×2	_____
	TOTAL SCORE		_____ %

SELECTION 18

DNA Fingerprinting: Cracking Our Genetic "Barcode"

Elaine N. Marieb

Contemporary Issues Reading

This selection is taken from a textbook titled *Essentials of Human Anatomy and Physiology*, by Elaine N. Marieb, published in 2009. Read the selection to find out about the process known as DNA fingerprinting.

PREVIEWING THE READING

Using the steps listed on page 36, preview the reading selection. When you have finished, complete the following items.

1. The topic of this selection is _____.

2. List at least three questions you expect to be able to answer after reading the selection.

   a. _____

   b. _____

   c. _____

MAKING CONNECTIONS

What do you already know about DNA fingerprinting? How is it like traditional fingerprinting? With a classmate, make a list of the ways that you think DNA fingerprinting is used in the world today.

READING TIP

As you read, highlight unfamiliar terms and their definitions. If a definition is not given, be sure to look up the term in a dictionary so that you can understand the passage.

DNA Fingerprinting: Cracking Our Genetic "Barcode"

1   The terrorist attacks on New York City's World Trade Center killed more than 3,000 people, their bodies buried in millions of tons of rubble. As weeks passed, it became clear that even if victims could be recovered from the wreckage, their bodies

would probably be mangled, burned, or decomposed to a point where even family members would not recognize them.

2   In a situation like this, how can we identify individuals with any certainty? The New York Medical Examiner's Office turned to **DNA** fingerprinting, a technique for analyzing tiny samples of DNA taken from semen, skin, blood, or other body tissues. DNA fingerprinting is based on the fact that no two human beings, except for identical twins, possess identical sets of genetic material. In effect, DNA fingerprinting creates a unique genetic "**barcode**" that distinguishes each of us from all other humans. Let's see how it works.

Creating a DNA Profile

3   Recall that DNA contains four **nucleotides**—A, G, C, and T—that form complementary base pairs. In members of the same species, 99.9 percent of DNA is identical. This means that only 0.1 percent of your DNA differs from that of other humans—even close relatives, but this is enough to make you genetically unique. In a DNA string 3 billion units long, that 0.1 percent translates into 3 million variations that differ slightly from everyone else's. Unless you're an identical sibling, your set of DNA is yours alone. DNA fingerprinting involves analyzing an individual's DNA, mapping its unique pattern, and comparing it to other DNA profiles to determine whether there's a match.

4   A standard technique for creating a DNA profile focuses on 13 specific sites on our chromosomes where short segments of nuclear DNA are arranged in a repeating sequence. Although it is theoretically possible that unrelated people could show identical repeats at all 13 sites, the odds are less than 1 in 1 trillion.

5   Sometimes it can be difficult to obtain sufficient nuclear DNA for analysis. DNA samples recovered from crime scenes or disaster sites, for example, are frequently contaminated with dirt, fibers, and debris, or badly decomposed, limiting the amount of testable tissue. DNA retrievel can become a race against time as microbes, enzymes, insects, and environmental factors such as heat and humidity accelerate the process of decomposition.

Sorting and Identifying DNA

6   For DNA to be profiled, it must first be cut into manageable fragments by *restriction enzymes,* enzymes that recognize a specific base sequence and cleave the DNA at this location. This breaks down chromosomes into millions of pieces of different sizes that are then subjected to *gel electrophoresis,* which sorts the pieces by length. The DNA is placed on a gel and positioned in an electric field. The negatively charged fragments of DNA are attracted to the positively charged electrode and migrate toward it. Because the smaller pieces move more quickly than the larger pieces, the fragments end up sorted by size.

7   To locate a specific repeating sequence, researchers make a *DNA probe* with a complementary sequence and tag it with a radioactive compound. Because their sequences are complementary, the probe binds to the site; and when exposed to X-ray film, the image shows dark bands where the probe bound to the DNA.

DNA
deoxyribonucleic acid, the long string of genetic material found in the nucleus of a cell

barcode
a series of vertical bars printed on consumer products to identify the item for pricing and inventory purposes

nucleotides
the basic structural units of nucleic acids such as DNA

DNA electrophoresis.
A scientist looking at DNA fragments in an electrophoresis gel.

8   A victim's DNA profile is then compared to known references to find one that matches. In the case of the World Trade Center attack, DNA references were obtained from victims' personal effects (such as toothbrushes and combs), entered into a computer, and sorted to find a match.

DNA Fingerprinting and Forensics

9   DNA fingerprinting has become a vital tool in forensic medicine (the application of medical knowledge to questions of law). For example, DNA fingerprinting is used to identify "John and Jane Does," unknown human remains. The U.S. military takes blood and saliva samples from every recruit so it can identify soldiers killed in the line of duty. DNA fingerprinting can also identify victims of mass disasters such as airplane crashes. The World Trade Center tragedy called for genetic analysis on an unprecedented scale.

10   DNA fingerprinting can prove that a suspect was actually at the scene of a crime. In the United States, some communities now require certain criminal offenders to provide DNA samples, which are classified and stored. DNA profiles can also establish innocence. At least 10 people in the United States have been released from death row after genetic evidence exonerated them.

11   DNA fingerprinting can also verify relationships in cases of disputed property, identify long-lost relatives, and establish paternity, even in paternity cases that are centuries old. For example, historians have fiercely debated whether Thomas Jefferson, our third president, fathered any children by his slave Sally Hemings. Modern DNA researchers entered the fray by profiling Jefferson's Y chromosome. A comparison of 19 genetic markers on the Jefferson Y chromosomes and those of Hemings's descendants found identical matches between the Jefferson line and Hemings's youngest son. Could it be chance? Hardly!

A. UNDERSTANDING THE THESIS AND OTHER MAIN IDEAS

Select the best answer.

_____ 1. The central thesis of this selection is that DNA fingerprinting is

    a. a legal tool primarily for use in the criminal justice system.

    b. a process that makes it possible to identify individuals through their genetic material.

    c. one of several methods used to analyze an individual's DNA.

    d. a new technology that may become useful in the future.

_____ 2. The author's primary purpose is to

    a. compare traditional and DNA fingerprinting.

    b. argue that DNA profiling should be against the law.

    c. describe the process and uses of DNA fingerprinting.

    d. discuss a variety of techniques used in forensic medicine.

_____ 3. The topic of paragraph 2 is

    a. the New York Medical Examiner's Office.

    b. DNA fingerprinting.

    c. identical twins.

    d. genetic barcodes.

_____ 4. According to the selection, DNA fingerprinting involves

    a. analyzing an individual's DNA.

    b. mapping the unique pattern of an individual's DNA.

    c. comparing an individual's DNA profile with others to find a match.

    d. all of the above.

_____ 5. The topic of paragraph 9 is expressed in the

    a. first sentence.

    b. second sentence.

    c. third sentence.

    d. last sentence.

_____ 6. The question that is answered in paragraph 9 is

    a. What is DNA fingerprinting?

    b. How is DNA fingerprinting used in forensic medicine?

    c. How is DNA obtained for matching purposes?

    d. Why is DNA fingerprinting important in criminal cases?

_____ 7. The main idea of paragraph 11 is expressed in the
   a. first sentence.
   b. second sentence.
   c. third sentence.
   d. fourth sentence.

_____ 8. According to the selection, DNA fingerprinting was used to find out whether Thomas Jefferson
   a. had an identical brother.
   b. died of natural causes.
   c. was the son of a slaveowner.
   d. fathered a child by Sally Hemings.

B. IDENTIFYING DETAILS

Complete each of the following statements by underlining the correct choice in parentheses.

1. DNA contains (4 / 100) nucleotides that form complementary base pairs.
2. In members of the same species, (0.1 / 99.9) percent of DNA is identical.
3. A DNA string is three (thousand / billion) units long.
4. A standard technique for creating a DNA profile focuses on (4 / 13) specific sites where DNA repeats.
5. The odds of unrelated people showing identical repeats are less than 1 in (3 million / 1 trillion).

C. RECOGNIZING METHODS OF ORGANIZATION AND TRANSITIONS

Select the best answer.

_____ 1. In paragraph 2, the author explains what DNA fingerprinting is by using the organizational pattern called
   a. cause and effect.
   b. definition.
   c. comparison and contrast.
   d. chronological order.

_____ 2. In paragraphs 6–8, the author describes how DNA is sorted and identified using the organizational pattern called
   a. process.
   b. listing.
   c. classification.
   d. comparison and contrast.

_____ 3. In paragraph 9, the transition indicating the author's organizational pattern is

    a. has become.

    b. for example.

    c. also.

    d. called for.

D. REVIEWING AND ORGANIZING IDEAS: SUMMARIZING

Use the following words and phrases to complete the summary of paragraphs 6–8.

size	restriction enzymes	probe
gel electrophoresis	X-rays	radioactive compound

The first step in profiling DNA is to break it down using _____.
The pieces of chromosomes are then subjected to _____,
which uses an electric field to sort the pieces by _____. To find
a specific repeating sequence, a DNA _____ with a complementary sequence is made and tagged with a _____. The
probe then binds to the complementary DNA site and _____
reveal dark bands where the probe and DNA are bound. Finally, this DNA
profile is compared to known references to find a match.

E. READING AND THINKING VISUALLY

Select the best answer.

_____ 1. The photo on page 441 makes it clear that the electrophoresis process makes use of

    a. glass.

    b. X-rays.

    c. solar energy.

    d. fingerprinting technology.

_____ 2. The primary purpose of the photograph on page 441 is to

    a. present evidence of the importance of DNA fingerprinting.

    b. illustrate how simple the DNA fingerprinting process is.

    c. show what DNA electrophoresis looks like.

    d. compare DNA fingerprinting to other identification techniques.

F. FIGURING OUT IMPLIED MEANINGS

Indicate whether each statement is true (T) or false (F).

_____ 1. Identifying some victims of the World Trade Center attacks would have been impossible without DNA fingerprinting.

_____ 2. The DNA profiles of siblings and other closely related family members are more similar than those of unrelated people.

_____ 3. The technique is called DNA fingerprinting because it relies primarily on fingerprints for identification.

_____ 4. It is extremely unlikely that unrelated people would have matching DNA profiles.

_____ 5. A person does not need any special training to conduct DNA profiling.

_____ 6. It is impossible to analyze DNA that is more than 100 years old.

_____ 7. In a criminal trial, DNA evidence can establish guilt, but cannot establish innocence.

G. THINKING CRITICALLY

Select the best answer.

_____ 1. The tone of the selection can best be described as

    a. grim.

    b. sympathetic.

    c. informative.

    d. cheerful.

_____ 2. The central thesis of "DNA Fingerprinting: Cracking Our Genetic 'Barcode'" is supported by

    a. facts.

    b. examples.

    c. descriptions.

    d. all of the above.

_____ 3. Of the following statements, the only one that is an *opinion* is

    a. "DNA samples recovered from crime scenes or disaster sites . . . are frequently contaminated with dirt, fibers, and debris . . . " (para. 5)

    b. "A victim's DNA profile is . . . compared with known references to find one that matches." (para. 8)

    c. DNA profiles can also establish innocence.

    d. "[H]istorians have fiercely debated whether Thomas Jefferson . . . fathered children by his slave Sally Hemings." (para. 11)

_____ 4. The author began the selection with a reference to the World Trade Center attacks in order to

    a. compare different types of historical events.

    b. illustrate the importance of DNA fingerprinting.

    c. introduce her own point of view.

    d. establish a setting for the selection.

H. BUILDING VOCABULARY

Context

Using context and a dictionary, if necessary, determine the meaning of each word as it is used in the selection.

_____ 1. accelerate (paragraph 5)

    a. affect

    b. speed up

    c. improve

    d. recover

_____ 2. cleave (paragraph 6)

    a. split

    b. appear

    c. cover

    d. harm

_____ 3. migrate (paragraph 6)

    a. match

    b. show

    c. move

    d. limit

_____ 4. exonerated (paragraph 10)

    a. attacked

    b. cleared

    c. removed

    d. identified

_____ 5. fray (paragraph 111)

    a. tool

    b. location

    c. proof

    d. fight

Word Parts

> ### A REVIEW OF PREFIXES AND SUFFIXES
>
> **DE-** means *away, from*
> **UN-** means *not*
> **PRE-** means *before*
> **-ANT** means *one who*

Use your knowledge of word parts and the review above to fill in the blanks in the following sentences.

1. Something that is *decomposed* (paragraph 1) or in the process of *decomposition* (paragraph 5) is breaking down; it is changing its composition _____ one form to another.

2. If an event happens on an *unprecedented* scale (paragraph 9), it is something that has _____ happened before to such an extent.

3. A person's *descendants* (paragraph 11) may include children, grandchildren, and so on down through a family line. A *descendant* is _____ comes from an ancestor or a race.

Unusual Words/Understanding Idioms

Use the meanings given below to write a sentence using the boldfaced word or phrase.

1. A **barcode** (paragraph 2) is usually an identification given to a product so that it can be priced or identified for inventory. In this selection it refers to our unique set of genetic material.

   Your sentence: _____

   _____

2. When there is a **race against time** (paragraph 5), an urgency exists that makes it important to complete a task before it is too late.

   Your sentence: _____

   _____

I. SELECTING A LEARNING/STUDY STRATEGY

Predict an essay question that might be asked on this selection.

J. EXPLORING IDEAS THROUGH DISCUSSION AND WRITING

1. Evaluate the introduction to the selection. Did it capture your interest? Why or why not?

2. Discuss the title of the selection, "DNA Fingerprinting: Cracking Our Genetic 'Barcode.'" Can you think of another title that would be as effective?

3. Do you think it would be interesting to work in DNA profiling or forensic medicine? Describe why it would or would not appeal to you.

4. Discuss the importance of DNA fingerprinting to the justice system. Do you think that all criminal offenders should be required to provide DNA samples?

K. BEYOND THE CLASSROOM TO THE WEB

Explore the applications of DNA research in online modules at **http://www.dnai. org/d/index.html.**

Using this site and the reading, write a paragraph that summarizes one way in which DNA is used.

TRACKING YOUR PROGRESS

Selection 18

Section	Number Correct		Score
A. Thesis and Main Ideas (8 items)	_____	×3	_____
B. Details (5 items)	_____	×3	_____
C. Organization and Transitions (3 items)	_____	×2	_____
E. Reading and Thinking Visually (2 items)	_____	×3	_____
F. Implied Meanings (7 items)	_____	×3	_____
G. Thinking Critically (4 items)	_____	×3	_____
H. Vocabulary			
Context (5 items)	_____	×2	_____
Word Parts (3 items)	_____	×2	_____
		TOTAL SCORE	_____ %

17 Health-Related Fields

"Nothing can be more important than your health." This is an overused saying, but it remains meaningful. As the medical field and health-care systems become more complex, as medical knowledge expands, and as technology plays an ever-increasing role in diagnosis and treatment, medical personnel, patients, and patients' families face new and difficult challenges, decisions, and dilemmas. In "Medical Technology and Ethical Issues," you will read about how a computer program is used to make decisions about who to treat first in emergency situations. In "When Living Is a Fate Worse Than Death," you will read about the question of whether to end the life of a critically ill child.

While the health field presents many challenges and issues, it also offers new and exciting innovations and opportunities for new treatment options. When reading "A Step Beyond Human," you will learn about changes in the field of prosthestics (artificial limbs) and see what one man has contributed to the field.

Use the following tips when reading in the health-related fields.

TIPS FOR READING IN HEALTH-RELATED FIELDS

- **Learn necessary terminology.** Each of the articles in this chapter uses some technical and specialized terms. Reading in the field and speaking with health-care professionals will be much easier if you have a mastery of basic terminology.

- **Learn the basics about human body systems.** You have to know how your body works in order to take care of it and to understand readings in the field. For example, in reading "When Living Is a Fate Worse Than Death," you need to know about brain functioning.

- **Read critically.** There are many different viewpoints, different proposed cures, numerous lose-20-pounds-in-a-week diets, and many "miracle" exercise programs. Read critically, ask questions, and look for supporting evidence. As you read "Medical Technology and Ethical Issues," for example, which is about using computers to make decisions about patient treatment and care, ask questions such as "How reliable are these programs?" and "What are the implications if a computer program makes a faulty recommendation?"

<table>
<tr><td>

SELECTION

19

</td><td>

Medical Technology and Ethical Issues

William E. Thompson and Joseph V. Hickey

</td></tr>
</table>

Contemporary
Issues Reading

This selection is taken from the health and medicine chapter of the textbook *Society in Focus: An Introduction to Sociology.* Read it to find out about the use of computer technology in determining a patient's treatment in the emergency room.

PREVIEWING THE READING

Using the steps listed on page 36, preview the reading selection. When you have finished, complete the following items.

1. The computer program that is the focus of this selection is referred to as

   _____.

2. The title indicates that the authors are interested in the relationship

   between _____ and _____.

 ### MAKING CONNECTIONS

What has been your experience with medical technology? Think about the last time you were in a doctor's office, clinic, or hospital and the different forms of technology that were used as part of your medical care.

READING TIP

As you read, highlight the arguments put forth by both critics and supporters of the RIP computer system.

Medical Technology and Ethical Issues

1   With sirens blaring and lights flashing, the ambulance skids to a halt in front of the hospital emergency room entrance. A swarm of medical personnel descend on the ambulance as its drivers and the paramedics who are aboard fling open its door and unload the cargo. The patient is wheeled through the automatic doors of the

triage
the area in a
hospital where a
patient's condition
is assessed
and the order
of treatment
for all patients
is determined
according to
urgency

hospital and rushed down the corridor toward the emergency room **triage**. While nurses and emergency room physicians monitor vital signs and start an intravenous solution, one doctor races over to a desk and hands a clipboard to a staff person who is sitting in front of a computer and who carefully begins to enter data.

2   The computer program is referred to simply as RIP. In emergency rooms across the country and around the world, this computer program is helping doctors make informed decisions about whether to administer life-saving treatments or simply allow patients to die. Using statistical probability, the program analyzes all of the input on a particular patient and makes a prognosis on the likelihood of survival. If the probability is 95 percent or better that the patient is going to die, regardless of treatment, it is recommended that treatment not be administered. However, if the odds are greater than 5 percent that the patient will survive, the computer not only indicates the probability of survival but also prints out recommended treatment procedures. All of this happens in milliseconds.

3   Critics of the new computerized system contend that it is a frightening example of overreliance on computer technology to make decisions that were once reserved for human judgment. Medical ethicist Arthur Caplan of Philadelphia argues that computers should not be used to make decisions about the allocation of medical resources to patients and points out that the computer will be wrong in about 5 percent of all cases. Supporters of the new technology insist that the computer does not make any decisions. Rather, it provides data and information that allow trained medical personnel to make more informed decisions about how to allocate very expensive treatment procedures and how to use most effectively limited medical resources, such as intensive care beds and organs for transplants. Armed with this information, doctors can better determine who should and should not be treated. David Bihari, a critical care specialist in England, points out that because of a lack of intensive care facilities, as many as one in four patients may have to be turned away from British hospitals. A computer program such as RIP provides physicians with vital information about who is most likely to benefit from treatment and who is not.

4   While medical doctors and ethicists debate the merits of using a computer program such as RIP, sociologists are more interested in the social ramifications of such procedures. Decisions about who to treat and how to treat them have always been part of the dynamics of emergency rooms. How important have social variables such as race, gender, age, and social class been in the past? Might a computer be less likely to discriminate on the basis of these and other social characteristics? However, what is lost when the human dimension is subordinated to computer technology in medical decision making? These and other sociological issues are likely to become even more pronounced as more sophisticated medical technology, combined with an increasing demand on medical services, forces physicians and health-care workers around the world to make even more decisions about who should and should not receive their services.

5   Less controversially, emergency rooms across the United States routinely use a doctor-friendly computerized database that, within 60 seconds of inputting symptoms provides a diagnosis and preferred method of treatment in pediatric emergency cases. And what contemporary doctor's office, medical clinic, or hospital would be complete today without computers, X-ray machines, and even sophisticated magnetic resonance imaging and laser technologies?

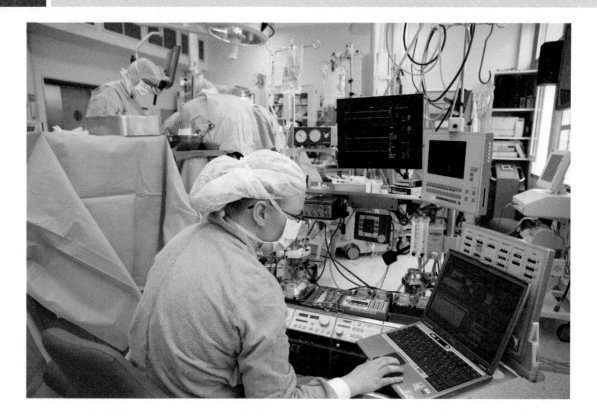

6   The question is not whether technology is going to alter the future course of health and medical care in the United States and around the world but, more important, where we draw the line. Medical ethicists today are debating issues ranging from the use of biogenetic engineering to create life, to the use of fetal organs for transplant and the treatment of Alzheimer's disease, to euthanasia and doctor-assisted suicides. The world was stunned when the parents of a teenage daughter who needed a kidney transplant but couldn't find a perfect match decided to have another child for the express purpose of providing an organ donor. Reports that starving people in developing nations may sell their organs on a black market, from which the organs eventually find their way to the United States and Europe for transplant, provide frightening science fiction-like scenarios for the future. The rapid development of medical knowledge and technology has created what some call an "ethical minefield." From a sociological viewpoint, these and other issues may be ruled on from medical, legal, and religious perspectives but will continue to be debated and ultimately decided in a larger social arena, where attitudes, values, beliefs, and important norms regarding technology, health, and medical care are created, transmitted, and transformed through the process of social interaction.

7   Sociologists have long understood that technology often develops at a much faster rate than the public's ability to grasp its consequences and to rethink the important values, attitudes, norms, and beliefs that surround its uses. Nowhere is this

cultural lag more evident than in the case of the revolutionary technological developments in medical and health care. As one sociologist noted, "medical ethics is an arena in which sociologists can revisit issues about the doctor–patient relationship . . . the meaning of death and dying, and the character of the medical profession."

SUMMING IT UP

TAKING A CLOSER LOOK

Some people contend that the major purpose of health care and medicine is to sustain and prolong life and that technological developments that allow us to do so should be used without hesitation. Others argue that medical technology has developed at such a rapid pace that the most important issue today is not whether we can sustain and prolong life almost indefinitely, but whether we *should*. On which side of this debate would you most closely align your position? Why? What do you think of computer programs such as RIP? How will they affect emergency room care? What ethical dilemmas are presented by this and other types of medical technology?

A. UNDERSTANDING THE THESIS AND OTHER MAIN IDEAS

Select the best answer.

_____ 1. The authors' primary purpose in this selection is to
   a. debate the use of computerized systems in hospital emergency rooms.
   b. describe the different types of technology used in medical situations.
   c. discuss sociological and ethical issues related to medical technology.
   d. compare critical care procedures in England with those in the United States.

_____ 2. The topic of paragraph 2 is
   a. emergency room care.
   b. the RIP computer program.
   c. health-care workers.
   d. medical technology.

_____ 3. The main idea of paragraph 4 is that sociologists are primarily interested in the
   a. merits of medical technology.
   b. increasing demand on medical services.

c. human dimension of decision making.

d. sociological implications of medical technology.

_____ 4. The main argument of supporters of the new computerized system is that it

a. allows untrained personnel to make high-level decisions.

b. makes more reliable decisions and fewer mistakes than humans.

c. provides data to help doctors make more informed decisions.

d. reduces the possibility of discrimination in treatment decisions.

_____ 5. The statement that best expresses the main idea of paragraph 6 is:

a. The development of medical technology has created debate about how it should be used.

b. Medical ethicists are debating the use of biogenetic engineering to create life.

c. Technology issues must be ruled on from medical, legal, and religious perspectives.

d. The process of social interaction transforms beliefs about technology and health care.

B. IDENTIFYING DETAILS

Indicate which of the following claims were made by medical ethicist Arthur Caplan (AC) and which were made by critical care specialist David Bihari (DB).

_____ 1. Computers should not be used to make decisions about the allocation of medical resources to patients.

_____ 2. As many as one in four patients may be turned away from British hospitals because of a lack of intensive care facilities.

_____ 3. The computer will be wrong in about 5 percent of all cases.

C. RECOGNIZING METHODS OF ORGANIZATION AND TRANSITIONS

Select the best answer.

_____ 1. In paragraph 1, the organizational pattern the authors use to describe a patient's arrival at the emergency room is

a. definition.

b. classification.

c. cause and effect.

d. time sequence.

_____ 2. In paragraph 3, the authors use the comparison and contrast pattern to discuss the difference between

      a. supporters and critics of the new computerized system.

      b. expensive treatment procedures and limited resources.

      c. health care in the United States and England.

      d. conventional medical treatment and new medical technology.

_____ 3. The transitional word or phrase in paragraph 3 that indicates examples will follow is

      a. rather.

      b. such as.

      c. as many as.

      d. because.

D. REVIEWING AND ORGANIZING IDEAS: MAPPING

Complete the map (p. 456) of the process described in paragraphs 1–2 by filling in the blanks.

E. READING AND THINKING VISUALLY

Answer the following questions.

1. What does the photograph show?

_____

2. What concepts in the selection are illustrated by the photograph?

_____

_____

3. What is the purpose of the box titled "Taking a Closer Look"?

_____

_____

F. FIGURING OUT IMPLIED MEANINGS

Each of the following boldfaced words has a strong positive or negative connotation. Make inferences by indicating whether the word creates a positive (P) or negative (N) image for the reader.

_____ 1. "With sirens **blaring** and lights flashing, the ambulance skids to a halt in front of the hospital emergency room entrance." (paragraph 1)

_____ 2. "Critics of the new computerized system contend that it is a **frightening** example of overreliance on computer technology . . ." (paragraph 3)

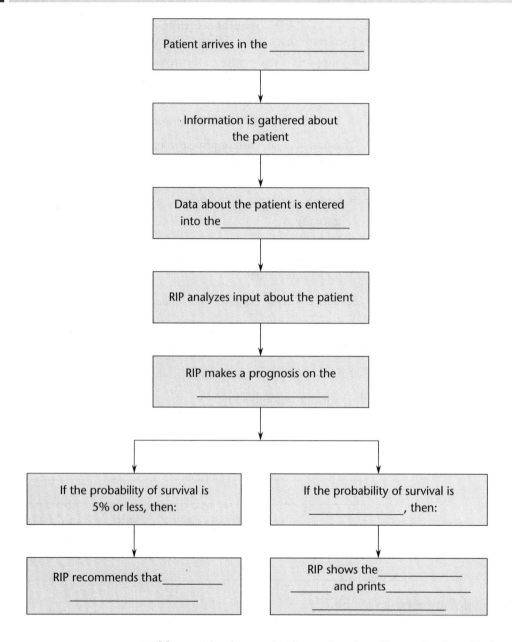

_____ 3. "[I]t provides data and information that allow trained medical
personnel to make more **informed** decisions . . ." (paragraph 3)

_____ 4. "[E]mergency rooms across the United States routinely use a
doctor-**friendly** computerized database . . ." (paragraph 5)

_____ 5. "Reports that **starving** people in developing nations may sell their
organs on a black market . . . provide frightening, science fiction–
like scenarios" (paragraph 6)

G. THINKING CRITICALLY

Select the best answer.

_____ 1. The authors begin the selection by describing a patient's arrival at the hospital in order to illustrate

a. the importance of each member of a medical team.

b. the authors' personal experience in an emergency room.

c. common mistakes in emergency room procedures.

d. how computerized technology is used in emergency rooms.

_____ 2. In the first paragraph of the selection, the authors are striving to create a sense of

a. detachment.

b. formality.

c. urgency.

d. enthusiasm.

_____ 3. The authors pose several questions in paragraph 4 primarily to

a. persuade the reader that the benefits of medical technology are worth the costs.

b. get the reader thinking about sociological issues related to medical technology.

c. demonstrate to the reader that discrimination exists in the health-care system.

d. remind the reader of the importance of technology in medical decision making.

_____ 4. The phrase "ethical minefield" in paragraph 6 refers to the

a. explosive growth in the field of medical technology.

b. hidden and unexpected ethical problems created by medical technology.

c. use of medical technology in a war setting.

d. belief that medical technology has caused more harm than good.

_____ 5. The intended audience for this selection is most likely to be

a. health care professionals.

b. hospital administrators.

c. sociology students.

d. medical ethicists.

H. BUILDING VOCABULARY

Context

Using context and a dictionary, if necessary, determine the meaning of each word as it is used in the selection.

_____ 1. prognosis (paragraph 2)
  a. prediction
  b. allowance
  c. oversight
  d. dismissal

_____ 2. contend (paragraph 3)
  a. nominate
  b. compete
  c. argue
  d. challenge

_____ 3. allocation (paragraph 3)
  a. distribution
  b. connection
  c. opposition
  d. dispute

_____ 4. merits (paragraph 4)
  a. concerns
  b. charges
  c. problems
  d. benefits

_____ 5. ramifications (paragraph 4)
  a. penalties
  b. consequences
  c. conclusions
  d. obstacles

_____ 6. lag (paragraph 7)
  a. region
  b. point
  c. delay
  d. rate

Word Parts

A REVIEW OF PREFIXES, ROOTS, AND SUFFIXES

INTRA- means *within, into, in*
MILLI- means *thousand*
SUB- means *under, below*
RE- means *back, again*
TRANS- means *cross, over*
SPECT means *look, see*
LOG means *study, thought*
-IST means *one who*

Use your knowledge of word parts and the review above to match each word in Column A with its meaning in Column B. Write your answers in the spaces provided.

Column A	Column B
_____ 1. intravenous	a. one who specializes in ethical issues
_____ 2. milliseconds	b. placed in a secondary or lower position
_____ 3. ethicist	c. consider again
_____ 4. sociologist	d. into the vein
_____ 5. subordinated	e. sent across
_____ 6. perspectives	f. thousandths of a second
_____ 7. transmitted	g. viewpoints
_____ 8. revisit	h. one who studies society and human behavior

Unusual Words/Understanding Idioms

Use the meanings given below to write a sentence using the boldfaced word or phrase.

1. A **swarm** (paragraph 1) means a large group, especially one that is in motion.

   Your sentence: _____

   _____

2. The term **black market** (paragraph 6) refers to the unlawful buying and selling of goods; in this selection, the "goods" are human organs.

   Your sentence: _____

   _____

I. SELECTING A LEARNING/STUDY STRATEGY

Discuss what method(s) you would use to learn this material in preparation for a multiple-choice test.

J. EXPLORING IDEAS THROUGH DISCUSSION AND WRITING

1. Reread the three questions posed by the authors in paragraph 4 and discuss your response to each one.

2. In the box titled "Taking a Closer Look," the authors ask several questions related to medical technology and ethical issues. Choose one of the questions and write an essay answering it.

3. Evaluate the introduction to this selection. How well did it capture your attention and introduce the topic?

K. BEYOND THE CLASSROOM TO THE WEB

Go to http://www.nlm.nih.gov/medlineplus/medicalethics.html, *the medical ethics section of the Web site for Medline Plus, which is the National Institutes of Health's site for patients and families. Read about some of the topics on the site and discuss the ethical dilemmas associated with those topics.*

TRACKING YOUR PROGRESS

Selection 19

Section	Number Correct		Score
A. Thesis and Main Ideas (5 items)	_____	× 4	_____
B. Details (3 items)	_____	× 5	_____
C. Organization and Transitions (3 items)	_____	× 5	_____
F. Implied Meanings (5 items)	_____	× 2	_____
G. Thinking Critically (5 items)	_____	× 4	_____
H. Vocabulary			
Context (6 items)	_____	× 2	_____
Word Parts (8 items)	_____	× 1	_____
	TOTAL SCORE		_____ %

SELECTION 20

When Living Is a Fate Worse Than Death

Christine Mitchell

Contemporary Issues Reading This reading first appeared in *Newsweek,* a weekly news magazine. The author, a medical ethicist, describes a dilemma faced by hospital staff in treating a young child.

PREVIEWING THE READING

Using the steps listed on page 36, preview the reading selection. When you have finished, complete the following statements.

1. The title indicates that the selection is about a situation in which living is worse than _____.

2. Most of the action in the selection takes place in a _____.

MAKING CONNECTIONS

Imagine that you are responsible for deciding whether to withhold further treatment from someone who is terminally ill. What factors would you consider in your decision?

trachea
the windpipe that carries air from the larynx to the lungs

coded
the action taken by medical professionals to restart a person's heart after it has stopped beating

ICU
the intensive care unit of a hospital

READING TIP

As you read, highlight reasons that support the child's right to die.

When Living Is a Fate Worse Than Death

1   The baby died last winter. It was pretty terrible. Little Charlotte (not her real name) lay on a high white bed, surrounded by nurses and doctors pushing drugs into her veins, tubes into her **trachea** and needles into her heart, trying as hard as they could to take over for her failing body and brain. She was being **coded**, as they say in the **ICU**. It had happened several times before, but this time it would fail. Her parents, who were working, weren't there.

2   Charlotte was born with too few brain cells to do much more than breathe and pull away from pain. Most of her malformed brain was wrapped in a sac that grew outside her skull and had to be surgically removed to prevent immediate death.

3   Her parents were a young, unmarried couple from Haiti. They loved Charlotte and wanted her to live. The nurses and doctors thought she should be allowed to

die peacefully. They recommended that a Do Not Resuscitate order be placed in Charlotte's chart. The new parents disagreed. Surely, they thought, medical care in the United States could save their baby. They bought their daughter a doll.

4   For 16 months Charlotte bounced back and forth—between hospital, home, the **ER** and pediatric nursing homes. Wherever she was, every time her body tried to die, nurses and doctors staved off death. Each time, Charlotte got weaker.

ER
the emergency room of a hospital

ethicist
a specialist in ethics, the rules or standards guiding the conduct and decisions of members of a profession

5   Charlotte's medical team at the hospital asked to talk with the Ethics Advisory Committee and, as the hospital's **ethicist**, I got involved. Is it right to keep doing painful things just to keep Charlotte alive a little longer, her doctors and nurses asked us. To whom are we most obligated: the patient or the family? The committee advised that in this case the parents' rights superseded the caregivers' beliefs about what was right. Painful procedures should be avoided, the panel believed, but the care that Charlotte's parents wanted for her should be provided unless there was a medical consensus that it would not prolong her life. Such a consensus was elusive. There's almost always another procedure that can be tried to eke out a little more time until the patient dies despite everything—as Charlotte did.

6   A week after Charlotte's death, I met with the doctors, nurses and therapists who had done everything they could for her and yet felt terrible about having done too much. We talked for almost two hours about how Charlotte had died.

7   "It was horrible," said a doctor. "We tried to resuscitate her for over an hour. It's the worst thing I've ever done. I actually felt sick." A nurse talked about the holes that were drilled in Charlotte's bones to insert lines they couldn't get in anywhere else.

8   Why didn't Charlotte's parents spare Charlotte—and us—the awfulness of her death? Because they were too young? Too hopeful? Because they were distrustful of white nurses and doctors who they thought might really be saying that their black baby wasn't worth saving? Or because they believed that a "good" death is one in which everything possible has been tried?

9   Why didn't the hospital staff, including the ethics committee, save Charlotte from that kind of death? Maybe we feared that her parents would take us to court, like the mother in Virginia who got a judge to order the hospital to provide lifesaving treatment for her anencephalic baby, who was born without most of her brain. Maybe we were afraid of seeing ourselves in the news—as the staff of a Pennsylvania hospital did when they withdrew life support, against the parents' wishes, from a comatose 3-year-old with fatal brain cancer. Maybe we were thinking about what was best for the parents, not just the child. Maybe we were wrong.

10   The nurse sitting next to me at the meeting had driven two hours from the nursing home where she used to care for Charlotte. She had attended the wake. She said the parents had sobbed; that Dad said he felt terrible because he wasn't there when his little girl died, that Mom still couldn't believe that she was dead.

11   It could have been different. They could have been there holding her. That's the way it happens most of the time in ICUs today. Family and staff make the decision together, machines are removed and death comes gently.

12   As a hospital ethicist, a large part of my job is helping staff and families distinguish between sustaining life and prolonging death. Sometimes I join the staff, as I did that night, in second-guessing decisions and drawing distinctions between

the dignified death of a child held by parents who accept their child's dying, and the death that occurs amid technologically desperate measures and professional strangers.

13   Sooner or later, every person will die. I wish, and the hospital staff I work with wishes, almost beyond telling, that people could know what they are asking when they ask that "everything" be done.

Source: From *The New York Times,* August 28, 2000 © 2000 The New York Times All rights reserved. Used by permission and protected by the Copyright Laws of the United States. The printing, copying, redistribution, or retransmission of the Material without express written permission is prohibited.

A. UNDERSTANDING THE THESIS AND OTHER MAIN IDEAS

Select the best answer.

_____ 1. The author's primary purpose is to
   a. describe the current technology used in hospitals to prolong life.
   b. explain that hospital personnel grieve along with a patient's family when the patient dies.
   c. contrast the rights of a patient's family with the beliefs of caregivers.
   d. argue that prolonging life is sometimes worse than letting the patient die peacefully.

_____ 2. The main idea of paragraph 3 is that
   a. Charlotte's parents were young and from another country.
   b. Charlotte's parents disagreed with the hospital staff about what was best for her.
   c. a Do Not Resuscitate order should have been placed in Charlotte's chart.
   d. Charlotte's parents believed that U.S. medical care should have been able to save her.

_____ 3. The Ethics Advisory Board ruled that
   a. the Ethics Advisory Committee made the wrong recommendation.
   b. there are many possible procedures that can be done to prolong life.
   c. the hospital staff would have to provide the care that Charlotte's parents wanted for her.
   d. it was difficult to reach a medical consensus about Charlotte's care.

_____ 4. The question that the author is asking in paragraph 9 is
   a. Would Charlotte's parents have taken the hospital staff to court?
   b. Would the hospital staff have been on the news because of their treatment of Charlotte?

        c. Was the staff thinking about what was best for the parents or for Charlotte?

        d. Why didn't the hospital staff do something to change the way that Charlotte died?

_____ 5. The main idea of paragraph 11 is expressed in the

        a. first sentence.

        b. second sentence.

        c. third sentence.

        d. fourth sentence.

B. IDENTIFYING DETAILS

Indicate whether each statement is true (T) or false (F).

_____ 1. Charlotte's parents were from Haiti.

_____ 2. Charlotte was in the hospital because she had developed brain cancer.

_____ 3. Charlotte lived her entire life in the hospital.

_____ 4. The hospital's Ethics Advisory Committee believed the staff should avoid painful procedures for Charlotte.

_____ 5. After Charlotte died, the hospital staff wished that they had tried more techniques to save her.

_____ 6. The nurse who attended the wake said the parents were angry at the hospital.

_____ 7. Charlotte's parents were not at the hospital with Charlotte when she died.

C. RECOGNIZING METHODS OF ORGANIZATION AND TRANSITIONS

Select the best answer.

_____ 1. The organizational pattern that the author uses to describe events in the order in which they occurred during Charlotte's brief life is

        a. time sequence.

        b. definition.

        c. enumeration.

        d. comparison and contrast.

_____ 2. Throughout the reading, the author uses the comparison and contrast organizational pattern to contrast the opinions of

        a. Charlotte's medical team and the Ethics Advisory Committee.

        b. Charlotte's parents and the hospital staff.

        c. Charlotte's parents and the Ethics Advisory Committee.

        d. the hospital ethicist and Charlotte's medical team.

D. REVIEWING AND ORGANIZING IDEAS: PARAPHRASING

Complete the following paraphrases of paragraphs 4 and 11 by filling in the missing words or phrases.

Paragraph 4: Charlotte was moved between the _____, her _____, the hospital's _____, and pediatric _____ for _____ months. Whenever she came close to _____, nurses and _____ were able to hold it off, but she grew _____ each time it happened.

Paragraph 11: Charlotte's _____ could have been different if her _____ had been there holding her. It usually happens like that now in _____. Together, the patient's _____ and the hospital _____ decide to remove the _____ and let _____ come peacefully.

E. READING AND THINKING VISUALLY

Select the best answer.

_____   Unlike many of the reading selections in this book, "When Living Is a Fate Worse Than Death" does not include any visual aids. What is the most likely explanation for why the author did not include a photo of baby Charlotte?

a. No photos were available of baby Charlotte.

b. The topic is very sensitive and the author felt that including a photo of baby Charlotte would not be tasteful or respectful of the baby's memory.

c. The hospital would not permit any photos to be taken of baby Charlotte.

d. The bereaved parents, doctors, and hospital would not allow any photos of baby Charlotte to be taken or printed.

F. FIGURING OUT IMPLIED MEANINGS

Indicate whether each statement is true (T) or false (F).

_____ 1. Charlotte's parents believed that the medical care in the United States was better than the medical care in Haiti.

_____ 2. Because of her condition at birth, Charlotte always would have been dependent on medical care even if she had survived longer.

_____ 3. It can be inferred that the white hospital staff was prejudiced against the black couple and their baby.

_____ 4. A hospital ethicist helps make decisions about removing life support for terminally ill patients.

_____ 5. The hospital Ethics Advisory Committee thought that Charlotte would eventually get better.

G. THINKING CRITICALLY

Select the best answer.

_____ 1. The author supports her central thesis with
  a. examples.
  b. descriptions.
  c. personal experience.
  d. all of the above.

_____ 2. The tone of the selection can best be described as
  a. angry.
  b. concerned.
  c. objective.
  d. optimistic.

_____ 3. The author wrote the first paragraph in order to
  a. gain sympathy for the baby's parents.
  b. explain why the lifesaving efforts failed.
  c. describe the awfulness of the baby's death.
  d. suggest that every effort had not been made to save the baby's life.

_____ 4. Of the following statements from paragraph 1, the only one that is an *opinion* is
  a. "The baby died last winter."
  b. "It was pretty terrible."
  c. "Charlotte . . . lay on a high white bed, surrounded by nurses and doctors."
  d. "She was being coded."

_____ 5. The author included the statement "They bought their daughter a doll" (paragraph 3) in order to indicate that
  a. the parents were not poor.
  b. Charlotte was able to play.
  c. the parents were hopeful that Charlotte would be all right.
  d. the hospital did not provide toys.

_____ 6. The author speculates that the parents let their child's death happen the way it did because they may have
  a. been too young and hopeful.

b. distrusted the commitment of white doctors and nurses toward their black baby.

c. believed that death should come only after every possible procedure had been tried.

d. all of the above.

_____ 7. In paragraph 12, the author considers the decisions that were made in this case by comparing

a. her responsibilities as an ethicist with those of the medical caregivers.

b. her beliefs with those of the parents.

c. the ICUs of today with the traditional ICUs of the past.

d. a peaceful, dignified death with the kind that occurs only after desperate medical efforts have failed.

H. BUILDING VOCABULARY

Context

Using context and a dictionary, if necessary, determine the meaning of each word as it is used in the selection.

_____ 1. resuscitate (paragraph 3)

a. disturb

b. revive

c. allow

d. review

_____ 2. elusive (paragraph 5)

a. difficult to reach

b. temporary

c. permanent

d. unlucky

_____ 3. eke (paragraph 5)

a. harm

b. leave out

c. draw out

d. hide

_____ 4. comatose (paragraph 9)

a. diagnosed

b. unconscious

c. terminally ill

d. recovering

Word Parts

> ### A REVIEW OF PREFIXES AND SUFFIXES
>
> **MAL-** means *poorly* or *wrongly*
> **SUPER-** means *above*
> **-IST** means *one who*

Use your knowledge of word parts and the review above to fill in the blanks in the following sentences.

1. The word *malformed* (paragraph 2) means _____.

2. The word *superseded* (paragraph 5) means to have been put _____ in importance.

3. A person who provides therapy is called a _____ (paragraph 6).

I. SELECTING A LEARNING/STUDY STRATEGY

Select the best answer.

_____ 1. If you were using this article as a source for a paper on the right-to-die issue, which of the following techniques would be most helpful?

    a. highlighting useful information and quotations

    b. drawing a time line

    c. rereading the article

    d. summarizing the parents' opinions

J. EXPLORING IDEAS THROUGH DISCUSSION AND WRITING

1. What do you consider a "good" death?

2. Do you agree more with the author or with those who would do everything possible to prevent, or delay, death?

3. What did the author mean by the phrase "almost beyond telling" (paragraph 13)?

K. BEYOND THE CLASSROOM TO THE WEB

Read this New York times blog post at **http://well.blogs.nytimes.com/2009/09/09/prolonging-death-at-the-end-of-life/.** *What comparisons can you make to this case and the one you read about Charlotte and her parents? How do you feel about the toll on doctors and patients families as a result of prolonged treatment? Do you think it is ethical?*

TRACKING
YOUR
PROGRESS

Selection 20

Section	Number Correct		Score
A. Thesis and Main Ideas (5 items)	_____	× 5	_____
B. Details (7 items)	_____	× 3	_____
C. Organization and Transitions (2 items)	_____	× 3	_____
E. Reading and Thinking Visually (1 item)	_____	× 3	_____
F. Implied Meanings (5 items)	_____	× 2	_____
G. Thinking Critically (7 items)	_____	× 3	_____
H. Vocabulary			
Context (4 items)	_____	× 2	_____
Word Parts (3 items)	_____	× 2	_____
	TOTAL SCORE		_____%

SELECTION 21

A Step Beyond Human

Andy Greenberg

Contemporary
Issues Reading

This selection first appeared in a December 2009 issue of *Forbes* magazine. Read the article to find out how and why one man is working to transform the field of artificial limbs.

PREVIEWING THE READING

Using the steps listed on page 36, preview the reading selection. When you have finished, complete the following items.

1. The subject of this selection is a man named _____.

2. List three questions you expect to be able to answer after reading the article.

   a. _____

   b. _____

   c. _____

 MAKING CONNECTIONS

Do you know anyone with a disability? Think about how you define "disability."

READING TIP

As you read, highlight descriptions of the different prosthetic devices developed and/or used by Hugh Herr.

A Step Beyond Human

1   On his way to a lunch meeting a few years ago Hugh Herr was running late. So he parked his Honda Accord in a handicapped parking spot, sprang out of the car and jogged down the sidewalk. Within seconds a policeman called out, asking to see his disability permit. When Herr pointed it out on his dashboard, the cop eyed him suspiciously. "What's your affliction?" he asked dryly.

2   Herr, a slim and unassuming 6-footer with dark, neatly parted hair, took a step toward the officer and responded in an even tone: "I have no [expletive] legs."

Cyborg evangelist: Herr wears a pair of his disability-defying PowerFoot devices.

3

biomechatronics
an applied
science
combining
elements
of biology,
mechanics,
and electronics,
as well as
robotics and
neuroscience

prosthetics
artificial limbs

crampons
spikes attached
to shoes for ice
climbing

4

5

Blurring the boundaries of disability is a trick that Herr, director of the **biomechatronics** group at MIT's Media Lab, has spent the last 27 years perfecting. At age 17 both of Herr's legs were amputated 6 inches below the knee after a rock climbing trip ended in severe frostbite. Today he's one of the world's preeminent **prosthetics** experts. His goal: to build artificial limbs that are superior to natural ones. His favorite test subject: himself. "I like to say that there are no disabled people," says Herr, 45. "Only disabled technology."

Herr swaps his feet out to suit his needs. He generally walks on flat carbon-fiber springs inside his shoes but sometimes replaces them with longer carbon bows for jogging. When he goes rock climbing—often scaling cliffs of expert-level difficulty—he switches to one of multiple pairs of climbing legs he's built himself, including small, rubber feet on aluminum poles that stretch his height beyond 7 feet, spiked aluminum claws that replace **crampons** for ice climbing or tapered polyethylene hatchets that wedge into crevices. "The fact that I'm missing lower limbs is an opportunity," he says. "Between my residual limb and the ground, I can create anything I want. The only limits are physical laws and my imagination."

Over the last several years that imagination has been working overtime. Late next year iWalk, a company Herr founded in 2006, plans to release the PowerFoot One, the world's most advanced robotic ankle and foot. Most prosthetic feet are fixed at a clumsy 90 degrees. The PowerFoot, equipped with three internal microprocessors

inertia
in physics, the tendency of a body to maintain its state of rest or uniform motion unless acted upon by an external force

6   and 12 sensors that measure force, **inertia** and position, automatically adjusts its angle, stiffness and damping 500 times a second. Employing the same sort of sensory feedback loops that the human nervous system uses, plus a library of known patterns, the PowerFoot adjusts for slopes, dips its toe naturally when walking down stairs, even hangs casually when the user crosses his or her legs.

   The PowerFoot is the only foot and ankle in the world that doesn't depend on its wearer's energy. With a system of passive springs and a half-pound rechargeable lithium iron phosphate battery, the foot—made of aluminum, titanium, plastic and carbon fiber—provides the same 20-joule push off the ground that human muscles and tendons do. It automatically adjusts the power to the walker's speed, but users can also dial that power up or down with a Bluetooth-enabled phone. (And soon, Herr says, with an iPhone application.) One test subject told Herr that his nonamputated leg often tires before his prosthetic-enhanced one. "This is the first time that the prosthesis is driving the human, instead of the other way around," says Herr.

7   Herr frequently wears a pair of his new creations. The next to try the PowerFoot will be the Department of Defense, which is looking for prostheses for the nearly 1,000 soldiers who have lost limbs in Iraq and Afghanistan. The Veterans Administration and the Army are among the investors who funded his MIT research. Veterans, he argues, also make the perfect early adopters, given their athletic, active lifestyles. "These are remarkable people," says Herr. "If the PowerFoot can work for them, it can work for anyone." iWalk hopes to put the PowerFoot on the general market in 2010, priced in the low five figures. The startup has raised $10.2 million from investors, including General Catalyst Partners and WFD Ventures.

8   Herr's motives extend beyond profit. In 1982 he and a friend climbed Mount Washington in New Hampshire, a place infamous for its unpredictable and nasty weather. They were caught in a snowstorm, losing their way in a near-complete whiteout and subzero temperatures. After three and a half days of crawling along a frozen river, Herr's lower legs were practically destroyed by cold. A member of the rescue team sent after them, 28-year-old Albert Dow, was killed in an avalanche. "I feel a responsibility to use my intellect and resources to do as much as I can to help people. That's Albert Dow's legacy for me," says Herr.

9   Within three months of his amputations Herr was rock climbing with simple prosthetics. Within six months he was in a machine shop, building new feet, using the skills he'd learned at a vocational high school in Lancaster, Pa., where he grew up.

10   While he had previously focused on merely working a trade, Herr became a nearly obsessive student, earning a master's in mechanical engineering at MIT and a Ph.D. in biophysics at Harvard. Once, when his hands suffered from repetitive stress disorder while he was writing his doctoral thesis, he attached a pencil to a pair of sunglass frames and typed with his head. "He's driven to the point of exhaustion, physical degradation," says Rodger Kram, a professor of integrative physiology at the University of Colorado at Boulder, who worked with Herr at Harvard. "Every step he takes, he's forced to think about making prosthetics better."

11   Herr wants to transform how people define disability. Last year he sat on a panel of scientists that confirmed that Oscar Pistorius, a South African sprinter with no legs below the knee, should be allowed to compete in the Olympics. Herr helped discredit arguments that Pistorius got a metabolic advantage from his carbon-fiber legs. (Pistorius missed qualifying by a fraction of a second.)

12   Herr has tasted athletic discrimination, too. Because he uses special climbing prosthetics, many dispute his claim to be the second in the world to free-climb a famously challenging pitch near Index Mountain, Wash. "When amputees partici-pate in sports, they call it courageous," he says. "Once you become competitive, they call it cheating." Herr even believes that in the coming decades **Paralympic** athletes will regularly outperform Olympic athletes. We may need special disability laws for humans who decline to have their bodies mechanically enhanced, he says.

Paralympic
related to an
international
competition for
athletes with
disabilities

13   "Disabled people today are the test pilots for technology that will someday be pervasive," Herr explains. "Eliminating disability and blurring man and machine will be one of the great stories of this century."

A. UNDERSTANDING THE THESIS AND OTHER MAIN IDEAS

Select the best answer.

_____ 1. The focus of this selection is on Hugh Herr's
   a. ice and rock climbing trips.
   b. athletic achievements.
   c. work with prosthetics.
   d. research at MIT.

_____ 2. The main idea of paragraph 4 is that Herr
   a. uses flat springs in his shoes for walking.
   b. has built his own pair of artificial legs.
   c. has created special prosthetics for ice climbing.
   d. uses different prosthetics for different tasks.

_____ 3. Herr's lower legs were amputated because of
   a. a war injury.
   b. severe frostbite.
   c. a car accident.
   d. bone disease.

_____ 4. The topic of paragraph 5 is
   a. Hugh Herr.
   b. iWalk.
   c. the PowerFoot One.
   d. robotics.

_____ 5. The main idea of paragraph 12 is that Herr
   a. has faced discrimination because of his use of prosthetics.
   b. wants to compete in the Paralympics.
   c. claims to be second in the world to climb Index Mountain.
   d. does not want special disability laws to be enacted.

B. IDENTIFYING DETAILS

Complete the sentences by filling in the blanks.

1. Hugh Herr was _____ years old when his legs were
   amputated _____ inches below the knee.

2. Herr earned a master's degree in _____ at
   _____ and a Ph.D. in _____ at
   _____.

3. Herr founded a company in _____ called iWalk, which
   has raised $ _____ million from investors.

4. The Department of _____ is considering the iWalk Power-
   Foot for _____ who have lost limbs.

C. RECOGNIZING METHODS OF ORGANIZATION AND TRANSITIONS

Complete the following statement by filling in the blanks.

In paragraphs 8–9, the author uses the time sequence pattern to describe
what happened after Herr and a friend climbed Mount Washington in 1982.
Three phrases that signal the passage of time are _____,
_____ , and _____ .

D. REVIEWING AND ORGANIZING IDEAS: OUTLINING

*Complete the following outline of paragraphs 5–6 by filling in the missing words
and phrases.*

The PowerFoot One

I. Most advanced robotic ankle and foot

  A. Equipped with:

    1. Three internal _____

    2. Twelve sensors measuring _____,
       _____ and position

  B. Automatically adjusts _____ times per second

    1. Angle

    2. _____

    3. _____

C. Makes use of:

   1. Sensory feedback loops

   2. Library of _____

D. Capable of adjusting for slopes and other natural actions

II. Not dependent on _____

A. Uses a system of passive springs and a rechargeable battery

B. Made of _____, _____, _____, and

   _____

C. Provides the same push as human muscles and tendons

   1. Automatically adjusts power to user's speed

   2. Users can _____ with a phone

E. READING AND THINKING VISUALLY

Complete each of the following items.

1. The purpose of the photograph that accompanies this reading is to

_____ .

2. The photograph caption refers to Herr as a "cyborg evangelist" because he

_____ .

F. FIGURING OUT IMPLIED MEANINGS

Indicate whether each statement is true (T) or false (F).

_____ 1. Herr was questioned by a policeman because he had parked illegally.

_____ 2. The policeman could not tell that Herr was disabled.

_____ 3. Herr wants to build prosthetics that are even better than natural limbs.

_____ 4. Herr did not think Oscar Pistorius should be allowed to compete in the Olympics.

_____ 5. According to Herr, Paralympic athletes will one day compete and win against Olympic athletes.

G. THINKING CRITICALLY

Select the best answer.

_____ 1. The tone of this selection can best be described as
   a. humorous.
   b. admiring.
   c. tragic.
   d. solemn.

_____ 2. The "trick" that the author refers to in paragraph 3 is Herr's ability to
   a. change prosthetics depending on his needs.
   b. climb up cliffs of expert-level difficulty.
   c. change people's ideas about what disability means.
   d. create prostheses that feature a variety of functions.

_____ 3. All of the following statements by Herr reveal his attitude toward his disability *except*
   a. "I like to say that there are no disabled people. Only disabled technology."
   b. "The fact that I'm missing lower limbs is an opportunity."
   c. "The only limits are physical laws and my imagination."
   d. "This is the first time that the prosthesis is driving the human."

_____ 4. As described in paragraph 8, the legacy of Albert Dow refers to
   a. an inheritance left to Herr by another disabled climber.
   b. a piece of property left to Herr by one of his distant relatives.
   c. the legal obligation Herr has to an investor in his company.
   d. a sense of responsibility that Herr feels toward a man who died trying to save him.

_____ 5. Of the following words in paragraph 12, the only one with a negative connotation is
   a. special.
   b. courageous.
   c. competitive.
   d. cheating.

H. BUILDING VOCABULARY

Context

Using context and a dictionary, if necessary, determine the meaning of each word as it is used in the selection.

_____ 1. affliction (paragraph 1)
    a. hurry
    b. disability
    c. purpose
    d. approach

_____ 2. preeminent (paragraph 3)
    a. top
    b. difficult
    c. unknown
    d. worst

_____ 3. residual (paragraph 4)
    a. automatic
    b. remaining
    c. unlimited
    d. effective

_____ 4. degradation (paragraph 10)
    a. breakdown
    b. assistance
    c. presentation
    d. reward

_____ 5. pervasive (paragraph 13)
    a. unusual
    b. widespread
    c. misunderstood
    d. expensive

Word Parts

A REVIEW OF PREFIXES AND ROOTS

UN- means *not*
RE- means *back, again*
SUB- means *under, below*
DIS- means *apart, away, not*
LOG means *study, thought*
CRED means *believe*

Use your knowledge of word parts and the review on the previous page to match each word in Column A with its meaning in Column B. Write your answers in the spaces provided.

Column A	**Column B**
_____ 1. unassuming	a. below zero
_____ 2. rechargeable	b. the study of the functions of living organisms
_____ 3. subzero	
_____ 4. physiology	c. take away belief in
_____ 5. discredit	d. modest, not pretentious
	e. able to be energized or charged again

Unusual Words/Understanding Idioms

Use the meanings given below to write a sentence using the boldfaced word.

1. Someone who has **tasted** (paragraph 12) discrimination has experienced it briefly.

   Your sentence: _____

   _____

2. The word **pitch** (paragraph 12) can refer to a throw, a sales talk, an element of sound, a playing field or, as it is used in this selection, a very steep piece of ground.

   Your sentence: _____

   _____

I. SELECTING A LEARNING/STUDY STRATEGY

Assume you will be tested on this article on an upcoming exam. Evaluate your highlighting as well as the outline you completed. How else might you prepare for a test on this material?

J. EXPLORING IDEAS THROUGH DISCUSSION AND WRITING

1. Discuss your initial impression of Herr after reading the opening paragraphs of the selection, and explain how that brief story contributes to your understanding of what kind of person he is. What words would you use to describe Herr?

2. Discuss the meaning of the title, "A Step Beyond Human." Can you think of other titles that might work for this selection?

3. What factors in Herr's life motivate him? Discuss how his life experiences and his attitude make him especially well suited to his work.

K. BEYOND THE CLASSROOM TO THE WEB

Read the profiles of some of the athletes on the U.S. Paralympic Team at the Web site **http://usparalympics.org/athletes/index.** *Which stories do you find most interesting or inspiring and why?*

Visit the Web site for iWalk, the company founded by Hugh Herr, at **http://www. iwalkpro.com/** *and read about the company's latest work in bionic limbs.*

TRACKING YOUR PROGRESS

Selection 21

Section	Number Correct		Score
A. Thesis and Main Ideas (5 items)	_____	× 2	_____
B. Details (10 items)	_____	× 2	_____
C. Organization and Transitions (3 items)	_____	× 5	_____
F. Implied Meanings (5 items)	_____	× 3	_____
G. Thinking Critically (5 items)	_____	× 4	_____
H. Vocabulary			
Context (5 items)	_____	× 2	_____
Word Parts (5 items)	_____	× 2	_____
		TOTAL SCORE	_____%

18 Life Sciences

The sciences investigate the physical world around us. The **life sciences** are concerned with living organisms—how they grow, develop, and function. The life sciences explore many important questions that affect our daily lives and are essential to our well-being. The study of science is fun and rewarding because you come to understand more about yourself and how you interact with other living things around you. "Volunteer Army" explores the impact of the Gulf oil spill and describes volunteer efforts to clean it up. "Species Extinction: One Found, Many Lost" explores species extinction, examining its leading causes. "Resolving the Debate: Adult vs. Embryonic Stem Cells" discusses the current issue of the use of stem cells.

Use the following suggestions for reading in the life sciences.

TIPS FOR READING IN LIFE SCIENCES

- **Adopt a scientific mind-set.** To read successfully in the sciences, get in the habit of asking questions and seeking answers, analyzing problems, and looking for solutions or explanations. For example, when reading "Species Extinction: One Found, Many Lost," focus on the problem and evidence presented.

- **Learn new terminology.** To read in the sciences, you have to learn the language of science. Science is exact and precise, and scientists use specific terminology to make communication as error free as possible. In "Resolving the Debate: Adult vs. Embryonic Stem Cells," for example, you will encounter biological terms that refer to cellular formation and reproduction.

- **Focus on cause and effect and process.** Since science is concerned with how and why things happen, cause and effect and process are almost always important. In "Species Extinction: One Found, Many Lost," for example, you will learn about the causes of species extinction.

SELECTION 22

Volunteer Army
Michele Wilson

Contemporary Issues Reading

This article originally appeared in *Audubon*, the magazine of the Audubon Society. The society is named in honor of John James Audubon, famous for his paintings of North American birds. *Audubon* magazine is devoted to environmental conservation and often features articles on birds.

PREVIEWING THE READING

Using the steps listed on page 36, preview the reading selection. When you have finished, complete the following items.

1. What is the topic of this reading?

   _____

2. Name at least three types of birds mentioned in the reading.

   _____

MAKING CONNECTIONS

Have you ever volunteered for a community or environmental cause? What motivated you to get involved? If you have never volunteered, what type of volunteer work might you consider doing in the future? Do you think one person can make a difference?

READING TIP

As you read, highlight the types of activities in which the volunteers are engaging. How must these efforts be coordinated on a larger scale? What are the long-term effects of the spill expected to be?

Volunteer Army

When the Gulf oil spill threatened birds and beaches, tens of thousands of citizens signed up to lend a hand. Five months later, they're still working hard.

marina
harbor for
small boats

1   On a blazing September day, Hopedale, Louisiana, teems with activity. Boats buy live bait and gas up in the **marina**. A white egret circles the boathouse, waiting for a handout or the stray forgotten fish. On an adjacent dirt-gravel road, trucks rumble

and crawl into a fenced-off compound, heading to one of dozens of tents and trailers organized into a temporary base for Gulf oil cleanup efforts.

2   Dockside, Sherri Lo Proto reads in the shade. After three-plus hours of silence, a U.S. Fish and Wildlife driver shows up to give her a 20-minute warning: The searchers are bringing in birds—dead and alive. When a fishing boat arrives with an oiled, injured white ibis and three dead laughing gulls, Lo Proto is ready, pad in hand. She records what's come in, then helps the driver lift the kennel-like crate onto his air-conditioned truck.

3   In real life, the 56-year-old Lo Proto teaches first grade in Covington, Louisiana, but this day she's a transport liaison, one of 34,500 volunteers the National Audubon Society has registered since April and one of 2,000 or so actually on the ground. Her work for Audubon includes hours of sitting around, but she doesn't seem to mind. "I wanted to not just talk the talk; I wanted to walk the walk. I wanted to do something," she says. "Life's fragile. You have to help the balance sometimes."

4   True to Lo Proto's words, volunteers wake up at any hour of the day to offer time, manpower, cars—anything to aid the oil-fouled animals and landscape. After the disaster, volunteers across the Gulf Coast, from Fort Worth, Texas, to Jacksonville, Florida, fed and monitored released pelicans, and transported non-oiled injured birds to rehab centers. They tied thousands of tiny knots to create noose mats, wire-and-mesh tools that gently capture shorebirds. They're still manning a call center three days a week. Some are counting birds and looking for oil on shore, while others are acting as beach stewards or attending training and workshops. Then there are the volunteers rebuilding habitat.

5   This network has cemented a unique partnership between Audubon and state and federal wildlife officials. Biologist Brac Salyers of the Louisiana Department of

Wildlife and Fisheries monitored pelicans for six weeks at a release site in Cameron, along the state's western coast. At least one Audubon participant accompanied his team most days, counting banded birds in masses of pelicans 1,500-strong. "You've got sometimes as many as 200 birds that you're trying to scan through at once," Salyers says. "It's very easy to not see a band or to overlook one. Having an extra set of eyes is just helpful."

6   Volunteers will also generate a year's worth of bird survey information about the Gulf Coast region—novel and crucial data for Audubon, says Tom Bancroft, the organization's chief scientist. "We don't have the staff capacity within Audubon to go to all these places on a regular basis," he says. "The only way to get to them is through the volunteers. We want to engage them in the monitoring to under-stand what's happening, but we'll be developing conservation plans, so we want the volunteers to also engage in implementation."

7   The sheer number of people taking action bodes well for the long term, says Sean Saville, director of Audubon's overall volunteer response. "About 90 percent who registered were not members of Audubon," he says. "We were one of the only ones who called them back. We heard that time and time again."

8   Most are simply grateful to lend a hand. Five months after the spill, some still tear up at the thought of it. "The first month around here, there wasn't anybody who wasn't crying," says artist Nancy Garrett, a volunteer from Biloxi, Mississippi, who is

painting a mural at the Moss Point call center. "I kept having this horrible thought of having to tell my grandchildren, 'Once upon a time the beaches were beautiful,' and then having to say we're responsible for what's happening."

9   To date, the full ramifications remain a question mark. An August report from the National Oceanic and Atmospheric Administration estimated that 75 percent of the oil had "either evaporated or been burned, skimmed, recovered from the wellhead, or dispersed." However, Woods Hole Oceanographic Institution researchers reported that a 1.2-mile-wide, 650-foot-high plume caused by the spill "had and will persist for some time." And University of Georgia scientists concluded that almost 80 percent of the released oil hadn't been recovered and "remains a threat to the ecosystem." In late September a team of Audubon scientists spent a week along the Gulf testing the beaches and just below the sand's surface for oil hydrocarbons and residue from **dispersants**.

dispersants
materials used 10
to break up
the oil

Until more is known (and likely, after that), volunteers like Sherri Lo Proto will continue counting birds, patrolling shorelines, or sitting on docks, awaiting instruction. "Luckily some people are still here for the long haul," she says. "Just because you don't see something or it's not headline news doesn't mean it's not there."

11   **Audubon in Action**

migrants
migrating birds

Don't live near the Gulf Coast but still want to help? To assist **migrants** passing through your area, create a bird-friendly habitat in your backyard. To help scientists gather data, enter the birds you see into eBird. Or write to Congress urging coastal wetlands and marsh restoration.

A. UNDERSTANDING THE THESIS AND OTHER MAIN IDEAS

Select the best answer.

_____ 1. The Gulf referred to in paragraph 1 is the
   a. Gulf of Tonkin.
   b. Gulf of Alaska.
   c. Gulf of Louisiana.
   d. Gulf of Mexico.

_____ 2. Which organization mobilized the 34,500 volunteers discussed in the article?
   a. National Audubon Society
   b. Louisiana Department of Wildlife and Fisheries
   c. Woods Hole Oceanographic Institution
   d. Gulf Coast Volunteer Association

_____ 3. The central thesis of the article is that
   a. environmentally conscious volunteers are patiently participating in a wide variety of activities following the oil spill.
   b. more people should take time off work to volunteer for an environmental organization.

c. the data collected by volunteers will provide valuable information for scientists.

d. volunteers often help a cause more than scientists and the government do.

_____ 4. Which of the following is not one of the author's purposes in writing "Volunteer Army"?

a. to describe some of the activities in which Audubon volunteers are taking part

b. to discuss the possible long-term effects of the oil spill

c. to criticize the Obama administration for its mishandling of the oil spill

d. to explain how the data collected by volunteers will benefit conservation efforts

_____ 5. The main idea of paragraph 9 is

a. a 1.2-mile-wide, 650-foot-high plume caused by the spill will persist for some time.

b. to date, the full ramifications of the Gulf oil spill remain a question mark.

c. almost 80 percent of the released oil has not been recovered yet.

d. oil hydrocarbons and residue from dispersants can be found just below the sand's surface.

_____ 6. The topic of paragraph 11 is

a. ways to volunteer even if you don't live near the Gulf Coast.

b. government agencies.

c. identifying birds in your neighborhood.

d. using the Internet to make a difference in the world.

B. IDENTIFYING DETAILS

Select the best answer.

_____ 1. In the second paragraph, how many birds does the fishing boat arrive with?

a. two

b. three

c. four

d. twelve

_____ 2. Sherri Lo Proto's full-time job is:

a. wildlife conservationist.

b. ornithologist.

c. employee of BP Oil Co.

d. first-grade teacher.

_____ 3. Which city is not mentioned in the reading?

a. Jacksonville, Florida

b. Baton Rouge, Louisiana

c. Forth Worth, Texas

d. Biloxi, Mississippi

_____ 4. According to the article, volunteers are doing all of the following jobs *except*

a. manning a call center.

b. creating noose mats to capture shorebirds.

c. staging protests against BP Oil and its plans to drill for oil in the Gulf.

d. transporting injured birds to rehab centers.

_____ 5. According to Brac Salyers, what type of bird has been observed in flocks of 1,500?

a. laughing gulls

b. pelicans

c. penguins

d. great egrets

_____ 6. The artist mentioned in the article is

a. Sherri Lo Proto.

b. Nancy Garrett.

c. Michele Wilson.

d. Tom Bancroft.

_____ 7. According to the August report from the National Oceanic and Atmospheric Administration, how much of the oil from the spill has evaporated or been burned, skimmed, recovered, or dispersed?

a. 34 percent

b. 56 percent

c. 75 percent

d. 80 percent

C. RECOGNIZING METHODS OF ORGANIZATION AND TRANSITIONS

Complete the sentences by filling in the blanks.

1. The pattern of organization used in paragraph 2 is _____ because it describes what Sherri Lo Proto did over a specific period of time.

2. Because paragraph 4 offers many examples of the activities in which volunteers take part, but in no particular order, it uses the _____ pattern.

3. In paragraph 9, which discusses the results of the oil spill, the overall organizational pattern used is _____. The transitional word used in the first sentence to indicate this pattern is _____, which is a synonym for a word in the name of the pattern.

4. Paragraph 9 also contrasts two different reports about the oil spill. The transitional word that emphasizes the contrast between the two reports is _____.

D. REVIEWING AND ORGANIZING IDEAS: MAPPING

The following conceptual maps are useful ways to organize the ideas presented in the article. Complete the maps by filling in the blanks.

Sherri Lo Proto's Day (paragraph 2)

Audubon Volunteer Activities (paragraph 4)

Volunteer Activities

↓

Feed and monitor released birds
_____
_____
Man the call center
_____
_____
_____
Attend training and workshops
_____

Results of Research (paragraph 9)

National Oceanic and Atmospheric Administration	Woods Hole Oceanographic Institution	University of Georgia
↓	↓	↓
_____	_____	_____
_____	_____	_____
_____		_____

E. READING AND THINKING VISUALLY

Select the best answer.

_____ 1. Look at the photos on pages 482 and 483. What do both photos have in common?

    a. Both were taken in Louisiana.

    b. Both feature wildlife and human beings.

    c. Both have a pessimistic tone.

    d. Both feature government employees.

_____ 2. The author most likely chose to include these photos to

    a. build the egos of the volunteers who helped to clean up the oil spill.

    b. represent the wide diversity of people in the article.

    c. emphasize that humans can be part of the solution rather than part of the problem.

    d. discourage people from volunteering due to the large numbers of volunteers who had to be turned away.

F. FIGURING OUT IMPLIED MEANINGS

Indicate whether each statement is true (T) or false (F).

_____ 1. Most of the volunteers in the article were kept constantly busy, with little time for rest.

_____ 2. Different reports reach vastly different conclusions about the amount of oil still unrecovered in the Gulf region.

_____ 3. The National Oceanic and Atmospheric Administration's report regarding the oil spill is much more optimistic than the University of Georgia report.

_____ 4. The director of volunteers at the Audubon Society was quite disappointed in the number of volunteers who turned out to help after the Gulf oil spill.

_____ 5. Many volunteers are motivated by the desire to get involved, rather than just sit back and wring their hands.

_____ 6. The state of Louisiana was resentful of having to work with the Audubon Society and its volunteers.

G. THINKING CRITICALLY

Select the best answer.

_____ 1. The overall tone of the selection can best be described as
   a. positive.
   b. sarcastic.
   c. grim.
   d. bitter.

_____ 2. When Sherri Lo Proto says "I wanted to walk the walk" (paragraph 3), she means that
   a. she wants to walk the beaches in search of wounded birds.
   b. she wants to back up her words with action.
   c. she wants to serve as a group leader on an environmental task force.
   d. she wants to get a job working for the Audubon Society.

_____ 3. What are the volunteers who are "rebuilding habitat" (paragraph 4) doing?
   a. building shelters for mammals left homeless by the oil spill
   b. re-creating natural conditions in which birds can live healthily
   c. crafting cages in which to house wounded birds
   d. putting up low-income housing for poor people

_____ 4. The tone of paragraph 8 of the selection can best be described as
   a. angry.
   b. ironic.
   c. formal.
   d. emotional.

_____ 5. What is eBird (paragraph 11)?
   a. a large egret native to Louisiana
   b. an adopt-a-wounded-bird program

c. a Web site at which birdwatchers can record bird sightings

d. a cartoon character that serves as a mascot for the Audubon Society

_____ 6. In the title "Volunteer Army," what is the connotation of the word *army*?

a. a large group of people committed to getting a job done

b. a military group that wages war against an enemy

c. an unofficial group that works against corporate interests

d. an international association of scientists committed to the environment

_____ 7. The author includes the last paragraph (11) to

a. populate her Facebook page with more friends.

b. provide an idea for a school project.

c. explain the importance of government programs.

d. encourage readers to get involved in environmental causes.

H. BUILDING VOCABULARY

Context

Using context and a dictionary, if necessary, determine the meaning of each word as it is used in the selection.

_____ 1. compound (paragraph 1)

a. animal shelter

b. cage

c. group of buildings

d. restricted area

_____ 2. liaison (paragraph 3)

a. go-between

b. assistant

c. facilitator

d. manager

_____ 3. stewards (paragraph 4)

a. flight attendants

b. polluters

c. speakers

d. caretakers

_____ 4. novel (paragraph 6)

    a. book   c. interesting

    b. new   d. personal

_____ 5. bodes (paragraph 7)

    a. foretells a particular outcome

    b. argues against a course of action

    c. prevents an action from occurring

    d. sings

Word Parts

> ### A REVIEW OF ROOTS
>
> **GEN** means _create_
> **ECO** often refers to the _Earth_

Use your knowledge of word parts and the review above to fill in the blanks in the following sentences.

1. The activities of the volunteers in paragraph 6 will _generate,_ or _____, large amounts of important new information.

2. A threat to the _ecosystem_ (paragraph 9) is a threat to the systems that make up the _____.

Unusual Words/Understanding Idioms

Use the meaning given below to write a sentence using the boldfaced word.

1. In ornithology (the study of birds), a **banded** bird (paragraph 5) is one with a harmless band attached to its leg. Banding birds helps ornithologists study them.

    Your sentence: _____

    _____

2. A **plume** usually refers to a bird's feather, but in the context of paragraph 9 it means a pollutant spreading from its original source.

    Your sentence: _____

    _____

I. SELECTING A LEARNING/STUDY STRATEGY

Assume you will be tested on this reading on an upcoming exam. Evaluate the usefulness of the conceptual maps you completed in Part D as a study tool. How would you use them to study?

J. EXPLORING IDEAS THROUGH DISCUSSION AND WRITING

1. Sherri Lo Proto says, "Just because you don't see something or it's not head-line news doesn't mean it's not there." What problem do you see in your local community that doesn't necessarily make the news, but is still a problem that should be addressed?

2. The BP oil spill was caused by drilling for oil in the Gulf of Mexico. Many environmentalists have argued that oil drilling should not be allowed so close to the U.S. coast. Do you agree or disagree? Why?

3. The oil spill resulted in more than 30,000 people volunteering to help. And yet most nonprofit organizations today suffer from a lack of volunteers. Suppose you were the director of a local charity or nonprofit organization. What cause would you choose, and how would you get the word out to recruit volunteers?

K. BEYOND THE CLASSROOM TO THE WEB

What qualities make a person effective as a volunteer? The reading points out a few good qualities, such as a positive attitude and a desire to get involved. For more information on the characteristics that organizations are seeking in their volunteers, visit **http://www.voluntaryworker.co.uk/.** *Click on "Becoming a Volunteer" and then on "What Organisations Look for in a Good Volunteer." You can also explore the site for other information on volunteering, including how to be a student volunteer.*

Alone or with a small group, create a list of the qualities that most organizations would not want in their volunteers. For example, most organizations would not benefit from lazy volunteers!

**TRACKING
YOUR
PROGRESS**

Selection 22

Section	Number Correct		Score
A Thesis and Main Ideas (6 items)	_____	×3	_____
B. Details (7 items)	_____	×2	_____
C. Organization and Transitions (5 items)	_____	×3	_____
E. Reading and Thinking Visually (2 items)	_____	×1	_____
F. Implied Meanings (6 items)	_____	×3	_____
G. Thinking Critically (7 items)	_____	×3	_____
H. Vocabulary			
Context (5 items)	_____	×2	_____
Word Parts (2 items)	_____	×1	_____
	TOTAL SCORE		_____%

SELECTION 23

Species Extinction: One Found, Many Lost

Teresa Audesirk, Gerald Audesirk,
and Bruce E. Byers

Textbook
Excerpt

This selection is taken from an introductory biology textbook used by many nursing, allied health, and biology majors. Read it to discover how and why animals and other life forms become extinct.

PREVIEWING THE READING

Using the steps listed on page 36, preview the reading selection. When you have finished, complete the following items.

1. The topic of this selection is _____.

2. List one question you expect to be able to answer after reading the selection.

_____

 MAKING CONNECTIONS

While extinction *is a scientific term, it is a concept that most people already understand. Perhaps the best-known mass extinctions are those of the dinosaurs, but can you think of any other, more modern examples?*

READING TIP

Some students find it difficult to read science textbooks because they contain so much unfamiliar vocabulary. While reading the selection, first try to determine the meaning of unknown words through context. If you get stuck on a particular word, check the meaning in a dictionary before you continue. Scientific knowledge builds on key concepts; if you don't understand the basics, you are unlikely to grasp the selection's main ideas. Make sure you understand the concept of adaptation.

Species Extinction: One Found, Many Lost

1   THE STEEP, rain-drenched slopes of Vietnam's Annamite Mountains are remote and forbidding, cloaked in tropical mists that lend an air of mystery and concealment to the forested peaks. As it turns out, this remote refuge conceals a most astonishing biological surprise: the saola, a hoofed, horned mammal that was unknown to science until the early 1990s. The discovery of a new species of large mammal at this late date was a complete shock. After centuries of human exploration and exploitation of every corner of the world's forests, deserts, and savannas, scientists were certain that no large mammal species could have escaped detection. As long ago as 1812, French naturalist Georges Cuvier wrote that "there is little hope of discovering new species of large quadrupeds." And yet, the saola–3 feet high at the shoulder, weighing up to 200 pounds and sporting 20-inch black horns—remained hidden in Annamite Mountain forests, outside the realm of scientific knowledge.

2   Ironically, we have discovered the lost world of Vietnamese animals at a moment when that world is in danger of disappearing. Economic development in Vietnam has brought logging and mining to ever more remote regions of the country; and Annamite Mountain forests are being cleared at an unprecedented rate. The increasing local human population means that animals are hunted heavily; most of our knowledge of the saola comes from carcasses found In local markets. All of the newly discovered mammals of Vietnam are quite rare, seen only infrquently even by local hunters. Fortunately, the Vietnamese government has established a number of national parks and nature preserves in key areas. Only time will tell if these measures are sufficient to ensure the survival of the mysterious mammals of the Annamiles.

What Causes Extinction?

3   Every living organism must eventually die, and the same is true of species. Just like individuals, species are "born" (through the process of speciation), persist for some period of time, and then perish. The ultimate fate of any species is extinction, the death of the last of its members. In fact, at least 99.9% of all the species that have ever existed are now extinct. The natural course of evolution, as revealed by **fossils**, is continual turnover of species as new ones arise and old ones become extinct.

fossil
the remains of a prehistoric organism preserved in rock

4   The immediate cause of extinction is probably always environmental change, in either the nonliving or the living parts of the environment. Environmental changes that

Sao La

The saola, unknown to science until 1992, is one of a number of previously undiscovered species recently found in the mountains of Vietnam.

Figure A: Very localized distribution can endanger a species. The Devil's Hole pupfish is found in only one spring-fed water hole in the Nevada desert. This and other isolated small populations are at high risk of extinction.

can lead to extinction include habitat destruction and increased competition among species. In the face of such changes, species with small geographic ranges or highly specialized adaptations are especially susceptible to extinction.

Localized Distribution Makes Species Vulnerable

5   Species vary widely in their range of distribution and, hence, in their vulnerability to extinction. Some species, such as herring gulls, white-tailed deer, and humans, inhabit entire continents or even the whole Earth; others, such as the Devil's Hole pupfish (Figure A), have extremely limited ranges. Obviously, if a species inhabits only a very small area, any disturbance of that area could easily result in extinction. "If" Devil's Hole dries up due to a drought or well drilling nearby, its pupfish will immediately vanish. Conversely, wide-ranging species will not succumb to local environmental catastrophes.

Overspecialization Increases the Risk of Extinction

6   Another factor that may make a species vulnerable to extinction is overspecialization. Each species evolves adaptations that help it survive and reproduce in its environment. In some cases, these adaptations include specializations that favor survival in a particular and limited set of environmental conditions. The Karner blue butterfly, for example, feeds only on the blue lupine plant (Figure B). The butterfly is therefore found only where the plant thrives. But the blue lupine has become quite rare because its habitat of sandy, open woods and clearings in northeast North America has been largely replaced by farms and development. If the lupine disappears, the Karner blue butterfly will surely become extinct along with it.

Figure B: Extreme specialization places species at risk. The Karner blue butterfly feeds exclusively on the blue lupine, found in dry forests and clearings in the northeastern United States. Such behavioral specialization renders the butterfly extremely vulnerable to any environmental change that may exterminate its single host plant species.

Interactions with Other Species May Drive a Species to Extinction

7   Interactions such as competition and predation serve as agents of natural selection. In some cases, these same interactions can lead to extinction rather than to adaptation.

8   Organisms compete for limited resources in all environments. If a species' competitors evolve superior adaptations and the species doesn't evolve fast enough to keep up, it may become extinct. A particularly striking example of extinction through competition occurred in South America, beginning about 2.5 million years ago. At that time, the **isthmus** of Panama rose above sea level and formed a land bridge between North America and South America. After the previously separated continents were connected, the mammal species that had evolved in isolation on each continent were able to mix. Many species did indeed expand their ranges, as North American mammmals moved southward and South American mammals moved northward. As they moved, each species encountered resident species that occupied the same kinds of habitats and exploited the same kinds of resources. The ultimate result of the ensuing competition was that the North American species diversified and underwent an adaptive radiation that displaced the vast majority of the South American species, many of which went extinct. Clearly, evolution had bestowed on the North American species some (as yet unknown) set of adaptations that enabled their descendants to exploit resources more efficiently and effectively than their South American counterparts could.

isthmus
a narrow strip of land with sea on both sides

HOW MANY SPECIES INHABIT THE PLANET?

One way to determine the number of species on Earth might be to simply count them. You could comb the scientific literature to find all the species that scientists have discovered and named, and then tally up the total number. If you did that, you'd end up with a count of roughly 1.5 million species. But you still wouldn't know how many species are on Earth.

Why doesn't counting work? Because most of the planet's species remain undiscovered. Relatively few scientists are engaged in the search for new species, and many undiscovered species are small and inconspicuous, or live in poorly explored habitats such as the floor of the ocean or the topmost branches of tropical rain forests. So, no one knows the actual number of species on Earth. But biologists agree that the number must be much higher than the number of named species. Estimates range from 2 million to 100 million or more.

Habitat Change and Destruction Are the Leading Causes of Extinction

9   Habitat change, both contemporary and prehistoric, is the single greatest cause of extinctions. Present-day habitat destruction due to human activities is proceeding at a rapid pace. Many biologists believe that we are presently in the midst of the fastest-paced and most widespread episode of species extinction in the history of life. Loss of tropical forests is especially devastating to species diversity. As many as half the species presently on Earth may be lost during the next 50 years as the tropical forests that contain them are cut for timber or to clear land for cattle and crops.

A. UNDERSTANDING THE THESIS AND OTHER MAIN IDEAS

Select the best answer.

_____ 1. The central thesis of the selection is that

    a. finding a new species is rare, but species extinction is very common for a number of reasons.

    b. extinction is the result of environmental destruction.

    c. mammals are more resilient species than birds and fish, especially the mammals that live in mountainous regions.

    d. competition for resources leads to evolution.

_____ 2. The authors' main purpose in "Species Extinction: One Found, Many Lost" is to

    a. explain how species adapt to their surroundings.

    b. relate their travel experiences in the mountains of Vietnam.

   c. get students involved in volunteer activities for environmental
      awareness.

   d. describe the finding of a new species as well as the causes of
      species extinction.

_____ 3. One of the "mysterious mammals of the Annamites" is the

   a. koala.

   b. blue lupine.

   c. saola.

   d. white-tailed deer.

_____ 4. The best estimate of the number of species found on
      Earth is

   a. 500,000.

   b. 2–100 million.

   c. 8–10 million.

   d. 1.5 million.

_____ 5. The ultimate fate of all species is

   a. extinction.

   b. evolution.

   c. habitat destruction.

   d. adaptation.

_____ 6. The leading causes of extinction are

   a. volcanic eruptions.

   b. asteroids striking the Earth.

   c. habitat change and destruction.

   d. global warming and flooding.

_____ 7. The main idea of paragraph 8 is found in the

   a. first sentence.

   b. second sentence.

   c. third sentence.

   d. last sentence.

B. IDENTIFYING DETAILS

Select the best answer.

_____ 1. Which species does not inhabit an entire continent or the whole Earth?

   a. humans   c. herring gulls

   b. pupfish   d. white-tailed deer

_____ 2. Which species relies on the blue lupine for its food?

    a. Karner blue butterfly

    b. pupfish

    c. saola

    d. cuvier

_____ 3. The immediate cause of species extinction is

    a. competition for food.

    b. human hunting practices.

    c. growth in human population.

    d. environmental change.

_____ 4. The authors provide the example of the Panamanian land bridge to explain

    a. how overspecialization leads to extinction.

    b. localized distribution.

    c. the death of species in the Amazon rain forest.

    d. extinction through competition.

_____ 5. All of the following can lead to extinction _except_

    a. overspecialization.

    b. localized distribution.

    c. high birth rates within a species.

    d. interaction with other species.

_____ 6. The natural habitat of the Karner blue butterfly is

    a. northeastern North America.

    b. South America.

    c. Vietnam.

    d. desert-like climates.

C. RECOGNIZING METHODS OF ORGANIZATION AND TRANSITIONS

Answer the following questions by filling in the blanks.

1. The overall organizational pattern used in paragraphs 3–9 is
   _____. _Now, considering your answer to question 1,
   answer questions 2 and 3._

2. The four _____ are localized distribution, overspecialization, interactions with other species, and habitat change and
   destruction.

3. The _____ is extinction.

4. Which boldfaced heading within the reading clearly signals the organizational pattern used? _____

D. REVIEWING AND ORGANIZING IDEAS: PARAPHRASING

Complete the following paraphrases by filling in the missing words or dates.

Paragraphs 1–2: As long ago as _____, scientists thought they had discovered all the _____ on Earth. But in the early _____ a horned mammal called a _____ was discovered in the _____ Mountains in _____. But the _____ of this species is not guaranteed because the _____ in which it lives are being cleared, and the animal is heavily _____.

Paragraphs 3–9: All species will become _____ at some point. Most species die out as a result of changes in the _____; the greatest cause of extinction is _____. _____ distribution makes some species vulnerable; if the species lives in one particular area, then the disturbance of that area can lead to _____. Species that are _____ to a particular environment are also vulnerable. Interactions such as _____ for resources and death at the hands of _____ can also lead to extinction.

E. READING AND THINKING VISUALLY

Select the best answer.

_____ 1. The author chose to include Figure A, the photo of the pupfish, in order to

a. provide an illustration of a species vulnerable to extinction due to localized distribution.

b. make the point that fish and other marine life are more in danger of extinction than land-based mammals.

c. illustrate a species that is already extinct as a result of habitat destruction or change.

d. show one of the few remaining members of a species that is already 99.9 percent extinct.

_____ 2. According to Figure A, which of the following is *not* the pupfish's native habitat?

    a. Nevada

    b. the rain forest

    c. the desert

    d. Devil's Hole

_____ 3. The author included Figure B, the photo of the Karner blue butterfly, as an example of

    a. the destruction of species as a result of habitat change.

    b. a species with localized distribution.

    c. competition for resources between the butterfly and the lupine.

    d. a species that has engaged in extreme specialization.

_____ 4. In Figure B, the caption refers to a "host" plant species. In this context, *host* means

    a. the dry forests in which the butterfly lives.

    b. an extremely specialized species limited to one geographic area.

    c. a species on which another species relies for its existence.

    d. the northeastern United States.

F. FIGURING OUT IMPLIED MEANINGS

Indicate whether each statement is true (T) or false (F).

_____ 1. Less than 1 percent of the species that have ever existed have not gone extinct.

_____ 2. The author implies that the Karner blue butterfly gets its color from the plant it feeds on.

_____ 3. In all environments, all resources are limited.

_____ 4. The authors imply that natural occurrences, such as volcanoes and earthquakes, are the major causes of habitat destruction.

_____ 5. About half of Earth's species live in tropical rain forests.

_____ 6. The saola's existence was not discovered until 1812.

_____ 7. Evolutionary processes provided South American species with a set of adaptations that gave them an advantage over North American species.

_____ 8. The authors imply that changes in the nonliving environment are more destructive to species than changes in the living environment.

_____ 9. Wide-ranging species tend to be heavily affected by local environmental disasters.

G. THINKING CRITICALLY

Select the best answer.

_____ 1. The tone of this selection is best described as

    a. angry.

    b. scientific.

    c. pessimistic.

    d. sympathetic.

_____ 2. Which word in paragraph 1 might hint at the authors' belief that humans pursue their own interests at the expense of all other species?

    a. concealment

    b. mystery

    c. exploitation

    d. shock

_____ 3. The authors use the quote from Georges Cuvier in paragraph 1 in order to

    a. describe how surprised scientists were by the discovery of the saola.

    b. hint that the scientific method is less than reliable.

    c. suggest that the saola must have evolved as a modern species after 1812.

    d. provide support for the idea that mountain wildlife must be preserved.

_____ 4. Based on paragraph 3, which of the following statements would the authors most likely agree with?

    a. Only the strongest species survive extinction.

    b. Insect and amphibian species (such as cockroaches and frogs) are likely to survive much longer than mammals.

    c. Humans will die out at some point.

    d. Life on Earth will eventually come to an end as a result of mass extinctions.

_____ 5. What is the best definition of *range* as the term is used in paragraph 5?

    a. a mountainous area

    b. a continent

    c. the area in which a species lives

    d. a landmass and the bodies of water it touches

_____ 6. When the authors say that "Interactions such as competition and predation serve as agents of natural selection" (paragraph 7), they mean that

    a. endangered species are best protected within natural wildlife preserves.

    b. modern zoos provide the re-creations of the natural environment that animals need in order to reproduce.

    c. the single most important influence on extinction is human-animal interaction.

    d. species can become extinct if they are weaker than other species that prey on them or other species eat all the available food.

_____ 7. Why have the authors included the box titled "How Many Species Inhabit the Planet?" with this selection?

    a. to fill up some additional space that otherwise would have been left empty on the page

    b. to explain why the answer to this question is much trickier than the average person would think

    c. to criticize scientists for severely undercounting the number of species left on Earth

    d. to encourage students to volunteer for causes that seek to protect endangered species

_____ 8. Which of the following is the best example of informed opinion?

    a. The discovery of a new species of large mammal at this late date was a complete shock. (paragraph 1)

    b. Each species evolves adaptations that help it survive and reproduce in its environment. (paragraph 6)

    c. Present-day habitat destruction due to human activities is proceeding at a rapid pace. (paragraph 9)

    d. Many biologists believe that we are presently in the midst of the fastest-paced and most widespread episode of species extinction in the history of life. (paragraph 9)

H. BUILDING VOCABULARY

Context

Using context and a dictionary, if necessary, determine the meaning of each word as it is used in the selection.

_____ 1. savannas (paragraph 1)

    a. oceans   c. islands

    b. icebergs   d. grasslands

_____ 2. unprecedented (paragraph 2)

    a. rapid

    b. surprising

    c. never happened before

    d. occurring quite soon

_____ 3. habitat (paragraph 4)

    a. jungle trees

    b. natural home

    c. urban location

    d. recurring event

_____ 4. drought (paragraph 5)

    a. prolonged dry spell

    b. hurricane

    c. earthquake

    d. high level of humidity

_____ 5. tally (see first paragraph in box on p. 498)

    a. kill

    b. divide

    c. estimate

    d. add

_____ 6. inconspicuous (see second paragraph in box on p. 498)

    a. in large numbers

    b. air-breathing

    c. not attracting attention

    d. gray-colored

Word Parts

A REVIEW OF PREFIXES

QUAD- means *four*
PRE- means *before*

Use your knowledge of word parts and the review above to fill in the blanks in the following sentences.

1. If the root PED means "foot," then a *quadruped* (paragraph 1) has _____ feet.

2. Something that occurred in *prehistoric* times (paragraph 9) took place _____ written history.

I. SELECTING A LEARNING/STUDY STRATEGY

Select the best answer.

_____   The best way to study and learn this reading would be to

a. create flash cards with key vocabulary.

b. outline the selection.

c. watch a video about the extinction of a particular species.

d. draw a diagram of the extinction process.

J. EXPLORING IDEAS THROUGH DISCUSSION AND WRITING

1. According to the selection, it is not uncommon for species to go extinct. But technologies can go extinct as well. For example, how many people still use telephones with cords? How many people own black-and-white TVs? Can you think of any other technologies that have become or are becoming extinct?

2. What do you think motivates people to want to protect endangered species? For example, most people would argue that the bald eagle, a longtime symbol of America, should be protected. But suppose we were to learn that cockroaches or bedbugs were about to go extinct. Would anyone care? Why or why not?

3. To what other areas of life or society might the concept of "extinction" be applied? For example, do words go extinct as new words are created? (Think, for example, about words that older people use. Will they still be in use 50 years from now?) Do certain social customs go extinct as society changes? (For example, do men still feel compelled to stand up when a woman leaves the table, the way they used to in the 1940s and 1950s?)

K. BEYOND THE CLASSROOM TO THE WEB

Two of the most common examples of extinct species are the dodo bird and the passenger pigeon. Visit **extinctanimal.com,** *an online database of extinct plants, birds, and animals. Choose one extinct species and do a Web search to find information and images. Prepare a paragraph describing the species, its original habitat, and the reasons suggested for its extinction.*

TRACKING YOUR PROGRESS

Selection 23

Section	Number Correct	Score
A. Thesis and Main Ideas (7 items)	_____ × 4	_____
B. Details (6 items)	_____ × 3	_____
C. Organization and Transitions (4 items)	_____ × 2	_____
E. Reading and Thinking Visually (4 items)	_____ × 1	_____
F. Implied Meanings (9 items)	_____ × 2	_____
G. Thinking Critically (8 items)	_____ × 2	_____
H. Vocabulary		
Context (6 items)	_____ × 1	_____
Word Parts (2 items)	_____ × 1	_____
	TOTAL SCORE	_____%

<table>
<tr><td>SELECTION 24</td><td>Resolving the Debate:
Adult vs. Embryonic Stem Cells</td></tr>
</table>

Resolving the Debate: Adult vs. Embryonic Stem Cells

Michael Bellomo

Textbook Excerpt
_____
Contemporary
Issues Reading

This selection is taken from a book titled *The Stem Cell Divide: The Facts, the Fiction, and the Fear Driving the Greatest Scientific, Political, and Religious Debate of Our Time,* by Michael Bellomo. Read the selection to find out more about the stem cell debate.

PREVIEWING THE READING

Using the steps listed on page 36, preview the reading selection. When you have finished, complete the following items.

1. The topic of this selection is _____.

2. List at least three questions you expect to be able to answer after reading the selection.

   a. _____

   b. _____

   c. _____

 MAKING CONNECTIONS

What do you already know about stem cells? How do you feel about stem cell research in general?

READING TIP

As you read, highlight sections that describe the benefits and limitations of each of the two types of stem cells.

Resolving the Debate: Adult vs. Embryonic Stem Cells

1   At the most basic level, the promise that stem cells hold is also the source of the controversy over them. The idea that replacement parts for our bodies might one day be as easy to create as ordering prescription medication from the local

regenerative medicine
the process of creating living, functional tissues to repair or replace damaged tissues and organs in the body

blastocyst
a stage of early embryonic development before cells have formed into specific types

stem cell line
a family of cells formed from a single parent group of stem cells and grown in laboratory cultures

venture capital
money invested or available for investment in new enterprises

pluripotent
capable of changing from a single cell into one of the many cell types that make up the body

immune reaction
a bodily defense reaction that recognizes an invading substance, such as a virus or transplanted tissue, and produces antibodies against it

drugstore is breathtaking. But if these same cells can only work their magic through the destruction of human embryos, then cure and curse will be one and the same to many people. To those who see a human being's life as starting from the moment of fertilization, **regenerative medicine** via stem cells is nothing more than *high-tech cannibalism.*

2   There is an alternative, imperfect though it may be. In recent years, scientists have discovered that similar kinds of cells can be found outside the holy sphere of the human embryo's **blastocyst**. These "adult" stem cells can be found in the blood, the pockets of our bone marrow, the umbilical cord, under the dermis of the skin, and, just perhaps, buried deep in the brain.

ASC Pros and Cons

3   Adult stem cells (ASCs) are the technology of choice among those who morally object to the use of embryonic stem cells. At a May 2005 White House press conference, President Bush reaffirmed his opposition to funding embryonic stem cell research outside of the existing **stem cell lines**, but praised the use of "alternative sources" of stem cells. The ones mentioned in the above paragraph, such as stem cells from bone marrow and umbilical cord blood, are classic examples of ASCs.

4   "With the right policies and the right techniques," Bush asserted, "we can pursue scientific progress while still fulfilling our moral duties." But is this indeed the case, or is it wishful thinking? As with many complex subjects, there is no clear-out answer.

5   The degree to which adult stem cells can be put to use often depends on who is being interviewed. However, if one sticks as closely as possible to what has been reliably reproduced in multiple laboratories over time, some hard facts do become available. That is, at least as "hard" as the facts can be, before the technology advances yet further and changes reality yet again.

6   A fair number of therapies involving adult stem cells are in human clinical trials at present, and the number continues to grow. It is likely that these therapies will make their appearance at the local hospital or health clinic long before embryonic stem cells can even begin to make it to human trials. At the third annual meeting of the International Society for Stem Cell Research, held in 2005, the clear majority of the presentations dealt with therapies related to adult stem cells. Clearly, the interest—and, not coincidentally, the private sector **venture capital**—lies in ASCs for now.

7   Adult stem cells have something of a trade-off in their makeup. They simply do not have the **pluripotent** ability to morph into any kind of cell. However, this one-track orientation allows them to be admirably well-suited building blocks for a limited number of therapies. For example, blood-specific illnesses such as leukemia stand to benefit from the use of adult stem cells collected from bone marrow.[1]

8   A major limitation of adult stem cells that their boosters fail to mention is that being a full-grown cell, the biological markers of an individual have matured. This means that an adult stem cell is more likely to cause a dangerous **immune reaction** if transplanted into another person. To avoid this, adult stem cell transplants could only be carried out using a patient's own cells.

_____

[1] These particular kinds of adult stem cells are also known as *hematopoietic* stem cells.

FIGURE A THE PROCESS FOR CULTURING ADULT STEM CELLS

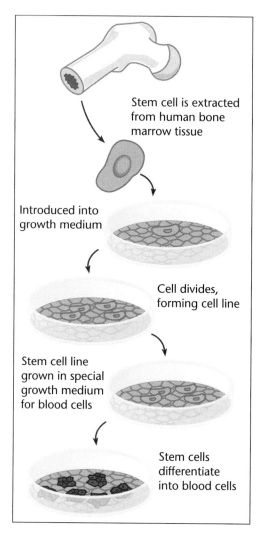

Stem cell is extracted from human bone marrow tissue

Introduced into growth medium

Cell divides, forming cell line

Stem cell line grown in special growth medium for blood cells

Stem cells differentiate into blood cells

9   Some researchers claim that adult stem cells do, in fact, have the ability to produce different kinds of cells. The trick, so the argument goes, is to get them to regress to the point that they become pluripotent, or developmentally plastic once again.

10   A few researchers, such as Dr. Catherine Verfaillie, the director of the University of Minnesota's Stem Cell Institute, have been able to persuade bone marrow stem cells to produce other types of organ tissue. However, until these results are replicated in many other labs, it is difficult to evaluate whether this can be done in a systematic way.

11   David Traver, a stem cell researcher at the University of California at San Diego, admits that there are no hard answers yet. "The more conservative thing to say is

12   that each human organ probably has a specific stem cell system behind it, and there probably isn't a lot of 'cross-talk' between them," says Traver.

Traver reiterates that more research has to be done, and that the field is not as advanced as many outside the scientific community would think. "The bottom line," he says, "is that we haven't learned much from studying human stem cells. Most of what we know comes from studying mice, fish, and flies."

13   Adult stem cells are also harder to study in some ways. Because they do not renew themselves indefinitely in the lab, as embryonic stem cells [ESCs] do, they must constantly be replenished if they are to be studied.

14   On the other hand, embryonic stem cells come with their own price tag in sweat and hard work. In order to keep them renewing themselves indefinitely, constant feeding and attention must be performed, or the relatively fragile embryonic stem cells will either die off or twist themselves into a grotesque **teratomatic** growth in the **petri dish**.

teratomatic
a tumor
consisting of
different types
of tissue

15   While scientists, admittedly, are still groping for ways to reliably "reprogram" the blank slate of the embryonic stem cell, the possibilities just seem too great to ignore. And embryonic stem cells, since they come from a point where the organism has yet to mature, simply provide much more insight into the complexities of stem cell function and development.

petri dish
a shallow
dish used in
laboratories to
grow cultures
of bacteria or
other micro-
organisms

16   Ironically, years of research spent on embryonic stem cells are very likely to teach scientists how to best reprogram an *adult* stem cell to make tissues as easily as an embryonic stem cell can. Put another way, embryonic stem cells may very well be needed . . . so that they will never be needed again.

17   In the meantime, it's worth moving beyond the sound bites of the researchers to review what both ASCs and ESCs are being used for at this time. Given how fast the field moves, the list is less a definitive catalog of therapies than a snapshot in time. In five years or less, the balance of treatments and knowledge between the two may have shifted, and the total number of treatments available will have expanded beyond belief.

A. UNDERSTANDING THE THESIS AND OTHER MAIN IDEAS

Select the best answer.

_____ 1. The central thesis of this selection is that
   a. stem cell research is controversial for many reasons.
   b. adult stem cells (ASCs) have too many limitations to be useful.
   c. embryonic stem cells (ESCs) are becoming more widely accepted.
   d. ASCs offer an imperfect alternative to ESCs.

_____ 2. The author's primary purpose is to
   a. argue that stem cell research should receive federal funding.
   b. compare traditional medical treatments with stem cell therapies.
   c. describe the pros and cons of ASCs and ESCs.
   d. present the most current medical applications for stem cells.

_____ 3. The topic of paragraph 3 is
    a. President Bush.
    b. ASCs.
    c. ESCs.
    d. funding for stem cell research.

_____ 4. The topic of paragraph 7 is expressed in the
    a. first sentence.
    b. second sentence.
    c. third sentence.
    d. last sentence.

_____ 5. According to the selection, a major limitation of ASCs is that they
    a. can be obtained only by destroying human embryos.
    b. produce too many different kinds of cells.
    c. are buried deep in the human brain.
    d. may cause a dangerous reaction if transplanted into another person.

B. IDENTIFYING DETAILS

Next to each of the following phrases, indicate whether it describes adult stem cells (ASCs) or embryonic stem cells (ESCs).

_____ 1. the type of stem cells found in the bone marrow and the umbilical cord

_____ 2. the type of stem cells used in therapies that are currently in human clinical trials

_____ 3. the only type of stem cells that are capable of changing into different kinds of cells

_____ 4. the type of stem cells that renew themselves indefinitely in the lab

_____ 5. the type of stem cells that have a "one-track" orientation useful for specific therapies

C. RECOGNIZING METHODS OF ORGANIZATION AND TRANSITIONS

Select the best answer.

_____ 1. In paragraph 7, the transitional word or phrase that indicates that the author will introduce a contrasting idea is
    a. any kinds.
    b. however.

    c. for example.

    d. such as.

_____ 2. In paragraph 8, the author describes a major limitation of ASCs using the organizational pattern called

    a. statement and clarification.

    b. comparison and contrast.

    c. classification.

    d. order of importance.

_____ 3. In paragraph 13, the author describes the difficulty of working with ASCs using the organizational pattern called

    a. classification.

    b. cause and effect.

    c. definition.

    d. spatial order.

_____ 4. In paragraph 14, the transitional word or phrase that indicates that a contrast is to follow is

    a. on the other hand.

    b. in order to.

    c. indefinitely.

    d. must be performed.

D. REVIEWING AND ORGANIZING IDEAS: OUTLINING

Complete the following outline of paragraphs 3–8 and 13.

Advantages and Disadvantages of ASCs

I. Advantages of ASCs

    A. Morally acceptable alternative to _____

        1. Do not require destruction of _____

    B. Therapies already being tested in _____

    C. Focus of current research and private funding

    D. _____ orientation well suited for specific therapies

II. Disadvantages of ASCs

    A. Unable to _____

    B. Biological markers have matured

1. Transplants may cause _____ in others

2. Transplants limited to patient's own cells

C. Hard to study in the lab

1. Do not _____ indefinitely

2. Must constantly be replenished

E. READING AND THINKING VISUALLY

Select the best answer.

_____ 1. The method of organization used in Figure A on page 510 is

a. enumeration.

b. process.

c. classification.

d. definition.

_____ 2. In Figure A, the fifth step is "Stem cells differentiate into blood cells." In this context, *differentiate* means

a. revert.

b. turn into.

c. overtake.

d. replace.

F. FIGURING OUT IMPLIED MEANINGS

Indicate whether each statement is true (T) or false (F).

_____ 1. Many people reject the idea of using stem cells from embryos because of moral or religious beliefs.

_____ 2. President Bush was opposed to all forms of stem cell research.

_____ 3. Researchers disagree about how successfully ASCs can be put to use.

_____ 4. Therapies based on ASCs will probably be available much sooner than those based on ESCs.

_____ 5. Most private funding for stem cell research is directed toward ASCs because of their unlimited potential.

_____ 6. Within the scientific community, most of the knowledge about stem cells has come primarily from studying human cells.

_____ 7. The field of stem cell research is rapidly changing.

G. THINKING CRITICALLY

Select the best answer.

_____ 1. The central thesis of this selection is supported by

    a. facts.

    b. examples.

    c. expert opinions.

    d. all of the above.

_____ 2. The primary question answered by Figure A is:

    a. How do adult stem cells differ from embryonic cells?

    b. How are stem cells extracted from bone marrow tissue?

    c. What is the process for culturing adult stem cells?

    d. At what point do stem cells differentiate into blood cells?

_____ 3. In paragraph 1, the author uses the phrase *high-tech cannibalism* in order to

    a. create a sense of fear and dread about the subject of stem cell research.

    b. indicate that his own attitude toward stem cell research is critical and disapproving.

    c. illustrate the viewpoint of many people that using embryonic cells in medicine is immoral and wrong.

    d. introduce a sense of humor and sarcasm into the discussion of stem cell research.

Indicate whether each of the following quotes from the selection is fact (F) or opinion (O).

_____ 4. "The idea that replacement parts for our bodies might one day be as easy to create as ordering prescription medication from the local drugstore is breathtaking." (paragraph 1)

_____ 5. "At the third annual meeting of the International Society for Stem Cell Research . . . the clear majority of the presentations dealt with therapies related to adult stem cells." (paragraph 6)

_____ 6. "A few researchers . . . have been able to persuade bone marrow stem cells to produce other types of organ tissue." (paragraph 10)

_____ 7. "While scientists . . . are still groping for ways to reliably 'reprogram' the blank slate of the embryonic stem cell, the possibilities just seem too great to ignore." (paragraph 15)

H. BUILDING VOCABULARY

Context

Using context and a dictionary, if necessary, determine the meaning of each word as it is used in the selection.

_____ 1. asserted (paragraph 4)

    a. questioned   c. disagreed

    b. claimed   d. removed

_____ 2. sector (paragraph 6)

    a. area   c. report

    b. number   d. technique

_____ 3. morph (paragraph 7)

    a. disappear   c. control

    b. harm   d. change

_____ 4. boosters (paragraph 8)

    a. critics   c. researchers

    b. supporters   d. markers

_____ 5. replicated (paragraph 10)

    a. prohibited   c. repeated

    b. abandoned   d. stolen

_____ 6. grotesque (paragraph 14)

    a. useful   c. limited

    b. simple   d. bizarre

_____ 7. groping (paragraph 15)

    a. feeling   c. starting

    b. searching   d. confusing

Word Parts

> ### A REVIEW OF PREFIXES AND SUFFIXES
>
> **IM-** means *not*
> **RE-** means *back, again*
> **-IVE** means *a state, condition,* or *quality*

Use your knowledge of word parts and the review above to fill in the blanks in the following sentences.

1. An alternative that is *imperfect* (paragraph 2) is one that has flaws or is somehow _____ perfect.

2. If a person has affirmed something, he or she has expressed commitment to it; when it is *reaffirmed* (paragraph 3), that commitment is expressed _____.

3. To make progress is to move forward, so to *regress* (paragraph 9) is to move _____.

4. When a person *reiterates* a statement (paragraph 12), he or she repeats it or says it _____.

5. Stem cells that do not renew themselves must be *replenished* (paragraph 13); in other words, the supply of cells must be filled up _____ or added to.

6. Something that is definite is known for certain, so a *definitive* list (paragraph 17) is one that has the _____ of being complete or certain.

Unusual Words/Understanding Idioms

Use the meanings given below to write a sentence using the boldfaced phrase.

1. The term **bottom line** (paragraph 12) refers to the last line of a financial statement, which shows net profit or loss. It is often used to indicate the main point or most important aspect of a topic of debate.

   Your sentence: _____

   _____

2. To describe stem cells as coming **with their own price tag** (paragraph 14) is to say that they have a cost associated with them. In the case of embryonic stem cells, the cost is the effort—"sweat and hard work"—required to study them.

   Your sentence: _____

   _____

3. The term **sound bites** (paragraph 17) refers to brief comments or statements taken from longer speeches or interviews; sound bites may be interesting excerpts, but they may also leave out important information.

   Your sentence: _____

   _____

I. SELECTING A LEARNING/STUDY STRATEGY

Suppose you were preparing for a class discussion on the pros and cons of differ-ent types of stem cell research. How would you use this selection to prepare for the discussion?

J. EXPLORING IDEAS THROUGH DISCUSSION AND WRITING

1. Discuss the title of the book from which this selection was taken *(The Stem Cell Divide: The Facts, the Fiction, and the Fear Driving the Greatest Scientific, Political, and Religious Debate of Our Time)*. Do you agree that stem cell research is the greatest debate of our time? Discuss each aspect of the debate cited in the title: scientific, political, and religious.

2. Evaluate the introduction. What captured your interest in the opening paragraphs?

3. What do you think the author meant by the phrase "holy sphere" in para-graph 2? Discuss his meaning and purpose in using that term.

4. The author is careful to present information about the advantages and disadvantages of both types of stem cells, but which type do you think he believes is preferable? Explain your answer with support from the selection.

5. Discuss some of the predictions the author makes in this selection. Together with a classmate, come up with your own list of predictions, either about medical treatments or another aspect of life such as transpor-tation, housing, work, and so on.

K. BEYOND THE CLASSROOM TO THE WEB

Read "Key Moments in the Stem-Cell Debate" at **http://www.npr.org/templates/ story/story.php?storyId=5252449.**

Using this site and the reading for inspiration, write a list of words to reflect your feelings about the stem cell debate. Use these words to create a short per-suasive speech for your side of the argument.

TRACKING YOUR PROGRESS

Selection 24

Section	Number Correct	Score
A. Thesis and Main Ideas (5 items)	_____ × 3	_____
B. Details (5 items)	_____ × 3	_____
C. Organization and Transitions (4 items)	_____ × 1	_____
E. Reading and Thinking Visually (2 items)	_____ × 2	_____
F. Implied Meanings (7 items)	_____ × 3	_____
G. Thinking Critically (7 items)	_____ × 3	_____
H. Vocabulary		
Context (7 items)	_____ × 2	_____
Word Parts (6 items)	_____ × 1	_____
	TOTAL SCORE	_____ %

19 Physical Sciences/Mathematics

The **physical sciences** are concerned with the properties, functions, structure, and composition of matter, substances, and energy. They include physics, chemistry, astronomy, physical geography, and geology. **Mathematics** is the study of relationships among numbers, quantities, and shapes using signs, symbols, and proofs (logical solutions of problems). Often mathematics and physical science work together to address interesting questions important to our life and well-being. "The Mathematics of Gambling: What's Luck Got to Do with It?" uses mathematics to examine a popular American pastime for some, an addiction for others—gambling. The reading "The Cultural Ecology of the City" explores environmental factors that influence cities. "Additional Renewable-Energy Options" examines new ways to harvest and channel energy.

Use the following suggestions for reading in the physical sciences and mathematics.

TIPS FOR READING IN PHYSICAL SCIENCES/ MATHEMATICS

- **Read slowly and reread if necessary.** Both mathematics and the physical sciences are technical and detailed. Do not expect to understand everything on your first reading. When reading "The Mathematics of Gambling: What's Luck Got to Do with It?" you might read it once to grasp the author's overall position on gambling and then reread, concentrating on the role mathematics plays in examining the issue.

- **Focus on new terminology.** To read mathematics and the physical sciences, you have to learn the language of science. Mathematics and physical sciences are exact and precise, using terminology to make communication as error free as possible. In "The Cultural Ecology of the City" you will encounter technical terms such as herbaceous plants, airborne particulates, and stream channels.

- **Use writing to learn.** Reading alone is often not sufficient for learning mathematics and physical sciences. While highlighting and annotating a text work well for many subjects, they do not for math and science textbooks, where everything seems important. Try writing; express ideas in your own words. This method will test your understanding, too. If you cannot explain an idea in your own words, you probably do not understand it. After reading "Additional Renewable-Energy Options," try to summarize in your own words each alternative energy option.

One of the most challenging things to read in mathematics textbooks is word problems. This task requires both reading skills and knowledge of mathematics, as well as reasoning skills. To read and solve word problems more effectively, use the following steps.

TIPS FOR READING WORD PROBLEMS

- **Identify what is being asked for.** You may need to read the problem several times in order to do so. Often the information asked for occurs at the end of the problem.

- **Locate the useful information contained in the problem.** Underline useful information. Many problems also contain irrelevant information that will not help you solve the problem; cross out this information. Also note what information you do not have.

- **Visualize the problem.** Draw a picture or diagram that will make the problem real and practical. Label its parts, and include measurements and any other relevant information.

- **Estimate your answer.** Decide what would and would not be a reasonable answer.

- **Decide how to solve the problem.** Recall formulas you have learned that are related to the problem. You may have to translate ordinary words into mathematical language. For example, the phrase *percent of* usually suggests multiplication; the words *decreased by* mean subtraction. Look for clue words that suggest a particular process. For example, the phrase *how fast* means *rate;* you may be able to use the formula $r = d/t$ to solve the problem.

- **Solve the problem.** Set up an equation and choose variables to represent unknown quantities.

- **Verify your answer.** Compare your answer with your estimate. If there is a large discrepancy, it is a signal that you have made an error. Be sure to check your arithmetic.

SELECTION 25

The Mathematics of Gambling: What's Luck Got to Do with It?

Helen Thompson

Contemporary Issues Reading This article originally appeared in *The New Scientist,* an international news magazine specializing in mathematical and scientific topics. Unlike many other scientific magazines, *The New Scientist* examines math and science within the context of society and culture.

PREVIEWING THE READING

Using the steps listed on page 36, preview the reading selection. When you have finished, complete the following items.

1. The title of this selection suggests that the author will be discussing

_____ .

2. List at least three questions that you might be able to answer after reading the selection.

    a. _____

    b. _____

    c. _____

MAKING CONNECTIONS

Have you ever played the lottery or some other game of chance? If so, did you feel you had a good chance of winning? If not, why not? If you did not win, how did you react?

READING TIP

As you read, note that the author is discussing probabilities *rather than* certainties. *Increasing your chances of winning is a very different matter from being guaranteed to win!*

The Mathematics of Gambling: What's Luck Got to Do with It?

Even if you can't beat the system, there are some cunning ways to get Lady Luck on your side

1   Five years ago, Ashley Revell sold all his possessions and cashed in his life savings. It raised $76,840. He flew to Las Vegas, headed to the roulette table, and put it all on red. The wheel was spun. The crowd held its breath as the ball slowed, bounced four or five times, and finally settled on number seven. Red seven.

2   Revell's bet was a straight gamble: double or nothing. But when Edward Thorp, a mathematics student at the Massachusetts Institute of Technology, went to the same casino some 40 years previously, he knew pretty well where the ball was going to land. He walked away with a profit, took it to the racecourse, the basketball court, and the stock market, and became a multimillionaire. He wasn't on a lucky streak. He was using his knowledge of mathematics to understand, and beat, the odds.

probability
mathematical
study of the extent
to which something
is probable, or likely
to happen

3   No one can predict the future, but the powers of **probability** can help. Armed with this knowledge, a high-school mathematics education and $50, I headed off to find some examples of the way Thorp, and others like him, have used math to beat the system. Just how much money could probability make me?

Tipping the Even Odds

4   When Thorp stood at the roulette wheel in the summer of 1961 there was no need for nerves—he was armed with the first "wearable" computer, one that could predict the outcome of the spin. Once the ball was in play, Thorp fed the computer information about the speed and position of the ball and the wheel using a microswitch inside his shoe. "It would make a forecast about a probable result, and I'd bet on neighboring numbers," he says. Thorp's device would now be illegal in a casino, and in any case getting a computer to do the work wasn't exactly what I had in mind. However, there is a simple and sure-fire way to win at the roulette table—as long as you have deep pockets and a faith in probability theory.

5   A spin of the roulette wheel (Figure A) is just like the toss of a coin. Each spin is independent, with a 50:50 chance of the ball landing on black or red. Contrary to intuition, a black number is just as likely to appear after a run of 20 consecutive black numbers as the seemingly more likely red.

6   This randomness means there is a way of using probability to ensure a profit: First, always bet on the same color.

Figure A: A typical Roulette Wheel

Figure B: A Standard Lotto Form

Second, if you lose, double your bet on the next spin. Because your color will come up eventually, this method will always produce a profit. The downside is that you'll need a big pot of cash to stay in the game; a losing streak can escalate your bets very quickly. Seven unlucky spins on a $10 starting bet will have you parting with a hefty $1280 on the next. Unfortunately, your winnings don't escalate in the same way. When you do win, you'll make a profit only equal to your original stake. So while the theory itself is sound, be careful. The roulette wheel is likely to keep on taking your money longer than you can remain solvent.

7   The theory is good, but in practice it's a lot of effort for a small return. It would be a lot easier if I could just win the lottery. How can I improve my chances there?

In It to Win It

8   January 14, 1995, was an evening that Alex White will never forget. He matched all six numbers on the lottery, with an estimated jackpot of a massive $16 million. Unfortunately, White won only $122,510 because 132 other people also matched all six numbers and took a share of the jackpot.

9   There are dozens of books that claim to improve your odds of winning the lottery. None of them works. Every combination of numbers has the same odds of winning as any other—1 in 13,983,816 in the case of the United Kingdom's "Lotto" game (Figure B). But, as White's story shows, the fact that you could have to share the jackpot suggests a way to maximize any winnings. Your chances of success may be tiny, but if you win with numbers nobody else has chosen, you win big.

10   So how do you choose a combination unique to you? You won't find the answer at Britain's National Lottery headquarters, because they don't give out any information about the numbers people choose. That didn't stop Simon Cox, a mathematician at the University of Southampton, from trying. Ten years ago, Cox worked out U.K. lottery players' favorite figures by analyzing data from 113 lottery draws. He compared the winning numbers with how many people had matched four, five, or six of them, and thereby inferred which numbers are most popular.

11   And what were the magic numbers? Seven was the favorite, chosen 25 percent more often than the least popular number, 46. Numbers 14 and 18 were also popular, while 44 and 45 were among the least favorite. The most noticeable preference was for numbers up to 31. "They call this the birthday effect," says Cox. "A lot of people use their date of birth."

12   Several other patterns emerged. The most popular numbers are clustered around the center of the form people fill in to make their selection, suggesting that players are influenced by its layout. Similarly, thousands of players appear to just draw a diagonal line through a group of numbers on the form. There is also a clear dislike of consecutive numbers. "People refrain from choosing numbers next to each other, even though getting 1, 2,

3, 4, 5, 6 is as likely as any other combination," says Cox. Numerous studies on the U.S., Swiss, and Canadian lotteries have produced similar findings.

13　　To test the idea that picking unpopular numbers can maximize your winnings, Cox simulated a virtual syndicate that bought 75,000 tickets each week, choosing its numbers at random. Using the real results of 224 lottery draws, he calculated that his syndicate would have won a total of 7.5 million—on an outlay of 16.8 million. If his syndicate had stuck to unpopular numbers, however, it would have more than doubled its winnings (*The Statistician,* Vol. 47, p. 629).

14　　So the strategy is clear: go for numbers above 31, and pick ones that are clumped together or situated around the edges of the form. Then if you match all six numbers, you won't have to share with dozens of others. Unfortunately, probability also predicts that you won't match all six numbers until the 28th century. I bought a ticket using some of Cox's least popular numbers: 26, 34, 44, 46, 47, and 49. Not one of them came up.

Cut Your Losses

15　　Gambling is addictive, and that's its problem—even when you have got math on your side, it's all too easy to lose sight of what you could lose. Fortunately, that's the final thing that probability can help you with: knowing when to stop.

16　　If you have trouble knowing when to quit, try getting your head around *diminishing returns*—the optimal stopping tool. The best way to demonstrate diminishing returns is the so-called *marriage problem.* Suppose you are told you must marry, and that you must choose your spouse out of 100 applicants. You may interview each applicant once. After each interview you must decide whether to marry that person. If you decline, you lose the opportunity forever. If you work your way through 99 applicants without choosing one, you must marry the 100th. You may think you have 1 in 100 chance of marrying your ideal partner, but the truth is that you can do a lot better than that.

17　　If you interview half the potential partners then stop at the next best one—that is, the first one better than the best person you've already interviewed—you will marry the very best candidate about 25 per cent of the time. Once again, probability explains why. A quarter of the time, the second best partner will be in the first 50 people and the very best in the second. So 25 per cent of the time, the rule "stop at the next best one" will see you marrying the best candidate. Much of the rest of the time, you will end up marrying the 100th person, who has a 1 in 100 chance of being the worst, but hey, this is probability, not certainty.

18　　You can do even better than 25 per cent, however. John Gilbert and Frederick Mosteller of Harvard University proved that you could raise your odds to 37 per cent by interviewing 37 people, then stopping at the next best. The number 37 comes from dividing 100 by *e*, the base of the natural **logarithms**, which is roughly equal to 2.72. Gilbert and Mosteller's law works no matter how many candidates there are—you simply divide the number of options by 2.72. So, for example, suppose you find 50 companies that offer car insurance but you have no idea whether the next quote will be better or worse than the previous one. Should you get a quote from all 50? No, phone up 18 (50 × 2.72) and go with the next quote that beats the first 18.

logarithm
in math, the exponent required to create a new number from a given number

19　　This can also help you decide the optimal time to stop gambling. Say you fancy placing some bets at the bookies. Before you start, decide on the maximum number of bets you will make—20, for example. To maximize your chance of walking away at the right time, make seven bets, then stop at the next one that wins you more than the previous biggest win. Sticking to this rule is psychologically difficult, however. According to psychologist JoNell Strough at West Virginia University, the more you invest, the more likely it is that you will make an unwise decision further down the line (*Journal of Psychological Science,* Vol. 19, p. 650). This is called the *sunk-cost fallacy,* and it reflects our tendency to keep investing resources in a situation once we have started, even if it's going down the drain. It's why you are more likely to waste time watching a bad movie if you paid to see it.

20   So if you must have a gamble, use a little math to give you a head start, or at least to tell you when to throw in the towel. Personally I think I'll retire. Overall I'm $11.50 up—a small win at the casino offset by losing $1 on my lottery ticket. It was a lot of effort for little more than pocket change.

21   Maybe I should have just put it all on red.

A. UNDERSTANDING THE THESIS AND OTHER MAIN IDEAS

Select the best answer.

_____ 1. The central thesis of "The Mathematics of Gambling" is
  a. those who play the lottery can earn larger jackpots by choosing numbers that reflect their birthday.
  b. careful use of mathematics guarantees profits for gamblers.
  c. gamblers can use mathematics to increase their chances of winning.
  d. casinos offer games of chance that minimize gamblers' chances of winning a large sum of money.

_____ 2. The author's primary purpose is to
  a. explore her decision to give up her writing career to become a professional gambler.
  b. expose the unfair practices in lotteries and other forms of state-sponsored gambling.
  c. provide a foolproof system for those who need to earn a large sum of money quickly.
  d. help average people understand some basic principles behind the odds of winning at games of chance.

_____ 3. According to the selection, the odds of winning at roulette are the same as winning
  a. the lottery.
  b. a coin toss.
  c. at the racetrack.
  d. a carnival game.

_____ 4. Which of the following pieces of advice is not offered in the selection?

  a. When playing roulette, always bet on the same color. If you lose, double your bet on the next spin.

  b. When choosing lotto numbers, maximize your winnings by choosing numbers that create a diagonal line on the form.

  c. When choosing lotto numbers, pick higher numbers (over 31).

  d. When visiting a bookie, decide on the maximum number of bets you'll make, multiply that number by 2.72, make that number of bets, then stop at the next one that wins you more than the previous biggest win.

_____ 5. Which of the following is an example of the sunk-cost fallacy in action?

  a. Boats are more likely to sink in stormy weather.

  b. A store offers a discount to bring customers in.

  c. You keep reading a book that you paid for but don't like.

  d. A gambler uses a wearable computer to cheat a casino.

_____ 6. The topic of paragraphs 11 and 12 is

  a. the numbers most frequently chosen by lottery players.

  b. the popularity of the number seven among gamblers.

  c. the U.S., Canadian, and Swiss lottery systems.

  d. the forms completed by people who want to play a lotto-type game.

_____ 7. The "magic number" that statisticians use in all situations to help determine when to stop gambling is

  a. 2.72.

  b. 11.50.

  c. 25.

  d. 37.

B. IDENTIFYING DETAILS

Indicate whether each statement is true (T) or false (F).

_____ 1. John Gilbert teaches at Harvard University.

_____ 2. The sunk-cost fallacy helps explain why gamblers who are losing money keep gambling.

_____ 3. The symbol used for the base of the natural logarithm is l_n.

_____ 4. The man who studied people's number choices in lotteries was Frederick Mosteller.

_____ 5. Lotto players' favorite number is seven.

_____ 6. The best time to stop gambling is based on the principle of diminishing returns.

C. RECOGNIZING METHODS OF ORGANIZATION AND TRANSITIONS

Select the best answer.

_____ 1. Because the selection offers a series of gambling examples to support the idea that a basic understanding of math can help gamblers, its overall pattern of organization is

a. definition.

b. generalization and example.

c. comparison and contrast.

d. classification.

_____ 2. The transition word used in paragraph 3 to signal the selection's overall pattern of organization is

a. predict.

b. probability.

c. knowledge.

d. examples.

_____ 3. Within each of the three headings, the author provides specific, step-by-step directions for increasing the gambler's chances of winning (or minimizing losses). So, in paragraphs 6 and 19, the author uses the _____ pattern of organization.

a. cause-and-effect

b. spatial order

c. process

d. comparison and contrast

_____ 4. The transitional words or phrases in paragraph 6 that point to its pattern of organization are

a. means.

b. first, second.

c. while.

d. keep on taking, you can remain.

D. REVIEWING AND ORGANIZING IDEAS: PARAPHRASING

Complete the following paraphrase of paragraphs 8–14 from the selection by filling in the blanks.

In a lotto game, every combination of numbers has the _____ chance of winning. But those who do win would rather have the _____ to themselves than _____ it. To increase the chances that you'll get to keep all the winnings, choose numbers that are less _____. For example, do not choose commonly chosen numbers like _____, _____, and _____. Choosing numbers over 31 will help you avoid _____. Do not choose numbers by drawing a _____ line through the numbers of the lotto card. And don't be reluctant to choose _____ numbers.

E. READING AND THINKING VISUALLY

Select the best answer.

_____ 1. Suppose you bet $2 on "red" in the game shown in Figure A. The wheel is spun and the result is shown in the figure. What happens to your bet?

a. You lose $2.

b. You win $4.

c. You win $2.

d. You lose $4.

_____ 2. Consider Figure A within the context of the reading. Suppose you bet $10 on black before the wheel is spun. What are your chances of winning?

a. You have a 1 in 2 chance of winning.

b. You have a 1 in 4 chance of winning.

c. You are almost guaranteed to win.

d. You are almost guaranteed to lose.

_____ 3. Consider the completed lotto card in the center of Figure B. Which statement is *not* true?

a. Due to the low numbers chosen, this card may exhibit the birthday effect.

b. If this card wins the jackpot, the owner will probably not have to share the winnings with other people.

c. The pattern of numbers chosen here is not uncommon, with several of the choices clustering around the center of the card.

d. The player has not selected the most commonly chosen number.

F. FIGURING OUT IMPLIED MEANINGS

Indicate whether each statement is true (T) or false (F).

_____ 1. If a roulette wheel is spun 50 times and comes up black each time, it is more likely to come up black (rather than red) on the 51st spin.

_____ 2. In playing roulette, losses tend to mount much more quickly than profits.

_____ 3. Ashley Revell lost his life savings on just one spin of a roulette wheel.

_____ 4. To win big at roulette, you need to have a large bank of money to sustain you through numerous losses.

_____ 5. Numbers in sequence (such as 8, 9, 10, 11, 12, 13) are much less likely to be the winning numbers in a lotto game.

_____ 6. The advice offered in the selection will increase a lottery player's chances of winning the jackpot.

_____ 7. According to the experts, it would take approximately 700 years for the average lotto player to win a jackpot.

_____ 8. The author of the selection won a large sum of money while conducting her research to write the article.

_____ 9. The author implies that it is easier to beat games of chance today than it was 40 years ago.

G. THINKING CRITICALLY

Select the best answer.

_____ 1. The tone of the selection can best be described as
   a. cynical.
   b. serious.
   c. abstract.
   d. informative.

_____ 2. The author uses all of the following to support her thesis and main ideas *except*
   a. research citations of scholarly source materials.
   b. real-world examples of people who have won games of chance.
   c. her advanced degree in mathematics.
   d. quotations from experts.

_____ 3. Suppose you were born on December 19th. Scientists would say you exhibit the birthday effect if you choose which two numbers on your lottery card?

    a. 45, 46

    b. 14, 18

    c. 12, 19

    d. 7, 31

_____ 4. A good piece of advice you can take away from paragraph 9 is

    a. Don't waste money on books that teach you how to win the lottery.

    b. Buy tickets to other countries' lotteries because the odds of winning are greater in countries with smaller populations than the United States.

    c. Play only games of chance that do not permit more than one winner.

    d. Each time you play the lottery, always choose the same numbers.

_____ 5. By including paragraphs 20 and 21, the author implies that

    a. her gambling efforts didn't have the payoff she'd hoped for.

    b. on a roulette table, red is more likely to win than black.

    c. readers should play only the games her article discusses, and avoid such games as blackjack or craps.

    d. academic mathematicians should leave their jobs and become professional gamblers.

_____ 6. With which of the following winning sets of numbers are you the least likely to have to share a large jackpot with other winners?

    a. 4, 8, 12, 16, 31, 45

    b. 7, 11, 18, 30, 42, 48

    c. 15, 16, 17, 18, 19, 20

    d. 7, 14, 18, 21, 30, 31

_____ 7. Which of the following opinions would Helen Thomas, author of this article, be _least_ likely to hold?

    a. Gambling is addictive, so people need to be very careful when they decide to gamble.

    b. If you need to make a lot of money quickly, cash in your life savings and head to the roulette wheel.

    c. Mathematics can give you a slight edge when you gamble, but not enough of an edge to allow you to take large risks with your money.

    d. At the end of the day, you may be better off saving your money than taking chances with it in a casino.

H. BUILDING VOCABULARY

Context

Using context and a dictionary, if necessary, determine the meaning of each word as it is used in the selection.

_____ 1. consecutive (paragraph 5)
   a. related to conscience
   b. in unbroken sequence
   c. criminal
   d. material

_____ 2. stake (paragraph 6)
   a. bet
   b. wooden spike
   c. beef
   d. land claim

_____ 3. solvent (paragraph 6)
   a. financially stable
   b. stain remover
   c. cleaning fluid
   d. correct answer

_____ 4. refrain (paragraph 12)
   a. sing
   b. repeat
   c. avoid
   d. insist

_____ 5. diminishing (paragraph 16)
   a. profitable
   b. stopping
   c. marrying
   d. decreasing

_____ 6. optimal (paragraph 19)
   a. latest
   b. best
   c. intermediate
   d. required

Word Parts

A REVIEW OF PREFIXES AND SUFFIXES

MICRO- means *small*
CONTRA- means *against* or *opposite*
-ABLE refers to a *state, condition,* or *quality*

Use your knowledge of word parts and the review above to fill in the blanks in the following sentences.

1. A *wearable* computer (paragraph 4) is a small computer than can be _____ on the body.

2. The *microswitch* (paragraph 4) in Edward Thorp's shoe was a very _____ switch that he could activate with his foot.

3. Something that is *contrary* (paragraph 5) to intuition is the _____ of common sense.

Unusual Words/Understanding Idioms

Use the meanings given below to write a sentence using the boldfaced word or phrase.

1. A **sure-fire** method (paragraph 4) is one that is guaranteed to work.

   Your sentence: _____

   _____

2. A lottery **draw** (paragraph 10) takes place when the winning numbers are chosen—are drawn—at random from a series of numbered balls.

   Your sentence: _____

   _____

3. A **virtual** syndicate (paragraph 13) is based on a computer simulation, much like virtual reality.

   Your sentence: _____

   _____

I. SELECTING A LEARNING/STUDY STRATEGY

Select the best answer.

_____   Suppose you were assigned this selection as a reading in your math class. For a class activity, you can most likely expect your math professor to ask you to

   a. read Simon Cox's original research.

   b. buy a lottery ticket and report on your process of choosing numbers.

   c. solve a word problem that asks you to calculate the odds of winning a particular game.

   d. take a field trip to a local casino or betting parlor and report on the behavior you observe there.

J. EXPLORING IDEAS THROUGH DISCUSSION AND WRITING

1. Some billboards that advertise the lottery show outrageous items that a person could buy with his or her winnings. Design a billboard that shows alternative uses for the money.

2. Compile a list of other types of "gambling" in which people engage (for example, church bingo).

3. Discuss what factors motivate people to gamble, despite the poor odds of winning.

4. Do you think it's easier to win with a scratch-off lottery game than with a lotto-type game? Why or why not?

K. BEYOND THE CLASSROOM TO THE WEB

1. *As a society, we love to hear stories about lottery winners. To read about lottery winners and the circumstances in which they found themselves, visit* **http:// www.cleveland.com/pdq/index.ssf/2010/02/for_these_lottery_winners_a_ dr.html.** *Write a paraphrase of one of the stories.*

2. *Carnival games are one form of gambling. Many people who attend carnivals do not know that most of the carnival games are rigged so that they have very little chance of winning. To understand how the games are rigged and to increase your chances of winning at them, visit* **http://www.blifaloo.com/info/beat–carnival– games.php.** *Which of the listed games do you think you have the best chance of beating? Why?*

TRACKING YOUR PROGRESS

Selection 25

Section	Number Correct		Score
A. Thesis and Main Ideas (7 items)	_____	× 3	_____
B. Details (6 items)	_____	× 2	_____
C. Organization and Transitions (4 items)	_____	× 2	_____
E. Reading and Thinking Visually (3 items)	_____	× 2	_____
F. Implied Meanings (9 items)	_____	× 2	_____
G. Thinking Critically (7 items)	_____	× 2	_____
H. Vocabulary			
Context (6 items)	_____	× 2	_____
Word Parts (3 items)	_____	× 3	_____
		TOTAL SCORE	_____ %

SELECTION 26 | The Cultural Ecology of the City

Mona Domosh, Roderick P. Neumann,
Patricia L. Price, and Terry G. Jordan-Bychkov

Textbook
Excerpt

This selection is taken from a human geography textbook titled *The Human Mosaic*. Read it to gain a better understanding of the way environmental conditions differ between large cities and the surrounding countryside.

PREVIEWING THE READING

Using the steps listed on page 36, preview the reading selection. When you have finished, complete the following items.

1. This selection is about _____.

2. List at least three topics that are discussed in the reading.

   a. _____

   b. _____

   c. _____

 ### MAKING CONNECTIONS

The topics of climate change and global warming are in the news constantly. In addition to burning fossil fuels, how do humans affect the environment? Are these effects positive or negative?

READING TIP

As you read, highlight to keep track of the key points. Be sure you understand the two key scientific processes discussed in the reading: evaporation and condensation.

The Cultural Ecology of the City

1   How can we understand the relationships between the urban mosaic and the physical environment? The physical environment affects cities, just as urbanization profoundly alters natural environmental processes. The study of cultural ecology helps us to organize information about these city-nature relationships.

Urban Weather and Climate

2   Cities alter virtually all aspects of local weather and climate. Temperatures are higher in cities; rainfall is increased; the incidence of fog and cloudiness is greater; and levels of atmospheric pollution are much higher.

3   The causes of these changes are no mystery. Because cities cover large areas of land with streets, buildings, parking lots, and rooftops, about 50 percent of the urban area is a hard surface. Rainfall is quickly carried into gutters and sewers, so that little standing water is available for **evaporation**. Because evaporation removes heat from the air, when moisture is reduced, evaporation is lessened and air temperatures are higher.

evaporation
process by which
liquid turns to vapor

4   Moreover, cities generate enormous amounts of heat. This heat comes not just from the heating systems of buildings but also from automobiles, industry, and even human bodies. One study showed that on a winter day in Manhattan, the amount of heat produced in the city is two and a half times the amount that reaches the ground from the sun. This results in a large mass of warmer air sitting over the city, called the urban heat island (Figure A). The heat island causes yearly temperature averages in cities to be 3.5°F (2°C) higher than in the countryside; during the winter, when there is more city-produced heat, the average difference can easily reach 7°F to 10°F (4°C to 5.6°C).

5   Urbanization also affects precipitation (rainfall and snowfall). Because of higher temperatures in the urban area, snowfall will be about 5 percent less than in the surrounding countryside. However, rainfall can be 5 to 10 percent higher. The increased

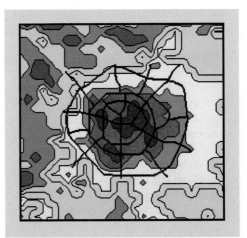

Figure A: Diagram of the urban heat island in Chengdu, China. The deep colors (purples and reds) indicate higher temperatures, while the shades of yellow and green indicate lower temperatures. Notice the marked contrast in temperature between the built-up part of the city and the surrounding rural areas. What might cause the center of the heat island to be located slightly east of the center of the city?

Source: Shangming and Bo, "Analysis of the Effects of Urban Heat Island by Satellite Remote Sensing," a paper presented at the 22nd Asian Conference on Remote Sensing, 5–9 November 2001, Singapore.

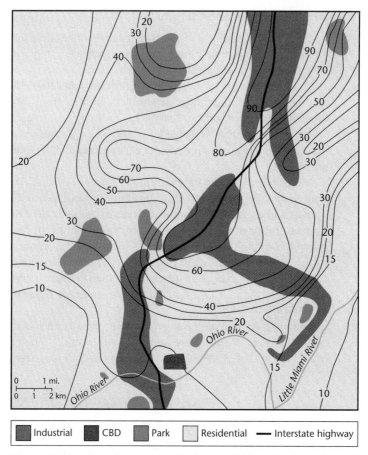

| ■ Industrial | ■ CBD | ■ Park | □ Residential | — Interstate highway |

Figure B: The dust dome over Cincinnati, Ohio. Numbers show the concentration of particulate matter in the air at an elevation of 3,000 feet (914 meters). The higher the value, the greater the amount of particulate matter. (After Bach and Hagedorn, 1971.)

condensation
process by which
water collects as
droplets

rainfall results from two factors: the large number of dust particles in urban air and the higher city temperatures. Dust particles are a necessary precondition for **condensation**, offering a nucleus around which moisture can adhere. An abundance of dust particles, then, facilitates condensation. That is why fog and clouds (dust domes) are usually more frequent around cities (Figure B).

Urban Hydrology

6   Not only is the city a great consumer of water, but it also alters runoff patterns in a way that increases the frequency and magnitude of flooding. Within the city, residential areas are usually the greatest consumers of water. Water consumption can vary, but generally each person in the United States uses about 60 gallons (264 liters) per day in a residence. Of course, residential demand varies. It is greater in drier climates as well as in middle- and high-income neighborhoods. Higher-income groups usually have a larger number of water-using appliances, such as washing machines, dishwashers, and swimming pools.

7   Urbanization can increase both the frequency and the magnitude of flooding because cities create large impervious areas where water cannot soak into the earth. Instead, precipitation is converted into immediate runoff. It is forced into gutters, sewers, and stream channels that have been straightened and stripped of vegetation, which results in more frequent high-water levels than are found in a comparable area of rural land. Furthermore, the time between rainfall and peak runoff is reduced in cities; there is more lag in the countryside, where water runs across soil and vegetation into stream channels and then into rivers. So, because of hard surfaces and artificial collection channels, runoff in cities is concentrated and immediate.

Urban Vegetation

8   Until a decade ago, it was commonly thought that cities were made up mostly of artificial materials: asphalt, concrete, glass, and steel. Studies, however, show that about two-thirds of a typical North American city is composed of trees and **herbaceous** plants (mostly weeds in vacant lots and cultivated grasses in lawns). This urban vegetation is usually a mix of natural and introduced species and is a critical component of the urban **ecosystem** because it affects the city's **topography**, hydrology, and meteorology.

herbaceous
related to fleshy plants

ecosystem
interacting community of organisms and their environment

topography
the physical features of the land

propagation
spread

9   More specifically, urban vegetation influences the quantity and quality of surface water and groundwater; reduces wind velocity and turbulence and temperature extremes; affects the pattern of snow accumulation and melting: absorbs thousands of tons of airborne particulates and atmospheric gases; and offers a habitat for mammals, birds, reptiles, and insects, all of which play some useful role in the urban ecosystem. Furthermore, urban vegetation influences the **propagation** of sound waves by muffling out much of the city's noise; affects the distribution of natural and artificial light; and, finally, is an extremely important component in the development of soil profiles—which, in turn, control hillside stability.

10   Our urban settlements are still closely tied to the physical environment. Cities change these natural processes in profound ways, and we must understand these disturbances in order to make better decisions about adjustments and control.

A. UNDERSTANDING THE THESIS AND OTHER MAIN IDEAS

Select the best answer.

_____ 1. The central thesis of the selection is found in
a. paragraph 2.   c. paragraph 7.
b. paragraph 5.   d. paragraph 10.

_____ 2. The authors' primary purpose in "The Cultural Ecology of the City" is to
a. describe patterns of rain runoff in U.S. cities.
b. explain how the natural environment affects cities and vice versa.
c. discuss the presence of vegetation in urban locations.
d. explore the process by which the temperature rises in cities.

_____ 3. The topic of paragraph 6 is

    a. appliances.   c. water.

    b. cities.   d. climate.

_____ 4. The main idea of paragraph 7 is that

    a. urbanization can increase the frequency and severity of flooding.

    b. water in urban areas is channeled quickly into runoff beds.

    c. urban sewers are home to unexpectedly large populations of animals and vegetation.

    d. the countryside has more natural water reservoirs than the city does.

_____ 5. Which of the following does *not* explain why cities are usually hotter than the suburbs and the country?

    a. In cities, less water is available for evaporation to cool the temperature.

    b. Many cities are located on or near bodies of water, which increase the temperature by magnifying the sun's rays.

    c. Cities generate more heat through their buildings and population than the countryside does.

    d. In cities, large amounts of the land are converted into hard surfaces that carry rainfall into sewers and gutters.

_____ 6. In general, the countryside

    a. receives less rainfall than the city.

    b. is warmer than the city.

    c. experiences more fog than the city.

    d. is more polluted than the city.

B. IDENTIFYING DETAILS

Indicate whether each statement is true (T) or false (F).

_____ 1. About two-thirds of a typical North American city is composed of artificial materials such as asphalt and steel.

_____ 2. Higher-income groups tend to use more water than lower-income groups.

_____ 3. On a winter day in New York City, the amount of heat generated by the city can be more than double the amount that reaches the ground from the sun.

_____ 4. The time between rainfall and peak water runoff is accelerated in the countryside due to the presence of irrigation ditches.

_____ 5. Most of the plants in cities are trees, weeds, or grasses.

_____ 6. The presence of dust domes helps explain why cities receive more rainfall than the countryside.

_____ 7. The average person in the United States uses about 264 gallons of water per day.

C. RECOGNIZING METHODS OF ORGANIZATION AND TRANSITIONS

Select the best answer.

_____ 1. The organizational pattern used in paragraph 2 is
   a. classification.
   b. enumeration or listing.
   c. time sequence.
   d. comparison and contrast.

_____ 2. The organizational pattern used in paragraph 3 is
   a. comparison and contrast.
   b. order of importance.
   c. cause and effect.
   d. classification.

_____ 3. Paragraph 4 uses a cause-and-effect pattern of organization. A transition word used in the paragraph to signal this pattern is
   a. generate.
   b. showed.
   c. results.
   d. during.

_____ 4. The organizational pattern used in paragraph 9 is
   a. order of importance.
   b. comparison and contrast.
   c. time sequence.
   d. cause and effect.

D. REVIEWING AND ORGANIZING IDEAS: MAPPING

Complete the following map of the main details in the reading.

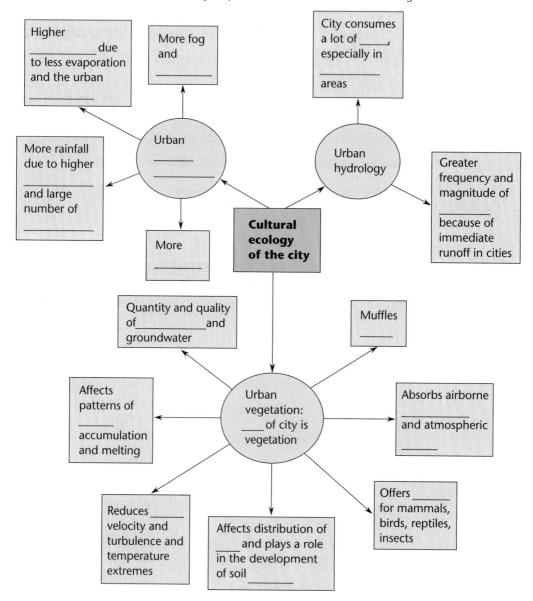

Higher _____ due to less evaporation and the urban _____

More fog and _____

City consumes a lot of _____, especially in _____ areas

More rainfall due to higher _____ and large number of _____

Urban _____

Urban hydrology

Greater frequency and magnitude of _____ because of immediate runoff in cities

More _____

Cultural ecology of the city

Quantity and quality of _____ and groundwater

Muffles _____

Affects patterns of _____ accumulation and melting

Urban vegetation: _____ of city is vegetation

Absorbs airborne _____ and atmospheric _____

Reduces _____ velocity and turbulence and temperature extremes

Affects distribution of _____ and plays a role in the development of soil _____

Offers _____ for mammals, birds, reptiles, insects

E. READING AND THINKING VISUALLY

Select the best answer.

_____ 1. Which statement is *not* true of Figure A?

   a. The green areas are most likely rural areas.

   b. The hottest temperatures are found in the center of the city.

c. The eastern side of the city is warmer than the western side of the city.

d. Hotter temperatures are associated with the presence of major roadways.

_____ 2. Consider Figure B. In which part of Cincinnati, as shown in the figure, are particulates at their highest level?

a. along the Ohio River and Little Miami River

b. surrounding the parks

c. in the northeastern industrial area

d. in the CBD (central business district)

F. FIGURING OUT IMPLIED MEANINGS

Indicate whether each statement is true (T) or false (F).

_____ 1. The authors imply that the presence of vegetation in a city makes the city less noisy.

_____ 2. In large urban areas, animal life (such as mammals, birds, and insects) plays a limited and not very useful role.

_____ 3. Cities are likely to receive more of all types of precipitation due to their higher temperatures.

_____ 4. The more vegetation a city has, the less polluted the city's air is likely to be.

_____ 5. Lower-income people tend to use less water because they cannot afford the appliances that typically consume large amounts of water.

_____ 6. Flooding results mainly when water accumulates too quickly to be absorbed into the earth.

_____ 7. Heat islands create more of a difference between city and countryside in summer than in winter.

G. THINKING CRITICALLY

Select the best answer.

_____ 1. The tone of the selection is best described as

a. optimistic.

b. worried.

c. humorous.

d. instructive.

_____ 2. Suppose the temperature is 72°F (Fahrenheit). The same temperature in degrees Celsius will be

    a. a lower number.

    b. a higher number.

    c. the same number.

    d. determined by the amount of humidity in the air.

_____ 3. Which U.S. city is likely to have the smallest heat island?

    a. Portland, Maine

    b. Boston, Massachusetts

    c. New York City, New York

    d. San Francisco, California

_____ 4. By an "introduced species" (paragraph 8), the authors mean

    a. species that are native to a region.

    b. species that are brought to a region by people who settle there.

    c. extinct species.

    d. herbivorous (plant-eating) species.

_____ 5. In which part of a city will the heat island be hottest?

    a. residential areas

    b. abandoned areas

    c. industrial/central business districts

    d. park areas

_____ 6. When the authors say "we must understand these disturbances in order to make better decisions about adjustments and control" (paragraph 10), they mean that

    a. the forces of nature are ultimately beyond anyone's control.

    b. coping with weather disturbances, such as snowstorms, requires most of the city's budget.

    c. modern technology can help cities control the amount of rain and snow they receive in a typical year.

    d. a fuller understanding of how cities and the environment affect one another helps city planners make better decisions.

H. BUILDING VOCABULARY

Context

Using context and a dictionary, if necessary, determine the meaning of each word as it is used in the selection.

_____ 1. urbanization (paragraph 1)
   a. the study of rainfall
   b. the systems used to prevent flooding
   c. the development of cities
   d. the creation of environmental awareness

_____ 2. incidence (paragraph 2)
   a. tragedy
   b. desire for
   c. occurrence
   d. lack

_____ 3. precipitation (paragraph 5)
   a. temperature
   b. rain, snow, sleet, or hail
   c. humidity
   d. size of the urban population

_____ 4. nucleus (paragraph 5)
   a. center
   b. summit
   c. warm area
   d. empty zone

_____ 5. magnitude (paragraph 6)
   a. timing
   b. magnetic properties
   c. size
   d. growth

_____ 6. impervious (paragraph 7)
   a. incapable of being shattered
   b. not allowing fluid to pass through
   c. spongelike and absorbent
   d. abnormal and unlikely

_____ 7. lag (paragraph 7)

    a. rain

    b. soil deposit

    c. sewer

    d. delay

_____ 8. velocity (paragraph 9)

    a. speed

    b. value

    c. possibility

    d. strength

Word Parts

> ### A REVIEW OF PREFIXES, ROOTS, AND SUFFIXES
>
> **PRE-** means _before_
> **FAC** means _make_ or _do_
> **-LOGY** means _study_

Use your knowledge of word parts and the review above to fill in the blanks in the following sentences.

1. A _precondition_ (paragraph 5) is a condition that must exist _____ something can occur.

2. When you _facilitate_ (paragraph 5) an action or process, you _____ it easier.

3. If hydro- means "water," then _hydrology_ (paragraph 8) is the _____ of water.

4. _Meteorology_ (paragraph 8) comes from a Greek root meaning "the atmosphere." Therefore _meteorology_ is the study of the _____.

I. SELECTING A LEARNING/STUDY STRATEGY

Select the best answer.

_____ Which of the following would be the _least_ effective way of studying for an essay exam on this selection?

    a. creating a map of the ideas in the selection

    b. memorizing the definitions of _precipitation, condensation,_ and _evaporation_

    c. visiting the downtown area in your town or city

    d. working with a classmate to quiz each other on the contents

J. EXPLORING IDEAS THROUGH DISCUSSION AND WRITING

1. Many squirrels in the parks of New York and other cities have become almost tame as a result of so many people feeding them by hand. This is just one example of the ways wildlife adapts to life in a city. Can you think of other ways that the wildlife in a city behaves differently from wildlife in the suburbs or rural areas?

2. In many cities, the battle lines are drawn between people who want to preserve parkland and people who want to build apartments or office buildings on open space. What are the pros and cons of each type of land use?

K. BEYOND THE CLASSROOM TO THE WEB

The New York Public Library sponsors a Web site, **http://urbanneighbors.nypl.org,** *designed to acquaint readers with the various kinds of wildlife that make New York City their home. Visit the Web site and look for a bird, animal, or fish of interest to you; then conduct a Web search to find more information about it. Share five interesting facts about that species with the class. (If you prefer, look for a similar Web site for your city and prepare some information about a species found in that city to present to the class.)*

TRACKING YOUR PROGRESS

Selection 26

Section	Number Correct		Score
A. Thesis and Main Ideas (6 items)	_____	× 3	_____
B. Details (7 items)	_____	× 2	_____
C. Organization and Transitions (4 items)	_____	× 2	_____
E. Reading and Thinking Visually (2 items)	_____	× 3	_____
F. Implied Meanings (7 items)	_____	× 2	_____
G. Thinking Critically (6 items)	_____	× 2	_____
H. Vocabulary			
Context (8 items)	_____	× 2	_____
Word Parts (4 items)	_____	× 3	_____
		TOTAL SCORE	_____ %

SELECTION 27

Additional Renewable-Energy Options

Richard T. Wright and Dorothy F. Boorse

Textbook Excerpt

Contemporary
Issues Reading

 This selection originally appeared in a textbook titled *Environmental Science: Toward a Sustainable Future*. Read it to learn about several options for renewable energy.

PREVIEWING THE READING

Using the steps listed on page 36, preview the reading selection. When you have finished, complete the following items.

1. This selection is about _____.

2. The three main types of renewable-energy options that are discussed in the selection are:

   a. _____

   b. _____

   c. _____

MAKING CONNECTIONS

Describe what the term "renewable energy" means to you. What renewable-energy options do you think are most worth pursuing? Why?

READING TIP

As you read, highlight descriptions of how different types of renewable-energy options are designed to work as well as any limitations of each option.

Additional Renewable-Energy Options

1   Aside from water, wind, biomass, and hydrogen energy, there are other renewable-energy options that are worth pursuing.

Geothermal Energy

2   In various locations in the world, such as the northwestern corner of Wyoming (now Yellowstone National Park), there are springs that yield hot, almost boiling,

water. Natural steam vents and other thermal features are also found in such areas. They occur where the hot, molten rock of Earth's interior is close enough to the surface to heat groundwater, particularly in volcanic regions. Using such naturally heated water or steam to heat buildings or drive turbogenerators is the basis of geothermal energy. In 2008, geothermal energy provided over 10,000 MW of electrical power (equivalent to the output of 10 large nuclear or coal-fired power stations) in countries as diverse as Nicaragua, the Philippines, Kenya, Iceland, and New Zealand. Today the largest single facility is in the United States at a location known as The Geysers, 70 miles (110 km) north of San Francisco (Figure A). With over 2,900 MW from geothermal energy, the United States is the world leader in the use of this energy source; new projects in the development stage will increase this to over 6,000 MW. As impressive as this application of geothermal energy is, nearly double the amount is being used to directly heat homes and buildings, largely in Japan and China.

3   A recent study by MIT suggested that the United States employ an emerging technology called enhanced geothermal systems (EGS). EGS involves drilling holes several miles deep into granite that holds temperatures of 400 degrees or more and injecting water under pressure into one hole where it absorbs heat from the rock and, as steam, flows up another shaft to a power plant where it generates electricity. Such plants already exist in Australia, Europe, and Japan. This underground heat is widespread in the United States, unlike the present limited geothermal sources. The MIT team proposed a $1 billion investment to exploit the EGS potential, predicting that by 2050 some 100 gigawatts (GW) of electrical power could be developed in this way.

Figure A: Geothermal energy. One of the 15 geothermal power plants operated by Calpine Corporation at The Geysers in Sonoma and Lake Counties, California. Calpine's geothermal plants at The Geysers are capable of producing 725 megawatts of power, or about 21 percent of California's non-hydroelectric green energy.

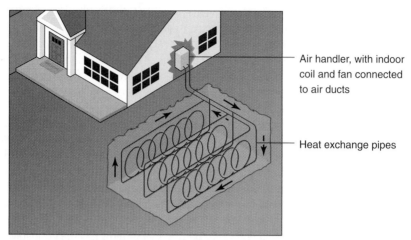

Figure B: Geothermal heat pump system. The pipes buried underground facilitate heat exchange between the house and the Earth. This system can either cool or heat a house and can be installed almost anywhere, although at a higher initial cost than a conventional heating, ventilation, and air-conditioning system.

Heat Pumps

4   A less spectacular, but far more abundant, energy source than the large geothermal power plants exists anywhere pipes can be drilled into the Earth. Because the ground temperature below six feet or so remains constant, the Earth can be used as part of a heat exchange system that extracts heat in the winter and uses the ground as a heat sink in the summer. Thus, the system can be used for heating and cooling and does away with the need for separate furnace and air-conditioning systems. As Figure B shows, a geothermal heat pump (GHP) system involves loops of buried pipes filled with an antifreeze solution, circulated by a pump connected to the air handler (a box containing a blower and a filter). The blower moves house air through the heat pump and distributes it throughout the house via ductwork.

5   Four elementary schools in Lincoln, Nebraska, installed GHP systems for their heating and cooling. Their energy cost savings were 57% compared with the cost of conventional heating and cooling systems installed in two similar schools. Taxpayers will save an estimated $3.8 million over the next 20 years with the GHP systems. According to the EPA, these systems are by far the most cost-effective energy-saving systems available. Although they are significantly more expensive to install than conventional heating and air-conditioning systems, they are trouble free and save money over the long run. New heat pump installations in the United Sates are growing at an annual rate of 20% per year, with almost 1 million installed by 2008.

turbines
machines which use rotating blades to convert a fast-moving flow of air, water, or other fluid into power

Tidal and Wave Power

6   A phenomenal amount of energy is inherent in the twice-daily rise and fall of the ocean tides, brought about by the gravitational pull of the Moon and the Sun. Many imaginative schemes have been proposed for capturing this limitless, pollution-free source of energy. The most straightforward idea is the tidal barrage, in which a dam is built across the mouth of a bay and turbines are mounted in the structure. The incoming

tide flowing through the turbines would generate power. As the tide shifted, the blades would be reversed so that the outflowing water would continue to generate power.

7   In about 30 locations in the world, the shoreline topography generates tides high enough—20 feet (6 m) or more—for this kind of use. Large tidal power plants already exist in two of those places: France and Canada. The only suitable location in North America is the Bay of Fundy, where the Annapolis Tidal Generating Station has operated since 1984, at 20-MW capacity. Thus, this application of tidal power has potential only in certain localities, and even there, it would not be without adverse environmental impacts. The barrage would trap sediments, impede the migration of fish and other organisms, prevent navigation, alter the circulation and mixing of saltwater and freshwater in estuaries, and perhaps have other, unforeseen ecological effects.

8   Other techniques are being explored that harness the currents that flow with the tides. For example, in 2006, Verdant Power installed six 15-foot-tall underwater turbines to harness the tidal energy of the East River in New York City; unfortunately, the currents were too strong for the blades and sheared off the tips. After another attempt also failed, Verdant has installed another turbine that has held up and is generating power for a nearby supermarket. The city plans to add many more turbines if all goes well, generating 10 MW of electricity. San Francisco is eyeing a similar scheme to tap the energy of the 400 billion gallons of water that flow under the Golden Gate Bridge with every tide.

Ocean Waves

9   Standing on the shore of any ocean, an observer would have to be impressed with the energy arriving with each wave, generated by offshore winds. It might be possible to harness some of this energy, but the technological challenge is daunting. The ideal location is one that receives the wave's force before it hits the shoaling sea floor, is close enough to shore to facilitate hookup with transmission cables, and is deep enough so that the equipment will not crash on the sea floor during storm turbulence. In the United States, the Pacific Northwest provides these conditions, and the Pacific Gas and Electric Company has contracted with Finavera Renewables to install the nation's first, admittedly small, wave power plant off the coast of northern California. Eight buoys will generate two MW of electricity as they bob up and down with the waves, expanding and contracting a hose that pumps pressurized water through a turbine. There are other proposed mechanisms for capturing wave energy, and it is fair to say that this technology is in the early research-and-development stage. The U.S. DOE is supporting research on ocean energy on a 50% cost-share basis.

Ocean Thermal-Energy Conversion

10   Over much of the world's oceans, a **thermal gradient** of about 20°C (36°F) exists between surface water heated by the Sun and the colder deep water. Ocean thermal-energy conversion (OTEC) is the name of an experimental technology that uses this temperature difference to produce power. The technology involves using the warm surface water to heat and vaporize a low-boiling-point liquid such as ammonia. The increased pressure of the vaporized ammonia would drive turbogenerators. The ammonia vapor leaving the turbines would then be recondensed by cold water pumped up from as much as 300 feet (100 m) deep and returned to the start of the cycle.

thermal gradient the rate of temperature change over a specified distance

11   Various studies indicate that OTEC power plants show little economic promise—unless, perhaps, they can be coupled with other, cost-effective operations. For example, in Hawaii, a shore based OTEC plant uses the cold, nutrient-rich water pumped from the ocean bottom to cool buildings and supply nutrients for vegetables in an aquaculture operation, in addition to cooling the condensers in the power cycle. Even so, interest in duplicating such operations is minimal at present.

Final Thoughts

12   Our look at current energy policy indicates that the United States is making a serious effort to address the need to develop renewable-energy sources and to improve the efficiency of current energy use. This policy also continues the effort to move toward a hydrogen economy. What about the global targets of achieving stable atmospheric levels of greenhouse gases and a long-term sustainable-energy policy? Unfortunately, current policy also promotes further use and development of fossil fuel energy. It's "business as usual" for the fossil fuel industries. How can that be changed?

13   One development that has caught everyone's attention in recent years is the rising price of gasoline. Until recently, the United States was the only industrialized country that has seen fit to keep gasoline prices remarkably low. Fuel in all other highly developed countries is so heavily taxed that it costs consumers upward of $6 per gallon—unlike U.S. prices, which were below $1.50 for 12 of the last 18 years. When gasoline rose to $3 a gallon in 2005, consumers began to turn away from gas-guzzling sport-utility vehicles and muscle cars and have been opting for the rising number of gasoline-electric hybrid cars appearing on the lots of many car manufacturers. This supports the suggestion of a number of economists and environmental groups that we should be paying more—much more—for gasoline (and other fossil fuels). To accomplish this, we would need a policy change: a carbon tax—that is, a tax levied on all fuels according to the amount of carbon dioxide that they produce when consumed. Such a tax, proponents believe, would provide both incentives to use renewable sources, which would not be taxed, and disincentives to consume fossil fuels. It is hard to imagine any step that would be more effective (or more controversial) in reducing greenhouse gas emissions in the United States. A number of European countries have already adopted such a tax.

14   Are the preceding developments, even the suggested carbon tax, enough to enable us to achieve a sustainable-energy system and to mitigate global climate change? Very likely, no. Yet many of them are moving us in the stewardly direction that is vital to the future of the global environment.

A. UNDERSTANDING THE THESIS AND OTHER MAIN IDEAS

Select the best answer.

_____ 1. The authors' primary purpose is to
   a. explain the importance of reducing the use of fossil fuels.
   b. identify factors that contribute to global climate change.
   c. suggest ways to improve energy conservation and efficiency.
   d. describe a variety of renewable-energy options.

_____ 2. The topic of paragraph 3 is
    a. renewable-energy options.
    b. enhanced geothermal systems (EGS).
    c. underground heat.
    d. emerging technologies.

_____ 3. The term **tidal barrage** describes a system in which
    a. holes are drilled several miles deep into granite.
    b. turbines are mounted in a dam built across the mouth of a bay.
    c. the warm surface water of the ocean is used to vaporize a low-boiling-point liquid.
    d. cold, nutrient-rich water is pumped from the ocean bottom.

_____ 4. The authors' purpose in paragraph 13 is to
    a. complain about the rising cost of gasoline.
    b. suggest ways to reduce greenhouse gas emissions.
    c. explain what a carbon tax is and why it is needed.
    d. compare the United States to other industrialized countries.

_____ 5. According to the selection, current energy policy in the United States is doing all of the following _except:_
    a. addressing the need to develop renewable-energy sources.
    b. attempting to improve the efficiency of current energy use.
    c. discouraging further use and development of fossil fuel energy.
    d. continuing the effort to move toward a hydrogen economy.

B. IDENTIFYING DETAILS

Indicate whether each statement is true (T) or false (F).

_____ 1. The largest single geothermal energy facility is located in the Philippines.

_____ 2. Power plants using enhanced geothermal systems (EGS) already exist in Australia, Europe, and Japan.

_____ 3. Geothermal heat pump (GHS) systems are being used to heat and cool four elementary schools in Lincoln, Nebraska.

_____ 4. GHS systems are much less expensive to install than conventional heating and cooling systems.

_____ 5. New heat pump installations are growing at a rate of 20% per year in the United States.

_____ 6. Large tidal power plants are being used in 30 locations around the world.

_____ 7. The only tidal power plant in North America is in the Bay of Fundy.

_____ 8. The first wave power plant in the United States will be installed off the coast of Alaska.

_____ 9. The U.S. Department of Energy shares the costs of ocean energy research.

_____ 10. The EPA considers ocean thermal-energy conversion (OTEC) the most cost-effective energy-saving system available.

C. RECOGNIZING METHODS OF ORGANIZATION AND TRANSITIONS

Select the best answer.

_____ 1. The overall pattern of organization in this selection is
   a. listing.
   b. cause and effect.
   c. comparison and contrast.
   d. order of importance.

_____ 2. In paragraph 4, the pattern the authors use to describe how a geothermal heat pump (GHP) system works is
   a. definition.
   b. process.
   c. classification.
   d. listing.

_____ 3. In paragraph 8, the pattern the authors use to describe other techniques for using tidal power is
   a. comparison and contrast.
   b. generalization and example.
   c. classification.
   d. chronological order.

_____ 4. In paragraph 11, the transition that indicates that the authors will illustrate an idea is
   a. unless.
   b. perhaps.
   c. For example.
   d. in addition.

D. REVIEWING AND ORGANIZING IDEAS: OUTLINING

Complete the following outline of paragraphs 2–11 of the selection by filling in the missing words or phrases.

I. Geothermal Energy

    A. Naturally heated water or steam

        1. Occurs where Earth's _____ is near the surface

    B. _____

        1. Holes drilled into hot granite

        2. Existing plants in _____

    C. Geothermal heat pumps

        1. Earth used as part of a _____

        2. Eliminate need for _____

II. Tidal and Wave Power

    A. _____

        1. Uses dam with turbines to harness power

        2. Limited to locations with tides over _____

        3. Adverse _____

    B. Ocean waves

        1. Early research-and-development stage

III. _____

    A. Uses temperature difference between _____

    B. Little economic promise

E. READING AND THINKING VISUALLY

Complete each of the following items.

1. The photograph in Figure A most closely corresponds to the material under the heading _____ .

2. According to the caption for Figure A, the Calpine Corporation operates _____ geothermal units in Sonoma and Lake Counties, California.

3. The purpose of Figure B is to illustrate a _____.

4. Figure B shows that heat exchange pipes are located _____.

F. FIGURING OUT IMPLIED MEANINGS

Indicate whether each statement is true (T) or false (F).

_____ 1. The study by MIT supports the idea that enhanced geothermal systems are a good potential source of electricity.

_____ 2. Geothermal heat pump (GHP) systems are not likely to gain acceptance in the United States.

_____ 3. The tidal barrage system may have several negative environmental effects.

_____ 4. Attempts to use the tidal energy of the East River to generate power have all failed.

_____ 5. The U.S. Department of Energy is supportive of research on ocean energy.

_____ 6. Ocean thermal-energy conversion power plants are too expensive unless they are part of other cost-effective operations.

G. THINKING CRITICALLY

Select the best answer.

_____ 1. The tone of the selection can best be described as
   a. informative.
   b. pessimistic.
   c. amused.
   d. sensational.

_____ 2. The title of this selection implies that
   a. the renewable-energy options in this selection are unlikely to succeed.
   b. solar and wind energy are the only realistic options for renewable energy.
   c. there are other renewable-energy options in addition to the ones described in this selection.
   d. the public prefers to continue using gasoline and other fossil fuels rather than renewable-energy options.

_____ 3. The central thesis of this selection is supported primarily by
   a. interviews with researchers.
   b. facts and statistics.
   c. expert opinions.
   d. the authors' personal experience.

_____ 4. The audience for this selection is most likely to be
   a. geothermal scientists.
   b. politicians.
   c. renewable-energy experts.
   d. students in environmental science.

H. BUILDING VOCABULARY

Context

Using context and a dictionary, if necessary, determine the meaning of each word as it is used in the selection.

_____ 1. molten (paragraph 2)
   a. surface
   b. deep
   c. melted
   d. variable

_____ 2. exploit (paragraph 3)
   a. complicate
   b. utilize
   c. expose
   d. waste

_____ 3. inherent (paragraph 6)
   a. part of
   b. prevented by
   c. separate from
   d. restricted

_____ 4. adverse (paragraph 7)
   a. pleasing
   b. accurate
   c. familiar
   d. harmful

_____ 5. impede (paragraph 7)

    a. attack

    b. improve

    c. obstruct

    d. promote

_____ 6. daunting (paragraph 9)

    a. careful

    b. intimidating

    c. limiting

    d. threatening

_____ 7. opting (paragraph 13)

    a. changing

    b. advancing

    c. choosing

    d. avoiding

_____ 8. mitigate (paragraph 14)

    a. make less severe

    b. remove

    c. build up

    d. prolong

Word Parts

A REVIEW OF ROOTS AND PREFIXES

GEO means _earth_

DICT means _tell, say_

ANTI- means _against_

GRAPH means _write_

PRE- means _before_

DU- means _two_

PRO- means _for, in favor of_

DIS- means _apart, away, not_

CONTRO- means _against, opposite_

VERS means _turn_

Match each word in Column A with its meaning in Column B. Write your answers in the spaces provided.

Column A

_____ 1. geothermal

_____ 2. predicting

_____ 3. antifreeze

_____ 4. topography

_____ 5. duplicating

_____ 6. proponents

_____ 7. disincentives

_____ 8. controversial

Column B

a. the physical features of a place or region

b. causing public dispute or debate

c. saying what will happen in the future

d. having to do with the Earth's temperature

e. factors intended to discourage or deter certain actions

f. a substance that lowers the freezing point of a liquid

g. making two of; copying

h. those in favor of an idea

I. SELECTING A LEARNING/STUDY STRATEGY

Discuss methods of studying the outline shown on page 555 in preparation for an exam that covers this reading.

J. EXPLORING IDEAS THROUGH DISCUSSION AND WRITING

1. What did you already know about different types of renewable energy? Which of the ones described in the selection seemed most likely to become a reality? Explain your answer.

2. What are the pros and cons of tidal power? Write a summary based on the information in the selection.

3. Why do the authors call the current energy policy "business as usual" for the fossil fuel industries? What do they mean by their use of the word "stewardly"? Reread the last three paragraphs of the selection and discuss what the authors reveal about their feelings toward U.S. energy policy, climate change, and the future of the global environment.

K. BEYOND THE CLASSROOM TO THE WEB

Visit the U.S. Department of Energy's Office of Energy Efficiency and Renewable Energy (EERE) Web site at **http://www.eere.energy.gov/.** *After you have spent some time exploring different aspects of the site, write a paragraph explaining which of the clean energy technologies described on the site seem to you most likely to succeed and why.*

**TRACKING
YOUR
PROGRESS**

Selection 27

Section	Number Correct		Score
A. Thesis and Main Ideas (5 items)	_____	× 4	_____
B. Details (10 items)	_____	× 2	_____
C. Organization and Transitions (4 items)	_____	× 2	_____
F. Implied Meanings (6 items)	_____	× 2	_____
G. Thinking Critically (4 items)	_____	× 2	_____
H. Vocabulary			
Context (8 items)	_____	× 2	_____
Word Parts (8 items)	_____	× 2	_____
		TOTAL SCORE	_____ %

20

Career Fields

Opportunities in a variety of career fields are rapidly expanding; new fields are being created and many existing fields are showing increased demand for workers. As the workplace changes, workers are often asked to shift to new fields, requiring them to adapt, retrain, and acquire new or updated skills.

In addition to the health-related fields (see Chapter 17), growing fields include education, criminal justice, and travel and tourism. The readings in this chapter are representative of these three career fields. As you read "Lift the Cell Phone Ban," you will see how teachers are encouraged to adapt new technology, specifically cell phones, to enhance classroom learning. "The CSI Effect" addresses a phenomenon increasingly found in the criminal justice field—the carryover of television crime scene programming to real-life situations. While reading "The Restaurant Dining Experience," you will learn about why people dine out and the factors that influence customer decision making.

TIPS FOR READING IN CAREER FIELDS

■ **Pay attention to processes and procedures.** Many career fields involve completing a task, such as teaching a lesson, filing a crime report, or writing a restaurant menu. Usually there are written rules and/or unwritten expectations about how things are done. Notice details, sequence, and format.

■ **Learn the terminology that is introduced in your readings.** You will need to be able to speak and write the language of your field in order to communicate with co-workers. When reading "The CSI Effect" you will see terms such as *forensic evidence, reasonable doubt,* and *DNA tests,* for example.

■ **Read slowly and reread as needed**. Textbooks in many career fields are highly factual and packed with information. Do not expect to understand or remember everything with only one reading.

■ **Use visualization to create mental images or pictures.** As you read descriptions, such as that of tangible and intangible reasons for dining out in "The Restaurant Dining Experience," visualize examples in each category.

SELECTION 28

Lift the Cell Phone Ban
David Rapp

Contemporary Issues Reading

This article originally appeared in *Administr@tor,* a magazine for teachers and administrators. Read it to discover how some schools are experimenting with the use of cell phones in the classroom.

PREVIEWING THE READING

Using the steps listed on page 36, preview the reading selection. When you have finished, answer the following questions.

1. This selection is primarily about _____

   _____.

2. Based on the four boldfaced headings, list four topics that will be discussed in the reading. The first one is provided for you.

   a. Cell phones as a solution to classroom problems or issues

   b. _____

   c. _____

   d. _____

   _____

MAKING CONNECTIONS

Do any of your instructors have specific policies regarding cell phone use in your classes? Do you find these policies fair, or do you think they are too restrictive? Can you think of any instances where a cell phone might be useful in a particular class?

READING TIP

As you read, keep track of the pros and cons of cell phone usage in the classroom.

Lift the Cell Phone Ban

Stop thinking classroom disruption. Start thinking powerful (and free) teaching tool.

Cell phones could become the next big learning tool in the classroom. So why have schools been so slow to embrace them?

1   Without a doubt, cell phones can cause serious disruption in the classroom. From urgent text messages flying across the room to lessons interrupted by rap-song ring-tones, these gadgets are responsible for nationwide frustration among educators. And, in extreme cases, students have used their cell phones to cheat on tests and harass other students, even during class time. While such disturbances are certainly a nuisance in school, not all teachers see cell phones as the enemy. In fact, for some, they've become a teaching solution.

Cell Phone Solution

2   Between the alarms, calls, and text-messaging, it's easy to see why some class-rooms have implemented a no-cell phone policy. But educators know that with students, cell phone use is inevitable, so why not use the devices for good? Many schools in Asia and the United Kingdom—where they've been using high-speed 3G, or third-generation, cellular networks years longer than the United States—have already turned cell phones into teaching tools. Recently, several school districts in North America have done the same. At the Craik School in Saskatchewan, Canada, such an experiment turned into an integral part of the **curriculum**.

curriculum
program of
study

3   Craik's program started with a discussion in the staff room between the school's principal, Gord Taylor, and teacher Carla Dolman. Many of the children had received cell phones for Christmas, and the phones had become a distraction. "So we tossed out the idea of rather than looking at them as an evil thing," says Taylor, "that we look at them as a tool for learning." They realized that the text message and alarm functions would be useful for reminding students of homework assignments and tests, for example. They decided to run a pilot project with eighth and ninth graders.

Testing the Waters

4   Initially, only about 40 percent of the class had cell phones, but kids who had them were willing to share. The text message function was mainly used at first, but as Dolman became more familiar with the myriad functions, it became clear that these gadgets had a lot more classroom potential. Video and sound recording came into play, and the phones' Bluetooth networking capabilities allowed for easy information sharing. Dolman found they worked perfectly for her classes' "lit circles," in which the students divide into smaller groups to discuss different aspects of a particular book. Previously, she found it difficult to monitor each of the different groups simultaneously. But kids who had video functions on their phones could record their discussions then Bluetooth them to Dolman's phone, and she could watch each individual discussion, without missing a moment.

minimal
small in number

5   Dolman says such problems like class disruption were **minimal**. "It's a stereotype of teenagers—that you can't trust them with a cell phone. Our experience was that if you give them the opportunity to use them, and you give them guidelines to go with that use, you won't have problems."

6   Principal Taylor agrees. "The one thing we really stressed with the kids was the whole idea of appropriate use," he says. "They make darn sure that the volume is turned off. A lot of adults need to learn that."

7   As for the kids, they loved using the phones for class work, but parents in the district have had mixed reactions, says Taylor. "Some thought we were crazy, and were very strongly opposed to it, and some embraced the idea initially. As time went on, about 90 percent came to say it was a good idea. They didn't see it as a gadget, or as a replacement for learning, they saw it as a tool for learning."

8   Taylor's colleagues have been more enthusiastic. "In our school division there are about 90 principals and about 600 teachers, and I would say that out of the principals, there were about 15 to 20 that really were gung-ho and wanted to know what we were doing." The rest, Taylor says, thought the program was innovative and at least worth a try. "There were no negative thoughts on it whatsoever."

Learning Curves

9   Taylor sees the cell phone as a necessary tool to teach to kids. "We would be burying our heads in the sand if we said that cell phones were not a part of everyday life," he says. "I don't know a businessman out there who doesn't carry a cell phone. I don't know a lawyer or accountant out there who doesn't carry a cell phone. Why wouldn't we have them in schools?"

10   Given the example of the Craik School, why haven't more American teachers embraced cell phone use in the classroom? In fact, few U.S. schools are even considering their use. Liz Kolb, author of the recently released book *Toys to Tools: Connecting Student Cell Phones to Education* (ISTE, 2008), says that Americans have traditionally seen cell phones as nothing more than a social toy. "We hear stories about students using cell phones in negative ways, like posting videos of teachers to YouTube, or cheating via text messaging," she says.

11   Many teachers simply don't know the teaching potential cell phones have, Kolb says. "There are some teachers who have never sent a text message, so the fear of

inhibiting
preventing

their students knowing more than them about a tool in the classroom is often very **inhibiting**." Professional development, Kolb says, is a necessity for normalizing the idea of classroom cell phones.

Corporate Help

12   Matt Cook, a math and science teacher in the Keller Independent School District, near Fort Worth, Texas, knows his cell phone inside and out. He's used it to document results in his classroom. In fact, his familiarity with cell phone tech sparked his imagination, and led him to get in touch with Verizon and AT&T, as well as software company GoKnow, based in Ann Arbor, Michigan. All three companies have agreed to donate technology to the district for a pilot program to use cell phones in fifth-grade classrooms. (Other cell phone companies are certainly interested in classroom possibilities. Qualcomm has a similar program in the works called K-Nect.)

13   "I firmly believe that to prepare kids for their future, we need to start speaking the language of kids," says Cook. "They're using this stuff anyway—let's teach them how to use it productively."

14   The GoKnow software turns the students' smartphones into computers, allowing students to use word processors, spreadsheets, and art programs, among others, on their cell phones. For example, every child learns the concept of the water cycle: how water moves on, above, and below Earth's surface through the processes of evaporation, condensation, precipitation, and so on. With GoKnow's cell-based applications, a student could draw a concept map showing the relationship between the processes, create an animation illustrating how it all looks, and write up a text report on what they've learned—all centralized on a desktop-like interface on the smartphone's screen.

15   At the end of the day, the students can upload all their work online. "The kids sync their phone up to the server. The parents can look at the work they've done, and the teachers can make annotations and grade the work, all online," says Cook.

16   Elliot Soloway, founder of GoKnow, sees the key to popularizing cell phone use in classrooms is to make it easy to integrate into a school's existing curriculum. GoKnow's software has been engineered to make the process as easy as possible, he says. "We can do this in eight minutes with a teacher. Sit down with your paper-and-pencil lesson, and we're going to show you how to transform that lesson into a cell phone–based lesson you can integrate with your existing curriculum."

17   Soloway says that if the Keller program is successful, smartphones could become a part of the curriculum in neighboring districts. "We've talked to other districts in Texas that are watching," he says. If cell phones in classrooms do catch on, the schools would, in effect, be getting low-cost computers into their students' hands.

harness
capture and use

18   Dolman thinks that the possibilities for cell phones will only increase as kids become more familiar with the technology. "The more we discover what we can do with them, the more valuable they are. If you can **harness** what students are interested in, you have massive amounts of potential. And if you can get that into the classroom, you're set."

A. UNDERSTANDING THE THESIS AND OTHER MAIN IDEAS

Select the best answer.

_____ 1. The central thesis of the selection is that

    a. cell phones in the classroom are annoying and disruptive.

    b. today's students enjoy using modern technologies.

    c. teachers who use cell phones in the classroom help their school districts save money.

    d. cell phones can be an effective teaching and learning tool when used properly.

_____ 2. The author's primary purpose is to

    a. discourage instructors from allowing cell phone use in the classroom.

    b. open up the minds of teachers, parents, and school administrators to the idea of using cell phones in the classroom.

    c. emphasize the way cell phones can be used in science education.

    d. describe the differing attitudes between the U.S. and Canadian educational systems with regard to cell phones.

_____ 3. The main idea of paragraph 8 is

    a. Overall, Canadian educators are open to or enthusiastic about the idea of using cell phones in the classroom.

    b. In general, teachers are more interested in the classroom use of cell phones than administrators are.

    c. The majority of principals are highly interested in finding ways to use cell phones in education.

    d. A great deal of negativity surrounds the idea of using cell phones in the grammar school classroom.

_____ 4. The topic of paragraph 10 is

    a. Liz Kolb's book, *Toys to Tools.*

    b. social media sites such as YouTube and Facebook.

    c. U.S. schools' attitudes toward cell phones in the classroom.

    d. cheating that occurs through text messaging.

_____ 5. The main idea of paragraph 14 is

    a. the water cycle is best illustrated through animations viewed on a cell phone.

    b. cell phones are best used for creating concept maps.

    c. GoKnow software turns students' smartphones into computers.

    d. the screens of cell phones are the ideal size for educational applications.

B. IDENTIFYING DETAILS

Select the correct answer.

_____ 1. Which Canadian province is discussed in the reading?

a. Alberta

b. Quebec

c. Saskatchewan

d. British Columbia

_____ 2. The staff of the Craik School discovered that cell phones' alarm functions can be used to

a. remind students about tests and homework assignments.

b. ensure that students arrive to class on time.

c. time experiments during scientific lab classes.

d. count down the amount of time left during tests.

_____ 3. Which statement best summarizes the attitude of the parents whose children attend the Craik School?

a. The parents were extremely supportive of the idea of using cell phones when the idea was first suggested.

b. While early attitudes varied from skeptical to enthusiastic, as time went on the vast majority of parents came to embrace the idea of cell phones as learning tools.

c. Parents were open to the idea of using cell phones in the classroom as long as companies such as GoKnow paid the associated costs.

d. The parents originally supported the idea of using cell phones for education, but have come to see the technology primarily as a "toy" used for socializing.

_____ 4. Which of the following companies did not donate technology to the Keller Independent School District in Fort Worth, Texas?

a. AT&T

b. Verizon

c. GoKnow

d. Qualcomm

_____ 5. Which of the following people does not work for a school district?

a. Carla Dolman

b. Gord Taylor

c. Elliot Soloway

d. Matt Cook

_____ 6. According to Liz Kolb, which factor is critical in helping U.S. teachers adjust to the idea of using cell phones in the classroom?

   a. professional development

   b. financial incentives

   c. free software donated by local companies

   d. parental support

C. RECOGNIZING METHODS OF ORGANIZATION AND TRANSITIONS

Select the best answer.

_____ 1. The reading examines educational practices in two countries, Canada and the United States, and finds that U.S. teachers tend to be less open to the idea of using cell phones as educational tools. For this reason, we might say one pattern of organization used in the reading is

   a. definition.

   b. comparison and contrast.

   c. spatial order.

   d. order of importance.

_____ 2. The transitional word or phrase used to signal the statement-and-clarification pattern in paragraph 1 is

   a. without a doubt.

   b. in extreme cases.

   c. for some.

   d. in fact.

D. REVIEWING AND ORGANIZING IDEAS

Complete the following outline of the reading by filling in the missing words and phrases.

Lift the Cell Phone Ban

A. Cell Phone Solution

   1. Reasons for no-cell-phone policy: alarms, calls, _____

   2. Some North American educators have begun using cell phones as teaching tools.

      Example: _____ in Saskatchewan, Canada

B. Testing the Waters

   1. At first only _____ % of students had cell phones, but students were willing to share

2. At first, _____ were the key function used

3. Later, _____ came into play

4. Teacher Dolman's experience: Few disruptions if students are given _____ for cell phone use

5. Parental reactions: At first _____, later more enthusiastic

6. Educator reactions: Very _____

C. _____

1. U.S. teachers don't embrace cell phones in classrooms because they see cell phones as _____

2. Many teachers don't understand the teaching potential of cell phones or have very little _____ with using cell phones

D. Corporate Help

1. Matt Cook got three companies to donate technology for a pilot program: _____, _____, and GoKnow

2. GoKnow software turns smartphones into _____ and allows students to upload their work online

3. Elliot Soloway believes that the key to successful cell phone use is _____ with the curriculum

E. READING AND THINKING VISUALLY

Select the best answer.

_____ 1. The author most likely chose to include the illustration shown on page 563 in order to
   a. stress that cell phones are an extremely common technology.
   b. illustrate the many education-based applications of cell phones.
   c. suggest that cell phones are a better choice than computers for the classroom.
   d. show the basic configuration of most cell phones.

_____ 2. Look closely at the illustration on page 563. Which of the following academic subjects or disciplines is not represented by the icons that appear alongside the cell phone?
   a. geography   c. psychology
   b. art   d. film making

F. FIGURING OUT IMPLIED MEANINGS

Indicate whether each statement is true (T) or false (F).

_____ 1. In general, cellular networks are more developed in Europe and Asia than they are in the United States.

_____ 2. Instructors have found that students are usually unwilling to share their cell phones with students who don't own cell phones of their own.

_____ 3. Principal Taylor implies that adults are just as guilty of rude cell phone use as students are.

_____ 4. The "lit circles" discussed in paragraph 4 were most likely part of a science class.

_____ 5. The title of the reading makes it clear that the author favors the use of cell phones in the classroom.

_____ 6 In general, the author believes that students cannot be trusted to use cell phones in an ethical and responsible manner.

_____ 7. Teachers can be trained to use GoKnow software in just a few minutes.

G. THINKING CRITICALLY

Select the best answer.

_____ 1. The tone of the reading can best be described as
   a. angry.
   b. optimistic.
   c. humorous.
   d. sarcastic.

_____ 2. A *rhetorical question* is a question a writer or speaker asks directly, often as a starting point for a discussion. Which of the following rhetorical questions is not found in the reading?
   a. So why have schools been slow to embrace them?
   b. But educators know that with students, cell phone use is inevitable, so why not use the devices for good?
   c. Why have parents in the United States been so unwilling to support the use of cell phones in the classroom?
   d. Given the example of the Craik School, why haven't more American teachers embraced cell phone use in the classroom?

_____ 3. What is a "lit circle" (paragraph 4)?
   a. a study group that meets at night
   b. a mathematical concept

c. a literary discussion group

d. an iPhone application

_____ 4. According to the reading, what is the primary purpose of Bluetooth technology?

a. tutoring in grammar and writing

b. networking and information sharing

c. simulating scientific phenomena

d. socializing and interpersonal communication

_____ 5. What does the author mean by the phrase *social toy* in paragraph 10?

a. communication device

b. overpriced electronic assistant

c. access point for entry into MySpace or Facebook

d. device used primarily for socializing rather than study or work

_____ 6. Liz Kolb implies that U.S. teachers do not want to use cell phones in the classroom as a result of

a. their own insecurities.

b. research suggesting that cell phones are not effective learning tools.

c. a sense of competition with Canadian teachers.

d. a fear of modern technology.

_____ 7. The author ends the reading with a(n)

a. fact.

b. statistic.

c. informed opinion.

d. example based on the author's experience.

H. BUILDING VOCABULARY

Context

Using context and a dictionary, if necessary, determine the meaning of each word as it is used in the selection.

_____ 1. nuisance (paragraph 1)

a. annoyance

b. forbidden item

c. highlight

d. noise

_____ 2. integral (paragraph 2)

    a. mathematical

    b. expensive

    c. essential

    d. technological

_____ 3. myriad (paragraph 4)

    a. complicated

    b. advanced

    c. multimedia

    d. many

_____ 4. colleagues (paragraph 8)

    a. students

    b. bosses

    c. co-workers

    d. principals

Word Parts

> **A REVIEW OF PREFIXES AND SUFFIXES**
>
> **-IZE** means *to make*
>
> **TRANS-** means *to change substantially*

Use your knowledge of word parts and the review above to fill in the blanks in the following sentences.

1. To *popularize* (paragraph 16) cell phone use in classrooms is to _____ cell phone use popular.

2. To *transform* (paragraph 16) a paper-and-pencil lesson into a cell-phone-based lesson is to _____ its format drastically from one based on paper to one based on technology.

Unusual Words/Understanding Idioms

Use the meanings given below to write a sentence using the boldfaced word or phrase.

1. To be **gung-ho** (paragraph 8) about something is to be very enthusiastic about it.

    Your sentence: _____

    _____

2. To **bury your head in the sand** (paragraph 9) is to deny reality.

Your sentence: _____

_____

3. A **pilot program** (paragraph 12) is a program that is being run on an experimental basis.

Your sentence: _____

_____

I. SELECTING A LEARNING/STUDY STRATEGY

_____ 1. In preparing for an class discussion based on this article, it would be most helpful to

a. reread it several times.

b. write a detailed outline

c. draw a map

d. write a list of questions and reactions

_____ 2. Which of the following would be the most likely essay exam question based on this article?

a. Compare and contrast cell phones and laptops as effective teaching tools.

b. Explain how and why cell phones are effective teaching tools

c. Justify distributing cell phones to all students who cannot afford them

d. Explain why the use of cell phones are often discouraged.

J. EXPLORING IDEAS THROUGH DISCUSSION AND WRITING

1. Describe an experience in which one of your instructors reacted to a student using a cell phone in class. How did your instructor handle the situation? What would you have done differently, if anything?

2. The reading specifies scientific simulations of the water cycle (paragraph 14) as one application that can be viewed on a cell phone. Alone or with a group, come up with a list of at least three additional suggestions for using cell phones in your college classes. For each suggestion, specify the course in which you would use it.

K. BEYOND THE CLASSROOM TO THE WEB

In many areas, cell phones are evolving into multimedia mini-computers that allow users not only to make phone calls, but also to surf the Web, make movies, and find their way around a city through satellite technology. These capabilities are made possible by computer applications, sometimes called "apps." Look at your cell phone provider's Web site and list three or four apps you find interesting and applicable to your college courses. Briefly describe how each works and what its benefits would be. If you don't own a cell phone, do a Web search for Apple's iPhone and describe some of its available apps.

**TRACKING
YOUR
PROGRESS**

Selection 28

Section	Number Correct	Score
A. Thesis and Main Ideas (5 items)	_____ × 4	_____
B. Details (6 items)	_____ × 4	_____
C. Organization and Transitions (2 items)	_____ × 2	_____
E. Reading and Thinking Visually (2 items)	_____ × 3	_____
F. Implied Meanings (7 items)	_____ × 2	_____
G. Thinking Critically (7 items)	_____ × 2	_____
H. Vocabulary		
Context (4 items)	_____ × 3	_____
Word Parts (2 items)	_____ × 3	_____
	TOTAL SCORE	_____%

SELECTION
29

The CSI Effect

Contemporary
Issues Reading

This reading appeared in *The Economist,* a highly respected international magazine known for its analysis of current issues. Read it to discover how television affects reality.

PREVIEWING THE READING

Using the steps listed on page 36, preview the reading selection. When you have finished, complete the following items.

1. The selection is about how the television drama _____

   _____.

2. List three questions you should be able to answer after reading the article.

   a. _____

   b. _____

   c. _____

MAKING CONNECTIONS

Do you watch any of the CSI *television shows? If so, which are your favorites? Why? Has watching these shows spurred your interest in forensic techniques and evidence?*

READING TIP

The selection's title may lead you to think you will be reading about a TV show, but you will actually be reading an article that is quite scientific and legal. Because the article summarizes research, keep track of the key conclusions reached by each researcher. These are the selection's main ideas.

The CSI Effect

Television dramas that rely on forensic science to solve crimes are affecting the administration of justice

forensic science
the application of scientific methods to investigate crime

What Is the "CSI Effect"?

1   Opening a new training centre in **forensic science** (see photo on p. 576) at the University of Glamorgan in South Wales recently, Bernard Knight, formerly one of

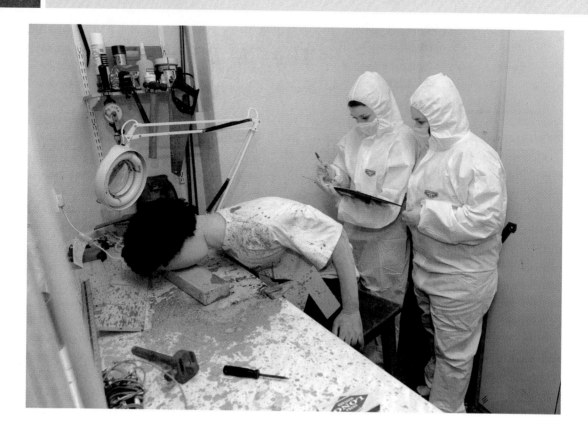

Britain's chief pathologists, said that because of television crime dramas, jurors today expect more categorical proof than forensic science is capable of delivering. And when it comes to the gulf between reality and fiction, Dr. Knight knows what he is talking about: besides 43 years' experience of attending crime scenes, he has also written dozens of crime novels.

2 The upshot of this is that a new phrase has entered the criminological lexicon: the "CSI effect," named for such TV shows as *CSI: Crime Scene Investigation.* In 2008 Monica Robbers, an American criminologist, defined it as "the phenomenon in which jurors hold unrealistic expectations of forensic evidence and investigation techniques, and have an increased interest in the discipline of forensic science."

3 Now another American researcher has demonstrated that the CSI effect is indeed real. Evan Durnal of the University of Central Missouri's Criminal Justice Department has collected evidence from a number of studies to show that exposure to television drama series that focus on forensic science has altered the American legal system in complex and far-reaching ways. His conclusions have just been published in *Forensic Science International.*

4 The most obvious symptom of the CSI effect is that jurors think they have a thorough understanding of science they have seen presented on television, when they do not. Mr. Durnal cites one case of jurors in a murder trial who, having noticed that a bloody coat introduced as evidence had not been tested for DNA, brought

this fact to the judge's attention. Since the defendant had admitted being present at the murder scene, such tests would have thrown no light on the identity of the true culprit. The judge observed that, thanks to television, jurors knew what DNA tests could do, but not when it was appropriate to use them.

Cops and Robbers: Results of the CSI Effect

5   The task of keeping jurors' feet on the ground falls to lawyers and judges. In one study, carried out by Dr. Robbers in 2008, 62% of defense lawyers and 69% of judges agreed that jurors had unrealistic expectations of forensic evidence. Around half of respondents in each category also felt that jury selection was taking longer than it used to, because they had to be sure that prospective jurors were not judging scientific evidence by television standards.

6   According to Mr. Durnal, prosecutors in the United States are now spending much more time explaining to juries why certain kinds of evidence are not relevant. Prosecutors have even introduced a new kind of witness—a "negative evidence" witness—to explain that investigators often fail to find evidence at a crime scene.

7   Defense lawyers, too, are finding that their lives have become more complicated. On the positive side, they can benefit from jurors' misguided notion that science solves crimes, and hence that the absence of crime-solving scientific evidence constitutes a reasonable doubt and grounds for acquittal. On the other hand, they also find themselves at pains to explain that one of television's fictional devices—an unequivocal match between a trace of a substance found at a crime scene and an **exemplar** stored in a database, whether it be fingerprints, DNA, or some other kind of evidence—is indeed generally just fiction.

exemplar
a typical example

8   In reality, scientists do not deal in certainty but in probabilities, and the way they calculate these probabilities is complex. For example, when testifying in court, a fingerprint expert may say that there is a 90% chance of obtaining a match if the defendant left the mark, and a one in several billion chance of a match if someone else left it. In general, DNA provides information of a higher quality or "individualizing potential" than other kinds of evidence, so that experts may be more confident of linking it to a specific individual. But DNA experts still deal in probabilities and not certainties. As a result of all this reality checking, trials are getting longer and more cases that might previously have resulted in quick convictions are now ending in acquittals.

The Guilty and the Innocent

9   Criminals watch television too, and there is evidence they are also changing their behavior. Most of the techniques used in crime shows are, after all, at least grounded in truth. Bleach, which destroys DNA, is now more likely to be used by murderers to cover their tracks. The wearing of gloves is more common, as is the taping shut—rather than the DNA-laden licking—of envelopes. Investigators comb crime scenes ever more finely for new kinds of evidence, which is creating problems with the tracking and storage of evidence, so that even as the criminals leave fewer traces of themselves behind, a backlog of cold-case evidence is building up.

10   The CSI effect can also be positive, however. In one case in Virginia, jurors asked the judge if a cigarette butt had been tested for possible DNA matches to the defendant in a murder trial. It had, but the defense lawyers had failed to introduce the DNA test results as evidence. When they did, those results exonerated the defendant, who was acquitted.

11   Mr. Durnal does not blame the makers of the television shows for the phenomenon, because they have never claimed their shows are completely accurate. (Forensic scientists do not usually wield guns or arrest people, for one thing, and tests that take minutes on television may take weeks to process in real life.) He argues that the CSI effect is born of a longing to believe that desirable, clever, and morally **unimpeachable** individuals are fighting to clear the names of the innocent and put the bad guys behind bars. In that respect, unfortunately, life does not always imitate art.

unimpeachable
completely
trustworthy and
reliable

A. UNDERSTANDING THE THESIS AND OTHER MAIN IDEAS

Select the best answer.

_____ 1. The central thesis of the selection is that
   a. criminals are becoming more aware of forensic techniques.
   b. the *CSI* television shows are affecting the administration of justice.
   c. forensic evidence makes acquittals more likely.
   d. trials are now taking longer due to huge amounts of forensic evidence.

_____ 2. The author's primary purpose is to
   a. argue for more funding for forensic labs in large urban areas.
   b. combat the idea that watching TV adequately prepares people to serve on a jury.
   c. explain what the CSI effect is and how it is affecting trials.
   d. describe the latest forensic techniques.

_____ 3. The main idea of paragraph 7 is
   a. the CSI effect has complicated the jobs of criminal defense attorneys.
   b. lawyers are now more likely to use forensic evidence than they used to be.
   c. much of the evidence presented in trials shown on television is fraudulent.
   d. defense lawyers now have a much easier time getting their clients acquitted.

_____ 4. The main idea of paragraph 8 is
   a. fingerprints are not always reliable evidence.
   b. trials are now longer than they used to be.

c. scientists do not deal in certainty but rather in probabilities, and the calculations for these probabilities are complex.

d. as a result of advanced DNA-profiling techniques, criminals are now more likely to be convicted than acquitted.

_____ 5. The topic of paragraph 9 is

a. criminals and the crimes they commit.

b. bleach and tape.

c. the tracking and storage of evidence.

d. changes in criminals' behavior as a result of the CSI effect.

_____ 6. Which of the following conclusions about the CSI effect is *not* supported by the reading?

a. As a result of the CSI effect, jurors now hold unrealistic expectations regarding forensic evidence.

b. The CSI effect has had many more positive effects than negative effects.

c. The task of countering the CSI effect falls to judges and lawyers.

d. As a result of the CSI effect, criminals are becoming more cautious about the types of evidence they leave behind.

B. IDENTIFYING DETAILS

Select the best answer.

_____ 1. Which of the following experts is not discussed in the selection?

a. Bernard Knight

b. Evan Durnal

c. Monica Robbers

d. Lee Child

_____ 2. The evidence presented at the trial described in paragraph 4 was a

a. bloody coat.

b. fingerprint.

c. licked envelope.

d. light bulb.

_____ 3. A new type of witness now called to testify as a result of the CSI effect is the

a. expert witness.

b. witness for the prosecution.

c. negative evidence witness.

d. forensic witness.

_____ 4. Which technique is *not* listed in the reading as an example of the way today's criminals are changing their behavior as a result of the CSI effect?

    a. They are using bleach to cover their tracks.

    b. They wear gloves more often.

    c. They wear caps to prevent leaving hair samples behind.

    d. They tape envelopes shut instead of licking them.

_____ 5. In the Virginia case in which a defendant was acquitted, what piece of evidence led to the acquittal?

    a. a fingerprint

    b. a bloody coat

    c. an envelope

    d. a cigarette butt

_____ 6. CSI stands for

    a. contemporary standards of intelligence.

    b. crime scene investigation.

    c. criminal systems interaction.

    d. classic sensory improvement.

C. RECOGNIZING METHODS OF ORGANIZATION AND TRANSITIONS

Select the best answer.

_____ 1. The title of the reading gives a hint regarding the reading's overall organizational pattern, which is

    a. cause and effect.

    b. order of importance.

    c. spatial order.

    d. comparison and contrast.

_____ 2. The reading makes use of all of the following organizational patterns and devices *except*

    a. listing/enumeration.

    b. examples.

    c. definition.

    d. spatial order.

_____ 3. The transitional word or phrase used in paragraph 2 to introduce the meaning of "CSI effect" is

    a. has entered.

    b. defined.

    c. hold.

    d. increased interest.

D. REVIEWING AND ORGANIZING IDEAS: OUTLINING

Complete the following outline of the selection by filling in the missing words and phrases.

I. What Is the CSI Effect?

    A. Bernard Knight: _____

        _____

    B. Monica Robbers coins phrase: _____

    C. _____: Summarizes studies showing CSI effect in America is real and far-reaching

        1. Example: bloody coat in Virginia; _____

        _____

II. Cops and Robbers: Results of the CSI Effect

    A. _____: responsible for teaching jurors about forensic evidence

    B. Prosecutors

        1. Spend more time explaining _____

        2. New type of witness: _____

    C. Defense Lawyers

        Pro: _____

        Con: _____

III. The Guilty and the Innocent

    A. Criminals change their behavior

        1. Use _____ to cover their tracks

        2. Wear _____

        3. _____

    B. Durnal's conclusion: _____

E. READING AND THINKING VISUALLY

Select the best answer.

_____ 1. Look closely at the photo on page 576. What is happening in the photo?

    a. Paramedics are learning CPR techniques.

    b. Researchers are re-creating a crime scene.

       c. Medical students are performing an analysis of the victim's blood type.

       d. Police officers are taking part in a simulation of a crime at the police academy.

_____ 2. The photo was taken in a

       a. garage.

       b. basement.

       c. attic.

       d. forensics lab.

_____ 3. The women in the photo are wearing plastic suits because

       a. they are ill and do not want to spread germs.

       b. they work in the sterilized "clean room" of an electronics factory.

       c. they must cover their bodies to prevent contaminating the scene.

       d. they wish to remain anonymous.

F. FIGURING OUT IMPLIED MEANINGS

Indicate whether each statement is true (T) or false (F).

_____ 1. South Wales is located in Great Britain.

_____ 2. In the last paragraph, the author implies that the CSI effect is the result of people's desire to see justice done.

_____ 3. Forensic scientists play the same role as police officers and detectives in the criminal justice system.

_____ 4. It is rare to find an exact match between an existing database and the trace of a substance at a crime scene.

_____ 5. The evidence collected by Evan Durnal focused on the CSI effect in the United States.

_____ 6. The author implies that the producers of *CSI*-type television shows are deliberately trying to mislead TV viewers.

_____ 7. TV shows often "speed up" processes that take much longer in the real world.

G. THINKING CRITICALLY

Select the best answer.

_____ 1. The tone of the reading can best be described as

       a. upset.

       b. enthusiastic.

    c. terrified.

    d. factual.

_____ 2. All of the following statements from the reading are facts *except*

    a. The task of keeping jurors' feet on the ground falls to lawyers and judges.

    b. [P]rosecutors in the United States are now spending much more time explaining to juries why certain kinds of evidence are not relevant.

    c. In reality, scientists do not deal in certainty but in probabilities.

    d. [Mr. Durnal] argues that the CSI effect is born of a longing to believe that desirable, clever, and morally unimpeachable individuals are fighting to clear the names of the innocent.

_____ 3. Which type of evidence is not used in the reading?

    a. expert opinion

    b. statistical data

    c. the author's personal experience

    d. quotations

_____ 4. Which heading in the reading contains a *pun,* which is a joke exploiting the different possible meanings of words that sound alike but have different meanings?

    a. The CSI Effect

    b. What Is the CSI Effect?

    c. Cops and Robbers: The Results of the CSI Effect

    d. The Guilty and the Innocent

_____ 5. The author closes the article by saying "life does not always imitate art." He means that

    a. fiction does not always reflect reality.

    b. real life is much uglier than artistic beauty.

    c. the best TV shows are also the most realistic.

    d. the criminal justice system is imperfect and unreliable.

_____ 6. In paragraph 8, the author notes that trials are getting longer. What is the most likely result of longer trials?

    a. increased funding for forensic research

    b. higher costs that must be borne by taxpayers

    c. the greater likelihood that a convicted criminal will get the death sentence

    d. an increase in the number of students attending medical school

H. BUILDING VOCABULARY

Context

Using context and a dictionary, if necessary, determine the meaning of each word as it is used in the selection.

_____ 1. fiction (paragraph 1)
   a. an unbelievable situation
   b. a true happening
   c. an imagined event
   d. a narrative

_____ 2. categorical (paragraph 1)
   a. definite
   b. classified
   c. nuanced
   d. medical

_____ 3. upshot (paragraph 2)
   a. murder
   b. crime
   c. cause
   d. result

_____ 4. prospective (paragraph 5)
   a. viewpoint
   b. potential
   c. biased
   d. unusual

_____ 5. laden (paragraph 9)
   a. invisible
   b. explosive
   c. loaded
   d. guilty

Word Parts

> ### A REVIEW OF PREFIXES, SUFFIXES, AND ROOTS
> **LEXIS** means *all the words in a language*
> **MIS-** means *wrong*
> **-IST** means *one who*

Use your knowledge of word parts and the review above to fill in the blanks in the following sentences.

1. *Pathos* means "suffering" and *ology* means "the study of," so a *pathologist* (paragraph 1) is _____.

2. A *lexicon* (paragraph 2) is a _____, a book listing words and their meanings.

3. A *misguided* notion (paragraph 7) is incorrect or _____.

Unusual Words/Understanding Idioms

Use the meanings given below to write a sentence using the boldfaced word or phrase.

1. To **comb** a crime scene (paragraph 9) is to search through it very carefully and systematically.

   Your sentence: _____

   _____

2. A **cold case** (paragraph 9) is a police investigation that was never solved.

   Your sentence: _____

   _____

I. SELECTING A LEARNING/STUDY STRATEGY

Discuss methods of studying the outline shown on page 581 in preparation for an exam that covers this reading.

J. EXPLORING IDEAS THROUGH DISCUSSION AND WRITING

1. Choose a television show that you watch regularly. In what ways is it realistic? In what ways is it unrealistic?

2. The reading lists several possible positive and negative results of the CSI effect. Can you think of any others?

3. Does your school offer any forensics-oriented courses, such as forensic chemistry or forensic psychology? (Consult your school's Web site or course catalog.) What is taught in each course? Would you have any interest in taking any of these courses?

4. Have you ever served on a jury? If so, describe the experience. Was it interesting, boring, provocative? What kinds of evidence did the prosecutor present, and was the evidence convincing? If you haven't served on a jury, suppose you are serving at a murder trial. What kinds of evidence would you need to see in order to find the defendant guilty?

K. BEYOND THE CLASSROOM TO THE WEB

Visit http://www.exploreforensics.co.uk/TypesofForensicsCategory.html, *which lists many careers in forensics, from computer forensics through forensic dentistry. Read through the descriptions. Which is most appealing to you? If you had to choose a career in one of these areas, which would you choose and why?*

Now visit http://www.exploreforensics.co.uk/AnalysingEvidenceCategory.html, *which explains the various types of forensic evidence. Read through the pages that interest you and list at least five facts about forensic evidence that you did not know.*

TRACKING YOUR PROGRESS

Selection 29

Section	Number Correct		Score
A. Thesis and Main Ideas (6 items)	_____	× 3	_____
B. Details (6 items)	_____	× 2	_____
C. Organization and Transitions (3 items)	_____	× 2	_____
E. Reading and Thinking Visually (3 items)	_____	× 3	_____
F. Implied Meanings (7 items)	_____	× 3	_____
G. Thinking Critically (6 items)	_____	× 3	_____
H. Vocabulary			
Context (5 items)	_____	× 2	_____
Word Parts (3 items)	_____	× 2	_____
	TOTAL SCORE		_____ %

SELECTION 30

The Restaurant Dining Experience

John R. Walker

Contemporary
Issues Reading

The following selection is taken from a textbook for those pursuing careers in the hospitality industry. Read it to learn about the different types of restaurants and understand the factors that motivate people to choose one restaurant over another.

PREVIEWING THE READING

Using the steps listed on page 36, preview the reading selection. When you have finished, complete the following items.

1. The selection is about _____.

2. List four questions you should be able to answer after reading the selection.

    a. _____

    b. _____

    c. _____

    d. _____

MAKING CONNECTIONS

What is your favorite place to eat away from home? What makes you go back to that place? Is it the food, price, service, atmosphere, or a combination of factors?

READING TIP

This selection makes use of many rhetorical questions—the author asks a series of questions and then answers them. As you read, use your own dining experiences to answer the questions posed by the author. Doing so will make the reading more enjoyable and interactive.

The Restaurant Dining Experience

1   The National Restaurant Association's figures indicate that Americans are spending an increasing number of food dollars away from home at various food-service operations. Americans are eating out more than ever—up to five times a

week—and on special occasions such as birthdays, anniversaries, Mother's Day, and Valentine's Day. The most popular meal eaten away from home is lunch, which brings in approximately 50 percent of fast-food restaurant sales. Restaurants fall into two general categories: individual restaurants and chain restaurants.

2   **Individual restaurants** (also called indies) are typically owned by one or more owners, who are usually involved in the day-to-day operation of the business. Even if the owners have more than one store (restaurant-speak for a "restaurant"), each usually functions independently. These restaurants are not affiliated with any national brand or name. They offer the owner independence, creativity, and flexibility, but are generally accompanied by more risk. For example, the restaurant may not be as popular as the owners hoped it would be, or the owners lacked the knowledge and expertise necessary for success in the restaurant business, or the owners did not have the cash flow to last several months before a profit could be made. You only have to look around your neighborhood to find examples of restaurants that failed for one reason or another.

franchised
owned
independently
as part of a
larger chain of
restaurants

3   **Chain restaurants** are a group of restaurants, each identical in market, concept, design, service, food, and name. Part of the marketing strategy of a chain restaurant is to remove uncertainty from the dining experience. The same menu, food quality, level of service, and atmosphere can be found in any one of the restaurants, regardless of location. Large companies or entrepreneurs are likely chain restaurant owners. For example, Applebee's is a restaurant chain; some stories are company owned but the majority are **franchised** by territory.

4   But what makes people choose one restaurant over another? Many factors are involved, as William Martin, a professor at Cal Tech-Monterey Bay, writes in the following article.

A couple dinning *al fresco* at a Greek taverna.

Restaurant Operations: The Challenge of the Intangibles

5   Does this situation sound familiar? You are sitting at home (studying, of course) and a friend or relative suggests that you should go out for dinner. That sounds good to you, so you say, "Okay." That is the easy part. Next comes the more difficult part. Where should you go? And so you ask, "Where do you want to go?" Your friend (or relative) responds, "I don't know. Where do you want to go?" And so it goes, back and forth until finally you arrive at a decision as to where you will go. Some time later, you arrive at your chosen destination. You experience whatever the restaurant has to offer. Afterward, consciously or unconsciously, you decide whether you will return to that particular restaurant.

6   As we can see from this common scenario, from a customer's point of view, dining out involves three critical questions: (1) To eat out or not? (2) Where to go? and (3) Whether to return? Let's take a closer look at typical restaurant consumer responses to each of these questions and see what we can learn.

To Eat Out or Not?

7   Why do people choose to dine out? What are the reasons? Multiple consumer surveys over the years have consistently reflected the following reasons. The rank order of importance may vary from survey to survey, but the reasons, themselves, remain fairly constant. The top ten reasons consumers tend to dine out in a full-service restaurant include to celebrate a special occasion, relax, avoid cooking, have a family night out, be waited on, enjoy the atmosphere, enjoy a familiar place, have menu choices, meet friends, and try foods not eaten at home.

8   The reasons consumers tend to dine out in a fast-food restaurant are surprisingly similar with two variations: to eat inexpensively and to eat quickly. All the other reasons for dining at a full-service restaurant are also cited for dining at a fast-food restaurant.

9   Now, let's take a minute and look carefully at this list of reasons for dining out—whether fast food or full service. What *don't* you see on this list? What is missing? What is missing is that the reason for dining out is "to eat." What does this tell us? What it tells us is that people choose to dine out for lots of reasons in addition to the need to eat. Eating comes along with the experience, but the choice to dine out in the first place is made for more complicated reasons—most of which are psychological and social reasons: to celebrate, to meet friends, to enjoy, to experience something new, to relax, and so forth.

10   How can we interpret this? What can we learn? First, we have to distinguish between tangibles and intangibles because in the restaurant business we deal with both, and both are very important to our success. *Tangibles* are those things that can be seen, smelled, touched, poked, prodded, weighed, or otherwise physically inspected. Food, of course, fits into this category. *Intangibles,* on the other hand, can't be so easily weighed and measured. They deal with human characteristics such as emotions, physiological states of mind, and sociological and cultural influences. They are indeed varied and complex—and often elusive because we can't inspect them, touch them, or smell them to know whether they are "right" or "wrong." Now here's the punch line: *The reasons that people decide whether or not to dine out are predominantly intangible in nature.* As you can see from the list, the reasons tend to be primarily psychologically and sociologically based.

Where to Go?

11   You have decided to go out. Now, how do you choose a restaurant? How it looks? Type of food? Location? The amount of money in your pocket (or purse)? Reputation? A recommendation? An advertisement? The answer is probably any one, all, or a combination of the preceding. If you have been to a restaurant before, you may choose to return for a combination of liking the food, the ambience, the value (what you get for your money), and the service. Choosing a restaurant for the first

12   time usually involves a different set of criteria, which usually includes type of food, location, and perceived pricing.

Whereas the reasons for choosing a particular restaurant are varied and complex, the type of *food* desired plays an important role, if not *the* role, in making a choice. Whether it is fast food or full service, we tend to choose a particular restaurant because we want to eat the style or type of food that the restaurant serves.

Whether to Return?

13   So, you have made a choice of where to eat. Among other factors, the type of food that is served has attracted you. Now, what determines whether you will return—or not?

14   Think about the last time you went out to eat in a restaurant. Once there, what happened? Was it a positive experience? How was the food? The service? The ambience? Did you have a good time? Would you go back? Why or why not?

15   If you had a bad or disappointing food experience, most likely you would tend not to go back. No doubt about it, food is a critical factor. But, there is more—much more. Let's go back to those *intangibles* that have influenced your decision to dine out in the first place. The decision to return is greatly influenced by how well your intangible expectations were met. Did you have a good time? Did you enjoy yourself? Were you treated well? These are questions that go way beyond food. They address your *total dining experience.* Simply put, when that *total* experience is positive, you tend to return. When it is not, you don't.

16   In short, a restaurant is much more than about food. Restaurant success is about creating a total positive atmosphere and dining experience.

17   We have addressed three questions: To eat out or not? Where to go? And whether to return? In two of the three questions, intangibles remain *the* critical decisive factor. That is why in the restaurant business managing the intangibles is just as important as managing the tangibles. As you can readily see, in the restaurant business it's the intangibles that can make or break you.

A. UNDERSTANDING THE THESIS AND OTHER MAIN IDEAS

Select the best answer.

_____ 1. The central thesis of the selection is that

a. intangibles matter more than tangibles when people are choosing a fine restaurant, but the opposite is true when people are choosing a casual restaurant.

b. intangibles are more important in individual restaurants than in chain restaurants.

    c. in both individual and chain restaurants, managers must pay careful attention to both the tangibles and intangibles.

    d. "eating" is the least common reason given for the desire to visit a restaurant.

_____ 2. The author's main purpose in the selection is to

    a. describe the differences between chain restaurants and independent restaurants.

    b. explain the three questions that people consciously ask themselves when they are trying to decide whether to go out for a meal.

    c. provide future restaurant managers with an overview of the restaurant industry and the necessary ingredients for restaurant success.

    d. discuss the reasons people prefer fast food to fine dining at lunchtime.

_____ 3. The topic of paragraph 2 is

    a. national brands.

    b. individual restaurants.

    c. failed restaurants.

    d. restaurant owners.

_____ 4. The main idea of paragraph 12 is

    a. the reasons for choosing a restaurant are complex.

    b. food plays an important role in the choice of a restaurant.

    c. it is difficult to measure intangibles accurately.

    d. tangibles are more easily measured in fast-food restaurants.

_____ 5. Which of the following is *not* an example of a tangible?

    a. portion size

    b. the smells coming from the restaurant's kitchen

    c. the desire to feel welcome at a local eatery

    d. the cleanliness of the restaurant's bathrooms

_____ 6. The reasons that people decide whether or not to dine out are primarily based on

    a. their need to eat and the size of their appetite.

    b. income and budgetary factors.

    c. their ability to juggle the demands of home and work.

    d. sociological and psychological factors.

B. IDENTIFYING DETAILS

Select the best answer.

_____ 1. In the context of this reading, *store* is a synonym for
   a. restaurant.
   b. food court in a mall.
   c. retail establishment.
   d. tangible.

_____ 2. In a restaurant chain, all the stores have the following elements in common *except*
   a. atmosphere.
   b. food quality.
   c. prices of menu items.
   d. level of service.

_____ 3. Most people who go to fast-food restaurants such as McDonald's desire to eat
   a. small portions of healthy foods.
   b. a meal with a significant amount of protein.
   c. quickly and inexpensively.
   d. in a local establishment close to their place of employment.

_____ 4. The term that the author uses to describe whether or not a person's tangible and intangible needs were met by eating at a particular restaurant is
   a. critical decisive factor.
   b. ambience.
   c. marketing strategy.
   d. total dining experience.

_____ 5. Which of the following is *not* one of the top ten reasons consumers choose to dine out in a full-service restaurant?
   a. to be waited on
   b. to eat
   c. to try food not eaten at home
   d. to meet friends

_____ 6. About half of all the meals eaten out are
   a. breakfasts.
   b. lunches.
   c. brunches.
   d. dinners.

_____ 7. In the box titled "Restaurant Operations: The Challenge of the Intangibles," which question does Professor Martin *not* discuss in detail?

    a. To eat out or not?

    b. How much to spend?

    c. Where to go?

    d. Whether to return?

C. RECOGNIZING METHODS OF ORGANIZATION AND TRANSITIONS

Select the best answer.

_____ 1. The overall organizational pattern used in paragraphs 1–3 is

    a. order of importance.

    b. spatial order.

    c. cause and effect.

    d. classification.

_____ 2. The transitional word or phrase used in paragraph 1 to signify the organizational pattern of the first part of the selection is

    a. figures.   c. popular.

    b. categories.   d. brings in.

_____ 3. The organizational pattern used in paragraph 5 is

    a. description.

    b. chronological order.

    c. comparison and contrast.

    d. classification.

_____ 4. Paragraph 10 uses all of the following methods of organization *except*

    a. definition.

    b. comparison and contrast.

    c. cause and effect.

    d. spatial order.

_____ 5. Which transitional word or phrase in the four paragraphs under the heading "Whether to Return?" signifies the use of the summary pattern?

    a. what happened? (paragraph 14)

    b. think about (paragraph 14)

    c. simply put (paragraph 15)

    d. in short (paragraph 16)

D. REVIEWING AND ORGANIZING IDEAS: MAPPING

Complete the following map of paragraph 10 by filling in the blanks.

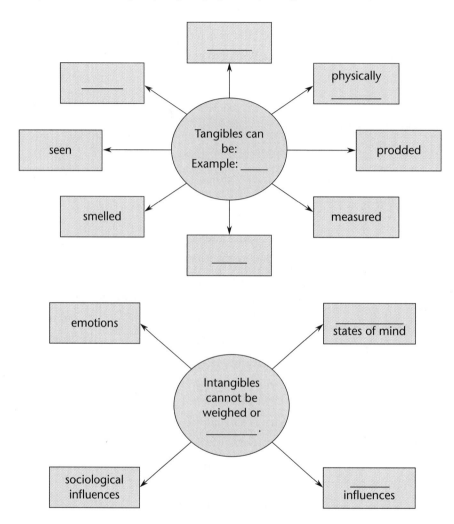

E. READING AND THINKING VISUALLY

Select the best answer.

_____ 1. Look closely at the photo of a Greek taverna on page 588. Which item pictured in the photo is an intangible?

a. the blue chairs

b. the menu

c. the bottle

d. the outdoor atmosphere

Paragraph 7 includes a discussion that can be summarized in an easy-to-read table. Complete the following table based on this paragraph.

TOP 10 REASONS PEOPLE GO TO FULL-SERVICE RESTAURANTS

1. Celebrate a special occasion
2. Relax
3.
4.
5. Be waited on
6. Enjoy the
7.
8.
9.
10. Try foods not eaten at home

F. FIGURING OUT IMPLIED MEANINGS

Indicate whether each statement is true (T) or false (F).

_____ 1. Though people like to go out to eat, most Americans still prefer to celebrate birthdays and anniversaries at home.

_____ 2. When people go to a chain restaurant, they usually know what to expect.

_____ 3. Dinner is the most popular meal eaten away from home.

_____ 4. Most chain restaurants are owned by large companies or entrepreneurs.

_____ 5. In the decision of where to go out to eat, the type of food desired usually plays the most important role.

_____ 6. In the photo caption on page 588, the phrase *al fresco* means "outdoors."

_____ 7. More people eat their meals out today than ever before.

_____ 8. An indie restaurant is usually a franchise.

G. THINKING CRITICALLY

Select the best answer.

_____ 1. The tone of the selection is best described as
   a. factual.
   b. solemn.
   c. concerned.
   d. dismissive.

_____ 2. The people most likely to find the box (paragraphs 5–17) useful are

    a. chefs.

    b. restaurant owners and managers.

    c. restaurant designers.

    d. waiters and bartenders.

_____ 3. By titling the box "Restaurant Operations: The Challenge of the Intangibles," the author implies that _____ is the most difficult part of operating a restaurant.

    a. having enough money to get through a restaurant's first few months in business

    b. getting the total dining experience right

    c. putting together the right combination of tangibles

    d. hiring a quality staff

_____ 4. When the author says that the reasons why people eat out remain "fairly constant" (paragraph 7), he means that

    a. these reasons don't change much from year to year.

    b. these reasons change constantly over the course of a year.

    c. these reasons are very dependent on the type of consumer and the state of the economy.

    d. these reasons are based on research that is probably biased.

_____ 5. The box in paragraphs 5–17 is a mixture of facts and

    a. research citations.

    b. expert opinion.

    c. uninformed opinion.

    d. quotations.

_____ 6. Based on this selection, what is the best single piece of advice you can give a restaurant owner?

    a. Create a total positive atmosphere and dining experience for your customers.

    b. Be sure that you offer quality food at good prices.

    c. Invest in an interior designer who can make your restaurant as friendly and inviting as possible.

    d. Offer a menu that gives customers a number of options for celebrating the special moments in their lives.

_____ 7. Mary and Oscar Gonzalez are opening a new Mexican restaurant that they plan to call "Mary and Oscar's." The décor is simple—just a few silver tables. They think that Mary's homemade traditional Mexican cooking will be the factor that draws people into the restaurant. What type of restaurant are the Gonzalezes operating?

      a. an indie

      b. a franchise

      c. a chain

      d. a fine-dining restaurant

_____ 8. Suppose that a new restaurant is opening in Hollywood. The owners want to attract a high-class clientele of models, actors, movie stars, and movie directors. Their advertisement reads "Come to Le Beau Monde—where the beautiful people meet to see and be seen." This advertisement is calling attention to the restaurant's

      a. menu.

      b. intangibles.

      c. location.

      d. tangibles.

H. BUILDING VOCABULARY

Context

Using context and a dictionary, if necessary, determine the meaning of each word as it is used in the selection.

_____ 1. affiliated (paragraph 2)

      a. fond of

      b. angry with

      c. understood by

      d. connected to

_____ 2. concept (paragraph 3)

      a. location

      b. idea

      c. funding

      d. strength

_____ 3. scenario (paragraph 6)

      a. problem

      b. concern

      c. situation

      d. question

_____ 4. cited (paragraph 8)

    a. given

    b. refused

    c. accumulated

    d. denied

_____ 5. predominantly (paragraph 10)

    a. rarely

    b. unquestionably

    c. ignorantly

    d. primarily

_____ 6. ambience (paragraph 14)

    a. atmosphere

    b. air

    c. design

    d. prices

Word Parts

A REVIEW OF PREFIXES AND ROOTS

PRE- means *before*
ANNO means *year*
LOGY means *study*
PRIM means *first*

Use your knowledge of word parts and the review above to fill in the blanks in the following sentences.

1. An *anniversary* (paragraph 1) takes place once a _____.

2. If *psych-* means "mind" and *soc-* means "society," then *psychology* (paragraph 9) is the _____ of the mind and *sociology* (paragraph 10) is the _____ of society.

3. Reasons that are *primarily* psychological and sociological (paragraph 10) would come _____ on a list of reasons.

4. If Event A *precedes* (paragraph 11) Event B, then Event A comes _____ Event B.

I. SELECTING A LEARNING/STUDY STRATEGY

Select the best answer.

_____ The best way to understand the differences between tangibles and intangibles in a restaurant is to

a. prepare vocabulary cards with the definitions of these terms.

b. go to a restaurant and make a list of its tangibles and intangibles.

c. write answers to the three questions found in the box's headings.

d. paraphrase paragraphs 1–3 of the selection.

J. EXPLORING IDEAS THROUGH DISCUSSION AND WRITING

1. Visit a fast-food restaurant in your area as well as a casual-dining restaurant (such as Applebee's, T.G.I. Friday's, and so on). How are the two restaurants similar? How are they different?

2. Suppose you are going out on a date with someone you really like (or the person you are already married to). Describe your ideal total dining experience on this date. For example, describe the restaurant's design, lighting, food, and service.

3. If you were to open a restaurant, would you prefer to own an independent restaurant or a chain? What are the pros and cons of each type?

4. This reading selection applies the ideas of tangibles and intangibles to restaurants, but these ideas can also be applied to education. What are the tangibles of your college education, and what are the intangible factors? Which psychological and sociological factors motivate you to go to college and study?

K. BEYOND THE CLASSROOM TO THE WEB

Most businesses today have a Web site, even chain restaurants. Select a chain restaurant you have been to and do a Google search for its Web site. Read the home page to find the restaurant's description ("About Us") or mission statement. How well does the restaurant deliver what it promises on its Web site? How might the restaurant improve? Be specific. For example, should it offer more nutritious foods? Extended hours? A bargain menu?

**TRACKING
YOUR
PROGRESS**

Selection 30

Section	Number Correct		Score
A. Thesis and Main Ideas (6 items)	_____	×3	_____
B. Details (7 items)	_____	×3	_____
C. Organization and Transitions (5 items)	_____	×1	_____
E. Reading and Thinking Visually (7 items)	_____	×1	_____
F. Implied Meanings (8 items)	_____	×2	_____
G. Thinking Critically (8 items)	_____	×2	_____
H. Vocabulary			
Context (6 items)	_____	×2	_____
Word Parts (5 items)	_____	×1	_____
	TOTAL SCORE		_____%

21 Workplace Issues

Work is a complex, important part of our lives and serves a number of different functions. It provides essential income to purchase life's necessities. It also offers an outlet for creative expression, helps us learn new skills, and allows us to explore new interests and talents. Jobs can be a source of personal satisfaction, a means of demonstrating that we are competent, self-sufficient individuals. Work can also make leisure time valuable and meaningful. Finally, work can lead to new friends, new relationships, new experiences, and new realizations.

The readings in this chapter provide several different perspectives on work and the workplace. The article "Interviewing for Success" offers suggestions and advice for interviewing for a job. In "Rx for Anger at Work" you will learn causes of anger on the job and discover ways to cope with anger. "What Will Be the Hot Jobs of 2018?" explores trends in the job market.

Use the following tips when reading about the workplace.

TIPS FOR READING IN WORKPLACE ISSUES	

- **Focus on practical information.** As you read the selections in this chapter, try to find techniques and strategies that you can use on the job or to find a better job. You may find some practical suggestions for coping with anger and frustrations on the job in "Rx for Anger at Work."

- **Pay attention to trends and projections.** The workplace is constantly changing and evolving. The job you have today may not exist in 20 years. Read to find out how to make yourself marketable and competitive. The article "What Will Be the Hot Jobs of 2018?" identifies growing fields and gives useful career planning advice.

- **Apply what you learn.** The information in the reading on anger management can be put to immediate use, both in the workplace and in the college environment.

SELECTION 31

Interviewing for Success

John V. Thill and Courtland L. Bovée

Textbook
Excerpt

This selection originally appeared in a business textbook titled *Excellence in Business Communication*. Read it to learn about the interview process, including how to prepare for a successful job interview.

PREVIEWING THE READING

Using the steps listed on page 36, preview the reading selection. When you have finished, complete the following items.

1. The subject of this selection is _____.

2. List at least four questions you should be able to answer after reading this selection.

   a. _____

   b. _____

   c. _____

   d. _____

 MAKING CONNECTIONS

If you had a job interview tomorrow, how would you prepare for it?

READING TIP

As you read, highlight specific actions you can take to improve your chances of having a successful job interview.

Interviewing for Success

1   Interviewing is stressful for everyone, so some nervousness is natural. However, you can take steps to feel more confident. Start by reminding yourself that you have value to offer the employer, and the employer already thinks highly enough of you to invite you to an interview.

2   If some aspect of your appearance or background makes you uneasy, correct it if possible or offset it by emphasizing positive traits such as warmth, wit, intelligence,

or charm. Instead of dwelling on your weaknesses, focus on your strengths. Instead of worrying about how you will perform in the interview, focus on how you can help the organization succeed. As with public speaking, the more prepared you are, the more confident you'll be.

Polishing Your Interview Style

3   Competence and confidence are the foundation of your interviewing style, and you can enhance them by giving the interviewer an impression of poise, good manners, and good judgment. You can develop an adept style by staging mock interviews with a friend. Record these mock interviews so you can evaluate yourself. Your career center may have computer-based systems for practicing interviews as well.

4   After each practice session, look for opportunities to improve. Have your mock interview partner critique your performance, or critique yourself if you're able to record your practice interviews, using the list of warning signs shown in Table A below. Pay close attention to the length of your planned answers as well. Interviewers want you to give complete answers, but they don't want you to take up valuable time or test their patience by chatting about minor or irrelevant details.

5   Evaluate your nonverbal behavior as well. In the United States and most other Western cultures, you are more likely to have a successful interview if you maintain eye contact, smile frequently, sit in an attentive position, and use frequent hand gestures. These nonverbal signals convince the interviewer that you're alert, assertive, dependable, confident, responsible, and energetic.

TABLE A WARNING SIGNS: 25 ATTRIBUTES THAT INTERVIEWERS DON'T LIKE TO SEE

1. Poor personal appearance
2. Overbearing, overaggressive, or conceited demeanor; a "superiority complex"; a know-it-all attitude
3. Inability to express ideas clearly; poor voice, diction, or grammar
4. Lack of knowledge or experience
5. Poor preparation for the interview
6. Lack of interest in the job
7. Lack of planning for career; lack of purpose or goals
8. Lack of enthusiasm; passive and indifferent demeanor
9. Lack of confidence and poise; appearance of being nervous and ill at ease
10. Insufficient evidence of achievement
11. Failure to participate in extracurricular activities
12. Overemphasis on money; interested only in the best dollar offer
13. Poor scholastic record; just got by
14. Unwillingness to start at the bottom; expecting too much too soon
15. Tendency to make excuses
16. Evasive answers; hedging on unfavorable factors in record
17. Lack of tact
18. Lack of maturity
19. Lack of courtesy; being ill mannered
20. Condemnation of past employers
21. Lack of social skills
22. Marked dislike for schoolwork
23. Lack of vitality
24. Failure to look interviewer in the eye
25. Limp, weak handshake

6   The sound of your voice can also have a major impact on your success in a job interview. Recording your voice can help you overcome voice problems. If you tend to speak too rapidly, practice speaking more slowly. If your voice sounds too loud or too soft, practice adjusting it. Work on eliminating speech mannerisms such as *you know, like,* and *um,* which make you sound hesitant or inarticulate.

Presenting a Professional Image

7   Clothing and grooming are important elements of preparation because they reveal something about a candidate's personality, professionalism, and ability to sense the unspoken "rules" of a situation. Your research into various industries and professions should give you insight into expectations for business attire.

8   Send a clear signal that you understand the business world and know how to adapt to it. You won't be taken seriously otherwise. You don't need to spend a fortune on interview clothes, but your clothes must be clean, pressed, and appropriate. The following conservative look will serve you well in just about any interview situation:

- Neat, "adult" hairstyle
- Conservative business suit (for women, that means no exposed midriffs, no short skirts, and no plunging necklines), in a dark solid color or a subtle pattern such as pinstripes
- White shirt for men; coordinated blouse for women
- Conservative tie (classic stripes or subtle patterns) for men
- Limited jewelry (men should wear very little jewelry)
- No visible piercings other than one or two earrings (for women only)
- No visible tattoos
- Stylish but professional-looking shoes (no high heels or casual shoes)
- Clean hands and nicely trimmed fingernails
- Little or no perfume or cologne (some people are allergic, and many people are put off by strong smells)
- Subtle makeup (for women)
- Exemplary personal hygiene

Being Ready When You Arrive

9   When you go to your interview, take a small notebook, a pen, a list of the questions you want to ask, several copies of your résumé (protected in a folder), an outline of what you have learned about the organization, and any past correspondence about the position. You may also want to take a small calendar, a transcript of your college grades, a list of references, and a portfolio containing samples of your work, performance reviews, and certificates of achievement. Carry all these items in a good-quality briefcase.

10   Be sure you know when and where the interview will be held. The worst way to start any interview is to be late. Verify the route and time required to get there, even if that means traveling there ahead of time. Plan to arrive early.

11   When you arrive, you may have to wait for a while. Use this time to review the key messages about yourself you want to get across in the interview. Conduct yourself professionally while waiting, and show respect for everyone you encounter. Avoid chewing gum, eating, or drinking. Anything you do or say at this stage may get back to the

interviewer, so make sure your best qualities show from the moment you enter the premises.

The Interview Process

12 At this point, you have a good sense of the overall process and know how to prepare for your interviews. The next step is to get familiar with the three stages of every interview: the warm-up, the question-and-answer session, and the close.

The Warm-Up

13 Of the three stages, the warm-up is the most important, even though it may account for only a small fraction of the time you spend in the interview. Studies suggest that many interviewers, particularly those who are poorly trained in interviewing techniques, make up their minds within the first 20 seconds of contact with a candidate. Don't let your guard down if the interviewer wants to engage in what feels like small talk; these exchanges are every bit as important as structured questions.

Make a positive first impression with careful grooming and attire. You don't need to spend a fortune on new clothes, but you do need to look clean, prepared, and professional.

14 Body language is crucial. Stand up or sit up straight, maintain regular but natural eye contact, and don't fidget. When the interviewer extends a hand, respond with a firm but not overpowering handshake. Repeat the interviewer's name when you're introduced ("It's a pleasure to meet you, Ms. Litton"). Wait until you're asked to be seated or the interviewer has taken a seat. Let the interviewer start the discussion and be ready to answer one or two substantial questions right away. Common openers include

- Why do you want to work here?
- What do you know about us?
- Tell me a little about yourself.

The Question-and-Answer Stage

15 Questions and answers will consume the greatest part of the interview. The interviewer will ask you about your qualifications and discuss many of the points mentioned in your résumé. You'll also be asking questions of your own.

Dealing with Questions

16   Let the interviewer lead the conversation and never answer a question before he or she has finished asking it. As much as possible, avoid one-word, yes-or-no answers. Use the opportunity to expand on a positive response or explain a negative response. If you're asked a difficult question, pause before responding. Think through the implications of the question; for instance, the recruiter may know that you can't answer a question and only want to see how you'll handle the situation.

17   Whenever you're asked if you have any questions, or whenever doing so naturally fits the flow of the conversation, ask a question from the list you've prepared. Probe for what the company is looking for in its new employees so that you can show how you meet the firm's needs. Also try to zero in on any reservations the interviewer might have about you so that you can dispel them.

Listening to the Interviewer

18   Paying attention when an interviewer speaks can be as important as giving good answers or asking good questions. The interviewer's facial expressions, eye movements, gestures, and posture may tell you the real meaning of what is being said. Be especially aware of how your comments are received. Does the interviewer nod in agreement or smile to show approval? If so, you're making progress. If not, you might want to introduce another topic or modify your approach.

The Close

19   Like the warm-up, the end of the interview is more important than its brief duration would indicate. These last few minutes are your last opportunity to emphasize your value to the organization and to correct any misconceptions the interviewer might have. Be aware that many interviewers will ask if you have any more questions this point, so save one or two from your list.

Concluding Gracefully

20   You can usually tell when the interviewer is trying to conclude the session. He or she may ask whether you have any more questions, check the time, sum up the discussion, or simply tell you that the allotted time for the interview is up. When you get the signal, be sure to thank the interviewer for the opportunity and express your interest in the organization. If you can do so comfortably, try to pin down what will happen next, but don't press for an immediate decision.

    If this is your second or third visit to the organization, the interview may end with an offer of employment. If you have other offers or need time to think about this offer, it's perfectly acceptable to thank the interviewer for the offer and ask for some time to consider it. If no job offer is made, the interview team may not have reached a decision yet, but you may tactfully ask when you can expect to know the decision.

A. UNDERSTANDING THE THESIS AND OTHER MAIN IDEAS

Select the best answer.

_____ 1. The authors' primary purpose is to
   a. explain hiring practices.
   b. identify employment trends.
   c. suggest interview questions.
   d. describe the interview process.

_____ 2. The topic of paragraph 5 is
   a. Western cultures.
   b. nonverbal behavior.
   c. eye contact.
   d. job interviews.

_____ 3. The main idea of paragraph 6 is expressed in the
   a. first sentence.
   b. second sentence.
   c. third sentence.
   d. last sentence.

_____ 4. The purpose of paragraph 8 is to
   a. list factors that can negatively affect an interview.
   b. compare business casual and business formal.
   c. explain how to research a company's dress code.
   d. describe the appropriate look for an interview situation.

_____ 5. All of the following statements about the interview process are true *except*
   a. The warm-up is the most important stage of the process.
   b. Questions and answers consume the greatest part of the interview.
   c. Only the interviewer asks questions during the question-and-answer stage.
   d. The close allows you to emphasize your value and correct misconceptions.

B. IDENTIFYING DETAILS

Indicate whether each statement is true (T) or false (F).

To prepare for a successful interview you should

_____ 1. focus on how you can help the organization succeed.

_____ 2. emphasize your positive traits.

_____ 3. dwell on your weaknesses.

_____ 4. practice by doing mock interviews.

_____ 5. record and evaluate your practice interviews.

During an interview you should

_____ 6. avoid eye contact.

_____ 7. smile frequently.

_____ 8. use hand gestures.

_____ 9. speak as quickly and loudly as possible.

_____ 10. dress in appropriate business attire.

C. RECOGNIZING METHODS OF ORGANIZATION AND TRANSITIONS

Select the best answer.

_____ 1. In paragraph 2, the transition that indicates that the authors will provide examples of positive traits is

    a. If.

    b. or.

    c. such as.

    d. Instead of.

_____ 2. In paragraph 8, the authors tell how to present a conservative appearance using the organizational pattern called

    a. definition.

    b. process.

    c. cause and effect.

    d. listing.

_____ 3. The transition that indicates the organizational pattern in paragraph 8 is

    a. how to.

    b. but.

    c. The following.

    d. just about.

_____ 4. In paragraph 12, the phrase "the three stages" indicates that the authors will discuss the parts of an interview using the organizational pattern called

    a. classification.

    b. process.

    c. order of importance.

    d. cause and effect.

D. REVIEWING AND ORGANIZING IDEAS: SUMMARIZING

Complete the following summary of paragraphs 12–20 by filling in the missing words or phrases.

The _____ involves three stages. The _____ stage is the most important because many interviewers decide on a _____ within the first _____ of contact. Body language is also crucial. The _____ stage is the longest. During this stage, you will answer and _____ questions. _____ carefully and notice the interviewer's _____. The _____ of the interview is brief but _____ because it is your last chance to emphasize your _____, correct _____, and ask questions.

E. READING AND THINKING VISUALLY

Complete each of the following items.

1. Its title indicates that Table A (p. 603) is a list of _____

   _____ .

2. Under the heading "Being Ready When You Arrive," the authors suggest items that you should _____ .

3. The photograph that accompanies the selection is intended to illustrate

   _____ .

F. FIGURING OUT IMPLIED MEANINGS

Each of the following statements contains two boldfaced words. Underline the boldfaced word that has a positive connotation or creates a positive image in the reader's mind.

1. Interviewing is **stressful** for everyone, so some nervousness is **natural.**

2. Build your **confidence** by removing as many sources of **anxiety** as you can.

3. Give complete answers without taking up **valuable** time chatting about **irrelevant** details.

4. Practice can help you **improve** the sound of your voice and **eliminate** mannerisms that make you sound hesitant.

5. For women, a **stylish** and professional business look does not include exposed midriffs or **plunging** necklines.

6. Clean hands and **nicely** trimmed fingernails are part of a professional image; **excessive** jewelry and cologne are not.

7. The worst way to start any interview is to be **late;** therefore, plan your route so you will arrive in a **timely** manner.

8. If you have to wait, conduct yourself professionally: show **respect** for everyone you meet and refrain from **rude** behavior, including chewing gum, eating, or drinking.

9. When you are introduced to the interviewer, respond with a **firm** but not **overpowering** handshake and repeat his or her name.

10. Body language is important during an interview, so be sure to sit in an **attentive** position and do not **fidget.**

G. THINKING CRITICALLY

Select the best answer.

_____ 1. The tone of the selection can best be described as
     a. informative and encouraging.
     b. condescending and critical.
     c. humorous and lighthearted.
     d. formal and detached.

_____ 2. Another accurate and descriptive title for this selection would be
     a. The Changing Workplace.
     b. Dressing for Success.
     c. Evaluating and Negotiating Job Offers.
     d. The Interview: Preparation, Practice, and Process.

_____ 3. The list of warning signs in Table A is intended primarily to
     a. help interviewers eliminate certain job candidates.
     b. show job candidates what they should try to avoid or correct.
     c. discourage employers from hiring unqualified applicants.
     d. persuade interviewers to overlook superficial mistakes.

_____ 4. The photograph with this selection best corresponds to the material under the heading
     a. Polishing Your Interview Style.
     b. Presenting a Professional Image.
     c. Being Ready When You Arrive.
     d. Dealing with Questions.

_____ 5. The audience for this selection is most likely to be

    a. executive recruiters.

    b. career counselors.

    c. human resources managers.

    d. students in business communication.

H. BUILDING VOCABULARY

Context

Using context and a dictionary, if necessary, determine the meaning of each word as it is used in the selection.

_____ 1. offset (paragraph 2)

    a. counterbalance

    b. increase

    c. disapprove

    d. consent

_____ 2. adept (paragraph 3)

    a. complex

    b. unusual

    c. skillful

    d. emotional

_____ 3. mock (paragraph 3)

    a. humorous

    b. simulated

    c. dishonest

    d. defiant

_____ 4. exemplary (paragraph 8)

    a. perfect

    b. fair

    c. secret

    d. distracting

_____ 5. dispel (paragraph 17)

    a. attract to

    b. provide for

    c. drive away

    d. allow

_____ 6. duration (paragraph 19)

      a. selection

      b. suggestion

      c. variety

      d. length

Word Parts

> **A REVIEW OF PREFIXES THAT MEAN *NOT***
>
> IR-
> NON-
> IN-
> MIS-

For each word in Column A, write the correct prefix (ir-, non-, in-, or mis-) in the blank before the word. Then match the new word with its meaning in Column B. Write your answers in the spaces provided.

Column A	Column B
_____ 1. _____relevant	a. not able to speak well
_____ 2. _____verbal	b. mistaken beliefs
_____ 3. _____articulate	c. not using words
_____ 4. _____conceptions	d. not important

Unusual Words/Understanding Idioms

Use the meanings given below to write a sentence using the boldfaced phrase.

1. To **zero in on** (paragraph 17) something means to focus your attention on it.

   Your sentence: _____

   _____

2. To **pin down** (paragraph 20) someone means to force him or her to come to a decision.

   Your sentence: _____

   _____

I. SELECTING A LEARNING/STUDY STRATEGY

Select the best answer.

_____   The best way to remember the tips described in this selection would be to

a. reread the selection and memorize each piece of advice.

b. create a chart or map detailing the stages of the interview process.

c. write a paragraph evaluating the advice given in the selection.

d. write a summary of what you have done in past job interviews.

J. EXPLORING IDEAS THROUGH DISCUSSION AND WRITING

1. Discuss whether any of the ideas in this selection were new or surprised you. How useful is the information in this selection as you prepare for your career?

2. Imagine that you are preparing for a job interview, and write a list of your strengths and weaknesses. Consider ways to address each of your weaknesses and practice how to express your strengths.

3. With a friend or a classmate, take turns conducting a mock interview following the suggestions in paragraphs 3–6. Be sure to offer each other a constructive critique after each practice interview.

K. BEYOND THE CLASSROOM TO THE WEB

*Visit the Web site **http://job–interview.net/**. After you have spent some time exploring different aspects of the site, write a review that includes a summary of the site's contents and resources as well as your evaluation of its usefulness. Would you use the site as part of your job search?*

**TRACKING
YOUR
PROGRESS**

Selection 31

Section	Number Correct		Score
A. Thesis and Main Ideas (5 items)	_____	× 2	_____
B. Details (10 items)	_____	× 2	_____
C. Organization and Transitions (4 items)	_____	× 5	_____
F. Implied Meanings (10 items)	_____	× 2	_____
G. Thinking Critically (5 items)	_____	× 2	_____
H. Vocabulary			
Context (6 items)	_____	× 2	_____
Word Parts (4 items)	_____	× 2	_____
		TOTAL SCORE	_____ %

SELECTION 32

Rx for Anger at Work

Kathy Simmons

Contemporary
Issues Reading

This reading appears on *Career Magazine*'s Web site. Read it to discover how anger works and how to control it.

Using the steps listed on page 36, preview the reading selection. When you have finished, complete the following items.

PREVIEWING THE READING

Using the steps listed on page 36, preview the reading selection. When you have finished, complete the following items.

1. The selection is about _____.

2. List three questions you should be able to answer after reading the article.

   a. _____

   b. _____

   c. _____

 MAKING CONNECTIONS

Have you ever gotten angry at work? Who or what provoked your anger? How did you express your anger?

READING TIP

This selection includes the work of several experts on the subject of anger. Keep track of who said what, and in what context (for example, three books are mentioned, and all three have a slightly different focus).

Rx
the abbreviation
for prescription   1

Rx for Anger at Work

A fable is told about a young lion and a cougar. The animals arrived at their usual water hole at the same time. They were both very thirsty, and immediately began to argue about who should take the first drink. The argument escalated rapidly. As they stubbornly clung to their anger, it quickly turned to rage. Their vicious attacks on each other were suddenly interrupted when they both looked up. Circling overhead was a flock of vultures waiting for the loser to fall. Quietly, the two beasts turned and walked away. The thought of being devoured was all they needed to end their quarrel.

2   Have you ever lost your cool at work? Warning: Seeing red too often might lead to seeing pink: the **pink slip**, that is. The workplace can be a regular breeding ground for anger, considering the amount of time we are around people of different value systems, deadlines, competitive co-workers, gossip and misunderstandings. The ugly consequences of mishandled anger include such "vultures" as lost credibility, damaged relationships, and stress.

pink slip
a notice of termination of employment

3   A solid understanding of anger is a giant leap toward mastering this "most misunderstood emotion." You can strengthen your anger IQ with the following information.

What Makes Us Angry at Work?

4   According to Dr. Hendrie Weisinger, author of *The Anger Work-Out Book,* there are five work situations that provoke anger.

5   **Being left out.** Not being accepted by your peers provokes anger for two reasons: 1) It severely limits how effective you can be on the job, and 2) It shakes your fundamental need for acceptance and a sense of belonging.

martyr
one who endures great suffering for the sake of a belief or principle, or one who makes a show of suffering in order to gain sympathy

6   **The critical boss.** Nit-picking bosses are infuriating. To add insult to injury, you are severely restricted in how much anger you can express toward him or her. Weisinger comments, "We tend to get back at our boss by taking a passive-aggressive stance. We do everything the job dictates, but not one iota more." This often makes the boss even more critical, and the vicious cycle continues.

7   **Not getting the promotion you deserve.** You bust your butt and it's not acknowledged. Who wouldn't feel cheated? Most people handle this perceived injustice poorly by becoming negative—and angry—**martyrs**.

8   **Being maligned by co-workers.** Dr. Weisinger points out that "being victimized by false rumors is a consistent anger arouser. It is abusive and unjust. And the rumors frequently cause irrevocable damage."

9   **Dealing with an incompetent boss.** Everyone has an innate need to admire their leader and follow their direction confidently and cheerfully. An incompetent boss can stifle your enthusiasm, and bring down the effectiveness of your organization.

Is There Such a Thing as Bad Anger?

10   Dr. Paul Meier, M.D., author of *Don't Let Jerks Get the Best of You,* offers three main causes of illegitimate anger: selfishness, perfectionism, and paranoia.

11   Selfishness carries the unrealistic expectation that people should never disagree with you, get to go first, or receive more recognition than you. You expect too much, and inevitably end up angry.

12   Perfectionists also have a difficult time with anger. According to Meier, "Some of the angriest people I know are perfectionists." When perfectionism rules your life, the person you are hardest on is yourself. Expecting flawless results causes continual anger, which accelerates as the same unrealistic demands are imposed on those with whom you work.

13   Paranoid people misinterpret situations—a glance from the boss or a co-worker passing by without saying hello, for instance. Too much energy is spent on insignificant and meaningless trivia, which can lead to a high anger level.

How Can You Avoid Feeling Out of Control When Angry?

Accept the Anger

14   Susanna McMahon, Ph.D., author of *The Portable Therapist,* points to the importance of acknowledging angry feelings. "Give yourself permission to feel angry. You do not always know when and why and how you will feel angry. Sometimes you may feel angry without knowing why. And sometimes, when you would expect to feel angry, you do not."

15   McMahon explains that anger lives inside of you along with your other feelings. Accepting anger does not mean you express it. You can control what you choose to do when you are angry. The reality is that most of us are afraid of what we might do when we are angry. As a result, we deny rage until it finally explodes into destructive behavior. You can be sure this will affect your career success.

16   A study by the Center of Creative Leadership indicates the primary reason executives were fired or forced to retire was their inability to handle anger—especially under pressure. Accepting the angry feeling as it occurs means that we do not accumulate the feelings until they become rage.

cathartic
producing
emotional
release

Acknowledge Your Choices

17   Don't repeat helpless statements like "I can't do anything about it." *The Anger Work-Out Book* encourages readers to keep one fact in mind: When angry, you must acknowledge that you want to keep your job. However **cathartic** it might be to "tell

someone off," the more rational choice is to avoid doing permanent damage to your career.

18   Weisinger explains, "This allows you to get angry and yet keep things in perspective as coming with the territory. 'I don't like it, but I will learn to deal with it' is much more productive than 'Nothing I can do about it, it's not that bad.' The latter statement denies the anger where the former is task oriented. You can then move on to workable solutions, in other words considering the fact I am angry, but I also want to keep my job, what is the best way to handle the situation?"

19   Your focus should be on keeping your job, *and* refusing to let unconstructive anger derail your career success. In the words of Roman philosopher Seneca, "The greatest cure of anger is delay."

Cool Your Anger with Humor

20   Steven Sultanoff, Ph.D., licensed psychologist and president of The American Association for Therapeutic Humor explains, "Anger and the experience of humor cannot occupy the same psychological space." Can you recall a situation when you were really angry with someone, and they spontaneously did something to make you laugh? In that moment you probably had a split second of disappointment—you wanted to be angry!

21   Sultanoff explains, "When we experience humor, distressing emotions like anger disappear. When we are angry, if we can look to our funny bone we will experience some relief." The root cause of anger at work is a belief that everything should be fair. Laughing at the "unfairness" will help you gain perspective and dissipate your anger.

Practice Forgiveness

22   When you are mistreated at work, the last thing you want to do is practice forgiveness. While it may be absolutely true that the offender does not deserve your kindness, remember this: *You do!*

23   By forgiving abusive jerks, you are actually giving yourself a break.

24   It has been said that recovering from wounds makes us extremely powerful. With this in mind, can you look at others' assaults against you that way? Rather than wallowing in despair and focusing on the inequity of the situation, can you view those painful wounds as growth opportunities?

25   Anger is a natural part of being human, but success-minded people have a healthy respect for—and control of—this emotion. By raising your awareness of what provokes your anger, and determining ways to handle it well, you can see clearly—even when you see red!

Ways to Deal with Your Anger

26   1. *Physically.* Get a tennis racquet and hit a pillow. Work out. Break something. I once broke all the dishes in my cabinet. It was a mess, but I felt good.

27   2. *Mentally.* Talk out your anger, with a confidante or with yourself. Ask yourself, "How is holding on to this anger serving me? Do I want to stay in this state?"

28   3. *Emotionally.* Underneath anger is pain, and underneath pain are tears. Have a good cry.

29   4. *Spiritually.* Seek guidance from a higher power. If you believe in God, pray for help. Ask that your anger be lifted, or imagine that your anger is like a lump of dough that you heave out into space. See your anger as something outside of you. Ask God to take it from you. (From: *Since Strangling Isn't an Option* by Sandra A. Crowe, M.A.)

A. UNDERSTANDING THE THESIS AND OTHER MAIN IDEAS

Select the best answer.

_____ 1. The central thesis of the selection is that

     a. employees who lose their temper at work often end up being fired.

     b. certain work situations can provoke anger that is justified.

     c. most anger in the workplace is based on misunderstandings that are easily resolved with proper communication.

     d. mishandled anger in the workplace can have serious consequences and workers can learn to manage their anger.

_____ 2. The author's primary purpose is to

     a. describe anger in the workplace and how to cope with it.

     b. compare various strategies for coping with disappointment at work.

     c. report on the best types of therapy for anger management.

     d. urge people who feel mistreated at work to express their emotions.

_____ 3. The topic of paragraph 12 is

     a. Paul Meier.

     b. illegitimate anger.

     c. perfectionism.

     d. paranoia.

_____ 4. The main idea of paragraph 15 is that

     a. angry feelings do not have to be expressed.

     b. most people are afraid of their anger.

     c. destructive behavior can ruin your career.

     d. denying rage is better than expressing it.

_____ 5. The method promoted by Steven Sultanoff in paragraphs 20 and 21 to deal with anger is

     a. delay.

     b. denial.

     c. humor.

     d. acceptance.

B. IDENTIFYING DETAILS

Indicate whether each statement is true (T) or false (F).

_____ 1. Kathy Simmons wrote *The Anger Work-Out Book*.

_____ 2. According to Dr. Hendrie Weisinger, not being accepted by peers at work severely limits a person's effectiveness.

_____ 3. The two main causes of illegitimate anger identified by Dr. Paul Meier are false rumors and an incompetent boss.

_____ 4. The author of *The Portable Therapist* emphasizes the importance of acknowledging angry feelings.

_____ 5. A study by the Center of Creative Leadership indicated that the primary reason executives were fired was their inability to adapt to the stress of new technology.

C. RECOGNIZING METHODS OF ORGANIZATION AND TRANSITIONS

Select the best answer.

_____ 1. In paragraph 2, the organizational pattern the author uses to describe the consequences of mishandled anger at work is

    a. time sequence.   c. problem and solution.

    b. cause and effect.   d. definition.

_____ 2. In paragraphs 4–9, the organizational pattern the author uses to describe the five anger-provoking work situations identified by Dr. Weisinger is

    a. time sequence.   c. enumeration.

    b. definition.   d. comparison and contrast.

D. REVIEWING AND ORGANIZING IDEAS: OUTLINING

Complete the following outline of the selection by filling in the missing words and phrases.

I. What Makes Us Angry at Work?

    A. Hendrie Weisinger—*The Anger Work-Out Book*

    B. _____

        1. Being left out by your peers

        2. _____

3. Not getting the _____ you deserve

4. _____

5. Dealing with an _____

II. Is There Such a Thing as Bad Anger?

A. _____ —*Don't Let Jerks Get the Best of You*

B. Main causes of _____

   1. Selfishness

   2. _____

   3. Paranoia

III. How Can You Avoid Feeling Out of Control When Angry?

A. Accept the anger

   1. Susanna McMahon— _____

B. Acknowledge your choices

   1. *The Anger Work-Out Book*

C. _____

   1. Steven Sultanoff—The American Association for Therapeutic Humor

D. Practice forgiveness

E. READING AND THINKING VISUALLY

Select the best answer.

_____ 1. The photograph used on p. 615 is appropriate to accompany the reading because it demonstrates the

   a. expression of anger

   b. paranoia that accompanies anger

   c. practice of forgiveness

   d. use of humor

_____ 2. Which of the following pieces of advice would the author *not* be likely to give to the man in the photo?

   a. Say to yourself, "I don't like it, but I'll deal with it."

   b. Deny the existence of your anger, which will make it go away.

   c. Go to the gym and work out with a punching bag.

   d. Pray for spiritual guidance.

F. FIGURING OUT IMPLIED MEANINGS

Indicate whether each statement is true (T) or false (F).

_____ 1. When the author refers to "your anger IQ," she means your understanding of what anger is.

_____ 2. It can be inferred that *The Anger Work-Out Book* is primarily a book about exercising and working out.

_____ 3. Taking a passive-aggressive stance is an effective way to express anger toward one's co-workers.

_____ 4. A lack of respect for one's boss can affect the success of the entire organization.

_____ 5. Perfectionists set impossible standards for themselves and others.

_____ 6. Humor can help people deal with other distressing emotions in addition to anger.

G. THINKING CRITICALLY

Select the best answer.

_____ 1. The central thesis of "Rx for Anger at Work" is supported primarily by
    a. the personal experience of the author.
    b. statistics from the Center of Creative Leadership.
    c. interviews with employees.
    d. evidence from authorities on anger.

_____ 2. The author begins with a fable in order to
    a. show that many work situations can be described in fable form.
    b. illustrate her point about the consequences of anger at work.
    c. introduce the idea that co-workers can be like vultures.
    d. appeal to very young readers.

_____ 3. The tone of the selection can best be described as
    a. humorous.
    b. encouraging.
    c. anxious.
    d. angry.

_____ 4. The author chose the title in order to
    a. advocate the use of prescription medication to cope with anger at work.

b. imply that the "ingredients" for anger are in the workplace.

c. indicate that the selection offers remedies or treatments for anger at work.

d. suggest that society's reliance on prescription medication is one of the causes of anger in the workplace.

_____ 5. The quote by Seneca (paragraph 19) means that

a. anger becomes even more intense with the passage of time.

b. letting time pass is the best way to get over anger.

c. the best way to make people angry is to make them wait.

d. it is impossible to hold people back from expressing their anger.

H. BUILDING VOCABULARY

Context

Using context and a dictionary, if necessary, determine the meaning of each word as it is used in the selection.

_____ 1. escalated (paragraph 1)

    a. provoked   c. avoided

    b. intensified   d. improved

_____ 2. fundamental (paragraph 5)

    a. basic   c. creative

    b. hidden   d. purposeful

_____ 3. infuriating (paragraph 6)

    a. harmful   c. maddening

    b. uncertain   d. humorous

_____ 4. accelerates (paragraph 12)

    a. improves   c. threatens

    b. increases   d. deflates

_____ 5. derail (paragraph 19)

    a. promote   c. cause questions

    b. speed up   d. go off course

_____ 6. dissipate (paragraph 21)

    a. dissolve   c. encourage

    b. spread   d. replace

_____ 7. wallowing (paragraph 24)

    a. wondering   c. recovering

    b. indulging   d. planning

Word Parts

> **A REVIEW OF PREFIXES THAT MEAN *NOT***
>
> IL-
> IN-
> IR-
> UN-

For each word in Column A, write the correct prefix (il-, in-, ir-, or un-) in the blank before the word. Then match the new word with its meaning in Column B. Write your answers in the spaces provided.

Column A

_____ 1. _____ justice

_____ 2. _____ revocable

_____ 3. _____ competent

_____ 4. _____ legitimate

_____ 5. _____ realistic

_____ 6. _____ evitable

_____ 7. _____ significant

_____ 8. _____ equity

Column B

a. not according to rules or laws

b. not qualified or effective

c. impossible to undo or take back

d. lack of fair treatment

e. not important or meaningful

f. lack of fairness

g. not reasonable or practical

h. impossible to avoid or prevent

Unusual Words/Understanding Idioms

Use the meanings given below to write a sentence using the boldfaced phrase.

1. To **lose your cool** (paragraph 2) is to lose your composure or self-control, in other words, to become angry.

   Your sentence: _____

   _____

2. Red is a color associated with rage, so when someone is **seeing red** (paragraph 2), that person has become angry.

   Your sentence: _____

   _____

3. A **nit-picking** person (paragraph 6) doesn't literally pick nits, which are the tiny eggs of lice; the person figuratively "picks nits" by focusing on minor or trivial details, usually in order to criticize.

Your sentence: _____

_____

4. When you **bust your butt** (paragraph 7) for someone or something, you put forth a lot of effort, or work very hard.

Your sentence: _____

_____

5. The **funny bone** (paragraph 21) in this case is not an actual bone, but an expression that means a sense of humor.

Your sentence: _____

_____

I. SELECTING A LEARNING/STUDY STRATEGY

Discuss methods of studying the outline shown on pages 619–620 in preparation for an exam that covers this reading.

J. EXPLORING IDEAS THROUGH DISCUSSION AND WRITING

1. Anger management is a timely topic in today's world, especially in light of the number of crimes committed in recent years by enraged employees at the workplace. Describe a situation in which you have observed anger expressed at work.

2. Discuss the author's tone. Does the author's language reveal her attitude toward the subject?

3. What does the author mean when she says, "By forgiving abusive jerks, you are actually giving yourself a break" (paragraph 23)?

K. BEYOND THE CLASSROOM TO THE WEB

Visit ITworld.com at **http://www.itworld.com/ITW0305joch/.**

Read the article "Defuse Workplace Anger." What factors does this article list as being the most likely causes of workplace anger?

TRACKING YOUR PROGRESS

Selection 32

Section	Number Correct		Score
A. Thesis and Main Ideas (5 items)	_____	× 4	_____
B. Details (5 items)	_____	× 3	_____
C. Organization and Transitions (2 items)	_____	× 1	_____
E. Reading and Thinking Visually (2 items)	_____	× 4	_____
F. Implied Meanings (6 items)	_____	× 3	_____
G. Thinking Critically (5 items)	_____	× 3	_____
H. Vocabulary			_____
Context (7 items)	_____	× 2	_____
Word Parts (8 items)	_____	× 1	_____
		TOTAL SCORE	_____%

<table>
<tr><td>

SELECTION 33

</td><td>

What Will Be the Hot Jobs of 2018?

Sue Shellenbarger

</td></tr>
</table>

This reading appeared in *The Wall Street Journal,* a newspaper geared toward businesspeople. Read it to learn about career opportunities you might consider as you choose your major and plan your studies.

PREVIEWING THE READING

Using the steps listed on page 36, preview the reading selection. When you have finished, complete the following items.

1. The topic of this selection is _____.

2. Name at least two industries discussed in the selection.

   a. _____

   b. _____

MAKING CONNECTIONS

Which factors did you take into account, or will you take into account, when choosing your major? How does your major tie into your career aspirations? Did you consider the job market when choosing your area of study?

READING TIP

This selection contains descriptions of several different industries. Create a two-column table as you read. In the left column, write the name of the industry. In the right column, list its jobs outlook and other relevant information.

What Will Be the Hot Jobs of 2018?

1   Kelley McDonald has always loved exploring new terrain. In home videos as early as age 3, "I'm always off by myself, looking under rocks or catching and studying bees," she says. Today, at 18, the Apple Valley, Minn., college student is studying for a science career in the fast-growing field of nanotechnology—working with materials at the molecular or atomic level. That makes her one of the

lucky ones—a young adult whose career passion is in sync with one of the hot jobs of the near future.

2   Predicting the jobs or skills that will be in demand years from now is a tricky task for many teens, young adults, and their parents. Luckily, there are rich sources of information on the Web, in books, and in most people's communities; the challenge is to sift through them all.

3   Ms. McDonald found her passion through a community-college nano-technology program funded by the National Science Foundation, where one official foresees hundreds of thousands of job openings in the field in the next five years. Other sources include government forecasts, school or college career counselors, and neighbors and friends employed in growing fields.

4   The richest vein of job-growth information is the Labor Department's 10-year forecast for demand, pay and

An artificial heart, just one of the many advances of biomedical engineering.

competition for more than 300 jobs in 45 categories. The department's latest biannual compilation, published last month as the "Occupational Outlook Handbook," is great for sizing up the long-term outlook for most fields. The forecasts have often been prescient—accurately predicting this decade's fast growth in special-education teaching jobs and the widening range of hot health-care careers, for example.

5   In the coming decade, engineering—already known for paying college graduates some of the highest starting salaries—is expected to offer the fastest-growing area: biomedical engineering. Jobs in this field, which centers on developing and testing health-care innovations such as artificial organs or imaging systems, are expected to grow by 72%, the Labor Department says.

6   Among other professions, job opportunities for physicians should be "very good," the guide says; health care dominates the list of the fastest-growing jobs, capturing 11 of the top 20 slots. While more attorneys and architects will be needed, competition for these jobs will be intense. Psychologists will be in demand, but growth will be fastest in industrial and organizational psychology.

macroeconomic 7   The forecasts have limitations. The Labor Department's **macroeconomic** a large-scale view of the economy model works on two noteworthy assumptions—that the economy will rebound to long-term growth and that there won't be any more big shocks like the 2007–2008 recession. Thus its forecasts don't predict the big job-market swings or sudden changes in the supply of workers that can easily happen in a volatile economy.

8   That means you could pick a job from the Labor Department's "fastest-growing" list when you enter college, only to find the field in a slump by the time you graduate. For example, a 2006 high-school graduate eyeing the government's 2004–2014 forecast for nursing at that time would have read about excellent job prospects, with "thousands of job openings" predicted because experienced nurses were expected to retire.

9   While that forecast is likely to hold for the long term, the job market for students graduating from college this year is headed in the opposite direction: Thousands of experienced nurses who had been inactive or retired have been re-entering the work force because of the **recession**. Similarly, a high-school grad in 2000 might have picked computer programming—No. 8 at the time on a government list of fast-growing, high-paying jobs—only to graduate to the aftermath of the dot-com collapse.

recession
economic
downturn

10   And finally, no economic model can forecast growth in jobs that are still evolving. While the government's latest handbook contains a supplement on "green occupations" in emerging industries such as biofuels and wind energy, it has no data on many of the jobs these industries are creating, such as fuel-cell technologists. "Right now, all the projections we have are about a world that existed" in the past, says David Passmore, director of The Pennsylvania State University's Institute for Research in Training & Development. "We are sitting on the precipice of the next big transformation" in energy production, "and no one in the occupational-projections area knows how to handle that."

11   All that leaves much to the resourcefulness, imagination and research skills of young people weighing a career choice. The first step is to explore and try out various fields in order to figure out what kind of work you love and can do well. The next is to learn about broad career fields that are likely to grow; the government's handbook lists job-by-job career-information contacts, such as professional associations or industry groups. Then, pick a field with this attitude: "I think I'll jump in and learn what I can learn," says Bob Templin, president of Northern Virginia Community College in Annandale, Va.

12   Networking with people in your target industries can help. Russell Wagner, a 20-year-old from Prior Lake, Minn., likes electronics and science, but when he tried robotics in high school, he found it boring. His mother contacted friends in the industry and learned nanoscientists are in demand in many industries, developing a wide range of products, from electronic memory devices and coatings for **stents** to mold-resistant shingle coatings. At Dakota County Technical College, Rosemount, Minn., where Mr. Wagner and Ms. McDonald are enrolled, program head Deb Newberry says employers contact her trying to fill more job openings than she has students.

stent
a medical device
used to unblock
an internal
system, such as
a blood vessel

13   All job markets are local, so it is important to check out job demand in the locale where you want to live. Community colleges tune into regional work-force needs and are often set up to provide counseling and work-force advice to the public. Also, ACT Inc. compiles state-by-state data comparing the career interests of students who have taken its college-entrance exams with the job outlook in each state. In Virginia, for example, student interest in computer-related jobs is falling far short of likely

demand; only 3% of Virginia students are interested in the field, which has projected growth of 23%. To see the data, go to ACT.org, click on "2009 College Readiness Report," and scroll down to the state list; work-force data is on page 10 of each "Readiness Report."

14   Of course, many people fare best by holding out for a job doing what they love. Careers in filmmaking are expected to grow very slowly in the coming decade, and competition for jobs will be keen. But that isn't stopping Kiel Greenfield. He has loved movies for so long—watching them, talking about them, and working with them as a video-rental store employee—that he has decided, at age 28, that filmmaking is the only career for him. He signed on for a filmmaking program at a respected school, the Zaki Gordon Institute, Sedona, Ariz., and plans to do whatever it takes to land a job in film photography. "It's going to be hard," he says, "but it's totally worth it."

Sue Shellenberger, "What Will Be the Hot Jobs of 2008?" WALL STREET JOURNAL, May 26, 2010. Reprinted with permission of THE WALL STREET JOURNAL, Copyright © 2010 Dow Jones & Company. All Rights Reserved Worldwide. License number 2633360179322/2633360350068.

A. UNDERSTANDING THE THESIS AND OTHER MAIN IDEAS

Select the best answer.

_____ 1. The central thesis of the selection is

    a. networking is key to finding a job in your field.

    b. national health care is expected to increase the number of jobs in the medical industry, while jobs in the film industry will remain scarce.

    c. all job markets are basically local, so students should be prepared to move quite far in order to find a job in their desired field.

    d. predicting the jobs that will be in demand years from now is tricky, but several sources of information are available to make the job a little easier.

_____ 2. The topic of paragraph 10 is that

    a. you cannot make any predictions about job growth.

    b. no economic model can forecast growth in evolving industries.

    c. "green occupations" are the jobs of the future.

    d. cell fuel technology is a growing source of jobs.

_____ 3. The main idea of paragraph 13 is found in

    a. the first sentence.

    b. the second sentence.

    c. the fourth sentence.

    d. the last sentence.

_____ 4. All of the following professions are discussed in the selection *except*

    a. biomedical engineering.

    b. psychology.

    c. law.

    d. accounting.

_____ 5. The author's primary purpose is to

    a. encourage students to choose a career that they will love instead of worrying about the money they will earn.

    b. tell several motivational stories regarding students who found exciting careers through campus sources.

    c. provide information regarding the pros and cons of different information sources regarding job growth.

    d. give investors an overview of industries that are likely to be successful in the coming decade, so that they can maximize their investment earnings.

Match each industry in Column A with the paragraph listed in Column B in which that industry is discussed.

Column A	Column B
_____ 6. filmmaking	a. paragraph 6
_____ 7. biofuels	b. paragraph 14
_____ 8. nanoscience	c. paragraph 9
_____ 9. health care	d. paragraph 10
_____ 10. computer programming	e. paragraph 12

B. IDENTIFYING DETAILS

Select the best answer.

_____ 1. Which of the following is *not* a drawback of the Labor Department's 10-year job forecast?

    a. It is based on the assumption that the economy will rebound to long-term growth.

    b. It does not account for the number of U.S. jobs that will be taken by immigrants.

    c. It assumes that the economy will not experience any shocks that set back job growth.

    d. It does not take into account the possibility of retirees re-entering the workforce.

_____ 2. Which field is expected to have the highest rate of job growth in the next decade?

    a. biomedical engineering

    b. hotel and restaurant management

    c. computer programming

    d. robotics and nanotechnology

_____ 3. In which area of psychology is the highest job growth rate expected?

    a. developmental psychology

    b. industrial psychology

    c. cognitive psychology

    d. abnormal psychology

_____ 4. Which organization compiles state-by-state data comparing the job interests of students with the job outlook in each state?

    a. the National Science Foundation

    b. the Labor Department

    c. Northern Virginia Community College

    d. ACT

_____ 5. More than half the jobs in the list of the top 20 fastest-growing jobs are in the field of

    a. health care.

    b. entertainment.

    c. accounting and finance.

    d. computers and computer information systems.

_____ 6. According to the selection, which of the following is *not* an emerging environmental industry?

    a. biofuels

    b. fuel-cell technology

    c. recycling plants

    d. wind energy

_____ 7. Which of the following sources of job information is not discussed in the selection?

    a. neighbors and friends employed in growing fields

    b. college career counselors

    c. government forecasts

    d. job recruitment fairs on campus

C. RECOGNIZING METHODS OF ORGANIZATION AND TRANSITIONS

Select the best answer.

_____ 1. The overall method of organization used in the selection is
   a. definition.
   b. cause and effect.
   c. generalization and example.
   d. comparison and contrast.

_____ 2. The organizational pattern used in paragraph 11 is
   a. process.   c. cause and effect.
   b. classification.   d. spatial order.

_____ 3. Which transitional word is *not* used in paragraph 11 to signal the organizational pattern?
   a. first   c. explore
   b. next   d. then

_____ 4. Suppose that the selection were composed of just paragraphs 5, 6, and 9. What pattern of organization would the selection have?
   a. narrative   c. spatial order
   b. comparison and contrast   d. listing

D. REVIEWING AND ORGANIZING IDEAS: MAPPING

Complete the following maps of the reading by filling in the blanks.

Sources of Information on Job Growth
School counselors
Neighbors and friends
Labor Department/Occupational Outlook Handbook
ACT data

Growing Fields	Information Provided About Them
_____ _____	Developing and testing health-care innovations Artificial organs/imaging systems
Physicians/Health care jobs	_____ of the top 20 slots
Attorneys and _____	Competition for jobs will be _____
Psychologists	Especially in _____ and _____ psychology
Emerging _____ occupations	Biofuels _____ _____

Making a Career Choice

Step 1: Explore and try out _____

Step 2: Learn about broad career fields that are likely to _____

Step 3: Choose a _____ with the goal of _____

E. READING AND THINKING VISUALLY

Select the best answer.

_____ 1. The author chose to include the photo on page 627 in order to

a. illustrate the technology that will lead to high job growth in the next decade.

b. encourage students to pursue careers in photography and filmmaking.

c. demonstrate her bias toward medical-related fields.

d. represent Russell Wagner's career choice.

_____ 2. Suppose the author wanted to provide a photo to illustrate a career path in which jobs have become harder to get. She would include a photo of

a. a doctor.

b. an attorney.

c. a nurse.

d. an industrial psychologist.

F. FIGURING OUT IMPLIED MEANINGS

Indicate whether each statement is true (T) or false (F).

_____ 1. The author implies that, despite a growing job market, only the best lawyers and architects will get jobs.

_____ 2. Most of the jobs in the environmental industry already exist and will need new graduates to fill them.

_____ 3. When the country experiences an economic downturn, there is more competition for fewer jobs.

_____ 4. Being highly motivated is enough to get you the job you want.

_____ 5. The Occupational Outlook Handbook's prediction regarding special-education teaching jobs was correct.

_____ 6. The predictions in this selection are less likely to be accurate if the U.S. economy does not improve.

_____ 7. In Virginia, competition for computer-related jobs is likely to be intense.

G. THINKING CRITICALLY

Select the best answer.

_____ 1. The tone of the selection can best be described as

    a. opinionated.

    b. informative.

    c. pessimistic.

    d. nervous.

_____ 2. Which of the following pieces of advice would the author *not* likely give to readers?

    a. Choose a career you love, but be aware of the job prospects in that industry.

    b. Pursue a job in green technologies, but understand that those jobs are limited.

    c. Use various sources of information about jobs, but be aware of the limitations of job predictions.

    d. Network as much as possible to find information about the career that is right for you.

_____ 3. The field of industrial and organizational psychology (paragraph 6) considers people's experiences and thought processes while they are

    a. at work.

    b. in school.

c. in hospitals or other care facilities.

d. at home.

_____ 4. When the author refers to the "dot-com collapse" (paragraph 9), she means

a. environmental disasters like earthquakes.

b. the tendency for people to work from their homes instead of commuting to an office.

c. the waves of bankruptcies faced by Internet companies in the early 2000s.

d. the restructuring of the American health-care system.

_____ 5. As used in the selection (paragraph 10), the word *green* is a synonym for

a. colorful.

b. high-paying.

c. environmental.

d. fast-growing.

_____ 6. To support her main points, the author uses all of the following *except*

a. personal experience.

b. expert opinion.

c. reliable sources and publications.

d. examples of real people and their experiences.

_____ 7. The author includes the last paragraph to

a. encourage students to pursue careers in the arts.

b. provide an example of a student who is a little older than the typical community college student.

c. help readers sympathize with the challenges faced by graduating seniors.

d. balance the logical tone of the selection with a positive, motivational story.

H. BUILDING VOCABULARY

Context

Using context and a dictionary, if necessary, determine the meaning of each word as it is used in the selection.

_____ 1. foresees (paragraph 3)

a. fears

b. visualizes

c. predicts

d. undertakes

_____ 2. prescient (paragraph 4)

    a. premature

    b. optimistic

    c. having foresight

    d. educational

_____ 3. volatile (paragraph 7)

    a. unpredictable

    b. tranquil

    c. growth-oriented

    d. developed

_____ 4. slump (paragraph 8)

    a. question

    b. tumor

    c. hill

    d. downturn

_____ 5. locale (paragraph 13)

    a. economy

    b. climate

    c. location

    d. population

Word Parts

A REVIEW OF ROOTS AND PREFIXES

TERR means *land* or *Earth*

BIO means *life*

NANO- means *extremely small*

BI- means *two*

RE- means *again, back*

Use your knowledge of word parts and the review above to fill in the blanks in the following sentences.

1. Exploring new *terrain* (paragraph 1) means exploring new

_____ .

2. *Nanotechnology* (paragraph 1) involves working with materials at the _____ level.

3. A *biannual* report (paragraph 4) is published _____ times a year.

4. If economists expect the economy to *rebound* (paragraph 7), they expect it to _____ to prior levels.

5. *Biofuels* (paragraph 10) come from sources that were once _____, such as corn or animals.

Unusual Words/Understanding Idioms

Use the meanings given below to write a sentence using the boldfaced word or phrase.

1. When two things are **in sync** (paragraph 1), they work well together.

   Your sentence: _____

   _____

2. Sitting on the **precipice** of the next big transformation (paragraph 10) means being on the edge of a new development or event that is likely to happen very soon.

   Your sentence: _____

   _____

3. **Keen** competition (paragraph 14) means many people competing for the same job.

   Your sentence: _____

   _____

I. SELECTING A LEARNING/STUDY STRATEGY

Select the best answer.

_____   The best way to study this selection would be to
   a. create vocabulary flash cards.
   b. write a paraphrase of it.
   c. memorize it.
   d. highlight and reread the selection.

J. EXPLORING IDEAS THROUGH DISCUSSION AND WRITING

1. Review Strategy 10 at the beginning of this book (page 30). How does that material work with the material in this selection to help you prepare for your major and chosen career?

2. The selection closes with the experience of Kiel Greenfield, who wants to pursue a career in filmmaking. What do you see as the advantages and disadvantages of working in that industry? What do you see as the advantages and disadvantages of working in the industry you are interested in?

3. What other advice might you add to the list of suggestions in this selection for researching possible career fields and their potential?

K. BEYOND THE CLASSROOM TO THE WEB

The Web contains a wealth of information about careers and career choices. Choose a career in which you are interested and conduct a Google search for information about it. Make a list of the five most interesting things you learned about that career and share it with the class.

Also check the ACT College Readiness Report (paragraph 13) to see if the job is listed there, and summarize the outlook for that job in your state. Finally, visit the updated Occupational Outlook Handbook (paragraph 4) at **http://www.bls.gov/oco/** *and summarize the job prospects for the career in which you're interested.*

TRACKING YOUR PROGRESS

Selection 33

Section	Number Correct		Score
A. Thesis and Main Ideas (10 items)	_____	× 2	_____
B. Details (7 items)	_____	× 2	_____
C. Organization and Transitions (4 items)	_____	× 3	_____
E. Reading and Thinking Visually (2 items)	_____	× 3	_____
F. Implied Meanings (7 items)	_____	× 2	_____
G. Thinking Critically (7 items)	_____	× 2	_____
H. Vocabulary			
Context (5 items)	_____	× 2	_____
Word Parts (5 items)	_____	× 2	_____
		TOTAL SCORE	_____%

PART THREE

Textbook Chapter Excerpt

This part of the book contains an excerpt from a psychology textbook chapter. Questions are included for the first two sections of the excerpt but these sets of questions appear at the end of the excerpt, not after each section.

To work through the excerpt, first turn to Psychology Selection 1 and note which pages in the chapter it covers. Then read Previewing the Section, Making Connections, and the Reading Tip. After you complete these exercises, turn to the appropriate section of the psychology chapter and read the material. After you have finished reading, go to the After Reading exercises, begin with Understanding Main Ideas, and work through the remainder of the questions. Work through the other section in the same way.

Please note that the page numbers mentioned in the exercises refer to the page numbering of the textbook excerpt itself, not to the pages of this book.

Psychology Textbook Excerpt

Excerpt from Chapter 9

Memory

From
PSYCHOLOGY

Lester A. Lefton
Linda Brannon

Memory

Chapter 8 pointed out that learning is a relatively permanent change in an organism that occurs as a result of experience and is often, but not always, expressed in overt behavior. *Memory* is the ability to recall past events, images, ideas, or previously learned information or skills. Memory is also the storage system that allows a person to retain and retrieve previously learned information. Learning and memory are two facets of the process of acquiring information, storing it, and using it. The acquisition part is learning, and the storage and accessing of learned information comprise memory.

Memory ■ The ability to recall past events, images, ideas, or previously learned information or skills; thestorage system that allows for retention and retrieval of previously learned information.

321

How Does the Memory Process Begin?

Traditionally, psychologists have considered memory as a type of storage and have sought to understand its structure and limits. Studies of memory at the beginning of the 20th century focused on factors related to how quickly people learned and forgot lists of nonsense words (Robinson-Riegler & Robinson-Riegler, 2004). Physiological psychologists sought to discover locations in the brain corresponding to the functions of memory. During the 1950s, research became more practical, focusing on variables such as how the organization of material affects retention. Today, research still focuses on understanding the complex processes of memory but also considers practical issues, including how people can code information and use memory aids, imagery, and other learning cues to retrieve information from memory more effectively. Researchers are also using brain-imaging techniques to pinpoint the specific areas in the brain that become more active when people are in the process of remembering.

The Brain as Information Processor

In this age of computers and information technology, it is not surprising that psychologists have likened the brain to a computer—an information processor. This analogy has influenced the study of memory since the 1960s and 1970s, when researchers began to recognize the brain's complex interconnections and information-processing abilities. Psychologists use the term *information processing* to refer to organizing, interpreting, and responding to information coming from the environment (Lachman, Lachman, & Butterfield, 1979). Of course, human brains are not computers—no computer has yet come close to the sophistication of the human brain. In addition, brains do not work exactly as computers do. Brains make mistakes, and they are influenced by biological, environmental, and interpersonal events. Computers complete some operations much faster than brains can, and they always get the same answer when they are given a problem repeatedly. Nevertheless, there are enough similarities between human brains and computers for psychologists to discuss perception, learning, and memory in terms of information processing.

The information-processing approach typically focuses on the flow of information, beginning with the sensory systems, where information from the outside world first impinges on the body. This approach describes and analyzes a sequence of stages for key memory processes and assumes that the stages and processes are related but separate. Although psychologists once considered memory a step-by-step, linear process, they now recognize that many of the steps take place simultaneously, in parallel (Rumelhart & McClelland, 1986).

Virtually every approach to understanding memory offered by researchers has proposed that memory involves three key processes. The names of these processes derive from information technology and will sound familiar to you if you know how computers work. The first process is *encoding*, the second is placement of information in some type of *storage* (either temporary or permanent), and the third is making the information available through *retrieval*. We'll use this three-process model to guide our exploration of memory.

Encoding

I (L.B.) tell my students to think of their memory as a filing cabinet, and I point out that how well a filing cabinet works depends on several factors. A filing cabinet can be very useful if you have a good system of organization so that when you put papers away, you will know how to retrieve them. You need folders and a system of labels that will allow you to find each folder in the cabinet. If you put papers in a folder and file it away in the cabinet without labeling it, your filing cabinet will be useful as a place to move folders off your desk, but little more. Labeling, or coding, the folders is critical.

The conversion of sensory stimuli into neural impulses is a type of coding, the first step of establishing a memory. *Encoding* is the organizing of sensory information so that the nervous system can process it, much as a computer programmer devises code that a computer can understand. The sensory information can be of any type: visual, auditory, olfactory, and so on. The type and extent of encoding affect what we remember. Encoding is not a discrete step that happens all at once. Rather, some levels of encoding happen quickly and easily, whereas others take longer and are more complex. Your brain may continue to encode information while storing previously encoded information.

Attention is important for encoding (Brown & Craik, 2000; Craik, 2002). In general, *attention* refers to the process of directing mental focus to some features of the environment and not to others. People can focus their attention on one idea, one event, one person, or one memory task, or they can shift their attention among several tasks or events. Dividing one's attention during encoding interferes with the process, and people who are forced to divide their attention during encoding tend to perform more poorly during retrieval—they experience a type of memory problem known as *encoding failure*. Such failures are very common, because many stimuli compete for a person's attention.

Encoding ■ The organizing of sensory information so that the nervous system can process it.

Levels of Processing

Does the human brain encode and process different kinds of information in different ways? Do thinking processes depend on different types of analysis? Researchers Fergus Craik and Robert Lockhart (1972) argued that the brain encodes and processes stimuli (information) in different ways, to different extents, and at different levels. They called their theory the *levels-of-processing approach*. According to this view of encoding, how information is processed determines how it will be stored for later retrieval.

Cognitive psychologists equate the level of processing with the depth of analysis involved. When the level of processing becomes more complex, they theorize, the code goes deeper into memory.

The levels-of-processing approach has generated an enormous amount of research (Craik, 2002). It explains why you retain some information, such as your family history, for long periods, whereas you quickly forget other information, such as the dry cleaner's phone number. It shows that when people are asked to encode information in only one way, they do not encode it in other ways. However, the levels-of-processing approach focuses on encoding and largely

Levels-of-processing approach ■ Theory of memory that suggests that the brain encodes and processes stimuli (information) in different ways, to different extents, and at different levels.

ignores retrieval, which led to the development of alternative views of how information is processed.

One variation is the idea of *transfer-appropriate processing*, which occurs when the processing for encoding of information is similar to the process for retrieval of the information. When there is a close relationship between the form of the information encoded (whether it is visual, auditory, or in some other form) and the processing required to retrieve it, retrieval improves. For example, when researchers give participants instructions to encode words for sound and then ask participants to recall the meaning of the words, performance is worse than when participants are asked to code for sound and to recall sound (Franks et al., 2000; Morris, Bransford, & Franks, 1977; Rajaram, Srinivas, & Roediger, 1998).

Other researchers also questioned the levels-of-processing approach, suggesting that differences in recall originate from how memories are elaborated on, or made distinctive. The *encoding specificity principle* explains the link between encoding and retrieval by stating that the effectiveness of a specific cue for retrieving information depends on how well it matches up with the originally encoded information (Tulving & Thompson 1973). The more sharply such cues are defined and the more closely they are paired with memory stores, the better your recall will be and the less likely you will be to experience retrieval failures. For example, my (L.B.'s) students sometimes fail to recognize me when they meet me in the grocery store or at the movies, but they always recognize me on campus. On campus, the circumstances in which we meet match those in which they first knew me, but off campus, the circumstances are different. Thus, some of them experience retrieval difficulties because of the type of encoding they have done.

The research on the levels-of-processing approach and its subsequent refinements and extensions have influenced the study of memory by emphasizing the importance of encoding. Researchers are aware that the encoding process is flexible. This process is affected by both the cues provided and the demands of the retrieval tasks, as well as by people's preconceived biases. Humans tend to notice and encode information that confirms beliefs they already hold—a tendency called *confirmation bias* (Jonas et al., 2001). This tendency to "see what you expect to see" is a powerful force in allowing people to retain inaccurate beliefs.

Neuroscience and Encoding

Memories are retained because they take some form in the brain. Many researchers are using brain-imaging techniques to explore the neurobiological bases of memory. Positron emission tomography (PET) and functional magnetic resonance imaging (fMRI) (described in Chapter 3) have allowed researchers to examine the brain during the process of encoding.

A general rule about brain functioning is that structures toward the top of the brain tend to control functions that are more complex and abstract. This principle has led researchers to concentrate on the cerebral cortex in their efforts to understand memory. Specifically, researchers have directed their attention to the prefrontal lobes with their overlying cortex—the large areas on the left and right at the top front of the brain, behind the forehead.

Transfer-appropriate processing ■ Processing of information that is similar for both encoding and retrieval of the information.

Encoding specificity principle ■ The principle that the effectiveness of a specific retrieval cue depends on how well it matches up with the originally encoded information.

In the view of Endel Tulving and his colleagues, the left prefrontal cortex is used more in the encoding of new information into memory, whereas the right prefrontal cortex is involved more in memory retrieval (Habib, Nyberg, & Tulving, 2003; Nyberg, Cabeza, & Tulving, 1996). Research using PET and FMRI imaging shows that when participants engage in various tasks, brain scans of the left and right hemispheres are quite different—that is, patterns of blood flow differ in different portions of the prefrontal cortex. These differences are generally consistent with Tulving's view—the left prefrontal cortex is more active when people encode information, especially meaningful verbal information (Otten, Henson, & Rugg, 2002). The left prefrontal cortex is also more active during encoding of information that is later recalled correctly than during encoding of information that is not recalled correctly (Casino et al., 2002; Reynolds et al., 2004).

Researchers have long known that the temporal lobes of the cerebral cortex are related to memory (Squire & Kandel, 1999), and brain-imaging studies have furnished more specific knowledge of how the temporal lobes interact with other brain structures. (Figure 9.1 shows several of the brain structures that are important to memory.) An FMRI study demonstrated that the anterior (front) part of the medial (middle) temporal lobes is activated during the process of successfully encoding information in memory (Jackson & Schacter, 2004). This type of association is critical for learning associations, for example, between a name and a face or a car and a parking space. Indeed, the medial temporal lobes may be important for encoding information about setting and context (Davachi, Mitchell, & Wagner, 2003).

One study that used PET scanning of the brain during encoding showed that more of the brain was activated when people encode fact-based information than when they merely listened to sentences (Maguire & Frith, 2004). The areas of greater activation included several regions of the prefrontal cortex, part of the thalamus, and the temporal cortex. Reasonably enough, your brain works harder when

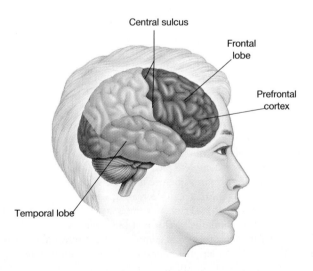

Central sulcus

Frontal lobe

Prefrontal cortex

Temporal lobe

Figure 9.1
Areas of the Brain Involved in Encoding
The prefrontal cortex and the temporal lobes are involved in the process of encoding.

you are encoding information than when you are listening passively. Just as the levels-of-processing approach predicts, people's brains are activated in different ways when they process information on a superficial level than when they process it on a deeper level (Weiser & Weiser, 2003).

Learners encode information to store it. If they do a good job of encoding, then they will be able to retrieve the information from storage. Thus, encoding is the first step in the flow of information through the memory system. Storage is the next step.

What Are the Types of Memory Storage?

Storage ■ The process of maintaining or keeping information readily available, as well as the locations where information is held, also known as *memory stores.*

If you think of memory as a filing cabinet, its storage capacity consists of the drawers of the cabinet. Once a folder is created and labeled, it is filed away in a drawer. *Storage* is the process of maintaining or keeping information readily available. It also refers to the locations where information is held, which researchers call memory stores. The duration of storage may be a few seconds or many years, but whenever people have access to information they no longer sense, memory is involved. For example, if you look up a telephone number, go to the telephone, and dial the number while no longer looking at it, then memory is involved, even if only for seconds.

Researchers have conceptualized a three-stage model for memory storage: (1) sensory memory, (2) short-term storage, and (3) long-term memory. Each type of storage has different characteristics and limits.

Sensory Memory

Sensory memory ■ The mechanism that performs initial encoding of sensory stimuli and provides brief storage of them; also known as the *sensory register.*

Sensory memory, sometimes called the *sensory register*, is the mechanism that performs initial encoding of sensory stimuli and provides brief storage of them. When you hear a song, see a photograph, or touch a piece of silk, sensory memory starts. This very brief storage allows the attention and coding processes to begin. The brief image of a stimulus appears the way lightning does on a dark evening: The lightning flashes, and you retain a brief visual image of it.

Research on sensory memory can be traced back to the early 1960s, when George Sperling (1960) briefly presented research participants with a visual display consisting of three rows of letters, which they saw for only a fraction of a second. He asked the participants to recite the letters, and they typically responded by reciting three or four letters from the first row. This limit on their performance suggests that they recorded only three or four items in their sensory register. But when Sperling cued them (with a tone that varied for each row), he found that participants were able to recall three out of four letters from *any* of the rows. This result suggests that the sensory register records a complete picture but that the image fades too rapidly for people to "read" the information before it fades. When Sperling delayed the cue that signaled which row to report, recall decreased, which again suggests a picture that fades rapidly (see **Figure 9.2**). From Sperling's studies and others that followed, researchers concluded that humans have a brief (250 milliseconds, or 0.25 second), rapidly fading sensory memory for visual stimuli. Current research on sensory memory concentrates on finding the underlying neural basis for the immediate processing of this type of stimuli (Schall et al., 2003; Ulanovsky, Lars, & Nelken, 2003).

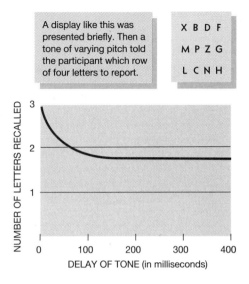

Figure 9.2
Sperling's
Discovery of a
Visual Sensory
Memory
The graph plots participants' accuracy in reporting a specified row of letters. At best, participants recalled about three out of the four letters in a row. As the tone was delayed, the accuracy of recall decreased. But note that there were no further decreases in accuracy when the tone was delayed more than 200 milliseconds. (Based on data from Sperling, 1960, p. 11.)

Sensory memory captures a visual, auditory, tactile, or chemical stimulus (such as an odor) in a form the brain can interpret. In the visual system, the initial coding usually contains information in the form of a picture stored for 0.25 second in a form almost like a photograph. This visual sensory representation is sometimes called an *icon*, and the storage mechanism is called *iconic storage*. For the auditory system, the storage mechanism is called *echoic storage*, which holds an auditory representation for about 3 seconds.

Sensory memory lasts very briefly. Once information is established there, it must be transferred elsewhere for additional encoding and storage, or it will be lost. For example, when you locate a phone number on a computer screen or phone book page, the number is established in your visual sensory memory (in iconic storage), but unless you quickly transfer it to short-term storage by repeating it over and over to yourself, writing it down, or associating it with something else in your memory, you will forget it. **Building Table 9.1** summarizes key processes in sensory memory.

Building Table 9.1

KEY PROCESSES IN SENSORY MEMORY

Stage	Encoding	Storage	Retrieval	Duration	Forgetting
Sensory Memory	Visual or auditory (iconic or echoic storage)	Brief, fragile, and temporary	Information is extracted from stimulus and transferred to short-term storage.	Visual stimuli: 250 milliseconds; auditory stimuli: about 3 seconds	Rapid decay of information; interference is possible if a new stimulus is presented.

Short-Term Storage

Once captured in sensory memory, stimuli either fade or are transferred to a second stage—short-term storage. This storage is similar to a computer's random access memory (RAM)—it is where information is held for processing. Another similarity between your memory and your computer's RAM is their fragility—information in short-term storage is easily lost, just as information in RAM is when the electricity goes off unexpectedly. Similarly, if you look up a telephone number but do not dial it immediately, you quickly lose that information. In terms of our filing cabinet analogy, short-term storage is equivalent to the process of creating folders for the papers on your desk, and deciding what to use as labels on the folders.

Initially, researchers spoke of *short-term memory*, to emphasize its brief duration. After extensive research demonstrated its active nature, however, some began to call it *working memory*. Both terms apply to the brief, fragile storage that occurs between sensory memory and long-term memory, but the two terms have slightly different meanings to some researchers in the field (Baddeley, 2002; Kail & Hall, 2001). This text uses *short-term storage* as a general term to refer to this type of brief memory; the terms *short-term memory* and *working memory* are used when discussing research on those specific topics.

Early Research on Short-Term Memory

Thousands of researchers have studied the components and characteristics of storage in short-term memory. Early research focused on its duration, its capacity, and its relationship to rehearsal. In 1959, Lloyd and Margaret Peterson presented experimental evidence for the existence of a separate memory store they called short-term memory. In a laboratory study, the Petersons asked participants to recall a three-consonant sequence, such as *xbd*, either immediately following its presentation or after a time interval ranging from 1 to 18 seconds. During the interval, the participants had to count backward by threes to prevent them from repeating (rehearsing) the consonant sequence. The Petersons wanted to examine recall when rehearsal was not possible. **Figure 9.3** shows that, as the interval between presentation and recall increased, accuracy of recall decreased until it fell to levels that could have been due to chance. The Petersons' experiment, like many others that followed, showed that information contained in short-term memory is available for 20–30 seconds at most. After that, the information must be transferred to long-term memory, or it will be lost.

In 1956, George Miller argued that human beings can retain about seven (plus or minus two) items in short-term memory. The number of items that a person can reproduce from short-term memory is the **memory span.** But what constitutes an "item" is not consistent. For example, a person can recall about five letters, about five words, and about five sentences. Therefore, people can group information in ways that expand short-term memory capacity. The groupings are called **chunks**—manageable and meaningful units of information organized in a familiar way for easy encoding, storage, and retrieval. Short-term memory will hold one or two chunks. Many people remember their Social Security number in three chunks (a really difficult task for short-term memory) and telephone numbers in two chunks (a much easier task). When ten-digit

Memory span ■ The number of items that a person can reproduce from short-term memory, usually consisting of one or two chunks.

Chunks ■ Manageable and meaningful units of information organized in a familiar way for easy encoding, storage, and retrieval.

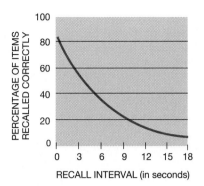

Figure 9.3
Results of
Peterson and
Peterson's
Classic
Experiment
Peterson and
Peterson (1959)
found that when
they delayed
the report of
three-letter syllables
by having participants
count backward,
accuracy of recall
decreased over the
first 18 seconds.

telephone numbers came into existence, people had trouble remembering them because of their short-term memory limit. But because they could think of the area code as a chunk, people got around that limit and dealt with ten-digit dialing. Chunks can be organized on the basis of meaning, past associations, rhythm, or some arbitrary strategy a person devises to help encode large amounts of data (Brown & Craik, 2000). Determining what constitutes a chunk is sometimes difficult, though, because it varies according to each individual's perceptual and cognitive groupings.

Psychologists agree that a key operation—rehearsal—is especially important in memory (Robinson-Riegler & Robinson-Riegler, 2004). *Rehearsal* is the process of repeatedly verbalizing, thinking about, or otherwise acting on or transforming information in order to keep that information active in memory. Rehearsal usually involves more than simply repeating information. Psychologists distinguish two important types of rehearsal: maintenance rehearsal and elaborative rehearsal. *Maintenance rehearsal* is the repetitive review of information with little or no interpretation. This shallow form of rehearsal focuses only on the physical stimuli, not their underlying meaning. It generally occurs just after initial encoding has taken place—for example, when you repeat a phone number just long enough to dial it. *Elaborative rehearsal* involves repetition plus analysis, in which the stimulus may be associated with (linked to) other information and further processed. When a grocery shopper attempts to remember the things he needs in order to make dinner, he may organize them in a meaningful mental pattern, such as the ingredients required for each recipe. Elaborative rehearsal, during which information is made personally meaningful, is especially important in the encoding processes. Maintenance rehearsal alone is usually not sufficient to allow information to be permanently stored, but elaborative rehearsal allows information to be transferred into long-term memory. In general, information held in short-term memory is either transferred to long-term memory or lost.

For example, you can repeat the term *suprachiasmatic nucleus* until you can recognize it and connect it with the regulation of circadian rhythms, but to remember this term and its meaning beyond the date of the test on Chapter 7, you need to do more. One strategy would be to analyze the term, breaking it down into parts and developing an understanding of each one. *Chiasm* means "intersection," and it refers to the place in the brain where the optic nerves from the two eyes come

Rehearsal ■ The process of repeatedly verbalizing, thinking about, or otherwise acting on or transforming information in order to keep that information active in memory.

Maintenance rehearsal ■ Repetitive review of information with little or no interpretation.

Elaborative rehearsal ■ Rehearsal involving repetition and analysis, in which a stimulus may be associated with (linked to) other information and further processed.

together. *Supra* means "above," and *nucleus* is a formation of neurons within the brain. So the term *suprachiasmatic nucleus* describes a brain structure that lies above the optic chiasm. Though it requires some work, this level of elaboration will boost memory for this information.

The Emergence of Working Memory

Working memory ■ The storage mechanism that temporarily holds current or recent information for immediate or short-term use.

Until the 1970s, psychologists used the term *short-term memory* to refer to memory that lasts for less than a minute. In the 1970s researchers Alan Baddeley and Graham Hitch (1974; Baddeley, 2002) began to reconceptualize short-term memory as a more complex type of brief storage they called ***working memory***, the storage mechanism that temporarily holds current or recent information for immediate or short-term use. Their model conceives of working memory as several substructures that operate simultaneously to maintain information while it is being processed. The concept of working memory goes beyond individual stages of encoding, storage, and retrieval to describe the active integration of both conscious processes (such as repetition) and unconscious processes. This model of memory emphasizes how human memory meets the demands of real-life activities such as listening to the radio, reading, and mentally calculating the sum of 74 plus 782.

In working memory, information is not simply stored; it is further encoded and then maintained for about 20–30 seconds while active processing takes place. A person may decide that a specific piece of information is important; if it is complicated or lengthy, the person will need to actively rehearse it to keep it in working memory. The addition of new information may interfere with the recall of other information in working memory. Baddeley and Hitch (1974) demonstrated the limited capabilities of several components, or subsystems, of working memory by having participants recall digits while doing some other type of reasoning task. If one subsystem is given a demanding task, the performance of the others will suffer.

One subsystem in working memory is the phonological loop, which encodes, rehearses, and holds auditory information such as a person's name or phone number. Another subsystem is a visual-spatial "scratchpad," which stores visual and spatial information, such as the appearance and location of objects, for a brief time and then is erased to allow new information to be stored. A third subsystem is an episodic buffer that holds integrated episodes or scenes and provides a limited-capacity storage system. Each of these subsystems also receives information from long-term memory. A fourth subsystem is a central executive mechanism; it balances the information flow, controlling attention. Research confirms the existence of these four separable components of working memory and also shows that they are functioning by the time a child is 6 years old (Gathercole et al., 2004).

Figure 9.4 illustrates the current form of the model of short-term storage as working memory (Baddeley, 2002). **Building Table 9.2** summarizes key processes in the first two stages of memory. Recent research on working memory has concentrated on the brain activity that underlies this type of processing (Bor et al., 2003) and on the episodic buffer, which allows a better explanation of how working memory relates to long-term memory (Baddeley, 2002).

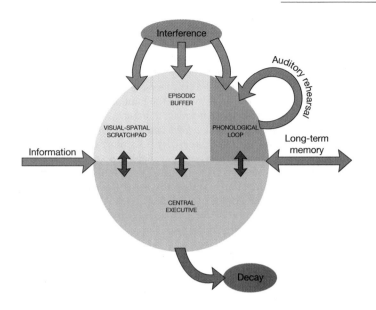

Figure 9.4
Working
Memory
Active processing
occurs in working
memory.
Information is held
in the visual-spatial
scratchpad, the
episodic buffer, or
the phonological
loop, depending on
the type of input.
This information is
monitored by the
central executive.

Building Table 9.2

KEY PROCESSES IN THE FIRST TWO STAGES OF MEMORY

Stage	Encoding	Storage	Retrieval	Duration	Forgetting
Sensory Memory	Visual or auditory (iconic or echoic storage)	Brief, fragile, and temporary	Information is extracted from stimulus and transferred to short-term storage.	Visual stimuli: 250 milliseconds; auditory stimuli: about 3 seconds	Rapid decay of information; interference is possible if a new stimulus is presented.
Short-Term Storage	Visual and auditory	Repetitive rehearsal maintains information in storage, in either visual or verbal form, so that further encoding can take place.	Maintenance and elaborative rehearsal can keep information available for retrieval; retrieval is enhanced through elaboration and further encoding.	No more than 30 seconds, probably less than 20 seconds; depends on specific task and stimulus	Interference and decay affect memory; new stimulation causes rapid loss of information unless it is especially important.

Long-Term Memory

In a computer, information is stored for long periods of time on the hard drive. In the brain, information is stored in *long-term memory*, the storage mechanism that keeps a relatively permanent record of information from which a person can recall, retrieve, and reconstruct previous experiences. Names, faces, dates, places, smells, and events are stored in long-term memory. In contrast to the limitations of sensory memory and short-term storage, long-term memory may last a lifetime, and its capacity seems unlimited. Using our filing cabinet analogy, we can say that long-term memory includes all the folders in the cabinet. Like folders in a filing cabinet, information in long-term memory can be lost (misfiled) or unavailable for some other reason (the drawers can get stuck). However, unlike a filing cabinet, human long-term memory is an active rather than a passive storage system that is subject to distortion—as if the information on the papers in the folders developed errors while in the filing cabinet.

A wide variety of information is stored in long-term memory—the words to "The Star-Spangled Banner," the meaning of the word *sanguine*, how to operate a CD player, where your psychology class meets, what you did to celebrate your high school graduation—the list is endless and, of course, unique for each individual. Different types of information seem to be stored and called on in different ways. Based on how information is stored and retrieved, psychologists have made a number of distinctions among types of long-term memories.

Procedural and Declarative Memory

Procedural memory is memory for skills, including the perceptual, motor, and cognitive skills required to complete complex tasks (see **Figure 9.5** on p. 333). Driving a car, riding a bike, or cooking a meal involves a series of steps that include perceptual, motor, and cognitive skills—and thus procedural memories. Acquiring such skills is usually time-consuming and difficult at first; but once the skills are learned, they are relatively permanent and automatic. *Declarative memory* is memory for specific information, such as what Abu Gharaib is (an American prison camp in Iraq), who tore off Janet Jackson's costume during halftime at the 2004 Superbowl (Justin Timberlake), and the meaning of the word *sanguine* (hopeful and confident). Declarative memories may be established quickly, but the information is more likely to be forgotten over time than is the information in procedural memory. Some researchers subdivide declarative memory into episodic memory and semantic memory.

Episodic and Semantic Memory

Episodic memory is memory for specific personal events and situations (episodes), tagged with information about time (Tulving, 1972, 2002). An episodic memory includes where and when the episode occurred; the chronological dating, or tagging, lets you know the sequence of events within your episodic memory. Examples of episodic memories include memories of having breakfast this morning, seeing a movie last night, and being on vacation two summers ago. Episodic memory is often highly detailed: You may recall not only the plot of the movie you saw last night and who starred in it, but also the temperature of

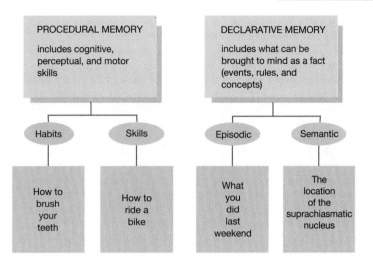

Figure 9.5
Procedural and Declarative Long-Term Memory

the theater, the smell of the popcorn, what you were wearing, who accompanied you, and many other details of the experience.

Episodic memories about ourselves—our own personal stories—are called *autobiographical memories*. In some sense, we *are* our autobiographical memories; we need these memories to construct our sense of self (Nelson & Fivush, 2004). Cognitive abilities such as understanding time are required for the development of autobiographical memory, and this capacity develops during early childhood. People's autobiographical memories can last for many years (Neisser & Libby, 2000), and when people lose autobiographical memory, they lose some of their sense of self. This type of long-term memory storage is durable and fairly easy to access if a helpful retrieval cue, such as a smell associated with an event, is available. These memories are also subject to a variety of distortions (which we'll consider in a later section).

Semantic memory is memory for ideas, rules, words, and general concepts about the world. It is your set of generalized knowledge, based on concepts about the world, about previous events, experiences, and learned information (Tulving, 1972, 2002). It is not time-specific. Semantic memory contains knowledge that may have been gathered over days or weeks, and it continues to be modified and expanded over a lifetime. Your knowledge of what a horse typically looks like comes from semantic memory, whereas your knowledge of your last encounter with a horse is episodic memory. Semantic memory develops earlier in childhood than does episodic memory (Wheeler, 2000).

Semantic memory ■
Memory for ideas, rules, words, and general concepts about the world.

Explicit and Implicit Memory

Explicit memory is conscious memory that a person is aware of, such as a memory of a word in a list or an event that occurred in the past. Both semantic and episodic memories are explicit, resulting from voluntary, active memory storage. When you tap semantic memory to recall, for example, the year the Declaration of Independence was signed, you are accessing explicit memory. In contrast, *implicit memory* is memory a

Explicit memory ■
Conscious memory that a person is aware of.

Implicit memory ■
Memory a person is not aware of possessing.

person is not aware that he or she possesses. Implicit memory is accessed automatically and sometimes unintentionally.

For example, you may remember things you are supposed to remember (explicit memories), but you are also likely to recall things you did not deliberately attempt to learn—the color of a book you are studying or the name of the book's publisher, the size of a piece of cake you were served, or perhaps the make of a computer in the office of a professor you have visited. Such implicit memories are formed without conscious awareness, which demonstrates that people can learn without intentional effort (Boronat & Logan, 1997). What they learn explicitly and how they are asked to recall it may affect their implicit memories (Nelson, McKinney, & Gee, 1998). The hippocampus and structures in the medial temporal lobe are necessary for the formation of most explicit memories but are not necessary for all implicit memories (Adeyemo, 2002). For example, people with damage to the hippocampus can still learn skills and motor associations. That different brain structures are required for forming explicit versus implicit memories confirms that these types of memory are separable.

The distinction between explicit and implicit memory adds another dimension to researchers' understanding of long-term memory, suggesting that this storage is varied and complex. The distinction also suggests that these different types of memory may have differing representations in the brain and that the functioning of each system is independent of others.

Practice

Obviously, practice is a factor in storage, but research indicates that the timing of practice is also an important factor. One early study (Baddeley & Longman, 1978) investigated which of two types of practice resulted in more optimal learning and retention: intensive practice at one time (massed practice) or the same amount of practice divided into several intervals (distributed practice). To answer this question, the researchers taught postal workers to type.

The participants were divided into four groups, each member of which practiced the same number of hours but spread over different numbers of days, to create either distributed practice or massed practice. One group practiced typing for 1 hour a day; the second practiced for 2 hours a day; the third practiced for 1 hour twice a day; the fourth practiced for 2 hours twice a day. Given the same total number hours of practice, did the distribution of those practice hours over days make a difference? The dependent variable was how well participants learned to type—that is, the number of accurate keystrokes per minute. A typing test showed that distributed practice (typing 1 hour a day for several days) was most effective. From this experiment and others, researchers have learned that the effectiveness of distributed practice depends on many variables, but it is typically more effective than massed practice. Distributed practice is especially effective for perceptual motor skills, where eye–hand coordination is important.

Neuroscience and Storage

Using both PET and fMRI, researchers can now monitor the neural machinery that underlies brain functions, and this technology has been applied to the study of both working memory and long-term memory. Brain-imaging studies of working memory reveal a complex pattern of activity in several different brain regions, which is compatible with the phonological loop and visual-spatial scratchpad of Baddeley's model (Wagner & Smith, 2003). Other research suggests that various parts of the frontal cortex as well as parts of the parietal cortex (see **Figure 3.9**) are activated when working memory is being used (Collette & Van der Linden, 2002). This diffusion of function is consistent with the concept of a central executive function that draws on several parts of the brain.

One patient with brain damage has been very important in understanding the brain mechanisms underlying the transition of information from short-term storage to long-term memory. Brenda Milner (1966) reported the case of H.M., a man whose brain was damaged as a result of surgery to control his epilepsy. His short-term storage was intact, but he was unable to form new long-term declarative memories. As long as H.M. was able to rehearse information and keep it in short-term storage, his recall performance was normal. For example, he could recall a telephone number as long as he kept repeating it. However, as soon as he could no longer rehearse, his recall became poor. His ability to shift information from short-term to long-term storage was impaired. He would have no memory that he had even heard the phone number 5 minutes after hearing it. (His procedural memory was not so severely affected, and he was able to learn new motor skills such as tracing and coordination tasks, but much more slowly than people with no brain damage.) Milner's account of this case provides support for a neurological distinction between short-term and long-term memory and focused researchers' attention on the role of the *hippocampus*, a brain structure in the medial (middle part of the) temporal lobes. Subsequent research has shown that this brain structure is an important component in memory formation, especially the transfer of information from short-term to long-term storage (Zeineh et al., 2003).

The process of changing a temporary memory to a permanent one is called *consolidation*. This concept plays an important role in one of the leading theories of storage, formulated by psychologist Donald Hebb. Hebb (1949) suggested that when groups of neurons are stimulated, they form patterns of neural activity. When specific groups of neurons fire frequently, this activity establishes regular neural circuits through the process of consolidation. According to Hebb, this process must occur for short-term memory to become long-term memory. When key neurons and neurotransmitters are repeatedly stimulated by various events, those events tend to be remembered and more easily accessed—this may be part of the reason that practiced behaviors are so easily recalled (Kandel, 2001).

Consolidation
[kon-SOL-ih-DAY-shun]
▪ The process of changing a temporary (short-term) memory to a permanent (long-term) one.

If a neuron is stimulated, the biochemical processes involved make it more likely to respond again later. This increase in responsiveness is referred to as *long-term potentiation*, and it is especially evident in areas of the brain such as the hippocampus. In addition, clear evidence exists that specific proteins are synthesized in the brain just after learning and that long-term memory depends on this synthesis (Kandel, 2001). Psychologists now generally accept the idea that synapses undergo structural changes after learning, and especially after repeated learning experiences. As Hebb (1949) said, "Some memories are both instantaneously established and permanent. To account for the permanence, some structural change seems necessary" (p. 62).

Long-term potentiation
▪ An increase in responsiveness of a neuron after it has been stimulated.

If the physical changes in the brain that form the basis for memory occur at the level of the synapse, then no particular brain structure should be specifically associated with long-term memory. This conclusion seems true. Researchers worked for years trying to find a structure in the cerebral cortex associated with the formation of memory. They failed (Lashley, 1950). Although complete agreement has not been reached, many researchers accept that memory is distributed throughout the brain rather than localized in one spot. As we have seen, structures in the medial temporal lobe, including the hippocampus, are critically important to long-term storage, but the temporal lobes are not the site of long-term memory (Markowitsch, 2000). Memories are distributed over the cerebral cortex and other brain structures, and their encoding and retrieval activate pathways that include the prefrontal cortex and the medial temporal lobes.

Building Table 9.3 summarizes key processes in the three stages of memory.

Building Table 9.3

KEY PROCESSES IN THE THREE STAGES OF MEMORY

Stage	Encoding	Storage	Retrieval	Duration	Forgetting
Sensory Memory	Visual or auditory (iconic or echoic storage)	Brief, fragile, and temporary	Information is extracted from stimulus and transferred to short-term storage.	Visual stimuli: 250 milliseconds; auditory stimuli: about 3 seconds	Rapid decay of information; interference is possible if a new stimulus is presented.
Short-Term Storage	Visual and auditory	Repetitive rehearsal maintains information in storage, in either visual or verbal form, so that further encoding can take place.	Maintenance and elaborative rehearsal can keep information available for retrieval; retrieval is enhanced through elaboration and further encoding.	No more than 30 seconds, probably less than 20 seconds; depends on specific task and stimulus	Interference and decay affect memory; new stimulation causes rapid loss of information unless it is especially important.
Long-Term Memory	Important information processed by short-term storage is transferred into long-term memory through elaborative rehearsal.	Storage is organized on logical and semantic lines for rapid recall; organization of information by categories, events, and other structures aids retrieval.	Retrieval is aided by cues and careful organization; errors in retrieval can be introduced: long-term memory is fallible.	Indefinite: many events will be recalled in great detail for a lifetime.	Both decay and interference contribute to retrieval failure.

How Does the Memory Process Begin?

(pages 322–326)

This set of questions refers to material from the beginning of the chapter up to the heading "What Are the Types of Memory Storage?" To locate a paragraph by number as referred to in an exercise, start counting with the first paragraph on the page, regardless of whether it is an incomplete paragraph continued from a preceding page or a new, full paragraph. Please note that page numbers refer to the pages of the textbook chapter, not to the pages of this book.

BEFORE READING

PREVIEWING THE SECTION

Using the steps listed on page 36, preview pages 322–326 of Psychology. *When you have finished, complete the following items.*

1. What is the topic of this section of the chapter? _____

2. List at least four questions you should be able to answer after reading this section of the chapter.

   a. _____

   b. _____

   c. _____

   d. _____

 MAKING CONNECTIONS

In what ways is your brain like a computer? What do you do to keep your brain working at its best?

READING TIP

As you read, highlight the findings of each of the studies described in this section.

VOCABULARY

neural (page 323, paragraph 2) related to a nerve or the nervous system

olfactory (page 323, paragraph 2) related to the sense of smell

cognitive psychologists (page 323, paragraph 5) psychologists whose approach emphasizes internal mental processes

positron emission topography (PET) (page 324, paragraph 5) a computerized radiographic technique used to examine metabolic and physiological functions in tissues

functional magnetic resonance imaging (fMRI) (page 324, paragraph 5) a form of magnetic resonance imaging that registers blood flow to functioning areas of the brain

AFTER READING

A. UNDERSTANDING MAIN IDEAS

Select the best answer.

_____ 1. The primary purpose of this section of the chapter is to
   a. identify sensory factors that affect memory.
   b. describe how the memory process begins.
   c. explain how short- and long-term memory work.
   d. discuss why we forget some things and remember others.

_____ 2. Most researchers propose that the three key processes involved in memory are
   a. encoding, interpreting, and responding.
   b. perception, learning, and memorizing.
   c. encoding, storage, and retrieval.
   d. organizing, analyzing, and processing.

_____ 3. The main idea of the levels-of-processing approach is that the brain
   a. has one level specifically for processing information and another level for retrieving it.
   b. encodes and processes information in different ways, to different extents, and at different levels.
   c. is constantly moving information from one level to another depending on its importance to the learner.
   d. uses only the large lobes in the top right and left areas behind the forehead for processing information.

B. IDENTIFYING DETAILS

Use the list of terms below to complete the following statements. One term will not be used.

confirmation bias	encoding	information processing
attention	retrieval	encoding failure

1. The organizing of sensory information so that the nervous system can respond to it is known as _____.

2. The process of directing mental focus to some features of the environment and not to others is called_____.

3. The human tendency to "see what you expect to see" is known as

   _____.

4. A type of memory problem that results when people divide their attention during encoding is known as _____.

5. The term that refers to organizing, interpreting, and responding to information coming from the environment is _____.

C. RECOGNIZING METHODS OF ORGANIZATION AND TRANSITIONS

Select the best answer.

_____ 1. In paragraph 2 of the section titled "The Brain as Information Processor" (page 322), the authors primarily use the organizational pattern called

   a. cause and effect.

   b. order of importance.

   c. comparison and contrast.

   d. classification.

_____ 2. The authors organize paragraphs 2 and 3 on page 324 in the same way, by using

   a. definition and example.

   b. comparison and contrast.

   c. chronological and spatial order.

   d. cause and effect.

D. REVIEWING AND ORGANIZING IDEAS: MAPPING

Complete the following map based on the section titled "Levels of Processing" (pages 323 and 324) by filling in the blanks.

How Information Is Processed

Levels-of-Processing Approach	Transfer-Appropriate Processing	Encoding Specificity Principle
How information is processed determines how _____ _____.	Occurs when the process for information encoding is similar to _____.	The effectiveness of a retrieval cue depends on how well it matches up with _____ _____.
The code goes deeper into memory when the level of processing becomes _____.	Retrieval improves when there is a close relationship between _____ _____ and the processing required to retrieve it.	Retrieval improves when cues are defined more sharply and paired more closely with _____.

E. READING AND THINKING VISUALLY

Select the best answer.

_____ 1. The purpose of Figure 9.1 on page 325 is to illustrate the
   a. different stages of memory.
   b. development of the brain.
   c. effects of PET and fMRI imaging on the brain.
   d. areas of the brain that are important to memory.

_____ 2. The authors include an analogy about a filing cabinet under the subheading
   a. The Brain as Information Processor.
   b. Encoding.
   c. Levels of Processing.
   d. Neuroscience and Encoding.

F. FIGURING OUT IMPLIED MEANINGS

Indicate whether each statement is true (T) or false (F) by making inferences based on the section "Neuroscience and Encoding" (pages 324–326).

_____ 1. It can be inferred that brain-imaging techniques such as PET and fMRI are harmful to the brain.

_____ 2. The functions of the cerebral cortex are probably limited to memory-related tasks only.

_____ 3. The left and right prefrontal cortexes are probably engaged in different ways during learning.

_____ 4. It can be inferred that people learn better when they actively encode information rather than passively listen to it.

_____ 5. It can be inferred from the selection that most headaches take place in a person's cerebral cortex.

G. THINKING CRITICALLY

Select the best answer.

_____ 1. The authors support the main ideas in this section of the chapter primarily with
   a. statistics.
   b. research evidence.
   c. analogies.
   d. personal experience.

_____ 2. In the introduction to the section, the authors describe how memory was studied in the past in order to
   a. illustrate how little early researchers understood about memory.
   b. provide evidence that past studies were based on faulty information.
   c. show how memory research has changed over the years.
   d. establish the parallels between computers and brains.

_____ 3. According to one of the authors, students sometimes fail to recognize her in off-campus settings because of
   a. the encoding specificity principle.
   b. confirmation bias.
   c. encoding failure.
   d. sensory stimuli.

H. BUILDING VOCABULARY

Context

Using context and a dictionary, if necessary, determine the meaning of each word as it is used in the selection.

_____ 1. impinges (page 322, paragraph 3)

    a. avoids   c. makes a sound

    b. has an effect   d. breaks apart

_____ 2. derive (page 322, paragraph 4)

    a. come from   c. improve

    b. contradict   d. complain

_____ 3. discrete (page 323, paragraph 2)

    a. unnoticeable   c. separate

    b. natural   d. sudden

_____ 4. stimuli (page 323, paragraph 4)

    a. problem

    b. information

    c. distraction

    d. barrier

_____ 5. anterior (page 325, paragraph 2)

    a. front

    b. inside

    c. middle

    d. behind

Word Parts

A REVIEW OF PREFIXES AND ROOTS

INTER- means *between*
PRE- means *before*
RE- means *back, again*
EX- means *from, out of*
IN- means *not*
SUPER- means *above*
AUD means *hear*
LOG means *study, thought*
TENT/TENS means *stretch* or *strain*

Match each word in Column A with its meaning in Column B. Write your answers in the spaces provided.

Column A	Column B
_____ 1. physiological	a. not correct
_____ 2. retention	b. additions to or expansions of a subject
_____ 3. interconnections	c. related to the study of living organisms
_____ 4. auditory	d. formed beforehand
_____ 5. extensions	e. on the surface only; not deep
_____ 6. preconceived	f. the ability to recall past experience (memory)
_____ 7. inaccurate	g. related to hearing
_____ 8. superficial	h. links between different parts

I. SELECTING A LEARNING/STUDY STRATEGY

Predict an essay question that might be asked on this section of the chapter.

J. EXPLORING IDEAS THROUGH DISCUSSION AND WRITING

1. Discuss the similarities and differences between the human brain and a computer or information processor.

2. Have you ever tried to improve your memory? Describe your technique and whether or not it was successful.

3. Evaluate Figure 9.1 in this section of the chapter. Was it helpful to you? Did it make you curious about the parts of the brain that were not labeled or depicted in this figure?

Psychology Selection 1

Section	Number Correct		Score
A. Main Ideas (3 items)	_____	× 4	_____
B. Details (5 items)	_____	× 4	_____
C. Organization and Transitions (2 items)	_____	× 2	_____
E. Reading and Thinking Visually (2 items)	_____	× 3	_____
F. Implied Meanings (5 items)	_____	× 3	_____
G. Thinking Critically (3 items)	_____	× 3	_____
H. Vocabulary			
Context (5 items)	_____	× 2	_____
Word Parts (8 items)	_____	× 3	_____
		TOTAL SCORE	_____%

PSYCHOLOGY SELECTION 2

What Are the Types of Memory Storage?

(pages 326–336)

To locate a paragraph by number as referred to in an exercise, start counting with the first paragraph on the page, regardless of whether it is an incomplete paragraph continued from a preceding page or a new, full paragraph. Please note that page numbers refer to the pages of the textbook chapter, not to the pages of this book.

BEFORE READING

PREVIEWING THE SECTION

Using the steps listed on page 36, preview pages 326–336 of Psychology. *When you have finished, complete the following items.*

1. What is the topic of this section of the chapter? _____

2. List the three types of memory that are discussed in this section of the chapter.

   a. _____

   b. _____

   c. _____

MAKING CONNECTIONS

How do you memorize information that you need to remember? Do you use different techniques for different types of information?

READING TIP

This section of the chapter has several graphic aids to help you understand the material you are reading. Be sure to take time to study the figures and tables as you read.

AFTER READING

A. UNDERSTANDING MAIN IDEAS

Select the best answer.

_____ 1. The primary purpose of this section of the chapter is to
   a. compare early studies on memory to more recent research using modern methods.
   b. discuss the relationship between learning and forgetting.
   c. describe the characteristics and limits of the different types of memory storage.
   d. explore the effects of brain damage on short-term and long-term memory.

_____ 2. The three-stage model for memory storage consists of
   a. storage, rehearsal, and memory span.
   b. sensory memory, sensory register, and working memory.
   c. sensory memory, short-term storage, and long-term memory.
   d. procedural memory, declarative memory, and long-term memory.

_____ 3. The difference between maintenance rehearsal and elaborative rehearsal is that *elaborative rehearsal*
   a. focuses only on the physical stimuli, not their underlying meaning.
   b. makes information meaningful so it can be transferred into long-term memory.
   c. repetitively reviews information with little or no interpretation.
   d. generally occurs just after initial encoding has taken place.

_____ 4. The type of memory that demonstrates that people can learn without intentional effort is called
   a. implicit memory.
   b. semantic memory.
   c. episodic memory.
   d. explicit memory.

_____ 5. According to the selection, the case of the patient with brain damage was important to understanding the
   a. effects of interference and decay during the encoding process.
   b. role of brain structures in the transfer of information from short-term to long-term storage.

    c. similarities between short-term storage and a computer's random access memory (RAM).

    d. use of retrieval cues, such as a smell associated with an event, in accessing long-term memory.

_____ 6. The process of changing a temporary memory to a permanent one is called

    a. iconic storage.

    b. long-term potentiation.

    c. echoic storage.

    d. consolidation.

B. IDENTIFYING DETAILS

Match the last names of the researchers in Column A with their corresponding research findings in Column B.

Column A

_____ 1. Sperling (1960)

_____ 2. Petersons (1959)

_____ 3. Miller (1956)

_____ 4. Baddeley/Hitch (1970s)

Column B

a. Humans can retain about seven items in short-term memory.

b. Working memory consists of substructures that operate simultaneously to maintain information while it is being processed.

c. Humans have a brief, rapidly fading sensory memory for visual stimuli.

d. Information contained in short-term memory is available for no more than 20–30 seconds before it must be transferred to long-term memory or lost.

C. RECOGNIZING METHODS OF ORGANIZATION AND TRANSITIONS

Select the best answer.

_____ 1. The primary organizational pattern in paragraph 1 on page 328 is

    a. comparison and contrast.

    b. process.

    c. order of importance.

    d. summary.

_____ 2. In paragraph 4 on page 330, the authors describe the subsystems in working memory using the organizational pattern called

    a. cause and effect.

    b. listing or enumeration.

    c. comparison and contrast.

    d. chronological order.

_____ 3. In paragraph 1 on page 332, the transitional words and phrases that indicate the authors' organizational pattern include

    a. In contrast.

    b. Like.

    c. However.

    d. all of the above.

_____ 4. The primary organizational pattern used in paragraphs 3 and 4 on page 335 is

    a. classification.

    b. chronological order.

    c. spatial order.

    d. cause and effect.

D. REVIEWING AND ORGANIZING IDEAS: OUTLINING

Complete the following outline based on the section "Long-Term Memory" (pages 332–334) by filling in the blanks.

Long-Term Memory

I. Procedural Memory

    A. For skills required to complete complex tasks

        1. Perceptual

        2. _____

        3. _____

    B. Memory acquisition

        1. Time-consuming, difficult

        2. Once acquired, permanent and automatic

II. Declarative Memory

    A. For specific information

        1. Episodic—events and situations

        2. _____—generalized knowledge

  B. Memory acquisition

   1. Established _____

   2. May be forgotten over time

 III. Explicit vs. Implicit Memory

  A. _____ —conscious memory

  B. _____ —formed without conscious awareness

  C. Different brain structures used for explicit and implicit

E. READING AND THINKING VISUALLY

Select the best answer.

_____ 1. The primary purpose of Figure 9.2 on page 327 is to
 a. illustrate the effects of chemical stimuli on recall and memory.
 b. show that people can remember words better than random letters.
 c. depict the results of a study on visual sensory memory.
 d. explain the importance of practice on short-term memory.

_____ 2. According to Tables 9.1–9.3 (pages 327, 331, 336), a sound stays in your sensory memory for about
 a. 250 milliseconds.
 b. 3 seconds.
 c. 20 seconds.
 d. 30 seconds.

F. FIGURING OUT IMPLIED MEANINGS

Complete each statement by underlining the correct answer in the parentheses.

1. The type of rehearsal you would need to remember a zip code just long enough to write it on an envelope is (elaborative / maintenance) rehearsal.

2. To learn a skill such as typing or playing guitar, it would probably be more effective to engage in (massed / distributed) practice.

3. Remembering the color of the hat your professor wore into class before a recent lecture is an example of an (implicit / explicit) memory.

4. Knowing what an ice cream cone looks like is an example of (semantic / episodic) memory, and remembering the last time you ate an ice cream cone is (semantic / episodic) memory.

G. THINKING CRITICALLY

Select the best answer.

_____ 1. According to Figure 9.3 on page 329, participants correctly recalled about 40 percent of test items after an interval of
   a. 18 seconds.
   b. 12 seconds.
   c. 6 seconds.
   d. 1 second.

_____ 2. The working memory subsystem that controls attention by balancing the flow of information is known as the
   a. phonological loop.
   b. visual-spatial scratchpad.
   c. episodic buffer.
   d. central executive mechanism.

_____ 3. An example of the type of information that would be stored in your semantic memory is
   a. how to ice-skate.
   b. the definition of the word *deluge*.
   c. what you did on your last birthday.
   d. what velvet feels like.

_____ 4. The units of information called "chunks" are helpful to learning because they allow a person to
   a. associate a retrieval cue with a memory.
   b. group information into more manageable segments.
   c. repeatedly review information without interpreting it.
   d. hold auditory information indefinitely in short-term memory.

H. BUILDING VOCABULARY

Context

Using context and a dictionary, if necessary, determine the meaning of each word as it is used in the selection.

_____ 1. duration (page 326, paragraph 3)
   a. property   c. difficulty
   b. length   d. storage

_____ 2. tactile (page 327, paragraph 1)

    a. related to sound

    b. related to vision

    c. related to smell

    d. related to touch

_____ 3. icon (page 327, paragraph 1)

    a. image

    b. tone

    c. letter

    d. character

_____ 4. fragility (page 328, paragraph 1)

    a. transparency

    b. urgency

    c. delicateness

    d. damage

_____ 5. arbitrary (page 329, paragraph 1)

    a. missing a part

    b. established by a judge

    c. based on individual preference

    d. limited by law

_____ 6. integrated (page 330, paragraph 4)

    a. combined

    b. awkward

    c. limited

    d. divided

_____ 7. distortion (page 332, paragraph 1)

    a. distraction

    b. interruption

    c. illustration

    d. change for the worse

_____ 8. monitor (page 334, paragraph 6)

    a. move

    b. observe

    c. agree

    d. alter

Word Parts

> ## A REVIEW OF PREFIXES AND ROOTS
>
> **RE-** means *again*
> **SUB-** means *under, below*
> **CAP** means *take*
> **PHONO** means *sound*
> **LOG** means *study, thought*
> **BIO** means *life*
> **GRAPH** means *write*

Match each word in Column A with its meaning in Column B. Write your answers in the spaces provided.

Column A

_____ 1. phonological

_____ 2. reproduce

_____ 3. capacity

_____ 4. autobiographical

_____ 5. substructures

Column B

a. the amount of information that can be taken in

b. related to stories about one's own life

c. related to sound

d. underlying or supporting parts

e. to create again

I. SELECTING A LEARNING/STUDY STRATEGY

Evaluate the usefulness of Table 9.3. How would you use this table to help you learn the material?

J. EXPLORING IDEAS THROUGH DISCUSSION AND WRITING

1. Discuss each of the graphic aids in this section of the chapter. Which ones were most helpful and which were least helpful? Explain your answers.

2. What is your earliest memory? Why do you think it has stayed in your long-term memory? Make a list of some of your autobiographical memories and any retrieval cues that accompany those memories.

3. Discuss the statements, "We need these memories to construct our sense of self" and "When people lose autobiographical memory, they lose some of their sense of self" (page 333, paragraph 2). How important are your memories to your own sense of self?

TRACKING
YOUR
PROGRESS

Psychology Selection 2

Section	Number Correct		Score
A. Main Ideas (6 items)	_____	× 4	_____
B. Details (4 items)	_____	× 3	_____
C. Organization and Transitions (4 items)	_____	× 3	_____
E. Reading and Thinking Visually (2 items)	_____	× 3	_____
F. Implied Meanings (4 items)	_____	× 2	_____
G. Thinking Critically (4 items)	_____	×	_____
H. Vocabulary			
Context (8 items)	_____	× 2	_____
Word Parts (5 items)	_____	× 2	_____
		TOTAL SCORE	_____%

Credits

Text Credits

6: "Metabolism," definition from THE RANDOM HOUSE WEBSTER'S UNABRIDGED DICTIONARY, 2nd Edition. New York: Random House, 2011; **17:** Tim Curry, Robert Jiobu, and Kent Schwirian, SOCIOLOGY FOR THE 21ST CENTURY, 3/e. Upper Saddle River, NJ: Pearson Education, 2001; **25:** Google™ search results for "British parliamentary system." © 2011 Google; **37:** Joseph A. DeVito, from THE INTERPERSONAL COMMUNICATION BOOK, 9/e, pp. 278–281, including Table 16.2. © 2001. Reproduced by permission of Pearson Education, Inc., Upper Saddle River, NJ; **40:** Joan O'C. Hamilton, "Treating Wounded Soldiers" as appeared in UTNE READER, edited from the original article titled "Mission Critical," STANFORD MAGAZINE, November/December 2009. Reprinted with permission from STANFORD MAGAZINE, published by Stanford Alumni Association, Stanford University. ; F. Philip Rice and Kim Gale Dolgin, THE ADOLESCENT: DEVELOPMENT, RELATIONSHIPS, AND CULTURE, 10/e, pp. 250–251. Boston: Allyn and Bacon, 2002; **52:** Teresa Audesirk, Gerald Audesirk, and Bruce E. Byers, LIFE ON EARTH, 3/e, pp. 622–624, 632. Upper Saddle River, NJ: Pearson Education, Inc., 2003; **54:** Mark C. Carnes and John A. Garraty, THE AMERICAN NATION: A HISTORY OF THE UNITED STATES, 11/e, p. 267. New York: Longman, 2003; **56:** Edward F. Bergman and William Renwick, INTRODUCTION TO GEOGRAPHY: PEOPLE, PLACES, AND ENVIRONMENT, 2/e, p. 263. Upper Saddle River, NJ: Pearson Education, 2002; **61:** William Germann and Cindy Stanfield, PRINCIPLES OF HUMAN PHYSIOLOGY, 1/e, p. 174. San Francisco: Benjamin Cummings, p. 174; **64:** Jeffrey Bennett, et al., THE COSMIC PERSPECTIVE, 2/e, p. 218. San Francisco: Addison-Wesley, 2002; **68:** Teresa Audesirk, Gerald Audesirk, and Bruce E. Byers, LIFE ON EARTH, 3/e, p. 237. Upper Saddle River, NJ: Pearson Education, Inc., 2003; **74:** Leon Baradat, UNDERSTANDING AMERICAN DEMOCRACY, p. 163. New York: HarperCollins College Publishers, 1992; **74:** Warren K. Agee et al., INTRODUCTION TO MASS COMMUNICATION, 12/e, p. 153. New York: Longman, 1997; **74:** Robert C. Nickerson, BUSINESS AND INFORMATION SYSTEMS, p. 30. Reading, MA: Addison-Wesley, 1998;

75: Laura Uba and Karen Huang, PSYCHOLOGY, p. 148. New York: Longman, 1999; **75:** Donald C. Mosley et al., MANAGEMENT: LEADERSHIP IN ACTION, 5/e, p. 317. New York: HarperCollins College Publishers, 1996; **76:** Warren K. Agee et al., INTRODUCTION TO MASS COMMUNICATION, 12/e, p. 225. New York: Longman, 1999; **77:** Joseph A. DeVito, from THE INTERPERSONAL COMMUNICATION BOOK, 9/e, p. 219. © 2001. Reproduced by permission of Pearson Education, Inc., Upper Saddle River, NJ; **78:** Josh R. Gerow, PSYCHOLOGY: AN INTRODUCTION, 5/e, p. 700. New York: Longman, 1997; **78:** Robert A. Wallace, BIOLOGY: THE WORLD OF LIFE, 6/e, p. 283. New York: HarperCollins College Publishers, 1992; **79:** James Coleman and Donald Cressey, SOCIAL PROBLEMS, 6/e, p. 277. New York: HarperCollins College Publishers, 1996; **79:** John D. Carl, from THINK SOCIOLOGY, 1/e, p. 122. © 2010. Reproduced by permission of Pearson Education, Inc., Upper Saddle River, NJ; **79:** Josh R. Gerow, PSYCHOLOGY: AN INTRODUCTION, 5/e, p. 250. New York: Longman, 1997; **79:** Karen Timberlake, CHEMISTRY: AN INTRODUCTION TO GENERAL, ORGANIC, AND BIOLOGICAL CHEMISTRY, 6/e, p. 30. New York: HarperCollins College Publishers, 1996; **80:** Michael C. Mix, Paul Farber, and Keith King, BIOLOGY: THE NETWORK OF LIFE, 2/e, p. 532. New York: HarperCollins College Publishers, 1992; **80:** Ronald J. Ebert and Ricky W. Griffin, adapted from BUSINESS ESSENTIALS, 7/e, p. 161. © 2009. Reproduced by permission of Pearson Education, Inc., Upper Saddle River, NJ; **80:** Joseph A. DeVito, from HUMAN COMMUNICATION: THE BASIC COURSE, 9/e, p. 217. Boston: Allyn and Bacon, 2003; **80:** George C. Edwards III et al., from GOVERNMENT IN AMERICA: PEOPLE, POLITICS, and POLICY, 14/e, p. 306. © 2009. Reproduced by permission of Pearson Education, Inc.; **81:** Ronald Ebert and Ricky Griffin, adapted from BUSINESS ESSENTIALS, 4/e, p. 64. © 2003. Reproduced by permission of Pearson Education, Inc., Upper Saddle River, NJ; **81:** Barbara Miller, CULTURAL ANTHROPOLOGY, 2/e, pp. 144–145. Boston: Allyn and Bacon, 2004; **81:** Paul G. Hewitt, CONCEPTUAL PHYSICS, 9/e, p. 39. San Francisco: Addison Wesley, 2002; **82:** Michael R.

HarperCollins College Publishers, 1991; **127:** Edward Greenberg and Benjamin Page, THE STRUGGLE FOR DEMOCRACY, Brief 2/e, p. 71. New York: Longman, 1999; **128:** William Germann and Cindy Stanfield, PRINCIPLES OF HUMAN PHYSIOLOGY, 1/e, pp. 606–607. San Francisco: Benjamin Cummings, p. 174; **128:** Leon Baradat, UNDER-STANDING AMERICAN DEMOCRACY, p. 202. New York: HarperCollins College Publishers, 1992; **129:** Rebecca Donatelle, from HEALTH: THE BASICS, 5/e, p. 324. © 2003. Reproduced by permission of Pearson Education, Inc., Upper Saddle River, NJ; **129:** Edward F. Bergman and William Renwick, INTRODUCTION TO GEOGRAPHY: PEOPLE, PLACES, AND ENVIRONMENT, 2/e, p. 185. Upper Saddle River, NJ: Pearson Education, 2002; **130:** Wilson Dizard, OLD MEDIA, NEW MEDIA, 3/e, p. 169. New York, Longman, 2000; **130:** Stephen F. Davis and Joseph J. Palladino, PSYCHOLOGY, 3/e, p. 210. Upper Saddle River, NJ: Prentice Hall, 2000; **130:** Wilson Dizard, OLD MEDIA, NEW MEDIA, 3/e, p. 169. New York, Longman, 2000; **131:** Edward F. Bergman and William Renwick, INTRODUCTION TO GEOGRAPHY: PEOPLE, PLACES, AND ENVIRONMENT, 2/e, p. 182. Upper Saddle River, NJ: Pearson Education, 2002; **132:** Rebecca J. Donatelle, ACCESS TO HEALTH, 7/e, p. 81. San Francisco: Benjamin Cummings/Pearson Education, 2002; **132:** James M. Henslin, SOCIAL PROBLEMS, 5/e, p. 93. Upper Saddle River, NJ: Pearson Education, 2000; **133:** James M. Henslin, SOCIAL PROBLEMS, 5/e, p. 91. Upper Saddle River, NJ: Pearson Education, 2000; **133:** Edward F. Bergman and William Renwick, INTRODUCTION TO GEOGRAPHY: PEOPLE, PLACES, AND ENVIRONMENT, 2/e, p. 197. Upper Saddle River, NJ: Pearson Education, 2002; **133:** Joseph A. DeVito, from HUMAN COMMUNICATION: THE BASIC COURSE, 7/e, p. 103. New York: Longman, 1997; **140:** Data in graph from Centers for Disease Control and Prevention, 2000; **142:** Table "Estimated Daily Calorie Needs" from The Center for Nutrition Policy and Promotion, April 2005, www.mypyramid.gov. An organization of the U.S. Department of Agriculture; **143:** Philip Kotler, from MARKETING:AN INTRODUCTION, 10/e, p. 346, Table 11.1. ©2011. Reproduced by permission of Pearson Education, Inc., Upper Saddle River, NJ; **145:** Jenifer Kunz, from THINK MARRIAGES AND FAMILIES, 1/e, p. 173. © 2011. Reproduced by permission of Pearson Education, Inc., Upper Saddle River, NJ; **146:** Jennifer Ehrle et al., data from "Who's Caring for Our Youngest Children? Child Care Patterns of Infants and Toddlers," Occasional Paper Vol. 42, 2001. Washington, DC: Urban Institute, 2001; **147:** George C. Edwards III et al., from GOVERNMENT IN AMERICA: PEOPLE, POLITICS, and POLICY, 14/e, p. 201. © 2009. Reproduced by permission of Pearson Education, Inc.; **150:** Michael R. Solomon et al., from BETTER BUSINESS, 1/e, p. 205, Fig. 7.5. © 2010. Reproduced by permission of Pearson Education, Inc.,

Upper Saddle River, NJ; **150:** J. David Bergeron, from FIRST RESPONDER, 8/e, p. 257, Fig. 9.5. © 2009. Reproduced by permission of Pearson Education, Inc., Upper Saddle River, NJ; **152:** Elaine Marieb, text and figure from ESSENTIALS OF HUMAN ANATOMY AND PHYSIOLOGY, 7/e, p. 106, Fig. 4.9. © 2003. Reproduced by permission of Pearson Education, Inc.; **154:** Map from U.S. Census Bureau, THE GEOGRAPHY OF AMERICAN POVERTY, 2008. www.census.gov; **155:** John D. Carl, from THINK SOCIOLOGY, 1/e, pp. 200–201. © 2010. Reproduced by permission of Pearson Education, Inc.; **157:** Rebecca Donatelle, from HEALTH: THE BASICS, Green Edition, 9/e, p. 130. © 2011. Reproduced by permission of Pearson Education, Inc., Upper Saddle River, NJ.; **162:** David Batstone, "Katja's Story: Human Trafficking Thrives in the New Global Economy" in SOJOURNER'S MAGAZINE, June 2006. Used by permission of the author. David Batstone is a professor at the University of San Francisco and co-founder and president of Not For Sale (www.NotForSaleCampaign.org); **165:** William Thompson and Joseph Hickey, from SOCIETY IN FOCUS: AN INTRODUCTION TO SOCIOLOGY, 4/e, p. 544. © 2002. Reproduced by permission of Pearson Education, Inc., Upper Saddle River, NJ; **166:** William Germann and Cindy Stanfield, PRINCIPLES OF HUMAN PHYSIOLOGY, 1/e, p. 185. San Francisco: Benjamin Cummings, p. 174; **166:** Joseph A. DeVito, from ESSENTIALS OF HUMAN COMMUNICATION, 4/e, pp. 36–37. Boston: Allyn and Bacon, 2002; **167:** Gini Stephens Frings, FASHION: FROM CONCEPTS TO CONSUMER, 6/e, p. 11. Upper Saddle River, NJ: Prentice Hall, 1999; **167:** Duane Preble and Sarah Preble, ARTFORMS: AN INTRODUCTION TO THE VISUAL ARTS, 7/e, p. 34. Upper Saddle River, NJ: Pearson Prentice Hall, 2002; **168:** James A. Fagin, from CRIMINAL JUSTICE, 2/e, pp. 245–246. © 2007. Reproduced by permission of Pearson Education, Inc., Upper Saddle River, NJ; **171:** Arlene Skolnick, THE INTIMATE ENVIRONMENT: EXPLORING MARRIAGE AND THE FAMILY, 6/e, p. 96. New York: Harper-Collins College Publishers, 1996; **172:** Robert Lineberry and George C. Edwards, III, GOVERNMENT IN AMERICA: PEOPLE, POLITICS, AND POLICY, 4/e, p. 540. Glenview, IL: Scott Foresman, 1989; **173:** Rebecca Donatelle, from HEALTH: THE BASICS, 5/e, p. 215. © 2003. Reproduced by permission of Pearson Education, Inc., Upper Saddle River, NJ; **173:** Rebecca J. Donatelle, ACCESS TO HEALTH, 8/e, pp. 372–373. San Francisco: Benjamin Cummings/Pearson Education, 2004; **173:** B. E. Pruitt and Jane Stein, HEALTH STYLES: DECISIONS FOR LIVING WELL, 2/e, pp. 572–573. Boston: Allyn and Bacon, 1999; **174:** William Thompson and Joseph Hickey, from SOCIETY IN FOCUS: AN INTRODUCTION TO SOCIOLOGY, 4/e, p. 364. © 2002. Reproduced by permission of Pearson Education, Inc., Upper Saddle River, NJ; **177:** Marge Thielman Hastreiter, excerpts from 'Not Every Mother Is Glad Kids Are Back at School,"

Photo Credits

Index